"The *Microsoft® Windows® Group Policy Guide* is a "must have" for any IT Professional looking to actively manage their desktops and servers! It contains a comprehensive collection of guidance on all aspects of Group Policy."

Michael Dennis
Lead Program Manager, Group Policy at Microsoft

D1489306

Microsoft® Windows® Group Policy Guide

Darren Mar-Elia

Derek Melber

William Stanek

The Microsoft Group Policy Team

PUBLISHED BY
Microsoft Press
A Division of Microsoft Corporation
One Microsoft Way
Redmond, Washington 98052-6399

Library of Congress Control Number: 2005922203
Printed and bound in the United States of America.

4 5 6 7 8 9   QWT   9 8 7

Distributed in Canada by H.B. Fenn and Company Ltd. A CIP catalogue record for this book is available from the British Library.

Microsoft Press books are available through booksellers and distributors worldwide. For further information about international editions, contact your local Microsoft Corporation office or contact Microsoft Press International directly at fax (425) 936-7329. Visit our Web site at www.microsoft.com/learning/. Send comments to *rkinput@microsoft.com*.

Acquisitions Editor: Martin DelRe
Project Editor: Karen Szall
Copy Editor: Ina Chang
Technical Editor: Mitch Tulloch
Indexer: Julie Bess
Compositor: Dan Latimer

Body Part No. X11-06980

Thanks to Karen for keeping me motivated and to Sid for walking
on top of my keyboard repeatedly as I tried to work.
— Darren Mar-Elia

Thanks to my family for being there in the
hard times and the good times.
— Derek Melber

To my wife and children, keeping
the dream alive.
— William R. Stanek

About the Authors

Darren Mar-Elia (*http://www.gpoguy.com*) is Quest Software's CTO for Windows Management and a Microsoft MVP for Group Policy. Darren has more than 18 years of experience in systems and network administration, design, and architecture. Darren is a contributing editor for *Windows IT Pro Magazine*. He has written and contributed to ten books on Windows NT and Windows 2000, including *Upgrading and Repairing Networks* (Que, 1996), *The Definitive Guide to Windows 2000 Group Policy* (NetIQ, FullArmor, and Realtimepublishers.com), and *Tips and Tricks Guide to Group Policy* (NetIQ, FullArmor, and Realtimepublishers.com). You can reach Darren by sending him e-mail at darren@gpoguy.com.

Derek Melber is a technical instructor, consultant, and author. Derek holds a Masters degree from the University of Kansas. He also has Microsoft Certified Systems Engineer (MCSE) certification and Certified Information Security Manager (CISM) certification. A Microsoft MVP with 15 years of experience in solution development, training, public speaking, and consulting, Derek has used his experience and knowledge to write numerous books on Windows Active Directory, Group Policy, security, auditing, and certifications. Derek offers both training and consulting on Group Policy, and he has developed and trained over 100,000 technical professionals around the world. To contact Derek for training, consulting, or questions, e-mail him at derekm@braincore.net.

William R. Stanek (*http://www.williamstanek.com*) has 20 years of hands-on experience with advanced programming and development. He is a leading technology expert, an award-winning author, and an exceptional instructor who teaches courses in Microsoft Windows, SQL Server, Exchange Server, and IIS administration. Over the years, his practical advice has helped millions of programmers, developers, and network engineers all over the world. His 50+ books have more than three million copies in print. Current and forthcoming books include *Microsoft Windows Server 2003 Inside Out* (Microsoft Press, 2004), *Microsoft Windows XP Professional Administrator's Pocket Consultant*, Second Edition (Microsoft Press, 2004), *Microsoft Windows Server 2003 Administrator's Pocket Consultant* (Microsoft Press, 2003), and *Microsoft IIS 6.0 Administrator's Pocket Consultant* (Microsoft Press, 2003). To contact William, visit his Web site (*http://www.williamstanek.com*) and send him an e-mail.

Thank you to those who contributed to the *Microsoft Windows Group Policy Guide*.

Group Policy Lead Program Manager: Michael Dennis

Technical Contributors: John Kaiser, Anshul Rawat, Mark Williams, Dan Fritch, Kurt Dillard, Adam Edwards, Stacia Snapp, Tim Thompson, Scott Cousins, Jennifer Hendrix, Gary Ericson, John Hrvatin, Drew Leaumont, Michael Surkan, Joseph Davies, David Beder, Mohammed Samji, Bill Gruber, Patanjali Venkatacharya, Mike Stephens, Michael Dennis, Paul Barr, Mike Jorden, Tarek Kamel, Mike Treit, Judith Herman, Rhynier Myburgh, Colin Torretta

From the Microsoft Press editorial team, the following individuals contributed to the *Microsoft Windows Group Policy Guide*:

Product Planner: Martin DelRe

Project Editor: Karen Szall

Technical Reviewer: Mitch Tulloch

Copy Editor: Ina Chang

Production Leads: Dan Latimer and Elizabeth Hansford

Indexer: Julie Bess

Art production: Joel Panchot and William Teel

Contents at a Glance

Part I   **Getting Started with Group Policy**

  1   Overview of Group Policy. 3

  2   Working with Group Policy 21

  3   Advanced Group Policy Management 53

Part II   **Group Policy Implementation and Scenarios**

  4   Deploying Group Policy 99

  5   Hardening Clients and Servers 135

  6   Managing and Maintaining Essential Windows Components 217

  7   Managing User Settings and Data 253

  8   Maintaining Internet Explorer Configurations 289

  9   Deploying and Maintaining Software Through Group Policy 317

  10   Managing Microsoft Office Configurations 369

  11   Maintaining Secure Network Communications 397

  12   Creating Custom Environments 439

Part III   **Group Policy Customization**

  13   Group Policy Structure and Processing 473

  14   Customizing Administrative Templates 515

  15   Security Templates. 553

Part IV   **Group Policy Troubleshooting**

  16   Troubleshooting Group Policy. 581

  17   Resolving Common Group Policy Problems 625

Part V   **Appendixes**

  A   Group Policy Reference 661

  B   New Features in Windows Server 2003 Service Pack 1 669

  C   GPMC Scripting 687

  D   Office 2003 Administrative Template Highlights. 705

Contents

Foreword xxvii
Introduction. xxix

Part I   Getting Started with Group Policy

1   Overview of Group Policy. 3

Understanding Group Policy. 4
    What It Does 4
    How It Works. 5
Using and Implementing Group Policy. 6
    Using Group Policy in Workgroups and Domains. 6
    Working with Group Policy Objects 6
Getting Started with Group Policy. 7
    Understanding Group Policy Settings and Options 7
    Using Group Policy for Administration 8
Understanding the Required Infrastructure for Group Policy 10
    DNS and Active Directory 10
    Applying Active Directory Structure to Inheritance 11
Examining GPO Links and Default GPOs 12
    Understanding GPO Links. 12
    Working with Linked GPOs and Default Policy 13
Summary 19

2   Working with Group Policy 21

Navigating Group Policy Objects and Settings 22
    Connecting to and Working with GPOs 22
    Applying Group Policy and Using Resultant Set of Policy 23
    RSoP Walkthrough 27
Managing Group Policy Objects 28
    Managing Local Group Policy 29
    Managing Active Directory–Based Group Policy. 32

What do you think of this book?
We want to hear from you!

Microsoft is interested in hearing your feedback about this publication so we can
continually improve our books and learning resources for you. To participate in a brief
online survey, please visit: *www.microsoft.com/learning/booksurvey/*

Creating and Linking GPOs 39

Creating and Linking GPOs for Sites. 39

Creating and Linking GPOs for Domains 41

Creating and Linking GPOs for OUs 43

Delegating Privileges for Group Policy Management 45

Determining and Assigning GPO Creation Rights 45

Determining Group Policy Management Privileges. 47

Delegating Control for Working with GPOs 49

Delegating Authority for Managing Links and RSoP. 50

Removing Links and Deleting GPOs 51

Removing a Link to a GPO 51

Deleting a GPO Permanently 51

Summary 52

3   Advanced Group Policy Management 53

Searching and Filtering Group Policy 54

Filtering Policy Settings. 54

Searching Policy Objects, Links, and Settings 56

Filtering by Security Group, User, or Computer 59

Managing Group Policy Inheritance 61

Changing Link Order and Precedence 62

Overriding Inheritance 64

Blocking Inheritance 65

Enforcing Inheritance 66

Managing Group Policy Processing and Refresh 68

Changing the Refresh Interval 70

Enabling or Disabling GPO Processing. 72

Changing Policy Processing Preferences 73

Configuring Slow Link Detection 75

Refreshing Group Policy Manually 80

Modeling and Maintaining Group Policy. 80

Modeling Group Policy for Planning Purposes. 81

Copying and Importing Policy Objects 85

Backing Up GPOs. 89

Restoring Policy Objects 91

Determining the Effective Group Policy Settings and Last Refresh 93

Summary 96

Part II   **Group Policy Implementation and Scenarios**

4   **Deploying Group Policy** **99**

Group Policy Design Considerations 100

Active Directory Design Considerations 100

Physical Design Considerations 104

Remote Access Connection Design Considerations 105

GPO Application Design Considerations 106

Additional GPO Design Considerations 113

Controlling GPO Processing Performance 115

Common Performance Issues 115

Performance Tips 117

Best Practices for Deploying GPOs 121

Choosing the Best Level to Link GPOs 121

Resources Used by GPOs 124

Software Installation 124

Designing GPOs Based on GPO Categories 125

Limit Enforced and Block Policy Inheritance Options 125

When to Use Security Filtering 126

When to Use WMI Filters 126

Network Topology Considerations 127

Limiting Administrative Privileges 128

Naming GPOs 129

Testing GPOs Before Deployment 129

Migrating GPOs from Test to Production 130

Migrating GPOs from Production to Production 130

Using Migration Tables 130

Summary 134

5   **Hardening Clients and Servers** **135**

Understanding Security Templates 136

Default Security Templates 136

Sections of the Security Template 142

Tools for Accessing, Creating, and Modifying Security Templates 150

Using the Security Configuration Wizard 152

Deploying Security Templates 161

Importing Security Templates into GPOs 161

Using the Security Configuration and Analysis Tool .162

Using the Secedit.exe Command-Line Tool. 162
Using the Security Configuration Wizard and the *scwcmd* Command. 163
General Hardening Techniques 164
Closing Unnecessary Ports. 164
Disabling Unnecessary Services. 165
Tools Used in Hardening Computers 166
Server Hardening. 168
Member Servers. 168
Domain Controllers 187
File and Print Servers. 190
Web Servers 191
Client Hardening 192
Ports Required for Clients. 205
Restricted Groups for Clients. 206
Client Computers for IT Staff and Administrators 206
Client Computers for Help Desk Staff. 208
Troubleshooting. 210
Security Areas and Potential Problems. 210
Tools. 213
Summary. 215

6   Managing and Maintaining Essential Windows Components 217
Configuring Application Compatibility Settings. 218
Optimizing Application Compatibility Through Group Policy 218
Configuring Additional Application Compatibility Settings. 219
Configuring Attachment Manager Settings 220
Working with Attachment Manager. 220
Configuring Risk Levels and Trust Logic in Group Policy. 221
Configuring Event Viewer Information Requests 224
Using Event Viewer Information Requests. 224
Customizing Event Details Through Group Policy 225
Controlling IIS Installation 225
Configuring Access to and Use of Microsoft Management Console. 226
Blocking Author Mode for MMC 227
Designating Prohibited and Permitted Snap-Ins 227
Requiring Explicit Permission for All Snap-Ins. 228
Optimizing NetMeeting Security and Features. 228
Configuring NetMeeting Through Group Policy 229

Enabling Security Center for Use in Domains 230

Managing Access to Scheduled Tasks and Task Scheduler 230

Managing File System, Drive, and Windows Explorer Access Options. 231

Hiding Drives in Windows Explorer and Related Views 232

Preventing Access to Drives in Windows Explorer and Related Views. 233

Removing CD-Burning and DVD-Burning Features in
Windows Explorer and Related Views. 234

Removing the Security Tab in Windows Explorer and Related Views 235

Limiting the Maximum Size of the Recycle Bin 235

Optimizing the Windows Installer Configuration 236

Controlling System Restore Checkpoints for Program Installations. 237

Configuring Baseline File Cache Usage. 237

Controlling Rollback File Creation 238

Elevating User Privileges for Installation. 239

Controlling Per-User Installation and Program Operation 240

Preventing Installation from Floppy Disk, CD, DVD,
and Other Removable Media 241

Configuring Windows Installer Logging. 241

Optimizing Automatic Updates with Windows Update. 243

Enabling and Configuring Automatic Updates 243

Controlling Auto Download and Notify for Install 246

Blocking Access to Automatic Updates 249

Designating an Update Server 249

Summary 251

7   Managing User Settings and Data **253**

Understanding User Profiles and Group Policy 254

Configuring Roaming Profiles. 257

Configuring the Network Share for Roaming Profiles 258

Configuring User Accounts to Use Roaming Profiles .258

Optimizing User Profile Configurations 260

Modifying the Way Local and Roaming Profiles Are Used 260

Modifying the Way Profile Data Is Updated and Changed. 265

Modifying the Way Profile Data Can Be Accessed 266

Limiting Profile Size and Included Folders. 269

Redirecting User Profile Folders and Data 271

Understanding Folder Redirection. 272

Configuring Folder Redirection 274

Managing Computer and User Scripts 281
    Working with Computer and User Scripts 282
    Configuring Computer Startup and Shutdown Scripts 283
    Configuring User Logon and Logoff Scripts 284
    Controlling Script Visibility 285
    Controlling Script Timeout 286
    Controlling Script Execution and Run Technique 287
Summary 287

8   Maintaining Internet Explorer Configurations 289

Customizing the Internet Explorer Interface 290
    Customizing the Title Bar Text 290
    Customizing Logos 291
    Customizing Buttons and Toolbars 292
Customizing URLs, Favorites, and Links 295
    Customizing Home, Search, and Support URLs 295
    Customizing Favorites and Links 296
Configuring Global Default Programs 299
Optimizing Connection and Proxy Settings 301
    Deploying Connection Settings Through Group Policy 301
    Deploying Proxy Settings Through Group Policy 303
Enhancing Internet Explorer Security 306
    Working with Security Zones and Settings 306
    Restricting Security Zone Configuration 308
    Deploying Security Zone Configurations 309
    Importing and Deploying the Security Zone Settings 313
Configuring Additional Policies for Internet Options 313
Summary 316

9   Deploying and Maintaining Software Through Group Policy 317

Understanding Group Policy Software Installation 318
    How Software Installation Works 318
    What You Need to Know to Prepare 319
    How to Set Up the Installation Location 320
    What Limitations Apply 321
Planning the Software Deployment 322
    Creating Software Deployment GPOs 322
    Configuring the Software Deployment 324

Deploying Software Through Group Policy 326
    Deploying Software with Windows Installer Packages. 326
    Deploying Software with Non–Windows Installer Packages 330
Configuring Advanced and Global Software Installation Options 334
    Viewing and Setting General Deployment Properties 334
    Changing the Deployment Type and Installation Options 335
    Defining Application Categories 338
    Adding, Modifying, and Removing Application Categories 339
    Adding an Application to a Category 340
    Performing Upgrades 340
    Customizing the Installation Package with Transforms 344
    Controlling Deployment by Security Group. 344
    Setting Global Deployment Defaults. 346
Deploying Microsoft Office and Service Packs 349
    Deploying Office Through Policy. 349
    Deploying Windows Service Packs Through Policy 354
Maintaining Deployed Applications 354
    Removing Deployed Applications 355
    Redeploying Applications 356
    Configuring Software Restriction Policies. 356
    Troubleshooting Software Installation Policy. 365
Summary 368

10 Managing Microsoft Office Configurations 369
Introducing Office Configuration Management 370
Customizing Office Configurations 371
    Downloading and Installing the Tools. 371
    Working with the Custom Installation Wizard. 372
    Working with the Custom Maintenance Wizard 375
    Preparing the Policy Environment 377
    Deploying Office Administrative Template Files 377
    Creating Office Configuration GPOs. 380
    Managing Multiple Office Configuration Versions 381
Managing Office-Related Policy. 383
    Working with Office-Related Policy. 383
    Examining Global and Application-Specific Settings 384

Configuring Office-related Policy Settings 385

Preventing Users from Changing Office Configurations................. 386

Controlling Default File and Folder Locations.......................... 391

Configuring Outlook Security Options................................. 393

Controlling Office Language Settings 394

Troubleshooting Office Administrative Template Policy 394

Summary... 396

11   Maintaining Secure Network Communications 397

Understanding IPSec Policy 398

How IPSec Works.. 398

How IPSec Policy Is Deployed 399

When to Use IPSec and IPSec Policy................................. 399

Managing and Maintaining IPSec Policy 401

Activating and Deactivating IPSec Policies 401

Create Additional IPSec Policies 402

Monitoring IPSec Policy 414

Deploying Public Key Policies 415

How Public Key Certificates Work.................................... 415

How Public Key Policies Are Used 416

Managing Public Key Policy... 418

Understanding Windows Firewall Policy 420

How Windows Firewall Works 420

How Windows Firewall Policy Is Used 421

Managing Windows Firewall Policy 424

Configuring IPSec Bypass.. 425

Enabling and Disabling Windows Firewall with Group Policy 425

Managing Firewall Exceptions with Group Policy...................... 426

Configuring Firewall Notification, Logging, and Response Requests 437

Summary... 438

12   Creating Custom Environments 439

Loopback Processing... 440

Replace Mode 441

Merge Mode... 442

Troubleshooting Loopback 443

Terminal Services 444

Controlling Terminal Services Through Group Policy
on an Individual Computer. 444
Controlling Terminal Services Through Group Policy in a Domain 445
Configuring Order of Precedence 446
Configuring Terminal Services User Properties 446
Configuring License Server Using Group Policy Settings. 447
Configuring Terminal Services Connections. 448
Managing Drive, Printer, and Device Mappings for Clients. 456
Controlling Terminal Services Profiles. 459
Group Policy over Slow Links 461
Default Policy Application over Slow Links 462
Slow Link Behavior for RAS Connections 463
Slow Link Detection Group Policy Settings 463
Additional Slow Link Detection Settings for Client-Side Extensions. 467
Summary 469

Part III   Group Policy Customization

13   Group Policy Structure and Processing 473

Navigating Group Policy Logical Structure. 474
Working with Group Policy Containers. 474
Examining Attributes of *groupPolicyContainer* Objects 476
Examining the Security of *groupPolicyContainer* Objects 477
Examining GPO Creation Permissions. 478
Viewing and Setting Default Security for New GPOs 479
Navigating Group Policy Physical Structure. 483
Working with Group Policy Templates 483
Understanding Group Policy Versioning 486
Understanding Group Policy Template Security 488
Navigating Group Policy Link Structure 488
Examining Group Policy Linking 488
Examining Inheritance Blocking on Links. 491
Understanding Group Policy Security and Links 491
Understanding Group Policy Processing. 492
Examining Client-Side Extension Processing 492
Examining Server-Side Extension Processing. 494
Understanding Policy Processing Events 501

Asynchronous vs. Synchronous Policy Processing 502
Tracking Policy Application 503
Tracking Slow Link Detection. 505
Modifying Security Policy Processing. 507
Group Policy History and State Data 507
Navigating Local GPO Structure 511
Understanding LGPO Creation and Application. 511
Understanding LGPO Structure. 512
Managing and Maintaining LGPOs. 512
Controlling Access to the LGPO 513
Summary. 514

14   Customizing Administrative Templates 515
What Is an Administrative Template? 516
Default .adm Files 516
Working with .adm Files. 518
Default Installed .adm Files 518
Tips for Importing .adm Files. 519
Adding .adm Files 520
Removing .adm Files 521
Managing .adm Files. 522
Policies vs. Preferences 524
Creating Custom .adm Files 525
A Simple .adm File 526
Using .adm File Language 527
Structure of an .adm File. 527
#if version 529
Syntax for Updating the Registry 530
Syntax for Updating the Group Policy Object Editor Interface 534
Additional Statements in the .adm Template 546
.adm File String and Tab Limits 549
Best Practices 550
Summary. 552

15   Security Templates. 553
Understanding the Security Template Structure 554
Account Policies. 554
Local Policies. 555

Event Log. 556

Restricted Groups. 557

System Services. 558

Registry 559

File System. 560

Where Security Template Settings Overlap with GPO Settings. 561

Working With Security Templates 562

Security Templates Snap-in. 562

Raw Security Template INF Files. 563

Customizing Security Templates. 563

Copying Templates. 563

Creating New Security Templates 564

Customizing Security Options 564

Structure of the Sceregvl.inf File 564

Customizing the Sceregvl.inf File. 570

Getting the Custom Entry to Show Up 571

Customizing Services in the Security Templates 572

Getting the Correct Service to Automatically Display 572

Acquiring the Service Syntax for the Security Template File. 572

Manually Updating Services in the Security Template File 573

Microsoft Solutions for Security Settings 574

Summary 577

Part IV   **Group Policy Troubleshooting**

16   **Troubleshooting Group Policy. 581**

Group Policy Troubleshooting Essentials 582

Verifying the Core Configuration. 582

Verifying Key Infrastructure Components 586

Verifying the Scope of Management 587

Essential Troubleshooting Tools 593

Working with Resultant Set Of Policy 593

Viewing RSoP from the Command Line 599

Verifying Server-Side GPO Health 600

Managing RSoP Logs Centrally 604

Group Policy Logging 609

Navigating the Application Event Logs 610

Managing Userenv Logging. 613

Managing Logging for Specific CSEs 617

Summary. 623

17   Resolving Common Group Policy Problems 625

Solving GPO Administration Problems. 626

Domain Controller Running the PDC Emulator Is Not Available. 626

Not All Settings Show Up in the Group Policy Editor 627

Delegation Restrictions Within the GPMC. 631

Group Policy Settings Are Not Being Applied Due to Infrastructure Problems. . . . 638

Domain Controllers Are Not Available. 639

Active Directory Database Is Corrupt. 640

Local Logon vs. Active Directory Logon. 641

SYSVOL Files Are Causing GPO Application Failure 642

Problems with Replication and Convergence
of Active Directory and SYSVOL 643

DNS Problems Causing GPO Application Problems. 645

Solving Implementation Problems 647

Tracking Down Incorrect GPO Settings 647

GPO Links Causing GPO Application Problems 650

Accounts Are Not Located in the Correct OU. 651

Trying to Apply Group Policy Settings to Groups. 652

Conflicting Settings in Two GPOs 653

Modifying Default GPO Inheritance. 654

Summary. 657

Part V   Appendixes

A   Group Policy Reference 661

Computer Configuration Reference 661

User Configuration Reference 664

B   New Features in Windows Server 2003 Service Pack 1. 669

Adprep. 670

Administrative Tools . . . . :. 671

Internet Explorer Feature Control Settings 672

Managing Feature Control Settings 673

Configuring Policies and Preferences 673

Internet Explorer Administration Kit/Internet Explorer Maintenance 673

Internet Explorer URL Action Security Settings 674

Changes to Internet Explorer URL Action Security Settings 675

Resultant Set of Policy 676

Changes to RSoP in SP1 676

Administering Remote RSoP with GPMC SP1 677

Delegating Access to Group Policy Results 678

Post-Setup Security Updates. 678

Security Configuration Wizard 679

Windows Firewall 681

Changes to Windows Firewall 681

Changes for Audit Logging 681

Changes for Netsh Helper. 682

Windows Firewall New Group Policy Support. 682

C   GPMC Scripting 687

GPMC Scripting Interface Essentials 687

Understanding the GPMC Scripting Object Model 687

Creating the Initial *GPM* Object. 689

Referencing the Domain to Manage. 689

Creating and Linking GPOs. 689

Automating Group Policy Security Management 693

Using the GPMC's Prebuilt Scripts 695

Creating GPOs. 696

Deleting GPOs. 696

Finding Disabled GPOs 696

Finding GPOs by Security Group 697

Finding GPOs Without Active Links. 697

Setting GPO Creation Permissions. 697

Setting Other GPO Permissions 698

Backing Up All GPOs 698

Backing Up Individual GPOs. 699

Copying GPOs. 699

Importing GPOs 700

Generating RSoP Reports 700

Mirroring Your Production Environment 701

GPMC Prebuilt Script Review 702

D   **Office 2003 Administrative Template Highlights. 705**

    Microsoft Access 2003. 706

    Microsoft Excel 2003 706

    Microsoft FrontPage 2003 708

    Microsoft Clip Organizer 2003. 708

    Microsoft InfoPath 2003 709

    Microsoft Office 2003 709

    Microsoft OneNote 2003 713

    Microsoft Outlook 2003 715

    Microsoft PowerPoint 2003 718

    Microsoft Project 2003 719

    Microsoft Publisher 2003 720

    Microsoft Visio 2003 721

    Microsoft Word 2003 722

    Index **725**

Foreword

The collection of writers for this book all have years of experience in using Group Policy, and, to write this book, they have all worked closely with those responsible for delivering the entire Group Policy feature set in Microsoft Windows. Their experience, coupled with their ability to explain complex concepts clearly, makes this book an invaluable resource for anyone looking to actively manage their desktops and servers. It starts by taking a scenario-based approach, introducing the concepts of Group Policy–based management and how it leverages the Active Directory. It then explores the various areas of Windows that are controllable via Group Policy, such as security, the Windows desktop, Microsoft Internet Explorer, networking components (like the Windows Firewall), and Microsoft Office. But it doesn't stop there; it also explores the more powerful capabilities of Group Policy, like using Group Policy–based Software Installation and how Group Policy can be extended to do even more.

Implementation of Group Policy can be done in a simple manner, and this book will make it even easier to get up and running in that regard. Group Policy is also very flexible and can be used in complex environments to solve complex management problems. This book is structured in a way that makes these more complex issues easier to understand. It also covers troubleshooting on multiple levels—from the common issues to the more complex to diagnose—and does so in a concise yet complete manner. The book rounds off by giving you pointers and links to those places where you can stay up-to-date on the latest information on Group Policy, from both Microsoft and others.

In these days of heightened security awareness and regulatory oversight, we all need to be more proactive about managing Windows desktops and servers. Group Policy gives you the power to do so, and this book makes using Group Policy a straightforward experience. So, whether you have rolled out Microsoft Active Directory or are thinking about it, this book is a must-have for you!

—*Michael Dennis, Lead Program Manager, Group Policy at Microsoft*

Introduction

Welcome to the *Microsoft® Windows® Group Policy Guide*. The *Microsoft Windows Group Policy Guide* covers the topic of Group Policy—quite possibly the most misunderstood product that Microsoft has ever introduced. Many system administrators, network engineers, and IT managers think of Group Policy as a complex behemoth within Active Directory® that they will never truly understand, and yet Group Policy is widely implemented because its benefits are well-known in areas of security, software distribution, and desktop lockdown. When you've widely implemented a product that you don't understand, you have a real problem and a frustrating experience for everyone involved, but it doesn't have to be that way. Group Policy is less complex, more configurable, and more manageable than you might have imagined—and step by step, chapter by chapter, you'll learn why as you read this book.

About This Book

Microsoft Windows Group Policy Guide covers Group Policy administration for Microsoft Windows Server™ 2003, Windows XP Professional, and Windows 2000. The book is designed for Windows system administrators, network engineers, and anyone else who wants to learn the ins and outs of Group Policy. If you currently support Active Directory or you want to learn more about Group Policy, this book is for you.

This book zeroes in on the essential information that you need to effectively deploy, manage, and troubleshoot Group Policy. To pack in as much information as possible, we're assuming that you have basic system administration skills and are familiar with Windows Server 2003 network environments. With this in mind, we don't devote entire chapters to understanding Active Directory, DNS, or Windows Server 2003. Other books cover those topics in depth and better than we ever could; they include *Microsoft Windows Server 2003 Inside Out* (Microsoft Press, 2004), *Microsoft Windows Server 2003 Administrator's Companion* (Microsoft Press, 2004), and *Microsoft Windows Server 2003 Administrator's Pocket Consultant* (Microsoft Press, 2003). What is this book, then? It is a guide to Group Policy, which explains everything you need to know to successfully deploy, manage, and troubleshoot Group Policy.

The book has five parts:

- **Part 1, "Getting Started with Group Policy,"** covers the fundamental tasks that you need for Group Policy administration. Chapter 1 provides an overview of Group Policy, discussing how it works, how it fits into a Windows network, and how you can use it. Chapters 3 and 4 examine techniques for managing Group Policy.

- **Part 2, "Group Policy Implementation and Scenarios,"** explains the essential tasks for deploying and using Group Policy. Chapter 4 discusses how you can deploy Group Policy in a wide variety of scenarios. Chapter 5 details how you can improve security through Group Policy. Chapter 6 shows how you can customize the Windows desktop and user interface using Group Policy. Chapter 7 shows how to manage user settings and data. You'll also learn about folder redirection, scripts, and profiles as they pertain to Group Policy. Chapter 8 discusses how to maintain Microsoft Internet Explorer configurations and how to customize browser security settings through Group Policy. Chapter 9 covers deploying software through Group Policy. Chapter 10 shows how to manage Microsoft Office configurations using Group Policy. Chapter 11 details how to use Group Policy to maintain network security and network communications settings. Chapter 12 examines techniques for creating custom environments for computer labs, kiosks, special-use computers, and more.

- **Part 3, "Group Policy Customization,"** digs into advanced customization of Group Policy. Chapter 13 examines Group Policy structure. You'll learn about Group Policy architecture, including how Group Policy is stored and processed. In Chapter 14, you learn about customizing administrative templates. Chapter 15 covers how to customize security templates. As you'll discover in these chapters, Group Policy is highly customizable, and you can do a lot to optimize your Active Directory environment.

- **Part 4, "Group Policy Troubleshooting,"** examines what to do when things go wrong. Chapter 16 covers troubleshooting tools and techniques. Chapter 17 provides solutions for common problems with Group Policy.

- **Part 5, "Appendixes,"** provides essential references and resources. Appendix A provides a quick lookup resource, which can be used in addition to the book's extensive table of contents and index. Appendix B looks at the new features of Windows Server 2003 Service Pack 1. Appendix C examines techniques for scripting Group Policy. Appendix D provides a reference for Office 2003 Administrative Templates.

Document Conventions

Reader alerts are used throughout the book to point out useful information.

	Reader Alert	Meaning
	Tip	Provides a helpful bit of inside information about specific tasks or functions
	More info	Points to other sources of information on the topic
	Note	Alerts you to supplementary information
	Caution	Contains important information about possible data loss, breaches of security, or other serious problems
	On the CD	Identifies tools or additional information available on the CD that accompanies the book

The following style conventions are used in documenting command-line tasks throughout this guide.

Element	Meaning
Bold font	Characters that you type exactly as shown, including commands and parameters. User interface elements also appear in boldface type.
Italic font	Variables for which you supply a specific value. For example, *Filename.ext* can refer to any valid file name.
`Monospace font`	Code samples.
`%SystemRoot%`	Environment variables.

Companion CD

The companion CD includes a variety of tools and scripts to help you work more efficiently with Group Policy on computers running Windows 2000, Windows XP Professional, and Windows Server 2003. Several of these tools are discussed in the book; many others are not. You can find documentation for each tool in the GroupPolicyGuideTools folder. Some of these tools are from the *Microsoft Windows Server 2003 Resource Kit*, so they are designed to be implemented with Windows Server 2003 operating systems.

 Note   The tools on the CD are designed to be used on Windows Server 2003 or Windows XP (or as specified in the documentation of the tool).

Support Policy

Microsoft does not support the tools supplied on the *Microsoft Windows Group Policy Guide* CD. Microsoft does not guarantee the performance of the tools or any bug fixes for these tools. However, Microsoft Press provides a way for customers who purchase *Microsoft Windows Group Policy Guide* to report any problems with the software and to receive feedback. To report any issues or problems, send an e-mail message to *rkinput@microsoft.com*. This e-mail address is only for issues related to *Microsoft Windows Group Policy Guide*.

Microsoft Press also provides corrections for books and companion CDs through the World Wide Web at *http://www.microsoft.com/learning/support/*. To connect directly to the Microsoft Knowledge Base and enter a query regarding a question or issue you have, go to *http://support.microsoft.com*. For issues related to the Microsoft Windows Server 2003 operating system, refer to the support information included with your product.

System Requirements

To use the tools, eBooks, and other materials on the CD, you need to meet the following minimum system requirements:

- Microsoft Windows Server 2003 or Windows XP operating system
- PC with 233-megahertz (MHz) or higher processor; 550-MHz or higher processor is recommended
- 128 megabytes (MB) of RAM; 256 MB or higher is recommended
- 1.5 to 2 gigabytes (GB) of available hard disk space

- Super VGA (800 x 600) or higher resolution video adapter and monitor
- CD or DVD drive
- Keyboard and Microsoft mouse or compatible pointing device
- Adobe Acrobat or Adobe Reader
- Internet connectivity for tools that are downloaded

Note   Actual requirements, including Internet and network access and any related charges, will vary based on your system configuration and the applications and features that you choose to install. Additional hard disk space might be required if you are installing over a network.

Part I
Getting Started with Group Policy

In this part:

Chapter 1: Overview of Group Policy 3
Chapter 2: Working with Group Policy 21
Chapter 3: Advanced Group Policy Management 53

Chapter 1
Overview of Group Policy

In this chapter:

Understanding Group Policy 4
Using and Implementing Group Policy 6
Getting Started with Group Policy 7
Understanding the Required Infrastructure for Group Policy 10
Examining GPO Links and Default GPOs 12
Summary 19

In this chapter, we will introduce Group Policy. You'll learn what Group Policy does, how it can be used in both domain and workgroup settings, and what infrastructure is required to implement it. If you're running an Active Directory® directory service network environment, you need Group Policy. Period. There's no doubt, no question at all. Your only real question should be how to make the most of what Group Policy has to offer, given your organization's structure and needs. Why? Because Group Policy is meant to make your life as an administrator easier. Microsoft coined the term *Group Policy* to describe the technology that allows you to group policy settings together and apply them in discrete sets. Group Policy is, in fact, a collection of policy settings that simplify administration of common and repetitive tasks as well as unique tasks that are difficult to implement manually but can be automated (such as deploying new software or enforcing which programs can be installed on computers).

Related Information

- For information about DNS architecture, see Chapter 26 in *Microsoft Windows Server 2003 Inside Out* (Microsoft Press, 2004).

- For information about Active Directory architecture, see Chapter 32 in *Microsoft Windows Server 2003 Inside Out*.

- For information on deploying Group Policy, see Chapter 4 in this book.

Understanding Group Policy

Group Policy provides a convenient and effective way to manage computer and user settings.

What It Does

With Group Policy, you can manage settings for thousands of users or computers in the same way that you manage settings for one user or computer—and without ever leaving your desk. To do this, you use one of several management tools to change a setting to a desired value, and this change is applied throughout the network to a desired subset of users or computers or to any individual user or computer.

One way to think of Group Policy is as a set of rules that you can apply to help you manage users and computers. Despite common misperceptions, Group Policy does this in a way that is more intuitive than was previously possible. Still a nonbeliever? Consider for a moment that before Group Policy, many of the administrative changes that Group Policy enables were possible only by hacking the Windows registry, and each change had to be made individually on each target computer. Time consuming, tricky to implement, prone to disastrous results? You betcha.

Enter Group Policy, whereby you can simply enable or disable a policy to tweak a registry value or other setting, and the change will apply automatically to every computer you designate the next time Group Policy is refreshed. Because changes can be modeled (through the Group Policy Management Console) before the modifications are applied, you can be certain of the effect of each desired change. Plus, if you don't like the results, you can undo a change by setting the policy back to its original or Not Configured state.

To take this scenario a step further, consider the case in which you've manually tweaked multiple Microsoft® Windows® registry settings on a number of machines and you start to have problems. Maybe users can't log on, they can't perform necessary actions, or computers aren't responding normally. If you documented every change on every computer, you might be able to undo the changes—if you are lucky and if you properly documented the original settings as well as the changes. In contrast, Group Policy allows you to back up ("save") the state of Group Policy before making changes. If something goes wrong, you can restore Group Policy to its original state. When you restore the state of Group Policy, you can be certain that all changes are undone with the next Group Policy refresh.

How It Works

Speaking of Group Policy refresh, you are probably wondering what this term means. While the nitty-gritty details are covered in Chapter 2, the basics of group policy application (initial processing) and refresh (subsequent processing) are straightforward. In Active Directory, two distinct sets of policies are defined:

- **Computer policies**   These apply to computers and are stored under Computer Configuration in Group Policy.

- **User policies**   These apply to users and are stored under User Configuration in Group Policy.

Initial processing of the related policies is triggered by two unique events:

- **Processing of computer policies is triggered when a computer is started.**   When a computer is started and the network connection is initialized, computer policy settings are applied and a history of the registry-based settings that were applied is written to %AllUsersProfile%\Ntuser.pol.

- **Processing of user policies is triggered when a user logs on to a computer.**   When a user logs on to a computer, user policy settings are applied and a history of the registry-based settings that were applied is written to %UserProfile%\Ntuser.pol.

Once applied, Group Policy settings are automatically refreshed to keep settings current and to reflect any changes that might have been made. By default, Group Policy on domain controllers is refreshed every 5 minutes. For workstations and other types of servers, Group Policy is refreshed every 90 to 120 minutes by default. In addition, Group Policy is refreshed every 16 hours regardless of whether or not any policy settings have changed in the intervening time.

Note   Officially, the default Group Policy refresh interval on workstations and member servers is every 90 minutes, but a delay of up to 30 minutes is added to avoid flooding domain controllers with multiple simultaneous refresh requests. This effectively makes the default refresh window from 90 to 120 minutes.

Tip   Other factors can affect Group Policy refresh, including how slow link detection is defined (per the Group Policy Slow Link Detection Policy under Computer Configuration\Administrative Templates\System\Group Policy) and policy processing settings for policies under Computer Configuration\Administrative Templates\System\Group Policy. You can check the last refresh of Group Policy using the Group Policy Management Console (GPMC). (See the section titled "Determining Policy Settings and Last Refresh" in Chapter 3.)

Using and Implementing Group Policy

Group Policy is so important to a successful Active Directory implementation that most administrators think of it as a component of Active Directory. This is mostly true—and it is okay to think of it this way—but you don't necessarily need Active Directory to use Group Policy.

Using Group Policy in Workgroups and Domains

You can use Group Policy to manage workstations running Microsoft Windows 2000 and Windows XP Professional as well as servers running Windows 2000 and Windows Server™ 2003. While you can't use Group Policy to manage Windows NT® workstations or servers, Windows 95, Windows 98, Windows Millennium Edition (Me), or Windows XP Home Edition, you can use Group Policy in both enterprise (domain) and local (workgroup) environments.

For enterprise environments where Active Directory is deployed, the complete set of policy settings is available. This policy set is referred to as domain-based Group Policy, Active Directory–based Group Policy, or simply Group Policy. In Active Directory, two important related elements are sites and organizational units (OUs). A site represents the physical architecture of your network. It is a group of TCP/IP subnets that are implemented to control directory replication traffic and isolate logon authentication traffic between physical network locations. OUs are used to group objects in a domain. An OU is a logical administrative unit within a domain that can be used to represent the structure of an organization or its business functions.

Working with Group Policy Objects

Group Policy is applied in discrete sets, referred to as Group Policy Objects (GPOs). GPOs contain settings that can be applied in a variety of ways to computers and users in a specific Active Directory domain, site, or OU. Because of the object-based hierarchy in Active Directory, the settings of top-level GPOs can also be inherited by lower-level GPOs.

For example, a setting for the cpandl.com domain can be inherited by the Engineering OU within that domain, and the domain settings will be applied to users and computers in the Engineering OU. If you don't want policy settings to be inherited, you can block these settings to ensure that only the GPO settings for the low-level GPO are applied.

Tip   With domain-based Group Policy, you might think that the forest or domain functional level would affect how Group Policy is used, but this is not the case. The forest and domain do not need to be in any particular functional mode to use Group Policy. The forest functional level can be Windows 2000, Windows Server 2003 Interim, or Windows Server 2003. The domain functional level can be Windows 2000 Mixed, Windows 2000 Native, Windows Server 2003 Interim, or Windows Server 2003.

For local environments, a subset of Group Policy called Local Group Policy is available. As the name implies, Local Group Policy allows you to manage policy settings that affect everyone who logs on to a local machine. This means Local Group Policy applies to any user or administrator who logs on to a computer that is a member of a workgroup as well as any user or administrator who logs on locally to a computer that is a member of a domain. Because Local Group Policy is a subset of Group Policy, there are some things you can't do locally that you can do in a domain setting. Generally speaking, the areas of policy that you can't manage locally have to do with Active Directory features that you can manage through Group Policy, such as software installation. Like Active Directory–based Group Policy, however, Local Group Policy is managed through a GPO. This GPO is referred to as the Local Group Policy Object (LGPO).

Beyond these fundamental differences between Local Group Policy and Active Directory–based Group Policy, both types of policy are managed in much the same way. In fact, you use the same tools to manage both. The key difference is in the GPO you work with. On a local machine, you work exclusively with the LGPO. If you have deployed Active Directory, however, you can also work with domain, site, and OU GPOs in addition to LGPOs.

Tip   Whether they are client workstations, member servers, or domain controllers, all Windows 2000, Windows XP Professional, and Windows Server 2003 computers have a Local Group Policy Object (LGPO). The LGPO is always processed. However, it has the least precedence, which means its settings can be superceded by site, domain, and OU settings. Although domain controllers have LGPOs, Group Policy for domain controllers is managed best through a default GPO called the Default Domain Controllers Policy. There's also a default GPO for domains called the Default Domain Policy. As you might imagine, these default GPOs have special purposes and are used in very specific ways. You'll learn more about these default GPOs later in this chapter in the section titled "Working with Linked GPOs and Default Policy."

Getting Started with Group Policy

So far we've discussed what group policy does, how it works, and how to use it, but we haven't discussed the specific ways in which it can help you better manage your network.

Understanding Group Policy Settings and Options

First of all, Group Policy might not be what you think it is. If you are moving from Windows NT 4.0 environments to Windows Server 2003 environments, you should know right up front that Group Policy is not the same as Windows NT System Policy. Windows NT System Policy is very limited and quite frankly not even on the same playing field as Group Policy. If you have worked with Windows 2000 or later versions of the Windows operating system, you might have already seen some of what

Group Policy can do and not realized it, or you might have heard someone incorrectly blame Group Policy for his woes.

The simple truth is that Group Policy does what you tell it to do. You manage Group Policy by configuring policy settings. A policy setting is an individual setting that you apply, such as restricting access to the Run dialog box. Most policy settings have three basic states:

- **Enabled**   The policy setting is turned on, and its settings are active. You typically enable a policy setting to ensure that it is enforced. Once enabled, some policy settings allow you to configure additional options that fine-tune how the policy setting is applied.

- **Disabled**   The policy setting is turned off, and its settings are not applied. Typically, you disable a policy setting to ensure that it is not enforced.

- **Not Configured**   The policy setting is not being used. No settings for the policy are either active or inactive and no changes are made to the configuration settings targeted by the policy.

By themselves, these states are fairly straightforward. But some people think Group Policy is complex because these basic states can be affected by inheritance and blocking (which we touched on briefly and will discuss in detail in Chapter 3). Keep these two rules about inheritance and blocking in mind, and you'll be well on your way to success with Group Policy:

- If inherited policy settings are strictly enforced, you cannot override them—the inherited policy setting is applied regardless of the policy state set in the current GPO.

- If inherited policy settings are blocked in the current GPO and not strictly enforced, the inherited policy setting is overridden—the inherited policy setting does not apply, and only the policy setting from the current GPO is applied.

Using Group Policy for Administration

Now that you know exactly how to apply individual policy settings, let's look at the administrative areas to which you can apply Group Policy. Whether you are talking about Local Group Policy or domain-based Group Policy, the areas of administration are similar, but you can do much more with domain-based Group Policy. As mentioned previously, however, you cannot use Local Group Policy to manage any features that require Active Directory; this restriction is the primary limiting factor in what you can and cannot do with Local Group Policy.

Using Group Policy, you can manage these key administrative areas:

- **Computer and user scripts**   Configuring logon/logoff scripts for users and startup/shutdown scripts for computers.

- **Folder redirection**   Moving critical data folders for users to network shares where they can be better managed and backed up regularly (domain-based Group Policy only).

- **General computer security**   Establishing security settings for accounts, event logs, restricted groups, system services, the registry, and file systems. (With Local Group Policy, you can only manage general computer security for account policies.)

- **Local security policies**   Setting policy for auditing, user rights assignment, and user privileges.

- **Internet Explorer maintenance**   Configuring the browser interface, security, important URLs, default programs, proxies, and more.

- **IP security**   Setting IP security policy for clients, servers, and secure servers.

- **Public key security**   Setting public key policies for autoenrollment, the Encrypting File System (EFS), enterprise trusts, and more.

- **Software installation**   Automated deployment of new software and software upgrades (domain-based Group Policy only).

- **Remote Installation Services**   Setting the options available during client installation.

- **Wireless networking (IEEE 802.11)**   Setting wireless network policies for access points, clients, and preferred networks (domain-based Group Policy only).

- **Software restriction**   Restricting the software that can be deployed and used. Local Group Policy does not support user-based software restriction policies, only computer-based software restriction policies.

Through a special set of policies called Administrative Templates, you can also manage just about every aspect of the Windows graphical user interface (GUI), from menus to the desktop, the taskbar, and more. The Administrative Template policy settings affect actual registry settings, so the available policies are nearly identical whether you are working with Local Group Policy or domain-based Group Policy. You can use Administrative Templates to manage:

- **Control Panel**   Controlling access to and the options of Control Panel. You can also configure settings for Add Or Remove Programs, Display, Printers, and Regional And Language Options.

- **Desktop**   Configuring the Windows desktop, the availability and configuration of Active Desktop, and Active Directory search options from the desktop.

- **Network**   Configuring networking and network client options, including offline files, DNS clients, and network connections.

- **Printers**   Configuring printer publishing, browsing, spooling, and directory options.

- **Shared folders**   Allowing publishing of shared folders and Distributed File System (DFS) roots.

- **Start menu and taskbar**   Configuring the Start menu and taskbar, primarily by removing or hiding items and options.

- **System**   Configuring policies related to general system settings, disk quotas, user profiles, logon, power management, system restore, error reporting, and more.

- **Windows components**   Configuring whether and how to use various Windows components, such as Event Viewer, Task Scheduler, and Windows Updates.

Understanding the Required Infrastructure for Group Policy

Local Group Policy is available on any computer running Windows 2000, Windows XP Professional, or Windows Server 2003. Domain-based Group Policy is available only if your network is running Active Directory. Because Active Directory in turn relies on TCP/IP and Domain Name System (DNS), you must implement TCP/IP networking, DNS, and Active Directory to use domain-based Group Policy.

DNS and Active Directory

DNS provides the naming context that allows one computer to find another computer. It is an Internet Engineering Task Force (IETF) standard name service that is described in detail in RFC 1034 and RFC 1035. DNS is installed automatically with TCP/IP on workstations and servers, and it provides for several types of forward lookup queries that allow a computer to resolve a host name to an IP address and reverse lookup queries that allow a computer to resolve an IP address to a host name.

Active Directory provides essential directory services for the domain and the many features that enable advanced controls through Group Policy. The primary communications protocol for Active Directory is Lightweight Directory Access Protocol (LDAP). LDAP is an industry-standard protocol for directory access that runs over TCP/IP. Clients can use LDAP to query and manage directory information, in accordance with the level of access they've been granted. Other communications protocols are supported as well, including the REPL interface, which is used for replication; Messaging Application Programming Interface (MAPI), which is used for older messaging clients; and Security Accounts Manager (SAM) interface, which allows Windows NT 4.0 clients to access Active Directory in a limited way. Together, these interfaces allow:

- Communication with LDAP, Active Directory Services Interface (ADSI), and newer Outlook clients for the purposes of authentication, access control, directory queries, and directory management

- Replication with other directory servers for the purposes of distributing directory changes to other domain controllers

- Communication with older (MAPI) Outlook clients, primarily for address book lookups

- Communication with Windows NT 4.0 clients for the purposes of authentication and access control

By using DNS with Active Directory, you can establish directory structures that give very specific naming contexts. Objects within the directory are logically grouped by domain. This makes the domain one of the basic building blocks in Active Directory. Two additional building blocks are sites and OUs, which we previously introduced.

Active Directory has very specific rules when it comes to domains, sites, and OUs. Every workstation or server on a network must be a member of a domain and be located in a site. A workstation or server can belong to only one domain and one site. OUs, on the other hand, are defined within domains and can be thought of as containers for subsets of a domain. For example, you might have Engineering, Marketing, Sales, and Support OUs within your domain. Like domains, OUs can be organized into a hierarchy. For example, you might have Printer Sales and Computer Sales OUs within your Sales OU.

> **Note**   With Windows NT, you often created additional domains to create clear separation between users, computers, and resources or to delegate administrator privileges while limiting administrative access. You can use Active Directory OUs for similar purposes—without the need to establish additional (and more complex) domain structures. Another reason for creating additional domains in NT was to reduce traffic between network segments, and this is where Active Directory sites come into the picture. You can use sites to gain better control over communications between network segments.

Applying Active Directory Structure to Inheritance

When you include the local computer within the basic structures we've discussed, a typical Active Directory network will have four distinct levels:

- Local computer
- Site
- Domain
- OU

When Group Policy is set at the local computer level, everyone who logs on to the local machine is affected by the policy settings (Local Group Policy). Domain-based

Group Policy is set within the actual directory structure, and Active Directory–based policy settings are applied in this basic order: site, domain, OU.

This structure is thought of as having four tiers. The top tier is the Local Group Policy, the second tier is the site, the third tier is the domain, and the fourth tier is the OU. OUs can be nested within each other, so you can create additional levels in the hierarchy as needed. By default, when policy is set at one level, the setting applies to all objects at that level and all objects in the levels below, via inheritance.

The inheritance of policy settings works as follows (unless inheritance is blocked):

- If a policy setting is applied at the site level, it affects all users and computers defined within domains and OUs that are part of the site. For example, if Main Site contains the tech.cpandl.com and sales.cpandl.com domains, any setting applied to the site will affect objects in both domains.

- If a policy setting is applied at the domain level, it affects all users and computers defined within OUs that are part of the domain. For example, if the tech.cpandl.com domain contains the Engineering and IT OUs, any setting applied to the tech.cpandl.com domain will affect objects in the Engineering and IT OUs.

- If a policy setting is applied at the OU level, it affects all users and computers defined within the OU as well as other OUs beneath it (child OUs). For example, if the Engineering OU contains the WebTeam and DevTeam child OUs, any setting applied to the Engineering OU will affect the WebTeam and DevTeam OUs.

Examining GPO Links and Default GPOs

Before you can move on to more advanced Group Policy topics, you must understand two fundamental concepts: GPO links and default GPOs. GPO links affect the way policy is applied. Default GPOs are special-purpose policy objects that Active Directory depends on to establish baseline security settings for domain controllers and domains.

Understanding GPO Links

As you know, the two types of Group Policy are Local Group Policy and Active Directory–based Group Policy. Local Group Policy applies to a local machine only, and there is only one Local GPO (LGPO) per local machine. Active Directory–based Group Policy, on the other hand, can be implemented at the site, domain, and OU levels, and each site, domain, or OU can have one or more GPOs associated with it. The association between a GPO and a site, domain, or OU is referred to as a *link*. For example, if a GPO is associated with a domain, the GPO is said to be linked to that domain.

All GPOs you create in Active Directory are stored in a container called Group Policy Objects. This container is replicated to all domain controllers in a domain, so by default all GPOs are also replicated to all domain controllers in a domain. The link (association) between a domain, site, or OU is what makes a GPO active and applicable to that domain, site, or OU.

Linking can be applied in two ways:

■ You can link a GPO to multiple levels in Active Directory. For example, a GPO can be linked to a site, a domain, and multiple OUs. In this case, the GPO applies to each of these levels within Active Directory.

■ You can link a GPO to a specific site, domain, or OU. For example, if a GPO is linked to a domain, the GPO applies to users and computers in that domain.

> **Tip**   When you work with GPOs, never forget about inheritance and its effects. In the two examples above, the linked GPO would also be inherited by lower-level objects because of inheritance. For example, the settings of the GPO linked to a domain would be inherited by any OUs in that domain. The reason for linking a GPO to multiple levels within Active Directory, then, is to create direct associations between a GPO and multiple sites, domains, or OUs or any combinations of sites, domains, and OUs.

> **Tip**   For more information on GPO linking and inheritance, see Chapter 3.

You can also unlink a GPO from a site, domain, or OU. This removes the direct association between the GPO and the level within Active Directory from which you've removed the link. For example, if a GPO is linked to a site called First Site and also to the cpandl.com domain, you can remove the link from the cpandl.com domain. Unlinking the GPO from the domain removes the association between the GPO and the domain. The GPO is then linked only to the site. If you later remove the link between the site and the GPO, the GPO is completely unlinked. A GPO that has been unlinked from all levels within Active Directory still exists within the Group Policy Objects container, but it is completely inactive.

Working with Linked GPOs and Default Policy

Several tools are available for working with Group Policy. The interfaces for these tools are very similar. When you want to work with security settings in Local Group Policy (for example, the Computer Configuration\Security Settings portion), you can use the Local Security Policy tool (which you can access by clicking Start, Programs or All Programs, Administrative Tools, and then Local Security Policy). When you want full access to Local Group Policy or want to work with Active Directory–based Group Policy, you can use the Group Policy Object Editor, which is included with a standard installation of Windows Server 2003, or the Group Policy Management Console (GPMC), which is available as a free download from the Microsoft Download Center (*http://www.microsoft.com/downloads*).

When you create a domain, two GPOs are created by default:

- **Default Domain Controllers Policy GPO**   A default GPO created for and linked to the Domain Controllers OU that is applicable to all domain controllers in a domain (as long as they aren't moved from this OU). This GPO is used to manage security settings for domain controllers in a domain.

- **Default Domain Policy GPO**   A default GPO created for and linked to the domain within Active Directory. This GPO is used to establish baselines for a wide variety of policy settings that apply to all users and computers in a domain.

Whether you are working with the Group Policy Object Editor or the GPMC, you'll have access to the linked Default Domain Policy GPO. For example, in GPMC, you simply select the Default Domain Policy node in the console root. The Default Domain Controllers Policy GPO, on the other hand, is accessed separately. On a domain controller, you can access the security settings for the Default Domain Controllers Policy GPO (for example, the Computer Configuration\Security Settings portion) by using the Domain Controller Security Policy console. (Click Start, Programs or All Programs, Administrative Tools, and then Domain Controller Security Policy.) If you want full access to the Default Domain Controllers Policy GPO, you can use Group Policy Object Editor or GPMC.

The default GPOs are essential to the proper operation and processing of Group Policy. By default, the Default Domain Controllers Policy GPO has the highest precedence among GPOs linked to the Domain Controllers OU, and the Default Domain Policy GPO has the highest precedence among GPOs linked to the domain. As you'll learn in the sections that follow, the purpose and use of each default GPO is a bit different.

Tip   The Default GPOs are so important for proper Group Policy operation that Microsoft created a recovery utility called DCGPOFIX that lets you easily restore the Default Domain Policy GPO, the Default Domain Controllers Policy GPO, or both. Simply run *DCGPOFIX fix* from the command line with the following options:

- */Target:Domain*   To restore the Default Domain Policy GPO
- */Target:DC*   To restore the Default Domain Controllers Policy GPO
- */Target:Both*   To restore the Default Domain Policy GPO and the Default Domain Controllers Policy GPO

> **More Info**   For more information on DCGPOFIX, see Chapters 16 and 17.

Working with the Default Domain Policy GPO

Under Windows 2000 or later, you create a domain by establishing the first domain controller in that domain. This typically means logging on to a standalone server as a local administrator, running DCPROMO, and then specifying that you want to establish a new forest or domain. When you establish the domain and the domain controller, the Default Domain Controllers Policy GPO and the Default Domain Policy GPO are created at the same time. The Default Domain Controllers Policy GPO is linked to the Domain Controllers OU, which is also automatically created for the new domain. The Default Domain Policy GPO is linked to the domain.

The Default Domain Policy GPO is a complete policy set that includes settings for managing the many policy areas we've discussed previously, but it isn't meant for general management of Group Policy. As a best practice, you should edit the Default Domain Policy GPO only to manage the default Account Policies settings and three specific areas of Account Policies:

- **Password Policy**   Determines default password policies for domain controllers, such as password history and minimum password length settings

- **Account Lockout Policy**   Determines default account lockout policies for domain controllers, such as account lockout duration and account lockout threshold

- **Kerberos Policy**   Determines default Kerberos policies for domain controllers, such as maximum tolerance for computer clock synchronization

To manage other areas of policy, you should create a new GPO and link it to the domain or an appropriate OU within the domain.

> **Note**   Wondering why configuring policy in this way is a recommended best practice? Well, there are two reasons. First, if Group Policy becomes corrupted and stops working, you can use DCGPOFIX to restore the Default Domain Policy GPO to its original state (which would mean that you would lose all the customized settings you've applied to this GPO). Second, some policy settings can only be configured at the domain level and configuring them in the Default Domain Policy GPO makes the most sense. However, no specific restrictions require you to follow this practice.

You can access the Default Domain Policy GPO in several ways. If you are using the GPMC, you'll see the Default Domain Policy GPO when you click the domain name in the console tree. Then right-click the Default Domain Policy node and select Edit to get full access to the Default Domain Policy GPO. If you want to work only with security settings in the Default Domain Policy GPO, you can use the Domain Security Policy console. In this case, follow these steps:

1. Log on to a domain controller as a Domain Administrator.

2. Access the Domain Security Policy console by clicking Start, Programs or All Programs, Administrative Tools, and then Domain Security Policy.

3. Any setting changes you make affect the entire domain.

> **Note**   Account Policies should be configured in the highest precedence GPO linked to a domain. By default, the highest precedence GPO linked to a domain is the Default Domain Policy GPO, and this is why most documentation tells you to configure Account Policies in the Default Domain Policy GPO. While this is a good practice, the bottom line is this: If you define Account Policies in multiple GPOs linked to a domain, the settings will be merged according to the link order of these GPOs. The GPO with a link order of 1 will always have the highest precedence.

Four policies are exceptions to the rule that the Default Domain Policy GPO (or the highest precedence GPO linked to the domain) is used only to manage Account Policies. These policies (located in Group Policy under Computer Configuration\Windows Settings\Security Settings\Local Policies\Security Options) are as follows:

- **Accounts: Rename Administrator Account**   Renames the built-in Administrator account on all computers throughout the domain and sets a new name for the account so that it is better protected from malicious users. Note that this policy affects the logon name of the account, not the display name. The display name remains Administrator or whatever you set it to. If an administrator changes the logon name for this account through Active Directory Users And Computers, it automatically reverts to what is specified in this policy setting the next time Group Policy is refreshed.

- **Accounts: Rename Guest Account**   Renames the built-in Guest account on all computers throughout the domain and sets a new name for the built-in Guest account so that it is better protected from malicious users. Note that this policy affects the logon name of the account, not the display name. The display name remains Guest or whatever else you set it to. If an administrator changes the logon name for this account through Active Directory Users And Computers, it automatically reverts to what is specified in this policy setting the next time Group Policy is refreshed.

- **Network Security: Force Logoff When Logon Hours Expire**   Forces users to log off from the domain when logon hours expire. For example, if you set the logon hours as 8 AM to 6 PM for the user, the user is forced to log off at 6 PM.

- **Network Access: Allow Anonymous SID/Name Translation**   Determines whether an anonymous user can request security identifier (SID) attributes for another user. If this setting is enabled, a malicious user could use the well-known Administrators SID to obtain the real name of the built-in Administrator account, even if the account has been renamed. If this setting is disabled, computers and applications running in pre–Windows 2000 domains may not be able to communicate with Windows Server 2003 domains. This communication issue specifically applies to Windows NT 4.0–based Remote Access Service servers, Microsoft SQL Servers that are running on Windows NT 3.x–based or on Windows NT 4.0–based computers, Remote Access Services that are running on Windows 2000–based computers that are located in Windows NT 3.x domains or in Windows NT 4.0 domains, SQL Servers that are running on Windows 2000–based computers that are located in Windows NT 3.x domains or in Windows NT 4.0 domains, and users in a Windows NT 4.0 resource domain who want to grant permissions to access files, shared folders, and registry objects to user accounts from account domains that contain Windows Server 2003 domain controllers.

You typically manage these four policy settings through the GPO that is linked to the domain level and has the highest precedence. As with Account Policies, this is the Default Domain Policy GPO by default.

Working with the Default Domain Controllers Policy GPO

Under Windows 2000 or later, you establish a domain controller by running DCPROMO and promoting a member server to domain controller status. When you do this, the server's computer object is moved to the Domain Controllers OU. As long as domain controllers remain in this Domain Controllers OU, they are affected by the Default Domain Controllers Policy GPO.

The Default Domain Controllers Policy GPO is designed to ensure that all domain controllers in a specified domain have the same security settings. This is important because all domain controllers in an Active Directory domain are equal, and if they were to have different security settings, they might behave differently and this would be bad, bad, bad. If one domain controller has a specific policy setting, this policy setting should be applied to all domain controllers to ensure consistent behavior across a domain.

> **Caution**   Moving a domain controller out of the Domain Controllers OU can adversely affect domain management. It can also lead to inconsistent behavior during logon and authentication. If you move a domain controller out of the Domain Controllers OU, you should carefully manage its security settings thereafter. For example, if you make security changes to the Default Domain Controllers Policy GPO, you should ensure that those security changes are applied to domain controllers stored in OUs other than the Domain Controllers OU.

You can access the Default Domain Controllers Policy GPO in several ways. If you are using the GPMC, you'll see the Default Domain Controllers Policy GPO when you click the Domain Controllers node in the console tree. Then right-click the Default Domain Controllers Policy and select Edit to get full access to the Default Domain Controllers Policy GPO. If you want to work only with security settings in the Default Domain Policy GPO, you can use the Domain Security Policy console. In this case, follow these steps:

1. Log on to a domain controller as a Domain Administrator.

2. Access the Domain Controller Security Policy console by clicking Start, Programs or All Programs, Administrative Tools, and then Domain Controller Security Policy.

3. You can now manage security settings for domain controllers. Any changes you make to settings will affect all domain controllers in the domain.

Because all domain controllers are placed in the Domain Controllers OU by default, any security setting changes you make will apply to all domain controllers by default. The key security areas that you should manage consistently include:

- Local Policies:

    - **Audit Policy**   Determines default auditing policies for domain controllers, such as logging event success, failure, or both

    - **User Rights Assignment**   Determines default user rights assignment for domain controllers, such as the Log On As Service and Allow Log On Locally rights

    - **Security Options**   These include the Domain Controller: Allow Server Operators To Schedule Tasks option

- Event log settings such as

    - Maximum log size for domain controllers

    - Preventing guest access of domain controller logs

    - Whether logs are retained and the retention method used

 Note   Microsoft recommends that you edit the Default Domain Controllers Policy GPO only to set user rights and audit policies—not to make any other changes. If something happens to this GPO, you can use DCGPOFIX to restore the default GPO.

Summary

Group Policy provides an effective and efficient way to manage computer and user settings. The real power of Group Policy is that you can manage settings for hundreds or thousands of users and computers as easily as you can manage settings for a single user or computer. Group Policy makes this possible by providing the necessary structures to seamlessly manage user and computer settings anywhere in the enterprise.

It is important to understand how Group Policy works in different environments. Regardless of whether you work with computers in workgroups, domains, or a combination of the two, you can use Group Policy to efficiently manage settings. There are, however, advantages to using Group Policy in a domain setting. Specifically, in Active Directory domains, Group Policy is extended to help you better manage computer security, wireless networking, software installation, and remote installation services.

Chapter 2
Working with Group Policy

In this chapter:

Navigating Group Policy Objects and Settings. 22
Managing Group Policy Objects 28
Creating and Linking GPOs 39
Delegating Privileges for Group Policy Management. 45
Removing Links and Deleting GPOs. 51
Summary 52

As you saw in the previous chapter, Group Policy is quite complex, with many structures that work together to ensure its proper operation. Not only does Group Policy
exist physically on disk, it also is represented logically in Microsoft® Active Directory®
directory service. Whether you are implementing Group Policy for the first time or are
planning to modify existing Group Policy, the techniques to use are the same. You
start by gathering information about settings and existing policy, and then you determine the steps needed to get Group Policy to work the way you want. This usually
means finding the policy settings you want to change and then making the changes.
Sometimes this also means modifying Group Policy behavior. For example, you might
need to modify the way Group Policy is processed or the way inheritance is applied.

Related Information

- For more information about Group Policy processing on clients and the physical
  structure of Group Policy on disk, see Chapter 13.

- For more information about managing Group Policy, see Chapter 3.

- For more information about automation and scripting Group Policy, see
  Appendix C.

Navigating Group Policy Objects and Settings

When you want to work with Group Policy Objects (GPOs) and settings, you use one of the two Group Policy management tools: the Group Policy Object Editor or the Group Policy Management Console (GPMC). Group Policy Object Editor is included with a standard Microsoft Windows Server™ 2003 installation. The GPMC is a free add-on that you can download from Microsoft at *www.microsoft.com/downloads/*. Whichever tool you use, the basic Group Policy management tasks of viewing, creating, editing, and linking GPOs are essentially the same. But beyond the basics, the tools are dramatically different. The GPMC has many advanced capabilities and features that aren't available in the Group Policy Object Editor. These advanced features make the GPMC the tool of choice for working with Group Policy.

Note   Our discussion of Group Policy management focuses on the GPMC rather than the Group Policy Object Editor. This chapter examines techniques for managing Group Policy in general and the behavior of Group Policy. Chapter 3 continues the discussion of the GPMC with a look at advanced techniques, including GPO backup and recovery, GPO copying and importing, and GPO modeling.

Tip   When you install the GPMC on a computer, options for managing Group Policy through the standard Microsoft Windows® interface are configured to access the GPMC rather than the Group Policy Object Editor. GPMC still uses Group Policy Object Editor as its editing tool when you are actually editing GPOs.

Connecting to and Working with GPOs

When you use the Group Policy Object Editor or the GPMC to work with GPOs, by default the corresponding changes are made on the domain controller that is acting as the primary domain controller (PDC) emulator. In this way, the PDC emulator is the central point of contact for GPO creation, modification, and deletion. Active Directory manages policy settings in this way to ensure that changes to the GPO structure can be implemented only on a single authoritative domain controller and that only one administrator at a time is granted access to a particular GPO. Because the PDC emulator role is specified at the domain level, there is only one PDC emulator in a domain and therefore only one place where policy settings are changed by default. If the PDC emulator is unavailable when you are trying to work with policy settings, you get a prompt that enables you to work with policy settings on the domain controller to which you are connected or on any available domain controller.

Any user who is a member of the Domain Admins or Enterprise Admins group can view and work with Active Directory–based Group Policy. Unlike Local Group Policy, which uses one LGPO per machine, Active Directory–based Group Policy can use multiple GPOs per site, domain, or organizational unit (OU). With Active Directory–based

Group Policy, GPO creation and linking are separate operations. First you create a GPO and define a group of policy settings to achieve desired results. Then you apply your GPO and make it "live" by linking it to the container or containers within Active Directory where it will be applied.

Although creating and linking GPOs are two distinct operations, the Group Policy management tools do allow you to create GPOs and simultaneously link them to a level within the directory. This means you have two options for creating and linking GPOs:

- Create a GPO and then later link it to a container or containers within the directory.

- Create a GPO and simultaneously link it to a container or containers within the directory.

Remember that it is the link that tells Active Directory to apply the settings specified by the GPO. For example, you can create a GPO called Main ADATUM.COM Domain Policy and then link it to the domain container for cpandl.com. To understand what settings will be applied when and to which users and computers throughout a domain, you need a strong understanding of inheritance and policy processing. According to the default (standard) inheritance and policy processing rules, once you link a GPO to a container, the related policy settings are applied to that container, and lower-level containers within the directory can also inherit the settings. This means that a linked GPO can affect every user and computer throughout the enterprise—or some subset of users and computers throughout the enterprise.

Applying Group Policy and Using Resultant Set of Policy

When GPOs are applied to users and computers, their effects are cumulative. These cumulative effects (the end result of inheritance and processing) on an individual computer or user are referred to as the Resultant Set of Policy (RSoP). When you work with Group Policy, you often must determine the RSoP for a particular user or group in order to troubleshoot and resolve problems. The GPMC also lets you be proactive by modeling the effects of GPOs before you deploy them. You can then determine the RSoP on a particular computer or user before deciding whether to deploy a specific GPO. For more information on modeling GPOs, see the section in Chapter 3 titled "Modeling and Maintaining Group Policy."

Within Active Directory, objects are organized using a hierarchical tree structure called a *directory tree*. The structure of the tree is derived from the schema and is used to define the parent-child relationships of objects stored in the directory. Figure 2-1 shows a representation of a directory tree for a domain. The domain object is the parent object of all objects in a domain; as such, it is at the root of the directory tree. The domain object in turn contains other objects, including other container objects such as subdomains or OUs and standard objects such as users, computers, and printers. In the figure, us.adatum.com is a subdomain of adatum.com, and this subdomain has two top-level OUs: Sales and Services.

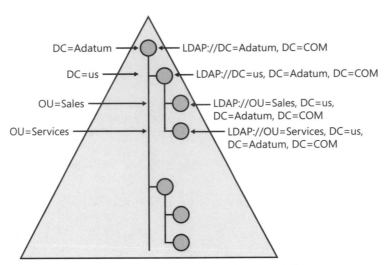

Figure 2-1   The adatum.com domain and its related directory tree

Active Directory uses Lightweight Directory Access Protocol (LDAP) for querying and managing objects in the directory. You can locate any object in the directory according to its LDAP path. The LDAP path to the Sales OU in the us.adatum.com domain is LDAP://OU=Sales,DC=us,DC=Adatum,DC=COM. Here *LDAP://* specifies that you are using LDAP, and *OU=Sales,DC=us,DC=Adatum,DC=COM* is the exact location of the Sales OU in the directory. Each component of the object's name is broken down into its component parts. (OU stands for organizational unit, and DC stands for domain component.) The exact path to an object, excluding the protocol designator, is the object's Distinguished Name (DN).

Objects in the directory also have a relative name, referred to as the Relative Distin-guished Name (RDN). The RDN includes only the name component of the object. For example, the RDN of the Sales OU is OU=Sales. Within the Sales OU, you might have a user, John, and a computer, JohnsPC. The RDN of these objects would be CN=John and CN=JohnsPC, respectively. (Here, CN stands for Common Name, and the DNs of these objects would be CN=John, OU=Sales,DC=us,DC=Adatum,DC=COM, and CN=JohnsPC,OU=Sales,DC=us,DC=Adatum,DC=COM, respectively.)

As you can see, the DN indicates an object's place within the directory. Not only does the DN tell you the exact containers in which the object is stored, but it also tells you the relationship of those containers to each other. The relationship of container objects is extremely important when it comes to applying Group Policy. When you know where an object is in the directory tree and in which container object it resides, you can determine most of the GPOs that would be applied to the object (in most instances). For example, JohnsPC would be affected by the following GPOs (and in the following order):

1. The local machine GPO for John's computer

2. The GPO for the adatum.com domain (if inheritance to child domains is enforced)

3. The GPO for the us.adatum.com subdomain

4. The GPO for the Sales OU

Note When you work with domains and OUs, it is important to remember that inheritance works differently within and between domains. Within a domain, top-level GPOs are inherited automatically by lower-level GPOs. The domain GPO is automatically inherited by OUs. The domain GPO and the GPO of a top-level OU are inherited by a second-level OU, and so on. Between domains, inheritance is *not* automatic, even for parent-to-child relationships. This means a child domain does not automatically inherit the GPO of the parent domain.

Caution Microsoft recommends that you avoid assigning Group Policy objects across domains. If Group Policy is obtained from another domain, the processing of Group Policy objects slows the startup and logon processes. Inheritance to child domains is rarely enforced.

The directory path tells you about most of the containers that might have GPOs that will affect a user or computer, but not all of them. One important piece is missing, and it has to do with sites. Figure 2-2 shows a deeper view of the us.adatum.com domain and the objects within it. As you can see, this domain has two sites associated with it:

- **Seattle Site** This site has two OUs—Sales and Support—and several resources that are physically located within it. Sales, a top-level OU, has two computer objects and one user object associated with it. Support, a child OU of Sales, has one computer object and one user object associated with it. CorpSvr01 is a domain controller. JohnsPC and EdsPC are workstations.

- **NY Site** This site has one OU, Services, and several resources physically located within it. Services, a top-level OU with no child OUs, has three computer objects and two user objects associated with it. CorpSvr02 is a domain controller. BethsPC and MikesPC are workstations.

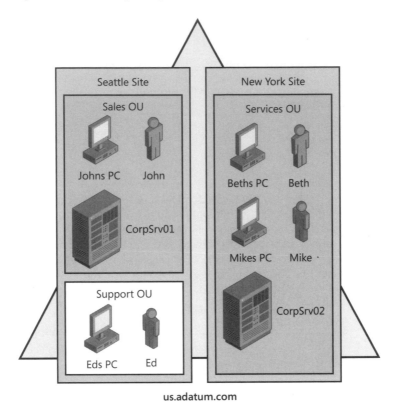

Figure 2-2   An example of objects within the us.adatum.com domain

Based on this diagram, you know exactly which objects are stored in the directory and in which containers. You also know which sites are associated with which objects, and this gives you the complete picture of which GPOs will be applied to which objects. Additionally, for this example and the examples that follow, there is no forced inheritance from the parent domain adatum.com to the child domain us.adatum.com. Since you know that computers and users are also affected by a local machine GPO (the LGPO), you now know that JohnsPC would be affected by the following GPOs (and in the following order):

1. The local machine GPO for the computer

2. The GPO for the Seattle Site

3. The GPO for the us.adatum.com subdomain

4. The GPO for the Sales OU

The user, John, would also be affected by the same GPOs, which would be applied in the same order to set permitted actions and limitations on his account.

RSoP Walkthrough

As you've seen, you can determine the complete picture for the accumulated set of GPOs that would be applied to any user or computer object in a domain by following the directory tree to see which domains, OUs, and sites (if any) would be applied and thereby determine the RSoP for a user or computer. Going back to the previous example and excluding the LGPO, you can determine that the GPOs have the following effects on computers and users:

- **At the site level:**
  - ❑ Seattle Site affects JohnsPC, John, CorpSvr01, EdsPC, and Ed.
  - ❑ NY Site affects BethsPC, Beth, MikesPC, Mike, and CorpSvr02.

- **At the domain level:**
  - ❑ us.adatum.com affects JohnsPC, John, CorpSvr01, EdsPC, Ed, BethsPC, Beth, MikesPC, Mike, and CorpSvr02.

- **At the OU level:**
  - ❑ Sales OU affects JohnsPC, John, and CorpSvr01.
  - ❑ Support OU affects EdsPC and Ed.
  - ❑ Services OU affects BethsPC, Beth, MikesPC, Mike, and CorpSvr02.

Another way to express this is to say that the RSoP for these objects is as follows (excluding LGPOs):

- **John**   The RSoP for John flows from Seattle Site to us.adatum.com and then Sales OU.
- **JohnsPC**   The RSoP for JohnsPC flows from Seattle Site to us.adatum.com and then Sales OU.
- **CorpSvr01**   The RSoP for CorpSvr01 flows from Seattle Site to us.adatum.com and then Sales OU.
- **Beth**   The RSoP for Beth flows from NY Site to us.adatum.com and then Services OU.
- **BethsPC**   The RSoP for BethsPC flows from NY Site to us.adatum.com and then Services OU.
- **Mike**   The RSoP for Mike flows from NY Site to us.adatum.com and then Services OU.
- **MikesPC**   The RSoP for MikesPC flows from NY Site to us.adatum.com and then Services OU.
- **CorpSvr02**   The RSoP for CorpSvr02 flows from NY Site to us.adatum.com and then Services OU.

- **Ed**   The RSoP for Ed flows from Seattle Site to us.adatum.com, Sales OU, and then Support OU.

- **EdsPC**   The RSoP for EdsPC flows from Seattle Site to us.adatum.com, Sales OU, and then Support OU.

When you look at RSoP, it's also important to consider what will happen if you move the furniture around a bit—for example, if Beth visits the Seattle office and logs on to JohnsPC or if Ed from Support goes to New York and logs on to MikesPC. Here is what happens with regard to Group Policy:

- **Beth in Seattle logging on to JohnsPC**   JohnsPC is subject to the Computer Configuration settings in the GPOs for Seattle Site, us.adatum.com, and the Sales OU. Beth (logging on to JohnsPC while in Seattle) is subject to the User Configuration settings in the GPOs for NY Site, us.adatum.com, and the Services OU. By default, the User Configuration settings in the GPOs that apply to Beth have precedence.

- **Ed in New York logging on to MikesPC**   MikesPC is subject to the Computer Configuration settings in the GPOs for NY Site, us.adatum.com, and the Services OU. Ed (logging on to MikesPC while in New York) is subject to the User Configuration settings in the GPOs for Seattle Site, us.adatum.com, Sales OU, and the Support OU. By default, the User Configuration settings in the GPOs that apply to Ed have precedence.

- **Moving CorpSvr01 into the Support OU**   CorpSvr01 (when it is moved into the Support OU) is subject to the GPOs for Seattle Site, us.adatum.com, Sales OU, and the Support OU. By default, the policy settings for the Support OU have precedence.

Managing Group Policy Objects

Group Policy applies only to users and computers. Group Policy settings are divided into two categories: Computer Configuration, which contains settings that apply to computers, and User Configuration, which contains settings that apply to user accounts. Each category can be divided further into three major classes of settings, each of which contains several subclasses of settings:

- **Software Settings**   For automated deployment of new software and software upgrades. Also used for uninstalling software.

- **Windows Settings**   For managing key Windows settings for both computers and users, including scripts and security. For users, you can also manage Remote Installation Services, Folder Redirection, and Microsoft Internet Explorer maintenance.

- **Administrative Templates** For managing registry settings that configure the operating system, Windows components, and applications. Administrative templates are implemented for specific operating system versions.

The Group Policy management tools provide access to these three top-level classes of settings and make use of a number of extensions that provide the functionality necessary to configure Group Policy settings. As we discussed previously, there are two types of Group Policy: Local Group Policy and Active Directory–based Group Policy. Local Group Policy applies to the local machine only, and there is only one local GPO per local machine. Active Directory–based Group Policy, on the other hand, can be implemented separately for sites, domains, and OUs. When you want to work with Group Policy, you can do so at the local machine level using the Local Security Policy tool or within Active Directory using the GPMC. The sections that follow examine the key techniques you'll use to access GPOs with these tools and to manage policy settings.

> **Note** You manage the Group Policy settings for domain controllers using the Domain Controller Security Policy tool (as long as the domain controllers are part of the Domain Controllers OU). For more information on managing Group Policy for domain controllers and the Domain Controller Security Policy tool, see the section in Chapter 1 titled "Working with Linked GPOs and Default Policy."

Managing Local Group Policy

To work with Local Group Policy, you must use an administrator account. In a domain, you can use an account that is a member of the Enterprise Admins, Domain Admins, or the Administrators domain local group. In a workgroup, you must use an account that is a member of the local Administrators group.

Accessing Local Group Policy on the Local Computer

You can access Local Group Policy in several ways. The fastest way is to type the following command at the command prompt:

```
gpedit.msc /gpcomputer:"%computername%"
```

This command starts the Group Policy Object Editor in an MMC and tells the Group Policy Object Editor to target the local computer. Here, *%ComputerName%* is an environment variable that sets the name of the local computer and must be enclosed in double quotation marks as shown. You can also access Local Group Policy in the Group Policy Object Editor snap-in by completing the following steps:

1. Click Start, Run. In the Run dialog box, type **mmc** in the Open field, and then click OK.

2. Choose Add/Remove Snap-In from the File menu in the main window. In the Add/Remove Snap-In dialog box, click Add.

3. In the Add Standalone Snap-In dialog box, click Group Policy Object Editor, and then choose Add. This starts the Group Policy Wizard.

4. The Select Group Policy Object page is displayed with the Local Computer selected as the Group Policy Object target. Click Finish.

5. In the Add Standalone Snap-In dialog box, click Close. Then, in the Add/Remove Snap-In dialog box, click OK.

If you want to work only with security settings in Local Group Policy, you can use the Local Security Policy console, shown in Figure 2-3. Click Start, Programs or All Programs, Administrative Tools, and then select Local Security Policy.

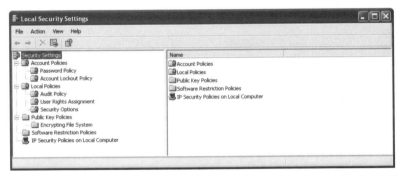

Figure 2-3   Accessing Local Group Policy using the Local Security Policy tool

In Group Policy Object Editor and Local Security Policy, you can configure security settings that apply to users and the local computer itself. Any policy changes you make are applied to that computer the next time Group Policy is refreshed. The settings you can manage locally depend on whether the computer is a member of a domain or a workgroup, and they include the following:

■ Account policies for passwords, account lockout, and Kerberos

■ Local policies for auditing, user rights assignment, and security options

■ Event logging options for configuring log size, access, and retention options for the application, system, and security logs

■ Security restriction settings for groups, system services, registry keys, and the file system

■ Security settings for wireless networking, public keys, and Internet Protocol Security (IPSec)

■ Software restrictions that specify applications that aren't allowed to run on the computer

You configure Local Group Policy in the same way that you configure Active Directory–based group policy. To apply a policy, you enable it and then configure any additional or optional values as necessary. An enabled policy setting is turned on and active. If don't want a policy to apply, you must disable it. A disabled policy setting is turned off and inactive. The enforcement or blocking of inheritance can change this behavior, as detailed in the section titled "Managing Group Policy Inheritance" in Chapter 3.

Accessing Local Group Policy on a Remote Machine

Often you'll want to access Local Group Policy on a remote machine. For example, if you are logged on to EdsPC, you might want to see how Group Policy is configured locally on JohnsPC. To access Local Group Policy on another computer, you use the Group Policy Object Editor snap-in.

One way to do this is to type the following command at the command prompt:

```
gpedit.msc /gpcomputer:"RemoteComputer"
```

where *RemoteComputer* is the host name or fully qualified DNS name of the remote computer. The remote computer name must be enclosed in double quotation marks, such as:

```
gpedit.msc /gpcomputer:"corpsvr04"
```

or

```
gpedit.msc /gpcomputer:"corpsvr04.adatum.com"
```

You can also access Local Group Policy on a remote computer by completing the following steps:

1. Click Start, Run. In the Run dialog box, type **mmc** in the Open field, and then click OK.

2. Choose Add/Remove Snap-In from the File menu in the main window. In the Add/Remove Snap-In dialog box, click Add.

3. In the Add Standalone Snap-In dialog box, click Group Policy Object Editor, and then choose Add. This starts the Group Policy Wizard.

4. The Select Group Policy Object page is displayed. Click Browse.

5. In the Browse For A Group Policy Object dialog box, click the Computers tab, select Another Computer, and then click Browse again.

6. In the Select Computer dialog box, type the name of the computer whose local group policy you want to access, and click Check Names. When you have the right computer, click OK twice and then click Finish.

7. In the Add Standalone Snap-In dialog box, click Close. Then, in the Add/ Remove Snap-In dialog box, click OK.

8. Repeat steps 2 through 7 as necessary to add other local computers whose policy you want to manage remotely. When you are finished, click File, Save As, and then use the Save As dialog box to save your custom MMC.

As Figure 2-4 shows, when you work with Local Group Policy through the Group Policy Object Editor snap-in, the nodes of the console root reflect the computers to which you are connected. In this example, the MMC is connected to a remote computer, CORPSVR04, and the local computer.

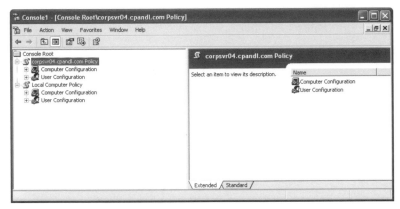

Figure 2-4   Accessing Local Group Policy using the Group Policy Object Editor snap-in

Managing Active Directory–Based Group Policy

The best way to manage Active Directory–based Group Policy is with the GPMC, which you must download and install. You can use the GPMC to manage policy settings in accordance with your administrative privileges. The account you use must be a member of the Enterprise Admins or Domain Admins group or must have been delegated permissions to work with specific aspects of Group Policy. When you work with the Enterprise Admins and Domain Admins groups, keep the following in mind:

■ Members of Enterprise Admins can manage policy settings for the specific forest of which they are a member. For example, if the user account WilliamS is a member of the Enterprise Admins group in the cpandl.com forest, WilliamS can manage the policy settings for any child domain in the cpandl.com domain as well as the parent domain (cpandl.com). This means he can manage the policy settings for tech.cpandl.com, cs.cpandl.com, and cpandl.com.

■ Members of Domain Admins can manage policy settings for the specific domain of which they are a member. For example, if the user account WilliamS is a member of the Domain Admins group in the tech.cpandl.com domain, WilliamS can manage the policy settings for the tech.cpandl.com domain. He cannot manage policy settings for cs.cpandl.com or cpandl.com. He can manage the policy settings for other domains only if he has Domain Admins privileges in those domains (or Enterprise Admins privileges for the forest).

When you work with delegated administrative permissions, keep in mind that the account has only the specific permissions that were delegated. Delegated permissions for Group Policy include permission to manage Group Policy links, generate RSoP for the purposes of logging, and generate RSoP for planning purposes. The sections that follow discuss how to install and use the GPMC. You'll learn techniques for delegating administration later in the chapter in the section titled "Delegating Privileges for Group Policy Management."

Installing the GPMC

The GPMC provides an integrated interface for working with policy settings. You can install this console on computers running Windows Server 2003 or Windows XP Professional Service Pack 1 with QFE 326469 or later (if the Microsoft .NET Framework is also installed). Because the .NET Framework in turn requires Internet Explorer version 5.01 or later, the minimum required components for working with GPMC are as follows:

■ Microsoft Internet Explorer 5.01 or later. Internet Explorer 6.0 SP1 or later is recommended. Computers running Windows XP Professional SP1 or Windows Server 2003 have Internet Explorer 6.0 or later installed already.

■ .NET Framework. Computers running Windows XP Professional do not have the .NET Framework installed by default. Computers running Windows Server 2003 have the .NET Framework installed by default.

■ GPMC with SP1 or later. Computers running Windows XP Professional or Windows Server 2003 do not have the GPMC installed by default. The GPMC is available as a download only (as of this writing).

Note Although you can use the GPMC to manage Group Policy on Windows Server 2003 and Windows 2000, you cannot install the GPMC on computers running Windows 2000 or earlier. Only Windows XP Professional and Windows Server 2003 are compatible with the extensions used by this console.

The key steps for downloading and installing the .NET Framework and the GPMC are as follows:

1. Download the .NET Framework 1.1 or later from Microsoft at *www.microsoft.com/ downloads/*. The installer file is named Dotnetfx.exe. Download Dotnetfx.exe and then double-click it to start the installation process.

2. Because the GPMC installation process updates the MMC, you must close any console-based tools that are running before you install the GPMC. If you don't do this, you'll see a warning when you try to run the installer telling you that the GPMC cannot be installed until you close the consoles that are open.

3. Download the GPMC with SP1 or later from the Microsoft Download Center at *www.microsoft.com/downloads/*. The installation package is Gpmc.msi. Double-click this file to start the installation process.

> **Caution**   Before installing the GPMC, you should think carefully about how you will manage Active Directory–based Group Policy. Installing the GPMC changes the way a computer works with Group Policy, and afterward you can manage Active Directory–based Group Policy only via the GPMC. This is, of course, a per-computer issue, and you have the option of using the existing Group Policy tools or installing and using the GPMC on other computers.

Using the GPMC

You can run the GPMC from the Administrative Tools menu. Click Start, Programs or All Programs, Administrative Tools, and then Group Policy Management Console. As shown in Figure 2-5, the left pane of the GPMC has two top-level nodes by default: Group Policy Management (the console root) and Forest (a node representing the forest to which you are currently connected, which is named after the forest root domain for that forest). When you expand the Forest node, you see the following nodes:

-   **Domains**   Provides access to the policy settings for domains in the forest being administered. You are connected to your logon domain by default; you can add connections to other domains. If you expand a domain, you can access Default Domain Policy, the Domain Controllers OU (and the related Default Domain Controllers Policy), and GPOs defined in the domain.

-   **Sites**   Provides access to the policy settings for sites in the related forest. Sites are hidden by default.

-   **Group Policy Modeling**   Provides access to the Group Policy Modeling Wizard, which helps you plan policy deployment and simulate settings for testing purposes. Any saved policy models are also available.

■ **Group Policy Results** Provides access to the Group Policy Results Wizard. For each domain to which you are connected, all the related GPOs and OUs are available to work with in one location.

Note GPOs found in domain, site, and OU containers in the GPMC are actually GPO links and not the GPOs themselves. The actual GPOs are found in the Group Policy Objects container of the selected domain. It is also helpful to note that the icons for GPO links have a small arrow at the bottom left, similar to shortcut icons.

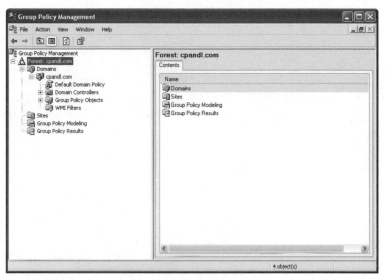

Figure 2-5 The GPMC provides access to the policy settings in domains, sites, and OUs

Connecting to Additional Forests

The GPMC is designed to work with multiple forests, domains, and sites. When you start the GPMC for the first time, you are connected to your logon domain and forest. You can connect to additional forests by completing the following steps:

1. Start the GPMC by clicking Start, Programs or All Programs, Administrative Tools, and then Group Policy Management Console. Or type **gpmc.msc** at a command prompt.

2. Right-click the Group Policy Management node in the console tree, and then select Add Forest.

3. In the Add Forest dialog box (shown in Figure 2-6), type the name of a domain in the forest to which you want to connect, and then click OK. As long as there is an external trust to the domain, you can establish the connection and obtain forest information—even if you don't have a forest trust with the entire forest.

From now on, when you start Group Policy Management Console, the additional forest should be listed.

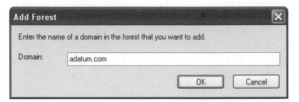

Figure 2-6   Entering the name of a domain in the forest to which you want to connect

Showing Sites in Connected Forests

The GPMC doesn't show the available sites by default. If you want to work with the sites in a particular forest, follow these steps:

1. Start the GPMC by clicking Start, Programs or All Programs, Administrative Tools, and then Group Policy Management Console. Or type **gpmc.msc** at a command prompt.

2. Expand the entry for the forest you want to work with, right-click the related Sites node, and then select Show Sites.

3. In the Show Sites dialog box (shown in Figure 2-7), select the check boxes for the sites you want to work with and clear the check boxes for the sites you don't want to work with. Click OK.

   From now on, when you start the GPMC, the additional site or sites should be listed.

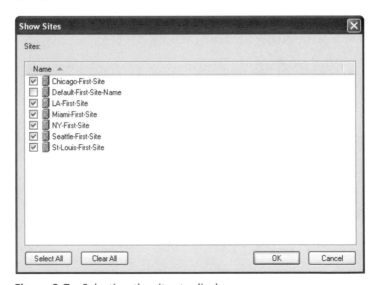

Figure 2-7   Selecting the sites to display

Accessing Additional Domains

In the GPMC, you can view the domains to which you are connected on a per-forest basis. You are connected to your logon domain and forest by default. To work with other domains in a particular forest, follow these steps:

1. Start the GPMC by clicking Start, Programs or All Programs, Administrative Tools, and then Group Policy Management Console. Or type **gpmc.msc** at a command prompt.

2. Expand the entry for the forest you want to work with, and then expand the related Domains node by double-clicking it.

    If the domain you want to work with isn't listed, right-click the Domains node in the designated forest, and then select Show Domains. Then in the Show Domains dialog box, select the check boxes for the domains you want to work with and clear the check boxes for the domains you don't want to work with. Click OK. From now on, when you start the GPMC, the additional domain or domains should be listed.

Setting Domain Controller Focus Options

When you start the GPMC, the console connects to Active Directory running on the domain controller that is acting as the PDC emulator for your logon domain and obtains a list of all GPOs and OUs in that domain. It does this using LDAP to access the directory store and the Server Message Block (SMB) protocol to access the Sysvol. If the PDC emulator isn't available for some reason, such as when the server is down or otherwise offline, the GPMC displays a prompt so you can choose to work with policy settings on the domain controller to which you are currently connected or on any available domain controller. If you want to force the GPMC to work with a domain controller other than PDC, you can configure this manually as well. This process is referred to as setting the *domain controller focus*.

You can choose the domain controller to work with on a per-domain basis by completing the following steps:

1. Start the GPMC by clicking Start, Programs or All Programs, Administrative Tools, and then Group Policy Management Console. Or type **gpmc.msc** at a command prompt.

2. Expand the entry for the forest you want to work with, and then expand the related Domains node by double-clicking it.

3. Right-click the domain for which you want to set the domain controller focus, and then select Change Domain Controller to open the Change Domain Controller dialog box shown in Figure 2-8.

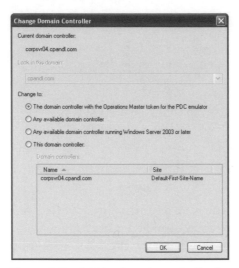

Figure 2-8   Set the domain controller focus

4. The domain controller to which you are currently connected is listed under Current Domain Controller. Use the following Change To options to set the domain controller focus, and then click OK.

- **The Domain Controller With The Operations Master Token For The PDC Emulator**   Choose this option if you aren't connected to the PDC Emulator for some reason and want to try to establish a connection with this server at this time. For example, if the PDC Emulator was offline for maintenance and is now online, you might want to try to reconnect with it.

- **Any Available Domain Controller**   Choose this option to connect to any available domain controller running Windows 2000 or later. Use this option if you don't need to work with a domain controller running a specific version of the Windows server operating system.

- **Any Available Domain Controller Running Windows Server 2003 Or Later**   Choose this option if you need to work with a domain controller that is running Windows Server 2003 or later.

- **This Domain Controller**   Choose this option and then make a selection in the Domain Controllers panel if you want to work with a specific domain controller. The site where each domain controller resides is listed as well so that you can work with a domain controller in a particular site if necessary.

Creating and Linking GPOs

As discussed previously, the GPMC allows you to create and link GPOs as separate operations or as a single operation on a selected domain, site, or OU. You can, for example, create a GPO without linking it to any domain, site, or OU. You can also create a GPO for a selected domain or OU and have the GPO linked automatically to that domain or OU. With sites, the only way to create and link a GPO is to do so with separate operations.

How you create GPOs is a matter of preference. There is no right or wrong way. Some administrators prefer to create a GPO first and then link it to a domain, site, or OU. Other administrators prefer to create a GPO and have it linked automatically to a specific domain, site, or OU. However, you should remember that a GPO can be linked to multiple containers (domains, sites, and OUs) and at multiple levels.

> **Note**   When you create and link a GPO to a site, domain, or OU, the GPO is applied to the user and computer objects in that site, domain, or OU according to the Active Directory options governing inheritance, the precedence order of GPOs, and other settings. In other words, these options can affect the way policy settings are applied. For details, see the section in Chapter 3 titled "Managing Group Policy Inheritance."

Creating and Linking GPOs for Sites

In an Active Directory forest, only Enterprise Admins and forest root Domain Admins can create and modify sites and site links. Similarly, only Enterprise Admins and forest root Domain Admins can create and manage GPOs for sites. Site-level GPOs aren't used that often, and when they are implemented, they are used primarily for managing network-specific policy settings—which is in keeping with the purpose of sites to help you better manage the physical structure of the network (your subnets). For example, you might want to use site-level GPOs to manage IP security, Internet Explorer configurations for proxies, wireless networking, or public key security on a per-subnet basis.

In the GPMC, you can create and link a new site GPO by completing the following steps:

1. Start the GPMC by clicking Start, Programs or All Programs, Administrative Tools, and then Group Policy Management Console. Or type **gpmc.msc** at a command prompt.

2. Expand the entry for the forest you want to work with, and then expand the related Domains node by double-clicking it.

3. Right-click Group Policy Objects, and then select New.

4. In the New GPO dialog box (shown in Figure 2-9), type a descriptive name for the new GPO, and then click OK. You'll see the new GPO listed in the Group Policy Objects container.

Figure 2-9   Entering a descriptive name for the new GPO

5. Right-click the new GPO, and then choose Edit. This opens the Group Policy Object Editor.

6. Configure the necessary policy settings, and then close the Group Policy Object Editor.

7. In the GPMC, expand the Sites node and select the site you want to work with. In the right pane, the Linked Group Policy Objects tab shows the GPOs that are currently linked to the selected site (if any).

8. Right-click the site to which you want to link the GPO, and then select Link An Existing GPO. Use the Select GPO dialog box (shown in Figure 2-10) to select the GPO to which you want to link, and then click OK.

> **Note**   Sites aren't listed automatically. If you don't see the site you want to work with, right-click Sites and then select Show Sites. You can then select the available sites that you want to display.

Figure 2-10   Selecting the GPO to which you want to link

The GPO is now linked to the site. In the right pane, the Linked Group Policy Objects tab should show the linked GPO. Once Group Policy is refreshed for computers and users in the site, the policy settings in the GPO will be applied. To learn how to manually refresh Group Policy, see "Refreshing Group Policy Manually" in Chapter 3.

Computer policy is refreshed during startup when the computer connects to the network. User policy is refreshed during logon when the user logs on to the network. Thus you can verify that computer policy settings have been applied as expected by restarting a workstation or server in the site and then checking the computer. To verify user policy settings, have a user who is logged on to a computer in the site log off and then log back on. You can then verify that user policy settings have been applied as expected.

Creating and Linking GPOs for Domains

In an Active Directory forest, only Enterprise Admins, Domain Admins, and those who have been delegated permissions can manage objects in domains. You must be a member of Enterprise Admins or Domain Admins or be specifically delegated permissions to be able to work with GPOs in a domain. With regard to Group Policy, delegated permissions are primarily limited to management of Group Policy links and RSoP for the purposes of logging and planning.

Unlike site GPOs, which aren't frequently used, GPOs are used widely in domains. In the GPMC, you can create and link a new GPO for a domain as two separate operations or as a single operation.

Creating and Then Linking a GPO for a Domain

To create a GPO and then link it separately for a domain, complete the following steps:

1. Start the GPMC by clicking Start, Programs or All Programs, Administrative Tools, and then Group Policy Management Console. Or type **gpmc.msc** at a command prompt.

2. Expand the entry for the forest you want to work with, and then expand the related Domains node by double-clicking it.

3. Right-click Group Policy Objects and then select New. In the New GPO dialog box, type a descriptive name for the new GPO and then click OK.

4. The new GPO is now listed in the Group Policy Objects container. Right-click the GPO, and then choose Edit.

5. In the Group Policy Object Editor, configure the necessary policy settings and then close the Group Policy Object Editor.

6. In the GPMC, expand the Domains node and then select the domain you want to work with. In the right pane, the Linked Group Policy Objects tab shows the GPOs that are currently linked to the selected domain (if any).

> **Note**   If you don't see the domain you want to work with, right-click Domains and then select Show Domains. You can then select the available domains that you want to display.

7. Right-click the domain to which you want to link the GPO, and then select Link An Existing GPO. Use the Select GPO dialog box to select the GPO to which you want to link, and then click OK.

   The GPO is now linked to the domain. In the right pane, the Linked Group Policy Objects tab should show the linked GPO as well.

When Group Policy is refreshed for computers and users in the domain, the policy settings in the GPO are applied. To verify that computer policy settings have been applied as expected, restart a workstation or server in the domain and then check the computer. To verify user policy settings, have a user who is logged on to a computer in the domain log off and then log back on. You can then verify that user policy settings have been applied as expected.

Creating and Linking a Domain GPO as a Single Operation

In the GPMC, you can create and link a domain GPO as a single operation by completing the following steps:

1. Start the GPMC by clicking Start, Programs or All Programs, Administrative Tools, and then Group Policy Management Console. Or type **gpmc.msc** at a command prompt.

2. Expand the entry for the forest you want to work with, and then expand the related Domains node by double-clicking it.

3. Right-click the domain you want to work with, and then select Create And Link A GPO Here.

4. In the New GPO dialog box, type a descriptive name for the new GPO and then click OK.

5. The GPO is created and linked to the domain. Right-click the GPO, and then choose Edit.

6. In the Group Policy Object Editor, configure the necessary policy settings and then close the Group Policy Object Editor.

When Group Policy is refreshed for computers and users in the domain, the policy settings in the GPO are applied. To verify that computer policy settings have been applied as expected, restart a workstation or server in the domain and then check the computer. To verify user policy settings, have a user who is logged on to a computer in the domain log off and then log back on. You can then verify that user policy settings have been applied as expected.

Creating and Linking GPOs for OUs

In an Active Directory forest, only Enterprise Admins, Domain Admins, and those that have been delegated permissions can manage objects in OUs. You must be a member of Enterprise Admins or Domain Admins or be specifically delegated permissions to be able to work with GPOs in OUs. With regard to Group Policy, delegated permissions are primarily limited to management of Group Policy links and RSoP for the purposes of logging and planning.

Unlike site GPOs, which aren't frequently used, GPOs are used widely in OUs. The GPMC is fairly versatile when it comes to OUs. Not only can you use it to create and link a new GPO for an OU, but you can also create any necessary OUs without having to work with Active Directory Users And Computers.

Creating OUs in the GPMC

To create an OU in the GPMC, follow these steps:

1. Start the GPMC by clicking Start, Programs or All Programs, Administrative Tools, and then Group Policy Management Console. Or type **gpmc.msc** at a command prompt.

2. Expand the entry for the forest you want to work with, and then expand the related Domains node by double-clicking it.

3. Right-click the domain in which you want to create the OU, and then select New Organizational Unit.

4. In the New Organizational Unit dialog box, type a descriptive name for the OU and then click OK.

Creating and Then Linking a GPO for an OU

To create a GPO for an OU and then link it separately, complete the following steps:

1. Start the GPMC by clicking Start, Programs or All Programs, Administrative Tools, and then Group Policy Management Console. Or type **gpmc.msc** at a command prompt.

2. Expand the entry for the forest you want to work with, and then expand the related Domains node by double-clicking it.

3. Right-click Group Policy Objects, and then select New. In the New GPO dialog box, type a descriptive name for the new GPO and then click OK.

4. The new GPO is now listed in the Group Policy Objects container. Right-click the GPO, and then choose Edit.

5. In the Group Policy Object Editor, configure the necessary policy settings and then close the Group Policy Object Editor.

6. In the GPMC, expand the Domains node and select the OU you want to work with. In the right pane, the Linked Group Policy Objects tab shows the GPOs that are currently linked to the selected OU (if any).

7. Right-click the OU to which you want to link the GPO, and then select Link An Existing GPO. Use the Select GPO dialog box to select the GPO to which you want to link, and then click OK.

8. The GPO is now linked to the OU. In the right pane, the Linked Group Policy Objects tab should show the linked GPO as well.

When Group Policy is refreshed for computers and users in the OU, the policy settings in the GPO are applied. To verify that computer policy settings have been applied as expected, restart a workstation or server in the OU and then check the computer. To verify user policy settings, have a user who is logged on to a computer in the OU log off and then log back on. You can then verify that user policy settings have been applied as expected.

Creating and Linking an OU GPO as a Single Operation

In the GPMC, you can create and link an OU GPO as a single operation by completing the following steps:

1. Start the GPMC by clicking Start, Programs or All Programs, Administrative Tools, and then Group Policy Management Console. Or type **gpmc.msc** at a command prompt.

2. Expand the entry for the forest you want to work with, and then expand the related Domains node by double-clicking it.

3. Right-click the OU you want to work with, and then select Create And Link A GPO Here.

4. In the New GPO dialog box, type a descriptive name for the new GPO and then click OK.

5. The GPO is created and linked to the OU. Right-click the GPO, and then choose Edit.

6. In the Group Policy Object Editor, configure the necessary policy settings and then close the Group Policy Object Editor.

When Group Policy is refreshed for computers and users in the OU, the policy settings in the GPO are applied. To verify that computer policy settings have been applied as expected, restart a workstation or server in the OU and then check the computer. To verify user policy settings, have a user who is logged on to a computer in the OU log off and then log back on. You can then verify that user policy settings have been applied as expected.

Delegating Privileges for Group Policy Management

In Active Directory, administrators are automatically granted permissions for performing different Group Policy management tasks. Other individuals can be granted such permissions through delegation. In Active Directory, you delegate Group Policy management permissions for very specific reasons. You delegate to allow a user who is not a member of Enterprise Admins or Domain Admins to perform any or all of the following tasks:

- View settings, change settings, delete a GPO, and modify security
- Manage links to existing GPOs or generate RSoP
- Create GPOs (and therefore also be able to manage any GPOs she has created)

The sections that follow explain how you can determine who has these permissions and how to grant these permissions to additional users and groups.

Determining and Assigning GPO Creation Rights

In Active Directory, administrators have the ability to create GPOs in domains, and anyone who has created a GPO in a domain has the right to manage that GPO. To determine who can create GPOs in a domain, follow these steps:

1. Start the GPMC by clicking Start, Programs or All Programs, Administrative Tools, and then Group Policy Management Console. Or type **gpmc.msc** at a command prompt.

2. Expand the entry for the forest you want to work with, expand the related Domains node, and then select the Group Policy Objects node.

3. As shown in Figure 2-11, the users and groups who can create GPOs in the selected domain are listed on the Delegation tab.

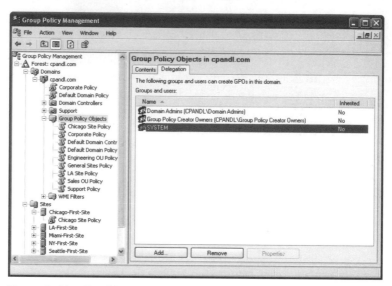

Figure 2-11 Checking permissions for GPO creation

You can allow a nonadministrative user or a group (including users and groups from other domains) to create GPOs (and thus implicitly grant them the ability to manage the GPOs they've created). To grant GPO creation permission to a user or group, follow these steps:

1. Start the GPMC by clicking Start, Programs or All Programs, Administrative Tools, and then Group Policy Management Console. Or type **gpmc.msc** at a command prompt.

2. Expand the entry for the forest you want to work with, expand the related Domains node, and then select the Group Policy Objects node.

3. In the right pane, select the Delegation tab. The current GPO creation permissions for individual users and groups are listed. To grant the GPO creation permission to another user or group, click Add.

4. In the Select User, Computer, Or Group dialog box, select the user or group and then click OK.

The options on the Delegation tab are updated as appropriate. If you want to remove the GPO creation permission in the future, access the Delegation tab, click the user or group, and then click Remove.

Determining Group Policy Management Privileges

The GPMC provides several ways to determine who has access permissions for Group Policy management. To determine Group Policy permissions for a specific site, domain, or OU, follow these steps:

1. Start the GPMC by clicking Start, Programs or All Programs, Administrative Tools, and then Group Policy Management Console. Or type **gpmc.msc** at a command prompt.

2. Expand the entry for the forest you want to work with, and then expand the related Domains or Sites node as appropriate.

3. When you select the domain, site, or OU you want to work with, the right pane is updated with several tabs. Select the Delegation tab (shown in Figure 2-12).

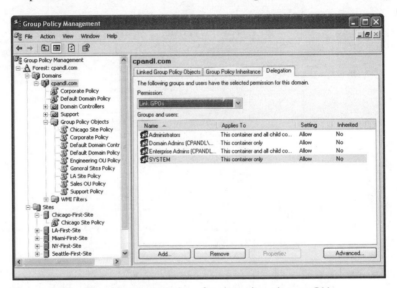

Figure 2-12   Checking permissions for sites, domains, or OUs

4. In the Permission list, select the permission you want to check. The options are:

   ❑ **Link GPOs**   The user or group can create and manage links to GPOs in the selected site, domain, or OU.

   ❑ **Perform Group Policy Modeling Analyses**   The user or group can determine RSoP for the purposes of planning.

   ❑ **Read Group Policy Results Data**   The user or group can determine RSoP that is currently being applied, for the purposes of verification or logging.

5. The individual users or groups with the selected permissions are listed under Groups And Users.

To determine which users or groups have access to a particular GPO and what permissions have been granted to them, follow these steps:

1. Start the GPMC by clicking Start, Programs or All Programs, Administrative Tools, and then Group Policy Management Console. Or type **gpmc.msc** at a command prompt.

2. Expand the entry for the forest you want to work with, expand the related Domains node, and then select the Group Policy Objects node.

3. When you select the GPO whose permissions you want to check, the right pane is updated with several tabs. Select the Delegation tab (shown in Figure 2-13).

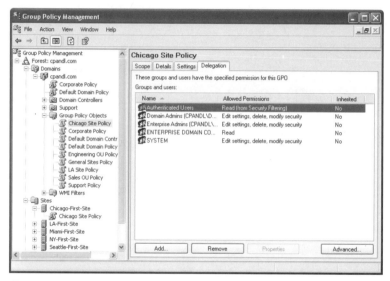

Figure 2-13   Checking permissions for specific GPOs

4. The permissions for individual users and groups are listed. You'll see three general types of allowed permissions:

   ❑ **Read**   The user or group can view the GPO and its settings.

   ❑ **Edit Settings**   The user or group can view the GPO and its settings. The user or group can also change settings—but not delete the GPO or modify security.

   ❑ **Edit Settings, Delete, Modify Security**   The user or group can view the GPO and its settings. The user or group can also change settings, delete the GPO, and modify security.

Delegating Control for Working with GPOs

You can allow a nonadministrative user or a group (including users and groups from other domains) to work with a domain, site, or OU GPO by granting one of three specific permissions:

- **Read**   Allows the user or group to view the GPO and its settings.
- **Edit Settings**   Allows the user or group to view the GPO and its settings. The user or group can also change settings—but not delete the GPO or modify security.
- **Edit Settings, Delete, Modify Security**   Allows the user or group to view the GPO and its settings. The user or group can also change settings, delete the GPO, and modify security.

To grant these permissions to a user or group, follow these steps:

1. Start the GPMC by clicking Start, Programs or All Programs, Administrative Tools, and then Group Policy Management Console. Or type **gpmc.msc** at a command prompt.

2. Expand the entry for the forest you want to work with, expand the related Domains node, and then select the Group Policy Objects node.

3. Select the GPO you want to work with in the left pane. In the right pane, select the Delegation tab.

4. The current permissions for individual users and groups are listed. To grant permissions to another user or group, click Add.

5. In the Select User, Computer, Or Group dialog box, select the user or group and then click OK.

6. In the Add Group Or User dialog box (shown in Figure 2-14), select the permission to grant: Read, Edit Settings, or Edit Settings, Delete, Modify Security. Click OK.

Figure 2-14   Granting permission to the user or group

The options of the Delegation tab are updated to reflect the permissions granted. If you want to remove this permission in the future, access the Delegation tab, click the user or group, and then click Remove.

Delegating Authority for Managing Links and RSoP

You can allow a nonadministrative user or a group (including users and groups from other domains) to manage GPO links and RSoP. The related permissions can be granted in any combination and are defined as follows:

- **Link GPOs**   Allows the user or group to create and manage links to GPOs in the selected site, domain, or OU.

- **Perform Group Policy Modeling Analyses**   Allows the user or group to determine RSoP for the purposes of planning.

- **Read Group Policy Results Data**   Allows the user or group to determine RSoP that is currently being applied, for the purposes of verification or logging.

To grant these permissions to a user or group, follow these steps:

1. Start the GPMC by clicking Start, Programs or All Programs, Administrative Tools, and then Group Policy Management Console. Or type **gpmc.msc** at a command prompt.

2. Expand the entry for the forest you want to work with, and then expand the related Domains or Sites node as appropriate.

3. In the left pane, select the domain, site, or OU you want to work with. In the right pane, select the Delegation tab.

4. In the Permission list, select the permission you want to grant. The options are Link GPOs, Perform Group Policy Modeling Analyses, and Read Group Policy Results Data.

5. The current permissions for individual users and groups are listed. To grant the selected permission to another user or group, click Add.

6. In the Select User, Computer, Or Group dialog box, select the user or group and then click OK.

7. In the Add Group Or User dialog box (shown in Figure 2-15), specify how the permission should be applied. To apply the permission to the current container and all child containers, select This Container And All Child Containers. To apply the permission only to the current container, select This Container Only. Click OK.

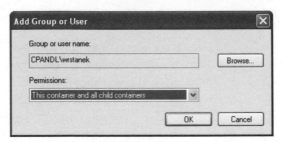

Figure 2-15 Granting the permission to this container only or to the container and its child containers

The options of the Delegation tab are updated to reflect the permissions granted. If you want to remove this permission in the future, access the Delegation tab, click the user or group, and then click Remove.

Removing Links and Deleting GPOs

In the GPMC, you can stop using a linked GPO in two ways. You can remove a link to a GPO but not the actual GPO itself, or you can permanently delete the GPO and all links to it.

Removing a Link to a GPO

Removing a link to a GPO stops the site, domain, or OU from using the related policy settings. It doesn't delete the GPO, however. The GPO remains linked to other sites, domains, or OUs as appropriate. If you remove all links to the GPO from sites, domains, and OUs, the GPO will continue to exist—it will still "live" in the Group Policy Objects container—but its policy settings will have no effect in your enterprise.

To remove a link to a GPO, right-click the GPO link in the container to which it is linked and then select Delete. When prompted to confirm that you want to remove the link, click OK.

Deleting a GPO Permanently

Deleting a GPO permanently removes the GPO and all links to it. The GPO will not continue to exist in the Group Policy Objects container and will not be linked to any sites, domains, or OUs. The only way to recover a deleted GPO is to restore it from a backup (if one is available).

To remove a GPO and all links to the object, expand the forest, the Domains node, and the Group Policy Objects node. Right-click the GPO, and then select Delete. When prompted to confirm that you want to remove the GPO and all links to it, click OK.

Summary

To work with Group Policy, the Group Policy Management Console (GPMC) should be your tool of choice. Not only does the GPMC provide a fairly intuitive interface for working with Group Policy, but it also provides an extended feature set, allowing you to do more with Group Policy than if you use the standard Group Policy Object Editor. When you work with the GPMC, the console connects by default to the PDC Emulator for your logon domain. This configuration ensures that there is a central location for managing changes to Group Policy. If the PDC Emulator is unavailable for any reason, you can choose the domain controller to which you will connect. You can also set the domain controller focus manually if necessary.

Generally speaking, Group Policy can be managed by members of the Domain Admins and Enterprise Admins groups. However, sites can be managed only by Enterprise Admins and forest root Domain Admins. Domains and OUs can be managed only by Enterprise Admins, Domain Admins, and those who have been delegated permissions. You can delegate privileges for Group Policy management in a few ways. First, you can assign GPO creation rights to users or groups. These users or groups can also manage the GPOs they've created. Second, you can delegate permission to link GPOs and work with Resultant Set of Policy (RSoP). Finally, you can delegate permission to read, edit settings, delete, and modify the security of GPOs.

Chapter 3

Advanced Group Policy Management

In this chapter:

Searching and Filtering Group Policy 54

Managing Group Policy Inheritance 61

Managing Group Policy Processing and Refresh 68

Modeling and Maintaining Group Policy 80

Determining the Effective Group Policy Settings and Last Refresh 93

Summary 96

The advanced management features of Group Policy can save you time and help you be more effective. For example, if you are looking for a specific policy object or a specific group of policy settings, you can search and filter policy. Or you might need to modify the way policy settings are inherited or processed, especially if you work in a large organization or one with one or more remote locations. As part of periodic maintenance, you might also need to copy, back up, or restore policy objects. This chapter covers all of these advanced management tasks.

Related Information

- For more information about customizing Group Policy and managing its structure, see Part III.

- For more information about copying policy settings and migrating Group Policy Objects, see Chapter 4.

- For more information about troubleshooting Group Policy, see Chapter 16.

Searching and Filtering Group Policy

One of the most challenging aspects of working with Group Policy is simply finding what you are looking for—whether it's a set of policies, a particular Group Policy Object (GPO), or an object that Group Policy is affecting. Some administrators have told us that they've gone through every single GPO and every related policy setting in those GPOs and still haven't found what they were looking for. You can save time and be much more effective by using one of several filtering techniques, including filtering policy settings to streamline the view, and searching for policy objects, links, and configuration settings for various conditions, values, and keywords.

Another type of filter you can apply to GPOs is a security filter to control the security groups to which a policy object is applied. By default, a linked GPO applies to all users and computers in the container to which it is linked. But sometimes you won't want a GPO to apply to a user or computer in a particular container. For example, you might want to apply a filter so that the Sales Policy GPO is applied to normal users in the Sales organizational unit (OU) but not to administrators in the Sales OU. Or you might want to apply a filter to Sales Policy GPO so that JoeS, a user in the Sales OU, doesn't get the policy settings from that OU at all.

Filtering Policy Settings

By default, all policy settings for all administrative templates are displayed in the Group Policy Object Editor. When you are viewing or editing a GPO, finding the policy settings you want to work with can be a daunting task because so many policy settings are available and many of them might not be applicable in your environment or might not be suited to your current needs.

Filtering Techniques for Policy Settings

To reduce the policy set and make it more manageable, you can filter the view so that only the policy settings you want to use are shown. Likewise, if you are looking for a particular group of policy settings, such as only those that are configured or those that can be used with computers running Microsoft® Windows® XP Professional with Service Pack 2 or later, you can filter the view to focus in on the policy settings you need.

Handy? You betcha. The one gotcha is that this type of filtering applies only to Administrative Templates policy settings. Anytime you are actively editing a GPO, you can filter the Administrative Templates policy settings in several key ways:

■ **Show only the policy settings that apply to a specific operating system, application or system configuration** For viewing only the policy settings that meet a specific set of requirements. By filtering policy settings in this way, you see only the policy settings that meet your specified operating system or application configuration requirements, such as only the policy settings that are supported by Windows XP Professional with Service Pack 2 or later.

■ **Show only the policy settings that are currently configured** Viewing currently configured policy settings is useful if you want to modify a configured policy setting. By filtering policy settings in this way, you see only policy settings that are either enabled or disabled. You don't see policy settings that are set as "not configured."

■ **Show only the policy settings that can be fully managed** For ensuring that you are working with nonlegacy policy settings. A legacy policy setting is one that was created in an administrative template written using the Microsoft Windows NT 4.0 administrative template format. Windows NT 4.0 administrative templates and their settings typically modify different sections of the Windows registry than do template settings for Windows 2000 or later. It is therefore recommended that you not use Windows NT 4.0 administrative templates. This filter option is selected by default. If you want to work with Windows NT 4.0 administrative templates and their settings, you must clear this filter option.

Note Filtering policy settings affects only their display in Group Policy Object Editor. Filtered policy settings are still applied as appropriate throughout the site, domain, or OU.

Filtering Policy Settings by Operating System and Application Configuration

In the Group Policy Management Console (GPMC), you can view or edit a GPO and its settings at any time by right-clicking the GPO and choosing Edit. When you work with the policy object, you can filter the related policy settings by completing the following steps.

Note Filtering of policy settings works only with Administrative Templates. You configure filtering separately for Computer Configuration and User Configuration.

1. In the Group Policy Editor, expand Computer Configuration or User Configuration as appropriate.

2. Right-click Administrative Templates and choose View, Filtering to open the Filtering dialog box (Figure 3-1).

Figure 3-1   Selecting the appropriate filter options

3. By default, all policy settings for all operating systems and application configurations that have Administrative Template files installed are shown in the Group Policy Editor.

   To filter by operating system and application configuration, select Filter By Requirements Information and then select or clear the items to be displayed.

> **Note**   Some of the Items To Be Displayed options are too long to read. You can see the complete description of an item by moving the mouse pointer over it. The complete description is then displayed as a ToolTip.

4. If you want to see only policy settings that are set as enabled or disabled, select Only Show Configured Policy Settings.

5. If you want to use the older-style policy settings from Windows NT 4.0 administrative templates, clear Only Show Policy Settings That Can Be Fully Managed.

6. Click OK.

Searching Policy Objects, Links, and Settings

When you have multiple policy objects with many configured settings, it can be a challenge to find the policy object or settings you need. The search feature of the GPMC can help. For example, if the Remove Add/Remove Programs policy is causing a problem that is preventing administrators from adding programs on users' computers and you don't know in which policy object this policy setting is enabled, the search feature can help. Or if you need to update the Wireless Networking policies but don't know which policy object has these settings, the search feature saves you from having to go through all the available policy objects in search of the one that has the Wireless

Networking Policies. To resolve these types of problems and many others, you can use the search feature of the Group Policy Management Console.

Search Techniques for Policy Objects, Links, and Settings

The GPMC search feature allows you to search Group Policy in a currently selected domain or in all the domains of a selected forest. You can search by any of the following criteria:

- **GPO Name** Allows you to search for a policy object by full or partial name. For example, if you know that a policy object has the word "Sales" in its name but you don't know in which domain the object exists, you can search for all policy object names that contain this keyword.

- **GPO Links** Allows you to search for policy objects that are either linked or not linked in a particular domain or in all domains of the current forest. For example, if you want to find all policy objects that are linked in a particular domain, you can search for all policy object links that exist in that domain. Or if you want to find all policy objects that aren't currently linked to a particular domain, you can search for all policy object links that do not exist in the domain.

- **Security Groups, Users or Computers** Allows you to search for security groups, users, or computers with specific Group Policy management privileges. For example, you might need to know whether the TechManagers group has explicit permission to edit Group Policy settings or whether the user JoeS has permission to read Group Policy settings in a particular domain or in any domain of the current forest. (Group Policy management privileges are discussed in Chapter 2 under "Delegating Privileges for Group Policy Management" and include Read; Edit Settings; and Edit Settings, Delete, Modify Security.)

- **Linked WMI Filter** Allows you to search for a linked WMI filter. You can search to find out whether a filter exists.

- **User Configuration** Allows you to quickly determine whether commonly used User Configuration settings are configured. The areas of User Configuration you can search for are Folder Redirection, Internet Explorer Branding, Internet Explorer Zonemapping, Registry, Scripts, and Software Installation. For example, you might need to find the policy object in a particular domain that has Folder Redirection configured, and you can use this search feature to do this.

- **Computer Configuration** Allows you to quickly determine whether commonly used Computer Configuration settings are configured. The areas of Computer Configuration you can search for are EFS Recovery, Internet Explorer Zonemapping, IP Security, Microsoft Disk Quota, QoS Pack Scheduler, Registry, Scripts, Security, Software Installation, and Wireless. For example, you might need to find the policy object in a particular domain that has Wireless Networking Policy configured, and you can use this search feature to do this.

■ **GUID**   Allows you to search for a policy object by its GUID. This is useful if you already know the full GUID of a policy object you need to locate so that you can work with it. A typical scenario in which you may know the GUID and not know the policy object location is when you are troubleshooting a problem with Group Policy and see errors that reference the GUID of a policy object.

Beginning Your Policy Object, Link, or Setting Search

To search Group Policy for any of the previously discussed search criteria, complete these steps:

1. Start the GPMC. Click Start, Programs or All Programs, Administrative Tools, and then Group Policy Management Console. Or type **gpmc.msc** at a command prompt.

2. If you want to search all the domains in a particular forest, right-click the entry for the forest you want to work with and then select Search. If you want to search a specific domain, expand the related forest node, right-click the domain, and then select Search.

3. In the Search For Group Policy Objects dialog box (Figure 3-2), use the Search Item list to choose the area of Group Policy to search, such as User Configuration.

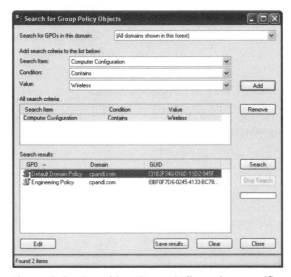

Figure 3-2   Searching Group Policy using specific search conditions and values

4. Use the Condition list to set the search condition. Conditions include:

    ❑ **Contains/Does Not Contain**   Allows you to search based on specific values that are either contained or not contained in the search item. For example, if you are sure the policy object you are looking for doesn't have the word *Current* in its name (while most other policy objects you've created do), you can search for a GPO Name that does not contain the value *Current*.

❑ **Is Exactly/Equals**   Allows you to search for an exact value associated with a search item. For example, if you are sure the policy object you are looking for is named Engineering Policy, you can search for a GPO Name that has that exact value.

❑ **Exist In/Does Not Exist In**   Allows you to search for GPO links that either exist in or do not exist in the selected domain or forest; it is used with GPO links.

❑ **Has This Explicit Permission/Does Not Have This Explicit Permission** Allows you to search for security groups, users, and computers that have or do not have an explicit permission in Group Policy. Explicit permissions are directly assigned. For example, if JohnS has been delegated permission to Edit Settings of the Engineering Policy GPO, he has explicit Edit Settings permission with regard to this object.

❑ **Has This Effective Permission/Does Not Have This Effective Permission**   Allows you to search for security groups, users, and computers that have or do not have an effective permission in Group Policy. Effective permissions are indirectly assigned. For example, a member of the Domain Administrators group has the effective permission to apply settings.

5. Select or enter a search value in the Value field.

6. As necessary, repeat steps 3 through 5 to add additional search criteria. Keep in mind that additional search criteria further restrict the result set. A policy object must match all search criteria to be displayed in the search results. Click Add to add the search criteria.

7. Click Search to search for policy objects that meet your search criteria. You can directly edit any policy object listed by selecting it in the Search Results list and clicking Edit.

Filtering by Security Group, User, or Computer

You'll often need to determine or control whether and how Group Policy applies to a particular security group, user, or computer. By default, GPOs apply to all users and computers in the container to which a particular GPO is linked. A linked GPO applies to all users and computers in this way because of the security settings on the GPO. Two GPO permissions determine whether a policy object applies to a security group, user, or computer:

■ **Read**   If this permission is allowed, the security group, user, or computer can read the policy for the purposes of applying it to other groups, users, or computers (not for the purposes of viewing policy settings; View Settings is an explicit permission that must be granted).

■ **Apply Group Policy**   If this permission is allowed, the GPO is applied to the security group, user, or computer. The settings of an applied GPO take effect on the group, user, or computer.

A security group, user, or computer must have both permissions for a policy to be applied. By default, all users and computers have these permissions for all new GPOs. They inherit these permissions from their membership in the implicit group Authenticated Users. An authenticated user is any user or computer that has logged on to the domain and been authenticated.

> **Note**   Additional permissions are also assigned to administrators and the operating system. All members of the Enterprise Admins and Domain Admins groups as well as the LocalSystem account have permission to edit or delete GPOs and manage their security.

When you've delegated Group Policy management permissions to users or have administrators whose accounts are defined at the domain or OU level, you might not want a policy object to be applied. Consider the following scenario: You've delegated administrator privileges and Group Policy management permissions to Sue. You want her to be able to install programs and perform other tasks that normal users cannot do because of restrictions in Group Policy. In this case, you must take special steps to ensure that Group Policy isn't applied to Sue. Rather than allowing Group Policy to be applied to Sue, you must configure permissions so that she is denied the Apply Group Policy Permission. This will ensure that the policy object isn't applied to Sue's account. If Sue should have permission to apply the Group Policy to other groups, users or computers, she must still have Read permission.

To view or change GPO permissions for a security group, user, or computer, complete these steps:

1. Start the GPMC. Click Start, Programs or All Programs, Administrative Tools, and then Group Policy Management Console. Or type **gpmc.msc** at a command prompt.

2. Expand the entry for the forest you want to work with, expand the related Domains node, expand the Group Policy Objects node, and then select the policy object you want to work with.

3. Click the Delegation tab to see a list of users and groups who have some level of permissions for the selected policy object.

4. Click Advanced to open the Security Settings dialog box (Figure 3-3).

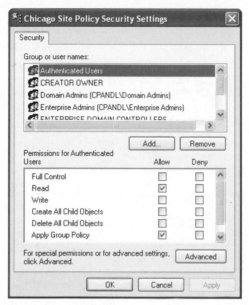

Figure 3-3 Viewing advanced permissions for security groups, users, and computers

5. Select the security group, user, or computer you want to work with. Or click Add to add a new security group, user, or computer. Then do one of the following:

    ❑ If the policy object should be applied to the security group, user, or computer, the minimum permissions should be set to allow Read and Apply Group Policy.

> **Caution** Don't change other permissions unless you are sure of the consequences. A better way to manage other permissions is to follow the techniques discussed in Chapter 2, in the section titled "Delegating Privileges for Group Policy Management."

    ❑ If the policy object should not be applied to the security group, user, or computer, the minimum permissions should be set to allow Read and deny Apply Group Policy.

6. Click OK to return to the GPMC.

Managing Group Policy Inheritance

Inheritance ensures that every computer and user object in a domain, no matter which container it is stored in, is affected by Group Policy. Most policies have three configuration options: Not Configured, Enabled, or Disabled. Not Configured is the default state for most policy settings. If a policy is enabled, the policy is enforced and is applied to all users and computers that are subject to the policy either directly or through inheritance. If a policy is disabled, the policy is not enforced and is not applied to users and computers that are subject to the policy either directly or through inheritance.

You can change the way inheritance works in four key ways. You can:

- Change link order and precedence
- Override inheritance (as long as there is no enforcement)
- Block inheritance (to prevent inheritance completely)
- Enforce inheritance (to supersede and prevent overriding or blocking)

The sections that follow cover managing Group Policy inheritance using these techniques.

Changing Link Order and Precedence

The order of inheritance for Group Policy goes from the site level to the domain level and then to each nested OU level. When multiple policy objects are linked to a particular level, the link order determines the order in which policy settings are applied. Linked policy objects are always applied in link ranking order. Lower-ranking policy objects are processed first, and then higher-ranking policy objects are processed.

To see how this works, consider Figure 3-4. These policies will be processed from the lowest link order to the highest. The Sales Desktop Policy (with link order 2) will be processed before the Sales Networking Policy (with link order 1).

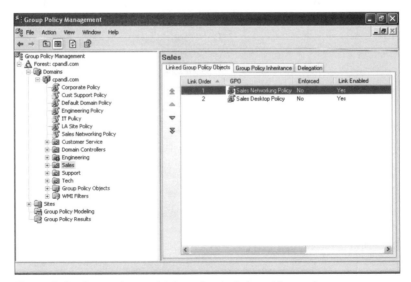

Figure 3-4   Processing multiple policy in link ranking order

What effect does this have on policy settings? Because Sales Networking Policy settings are processed after Sales Desktop Policy settings, Sales Networking Policy settings have precedence and take priority. You can confirm this by clicking the Group Policy Inheritance tab (Figure 3-5).

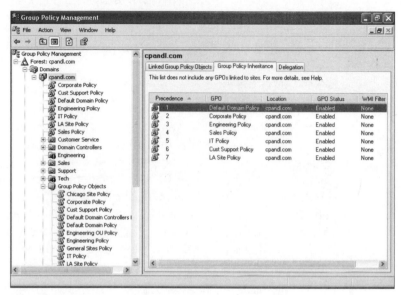

Figure 3-5   The precedence order

The precedence order shows exactly how policy objects are being processed for a site, domain, or OU. As with link order, lower-ranking policy objects are processed before higher-ranking policy objects. Here the LA Site Policy (with precedence 7) will be processed first, and then Cust Support Policy (with precedence 6), and so on. Default Domain Policy is processed last, so any policy settings configured in this policy object are final and will override those of other policy objects (unless inheritance blocking or enforcing is used).

When multiple policy objects are linked at a specific level, you can easily change the link order (and thus the precedence order) of policy objects linked at that level. To do so, complete these steps:

1. In the GPMC, select the container for the site, domain, or OU with which you want to work.

2. In the right pane, the Linked Group Policy Objects tab should be selected by default. Select the policy object with which you want to work by clicking it.

3. Click the Move Link Up or Move Link Down buttons as appropriate to change the link order of the selected policy object.

4. When you are done changing the link order, confirm that policy objects are being processed in the expected order by checking the precedence order on the Group Policy Inheritance tab.

Overriding Inheritance

As you know, Group Policy settings are inherited from top-level containers by lower-level containers. If multiple policy objects modify the same settings, the order in which the policy objects are applied determines which policy settings take effect. Essentially, the order of inheritance goes from the site level to the domain level to the OU level. This means Group Policy settings for a site are passed down to domains, and the settings for a domain are passed down to OUs.

You can override policy inheritance in two key ways:

- **Disable an enabled (and inherited) policy**   When a policy is enabled in a higher-level policy object, you can override inheritance by disabling the policy in a lower-level policy object. You thus override the policy that is enabled in the higher-level container. For example, if the user policy Prohibit Use Of Internet Connection Sharing On Your DNS Domain is enabled for a site, users in the site should not be able to use Internet Connection Sharing. However, if domain policy specifically disables this user policy, users in the domain can use Internet Connection Sharing. On the other hand, if the domain policy is set to Not Configured, that setting will not be modified and will be inherited as normal from the higher-level container.

- **Enable a disabled (and inherited) policy**   When a policy is disabled in a higher-level policy object, you can override inheritance by enabling the policy in a lower-level policy object. By enabling the policy in a lower-level policy object, you override the policy that is disabled in the higher-level container. For example, if the user policy Allow Shared Folders To Be Published is disabled for a domain, users in the domain should not be able to publish shared folders in Active Directory® directory service. However, if the Support Team OU policy specifically enables this user policy, users in the Support Team OU can publish shared folders in Active Directory. Again, if the OU policy is set to Not Configured instead, the policy setting will not be modified and will be inherited as normal from the higher-level container.

Note   Overriding inheritance is a basic technique for changing the way inheritance works. As long as a policy is not blocked or enforced, this technique will achieve the desired effect.

Blocking Inheritance

Sometimes you will want to block inheritance so that no policy settings from higher-level containers are applied to users and computers in a particular container. When inheritance is blocked, only configured policy settings from policy objects linked at that level are applied. This means all GPOs from all high-level containers are blocked (as long as there is no policy enforcement).

Domain administrators can use inheritance blocking to block inherited policy settings from the site level. OU administrators can use inheritance blocking to block inherited policy settings from both the domain and the site level. Here are some examples of inheritance blocking in action:

- Because you want a domain to be autonomous, you don't want a domain to inherit any site policies. You configure the domain to block inheritance from higher-level containers. Because inheritance is blocked, only the configured policy settings from policy objects linked to the domain are applied. Blocking inheritance of site policy doesn't affect inheritance of the domain policy objects by OUs, but it does mean that OUs in that domain will not inherit site policies either.

- Because you want an OU to be autonomous, you don't want an OU to inherit any site or domain policies. You configure the OU to block inheritance from higher-level containers. Because inheritance is blocked, only the configured policy settings from policy objects linked to the OU are applied. If the OU contains other OUs, inheritance blocking won't affect inheritance of policy objects linked to this OU, but the child OUs will not inherit site or domain policies.

Note By using blocking to ensure the autonomy of a domain or OU, you can ensure that domain or OU administrators have full control over the policies that apply to users and computers under their administration. Keep in mind also that the way blocking or enforcement is used depends largely on your organizational structure and how much control is delegated. Some organizations may choose to centrally manage Group Policy. Others may delegate control to divisions, branch offices, or departments within the organization. There is no one-size-fits-all solution. A balance between central management and delegation of control might work best.

Using the GPMC, you can block inheritance by right-clicking the domain or OU that should not inherit settings from higher-level containers and then selecting Block Inheritance. If Block Inheritance is already selected, selecting it again removes the setting. When you block inheritance in the GPMC, a blue circle with an exclamation point is added to the container's node in the console tree, as shown in Figure 3-6. The notification icon provides a quick way to tell whether any domain or OU has the Block Inheritance setting enabled.

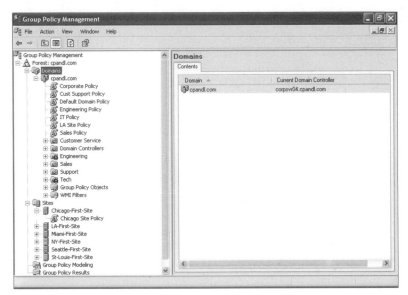

Figure 3-6   A notification icon indicates that inheritance blocking enabled

Enforcing Inheritance

To prevent administrators who have authority over a container from overriding or blocking inherited Group Policy settings, you can enforce inheritance. When inheritance is enforced, all configured policy settings from higher-level policy objects are inherited and applied regardless of the policy settings configured in lower-level policy objects. Thus, enforcement of inheritance is used to supersede overriding and blocking of policy settings.

Forest administrators can use inheritance enforcement to ensure that configured policy settings from the site level are applied and prevent overriding or blocking of policy settings by both domain and OU administrators. Domain administrators can use inheritance enforcement to ensure that configured policy settings from the domain level are applied and prevent overriding or blocking of policy settings by OU administrators. Here are some examples of inheritance enforcement in action:

■   As a forest administrator, you want to ensure that domains inherit a particular site policy, so you configure the site policy to enforce inheritance. All configured policy settings from the site policy are thus applied regardless of whether domain administrators have tried to override or block policy settings from the site level. Enforcement of the site policy also affects inheritance for OUs in the affected domains. They will inherit the site policy regardless of whether overriding or blocking has been used.

- As a domain administrator, you want to ensure that OUs within the domain inherit a particular domain policy, so you configure the domain policy to enforce inheritance. All configured policy settings from the domain policy are thus applied regardless of whether OU administrators have tried to override or block policy settings from the domain level. Enforcement of the domain policy also affects inheritance for child OUs within the affected OUs. They will inherit the domain policy regardless of whether overriding or blocking has been used.

Using the GPMC, you can enforce policy inheritance by expanding the container to which the policy is linked, right-clicking the link to the GPO, and then selecting Enforced. If Enforced is already selected, selecting it again removes the enforcement. In the GPMC, you can determine which policies are inherited and which policies are enforced in several ways:

- Select a policy object anywhere in the GPMC, and then view the related Scope tab in the right pane (Figure 3-7). If the policy is enforced, the Enforced column under Links will have a Yes entry.

> **Tip**   After you select a policy object, you can right-click a location entry on the Scope tab to display a shortcut menu. This shortcut menu allows you to manage linking and policy enforcement.

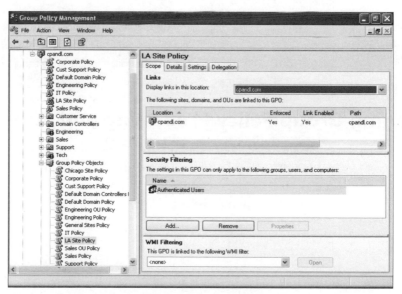

Figure 3-7   Viewing the Scope tab to determine which policies are enforced

- Select a domain or OU container in the GPMC, and then view the related Group Policy Inheritance tab in the right pane (Figure 3-8). If the policy is enforced, you'll see an (Enforced) entry in the Precedence column.

Caution   Enforcing group policy inheritance dramatically affects the way Group Policy is processed and applied. By default, a site policy has the lowest precedence and as such is the first policy processed. Any of the other policy objects can override or block its settings because they are processed later. On the other hand, an enforced site policy can have the highest precedence and as such will be the last policy processed. This means that no other policy objects can override or block its settings.

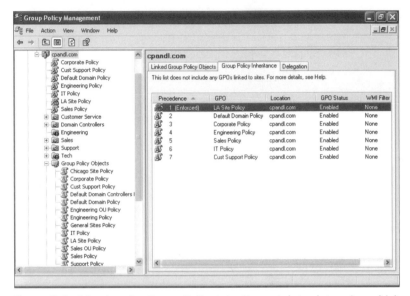

Figure 3-8   Viewing the Group Policy Inheritance tab to determine which policies are enforced

Managing Group Policy Processing and Refresh

In Group Policy, policy settings are divided into two categories: Computer Configuration and User Configuration. Computer Configuration settings are applied during startup of the operating system. User Configuration settings are applied when a user logs on to a computer. Because User Configuration settings are applied after Computer Configuration settings, User Configuration settings have precedence over Computer Configuration settings by default. This means that if there is a conflict between computer and user settings, user settings have priority and take precedence.

Once policy settings are applied, the settings are refreshed automatically to ensure they are current. During Group Policy refresh, the client computer contacts an available domain controller in its local site. If one or more of the policy objects defined in the domain have changed, the domain controller provides a list of all the policy objects that apply to the computer and to the user who is currently logged on, as appropriate. The domain controller does this regardless of whether the version numbers on all the listed policy objects have changed. By default, the computer processes the policy objects only if the version number of at least one of the policy objects has changed. If any one of the related policies has changed, all of the policies have to be processed again because of inheritance and the interdependencies within policies.

Security settings are a notable exception to the processing rule. By default, these settings are refreshed every 16 hours (960 minutes) regardless of whether policy objects contain changes. A random offset of up to 30 minutes is added to reduce impact on domain controllers and the network during updates (making the effective refresh window 960 to 990 minutes). Also, if the client computer detects that it is connecting over a slow network connection, it informs the domain controller and only the Security Settings and Administrative Templates are transferred over the network, which means that by default only the security settings and Administrative Templates are applied when a computer is connected over a slow link. The way slow link detection works is configurable in policy.

Note A major factor affecting the way refresh works is link speed. If the computer detects that it is using a slow connection (the exact definition of which is configurable in Group Policy), the computer modifies the way policy changes are processed. Specifically, if a client computer detects that it is using a slow network connection, only the security settings and administrative templates are processed. Although there is no way to turn off processing of security settings and administrative templates, you can configure other areas of policy so that the related settings are processed even across a slow network connection.

You have many options for customizing or optimizing Group Policy processing and refresh in your environment. Key tasks you might want to perform include the following:

- Changing the default refresh interval
- Enabling or disabling policy object processing completely or by setting category
- Changing the processing preference for user and computer settings
- Configuring slow link detection and subsequent processing
- Manually refreshing Group Policy

We will explore these techniques in the sections that follow.

Tip When you work with Group Policy processing and refresh, you might also want to know which policy objects have been applied and when the last policy refresh occurred on a particular computer. For details, see the section titled "Determining the Effective Group Policy settings and Last Refresh" later in this chapter.

Changing the Refresh Interval

Once Group Policy is applied, it is periodically refreshed to ensure that it is current. The default refresh interval for domain controllers is 5 minutes. For all other computers, the default refresh interval is 90 minutes, with up to a 30-minute variation to avoid overloading the domain controller with numerous concurrent client requests. This means an effective refresh window for non-domain controller computers of 60 to 120 minutes.

Wondering when you might want to change the refresh interval? In a large organization with many computers, you might want to reduce policy-related resource usage on your domain controllers or you might want to reduce policy-related traffic on your network. There is a careful balance to be found between the update frequency and the actual rate of policy change. If policy is changed infrequently, you might want to increase the refresh window to reduce resource usage. For example, you might want to use a refresh interval of 15 minutes on domain controllers and 120 minutes on other computers.

You can change the Group Policy refresh interval on a per-policy object basis. To set the refresh interval for domain controllers, complete the following steps:

1. In the GPMC, right-click the Group Policy Object you want to modify, and then select Edit. This should be a GPO linked to a container that contains domain controller computer objects.

2. Double-click the Group Policy Refresh Interval For Domain Controllers policy in the Computer Configuration\Administrative Templates\System\Group Policy folder. This displays a Properties dialog box for the policy, as shown in Figure 3-9.

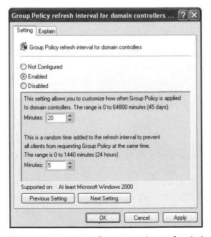

Figure 3-9   Configuring the refresh interval for domain controllers

3. Define the policy by selecting Enabled.

4. Use the first Minutes combo box to set the base refresh interval. You will usually want this value to be between 5 and 59 minutes.

> **Tip**   A faster refresh rate reduces the possibility that a domain controller won't have the most current policy configuration. A slower refresh rate reduces the frequency of policy refresh (which can also reduce overhead with regard to resource usage) but it also increases the possibility that a domain controller won't have the most current policy configuration.

5. Use the other Minutes combo box to set the minimum and maximum time variation for the refresh interval. The variation effectively creates a refresh window with the goal of avoiding overload because of numerous simultaneous client requests for Group Policy refresh.

6. Click OK.

To set the refresh interval for non-domain controller computers (member servers and workstations), complete the following steps:

1. In the GPMC, right-click the Group Policy Object you want to modify, and then select Edit. This should be a GPO linked to a container that contains computer objects.

2. Double-click the Group Policy Refresh Interval For Computers policy in the Computer Configuration\Administrative Templates\System\Group Policy folder. This displays a Properties dialog box for the policy, as shown in Figure 3-10.

Figure 3-10   Configuring the refresh interval for member servers and workstations

3. Define the policy by selecting Enabled.

4. Use the first Minutes combo box to set the base refresh interval. You will usually want this value to be between 60 and 180 minutes.

> **Tip**   A faster refresh rate reduces the possibility that a computer won't have the most current policy configuration. A slower refresh rate reduces the frequency of policy refresh (which can also reduce overhead with regard to resource usage) but it also increases the possibility that a computer won't have the most current policy configuration.

5. Use the other Minutes combo box to set the minimum and maximum time variation for the refresh interval. The variation effectively creates a refresh window with the goal of avoiding overload because of numerous simultaneous client requests for Group Policy refresh.

6. Click OK.

Enabling or Disabling GPO Processing

You can enable or disable processing of policy objects either completely or partially. Completely disabling a policy object is useful if you no longer need a policy but might need to use it again in the future, or if you're troubleshooting policy processing problems. Partially disabling a policy object is useful when you want the related policy settings to apply to either users or computers but not both.

> **Tip**   By partially disabling policy, you can ensure that only the per-computer policy settings or only the per user policy settings are applied. In cases in which you are trying to speed up policy processing, you might also want to disable user or computer settings. However, you should only do this when you've fully determined the impact of this change on your environment.

You can enable and disable policies partially or entirely by completing the following steps:

1. In the GPMC, select the container for the site, domain, or OU with which you want to work.

2. Select the policy object you want to work with, and then click the Details tab in the right pane (Figure 3-11).

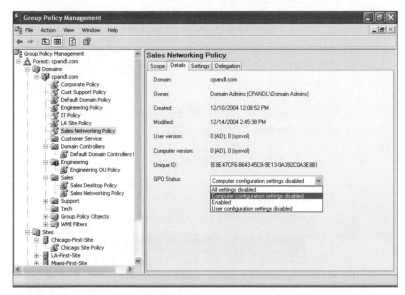

Figure 3-11   The current GPO status is shown on the Details tab

3. Use the GPO Status list to choose one of the following status settings:

- ❑ **Enabled**   Allows processing of the policy object and all its settings

- ❑ **All Settings Disabled**   Disallows processing of the policy object and all its settings

- ❑ **Computer Configuration Settings Disabled**   Disables processing of Computer Configuration settings; this means only User Configuration settings are processed

- ❑ **User Configuration Settings Disabled**   Disables processing of User Configuration settings; this means only Computer Configuration settings are processed

4. When prompted to confirm that you want to change the status of this GPO, click OK.

Changing Policy Processing Preferences

In Group Policy, Computer Configuration settings are processed when a computer starts and accesses the network. User Configuration settings are processed when a user logs on to the network. When there is a conflict between settings in both Computer Configuration and User Configuration, the Computer Configuration settings win. It is also important to point out that computer settings are applied from the computer's GPOs and the user settings are applied from the user's GPOs.

In some special situations, you might not want this behavior. In a secure lab or kiosk environment, you might want the user settings to be applied from the computer's

GPOs to ensure compliance with the strict security rules and guidelines for the lab. On a shared computer, you might want the user settings to be applied from the computer's GPOs but also allow the user settings from the user's GPOs to be applied. Using loopback processing, you can allow for these types of exceptions and obtain user settings from a computer's GPOs.

While specific scenarios and additional details are covered in Chapter 12, you can change the way loopback processing works by completing the following steps:

1. In the GPMC, right-click the Group Policy you want to modify, and then select Edit.

2. Double-click the User Group Policy Loopback Processing Mode policy in the Computer Configuration\Administrative Templates\System\Group Policy folder. This displays a Properties dialog box for the policy (Figure 3-12).

Figure 3-12   Enabling the policy and then setting the mode to either Replace or Merge

3. Define the policy by selecting Enabled, and then use the Mode list to select one of these processing modes:

   ❑ **Replace**   When you use the Replace option, the user settings from the computer's GPOs are processed, and the user settings in the user's GPOs are not processed. The user settings from the computer's GPOs replace the user settings normally applied to the user.

   ❑ **Merge**   When you use the Merge option, the user settings in the computer's GPOs are processed first, the user settings in the user's GPOs are processed next, and then the user settings in the computer's GPOs are processed again. This processing technique serves to combine the user settings in both the computer and user GPOs. If there are any conflicts, the user settings in the computer's GPOs have preference and overwrite the user settings in the user's GPOs.

4. Click OK.

> **Tip**   When you work with Group Policy, it is important to note the level of support for the policies you are working with. The User Group Policy Loopback Processing Mode policy is supported by all computers running Windows 2000 or later. This means computers running Windows 2000, Windows XP Professional, Microsoft Windows Server™ 2003, and later versions of the Windows operating system support this policy.

Configuring Slow Link Detection

Active Directory uses slow link detection to help reduce network traffic during periods of high latency. This feature is used by Group Policy clients to detect when there is increased latency and reduced responsiveness on the network and to take corrective action to reduce the likelihood that processing of Group Policy will further saturate the network. Once a slow link is detected, Group Policy clients reduce their network communications and requests to reduce the overall network traffic load by limiting the amount of policy processing they do.

Slow Link Detection

Client computers use a specific technique to determine whether they are using a slow network connection. In most cases, the client computer sends a ping to the domain controller to which it is connected. The response time from the domain controller (which is an indicator of latency) determines the next step. If the response time from any of the pings is 10 milliseconds or less, the client maintains or resumes processing of Group Policy following normal (full) procedures. If the response time from the domain controller is more than 10 milliseconds, the computer does the following:

1. Pings the domain controller three times with a 2-KB message packet

2. Uses the average response time to determine the network speed

By default, if the connection speed is determined to be less than 500 kilobits per second (which could also be interpreted as high latency/reduced responsiveness on a fast network), the client computer interprets this as indicating a slow network connection and notifies the domain controller. As a result, only security settings and administrative templates in the applicable policy objects are sent by the domain controller during policy refresh.

You can configure slow link detection using the Group Policy Slow Link Detection policy, which is stored in the Computer Configuration\Administrative Templates\System\ Group Policy folder. If you disable this policy or do not configure it, clients use the default value of 500 kilobits per second to determine whether they are on a slow link. If you enable this policy, you can set a specific slow link value, such as 256 kilobits per second.

> **Tip**   The only way to disable slow link detection completely is to enable the Group Policy Slow Link Detection policy and then set the Connection Speed option to 0. This setting effectively tells clients not to detect slow links and to consider all links to be fast.

You can optimize slow link processing for various areas of Group Policy as well. To do this, you use the following policies also found in the Computer Configuration\Administrative Templates\System\Group Policy folder:

- **Disk Quota Policy Processing**   By default, updates to policy settings for disk quotas are not processed over slow links. This doesn't, however, change the meaning of or enforcement of any current disk quotas defined in policy. Previously obtained policy settings for disk quotas are still enforced.

- **EFS Recovery Policy Processing**   By default, updates to policy settings for EFS recovery are not processed over slow links. This doesn't, however, change the meaning of or enforcement of any current EFS recovery options defined in policy. Previously obtained policy settings for EFS recovery are still valid and enforced. Note that some documentation states that the only time EFS recovery policy is not refreshed is when you specifically elect not to apply the related policy settings during periodic refresh. Based on testing, this appears to be the case, but future service packs and changes to Group Policy might modify this behavior.

- **Folder Redirection Policy Processing**   By default, updates to policy settings for folder redirection are not processed over slow links. Note that folder redirection settings are only read and applied during logon. Thus, if a user connects over a slow network during logon, the folder redirection settings will not apply by default, and the user's folders will not be subsequently redirected. This is typically the desired behavior, especially if users are connecting via dial-up or another slow remote connection.

- **Internet Explorer Maintenance Policy Processing**   By default, updates to policy settings for Microsoft Internet Explorer maintenance are not processed over slow links. If it is important to the safety and security of the network to always have the most current Internet Explorer maintenance settings, you can allow processing across a slow network connection. This ensures that the settings are the most current possible given the current Group Policy refresh rate.

- **IP Security Policy Processing**   By default, updates to policy settings for IP Security are not processed over slow links. This doesn't, however, change the meaning of or enforcement of any current IP Security policies. Previously obtained policy settings for IP Security are still valid and enforced. Note that some documentation states that the only time IP Security policy is not refreshed is when you specifically elect not to apply the related policy settings during periodic refresh. Based on testing, this appears to be the case, but future service packs and changes to Group Policy might modify this behavior.

- **Scripts Policy Processing** By default, updates to policy settings for scripts are not processed over slow links. Note that policy-defined scripts are executed only when specific events occur, such as logon, logoff, shutdown, or startup.

- **Security Policy Processing** Updates to policy settings for security are always processed regardless of the type of link. By default, security policy is refreshed every 16 hours even if security policy has not changed. The only way to stop the forced refresh is to configure security policy processing so that it is not applied during periodic background refresh. To do this, select the policy setting Do Not Apply During Periodic Background Processing. Because security policy is so important, however, the Do Not Apply setting only means security policy processing is stopped when a user is logged on and using the machine. One of the only reasons you'll want to stop security policy refresh is if applications are failing during refresh.

- **Software Installation Policy Processing** By default, updates to policy settings for software installation are not processed over slow links. This means new deployments of or updates to software are not made available to users who connect over slow links. This is typically a good thing because deploying or updating software over a slow link can be a very long process.

- **Wireless Policy Processing** By default, updates to policy settings for wireless networking are not processed over slow links. This doesn't, however, change the meaning of or enforcement of any current wireless policies. Previously obtained policy settings for wireless networking are still valid and enforced.

> **Note** Background processing (periodic refresh) can also be controlled for some of these policy areas. See the "Managing Group Policy Processing and Refresh" section in this chapter.

Configuring Slow Link Detection and Slow Link Policy Processing

You can configure slow link detection and related policy processing by completing the following steps:

1. In the GPMC, right-click the policy object you want to modify, and then select Edit.

2. Double-click the Group Policy Slow Link Detection policy in the Computer Configuration\Administrative Templates\System\Group Policy folder.

3. Select Enabled to define the policy, as shown in Figure 3-13, and then use the Connection Speed combo box to specify the speed that should be used to determine whether a computer is on a slow link. For example, if you want connections of less than 256 kilobits per second to be deemed as slow, type **256**. If you want to disable slow link detection completely for this policy object, type **0**.

Figure 3-13   Enabling and configuring the Group Policy Slow Link Detection policy

4. Click OK.

Configuring Slow Link and Background Policy Processing

You can optimize slow link and background processing (refresh) of key areas of Group Policy using policies in the Computer Configuration\Administrative Templates\System\Group Policy folder. The key configuration options available include:

■ **Allow Processing Across A Slow Network Connection**   Ensures that the extension settings are processed even on a slow network

■ **Do Not Apply During Periodic Background Processing**   Overrides refresh when extension settings change after startup or logon

■ **Process Even If The Group Policy Objects Have Not Changed**   Forces the client computer to process the extension settings during refresh even if the settings haven't changed

Tip   Although the security area of Group Policy is refreshed in full every 16 hours by default, the other areas of Group Policy are not. For these areas, only policy settings that have changed are refreshed. It is therefore sometimes necessary to force clients to reprocess policy settings even if they haven't changed on the server. Consider the case in which a local OU administrator has made changes to a local computer that might affect how the computer operates. If the local admin has modified the registry or another area of the operating system directly, these changes won't be reflected as changes to Group Policy. To try to overwrite and fix these types of changes, you might want to reapply Group Policy from a domain controller as discussed in the next section. As long as Group Policy writes to the related area of the registry or the operating system configuration in general, the problem will be resolved.

To configure slow link and background policy processing of key areas of Group Policy, complete these steps:

1. In the GPMC, right-click the policy object you want to modify, and then select Edit.

2. Expand Computer Configuration\Administrative Templates\System\Group Policy.

3. Double-click the policy you want to configure. The key policies for controlling slow link and background policy processing include:

   ❏ Disk Quota Policy Processing

   ❏ EFS Recovery Policy Processing

   ❏ Folder Redirection Policy Processing

   ❏ Internet Explorer Maintenance Policy Processing

   ❏ IP Security Policy Processing

   ❏ Scripts Policy Processing

   ❏ Security Policy Processing

   ❏ Software Installation Policy Processing

   ❏ Wireless Policy Processing

4. Select Enabled to define the policy, as shown in Figure 3-14, and then make your configuration selections. The options will differ slightly depending on the policy selected and might include the following:

   ❏ Allow Processing Across A Slow Network Connection

   ❏ Do Not Apply During Periodic Background Processing

   ❏ Process Even If The Group Policy Objects Have Not Changed

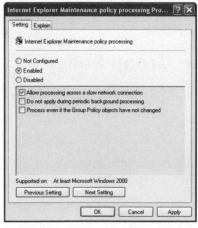

Figure 3-14   Enabling the policy and then configuring it

5. Click OK.

Refreshing Group Policy Manually

As an administrator, you might often need or want to refresh Group Policy manually. For example, you might not want to wait for Group Policy to refresh at the automatic periodic interval or you might be trying to resolve a problem with refresh and want to force Group Policy refresh. You can refresh Group Policy manually using the Gpupdate command-line utility.

Note   If you've been using SECEDIT /refreshpolicy tool provided in Windows 2000, you should now use Gpupdate. Gpupdate replaces the SECEDIT /refreshpolicy tool provided in Windows 2000.

You can initiate refresh in several ways. If you type **gpupdate** at a command prompt, both the Computer Configuration settings and the User Configuration settings in Group Policy are refreshed on the local computer. You can also refresh user and computer configuration settings separately. To refresh only Computer Configuration settings, type **gpupdate /target:computer** at the command prompt. To refresh only User Configuration settings, type **gpupdate /target:user** at the command prompt.

Note   Only policy settings that have changed are processed and applied when you run Gpupdate. You can change this behavior using the */Force* parameter. This parameter forces a refresh of all policy settings.

Tip   You can also use Gpupdate to log off a user or restart a computer after Group Policy is refreshed. This is useful because some group policies are applied only when a user logs on or when a computer starts up. To log off a user after a refresh, add the */Logoff* parameter. To restart a computer after a refresh, add the */Boot* parameter.

Modeling and Maintaining Group Policy

Group Policy modeling and maintenance tasks often go hand in hand. Typically, you will:

1. Use Group Policy modeling to plan a Group Policy implementation or update.

2. Perform maintenance tasks, including copying and backup of Group Policy objects, to safeguard the Group Policy configuration before changes are made.

3. Implement your Group Policy plan or update.

4. Use Group Policy Results to determine the effective Group Policy settings for a user logging on to the network from a specific computer, and make any necessary changes after your review.

5. Perform maintenance tasks, including copying and backing up Group Policy objects, to safeguard the Group Policy configuration after changes are made.

You won't always need to perform each of these steps, but you will usually want to perform them in the order listed. Simply put, before you change Group Policy, you should model Group Policy and back up the current Group Policy configuration. After you implement Group Policy or perform updates to Group Policy, you should log and review the results. If necessary, you should make changes and then, when you are finished with the update/review process, back up the Group Policy configuration.

Modeling Group Policy for Planning Purposes

Modeling Group Policy for planning is useful when you want to test various implementation and configuration scenarios. For example, you might want to model the effect of a slow link or the use of loopback processing mode. You can also model the effect of moving users or computers to another container in Active Directory or the effect of changing security group membership for users and computers.

All domain and enterprise administrators have permission to model Group Policy for planning, as do those who have been delegated the Perform Group Policy Modeling Analyses permission. To model Group Policy and test various implementation and update scenarios, complete these steps:

1. In the GPMC, right-click the Group Policy Modeling node, and then select Group Policy Modeling Wizard.

2. When the Group Policy Modeling Wizard starts, click Next. The Domain Controller Selection page, shown in Figure 3-15, is displayed.

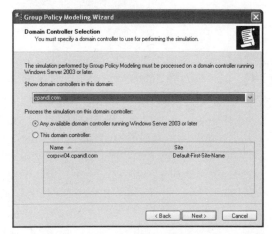

Figure 3-15   Selecting the domain controller on which the simulation will run

3. Under Show Domain Controllers In This Domain, select the domain for which you want to model results.

4. Under Process The Simulation On This Domain Controller, the Any Available Domain Controller option is selected by default. If you want to use a specific domain controller, select This Domain Controller and then choose a specific domain controller. Click Next.

5. On the User And Computer Selection page, shown in Figure 3-16, select the modeling options for users and computers. In most cases, you'll want to model policy for a specific container using user and computer information. In this case, the following steps apply:

   ❑ Under User Information, select Container, and then click Browse to display the Choose User Container dialog box. Choose any of the available user containers in the selected domain. For example, you can simulate policy settings for users in the Engineering OU.

   ❑ Under Computer Information, select Container, and then click Browse to display the Choose Computer Container dialog box. Choose any of the available computer containers in the selected domain. For example, you can simulate policy settings for computers in the Engineering OU.

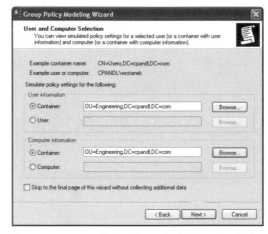

Figure 3-16   Defining the simulation criteria for users, computers, or both

6. Click Next. The Advanced Simulation Options page, shown in Figure 3-17, is displayed. The advanced options allow you to modify the simulation for network and subnet variations, such as slow link detection, loopback processing, and accessing the network from a particular site. Select any advanced options for slow network connections, loopback processing, and sites as necessary.

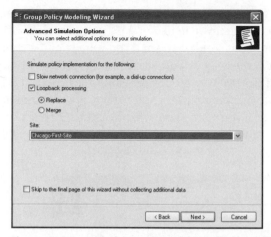

Figure 3-17 Specifying advanced simulation criteria

7. Click Next. If you are modeling user information, the User Security Groups page, shown in Figure 3-18, is displayed. Use the options on this page to simulate what would happen if you were to add a user to a designated security group. By default, the simulation is for a user who is a member of the implicit security groups Authenticated Users and Everyone. If you want to simulate membership in additional groups, you can add the groups here. For example, if you want to see what would happen if a user in the designated container were a member of the Engineering security group, you can add this group to the Security Groups list.

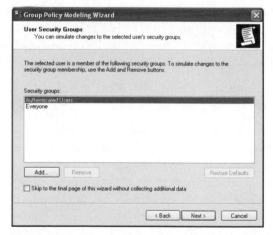

Figure 3-18 Simulating user membership in various security groups

8. Click Next. If you are modeling computer information, the Computer Security Groups page, shown in Figure 3-19, is displayed. Use the options on this page to simulate what would happen if you were to add a computer to a designated security group. By default, the simulation is for a computer that is a member of the implicit security groups Authenticated Users and Everyone. If you want to simulate membership in additional groups, you can add the groups here. For example, if you want to see what would happen if a computer in the designated container were a member of the Domain Controllers security group, you can add this group to the Security Groups list.

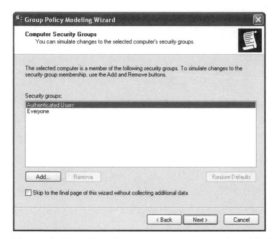

Figure 3-19   Simulating computer membership in various security groups

9. WMI filters can be linked to policy objects. By default, it is assumed that the selected users and computers meet all the WMI filter requirements, which is what you want in most cases for modeling, so click Next twice to skip past the WMI Filters For Users and WMI Filters For Computers pages.

10. To complete the modeling, click Next, and then click Finish. The wizard generates a report, the results of which are displayed in the Details pane.

11. As shown in Figure 3-20, the name of the modeling report is generated based on the containers you chose. Click on the name to highlight it for editing. Type a descriptive name for the modeling report, and then press Tab. On the report, click Show All to display all of the policy information that was modeled. You can then work through the various nodes of the report to view the effective settings for users, computers, or both in the selected container and for the selected modeling options.

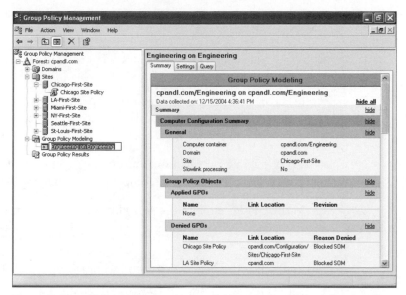

Figure 3-20 Giving the report a descriptive name and then viewing the report details

Copying and Importing Policy Objects

The GPMC features built-in copy and import operations. The copy feature allows you to copy existing policy objects from one domain to another. The import operation allows you to restore a backup copy of policy objects from one domain and then later import them into another domain. No trust is necessary for the copy and import operation to work. This means the target domain for the import operation can be a parent domain, a child domain, a domain in a different tree or forest, or even an external domain for which no trust exists.

> **Note** Copy and import operations are only for the policy settings within a policy object. These operations don't copy a policy object's links or any WMI filters that might be associated with a policy object.

Copying Policy Objects and Their Settings

Using the GPMC copy feature is fairly straightforward. You can copy a policy object and all its settings in one domain and then navigate to the domain into which you want to paste the copy of the policy object. The source and target domains can be any domains to which you can connect in the GPMC and for which you have permission to manage their related policy objects. The specific permissions you need are as follows:

- In the source domain, you need Read permission to create the copy of the policy object.

- In the target domain, you need Write permission to write the copied policy object. Administrators have this privilege, as do those who have been delegated permission to create policy objects.

You can copy a policy object from one domain to another domain to which you have connectivity and permissions by completing the following steps:

1. In the GPMC, expand the entry for the forest you want to work with, expand the related Domains node, and then expand the related Group Policy Objects node.

2. Right-click the policy object you want to copy, and then select Copy.

3. Access the target domain. Expand the entry for the forest, expand the related Domains node, and then expand the related Group Policy Objects node.

4. Right-click the target domain's Group Policy Objects node, and then select Paste.

5. If the source and target domain for the copy operation are the same, you'll see a dialog box like the one shown in Figure 3-21. Otherwise, the Cross-Domain Copying Wizard starts, and when you click Next, you see a wizard page with similar options.

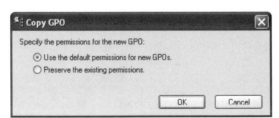

Figure 3-21   Specifying how permissions should be applied

6. You can now choose to create a copy of the policy object with the default permissions for the selected domain or copy the existing permissions to the new policy object. In most cases, you'll want to use the default permissions for new GPOs to ensure that administrators in the target domain can access and work with the copied policy object.

7. Click OK or Next as appropriate. The rest of the wizard pages have to do with migration tables, which allow you to refine the copied settings so that the proper security groups and UNC paths are used (based on the local

environment). For example, you might need to specify that the permissions for EngSec group should be migrated to the EngTeam group in the new policy object, or you might need to specify new locations for folder redirection in the new domain.

> **More Info**   You'll find detailed information on migration tables in Chapter 4, which also provides additional examples of copying and importing policy objects.

Importing Policy Objects and Their Settings

Copying policy objects between domains works fine when you have connectivity between domains and the appropriate permissions. If you are an administrator at a remote office or have been delegated permissions, however, you might not have access to the source domain to create a copy of a policy object. In this case, another administrator can make a backup copy of a policy object for you and then send you the related data. When you receive the related data, you can import the backup copy of the policy object into your domain to create a new policy object with the same settings.

Anyone with the Edit Settings Group Policy management privilege can perform an import operation. To import a backup copy of a policy object into a domain, complete the following steps:

1. Start the GPMC. Click Start, Programs or All Programs, Administrative Tools, and then Group Policy Management Console. Or type **gpmc.msc** at a command prompt.

2. Expand the entry for the forest you want to work with, and then expand the related Domains node by double-clicking it.

3. Right-click Group Policy Objects, and then select New. In the New GPO dialog box, type a descriptive name for the new GPO and then click OK.

4. The new GPO is now listed in the Group Policy Objects container. Right-click the GPO, and then choose Edit. This opens the Group Policy Object Editor.

5. Right-click the New policy object, and choose Import Settings. This starts the Import Settings Wizard.

6. Click Next. Because the import operation overwrites all the settings of the policy object you select, you are given the opportunity to back up the policy object before continuing, as shown in Figure 3-22.

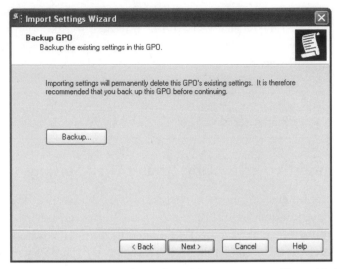

Figure 3-22   Back up the policy object you are working with, if necessary

7.   Click Next. Use the options on the Backup Location page to type or browse for the name of the folder containing the backup copy of the policy object you want to import. This is a bit confusing because you were just given the opportunity to back up the current policy object, but what is meant here is the backup folder for the policy object you want to import.

8.   Click Next. If there are multiple backups stored in the designated backup folder, you'll see a list of them on the Source GPO page, as shown in Figure 3-23. Select the one you want to use by clicking it.

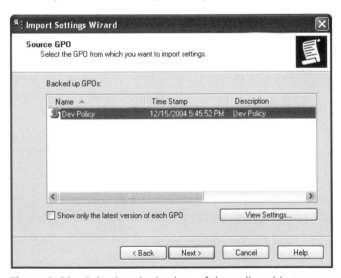

Figure 3-23   Selecting the backup of the policy object you want to use

9.   Click Next. The Import Settings Wizard scans the policy object for references to security principals and UNC paths that might need to be migrated. If any are found, you are given the opportunity to create migration tables or use existing migration tables. (You'll find detailed information on migration tables in Chapter 4.)

10.   Continue through the wizard by clicking Next, and then click Finish. The import process begins. When it is completed, click OK.

Backing Up GPOs

Just as you back up other types of critical data, you should back up your policy objects. In fact, we'll go so far as to say that backing up policy objects should be part of your periodic maintenance routine. Typically, you'll want to create two types of backups for your policy objects:

- Policy object backups that are stored on a designated domain controller and then backed up as part of that computer's routine system backup

- Policy object backups that are stored on removable media, CD-ROM or DVD, or other location that can be stored in a lock box and rotated periodically to storage off site

As with any backup process, you should develop a specific backup strategy for policy objects. Here is an example strategy:

1.   Designate a domain controller in each domain as the policy backup computer. In most cases, you will want this computer to be the PDC emulator for the domain because this is the default domain controller to which the GPMC connects.

2.   Before backing up the designated domain controller using the normal system backup process, create a backup of your domain's policy objects. You should create a new backup periodically (weekly or monthly, in most cases). Before you change policy settings, you should also create a backup, and then after you've finalized policy, you should create another backup.

3.   You should periodically create media backups of your policy objects. This means storing the backups on removable media, CD-ROM or DVD, or another location. You should have designated secure storage on site and periodically rotate backup sets off site.

Using the GPMC, you can back up individual policy objects in a domain or all policy objects in a domain by completing the following steps:

1.   In the GPMC, navigate to the Group Policy Objects container for the domain with which you want to work. Expand the forest, the Domains node, and the related Group Policy Objects node.

2. If you want to back up all policy objects in the domain, right-click the Group Policy Objects node, and then select Back Up All.

3. If you want to back up a specific policy object in the domain, right-click the policy object, and then select Back Up.

4. In the Back Up Group Policy Object dialog box, shown in Figure 3-24, click Browse, and then use the Browse For Folder dialog box to set the location in which the GPO backup should be stored.

Figure 3-24   Specifying the backup location and description

5. In the Description field, type a clear description of the contents of the backup.

6. Click Backup to start the backup process.

7. The Backup dialog box, shown in Figure 3-25, shows the progress and status of the backup. Click OK when the backup completes.

> **Tip**   When doing a full backup, you should be able to back up all policy objects successfully. If a backup fails, check the permissions on the policy and the folder to which you are writing the backup. You need Read permission on a policy and Write permission on the backup folder to create a backup. By Default, members of the Domain Admins and Enterprise Admins groups should have these permissions.

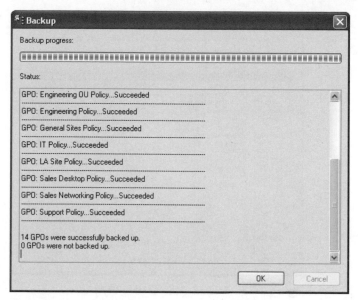

Figure 3-25   Tracking the status of the backup

Restoring Policy Objects

Using the GPMC, you can restore a policy object to the exact state it was in when it was backed up. The GPMC tracks the backup of each policy object separately, even if you back up all policy objects at once. Because version information is also tracked according to the backup time stamp and description, you can restore the last version of each policy object or a particular version of any policy object.

To restore a GPO, you need Edit Settings, Delete, and Modify Security permissions on the policy object and Read permission on the folder containing the backup. By default, members of the Domain Admins and Enterprise Admins groups should have these permissions. You can restore a policy object by completing the following steps:

1. In the GPMC, navigate to the Group Policy Objects container for the domain with which you want to work. Expand the forest and the related Domains node.

2. Right-click the Group Policy Objects node and then select Manage Backups. This displays the Manage Backups dialog box, shown in Figure 3-26.

3. In the Backup Location field, type the folder path to the backup or click Browse to use the Browse For Folder dialog box to find the folder.

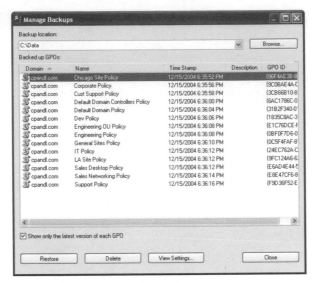

Figure 3-26   Selecting the backup to restore

4. All policy object backups in the designated folder are listed under Backup Policy objects. To show only the latest version of the policy objects according to the time stamp, select Show Only The Latest Version Of Each GPO.

5. Select the GPO you want to restore. If you want to confirm its settings, click View Settings, and then verify that the settings are as expected by using Internet Explorer. When you are ready to continue, click Restore.

6. Confirm that you want to restore the selected policy object by clicking OK. The Restore dialog box, shown in Figure 3-27, shows the progress and status of the restore.

> **Tip**   If a restore fails, check the permissions on the policy object and the folder from which you are reading the backup. To restore a GPO, you need Edit Settings, Delete, and Modify Security permissions on the policy object and Read permission on the folder containing the backup.

7. Click OK, and then restore additional Policy objects as necessary or click Close.

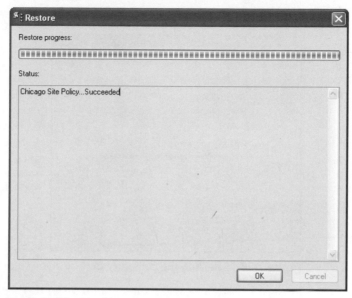

Figure 3-27   Tracking the restore status

Determining the Effective Group Policy Settings and Last Refresh

Previously we mentioned using Group Policy modeling for logging Resultant Set of Policy (RSoP). When you use Group Policy modeling in this way, you can review:

- All of the Policy objects that apply to a computer
- The last time the applicable policy objects were processed (refreshed)
- The user currently logged on to that computer (if any)

All domain and enterprise administrators have permission to model Group Policy for logging, as do those who have been delegated permission to Read Group Policy Results Data. To model Group Policy for the purpose of logging RSoP, complete these steps:

1. In the GPMC, right-click the Group Policy Results node, and then select Group Policy Results Wizard.

2. When the Group Policy Results Wizard starts, click Next. On the Computer Selection page, shown in Figure 3-28, select This Computer to view information for the local computer.

   If you want to view information for a remote computer, select Another Computer and then click Browse. In the Select Computer dialog box, type the name of the computer, and then click Check Names.

After you select the correct computer account, click OK.

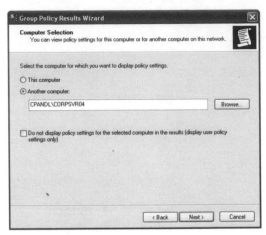

Figure 3-28   Selecting the computer for which you want to log RSoP

3. By default, both user and computer policy settings are logged. If you want to see results only for user policy settings, select Do Not Display Policy Settings For The Selected Computer.

4. In the Group Policy Results Wizard, click Next. On the User Selection page, shown in Figure 3-29, select the user whose policy information you want to view. You can view policy information for any user who has logged on to the computer.

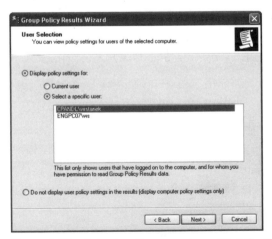

Figure 3-29   Selecting the user whose RSoP for this computer you want to view

If you want to see results only for computer policy settings, select Do Not Display User Policy Settings.

5. To complete the modeling, click Next twice, and then click Finish. The wizard generates a report, the results of which are displayed in the Details pane.

6. As shown in Figure 3-30, the name of the modeling report is generated based on the user and computer you chose. Click on the name to highlight it for editing. Type a descriptive name for the modeling report, and then press Tab.

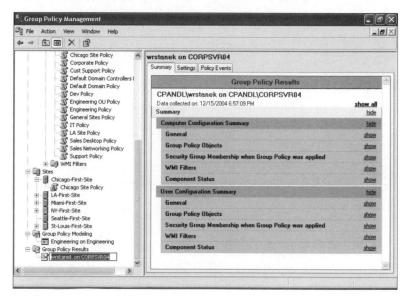

Figure 3-30   Giving the report a descriptive name and then viewing the report details

7. On the report, click Show All to display all of the policy information that was modeled. You can then work through the various nodes of the report to view the effective settings for the selected user, computer, or both. Keep the following in mind:

   ❑ To view the last time the computer or user policy was refreshed, look under Computer Configuration Summary, General for the Last Time Group Policy Was Processed or User Configuration Summary, General for the Last Time Group Policy Was Processed as appropriate.

   ❑ To view applied policy objects for the computer or user, look under Computer Configuration Summary, Group Policy Objects, Applied GPOs or User Configuration Summary, Group Policy Objects, Applied GPOs as appropriate.

   ❑ To view denied policy objects for the computer or user, look under Computer Configuration Summary, Group Policy Objects, Denied GPOs or User Configuration Summary, Group Policy Objects, Denied GPOs as appropriate.

> **Note**   The entries under Denied Policy objects show all Policy objects that should have been applied but weren't. This typically occurs because the policy objects were empty or did not contain any computer or user policy settings. The policy object also might not have been processed because inheritance was blocked. If so, the Reason Denied is stated as Blocked SOM.

Summary

As you've learned in this chapter, there are many ways you can customize and optimize the way Group Policy works. If you are looking for specific policy settings or specific values within Group Policy, you can use filters to help make your job easier. Another type of filter, called a security filter, that you can apply to Group Policy is one that changes the way Group Policy is processed with respect to security groups as well as individual computers and users. For example, if you don't want a policy object to apply to a user whose account is located in an OU, you can filter policy to achieve this.

Also, many factors affect the way policy settings are applied, including inheritance, processing order, and refresh. You can change the way inheritance works by changing the link order and precedence of link objects, overriding inheritance (as long as there is no enforcement), blocking inheritance to prevent inheritance, or enforcing inheritance to supersede other modifications to the way inheritance works. Policy processing and refresh also have major effects on the way policy settings are applied. Not only can you modify policy processing by changing the refresh interval, enabling or disabling GPO processing, and configuring slow link detection, but you can also force background refresh or manually refresh Group Policy.

Finally, to maintain policy and ensure that you can manage it over time, you can perform a number of maintenance procedures. You can model policy for the purposes of planning and tracking Resultant Set of Policy (RSoP). You can copy policy objects within and between domains. You can also back up policy objects and restore them as necessary to recover policy objects if problems occur.

Part II
Group Policy Implementation and Scenarios

In this part:

Chapter 4: Deploying Group Policy 99

Chapter 5: Hardening Clients and Servers. 135

Chapter 6: Managing and Maintaining Essential
Windows Components 217

Chapter 7: Managing User Settings and Data 253

Chapter 8: Maintaining Internet Explorer Configurations 289

Chapter 9: Deploying and Maintaining Software Through
Group Policy. 317

Chapter 10: Managing Microsoft Office Configurations 369

Chapter 11: Maintaining Secure Network Communications 397

Chapter 12: Creating Custom Environments 439

Chapter 4
Deploying Group Policy

In this chapter:

Group Policy Design Considerations 100

Controlling GPO Processing Performance. 115

Best Practices for Deploying GPOs. 121

Testing GPOs Before Deployment. 129

Summary 134

You must consider many issues and details before deploying Group Policy in your environment. This chapter will help you make the best decisions possible. We will first discuss where the concepts of Active Directory® design meet the essential concepts of linking and implementing Group Policy objects (GPOs) within the Active Directory structure. We will then consider where GPOs can be linked within Active Directory, as well as the pros and cons of linking GPOs to different Active Directory containers.

We will also discuss when and where to use the Enforce (No Override), Block Policy Inheritance, GPO Filtering, and WMI Filtering settings. These settings are extremely powerful and useful, but they can be overused, to the detriment to the overall GPO design.

At the core of all Group Policy deployment discussion is the issue of performance. If you have too many GPOs, with too many settings deployed to a target object, it will take far too long to apply the policies. This chapter will introduce techniques for improving the performance of GPO design and deployment.

Finally, we will offer an extensive list of best practices to help you in every aspect of GPO deployment—including overall design, testing of GPOs, structuring of GPOs, and linking GPOs.

Related Information
- For information on the Active Directory database and Group Policy, see Chapter 13.

Group Policy Design Considerations

A well-considered Group Policy design is essential to a stable and successful Active Directory infrastructure. When you design your Group Policy infrastructure and deploy GPOs, you must consider more than just the settings in the GPOs. Because Group Policy is an integral part of every Active Directory domain, you must also consider its interaction with all of the networks, computers, and services related to Active Directory.

The most important consideration is the design of Active Directory itself. Many facets of Active Directory design affect Group Policy, so your Group Policy design should be integrated into every step of your Active Directory design process. If you don't consider Group Policy when you design your Active Directory implementation, you could end up making major changes to one or the other to make everything work. The following section provides some design guidelines to help you avoid this kind of situation.

Active Directory Design Considerations

Group Policy depends on Active Directory for almost every aspect of how it operates. It is easier to list what aspects of Group Policy don't rely on Active Directory than list what aspects do rely on Active Directory. In fact, the former list has only one item: the local GPO. Every computer in a domain has a local GPO. This LGPO is responsible for controlling the security, environment, and software on the computer where it is located. The LGPO on a local computer is the only aspect of Group Policy that is not directly dependent on Active Directory, although the LGPO is involved in how Group Policy is processed in an Active Directory environment.

Let's now look at the Active Directory–related functions, features, and services that directly affect Group Policy:

Active Directory Database Storage Location

Some components of Group Policy are stored in the Active Directory database, and the location of that database is important for Group Policy for two reasons. First, the database must be protected so it can't be altered or accessed by an attacker or negligent user. Second, the database must be located on a hard drive with enough room to allow the database to grow, as some GPOs can become rather large as additional templates and configurations are added to them.

> **More Info**   For more information about what is stored in the Active Directory database that affects Group Policy, see Chapter 13.

Active Directory Operating System File Storage Location

Group Policy also stores some information in the system file on domain controllers. This file system includes a SYSVOL folder, which in turn includes a subfolder named Policies where GPO configurations are actually stored. The location of these files is only important when an administrator needs to troubleshoot or fix issues concerning the files stored in the Policies folder—Group Policy tools automatically find this location when you use them.

> **More Info** For more information about what is stored in the Active Directory system files (SYSVOL folder) that affects Group Policy, see Chapter 12.

Replication

A key aspect of designing Active Directory and Group Policy is directory replication between domain controllers. Replication ensures that the entire Active Directory database and the contents of the SYSVOL share are copied to all domain controllers in a domain. This is essential because domain members can communicate with any domain controller within a domain. If the domain controller that communicates back to the domain member does not have the latest Active Directory information or Group Policy settings, that computer cannot receive the correct information. Convergence means making sure that all domain controllers receive updated information related to Active Directory objects and Group Policy. Convergence depends on several things, including intersite and intrasite replication topologies. Unless you have considered convergence time when you designed your Active Directory implementation, the changes you make to Active Directory and within Group Policy may never converge to all domain controllers. Although this is unlikely, it is possible.

> **Tip** For more information about Active Directory replication, convergence, and site design, see "What is the Active Directory Replication Model?" at *http://www.microsoft.com/resources/documentation/WindowsServ/2003/all/techref/en-us/Default.asp?url=/resources/documentation/WindowsServ/2003/all/techref/en-us/w2k3tr_repup_what.asp*.

Organizational Unit Design

By far the most important aspect of Active Directory design that affects Group Policy is the design of the organizational units (OUs) within Active Directory. Because Active Directory is used mainly as a tool to organize, manage, and control user, group, and computer accounts, the design of OUs is integral to the design of Active Directory also.

When you consider the design of OUs, you should focus on two essential aspects: delegation of administration and Group Policy deployment.

■ **Delegation of administration** This powerful feature of Active Directory should receive the majority of your attention during the design phase. Delegation of administration within Active Directory refers to the administrator of Active Directory "delegating" the tasks of controlling objects within Active Directory to other administrators and users. Examples of administrative tasks that could be delegated might include:

❑ Resetting passwords for user accounts in the Sales department only

❑ Adding user accounts to security groups that are associated only with the Marketing department

❑ Controlling the ability for computer accounts to be joined to the domain and added to a specific OU

Delegation of administration can be configured at any level within Active Directory, but it is best to use it at the OU level. This requires that you incorporate the following in your OU design:

❑ Define the administrative model of controlling user, group, and computer accounts.

❑ Define which administrators and users will have control over specific user, group, and computer accounts.

❑ Define the specific tasks that administrators and users will be delegated authority over for their respective user, group, and computer accounts.

❑ Do not create OUs that do not facilitate delegation of administration or Group Policy deployment.

■ **Group Policy deployment** Almost as important as delegation of administration to your OU design is Group Policy deployment. (GPO deployment has somewhat lower priority because it is more flexible than delegation of administration.) When you do think about OU design and how to deploy Group Policy, keep these points in mind:

❑ Group Policy applies only to user and computer accounts. (GPOs don't apply to group accounts.)

❑ GPOs affect the level in Active Directory at which they are applied, as well as all subordinate levels.

❑ GPOs affect all objects at the level at which they are deployed, including domain controllers, administrative groups, and administrative user accounts

❑ GPOs can be limited in their scope of influence by an administrator configuring Block Policy Inheritance, Security filtering, and WMI filters

Once you begin to interweave the concepts of delegation of administration and Group Policy deployment into your OU design, you might find that the OU structure can become quite large. As a best practice, you should limit your OU structure to no more than 10 levels deep. This guideline is based on the premise that there will be at least one GPO linked to each OU, combining for approximately 10 GPOs. Performance will suffer if too many GPOs are applied to a computer or user account at logon.

> **More Info**   For more information on other factors that can affect computer and user logon performance due to GPO configurations, see the "Controlling GPO Processing Performance" section in this chapter.

Site Design

You must consider several aspects of Active Directory sites during the design phase. First, sites are created to control replication between domain controllers in different geographical locations. Second, sites can differentiate domain controllers that are "poorly connected" (which typically means using any network connection that is less than 10 Mbps). Third, sites control client and server access to Active Directory–aware resources and functions. Active Directory–aware resources and functions include:

- Authentication of computer and user accounts
- Renewal of Kerberos tickets
- Distributed File System
- Group Policy application

> **More Info**   For more information about the process a computer goes through when applying GPOs, see Chapter 13.

Sites control other aspects of Active Directory and Group Policy administration and management. When you design the replication topology and the site itself, it is important to remember that sites are designed and implemented to control replication. The replication topology that you configure within the site determines what the convergence time will be for all Active Directory and Group Policy changes. (The "Replication" section in this chapter explains convergence time.)

Sites also indirectly control the administration of Group Policy. By default, the domain controller running the Primary Domain Controller (PDC) master operator role is referenced for administration of Group Policy. Therefore, when you create, edit, or manage GPOs, the updates are made on the domain controller responsible for the PDC role. However, this behavior can be changed in the Group Policy Management Console (GPMC).

> **Tip**   To change the domain controller that the GPMC references, right-click the domain name in the GPMC console and select Change Domain Controller. In the dialog box that appears, select Any Available Domain Controller. The GPMC will first try to pick a domain controller in your site, and then it will move to domain controllers in other sites.

> **More Info**   For more information on the GPMC, see Chapter 3. For more Active Directory design tips, see "Best Practice Active Directory Design for Managing Windows Networks" at *http://www.microsoft.com/technet/prodtechnol/windows2000serv/technologies/activedirectory/plan/bpaddsgn.mspx*.

As you can see, Group Policy and Active Directory are highly dependent on one another. Make sure that all Group Policy considerations are carried throughout the entire Active Directory design process. Forgetting Group Policy issues and needs can cause serious problems.

Physical Design Considerations

You must consider a few physical aspects of your network in conjunction with your overall Group Policy design. We have already identified one of these aspects, which is directly tied to the network topology: Active Directory site design. The site design controls which domain controllers the target computer will communicate with during the authentication process. The site also directs the computer to the nearest domain controller and resource server when it needs to obtain resources that are Active Directory site-aware.

Another important consideration is the link speed of the connection between the target computer and the domain controller that is servicing it. GPOs make a distinction between slow and fast link speeds. By default, the cutoff between fast and slow links is 500 Kbps. This means that any connection with a speed of less than 500 Kbps is considered a slow connection and some GPO settings might not apply. Several situations can cause the computer to have a slow network connection to the domain controller:

- A connection with speed degradation due to poor network configuration or interference
- A connection to the domain controller over a slow link from a branch office
- A congested network, which causes the computer connection to slow down

You can control what connection speed is considered slow for each GPO. This means you also have control over whether the settings in a GPO apply to computers that don't have very good connections to domain controllers.

Note   The GPO settings that control the connection speed are located under both the Computer Configuration and User Configuration nodes in a GPO. Here are the paths to each of the settings:

■ *Computer Configuration\Administrative Templates\System\Group Policy\Group Policy slow link detection*

■ *User Configuration\Administrative Templates\System\Group Policy\Group Policy slow link detection*

More Info   For more information on the slow-link detection process, see Chapter 13.

You also have control over which major components of the GPO are processed over slow connection links. Some GPO components are always processed, regardless of the connection speed:

■ Administrative template settings

■ Security policies

The following are other settings that are processed over slow connection links by default but can be configured to not be processed over slow links:

■ EFS Recovery policies

■ IP Security policies

■ Software restrictions policies

■ Wireless policies

■ Internet Explorer Maintenance policies

The following components of a GPO aren't processed over slow links by default but can be configured to be processed over slow connection links:

■ Application deployment

■ Logon/logoff scripts

■ Folder redirection

■ Disk quotas

Remote Access Connection Design Considerations

When a computer connects to the network over a remote access connection, Group Policy is processed differently from a slow link connection. The main reason for this is that the computer policy is processed before the logon screen appears. In a remote access connection scenario, however, the computer is already at the logon screen when an attempt to communicate with the remote access server is initiated.

To control the behavior of Group Policy during a remote access connection, you can select the Logon Using Dial-up Connection check box at the logon prompt. This triggers the applicable computer and user Group Policy settings to apply if the computer is a member of the domain that the authenticating remote access server belongs to or trusts. The computer settings are applied as a background refresh during the logon process. However, computer-based software installation settings and startup scripts are not processed at this point because these computer settings are normally processed before the logon screen appears. The user Group Policy settings are applied as a foreground process during the logon.

If you decide not to select the Logon Using Dial-up Connection check box for your remote access connection but you still authenticate to the domain through the remote access server, you still receive Group Policy settings. The settings are applied during the background refresh interval for the computer and user Group Policy settings. This means the computer-based software installation settings and startup scripts do not run. It also means that the user-based software installation settings, logon scripts, and folder redirection policy settings do not run because these user-based Group Policy settings can be run only during a foreground application period, which is at the initial logon.

The other components of Group Policy behave in a similar manner to that of a typical slow link connection. This means that registry settings and security settings are always applied, either at logon or during a background refresh. Other Group Policy components can be controlled according to the link speed, as described in the "Physical Design Considerations" section of this chapter.

> **More Info**   For more information about best-practice configurations for slow link settings that apply to remote access clients, see Chapter 11. For more information about how remote access clients process Group Policy at logon, see Chapter 13.

GPO Application Design Considerations

The design criteria for your overall Group Policy deployment plan should include details regarding GPO application—how GPOs are created, linked, configured, processed, and controlled. Many of these GPO controls allow the administrator to control key aspects of the target computer and user accounts within Active Directory. These settings also allow users to access their desktop and network resources without having to wait for their computer to load all of the scripts, applications, and settings. However, these settings can also be configured too tightly. You must find a balance that does not leave the computer and user environment insecure while not forcing users to wait a long time for Group Policy processing to complete before they can use their computers.

Here are four key points that you need to consider for the design, configuration, and implementation of your GPOs:

- Group Policy affects only computer accounts and user accounts.

- GPOs do not apply to security groups.

- GPOs can be linked to sites, domains, or OUs.

- Multiple GPOs can be linked to a single site, domain, or OU.

> **More Info** For more information about the basics of Group Policy, GPO processing, and GPO linking, see Chapter 2.

Site, Domain, and OU Linking

Two important design considerations come into play when you consider linking GPOs to sites, domains, or OUs. By the time your sites and OUs have been created, your Active Directory design is already done, and you finalize your GPO deployment by linking your GPOs to these objects in Active Directory.

However, before you link GPOs to sites, domains, or OUs, you must think about the objects the GPO settings will affect, as well as the interaction between the different GPOs. You need to be aware of two main considerations with regard to linking GPOs to sites, domains, and OUs:

- GPOs have two distinct sections.

- GPOs interact with sites, domains, and OUs

GPOs Have Two Distinct Sections Although the Group Policy Object Editor shows two completely different sections in a GPO, administrators often tend to forget this simple fact. The two sections of a GPO are Computer Configuration and User Configuration, as shown in Figure 4-1. This is important to remember because the policy settings located under the Computer Configuration section apply only to computer accounts, while the policy settings located under the User Configuration section affect only user accounts.

Figure 4-1 Computer Configuration and User Configuration sections of a standard GPO

Take a look at an example of when this design consideration might come into play. In our scenario, there are two OUs: Sales_employees and Sales_computers. The Sales_employees OU contains all user accounts for employees in the Sales department. The Sales_computers OU contains all of the computer accounts for the Sales employees. A GPO named Security Message is linked to the Sales_computers OU. The Security Message GPO has both the Message Title and Message Text policies configured, to show a security warning to the user when she attempts to log on to the computer. When any Sales employee attempts to log on to any sales computer, he will see this security message.

There are two other OUs in this scenario: IT_employees and IT_computers. User accounts are in the IT_employees OU, and computer accounts reside in the IT_computers OU. No GPOs are linked to these OUs. You need to consider whether a security message will appear when an employee from Sales logs on to a computer in IT. Similarly, you need to consider whether a security message will appear when an employee from IT logs on to a computer in Sales.

To determine the results in each case, you must remember that the Message Title and Message Text policies are "computer-based" because they reside in the Computer Configuration section. Therefore, when *any* user logs on to a computer in Sales, she will receive the security message. However, because the policy doesn't apply to computers in IT, *no* user will see a security message when logging on to a computer in IT.

To ensure that you keep these settings straight, here are some tips to keep in mind when you design OUs, place accounts in OUs, and link GPOs to OUs:

- Place user accounts in different OUs than those where computer accounts reside.
- When creating GPOs, keep computer account settings in different GPOs than user account settings.
- Make sure all of the desired accounts you want to target by a GPO are located in an OU to which that GPO is linked.
- When troubleshooting processing of some specific policy setting, be aware of whether that policy setting applies to computer accounts or user accounts.

 More Info For more information about linking GPOs to sites, the domain, and OUs, see Chapter 2 and Chapter 3.

Interaction of GPO Application When Linked to Sites, Domains, and OUs

Another key design consideration is how GPOs linked to sites, domains, and OUs interact when Group Policy is applied. You must remember that GPOs follow inheritance rules down through the Active Directory structure. For example, any GPO that is linked to the domain will affect all accounts within the domain by default. This includes domain controllers, servers, IT staff, the Administrator account, executives, and service accounts.

If two GPOs are linked to the same domain, they are processed according to the link order specified in the GPMC, as shown in Figure 4-2.

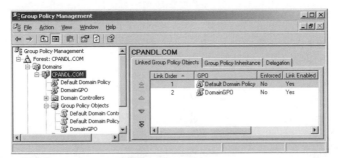

Figure 4-2   Link order of multiple GPOs linked to the same level in Active Directory

 Important   GPO precedence works in the opposite direction from the link order numbering. In other words, a GPO with a lower link-order number has precedence over a GPO with a higher link-order number. The result of this ordering can be seen when the same policy setting is configured in two GPOs linked to the same level. In this situation, the policy setting configured in the GPO with the lower link number takes precedence over the policy setting configured in the GPO with the higher link number.

 More Info   For more information on GPOs linked at the same level within Active Directory, see Chapter 2.

The behavior of multiple GPOs linked to a single level in Active Directory becomes more complicated when you consider the larger picture of having additional GPOs linked to sites, the domain, and OUs. As we have already seen, the overall GPO precedence order is as follows, from lowest to highest:

- Local GPO
- GPO linked to site
- GPO linked to domain
- GPO linked to OU

As you consider where GPOs will be linked within Active Directory, you must consider what the final policy settings will be on the target object. Like GPOs linked at the same level, GPOs linked to sites, domains, and OUs, as well as the local GPO, must resolve conflicting policy settings. The GPO with the highest precedence will always have control over a GPO with lower precedence when there is a conflicting policy setting.

Cross-Domain GPO Linking

If your Active Directory design and infrastructure includes multiple domains, you will have still more options than just linking GPOs to sites, the domain, and OUs. You will also be able to link a GPO from one domain to the domain node or an OU in a different domain. At first glance, this feature appears to offer an avenue for streamlining the number of required GPOs, by having one domain use an existing GPO in another domain that meets the GPO design and security requirements. However, linking GPOs across domains has drawbacks in three areas: performance, administration, and troubleshooting.

- **Performance**   When a GPO is linked from one domain to another, communication is required between domain controllers in the two domains when the GPO is referenced—for both the computer and user portions of the GPO. This additional communication is needed because of the trust relationship between the two domains, which forces the domain controllers to pass credentials back and forth to authenticate computer and user accounts. This additional communication slows down the GPO processing for the domain that does not contain the GPO.

- **Administration**   When a forest has more than one domain, it is common to have separate administrative staff responsible for each domain, including separate administration for linking GPOs to OUs, creating GPOs, and managing GPOs. This separation makes it difficult for administrators in the remote domain to be aware of how GPOs are managed in the originating domain and what functionality they contain.

> **More Info**   For more information on managing GPOs, see Chapter 2.

- **Troubleshooting**   Once a GPO is linked across domains, the complexity of the GPO design increases, making the task of troubleshooting Group Policy processing more difficult. This issue, which can be further complicated by use of GPO permissions, enforcing GPOs, WMI filters, and disabling sections of GPOs can make cross-domain GPO linking scenarios extremely difficult to troubleshoot.

Synchronous and Asynchronous Processing

One key design decision is whether the GPOs should be processed synchronously or asynchronously. These two processing methods have a very different effect on how GPOs are processed. You must understand what each of these processing methods does to the application of GPO settings before you can make a prudent design decision.

- **Synchronous**   Each process that applies policy must finish running before the next one begins. Applying all of the GPO settings to the target object can take a long time. However, if you choose this approach then you are guaranteed that the policies will be applied before the user gains access to the network. This increases security and ensures that the user's desktop environment is configured properly before he can use the computer.

- **Asynchronous**   Multiple processes can run at the same time. With this approach, the user gains access to her computer faster than with synchronous processing. However, it is possible for the user to gain access to her computer before all of the policy settings have been applied to the computer. This can lead to strange consequences. For example, if the policy that removes the Run command from the Start menu is enabled, asynchronous processing might allow the user to access to computer before this policy takes effect. The result is that the user can then access the Run command for a brief moment before the policy effectively takes the Run command away.

More Info   For more information on how GPOs are processed, see Chapter 13. For more information on network communication and security scenarios, see Chapter 11.

Fast Logon Optimization

Similar to the synchronous/asynchronous policy processing, there is a policy setting that can affect the startup behavior with regard to applying GPO settings. The Fast Logon Optimization policy is named Always Wait For The Network At Computer Startup And Logon. This policy applies policy settings asynchronously when the computer starts and when the user logs on. The result is that users can begin working on their computer faster than if synchronous processing were enabled. Fast Logon Optimization is enabled for Windows XP by default for both domain and workgroup members. Fast Logon Optimization is always off during logon under the following conditions:

- When a user first logs on to a computer
- When a user has a roaming user profile or a home directory for logon purposes
- When a user has synchronous logon scripts

Fast Logon Optimization is supported only by Windows XP Professional. Windows 2000 and Windows Server 2003 computers are still controlled by the synchronous and asynchronous policy setting, even though the results are similar. The policy setting for enabling or disabling Fast Logon Optimization can be found at:

Computer Configuration\Administrative Templates\System\Logon\Always wait for the network at computer startup and logon

Enabling this policy setting forces the computer to process Group Policy synchronously in the foreground when logging on. (Background processing during Group Policy refresh is always asynchronous.). However, it makes the computer appear to be working more slowly and does not give the user access to their desktop as quickly. Disabling this policy setting forces the computer to process policy asynchronously in the foreground. The user then gets access to the computer faster, but not all policies may apply until processing completes.

More Info   For more information on how GPOs are processed, see Chapter 13.

GPO Inheritance Modification

The default GPO inheritance scheme (GPOs at higher levels apply to lower levels) will suffice in most cases. However, in some cases such inheritance might conflict with your overall Active Directory design. This might be due either to administrative requirements or because inheritance might need to be uniquely controlled for a few accounts in an OU based on the user's needs, application requirements, or security requirements.

You can alter the default GPO inheritance in four ways. Each option gives you ultimate control over which policy settings affect specific accounts. These options are:

- Enforce (No Override)
- Block Policy Inheritance
- Security Filtering
- WMI Filters

These options let you be very specific about exactly which user and computer accounts the GPOs and their settings will ultimately affect. However, overusing these options can lead to problems with the following aspects of GPO deployment:

- Determining the Resultant Set of Policies
- Logon performance
- Troubleshooting GPO application

As a result, you should generally try to avoid these four inheritance-altering options. Later in this chapter, you will look at when and how you should use these options when deploying GPOs.

More Info   For more information on Enforce (No Override), Block Policy Inheritance, security filtering, and WMI Filtering, see Chapter 3.

Additional GPO Design Considerations

We have considered where GPOs can be linked, as well as some specific settings that can be made in a GPO to control how Group Policy is processed and applied. However, we also need to consider the structure of the GPOs with regard to the number of settings per GPO, the type of settings per GPO, and additional settings that can be placed in a GPO. Failure to take these considerations into account can result in slower startup times and longer logon times.

Monolithic vs. Functional

When you consider the types of computers and users that will be receiving policy settings, you must decide how to organize these policy settings into GPOs. You will inevitably have many different categories of policy settings for each type of computer. Here are examples of some commonly used types of computers:

- Domain controller
- File server
- SQL server
- IT staff client
- Developer client
- Executive client

We will investigate additional types throughout this chapter. As a reminder, here are some of the categories of policy settings that are possible within a GPO:

- Security
- Application deployment
- Internet Explorer maintenance
- Scripts

It is common during the design phase to develop a matrix based on the type of computer and listing the policy settings by categories. One intuitive design approach places all of the policy settings for each type of computer into a single GPO. This is called the *monolithic* approach. As you can imagine, this produces a GPO implementation that yields one GPO for each type of computer. However, the monolithic approach is typically the least flexible for working into your Active Directory design. This approach is also harder to delegate administrative control over and is more difficult to troubleshoot.

The other approach for implementing GPO policies is the *functional* approach. Instead of placing all of the GPO settings into a single GPO for each computer type, you set up the GPOs based on the category for each computer type. This yields more GPOs, but they are typically easier to work into your Active Directory design, simpler to delegate administrative control over, and easier to troubleshoot.

Additional GPO Settings

Even though a typical GPO includes thousands of possible settings, you might have certain applications or services that require additional or custom GPO settings. You should consider these additional settings as their own category within your matrix.

For example, the Microsoft Office suite has many component applications that can be installed individually or all together. Office also has a set of administrative templates (.adm files) that provide additional GPO settings to configure how Office works. You can install these templates for the individual Office components or all at once. The Office components with their own .adm file include:

- Access
- Excel
- FrontPage
- Outlook
- Word

Other components and features of Windows also have special .adm files. They include:

- Internet Explorer security
- Outlook Express
- Windows Media Player

> **More Info**   For more information on .adm files for Office, see Chapter 10.

There are more areas where you might encounter additional GPO settings. You can consider each area as its own category as you develop the design matrix for what settings each type of computer will include in its GPO. These additional areas can include:

- Applications (Microsoft or third-party)
- Custom .adm file settings (registry values)
- Custom security template settings

> **More Info**   For more information about developing custom .adm files, see Chapter 14. For more information on developing custom security template settings, see Chapter 15.

Controlling GPO Processing Performance

A key consideration during the design and implementation of GPOs is performance–not only the speed at which GPO settings are applied to computers and users, but also the potential performance degradation of the network, servers, and domain controllers that are all associated with Group Policy. The degradation to the network and servers can be attributed to replication of numerous GPO changes and the application of many GPO settings (especially software installation).The speed at which GPOs are applied can also be affected by many settings and implementation flaws.

Common Performance Issues

Although the design considerations described earlier can all contribute to the degradation of performance when GPOs are applied, certain factors are most influential–the network topology, the number of GPO settings that need to be applied, the complexity of scripts, and so on. You must be aware of these factors and try to design your GPO implementation to reduce their effects.

- **Too many settings in a single GPO** If there are too many policies configured in a single GPO, it can lead to slow response times for the computer startup and user logon. This slow response time is common for many implementation of GPOs, but you should be aware of it when you consider the policy settings to implement and you should make users aware of the potential lag time in accessing their computer. Another facet of having too many GPO settings in a single GPO is if too many settings have to be reversed in other GPOs. It is best to not reverse or negate too many GPO settings when policy settings are applied at the local, site, domain, and OU levels.

- **Too many GPOs** A similar problem to having too many settings in a single GPO is having too many GPOs. The result can be the same as having too many settings overall, but with too many GPOs the processing time is multiplied because each GPO must be evaluated for the computer or user account's access control list (ACL). If there are WMI filters or scripts in each GPO, this also can significantly increase the time it takes for GPOs to be applied.

> **More Info**   For more information on GPO processing, see Chapter 13.

- **Slow links** Sometimes several physical networks are traversed when a single GPO is applied. Not only does the domain controller need to communicate with the computer, but other servers might be involved that store applications or updates. If any of the networks between the client and servers involved with the application of GPO settings and configurations have slow links, application of Group Policy will be slower.

■ **Too many scripts** Sometimes you need to configure a user's environment, applications, and other features through scripts. If these scripts become large or complex, it can take a long time to apply the settings to the computer. In some cases, the computer might appear to be not responding, which might lead the user to manually shut down her computer and restart it. Because the script goes through the same process at the next startup, the user will still see the same "problem." The solution is to make sure that scripts are optimized and users are well educated.

■ **Software installation** When GPOs are used to install software, startup and logon times can be affected dramatically. When software is deployed to computer accounts, the software installs automatically the next time the computer starts up. For user accounts, this behavior can be controlled to install the application when the GPO setting is applied or when the user triggers the need to use the application. These triggers can be an attempt by the user to open a file that has an extension associated with the application, or an attempt to access a shortcut to the application's EXE file. We will offer some tips for optimizing the deployment of applications using GPOs later in this chapter.

More Info For more information on installing applications using GPOs, see Chapter 9.

■ **File system and registry entries are slow on deep trees** If you are controlling permissions on files, folders, and registry keys using the Security Settings section within a GPO, this can slow down the application of the GPO settings to the target computer. The settings that control the files, folders, and registry keys can be found in one of two nodes within a GPO: File System or Registry, as shown in Figure 4-3.

Figure 4-3 A typical GPO showing the location of the File System and Registry nodes

Performance Tips

Your best intentions in deploying Group Policy settings can be negated if the user experiences too much delay during startup or logon. This section provides you with some tips for speeding up Group Policy processing.

Reduce the Number of Group Policy Objects

The GPO design stage is a great place to start optimizing GPO application. A design matrix that depicts which policy settings apply to each type of computer can help. Once you have the matrix, you can decide which settings to place in specific GPOs. Remember that each GPO must be evaluated for each account that it applies to.

Let's look at a simple scenario. You have five types of computers, and you have broken down the GPO settings into 20 categories. Your options range from using 100 different GPOs based on category, or 5 different GPOs based on computer type. The best approach will probably fall somewhere in the middle.

The first option of using 100 different GPOs would require that each type of computer apply 20 different GPOs. While this approach has the most flexibility from the design point of view, it is likely to result in users experiencing extremely slow startup times and logons. The second option of using only 5 different GPOs means that each type of computer will apply only one GPO. Even though this second option is ideal from the performance point of view, troubleshooting this scenario would be difficult. With the GPO settings separated into different GPOs, it is easier to find the settings, as well as enable and disable entire GPOs to try to identify where problems in the GPO processing are occurring.

Thus, you generally need to consider a solution that falls somewhere in the middle. How you break up the GPO settings into different GPOs is up to you, and your solution should take into consideration all of the GPO design considerations that we looked at earlier in this chapter. Your solution should also try to facilitate delegation of administration for tasks like GPO creation, linking, editing, and viewing. Finally, your final GPO structure should be designed to simplify troubleshooting.

Link GPOs to Organizational Units

You might decide to link your GPOs to the domain level to reduce the total number of GPOs required. However, in the long run this can cause more work once you evaluate all the types of computers you will deploy, plus the work that it will take to design your GPO filtering requirements to ensure that only the proper accounts receive certain GPOs.

One important factor in linking GPOs is to only have the target accounts that need to apply the GPO settings evaluate them for application. If you link all of the GPOs to the domain and use GPO filtering, all GPOs will need to be evaluated by all accounts in the domain. This will slow down the processing of GPOs for all accounts in the domain.

The alternative is to link GPOs to OUs that are as close to the target accounts as possible. This reduces the load on all accounts, forcing only the target accounts to evaluate the GPOs for processing.

Disable Unused Sections of GPOs

In most Active Directory implementations, the computer and user accounts are separated into different OUs. This is not a requirement of Active Directory design, but it is common practice to separate the different types of computer accounts (domain controllers, file servers, Web servers, SQL servers, and so on) and user accounts (IT staff, executives, developers, service accounts, employees, and others) and place each type of computer or user account in a different OU.

With computer accounts in their own OUs and user accounts in separate OUs, the GPOs that are linked to each of these OUs will be specific to each type of account. For example, if a GPO is linked to the OU that contains only file servers, there is no need to have any of the User Configuration settings configured. If the User Configuration settings were configured, they would not affect any users anyway because there are no user accounts in an OU that contain only file servers.

Because the GPO settings associated with user accounts will not be useful in this scenario, you should disable the User portion of the GPO to reduce the overall processing required by computer accounts in the OU. Doing this for a single GPO won't make much difference, but if you disable the User section of every GPO that computer accounts need to process, it can make a significant difference in the total processing time.

> **More Info**   For more information on how to disable the Computer or User section of a GPO, see Chapter 2.

Optimize the Background Refresh Interval

You can change the background refresh interval to modify the time it takes to reassess whether new GPO settings have been made. The default refresh interval is different for domain controllers, domain members, and user accounts.

The interval can be set anywhere from 7 seconds to 45 days. A longer interval reduces how often a computer or user refreshes new GPO settings; 45 days is a long time to wait between GPO updates. If you configure the refresh interval too low, however, network traffic will increase and the user's work can be adversely affected.

The default refresh interval for domain members and user accounts is 90 minutes, which is an efficient interval for most organizations. This value should be modified only if a smaller interval is required or the bandwidth is too small to support even the 90-minute default setting.

Domain controllers update GPO settings every 5 minutes by default. The interval for domain controllers is lower to increase security on these computers and to ensure that critical settings are pushed down to these computers as quickly as possible. Again, this is a reasonable setting unless your environment warrants a smaller interval. For domain controllers, a larger interval is typically not recommended for security reasons.

> **More Info**   For more information on how to configure the refresh interval for domain controllers, domain members, or user accounts, see Chapter 3.

Configure a Reasonable Timeout for Scripts

Because scripts can configure the user's environment in important ways, they are often used in enterprise environments. It is common to have scripts map drives, configure printer ports, modify services, and more. In some cases, the scripts that run against computer or user accounts can become too large or complex, causing the logon time to become too long.

Sometimes startup or logon scripts can only finish their work when the network and key servers are available. In this case, when the network or a server resource is temporarily unavailable, the processing time for the scripts slows down and can make the user wait an unreasonable amount of time to start using her computer. In this situation, you should consider configuring a reasonable timeout for scripts, both startup and logon. If your scripts typically take 2 to 3 minutes to run, you might want to add 1 to 2 additional minutes to allow for slow response times or network congestion.

> **More Info**   For more information on how to configure the timeout for scripts, see Chapter 7.

Configure Asynchronous Processing

When GPO settings take too long to apply, the problem might be due to an abundance of security settings, desktop environment settings, Internet Explorer settings, and so on. In this case, you might want to consider configuring GPOs to apply asynchronously. By default, GPOs apply synchronously (except for Windows XP, which takes advantage of the Fast Logon configuration described above), which means the user cannot access the desktop and applications until all GPO settings have been successfully applied.

Asynchronous application of GPOs speeds up the user's access to his computer but also leaves the computer vulnerable for a brief amount of time between when the user has access to his desktop and when all of the GPO settings have successfully been applied.

> **More Info**   For more information on how to configure synchronous and asynchronous policy processing, see Chapter 13.

Limit Use of Loopback

Configuring the use of loopback processing for a GPO can hurt performance on the computer it applies to. If the computer needs to evaluate the GPO settings within the User Configuration section in the GPOs for both the computer account and the user account, this can take extra time.

Loopback processing has two modes. The first is *Replace* mode, which takes only the settings for the user account from the User Configuration section of the GPO and applies those settings to the computer account. Because this is a simple replacement of the user-based GPO settings, the processing time required is not great. However, if you have configured loopback processing for *Merge* mode, the computer must evaluate the User Configuration sections in multiple GPOs, determining which settings should have precedence. This additional processing causes a slower response time for the user's access to his desktop. As a result, you should limit your use of loopback processing to computers that need the additional control that this feature can provide.

> **More Info**   For more information on how to configure loopback processing, see Chapter 12.

Filter GPOs Based on Group Membership

A new GPO is configured to apply to all computer and user accounts by having the Authenticated Users group configured on the ACL of all GPOs by default. In most cases, this is the best configuration because there is no need to administer the ACL on the GPO.

If you have GPOs linked to OUs that contain both accounts that need to have the GPO settings applied and accounts that should bypass the GPO settings, you should filter the GPOs. This filtering reduces the time that it takes to process GPOs because the accounts do not evaluate the GPOs for which they are not listed on the ACL.

In this case, the best method for filtering your GPOs is to remove the Authenticated Users group and add the specific security groups that contain the accounts for which the GPO settings should apply. These entries in the ACL must have both the Read and Apply Group Policy permissions.

> **More Info**   For more information on how to filter GPOs, see Chapter 3.

Best Practices for Deploying GPOs

Deploying GPOs efficiently and effectively requires careful attention. As we have seen in this chapter, you must consider many factors when you design and implement Group Policy in your enterprise. How you design your GPOs depends on your Active Directory structure, replication, site design, and more—and that's a lot of information to evaluate. If you do not evaluate these factors, troubleshooting Group Policy can be much more difficult, and Group Policy processing can suffer performance degradation as well.

There is no secret recipe or procedure that you can follow to bypass all possible issues involved in deploying Group Policy, but the following best practices can help you avoid many pitfalls.

Choosing the Best Level to Link GPOs

You can link GPOs to sites, domains, and OUs: which level is best when deploying GPOs? As a general rule, there are more ramifications when linking GPOs to sites and domains due to the scope of the accounts that are affected. Also, GPOs that are linked to sites and domains typically contain generic settings, whereas the GPOs that are linked down through the OU structure usually contain specific settings that are based on the type of computer or user. Let's look at some general rules and guidelines for each level.

GPOs Linked to Sites

It is rare to have a lot of GPOs linked to sites in a typical Active Directory implementation. When you link a GPO to a site, it affects computers and users based on the IP address of the computer. In most cases, Active Directory administration, computer types, and user types don't follow the network topology, so it is difficult to organize GPO settings in such a way that they can be deployed to sites. Here are a few scenarios where you might decide to link a GPO to a site:

- **IPSec settings**   A branch office or other network segment might need to have IPSec security configurations for all computers on that network.

- **Software Update Services (SUS)**   When clients and servers receive information from Group Policy about SUS, they are typically directed to a SUS server. Since they are targeted to a SUS server to receive their updates, the GPOs containing SUS settings can be linked to sites to automatically affect all computers within a specific range of IP addresses. This will lead to computers being directed to the SUS server that is nearest them, increasing performance of applying the updates and reducing network traffic across the slower links.

- **Remote Access Services (RAS)**   If you have your RAS server configured to use a specific range of IP addresses, it is a good design decision to link a GPO to a site to configure the RAS clients. You can target computer and user accounts based on whether the computer is coming in over dial-up or VPN. You can thus control software installation, profiles, security configurations, and more. In most cases, the RAS clients must have increased security configurations and decreased network access privileges.

GPOs Linked to Domains

By default, a GPO named the Default Domain Policy is linked at the domain level and is typically used to configure account policies for all domain users. Additional GPOs can be linked to the domain level as well however. You might be tempted to link numerous GPOs to the domain level or configure numerous GPO settings at this level, but you will find that only a few GPO settings can be successfully configured at the domain level because these GPO settings affect all computer and user accounts in the domain.

When you consider linking GPOs at the domain level, evaluate the computer and user settings configured in the GPOs to determine whether they should be applied to every account in the domain. For computers, this would include domain controllers, file servers, print servers, application servers, SQL Servers, executive clients, IT staff clients, and developer clients. For users, this would include executives, power users, IT staff, developers, and service accounts.

Here are some best practices for configuration at the domain level:

- **Account policies**   Although account policies are already configured in the default GPO, they are worth mentioning again. The only GPOs that can establish the account policies for domain user accounts are those that are linked to the domain level.

- **Legal notice**   Display a legal notice at logon on all computers of any type in the organization.

- **Screen saver**   Many companies require that computers be configured to use a standardized company screen saver. You should configure each user account to password-protect the screen saver after a set amount of idle time. Set a reasonable idle time for your environment, but the shorter the idle time, the better the security. In many companies, the idle time is set between 15 to 30 minutes.

- **Scripts**   Some scripts configure drive mappings, printers, and other settings that are required for all computers and users throughout the domain.

- **Security settings**   Many security settings such as SMB signing, authentication protocols, and anonymous access, can be configured for all computers in the domain.

- **Software installation**   Your organization might have anti-virus or patch agent software that runs on all computers in the domain and can be deployed from the domain level. It is common to also deploy administrative tools to all computers for when administrators need to troubleshoot problems directly from a client or a server.

- **Internet Explorer**   Because Internet Explorer is the main tool for Internet and intranet resource access, these settings are typically required for all computers in the domain. These settings might include proxy, caching, or security settings.

- **GPO processing**   Ensure that all computers and users process GPOs in the same way, to eliminate working with different GPO implementation designs during the troubleshooting process. Configuring settings for GPO processing at the domain level ensures that all computer and user accounts are configured consistently across the forest. Settings such as synchronous/asynchronous, refresh intervals, and script timeouts are all usually appropriate to configure at the domain level.

GPOs Linked to OUs

Besides configuring the recommended GPO settings above at the site and domain levels, all other GPO settings should generally be applied at the OU level. This includes most GPO settings, which proves how important it is to design the OU structure of each domain with GPO deployment in mind.

You will typically have multiple levels of OUs within a domain, with some OUs toward the top of the structure and some OUs lower down. It is common to have fewer computer and user accounts in the higher-level OUs, while most of these accounts will reside in the lower-level OUs.

The same can be said of the GPOs linked to your OUs. Try to have fewer GPOs linked to higher-level OUs because too many accounts would be affected at this level. If any GPOs are linked at the higher-level OUs, their settings are typically generic enough to span multiple computer or user types.

Most GPOs are linked to lower-level OUs. These OUs typically contain accounts based on type, department, security needs, software requirements, or delegation of administration requirements.

Resources Used by GPOs

When you have software that is being deployed using GPOs, organize your source files on servers that are on the same network as the target machines. The shares that contain application source files are specified within the software packages created in a GPO. You should specify shares that reside on file servers with fast network connections to the target accounts.

The same goes for SUS servers that are configured through GPOs. You should have multiple SUS servers provide updates for clients throughout the enterprise. The GPOs should be designed to lead target computers to SUS servers that have fast network connections to them.

Finally, you can combine domain-based DFS links with the specific shares that you need to specify for software and SUS server configurations in your GPOs. Domain-based DFS links allow multiple servers to respond to a single shared folder. Clients are directed to the share on the server that is within their site, providing fast, reliable access to software and SUS update resources.

 More Info   For more information on DFS, go to *http://www.microsoft.com/ windowsserver2003/techinfo/overview/dfs.mspx.*

Software Installation

When you deploy software based on a computer and user accounts, you have a choice of when you install the software and how the user will access the software for use or installation. The options are different for deploying software based on computer accounts versus user accounts.

For computer accounts, your options are limited because a computer can't interact with itself to install or initialize some behavior to start the installation. Therefore, if you deploy software based on a computer account, your only option is to have the software install automatically when the computer starts.

For user accounts, you have three options:

- **Publish**   When you publish software, it shows up only in the Add/Remove Programs list. The user is not even aware that the software is available unless she checks this list. This option is appropriate if you want to provide software to users but not have the software available to them until they need it. You can also choose to install the software when the user attempts to open a file associated with the software—for example, if Microsoft Excel has been published and the user opens a file with an .xls file extension. In this case, Excel is installed when the user attempts to open the file.

- **Assign, But Don't Automatically Install At Logon**   Assigning software to users makes the software available on the Start menu as a shortcut. This means the software is available for installation but is only installed when the user clicks the shortcut on the Start menu for the application or attempts to open a file associated with that software. This is a good approach if you plan to deploy software to a large group of people because it spreads the installation load across the network and source servers and across multiple hours and days rather than concentrating it at a time like early morning when all of users typically log on.

- **Assign And Install When User Logs On**   This option is identical to the previous one except that the software is installed when the user logs on. This is a good option when the software is being deployed to only a few people or when the software (such as HR applications or security applications) need to be installed when the user accesses the desktop after logon.

More Info   For more information on deploying software using Group Policy, see Chapter 9.

Designing GPOs Based on GPO Categories

When you organize your GPOs based on the kinds of settings they contain, they become easier to manage. Depending on the overall requirements of your organization, you could typically use security, software deployment, desktop control, Internet Explorer, scripts, Windows components, system configurations, and network settings as initial categories. Using such categories makes the following management tasks much easier:

- Documentation of GPO settings

- Troubleshooting of GPO processing

- Multi-user administration of GPOs

- Delegation of administration within Active Directory

Limit Enforced and Block Policy Inheritance Options

You should allow GPOs to be processed according to their default inheritance behavior as much as possible. This means that when you link a GPO to the domain level, it should affect all accounts in the domain. Likewise, when you link a GPO to an OU of Sales employees, all Sales employee user accounts will be affected.

The Enforced option can push the settings in a GPO down through the Active Directory structure even if another GPO with higher precedence attempts to override the settings in the Enforced GPO. The Block Policy Inheritance option allows you to stop all lower-precedence GPO settings from applying to accounts at a certain level in the Active Directory structure. Both the Enforce setting and the Block Policy Inheritance setting should be used only when other recommended design options are not available. Here are some best practices for using these options:

- **Enforced** This is a good configuration option for the Default Domain Policy. It ensures that all settings related to the account policies and other miscellaneous security settings always override weaker settings farther down in the Active Directory structure.

- **Block Policy Inheritance** The Domain Controllers OU contains all domain controllers for the specified domain. It is a good idea to use the Block Policy Inheritance option here so no surprises are configured on domain controllers if an errant GPO is configured at the site or domain level.

> **Tip** If you configure account policy settings in a GPO linked to an OU, these settings will affect local user accounts for computers in that OU. To prevent this from happening, set the Default Domain Policy GPO link to Enforced.

When to Use Security Filtering

By default a GPO has an ACL that allows it to affect all accounts in the container to which the GPO is linked. This should not be changed unless security filtering of the GPO's ACL becomes necessary. The reason you should avoid modifying a GPO's ACL is because it is hard to document and troubleshoot such detailed configurations. However, in some situations using security filtering on a GPO's ACL is preferred:

- **When Active Directory delegation is more important** As you design your Active Directory structure, you might find areas where you need to place two types of user accounts in the same OU even though the user accounts need to have different GPO settings. In this case, you can use security filtering to control which user accounts receive the proper GPO settings.

- **GPOs are linked higher in the OU structure** When you link GPOs high in the OU structure, you will find that the GPO settings can affect too many accounts. You are forced to configure the GPO ACL to indicate which accounts should apply these settings.

When to Use WMI Filters

WMI filters are very useful, but they can cause more harm than good if they are overused or configured improperly. The main problem with WMI filters is that they are expensive to process and therefore lead to slow response times and poor logon performance for users. It is best to design your OU structure to eliminate the need for WMI filters wherever possible. However, in some situations WMI filters are the only way to control which accounts receive the settings configured in the GPOs where the WMI filter is linked.

You might want to limit the use of WMI filters the following situations:

- When software installation takes a large amount of hard disk space but not all target computers have sufficient disk space.

- When a setting or application depends on the current service pack or update level.

- When you are installing software or updates that rely on a certain operating system or operating system version.

- When you need to verify memory installed on a computer.

Network Topology Considerations

Whether you are rolling GPO settings out to accounts or are updating a critical security setting, you must consider network topology, replication, and convergence when you make these changes. You should make sure that your Group Policy infrastructure is well documented so you know how to get updates from one domain controller to all domain controllers.

Here are some guidelines on updating GPOs with consideration for network topology:

- **GPO updates**   By default, all GPO updates occur on the domain controller that houses that PDC emulator role. You can modify which domain controller updates Group Policy, but you still need to know where these changes occur.

> **More Info**   For more information about how to control which domain controller updates Group Policy changes, see Chapter 2.

- **Convergence of GPO changes**   When a change is made to a GPO, that change must be replicated to all domain controllers in the domain. When a computer or user attempts to apply GPO updates, the domain controller that authenticates the account must have the GPO changes or else the account will not be updated. Knowing how to force replication and check for convergence of GPO changes on all domain controllers is essential.

> **More Info**   For more information about how to control replication of GPOs and verify convergence of GPO changes on all domain controllers, see Chapter 13.

- **Slow links**   Because so many GPO settings are affected by slow links, you must know the link speed from the computer to the domain controller and resource servers when you configure certain GPO settings. Settings that control software application, SUS updates, scripts, and user profiles should have fast connections to the servicing servers to ensure that the user can use his computer in a reasonable amount of time. This requires limiting all of these settings to fast links and omitting these settings for computers that connect across slow links; as a result, you must develop solutions for controlling these settings in some other way.

Limiting Administrative Privileges

You must protect your GPO implementation and the management of your Group Policy infrastructure by controlling which users have permissions to manage GPOs and their settings. You should determine which administrators should have control over the creation, modification, and management of GPOs at every level within that Active Directory structure. Here are some recommendations for tasks related to GPO management:

- **Creating GPOs**   This ability should be limited to a few administrators within your organization—perhaps two to five—but not to a single person only. This limitation protects against errant GPOs from being created throughout your enterprise.

- **Editing GPOs**   You should delegate configuration of GPO settings to the administrators who are responsible for the computer and user accounts that are affected by each GPO. In this way, there typically is not a large number of administrators per GPO—perhaps 2 to 10 administrators. You don't want too many administrators to be able to modify the contents of GPOs because this might cause conflicting settings and errant configurations.

- **Modifying security**   The list of administrators who have the ability to modify the ACL on a GPO as well as establish delegation to the GPO should limited to two to five administrators.

- **Linking GPOs to a level**   When a GPO is linked to a site, domain, or OU, all of the accounts are immediately affected by the settings in that GPO. Therefore, the ability to link GPOs to a level is a very powerful one. You should limit the number of administrators who can link GPOs to any given level to between two and five.

- **Viewing GPO settings**   By giving help desk employees, and some power users the ability to view GPO settings, you can help offload some of the administrative responsibilities around resolving and troubleshooting GPO issues from the shoulders of administrators. This might mean delegating a number of groups the ability to view GPO settings. It is reasonable to allow up to 100 users the ability to view GPO settings.

Naming GPOs

After you complete your final GPO design, you should develop a method for naming and documenting your GPOs. You shouldn't have any duplicate GPO names because it would then be difficult to track which settings were within each GPO. You must come up with a naming scheme that makes sense to you yet is flexible enough for easy implementation.

Here are some best practices for naming your GPOs:

- **Don't name GPOs after sites, domains, or OUs.** This will only make your Group Policy design rigid and more complex.

- **Name GPOs based on the types of settings they contain.** These might include the different GPO categories, such as security, software applications, scripts, and so forth.

- **Organize your GPO settings based on the account types they will service.** This is also a good way to refer to your GPO names—for example, IT, developer, Help-Desk, file_server, SQL_server, and so forth.

- **Add a version number to the GPO name.** In a large organization, documentation and management of Group Policy can be difficult to control. In this case, you can add a version number to the GPO name to help you track and document the GPOs and the current version of the settings. This is also an excellent way to create an archive of your old GPO settings, in case you need to refer back to them for troubleshooting purposes.

Testing GPOs Before Deployment

Whether you have been running Active Directory for a long time or are just deploying Active Directory in your enterprise, you must consider the effects of GPOs within the organization. We have spent the majority of this chapter talking about what to consider and have outlined some best practices for Group Policy design and deployment.

Before you deploy any Group Policy settings to production computers, you must develop a strategy to test the settings to ensure that they produce the desired results. Ideally, you should have a test environment that closely resembles your production environment—including domain controllers, domain members, operating systems, resource servers, network bandwidth, and so forth. You use the test network to try out your Group Policy settings before they go into production.

Migrating GPOs from Test to Production

Your test network should be in a separate forest from the production forest. The test forest should be a mirror image of the production forest to allow for full interaction between operating systems, servers, services, applications, and network devices. For security reasons, there should not be a trust relationship between the test forest and the production forest.

Because the two forests may contain multiple domains, you should track which domain the GPO is tested in. You should also test GPOs with the correct computer account, user account, and group accounts in mind. Many GPO settings rely on these accounts to allow access or configure restrictions. This tracking is essential during the testing and migration phase because these objects have security identifiers (SIDs) associated with them, and the computer uses this value to track the accounts throughout the entire forest. Because the two forests have different SIDs, you must ensure that test domain accounts are translated into the production domain accounts as you migrate GPOs from one domain to the other.

 More Info   For more information on using the GPMC to migrate GPOs from one domain or forest to another, see Chapter 3.

Migrating GPOs from Production to Production

In some instances, you may have a GPO in one of your domains that you want to migrate to another domain or forest. This is common because GPOs are initially tested and placed into production for one domain. After the GPO has proven to be stable and provides the correct settings, you can deploy it in other domains and forests.

Because the GPO is migrated from one domain to another, the SIDs for the accounts must also be translated, even if the GPO is being migrated from one domain to another within the same forest. The reason for this is that each domain has its own unique list of accounts with unique SIDs.

Using Migration Tables

Migration tables are used to tell the GPMC how domain-specific data should be treated during migration of GPOs. Migration tables are required because some of the data in a GPO is unique to the domain and might not be valid if copied directly to another domain. The tables are stored with the file extension .migtable and are formatted as XML files.

Within the migration table, the computer, user, group, and UNC paths are mapped from the old value to a new value specific to the target domain. Migration tables require at least one mapping entry, but typically have more than one. Each mapping entry consists of a source type, source reference, and destination reference. The migration table is referenced when a GPO is imported or copied; each reference to a source entry is replaced with the destination entry when the settings are written into the destination GPO.

Domain-Specific GPO Settings

The GPMC makes it easy to import or copy GPOs from one domain to another. The key challenge when migrating GPOs is that some information in the GPO is unique to the domain in which the GPO was originally defined. This can cause issues in the target domain if these settings are not modified beforehand in some manner to reference the new domain. Items that can be specific to a domain include user, group, and computer accounts, as well as UNC paths.

The following GPO settings may contain computer, user, or group references and should be translated during migration:

- **Security policy settings**
    - ❏ User Rights Assignment
    - ❏ Restricted Groups
    - ❏ System Services
    - ❏ File System
    - ❏ Registry
- **Advanced folder redirection policy settings**
- **DACL on the GPO**
    - ❏ Only if you are using security filtering and want to preserve it during the migration
- **DACLs on software installation packages**
    - ❏ Only if the DACL has been configured from the default.
    - ❏ These DACLs are preserved only if the option to copy the GPO DACL is specified.

In addition, the following settings might contain UNC paths. The UNC paths from one domain to the next differ based on server name and share name.

- Folder redirection policy settings
- Software installation policy settings
- Scripts
    - ❏ Logon and logoff
    - ❏ Startup and shutdown

> **Caution**   A few GPO settings under the administrative template section of a GPO can't be mapped using migration tables. These settings must be migrated as is and then modified after the migration. To get more information on these settings and migration tables, refer to *http://www.microsoft.com/windowsserver2003/gpmc/ migrgpo.mspx.*

Migration Table Structure

Migration tables store mapping information for GPO settings as XML files having the file extension .migtable. You can create migration tables manually, but it is more efficient to use the Migration Table Editor, a component of the GPMC. The Migration Table Editor allows you to create, view, and edit migration tables for migration of any GPO.

The migration table files contain only three variables for you to enter: source name, source type, and destination name. Figure 4-4 shows a migration table in the Migration Table Editor using the GPMC.

Figure 4-4   The Migration Table Editor

Source Type   The source type describes the type of domain-specific information for the source GPO. The following source types are supported in migration tables:

- User
- Computer
- Domain local group
- Domain global group
- Universal Group
- UNC Path
- Free Text or SID (This category is for use only with security principals that are specified as free text or raw SIDs.)

> **Note**   The built-in groups (such as Administrators and Account Operators) that are common to all domains have the same SID regardless of the domain. If references to built-in groups are stored in the GPO using their underlying SID, they cannot be mapped in a migration table. If the references to built-in groups are stored as free text, they can be mapped using the Free Text or SID source type.

Source Name The source name indicates which setting exists in the GPO as the GPO is migrated from one domain to another. The source reference is the specific name of the computer, user, group, or UNC path used in the source GPO. The source name format must match the source type for each entry in the migration table. Table 4-1 contains examples of source names and their syntax.

Table 4-1 Source Reference Syntax

Source Name	Syntax
UPN	bruno@contoso.com
SAM	CONTOSO\Bruno
DNS	Contoso.com\bruno
Free text	bruno (must be specified as the unknown type)
SID	S-1-11-111111111-111111111-1111111111-1112 (must be specified as the unknown type)

Destination Name The destination name is the final entry in the migration table. It specifies how the name of the computer, user, group, or UNC path in the source GPO should be treated upon transfer to the destination GPO. Table 4-2 shows some descriptions of destination names.

Table 4-2 Destination Names

Destination Name	Description
Same as source	Copy without changes. Equivalent to not putting the source value in the migration table.
None	Removes the user, computer or group from the GPO. This option cannot be used with UNC paths.
Map by relative name	For example, map SourceDomain\Group1 to TargetDomain\Group1. This option cannot be used with UNC paths.
Explicitly specify value	In the destination GPO, replace the source value with the exact literal value you specify.

Note You can specify security principals for destination names using any of the formats described above in the source reference table, except for using a raw SID. You can never use a raw SID for the destination name.

More Info For more information on the steps required to migrate GPOs using the GPMC and migration tables, see "Testing GPOs Before Deployment" in this chapter.

Summary

Deploying GPOs is not a simple task. Effective deployment involves factors well beyond the settings that are configured in the GPOs. These factors include Active Directory design, delegation considerations, replication, and convergence of Active Directory to all domain controllers.

You must also consider Group Policy inheritance and application controls to ensure that the deployment of the production GPOs is stable, secure, and efficient. Default inheritance should be left in place unless you absolutely need to implement GPO filtering, enforce GPOs, or use No Override. WMI filters should also be avoided if possible because they can degrade the performance of GPO application.

Finally, all GPO settings should be tested in a nonproduction environment before being migrated to production.

Chapter 5
Hardening Clients and Servers

In this chapter:

Understanding Security Templates 136
Deploying Security Templates 161
General Hardening Techniques 164
Server Hardening 168
Client Hardening 192
Troubleshooting 210
Summary 215

This chapter discusses the philosophy behind protecting clients and servers in the Active Directory® domain and the methods and tools for doing so. We will investigate security templates, which are the main mechanism used to configure security on computers running Microsoft® Windows®. We will look at the uses and roles of the default security templates, as well as how to create, import, change, export, and apply security templates. We will examine the various sections of a security template, along with the key settings in each section.

We will also look at the Security Configuration Wizard, a new tool in Microsoft Windows Server™ 2003 Service Pack 1. The wizard works in conjunction with your security templates, but it also incorporates "role-based" security and application security. The wizard generates security policies, which can include security template settings. We will look at how to deploy security templates and security policies to ensure secure clients and servers, and we will investigate using the new Security Configuration Wizard to harden clients and servers.

We will finish up the chapter with a section on troubleshooting situations that occur when trying to harden computer security on a network. We will discuss troubleshooting security templates, the template application process, and additional tools that can be used to analyze and track security configurations.

Related Information

■ For detailed information about prescriptive security settings, see the *Windows Server 2003 Security Guide* at *http://www.microsoft.com/technet/security/ prodtech/windowsserver2003/w2003hg/sgch00.mspx*.

- For more information about security settings, see the *Threats and Countermeasures Guide* at *http://www.microsoft.com/technet/security/topics/serversecurity/tcg/tcgch00.mspx*.

- For more information about customizing security templates, refer to the "Customizing Security Templates" section in Chapter 15.

- For more information about creating and configuring security templates, see the *Microsoft Windows Security Resource Kit*, Second Edition (Microsoft Press, 2005).

Understanding Security Templates

Security templates are text files that are used to organize, configure, and manage security on computers throughout a Windows–based enterprise. These templates are organized into logical sections based on the various categories of security policies on all Windows–based computers. Once a security template is configured, you can use it to configure a single computer or multiple computers on the network. Security templates offer a method for centralizing the configuration and deployment of security configurations to computers.

Security templates are basic text files that are accessed through the Security Templates snap-in using the Microsoft Management Console (MMC), as shown in Figure 5-1.

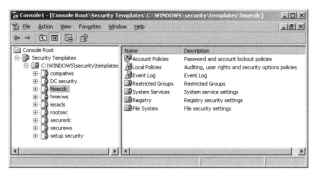

Figure 5-1   Security Templates snap-in allows quick access to security templates

Default Security Templates

Windows Server 2003 comes with a number of default security templates that are designed to help meet the needs of different computer security levels and functions. These templates can be used as is, or they can be modified to meet the needs of the computers on your network. All of the default security templates can be found in the C:\Windows\Security\Templates folder. This following sections describe the default security templates and their functions.

Compatws.inf

The Compatws.inf template relaxes the default permissions for the Users group so that you don't have to make end users members of the Power Users group. Limiting the number of Power Users makes computers more secure when they run legacy applications.

In practice, the default permissions for workstations and servers are primarily granted to three local groups: Administrators, Power Users, and Users. Administrators have the most privileges and Users have the least. As a result, it is a best practice to put most user accounts in the Users group—not the Administrators group—assuming that applications can be successfully run by members of the Users group. For each application that requires more than Users group membership, there are two options: The users can be placed in the Power Users group or the permissions for the Users group can be relaxed to allow the Users group to run the application.

The Compatws.inf security template changes the default file and registry permission for the Users group so that its members can run the application, and it removes the Power Users group from running the application. Because Power Users have inherent capabilities, such as creating users, groups, printers, and shares, some administrators would rather relax the default User permissions than allow end users to be members of the Power Users group.

> **Warning**   This security template should not be used for domain controllers because it will reduce security dramatically; it is designed for a local SAM, not Active Directory.

DC security.inf

This template is created when a server is promoted to a domain controller. It reflects file, registry, and system service default security settings. Reapplying it resets these areas to the default values, but it might overwrite permissions on new files, registry keys, and system services created by other applications.

Iesacls.inf

The Iesacls.inf template is designed to establish auditing for Registry keys that are associated with Microsoft Internet Explorer. The permissions for these keys are set using the security template to allow the built-in Everyone group Full Control access to the keys. Then, the auditing is configured to track when anyone attempts to modify the values located in the keys.

Securedc.inf

The Secure templates (Secure*.inf) define enhanced security in ways that are least likely to affect application compatibility. The security settings include stronger passwords, lockout, and audit settings. Both Secure templates also limit the use of LAN Manager and NTLM authentication protocols by configuring clients to send only NTLMv2 responses and configuring servers to refuse LAN Manager responses. The Secure templates also further restrict anonymous users by preventing those users (such as users from untrusted domains) from enumerating account names and shares, as well as performing SID-to-name or name-to-SID translations.

> **Important**   If the Securedc.inf security template is applied to a domain controller, a user with an account in that domain cannot connect to any member server from a client computer configured to use only LAN Manager authentication when using that domain account.

Securews.inf

This template provides the same configurations as the Securedc.inf template, but it is designed to be applied to clients and member servers. The template enables server-side Server Message Block (SMB) packet signing, which is disabled by default for servers. Because client-side SMB packet signing is enabled by default, SMB packet signing is always negotiated when workstations and servers are operating at the Secure level.

If the Securews.inf security template is applied to a domain member, the following limitations apply:

- All of the domain controllers that contain the accounts of all users who log on to the client must run Microsoft Windows NT® 4.0 Service Pack 4 or later.

- If the domain member is joined to a domain that contains domain controllers running Windows NT 4.0, the clocks of the domain controllers running Windows NT 4.0 and the member computers must be within 30 minutes of each other.

- Clients cannot connect to servers that use only the LAN Manager authentication protocol or that run Windows NT 4.0 before Service Pack 4 using a local account defined on the target server.

- Clients cannot connect to servers running Windows 2000 or Windows NT 4.0 using a local account defined on the target server unless the clock on the target server is within 30 minutes of the clock on the client.

- Clients cannot connect to a computer running Windows XP or later using a local account defined on the target server unless the clock on the target server is within 20 hours of the clock on the client.

- Clients cannot connect to servers configured to use LAN Manager authentication that are running in share-level security mode.

- A user with a local account on a configured server cannot connect to it from a client computer running only LAN Manager that is using that local account.

- A user with a local account on a configured Windows Server 2003 server that is also configured to use NTLMv2 authentication cannot connect unless the clocks on the two machines are within 20 hours of each other.

Hisecdc.inf

The Highly Secure templates (Hisec*.inf) are supersets of the Secure templates that impose further restrictions on the levels of encryption and signing that are required for authentication and for the data that flows over secure channels and between Server Message Block (SMB) clients and servers. For example, the Secure templates cause servers to refuse LAN Manager responses, while the Highly Secure templates cause servers to refuse both LAN Manager and NTLM responses. The Secure templates enable server-side SMB packet signing, while the Highly Secure templates require it. Also, the Highly Secure templates require strong encryption and signing for the secure channel data that constitutes domain-to-member and domain-to-domain trust relationships.

If the Hisecdc.inf security template is applied to a domain controller, the following limitations apply to the domain controllers:

- All of the domain controllers in all trusted or trusting domains must run Windows 2000 or Windows Server 2003.

- A user with an account in that domain cannot connect to member servers using that domain user account if the connection is being attempted from a client that uses only the LAN Manager authentication protocol.

- A user with an account in that domain cannot connect to member servers using that domain account unless the client and target server are both running Windows 2000 or later. Users can also use Kerberos-based authentication rather than LAN Manager–based authentication, unless the client is configured to send NTLMv2 responses.

- Lightweight Directory Access Protocol (LDAP) clients cannot bind with the Active Directory LDAP server unless data signing is negotiated. By default, all Microsoft LDAP clients that ship with Windows XP request data signing if Transport Layer Security/Secure Sockets Layer (TLS/SSL) is not already being used. If TLS/SSL is being used, data signing is considered to be negotiated.

Hisecws.inf

The Hisecws.inf template works on the same premise as the Hisecdc.inf template, with some minor modifications. It removes all members of the Power Users group and ensures that only Domain Admins and the local Administrator account are members of the local Administrators group.

If the Hisecws.inf security template is applied to a domain member, the following limitations apply:

- All of the domain controllers that contain the accounts of all users that will log on to the client must be running Windows NT 4.0 Service Pack 4 or later.

- All of the domain controllers for the domain that the client is joined to must be running Windows 2000 or later.

- Clients cannot connect to computers that run only LAN Manager or computers that are running Windows NT 4.0 Service Pack 3 or earlier using a local account defined on the target server.

- Clients cannot connect to servers running Windows 2000 or Windows NT 4.0 Service Pack 4 using a local account defined on the target server unless the clock on the target server is within 30 minutes of the clock on the client.

- Clients cannot connect to computers running Windows XP or later using a local account defined on the target computer unless the clock on the target computer is within 20 hours of the clock on the client.

- Clients cannot connect to LAN Manager servers operating in share-level security mode.

- A user with a local account on a configured server cannot connect to the server from a client that does not support NTLMv2.

- A client with a local account on a configured server cannot connect to the server unless the client's computer is configured to send NTLMv2 responses.

- All clients that want to use SMB to connect to a configured server must enable client-side SMB packet signing. All computers running Windows 2000 and Windows XP operating systems enable client-side SMB packet signing by default.

Notssid.inf

The Notssid.inf template weakens security to allow older applications to run on Windows Terminal Services. The default file system and registry access control lists (ACLs) that are on servers grant permissions to a Terminal Server security identifier (SID). The Terminal Server SID is used only when Terminal Server is running in application compatibility mode. If Terminal Services is not being used, this template can be applied to remove the unnecessary Terminal Server SIDs from the file system and registry locations. However, removing the access control entry for the Terminal Server SID from these default file system and registry locations does not increase the security of the system. Instead of removing the Terminal Server SIDs, a better approach is to run Terminal Server in Full Security mode. In this mode, the Terminal Server SID is not used.

Rootsec.inf

The Rootsec.inf template establishes the security for the root of the system drive. The best use of this template is to reapply the root directory permissions if they have been changed accidentally or where the system is broken. The template will not overwrite explicit permissions for any child object; it will only establish permissions for the parent objects, with the default inheritance configuring the child objects.

Setup Security.inf

The Setup Security.inf template is created during installation for each computer. It can vary from computer to computer, depending on whether the installation was a clean installation or an upgrade. This template represents the default security settings that are applied during installation of the operating system, including the file permissions for the root of the system drive. It can be used on servers and client computers; it cannot be applied to domain controllers. You can apply portions of this template for disaster-recovery purposes.

Tip Setup Security.inf should never be applied using Group Policy. It contains a large amount of data and can seriously degrade performance if it is applied through Group Policy because policy is periodically refreshed and a large amount of data would move through the domain.

It is a best practice to apply the Setup Security.inf template in parts, and the Secedit command-line tool is a good choice for doing this.

Caution The default security templates are meant to be applied to computers that already use the default security settings. You should use these templates to incrementally modify the default security settings you configure on the computers. These security templates do not install the default security settings before performing the modifications. This means you should also test these security templates in a nonproduction environment to ensure that the right level of application functionality is maintained for your network and system architecture.

Sections of the Security Template

A security template has many sections, each with a specific role in protecting, securing, and hardening the computer it will be deployed to. Knowing the role of each section will help you move forward as you decide which security settings to configure for each type of computer in your organization.

Descriptions of the sections within the security template follow, along with some best practices for using them.

Account Policies

The Account Policies section controls areas of authentication for user accounts and is configured at the domain policy level. Account Policies has three subsections:

- **Password policy**   Controls the password for user accounts—the time period that a password is valid, the length of the password, and the complexity of the password
- **Account Lockout policy**   Controls how the authenticating computer will behave when incorrect passwords are typed multiple times
- **Kerberos policy**   Controls the ticketing that the Kerberos authentication protocol uses for domain communication and authorization

Table 5-1 lists some best practices for configuring these settings for domain policy in enterprise client environments—that is, where client computers are running Windows 2000 Professional or Windows XP Professional and where all domain controllers are running Windows 2000 or later.

> **More Info**   For more information on these recommended domain policy settings in enterprise client environments, and for additional recommendations for configuring these settings in legacy client and high security client environments, refer to the *Windows Server 2003 Security Guide* found at *http://www.microsoft.com/downloads/ details.aspx?FamilyID=8a2643c1-0685-4d89-b655-521ea6c7b4db&displaylang=en*. Additional recommendations for securing client computers can be found in the *Windows XP Security Guide v2* found at *http://www.microsoft.com/downloads/ details.aspx?FamilyId=2D3E25BC-F434-4CC6-A5A7-09A8A229F118&displaylang=en*.

Table 5-1   **Best-Practice Account Policies Settings**

Account Policies Setting	Subsection	Best Practice Setting
Enforce Password History	Password Policy	24
Maximum Password Age	Password Policy	42 days
Minimum Password Age	Password Policy	2 days

Table 5-1   **Best-Practice Account Policies Settings**

Account Policies Setting	Subsection	Best Practice Setting
Minimum Password Length	Password Policy	8
Password Must Meet Complexity Requirements	Password Policy	Enabled
Store passwords using reversible encryption	Password Policy	Disabled
Account Lockout Duration	Account Lockout Policy	30 minutes
Account Lockout Threshold	Account Lockout Policy	50 invalid logon attempts
Reset account lockout counter after	Account Lockout Policy	30 minutes
Any policy settings	Kerberos Policy	Leave at defaults

Important   These Account Policy best practices will depend on your network, your corporate security policy, and your overall security needs. Therefore, be sure to consult your security staff before applying these security settings.

Local Policies

The Local Policies section of the security template controls the local security settings that reside on each computer. It has three subsections:

- **Audit Policy**   Triggers events to be logged in the Security log that resides in the Event Viewer. Each Audit Policy setting can be set to Log Successful, Failed, or to both types of attempts. There are different categories within the Audit Policy that you can configure. On member servers and workstations that are joined to a domain, auditing settings for the event categories are undefined by default. On domain controllers, auditing is enabled for most of the audit policy settings. By defining auditing settings for specific event categories, you can create an auditing policy that suits the security needs of your organization.

- **User Rights Assignment**   Determines what a user or group can do on a server or client. These settings are computer-specific but can be defined through a GPO. In many cases, the default user rights are too open and need to be limited.

- **Security Options**   Enables or disables security settings for the computer, such as digital signing of data, Administrator and Guest account names, floppy drive and CD-ROM access, driver installation, and logon prompts.

Table 5-2 lists some best practices for configuring these settings in policy that applies to domain controllers and member servers in enterprise client environments—that is, where client computers are running Windows 2000 Professional or Windows XP Professional and where all domain controllers are running Windows 2000 or later.

More Info   For more information on these recommended settings in enterprise client environments, and for additional recommendations for configuring these settings in legacy client and high security client environments, refer to the *Windows Server 2003 Security Guide* found at *http://www.microsoft.com/downloads/details.aspx? FamilyID=8a2643c1-0685-4d89-b655-521ea6c7b4db&displaylang=en*. Additional recommendations for securing client computers can be found in the *Windows XP Security Guide v2* found at *http://www.microsoft.com/downloads/details.aspx? FamilyId=2D3E25BC-F434-4CC6-A5A7-09A8A229F118&displaylang=en*.

Note   The Local Policies section has nearly 75 security option settings. Table 5-2 lists best practice settings for only the settings that are very important for most computers on the network. For more information on all recommended settings as well as recommended values, refer to the Security Template snap-in and Security Configuration Wizard and the appropriate files that these tools generate. For help on this procedure, refer to Chapter 15 in this book. Also see the sections later in this chapter on hardening servers and hardening clients, which cover best practice configurations for various server and client scenarios.

Table 5-2   Best-Practice Local Policies Settings

Local Policies Setting	Subsection	Best Practice Setting
Account logon events	Audit Policy	Success: Yes
		Failure: Yes
Account management events	Audit Policy	Success: Yes
		Failure: Yes
Directory service access	Audit Policy	Success: Yes
		Failure: Yes
Logon events	Audit Policy	Success: Yes
		Failure: Yes
Object access	Audit Policy	Success: Yes *
		Failure: Yes
Policy change	Audit Policy	Success: Yes
		Failure: No
Privilege use	Audit Policy	Success: No
		Failure: Yes
Process tracking	Audit Policy	Success: No
		Failure: No
System events	Audit Policy	Success: Yes
		Failure: No

Table 5-2   Best-Practice Local Policies Settings

Local Policies Setting	Subsection	Best Practice Setting
Act as part of the operating system	User Right Assignment	Limit to privileged accounts
Add workstations to domain	User Right Assignment	Limit to privileged accounts
Back up files and directories	User Right Assignment	Limit to privileged accounts
Change the system time	User Right Assignment	Limit to privileged accounts
Force shutdown from a remote system	User Right Assignment	Limit to privileged accounts
Log on as a service	User Right Assignment	Limit to privileged accounts
Log on locally	User Right Assignment	Limit to privileged accounts
Replace a process level token	User Right Assignment	Limit to privileged accounts
Restore files and directories	User Right Assignment	Limit to privileged accounts
Shut down the system	User Right Assignment	Limit to privileged accounts
Take ownership of files or other objects	User Right Assignment	Limit to privileged accounts
Accounts: Guest account status	Security Options	Disabled
Audit: Audit the access of global system objects	Security Options	Disabled
Devices: Prevent users from installing printer drivers	Security Options	Enabled
Domain member: Digitally encrypt or sign secure channel data (always)	Security Options	Enabled
Domain member: Digitally sign secure channel data (when possible)	Security Options	Enabled
Interactive logon: Do not display last user name	Security Options	Enabled
Interactive logon: Message text for users attempting to log on	Security Options	Specify as needed
Interactive logon: Message title for users attempting to log on	Security Options	Specify as needed
Interactive logon: Number of previous logons to cache (in case domain controller is not available)	Security Options	0
Interactive logon: Require Domain Controller authentication to unlock workstation	Security Options	Enabled

Table 5-2   Best-Practice Local Policies Settings

Local Policies Setting	Subsection	Best Practice Setting
Network access: Allow anonymous SID/Name translation	Security Options	Disabled**
Network access: Do not allow anonymous enumeration of SAM accounts and shares	Security Options	Enabled
Network access: Let Everyone permissions apply to anonymous users	Security Options	Disabled
Network security: Do not store LAN Manager hash value on next password change	Security Options	Enabled
Network security: LAN Manager authentication level	Security Options	Send NTLMv2 response only/refuse LM & NTLM
Network security: LDAP client signing requirements	Security Options	Negotiate signing

 * When establishing your object access audit, be careful of the amount of information that can be generated from this setting. As a best practice, you can enable both Success and Failure events for object access in the baseline audit policy and then be very careful and selective in enabling the SACL on the objects whose access you want to audit.

** Must be specified in domain policy.

Event Log

The Event Log security area defines attributes related to the application, security, and system logs: maximum log size, access rights for each log, and retention settings and methods. The application log records events generated by programs; the security log records security events, including logon attempts, object access, and changes to security, depending on what is audited; and the system log records operating system events.

Table 5-3 lists some best practice configurations for configuring these settings in policy that applies to domain controllers and member servers in enterprise client environments—that is, where client computers are running Windows 2000 Professional or Windows XP Professional and where all domain controllers are running Windows 2000 or later.

More Info   For more information on these recommended settings in enterprise client environments, and for additional recommendations for configuring these settings in legacy client and high security client environments, refer to the *Windows Server 2003 Security Guide* found at *http://www.microsoft.com/downloads/details.aspx?FamilyID=8a2643c1-0685-4d89-b655-521ea6c7b4db&displaylang=en*. Additional recommendations for securing client computers can be found in the *Windows XP Security Guide v2* found at *http://www.microsoft.com/downloads/details.aspx?FamilyId=2D3E25BC-F434-4CC6-A5A7-09A8A229F118&displaylang=en*.

Table 5-3   Best-Practice Event Log Settings

Event Log Setting	Best Practice Setting
Prevent local guests group from accessing application log	Enabled
Prevent local guests group from accessing security log	Enabled
Prevent local guests group from accessing system log	Enabled
Retention method for security log	Overwrite events as needed

Restricted Groups

The Restricted Groups security setting allows an administrator to define two properties for security-sensitive groups ("restricted" groups): Members and Member Of. The Members list defines who does and does not belong to the restricted group. The Member Of list specifies which other groups the restricted group belongs to.

When Restricted Groups are configured, the existing members of that group are removed. After the policy is completed, the members of the group will be only those users and groups that are listed on the Members list.

Caution   If a Restricted Groups policy is defined and Group Policy is refreshed, any current member not on the Restricted Groups policy members list is removed. This can include default members, such as administrators.

Note   Restricted Groups are an excellent solution to configure clients and member servers, but should not be used for Active Directory groups. If the Members list is empty, the group will have no members—not even those that are currently configured in the group. On the other hand, if the Members Of list is empty, it just means that the policy setting is not specifying any additional groups in which the group should be a member.

As a best practice, you should control the membership of local groups that reside on member servers and clients within the Active Directory domain. Some of the groups you will want to control include those with advanced or administrative privileges, as shown in Table 5-4.

More Info   For additional information on using Restricted Groups to secure domain controllers and member servers running Windows 2000 or later in enterprise environments, see the *Windows Server 2003 Security Guide* found at *http://www.microsoft.com/downloads/details.aspx?FamilyID=8a2643c1-0685-4d89-b655-521ea6c7b4db&displaylang=en*.

Table 5-4   **Best-Practice Restricted Groups Configurations**

Group	Best Practice Group Members
Administrators	Administrator
	Domain Admins
Power Users	Domain user accounts that need this privilege on the server or client
Backup Operators	Domain administrators or local administrators, not standard domain user accounts

System Services

The System Services section of the security template allows you to define the behavior of system services on all computers in the enterprise. You can first specify how the system service will start when the computer starts:

- Manual
- Automatic
- Disabled

Specifying how the system service will start does not affect whether the user of the computer can start or stop the service. As a result, this section of the template also allows the administrator to control the access permissions for each service. This includes the permissions to start, stop, or pause the service.

Some services are commonly controlled to harden the server or client. These services either have well-known exploits or are routinely targeted by attackers due to the access the attacker would gain if he could exploit the service. The following services are commonly secured for servers and clients:

- Alerter
- Computer Browser
- IIS Admin Service
- Messenger
- Microsoft NetMeeting® Remote Desktop Sharing
- Remote Access Auto Connection Manager
- Remote Access Connection Manager
- Remote Desktop Help Session Manager
- Remote Registry
- Routing and Remote Access

- Telnet
- Terminal Services
- World Wide Web Publishing Service

In addition to controlling these services, you should also consider the following best practices with regard to system services:

- Test all services that you disable using this section of the security template. Some services are required for the operating system or applications to function properly.

- If you choose to set the system service startup to Automatic, perform adequate testing to verify that the service can start without user intervention.

- For performance optimization, set unnecessary or unused services to start as Manual.

> **More Info**   For more information on securing system services on domain controllers and member servers running Windows 2000 or later in enterprise environments, see the *Windows Server 2003 Security Guide* found at *http://www.microsoft.com/downloads/details.aspx?FamilyID=8a2643c1-0685-4d89-b655-521ea6c7b4db&displaylang=en*.

Registry

The Registry section allows you to define access permissions and audit settings for registry keys, including the discretionary access control list (DACL) and the system access control list (SACL) on any registry key. You also use this section to control all domain members—servers and clients alike. To take full advantage of the power of this section, you must also consider the best way to implement these new access permissions for registry keys. Here are some general and specific best practices to consider as you implement your registry changes:

- **Always make a backup of the registry before making changes.**   For Windows XP and Windows Server 2003 computers, you do this by updating your Automated System Recovery (ASR) feature.

- **Do not intermix registry keys or permissions on different operating systems.**   Windows NT, Windows 9x, Windows 2000, Windows XP, and Windows Server 2003 operating systems are not identical with regard to the registry. You must configure the registries correctly for the specific operating system you are targeting.

- **Limit the number of users and groups that have access to the registry.**   This is the key benefit of this section of the security template. You can add or remove any user or group account to the DACL or SACL of any registry key.

- **Don't be too restrictive.**   Although you have ultimate power to control permission to the registry, you must be careful not to break applications and services. It is always best to test configurations in a non-production environment and then deploy the settings to production computers after you know that your settings will not cause problems.

File System

The File System section allows you to define access permissions and audit settings for files and folders. This includes both the DACL and SACL on any file and folder. You also use this section to control all domain members—servers and clients alike. To take full advantage of the power of this section, you must also consider the best way to implement these new access permissions for these resources. Consider the following general and specific best practices as you implement your changes:

- **Assign permissions to groups rather than to users.**   It is more efficient to configure DACLs and SACLs for groups than it is for individual accounts.

- **Use Deny permissions for special cases only.**   Troubleshooting and tracking access issues related to Deny configurations is difficult, so you should use Deny permissions for two reasons only. First, use the Deny permission to exclude a subset of a group that has Allowed permissions. Second, if you want to exclude one special permission when you have already granted full control to a user or a group, you can use the Deny permission.

- **Don't be too restrictive.**   Avoid changing the default permissions on file system objects, especially system folders and root folders. Changing these permissions can be too restrictive, causing unexpected access problems for applications or the operating system.

- **Never deny the Everyone group access to an object.**   The Everyone group includes all users, including the Administrator.

- **Configure permissions as high up in the folder structure as possible.**   This reduces the overall complexity of your permissions and reduces the need to troubleshoot access issues. This approach relies on the inheritance built in to the folder permissions to propagate your permissions down through the folder and file structure.

Tools for Accessing, Creating, and Modifying Security Templates

Security templates are just text files, but you should not modify them using Microsoft Word or Notepad on a regular basis. The files can become quite large, and it can be hard to figure out the syntax used within each section of the template file. Some built-in tools are available that can help you access, create, and modify these templates.

Security Templates Snap-in

The Security Templates snap-in is one of the many tools available within the MMC, which we introduced earlier in the chapter. The tool opens at the default storage location for security templates, C:\Windows\Security\Templates.

Follow these steps to open the Security Template snap-in:

1. Click Start, Run, type **mmc** in the Run dialog box, and then click OK.
2. On the File menu, click Add/Remove Snap-In, and then click Add.
3. Scroll down to the Security Templates snap-in and select it.
4. In the Add Standalone Snap-in dialog box, click Add.
5. In the Add Standalone Snap-in dialog box, click Close.
6. In the Add/Remove Snap-in dialog box, click OK.

The Security Templates snap-in is the primary tool used to create and manipulate security templates. It allows you to perform the following tasks:

- View security template settings
- Modify security template settings
- Copy and paste security settings from one template to another
- Copy a security template
- Create a new, unconfigured security template
- Configure new search paths for stored security templates

More Info For more information about how to use the Security Templates snap-in to manage security templates, see Chapter 15.

Note Instead of modifying the default security templates, it is always best to copy the one that you like and work from the new template. This allows you to refer back to the default templates at a later time.

Security Configuration and Analysis Snap-in

The Security Configuration and Analysis snap-in is a tool that uses the security templates created by the Security Templates snap-in. As the name suggests, the Security Configuration and Analysis snap-in is responsible for configuring and analyzing security on a computer. Both of these tasks are accomplished by using a security template. You access and launch this snap-in in the same way that you access and launch the Security Templates snap-in, except that you select the Security Configuration and Analysis snap-in in step 3 in the procedure under "Security Templates Snap-In" in this chapter.

 More Info   For more information about how to use the Security Configuration and Analysis snap-in to configure and analyze security on a computer using security templates, see Chapter 15.

Security Configuration Wizard

The Security Configuration Wizard is a new tool provided with Windows Server 2003 Service Pack 1. It does not create and manipulate security templates—rather, it uses security templates to help generate security policies. The next section explains how to access and use this wizard.

Using the Security Configuration Wizard

The Security Configuration Wizard is a new tool in Windows Server 2003 Service Pack 1 that uses security templates to help generate security policies. It is similar to the intentions of both the Security Templates snap-in and Security Configuration and Analysis snap-in, but with distinctly different results. The tool is also similar to the Configure Your Server Wizard, which is also available on all Windows Server 2003 computers, in that it relies on roles.

Accessing the Security Configuration Wizard

The Security Configuration Wizard is not installed by default when you install SP1 on your Windows Server 2003 computers. To install the wizard, follow these steps:

1. Click Start, Control Panel, and Add Or Remove Programs.

2. Click the Add/Remove Windows Components icon in the left pane.

3. Scroll down and select the Security Configuration Wizard check box in the Components area. The wizard now appears on the Administrative Tools menu.

The wizard also comes bundled with the SCW Viewer, which allows you to view security policies in much the same way that the Security Templates snap-in allows you to view security templates. The SCW Viewer can be accessed from within the wizard, or you can just run the SCW Viewer from the command line.

Sections of the Security Configuration Wizard

The Security Configuration Wizard has the following sections:

- Role-based service configuration
- Network security
- Registry settings
- Audit policy

> **Note**   The Security Configuration Wizard might have additional sections if other server components have been installed. For example, if the Application Server role has been installed, the wizard has an additional section called Internet Information Services, which you can use to harden your Web server.

Role-Based Service Configuration   The most important concept that the Security Configuration Wizard uses is server roles. Server roles are logical functions that a Windows Server 2003 computer can host and provide services for. The concept of server roles is not new—it was first introduced in the Configure Your Server Wizard, which was first introduced with Windows 2000 Server.

You can choose from approximately 60 server roles within the Security Configuration Wizard. Here are a few of them, to give you an idea of how the functions are broken down:

- Application server
- Certificate server
- DFS server
- DHCP server
- DNS server
- Domain controller
- File server
- Message queuing server
- Microsoft Operations Manager 2005 server
- Print Server for UNIX (LDP)
- Remote Storage server
- SMTP server
- Microsoft Windows SharePoint® Services

These server roles are designed to help you choose which functions your server or servers will support. You choose these functions so the Security Configuration Wizard can help you configure services, open ports, and include other server roles that need to function on the server that is updated by the policy. Figure 5-2 illustrates how the wizard organizes these roles and provides information to help you understand each role and what the wizard will do with regard to services, ports, and other roles.

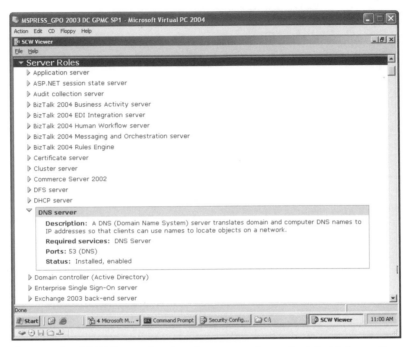

Figure 5-2   SCW Viewer showing the server roles and related information

The Security Configuration Wizard is not responsible for installing the server roles that you configure and store in the security policies. This task is left to the Configure Your Server Wizard. Instead, the Security Configuration Wizard security policy, when applied to a computer, enables the services and open the ports that are associated with the roles you specified. It also disables services and closes ports that are not associated with the roles you specified.

Caution   If you omit a server role when you create the security policy using the Security Configuration Wizard, the server might not function properly after the security policy is applied. You can fix this by enabling the appropriate services and opening the correct ports or by rolling back the security policy using the Security Configuration Wizard. You can then modify the security policy and reapply it to the server so that it will function properly. It is always a good idea to test your security policies for incorrect settings or incompatible configurations before you deploy them.

The server roles are the largest portion of the Security Configuration Wizard. However, the wizard and the security policy also have other server role–dependent and server role–independent sections. These areas help you create a secure foundation for the computers on the network. Here is a list of those additional areas and some information to help you understand best practices for hardening computers.

- **Client Features** A subset of the Server Roles section of the wizard. It might seem a bit odd to have a section named "Client Features" on a server, but servers perform many client activities on the network. This section of the wizard enables services that are related to the client features you select. Figure 5-3 shows the Select Client Features page. Table 5-5 specifies which services are associated with each of the available client features.

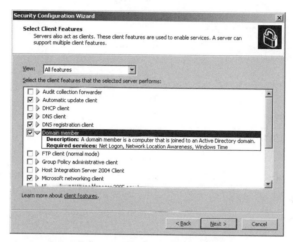

Figure 5-3   Client Features page

Table 5-5   Client Features and Their Required Services

Client Feature	Required Services
Automatic update client	Background Intelligent Transfer Service
	Automatic Updates
DHCP client	DHCP client
DNS client	DNS Client
DNS registration client	DNS Client
Domain member	Net Logon
	Network Location Awareness
	Windows Time
Microsoft networking client	Workstation, TCP/IP NetBIOS helper
Remote access client	Remote Access Connection Manager
	Telephony
WINS client	Server
	TCP/IP NetBIOS helper

■ **Administration And Other Options**   A subset of the server roles that you specify for the server. These options are used to enable services and open ports. When you think "administration," you typically think of tools or applications. This section offers more than that—it targets the Windows services and features that help support the tools and applications you want to use. Table 5-6 lists some of the options in this section and specific services that are associated with each option.

Table 5-6   Administration And Other Options Settings

Option	Required Services
Alerter	Alerter
	Messenger
	Workstation
	TCP/IP NetBIOS helper
Browse master	Computer Browser
	Server
	Workstation
	TCP/IP NetBIOS helper
Remote Desktop administration	Terminal Services
	Server
RSoP planning mode	Resultant Set of Policy Provider
Shadow copying	MS Software Snapshot Provider
	Volume Snapshot
Time synchronization	Windows Time
Windows firewall	Windows Firewall / Internet Connection Sharing (ICS)
Wireless networking	Wireless Zero Configuration
	Network Location Awareness
	Network Provisioning Service

■ **Additional Services**   Other server role–independent services might be installed on the server that is being used as the baseline for the wizard. You can control these additional services within the wizard to enable or disable the service when the security policy is deployed.

■ **Unspecified Services**   The wizard creates the security policy based solely on a baseline server. Therefore, the only services the wizard is aware of are those that are configured on the server or stored in the security policy from a different baseline server. The servers that receive the security policy might have additional services that are not associated with server roles or listed under Additional

Services. The wizard gives you an opportunity to control these services in one of two ways:

- Do not change the startup mode for the service
- Disable the service

Network Security   This section allows you to configure inbound ports using Windows Firewall. The ports you configure are based on the roles and administrative options selected earlier in the wizard. The configurations also allow you to restrict access to ports and indicate whether port traffic is signed or encrypted using Internet Protocol Security (IPSec).

> **Caution**   Configuring the network protocols, ports, and services incorrectly can prevent the server from communicating on the network. Be sure to test the settings on a non-production server before you configure the security policy on an important production server in your environment.

Registry Settings   This section allows you to configure protocols used to communicate with other computers on the network. You can disable use of earlier versions of communication protocols needed to communicate with older Windows operating systems. These earlier communication protocols are vulnerable to exploits such as password cracking and man-in-the-middle attacks. The wizard allows you to configure and control the following aspects of authentication and communication on the network:

- Named Pipe Firewall
- Server Message Block (SMB) security signatures
- LDAP signing
- LAN Manager authentication protocol and levels

> **Caution**   Configuring the network communication protocols incorrectly can prevent the server from communicating on the network. Be sure to test the settings on a non-production server before you configure the security policy on an important production server in your environment.

Audit Policy   This section allows you to configure the auditing of the events that occur on the server. You can set the following configurations for auditing on the selected server:

- Do not audit
- Audit successful activities
- Audit successful and unsuccessful activities

Incorporating Security Templates into Security Policies

After you work through all of the sections of the Security Configuration Wizard, you can save the security policy to the local computer or a centralized network location. Figure 5-4 shows the wizard page where you save the file, as well as the default location where security policies are stored.

> **Important** Remember that the security policy file is saved with an .xml extension. This is important to remember because you might need to find these files at a later time. Also, the .xml file extension is not supported in a GPO, so a native security policy is not compatible with GPOs. The next section discusses how to convert security policies to a format that is compatible with deployment using GPOs.

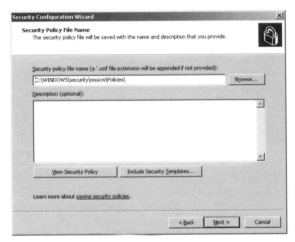

Figure 5-4 Security Policy File name page

You can also click the Include Security Templates button on that wizard page to include one or more existing security templates (generated by the Security Templates snap-in) in your security policy. If you add more than one security template, you can prioritize them in case any configuration conflicts occur between them. However, the security settings configured in the wizard will have precedence over all security templates included in the final security policy file. Figure 5-5 shows the wizard page for adding security templates to security policies and prioritizing them.

> **Note** The Security Configuration Wizard uses two security templates by default: DefaultSACLs.inf and SCWAudit.inf. These files establish permissions on registry keys and the file system. You might see these security templates listed with the other security templates that you import to the security policy during this final stage of creating the policy.

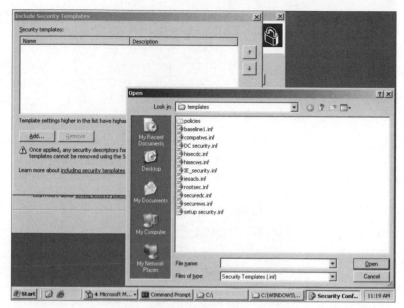

Figure 5-5 Importing and prioritizing security templates with the Security Configuration Wizard

Best Practices for Using the Security Configuration Wizard

To harden servers by using the Security Configuration Wizard and the associated security policies, you must consider the areas that the wizard covers and how they fit into your overall scheme for securing and protecting your servers. The wizard can help reduce the attack surface of servers by allowing you to design security policies based on the server's specific role. Here are some best practices for using the wizard to optimize the hardening of your servers:

- **Identify, organize, and target similar servers.** The wizard is designed to work with other methods that are typically used to harden servers, which are based on server roles. Take advantage of this relationship as you develop and author security polices and distribute them to servers in the organization. Here are some ways you can do this:
  - ❑ **Author only one security policy for a group of servers.** Administrators can use the wizard once to author a security policy, save the policy, and then apply it to all servers that perform the job function. Others servers that perform the same, or similar, functions can be configured with the same security policy.

❑ **Group servers with similar functions into one organizational unit (OU).** Administrators can use the same security policy for servers that perform similar job functions by grouping those servers into a single OU. They can then use the wizard's transform operation to quickly and easily distribute the new security policy to the OU containing the servers. The transform operation can apply the security policy to a domain or an OU.

❑ **Select a prototype server with similar services as the target servers.** The administrator must select a server from which the security policy will be derived. Make sure this server matches the target servers at the service level as much as possible. The security policy disables any service on the server that is contained in the Security Configuration Database but was not present on the prototype server when the policy was created.

Tip You can use the Security Configuration Wizard to configure any unnecessary service that is not in the Security Configuration Database and is therefore not defined in the security policy that you created with the Security Configuration Wizard. You can disable the service or leave the startup mode of the service unchanged.

■ **Test new security policies offline before deployment.** Given the wide variety of security settings included in a standard security policy, it is essential that you test the policies on a server that is configured as closely to the target servers as possible. The settings configured in the new security policies might cause compatibility issues with applications or services. Do this testing on a nonproduction computer that can't hinder or adversely affect the production network before you apply the policies to production servers.

■ **Create one complete security policy.** Use the Security Configuration Wizard to author a single security policy that contains all desired security settings for a server. This simplifies configuration, rollback, and analysis. For simple configuration and rollback, a single security policy for a machine, or set of machines, is much easier to understand and update than a series of policies. If a security policy defines all the desired settings for a server, you can generate a compliance report by executing one scan, which facilitates analysis when you use the *scwcmd /analyze* command.

Note For more information about the Security Configuration Wizard command-line option, *scwcmd*, type **scwcmd /?** on the command line on a computer that has the Security Configuration Wizard installed.

Deploying Security Templates

Once you have the perfect security template—either a default security template or a custom one that you designed—you can apply it to the computer or computers it was designed for. Keep in mind that the overall design of the OUs, including the placement of computer accounts, plays a key role in how and where you can deploy these security templates.

 Note For more information on designing Active Directory and OUs for deploying GPOs, security, and other control mechanisms, see Chapter 4.

You have four options at your disposal for deploying security templates. Only one option is related to GPOs, and it is the most popular option. The other options are valid but are not related to GPOs. The non-GPO options are:

- Importing Security Templates Into GPOs
- Using the Security Configuration and Analysis tool
- Using the Secedit.exe command-line tool
- Using the Security Configuration Wizard and the *scwcmd* command

Importing Security Templates Into GPOs

A best practice for deploying security templates is to import them into a GPO, which will then push out the security settings that you initially configured in the security template. This method relies on the Active Directory and OU design accommodating this rollout.

Before you can implement this method, you must complete the following steps. First, create OUs for the different types of computers that will receive a different security template. Second, move the computer accounts for these computers into the appropriate OU. Third, create and link a GPO for each of the computer OUs that you created in the first step. Now, you are ready to include the security templates into the GPOs.

To import a security template into a GPO, complete these steps:

1. Open the target GPO using the Group Policy Object Editor.
2. Expand the GPO to the following node: Computer Configuration\Windows Settings\Security Settings.
3. Right-click Security Settings and select the Import Policy from the shortcut menu.

4. Browse and select the security template (.inf file) that you want to include and click Open.

5. Verify that some of the configurations from the security template are correct in the GPO, and then close the Group Policy Object Editor.

6. Repeat these steps for each security template that you create. The settings that have been imported into the GPO will take approximately 90 minutes to reach the target computer, not considering any intersite replication considerations.

More Info   For more information about intersite replication, refer to Chapter 13, "Group Policy Structure and Processing."

Using the Security Configuration and Analysis Tool

The Security Configuration and Analysis tool performs two tasks: configuring and analyzing security. The tool works with security templates only to perform these duties. Therefore, once you have a security template, you can use this tool to deploy the settings. The drawback of the tool is that it is not capable of configuring multiple computers at once—it can configure only the computer on which it is running. You must therefore visit each computer that should receive the security template settings. Of course, this is not feasible in most environments, even those with only a few dozen computers. Therefore, this method is best suited to hardening standalone servers that are not part of an Active Directory domain.

Using the Secedit.exe Command-Line Tool

The Secedit.exe tool can perform the same functions as the Security Configuration and Analysis tool. Because the Secedit.exe tool can be scripted, it can be used in a logon or startup script. This allows for multiple computers to be configured with a single script. The Secedit.exe tool was also used in Windows 2000 to refresh GPOs. However, Windows Server 2003 and Windows XP don't use Secedit.exe to refresh GPOs, so the tool is now used almost solely for deploying security templates.

Tip   The Secedit.exe command-line tool is commonly used in a startup script to ensure that the security configurations are applied to computers. The local administrator can modify the registry values included in the security template configurations so that the script can ensure that these values are restored when the computer is restarted.

Tip   To refresh GPOs in Windows Server 2003, you can use the Gpupdate.exe command-line tool.

Using the Security Configuration Wizard and the *scwcmd* Command

A new option for deploying security templates is to use the Security Configuration Wizard together with the *scwcmd* command. The wizard produces security policies, which can include security templates as discussed earlier. The wizard can accept a single security template or multiple templates. When you include the security templates, you can prioritize them to ensure that the correct settings take precedence because the settings within each security template update the security policy. This wizard page can be seen in Figure 5-6.

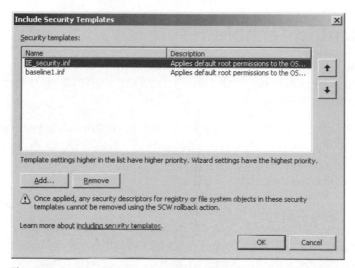

Figure 5-6   Prioritizing security templates that are imported into the Security Configuration Wizard

 Note   To configure multiple servers with a security policy, you can use the Security Configuration Wizard command-line suite of tools. The *scwcmd configure* command allows you to specify the security policy and create a list of servers that the policy will affect. For more information on this option, type **scwcmd configure** at the command prompt.

After you create your security policy using the Security Configuration Wizard, you need to deploy them efficiently to the appropriate servers on the network. By using Group Policy to deploy security policies created using the Security Configuration Wizard you can optimize the deployment of the security settings. Use the *scwcmd transform* command to create a Group Policy object that includes the settings that you configured within the security policy. Use the following syntax to convert a security policy to a GPO:

```
Scwcmd transform /p:PathAndPolicyFileName /g:GPODisplayName
```

In this example, *PathAndPolicyFileName* is the security policy that you created earlier using the Security Configuration Wizard. This must include the .xml filename extension. *GPODisplayName* is the name that the GPO will show when you view it in the Group Policy Object Editor or in the Group Policy Management Console (GPMC).

> **Important**   The GPO that you create based on the security policy is immediately available in Active Directory. However, the GPO will not apply to any server until it is linked to a site, the domain, or an OU containing server accounts.

General Hardening Techniques

Many techniques are available for hardening clients and servers. Here we'll focus on commonly used tools, techniques related to Group Policy, and security capabilities of security templates.

Two of the most important areas that need attention when you harden computers are ports and services. We will discuss various ways to control these areas on a computer and also look at some tools that can help you investigate the current state of a computer for which ports are being used.

Closing Unnecessary Ports

Ports are used by services and other applications to allow two computers to communicate. These ports are doorways into a client or server. Over the years, attackers have exploited ports to gain access to Windows–based computers. Therefore, if a port is open that is not being used by the computer, the port should be closed to help protect the computer from an attacker.

Many approaches are available for closing these ports. Some are manual and can be time consuming and cumbersome when you consider the number of clients and servers in your organization. The following three other approaches are efficient and provide ease of administration and persistence of the configurations:

■ **Windows Firewall**   Windows Firewall is designed to control the inbound and outbound communication of a computer. When you configure Windows Firewall, you have a set list of services that you can allow or deny. These services are associated with ports within Windows Firewall. If you have a special port that is not listed through a service, you can add individual ports and services that can be controlled.

> **More Info**   For more information on Windows Firewall and how to configure these settings, see Chapter 11.

■ **Security Configuration Wizard**   The Security Configuration Wizard provides a seamless method for configuring ports for servers. It uses server roles, administrative options, and Windows Firewall to open and close ports to protect the server. Within the wizard, you have the option to add specific UDP and TCP ports, as well as add approved applications. (You need not know the ports that the application uses.) You can apply these port restrictions using the wizard, or you can export the security policy to a GPO for deployment through Active Directory.

> **Note**   For more information on the Security Configuration Wizard and how to configure these settings, see the "Using the Security Configuration Wizard" section in this chapter.

■ **IPSec policies**   IPSec filters can provide an effective method for controlling communication to ports on clients and servers. An IPSec filter contains information about the source port, destination port, protocol, and the action that should be taken when any communication occurs for each port. These IPSec policies and filters can be deployed to clients and servers manually or deployed using Group Policy. For the most efficient and stable results, using Group Policy is the best choice.

> **More Info**   For more information on IPSec policies and filters, as well as how to configure these settings, see Chapter 11.

Disabling Unnecessary Services

Many services are installed and started on a default installation of Windows Server 2003, Windows XP, and Windows 2000. These services are meant to give your computer the most flexibility and functionality possible, but some of them can also expose your computer and make it vulnerable to attack.

To reduce the vulnerability of your computer, you should remove or disable unnecessary services whenever possible. You can disable services using some automated approaches; removal of services is typically done manually. The following automated methods allow you to efficiently control the services, while also ensuring that the settings are consistent for multiple computers in your organization.

■ **Security templates**   An entire section in security templates is dedicated to system services. This section allows you to control the startup mode for the services that are running on the computers in your environment. Once you have the security template configured for the selected services, you can use the *secedit* command or a GPO to deploy the settings to your computers.

> **More Info**   For more information on security templates and how to deploy them, see the "Deploying Security Templates" section in this chapter.

- **Security Configuration Wizard**   The Security Configuration Wizard allows you to control every service that is running on a server. You do this by selecting the server role and administrative features and specifying how to manage services that are not included in these two categories. The wizard controls every service that is running on the servers that you target with the security policy that is generated from the wizard. You can deploy these service restrictions to servers using the wizard, or you can export the security policy to a GPO for deployment through Active Directory.

> **More Info**   For more information about the Security Configuration Wizard and how to configure these settings, see the "Using the Security Configuration Wizard" section in this chapter.

- **Group Policy**   You have three options for using Group Policy to control services. First, you can import a security template into an existing GPO. Second, you can convert a security policy generated with the Security Configuration Wizard into a GPO, which then can be linked to a site, the domain, or an OU. Finally, a standard GPO has a section on system services, which you can configure to control computers in the organization.

Tools Used in Hardening Computers

Many tools are available for querying, investigating, probing, configuring, troubleshooting, and assisting with security configurations. However, two particular tools come to mind when it comes to general hardening of clients and servers: Netstat and Portqry.

Netstat

Netstat (Netstat.exe) is a command-line tool that displays TCP/IP protocol statistics and active connections to and from your computer. Netstat can also display the number of bytes sent and received, as well as network packets dropped (if any). The tool is useful if you want to quickly verify that your computer can send and receive information over the network. It can also be used to identify all ports and their state on a computer.

To identify the ports and the process ID for each port, complete these steps:

1. Click **Start**, **Run**, and then type **cmd** in the **Open** box. Click **OK**.

2. Obtain a list of all listening ports by typing the following at a command prompt and then pressing Enter:

   ```
   netstat -ano > c:\netstat.txt
   ```

3. Obtain the process identifiers for the processes that are running by typing the following command at the command prompt and then pressing Enter:

   ```
   tasklist > tasklist.txt
   ```

> **Note** If the program in question is running as a service, add the **/svc** switch to the list the services that are loaded in each process:
>
> ```
> tasklist /svc > tasklist.txt
> ```

4. Open Tasklist.txt, and locate the program you are troubleshooting. Note the process identifier for the process.

5. Open Netstat.txt, and note any entries that are associated with that process identifier. Also note the protocol in use (TCP or UDP).

Portqry

The Portqry command-line tool reports the status of TCP and UDP ports on a target computer. You use it to troubleshoot TCP/IP connectivity issues. It provides an additional level of detail on port status not provided by other port scanning tools. You can use PortQry to query a single port, an ordered list of ports, or a sequential range of ports.

If the target port does respond, it is characterized as "listening." If an "ICMP destination unreachable" message is returned from the port, the port is characterized as "not listening." However, some port scanning utilities will report that a port is listening simply if an "ICMP destination unreachable" message is *not* returned from a target port. This might actually be inaccurate because no response to a directed datagram might also indicate that the target port is being filtered.

To get a listing of the ports and their state using Portqry, type the following at a command prompt, and then press Enter:

```
Portqry -n <IP address> -r <port range> -p both -l <file path>
```

> **Tip** For more information on the switches and syntax used by the Portqry command, you can type **portqry /?** at a command prompt.

Server Hardening

Server hardening consists of creating a baseline for the security on your servers in your organization. The default configurations of a Windows Server 2003 computer are not designed with security as the primary focus. Rather, a default installed computer is designed for communication and functionality. To protect your servers, you must establish solid and sophisticated security policies for all types of servers in your organization.

In this section, we will discuss the basic security baseline for a member server that is running in a Windows Server 2003 Active Directory domain. We will also discuss the best-practice security configurations in the security templates, starting with the generic best practices that apply to most member servers in the organization. We will then move on to the specific types of member servers, as well as domain controllers. We will discuss which services, ports, applications, and so forth need to be hardened for different server roles, and compare this to the baseline security for simple member servers.

Member Servers

You must establish a baseline of security for all members servers before creating additional security templates and policies to tailor security for specific types of servers. One of the most important aspects of applying hardening settings to member servers is developing the OU hierarchy that will support the security template and policies that you develop. You must also understand the various levels of security that are routinely used to develop and deploy security to all servers.

OU Design Considerations

The only way to efficiently and successfully deploy security to the different server roles in your enterprise is to design Active Directory to support those roles. The design should not only provide an efficient method to deploy security, but it should also organize the computer accounts into OUs for easier management and troubleshooting.

Although Active Directory design is extremely flexible, you must consider a number of factors when organizing servers into OUs based on server role. The first factor is Group Policy application. For example, if you have two server roles that each need different security policy settings, you should separate the computer accounts into different OUs. The second factor is administration of the computer accounts within Active Directory. Even though you have only two different server roles, you might have two different administrators controlling the same type of server role. This might force you to have OUs not only for server roles, but also for server roles based on the administrator in charge.

Figures 5-7 illustrates an OU structure that does not consider location or administrative needs but does consider server roles. Figure 5-8 illustrates an OU structure that has a different set of administrators for the Main Office and Branch Office, where each office also has the same types of server roles.

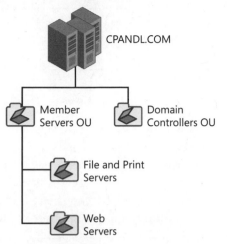

Figure 5-7   An OU structure based on server roles only

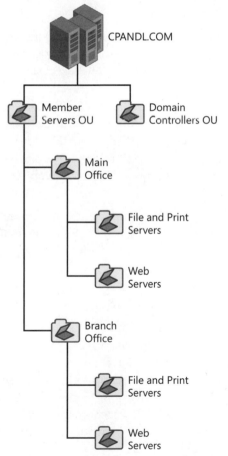

Figure 5-8   An OU structure that considers location and administrative needs as well as server roles

> **Tip**   OUs are also commonly organized by physical location—for example, the Main Office and Branch Office model. For more information on organizing OUs based on GPO deployment, see Chapter 4.

Member Server Security Environment Levels

Member server security environments are based on the operating systems of the clients and servers in your enterprise. Legacy clients and servers can't take advantage of the robust features and functions that Active Directory provides, such as Group Policy, Kerberos, and other security features. As the operating systems of domain members rise to levels that support all Active Directory functions and features, it becomes possible to raise the overall security for the enterprise and thus create a solid security environment.

There are three different security environment levels typically found in an enterprise environment:

- **Legacy Client**   When you have a mixed operating system environment of new and older versions, you must provide adequate security that will not constrain the operation of legacy clients. This is the lowest security level, but it needs to be that way for communication to occur and legacy applications to work properly. This business environment might include legacy clients such as Windows 95, Windows 98, or Windows NT 4.0 Workstation. You should limit this environment to having only Windows 2000 Server and Windows Server 2003 domain controllers. You should not support Windows NT 4.0 Server domain controllers, although you can have Windows NT Server computers configured as member servers.

- **Enterprise Client**   This security level removes the legacy operating systems and uses only those that support the features and functions that Active Directory offers. This includes clients running Windows 2000 Professional and Windows XP Professional. These clients all support Group Policy, Kerberos authentication, and new security features that the legacy clients don't support. The domain controllers must be Windows 2000 Server or later. There will not be any Windows NT Server computers, even as member servers.

- **High Security**   This security level is basically the same as for Enterprise Client—it changes only the level of security that is implemented. This level enhances security standards so that all computers conform to stringent security policies for both clients and servers. This environment might be constrictive enough that loss of functionality and manageability occurs. However, this must be acceptable because the higher security levels are a good tradeoff for the functionality and manageability that you are losing.

Windows Server 2003 Security Guide

The three enterprise environments described earlier and the procedures outlined in this chapter for hardening different server roles in each environment are discussed more fully in the *Windows Server 2003 Security Guide*, which can be found at *http://www.microsoft.com/downloads/details.aspx?FamilyID=8a2643c1-0685-4d89-b655-521ea6c7b4db&displaylang=en*. The Security Guide also includes a set of additional security templates that can be imported into GPOs to harden different server roles in legacy client, enterprise client, and high security environments. It also includes additional procedures for hardening security settings that cannot be configured using Group Policy. Using these additional security templates can simplify the hardening of different server roles on your network, and you can further customize these security templates to meet the specific needs of your Active Directory environment.

Security Settings for Member Servers

This section will cover some common security settings that apply to standard member servers in the domain. These settings are best created in a GPO that is then linked to the top-level server OU. In Figure 5-7 or 5-8, this would be the Member Servers OU.

Table 5-7 provides a full list of security settings for a member server.

> **Note** Account Policies, which include Password Policy, Account Lockout Policy, and Kerberos Policy, are not specified in the member servers security baseline outlined here. This is because Account Policies must be defined at the domain level in Active Directory, while the member servers security baseline is defined in GPOs linked to OUs where member servers are found. For best practices concerning domain Account Policies, see "Account Policies" under "Sections of the Security Template" earlier in this chapter, and also refer to the *Windows Server 2003 Security Guide* described in the "Windows Server 2003 Security Guide" sidebar.

Table 5-7   Security Settings for Member Servers

Security Setting	Legacy Client Configuration	Enterprise Client Configuration	High Security Configuration
Auditing			
Account Logon Events	Success	Success	Success
	Failure	Failure	Failure
Account Management	Success	Success	Success
	Failure	Failure	Failure
Directory Service Access	Success	Success	Success
	Failure	Failure	Failure

Table 5-7   Security Settings for Member Servers

Security Setting	Legacy Client Configuration	Enterprise Client Configuration	High Security Configuration
Auditing			
Logon Events	Success	Success	Success
	Failure	Failure	Failure
Object Access	Success	Success	Success
	Failure	Failure	Failure
Policy Change	Success	Success	Success
Privilege Use	No Auditing	Failure	Success
			Failure
Process Tracking	No Auditing	No Auditing	No Auditing
System Events	Success	Success	Success
User Rights			
Access this computer from the network	Not Defined (Use defaults)	Not defined (Use defaults)	Administrators, Authenticated Users
Act as part of the operating system	Not Defined (Use defaults)	Not Defined (Use defaults)	Revoke all security groups and accounts
Add workstations to domain	Not Defined (Use defaults)	Not Defined (Use defaults)	Administrators
Adjust memory quotas for a process	Not Defined (Use defaults)	Not Defined (Use defaults)	Administrators, NETWORK SERVICE, LOCAL SERVICE
Allow log on locally	Administrators, Backup Operators, Power Users	Administrators, Backup Operators, Power Users	Administrators, Backup Operators, Power Users
Allow log on through Terminal Services	Administrators, Remote Desktop Users	Administrators, Remote Desktop Users	Administrators
Change the system time	Not Defined (Use defaults)	Not Defined (Use defaults)	Administrators
Debug programs	Revoke all security groups and accounts	Revoke all security groups and accounts	Revoke all security groups and accounts
Deny access to this computer from the network	ANONYMOUS LOGON; Built-in Administrator, Guests; SUPPORT_ 388945a0; Guest; all NON-Operating System service accounts	ANONYMOUS LOGON; Built-in Administrator, Guests; SUPPORT_ 388945a0; Guest; all NON-Operating System service accounts	ANONYMOUS LOGON; Built-in Administrator, Guests; SUPPORT_ 388945a0; Guest; all NON-Operating System service accounts

Table 5-7   Security Settings for Member Servers

Security Setting	Legacy Client Configuration	Enterprise Client Configuration	High Security Configuration
User Rights			
Deny log on as a batch job	Guests; Support_388945a0; Guest	Guests; Support_388945a0; Guest	Guests; Support_388945a0; Guest
Deny log on through Terminal Services	Built-in Administrator; Guests; Support_388945a0; Guest; all NON-operating system service accounts	Built-in Administrator; Guests; Support_388945a0; Guest; all NON-operating system service accounts	Built-in Administrator; Guests; Support_388945a0; Guest; all NON-operating system service accounts
Enable computer and user accounts to be trusted for delegation	Not Defined (Use defaults)	Not Defined (Use defaults)	Revoke all security groups and accounts
Force shutdown from a remote system	Not Defined (Use defaults)	Not Defined (Use defaults)	Administrators
Generate security audits	Not Defined (Use defaults)	Not Defined (Use defaults)	NETWORK SERVICE, LOCAL SERVICE
Impersonate a client after authentication	Not Defined (Use defaults)	Not Defined (Use defaults)	Local Service; Network Service
Increase scheduling priority	Not Defined (Use defaults)	Not Defined (Use defaults)	Administrators
Load and unload device drivers	Not Defined (Use defaults)	Not Defined (Use defaults)	Administrators
Lock pages in memory	Not Defined (Use defaults)	Not Defined (Use defaults)	Administrators
Log on as a batch job	Not Defined (Use defaults)	Not Defined (Use defaults)	Revoke all security groups and accounts
Manage auditing and security log	Not Defined (Use defaults)	Not Defined (Use defaults)	Administrators
Modify firmware environment values	Not Defined (Use defaults)	Not Defined (Use defaults)	Administrators
Perform volume maintenance tasks	Not Defined (Use defaults)	Not Defined (Use defaults)	Administrators
Profile single process	Not Defined (Use defaults)	Not Defined (Use defaults)	Administrators
Profile system performance	Not Defined (Use defaults)	Not Defined (Use defaults)	Administrators
Remove computer from docking station	Not Defined (Use defaults)	Not Defined (Use defaults)	Administrators

Table 5-7   Security Settings for Member Servers

Security Setting	Legacy Client Configuration	Enterprise Client Configuration	High Security Configuration
User Rights			
Replace a process level token	Not Defined (Use defaults)	Not Defined (Use defaults)	LOCAL SERVICE, NETWORK SERVICE
Restore files and directories	Not Defined (Use defaults)	Administrators	Administrators
Shut down the system	Not Defined (Use defaults)	Not Defined (Use defaults)	Administrators
Synchronize directory service data	Not Defined (Use defaults)	Not Defined (Use defaults)	Revoke all security groups and accounts
Take ownership of files or other objects	Not Defined (Use defaults)	Not Defined (Use defaults)	Administrators
Security Options			
Accounts: Guest account status	Disabled	Disabled	Disabled
Accounts: Limit local account use of blank passwords to console logon	Enabled	Enabled	Enabled
Audit: Audit the access of global system objects	Disabled	Disabled	Disabled
Audit: Audit the use of Backup and Restore privilege	Disabled	Disabled	Disabled
Audit: Shut down system immediately if unable to log security audits	Disabled	Disabled	Enabled
Devices: Allow undock without having to log on	Disabled	Disabled	Disabled
Devices: Allowed to format and eject removable media	Administrators	Administrators	Administrators
Devices: Prevent users from installing printer drivers	Enabled	Enabled	Enabled
Devices: Restrict CD-ROM access to locally logged—on user only	Not Defined (Use defaults)	Not Defined (Use defaults)	Enabled

Table 5-7   Security Settings for Member Servers

Security Setting	Legacy Client Configuration	Enterprise Client Configuration	High Security Configuration
Security Options			
Devices: Restrict floppy access to locally logged—on user only	Not Defined (Use defaults)	Not Defined (Use defaults)	Enabled
Devices: Unsigned driver installation behavior	Warn but allow installation	Warn but allow installation	Warn but allow installation
Domain controller: Allow server operators to schedule tasks	Disabled	Disabled	Disabled
Domain controller: LDAP server signing requirements	Not Defined (Use defaults)	Not Defined (Use defaults)	Require Signing
Domain controller: Refuse machine account password changes	Disabled	Disabled	Disabled
Domain member: Digitally encrypt or sign secure channel data (always)	Disabled	Enabled	Enabled
Domain member: Digitally encrypt secure channel data (when possible)	Enabled	Enabled	Enabled
Domain member: Digitally sign secure channel data (when possible)	Enabled	Enabled	Enabled
Domain member: Disable machine account password changes	Disabled	Disabled	Disabled
Domain member: Maximum machine account password age	30 days	30 days	30 days
Domain member: Require strong (Windows 2000 or later) session key	Enabled	Enabled	Enabled
Interactive logon: Do not display last user name	Enabled	Enabled	Enabled

Table 5-7   **Security Settings for Member Servers**

Security Setting	Legacy Client Configuration	Enterprise Client Configuration	High Security Configuration
Security Options			
Interactive logon: Do not require CTRL+ALT+DEL	Disabled	Disabled	Disabled
Interactive logon: Message text for users attempting to log on	This system is restricted to authorized users. Individuals attempting unauthorized access will be prosecuted. If unauthorized, terminate access now! Clicking on OK indicates your acceptance of the information in the background.	This system is restricted to authorized users. Individuals attempting unauthorized access will be prosecuted. If unauthorized, terminate access now! Clicking on OK indicates your acceptance of the information in the background.	This system is restricted to authorized users. Individuals attempting unauthorized access will be prosecuted. If unauthorized, terminate access now! Clicking on OK indicates your acceptance of the information in the background.
Interactive logon: Message title for users attempting to log on	IT IS AN OFFENSE TO CONTINUE WITHOUT PROPER AUTHORIZATION	IT IS AN OFFENSE TO CONTINUE WITHOUT PROPER AUTHORIZATION	IT IS AN OFFENSE TO CONTINUE WITHOUT PROPER AUTHORIZATION
Interactive logon: Number of previous logons to cache (in case domain controller is not available)	1	0	0
Interactive logon: Prompt user to change password before expiration	14 days	14 days	14 days
Interactive logon: Require Domain Controller authentication to unlock workstation	Enabled	Enabled	Enabled
Interactive logon: Smart card removal behavior	Not Defined (Use defaults)	Lock Workstation	Lock Workstation
Microsoft network client: Digitally sign communications (always)	Disabled	Enabled	Enabled

Table 5-7   **Security Settings for Member Servers**

Security Setting	Legacy Client Configuration	Enterprise Client Configuration	High Security Configuration
Security Options			
Microsoft network client: Digitally sign communications (if server agrees)	Enabled	Enabled	Enabled
Microsoft network client: Send unencrypted password to third-party SMB servers	Disabled	Disabled	Disabled
Microsoft network server: Amount of idle time required before suspending session	15 minutes	15 minutes	15 minutes
Microsoft network server: Digitally sign communications (always)	Disabled	Enabled	Enabled
Microsoft network server: Digitally sign communications (if client agrees)	Enabled	Enabled	Enabled
Microsoft network server: Disconnect clients when logon hours expire	Enabled	Enabled	Enabled
Network access: Do not allow anonymous enumeration of SAM accounts	Enabled	Enabled	Enabled
Network access: Do not allow anonymous enumeration of SAM accounts and shares	Enabled	Enabled	Enabled
Network access: Do not allow storage of credentials or .NET Passports for network authentication	Enabled	Enabled	Enabled
Network access: Let Everyone permissions apply to anonymous users	Disabled	Disabled	Disabled
Network access: Named Pipes that can be accessed anonymously	None	None	None

Table 5-7   Security Settings for Member Servers

Security Setting	Legacy Client Configuration	Enterprise Client Configuration	High Security Configuration
Security Options			
Network access: Remotely accessible registry paths	System\Current ControlSet\Control\ ProductOptions; System\Current ControlSet\Control\ Server Applications; Software\Microsoft\ Windows NT\ CurrentVersion	System\Current ControlSet\ Control\ ProductOptions; System\Current ControlSet\ Control\Server Applications; Software\ Microsoft\ Windows NT\ CurrentVersion	System\Current ControlSet Control\Product-Options; System\Current ControlSet\ Control\Server Applications; Software\ Microsoft\ Windows NT\ CurrentVersion
Network access: Remotely accessible registry paths and sub-paths	System\Current ControlSet\Control\ Print\Printers _____ System\Current ControlSet\ Services\Eventlog _____ System\Current ControlSet\Services\ Eventlog Software\Microsoft\ OLAP Server _____ Software\Microsoft\ Windows NT\ CurrentVersion\Print _____ Software\Microsoft\ Windows NT\ CurrentVersion\ Windows _____ System\Current ControlSet\Control\ ContentIndex _____	System\Current ControlSet\ Control\ Print\Printers _____ System\Current ControlSet\ Services\Eventlog _____ System\Current ControlSet\ Services\Eventlog Software\ Microsoft\ OLAP Server _____ Software\ Microsoft\ Windows NT\ CurrentVersion\ Print _____ Software\ Microsoft\ Windows NT\ CurrentVersion\ Windows _____	System\ Current ControlSet\ Control\Print\ Printers _____ System\Current ControlSet\ Services\Eventlog _____ System\Current ControlSet\ Services\Eventlog Software\ Microsoft\ OLAP Server _____ Software\ Microsoft\ Windows NT\ CurrentVersion\ Print _____ Software\ Microsoft\ Windows NT\ CurrentVersion\ Windows _____

Table 5-7   **Security Settings for Member Servers**

Security Setting	Legacy Client Configuration	Enterprise Client Configuration	High Security Configuration
Security Options			
Network access: Remotely accessible registry paths and sub-paths	System\Current ControlSet\Control\ Terminal Server	System\Current ControlSet\ Control\ ContentIndex	System\Current ControlSet\ Control\ ContentIndex
	System\Current ControlSet\Control\ Terminal Server\ UserConfig	System\Current ControlSet\ Control\Terminal Server	System\Current ControlSet\ Control\ Terminal Server
	System\Current ControlSet\Control\ Terminal Server\ DefaultUser Configuration	System\Current ControlSet\ Control\Terminal Server\UserConfig	System\Current ControlSet\ Control\ Terminal Server\ UserConfig
	Software\ Microsoft\ Windows NT\ CurrentVersion\ Perflib	System\Current ControlSet\ Control\Terminal Server\DefaultUser Configuration	System\Current ControlSet\ Control\Terminal Server\Default User Configuration
	System\Current ControlSet\Services\ SysmonLog	Software\ Microsoft\ Windows NT\ CurrentVersion\ Perflib	Software\ Microsoft\ Windows NT\ CurrentVersion\ Perflib
		System\Current ControlSet\ Services\ SysmonLog	System\Current ControlSet\ Services\ SysmonLog
Network access: Restrict anonymous access to Named Pipes and Shares	Enabled	Enabled	Enabled
Network access: Shares that can be accessed anonymously	None	None	None

Table 5-7   Security Settings for Member Servers

Security Setting	Legacy Client Configuration	Enterprise Client Configuration	High Security Configuration
Security Options			
Network access: Sharing and security model for local accounts	Classic—local users authenticate as themselves	Classic—local users authenticate as themselves	Classic—local users authenticate as themselves
Network security: Do not store LAN Manager hash value on next password change	Enabled	Enabled	Enabled
Network security: LAN Manager authentication level	Send NTLMv2 responses only	Send NTLMv2 response only/ refuse LM	Send NTLMv2 response only/ refuse LM and NTLM
Network security: LDAP client signing requirements	Negotiate signing	Negotiate signing	Negotiate signing
Network security: Minimum session security for NTLM SSP based (including secure RPC) clients	No minimum	Enabled all settings	Enabled all settings
Network security: Minimum session security for NTLM SSP based (including secure RPC) servers	No minimums	Enabled all settings	Enabled all settings
Recovery console: Allow automatic administrative logon	Disabled	Disabled	Disabled
Recovery console: Allow floppy copy and access to all drives and all folders	Enabled	Enabled	Disabled
Shutdown: Allow system to be shut down without having to log on	Disabled	Disabled	Disabled
Shutdown: Clear virtual memory page file	Disabled	Disabled	Enabled
System cryptography: Force strong key protection for user keys stored on the computer	User is prompted when the key is first used	User is prompted when the key is first used	User must enter a password each time they use a key

Table 5-7   Security Settings for Member Servers

Security Setting	Legacy Client Configuration	Enterprise Client Configuration	High Security Configuration
Security Options			
System cryptography: Use FIPS compliant algorithms for encryption, hashing, and signing	Disabled	Disabled	Disabled
System objects: Default owner for objects created by members of the Administrators group	Object creator	Object creator	Object creator
System objects: Require case insensitivity for non-Windows subsystems	Enabled	Enabled	Enabled
System objects: Strengthen default permissions of internal system objects (such as Symbolic Links)	Enabled	Enabled	Enabled
System settings: Optional subsystem	None	None	None
Event Log			
Maximum application log size	16,384 KB	16,384 KB	16,384 KB
Maximum security log size	81,920 KB	81,920 KB	81,920 KB
Maximum system log size	16,384 KB	16,384 KB	16,384 KB
Prevent local guests group from accessing application log	Enabled	Enabled	Enabled
Prevent local guests group from accessing security log	Enabled	Enabled	Enabled
Prevent local guests group from accessing system log	Enabled	Enabled	Enabled
Retention method for application log	As needed	As needed	As needed
Retention method for security log	As needed	As needed	As needed
Retention method for system log	As needed	As needed	As needed

Table 5-7   Security Settings for Member Servers

Security Setting	Legacy Client Configuration	Enterprise Client Configuration	High Security Configuration
System Services			
Alerter	Disabled	Disabled	Disabled
Application Layer Gateway Service	Disabled	Disabled	Disabled
Application Management	Disabled	Disabled	Disabled
ASP.NET State Service	Disabled	Disabled	Disabled
Automatic Updates	Automatic	Automatic	Automatic
Background Intelligent Transfer Service	Manual	Manual	Manual
Certificate Services	Disabled	Disabled	Disabled
MS Software Shadow Copy Provider	Manual	Manual	Manual
Client Service for Netware	Disabled	Disabled	Disabled
ClipBook	Disabled	Disabled	Disabled
Cluster Service	Disabled	Disabled	Disabled
COM+ Event System	Manual	Manual	Manual
COM+ System Application	Disabled	Disabled	Disabled
Computer Browser	Automatic	Automatic	Automatic
Cryptographic Services	Automatic	Automatic	Automatic
DHCP Client	Automatic	Automatic	Automatic
DHCP Server	Disabled	Disabled	Disabled
Distributed Link Tracking Client	Disabled	Disabled	Disabled
Distributed Link Tracking Server	Disabled	Disabled	Disabled
Distribution Transaction Coordinator	Disabled	Disabled	Disabled
DNS Client	Automatic	Automatic	Automatic
DNS Server	Disabled	Disabled	Disabled
Error Reporting Service	Disabled	Disabled	Disabled
Event Log	Automatic	Automatic	Automatic
Fax Service	Disabled	Disabled	Disabled
File Replication	Disabled	Disabled	Disabled

Table 5-7 Security Settings for Member Servers

Security Setting	Legacy Client Configuration	Enterprise Client Configuration	High Security Configuration
System Services			
File Server for Macintosh	Disabled	Disabled	Disabled
FTP Publishing	Disabled	Disabled	Disabled
Help and Support	Disabled	Disabled	Disabled
HTTP SSL	Disabled	Disabled	Disabled
Human Interface Device Access	Disabled	Disabled	Disabled
IAS Jet Database Access	Disabled	Disabled	Disabled
IIS Admin Service	Disabled	Disabled	Disabled
IMAPI CD–Burning COM Service	Disabled	Disabled	Disabled
Indexing Service	Disabled	Disabled	Disabled
Infrared Monitor	Disabled	Disabled	Disabled
Internet Authentication Service	Disabled	Disabled	Disabled
Internet Connection Firewall (ICF)/Internet Connection Sharing (ICS)	Disabled	Disabled	Disabled
Intersite Messaging	Disabled	Disabled	Disabled
IP Version 6 Helper Service	Disabled	Disabled	Disabled
IPSec Policy Agent (IPSec Service)	Automatic	Automatic	Automatic
Kerberos Key Distribution Center	Disabled	Disabled	Disabled
License Logging Service	Disabled	Disabled	Disabled
Logical Disk Manager	Manual	Manual	Manual
Logical Disk Manager Administrative Service	Manual	Manual	Manual
Message Queuing	Disabled	Disabled	Disabled
Message Queuing Down Level Clients	Disabled	Disabled	Disabled
Message Queuing Triggers	Disabled	Disabled	Disabled
Messenger	Disabled	Disabled	Disabled
Microsoft POP3 Service	Disabled	Disabled	Disabled

Table 5-7   **Security Settings for Member Servers**

Security Setting	Legacy Client Configuration	Enterprise Client Configuration	High Security Configuration
System Services			
MSSQL$UDDI	Disabled	Disabled	Disabled
MSSQLServerADHelper	Disabled	Disabled	Disabled
.NET Framework Support Service	Disabled	Disabled	Disabled
Netlogon	Automatic	Automatic	Automatic
NetMeeting Remote Desktop Sharing	Disabled	Disabled	Disabled
Network Connections	Manual	Manual	Manual
Network DDE	Disabled	Disabled	Disabled
Network DDE DSDM	Disabled	Disabled	Disabled
Network Location Awareness (NLA)	Manual	Manual	Manual
Nework News Transport Protocol (NNTP)	Disabled	Disabled	Disabled
NTLM Support Provider	Automatic	Automatic	Automatic
Performance Logs and Alerts	Manual	Manual	Manual
Plug and Play	Automatic	Automatic	Automatic
Portable Media Serial Number	Disabled	Disabled	Disabled
Printer Server for Macintosh	Disabled	Disabled	Disabled
Print Spooler	Disabled	Disabled	Disabled
Protected Storage	Automatic	Automatic	Automatic
Remote Access Auto Connection Manager	Disabled	Disabled	Disabled
Remote Access Connection Manager	Disabled	Disabled	Disabled
Remote Administration Service	Manual	Manual	Manual
Remote Desktop Helper Session Manager	Disabled	Disabled	Disabled
Remote Installation	Disabled	Disabled	Disabled
Remote Procedure Call (RPC)	Automatic	Automatic	Automatic
Remote Procedure Call (RPC) Locator	Disabled	Disabled	Disabled
Remote Registry Service	Automatic	Automatic	Automatic

Table 5-7   Security Settings for Member Servers

Security Setting	Legacy Client Configuration	Enterprise Client Configuration	High Security Configuration
System Services			
Remote Server Manager	Disabled	Disabled	Disabled
Remote Server Monitor	Disabled	Disabled	Disabled
Remote Storage Notification	Disabled	Disabled	Disabled
Remote Storage Server	Disabled	Disabled	Disabled
Removable Storage	Manual	Manual	Manual
Resultant Set of Policy Provider	Disabled	Disabled	Disabled
Routing and Remote Access	Disabled	Disabled	Disabled
SAP Agent	Disabled	Disabled	Disabled
Secondary Logon	Disabled	Disabled	Disabled
Security Accounts Manager	Automatic	Automatic	Automatic
Server	Automatic	Automatic	Automatic
Shell Hardware Detection	Disabled	Disabled	Disabled
Simple Mail Transport Protocol (SMTP)	Disabled	Disabled	Disabled
Simple TCP/IP Services	Disabled	Disabled	Disabled
Single Instance Storage Groveler	Disabled	Disabled	Disabled
Smart Card	Disabled	Disabled	Disabled
SNMP Service	Disabled	Disabled	Disabled
SNMP Trap Service	Disabled	Disabled	Disabled
Special Administration Console Helper	Disabled	Disabled	Disabled
System Event Notification	Automatic	Automatic	Automatic
Task Scheduler	Disabled	Disabled	Disabled
TCP/IP NetBIOS Helper Service	Automatic	Automatic	Automatic
TCP/IP Print Server	Disabled	Disabled	Disabled
Telephony	Disabled	Disabled	Disabled
Telnet	Disabled	Disabled	Disabled
Terminal Services	Automatic	Automatic	Automatic

Table 5-7   Security Settings for Member Servers

Security Setting	Legacy Client Configuration	Enterprise Client Configuration	High Security Configuration
System Services			
Terminal Services Licensing	Disabled	Disabled	Disabled
Terminal Services Session Directory	Disabled	Disabled	Disabled
Themes	Disabled	Disabled	Disabled
Trival FTP Daemon	Disabled	Disabled	Disabled
Uninterruptible Power Supply	Disabled	Disabled	Disabled
Upload Manager	Disabled	Disabled	Disabled
Virtual Disk Service	Disabled	Disabled	Disabled
Volume Shadow Copy	Manual	Manual	Manual
WebClent	Disabled	Disabled	Disabled
Web Element Manager	Disabled	Disabled	Disabled
Windows Audio	Disabled	Disabled	Disabled
Windows Image Acquisition (WIA)	Disabled	Disabled	Disabled
Windows Installer	Automatic	Automatic	Automatic
Windows Internet Name Service (WINS)	Disabled	Disabled	Disabled
Windows Management Instrumentation	Automatic	Automatic	Automatic
Windows Management Instrumentation Driver Extensions	Manual	Manual	Manual
Windows Media Services	Disabled	Disabled	Disabled
Windows System Resource Manager	Disabled	Disabled	Disabled
Windows Time	Automatic	Automatic	Automatic
WinHTTP Web Proxy Auto—Discovery Service	Disabled	Disabled	Disabled
Wireless Configuration	Disabled	Disabled	Disabled
WMI Performance Adapter	Manual	Manual	Manual
Workstation	Automatic	Automatic	Automatic
World Wide Publishing Service	Disabled	Disabled	Disabled

Ports Required for Member Servers

For a member server to function on the network with other computers, specific ports must be opened. Table 5-8 presents a list of those critical ports. As we investigate specific server roles, additional ports will need to be added to ensure the server functions properly.

Table 5-8 Ports for Member Servers

Port	Description
137 (NetBIOS name service)	Used by the browse master service. This must be open for WINS and browse master servers.
138 (NetBIOS datagram service)	Must be open to accept inbound datagrams from NetBIOS applications such as the Messenger service or the Computer Browser service.
139 (NetBIOS session service)	Must be closed unless you run applications or operating systems that need to support Windows networking (SMB) connections. If you run Windows NT 4.0, Windows Millennium Edition, Windows 98, or Windows 95, this port must be open on your servers.
445 (CIFS/SMB server)	Used by basic Windows networking, including file sharing, printer sharing, and remote administration.
3389 (Remote Desktop Protocol)	Must be open if you are using Terminal Services for application sharing, remote desktop, or remote assistance.

Domain Controllers

Domain controllers are the heart of any environment that runs Active Directory. These computers must be stable, protected, and available to provide the key services for the directory service, user authentication, resource access, and more. If there is any loss or compromise of a domain controller in the environment, the result can be disastrous for clients, servers, and applications that rely on domain controllers for authentication, Group Policy, and the LDAP directory.

Not only should these domain controllers be hardened with security configurations, they must also be physically secured in locations that are accessible only to qualified administrative staff. If domain controllers are stored in unsecured locations due to limitations of the facility (such as in a branch office), you should apply additional security configurations to limit the potential damage from physical threats against the computer.

Domain Controller Security Environment Levels

Along the same lines as the Member Server hardening guidelines, domain controllers also have different levels of security based on the environment in which they are deployed. These levels are the same as those defined in the "Member Servers" section in this chapter: Legacy Client, Enterprise Client, and High Security.

Security Settings for Domain Controllers

Security settings that apply specifically to domain controllers are best created in a GPO that is then linked to the Domain Controllers OU. The settings for domain controllers should be based on those we reviewed in the earlier "Member Servers" section. Of course, a domain controller also has additional functions or features compared to a member server, and this requires additional open ports and security configuration. You must review the security settings list to ensure that you are not restricting a key feature for your domain controller.

Table 5-9 lists the settings that differ from those specified in Table 5-7. In other words, the baseline security settings for domain controllers as outlined below should be incrementally added to the baseline security settings for member servers described previously.

> **More Info**   For more information on hardening domain controllers in different enterprise environments, see the *Windows Server 2003 Security Guide* found at *http:// www.microsoft.com/downloads/details.aspx?FamilyID=8a2643c1-0685-4d89-b655- 521ea6c7b4db&displaylang=en.*

Table 5-9   Security Settings for Domain Controllers

Security Setting	Legacy Client Configuration	Enterprise Client Configuration	High Security Configuration
User Rights			
Access this computer from the network	Not Defined (Use defaults)	Not Defined (Use defaults)	Administrators, Authenticated Users, ENTERPRISE DOMAIN CONTROLLERS
Add workstations to domain	Administrators	Administrators	Administrators
Allow log on locally	Administrators	Administrators	Administrators
Allow log on through Terminal Services	Administrators	Administrators	Administrators
Change the system time	Administrators	Administrators	Administrators
Enable computer and user accounts to be trusted for delegation	Not Defined (Use defaults)	Not Defined (Use defaults)	Administrators

Table 5-9   Security Settings for Domain Controllers

Security Setting	Legacy Client Configuration	Enterprise Client Configuration	High Security Configuration
User Rights			
Load and unload device drivers	Administrators	Administrators	Administrators
Restore files and directories	Administrators	Administrators	Administrators
Shutdown the system	Administrators	Administrators	Administrators
Security Options			
Network security: Do not store LAN Manager hash value on next password change	Disabled	Enabled	Enabled
System Services			
Distributed File System	Automatic	Automatic	Automatic
DNS Server	Automatic	Automatic	Automatic
File Replication	Automatic	Automatic	Automatic
Intersite Messaging	Automatic	Automatic	Automatic
Kerberos Key Distribution Center	Automatic	Automatic	Automatic
Remote Procedure Call (RPC) Locator	Automatic	Automatic	Automatic

Ports Required for Domain Controllers

Domain controllers are responsible for specific functions, as seen in the different settings listed in Table 5-9. Many of these different security template settings are due to required services to authenticate users and maintain consistency of the Active Directory database between other domain controllers. Table 5-10 lists additional ports that you must open for domain controllers.

Table 5-10   Ports for Domain Controllers

Ports	Description
88 (Kerberos)	The Kerberos protocol is used by Windows 2000 and later operating systems to log on and retrieve tickets for accessing other servers.
123 (NTP)	This port provides time synchronization for network clients using the Network Time Protocol (NTP).

Table 5-10   **Ports for Domain Controllers**

Ports	Description
135 (RPC endpoint mapper/DCOM)	This port allows RPC clients to discover the ports that the RPC server is listening on.
389 (LDAP)	This port the primary way that clients access Active Directory to obtain user information, e-mail addresses, services, and other directory service information.
464 (Kerberos Password Changes)	This port provides secure methods for users to change passwords using Kerberos.
636 (LDAP over SSL)	This port is needed if LDAP will use SSL to provide encryption and mutual authentication for LDAP traffic.
3268 (Global Catalog)	This port provides the means for clients to search Active Directory information that spans multiple domains.
3269 (Global Catalog over SSL)	This port is needed because the Global Catalog uses SSL to provide encryption and mutual authentication for Global Catalog traffic.

Note   If your domain controller is running DNS, you will need to also open port 53.

File and Print Servers

File and print servers are responsible for resource storage and controlling access to these resources throughout the enterprise. These servers house the company's documents, trade secrets, financial data, and much more. If these computers are not protected, the entire company might be in jeopardy. These computers must be stable, protected, and available to provide users and applications access to resources stored on these computers.

Like the domain controllers, these servers must be physically protected. If someone were to get hold of a file server, they could potentially use other tools to gain access to the resources on the server. You should take action to protect against this.

Table 5-11 lists security settings for file and print servers that differ from the settings in the Member Servers section earlier in the chapter. In other words, the baseline security settings for file and print servers as outlined here should be incrementally added to the baseline security settings for member servers described previously. These settings are best created in a GPO that is then linked to the OU that contains the file servers.

More Info   For more information on hardening file and print servers in different enterprise environments, see the *Windows Server 2003 Security Guide* found at *http://www.microsoft.com/downloads/details.aspx?FamilyID=8a2643c1-0685-4d89-b655-521ea6c7b4db&displaylang=en*.

Table 5-11   Security Settings for File and Print Servers

Security Setting	Legacy Client Configuration	Enterprise Client Configuration	High Security Configuration
Security Options			
Microsoft network server: Digitally sign communications (always)	Disabled (Print Servers only)	Disabled (Print Servers only)	Disabled (Print Servers only)
System Services			
Distributed File System	Disabled	Disabled	Disabled
File Replication	Disabled	Disabled	Disabled
Print Spooler	Automatic (Print Servers only)	Automatic (Print Servers only)	Automatic (Print Servers only)

Web Servers

Microsoft Internet Information Services (IIS) is the service that provides Web services on a Windows server. Web servers must be properly secured from malicious attackers, while still allowing legitimate clients to access intranet or public Web sites hosted on the server.

IIS is not installed by default on the Windows Server 2003 family of servers, and when you do install IIS, it installs in "locked" mode—a highly secure mode that protects IIS against threats. Beyond the best-practice security settings presented in this section for IIS, be sure to protect your Web servers by monitoring security using some form of intrusion detection system, and by implementing proper incident response procedures.

Security Settings for Web Servers

Security settings for Web servers are best created in a GPO that is then linked to the OU that contains the Web servers. Table 5-12 lists only the settings that differ from those in the Table 5-7. In other words, the baseline security settings for Web servers as outlined here should be incrementally added to the baseline security settings for member servers described previously.

> **More Info**   For more information on hardening Web servers in different enterprise environments, see the *Windows Server 2003 Security Guide* found at *http://www.microsoft.com/downloads/details.aspx?FamilyID=8a2643c1-0685-4d89-b655-521ea6c7b4db&displaylang=en.*

Table 5-12   Security Settings for Web Servers

Security Setting	Legacy Client Configuration	Enterprise Client Configuration	High Security Configuration
User Rights			
Deny access to this computer from the network	ANONYMOUS LOGON; Built— in Administrator; Support_ 388945a0; Guest; all NON— Operating System service accounts	ANONYMOUS LOGON; Built— in Administrator; Support_ 388945a0; Guest; all NON— Operating System service accounts	ANONYMOUS LOGON; Built— in Administrator; Support_ 388945a0; Guest; all NON— Operating System service accounts
System Services			
HTTP SSL	Automatic	Automatic	Automatic
IIS Admin Service	Automatic	Automatic	Automatic
World Wide Web Publishing Service	Automatic	Automatic	Automatic

Ports Required for Web Servers

Web servers should have limited ports available, to reduce their exposure to attacks from the local network and the Internet. The fewer the ports that are open, the better. Table 5-13 is a list of additional ports that you will need to open for Web servers.

Table 5-13   Ports for Web Servers

Ports	Description
80 (HTTP)	The standard HTTP port for providing Web services to users. This can be easily changed and is not required. If you do change the port for HTTP, be sure to add that new port to this list and configure that setting within IIS.
443 (HTTPS)	Allows HTTP to have a higher level of security that provides integrity, encryption, and authentication for Web traffic.

Client Hardening

Not only should servers be hardened to protect against outside intruders, but clients need the same attention. Clients also need to have services, ports, applications, groups, and so on locked down to reduce security risks as much as possible. This reduction in security risk should not compromise functionality in most cases. If the security on a client is too tight, users might not be able to use applications and network communications as needed.

To show a wide range of client configuration best practices, we will look at four common environments. The best practices focus on creating and maintaining a secure environment for desktops and laptops running Windows XP Professional. We will break down clients into two more categories: enterprise and high security:

- **Enterprise**   The enterprise environment consists of a Windows 2000 or Windows Server 2003 Active Directory domain. The clients in this environment will be managed using Group Policy that is applied to containers, sites, domains, and OUs. Group Policy provides a centralized method of managing security policy across the environment.

- **High security**   The high-security environment has elevated security settings for the client. When high-security settings are applied, user functionality is limited to functions that are required for the necessary tasks. Access is limited to approved applications, services, and infrastructure environments.

It would be impossible to cover every possible scenario or environment. However, we will suggest security settings that have been reviewed, tested, and approved by Microsoft engineers, consultants, and customers in a production environment. Table 5-14 lists settings that are available within a standard security template and the best-practice configurations for the following four scenarios:

- Enterprise desktop computers
- Enterprise laptop computers
- High-security desktop computers
- High-security laptop computers

More Info   For more information on the below security settings for hardening Windows XP clients in each of these four environments, see the *Windows XP Security Guide v2* found at *http://www.microsoft.com/downloads/details.aspx?FamilyId=2D3E25BC-F434-4CC6-A5A7-09A8A229F118&displaylang=en*. For a thorough discussion of *all* security settings available in Windows XP Service Pack 2, see the *Threats and Countermeasures Guide* at *http://go.microsoft.com/fwlink/?LinkId=15159*.

Important   Before you implement any security settings or best-practice configurations for your production clients, be sure to test the settings for your environment. Applications, operating systems, and other network constraints can cause issues with these best-practice settings in some instances.

Table 5-14   Best Practice Security Settings for the Four Types of Clients

Security Setting	Enterprise Desktop	Enterprise Laptop	High Security Desktop	High Security Laptop
Auditing				
Account Logon Events	Success Failure	Success Failure	Success Failure	Success Failure
Account Management	Success Failure	Success Failure	Success Failure	Success Failure
Directory Service Access	No Auditing	No Auditing	No Auditing	No Auditing
Logon Events	Success Failure	Success Failure	Success Failure	Success Failure
Object Access	Success Failure	Success Failure	Success Failure	Success Failure
Policy Change	Success	Success	Success	Success
Privilege Use	Failure	Failure	Failure	Failure
Process Tracking	No Auditing	No Auditing	No Auditing	No Auditing
System Events	Success	Success	Success Failure	Success Failure
User Rights				
Access this computer from the network	Administrators, Backup Operators, Power Users, Users	Administrators, Backup Operators, Power Users, Users	Administrators, Users	Administrators, Users
Act as part of the operating system	No one	No one	No one	No one
Adjust memory quotas for a process	Not Defined (Use defaults)	Not Defined (Use defaults)	Administrators, Local Service, Network Service	Administrators, Local Service, Network Service
Allow log on locally	Users, Administrators	Users, Administrators	Users, Administrators	Users, Administrators
Allow log on through Terminal Services	Administrators, Remote Desktop Users	Administrators, Remote Desktop Users	No one	No one
Backup files and directories	Not Defined (Use defaults)	Not Defined (Use defaults)	Administrators	Administrators
Change the system time	Not Defined (Use defaults)	Not Defined (Use defaults)	Administrators	Administrators

Table 5-14   Best Practice Security Settings for the Four Types of Clients

Security Setting	Enterprise Desktop	Enterprise Laptop	High Security Desktop	High Security Laptop
User Rights				
Create a pagefile	Not Defined (Use defaults)	Not Defined (Use defaults)	Administrators	Administrators
Create a permanent shared object	Not Defined (Use defaults)	Not Defined (Use defaults)	No one	No one
Create a token object	Not Defined (Use defaults)	Not Defined (Use defaults)	No one	No one
Debug programs	Administrators	Administrators	Administrators	Administrators
Deny access to this computer from the network	Not Defined (Use defaults)	Not Defined (Use defaults)	Everyone	Everyone
Deny log on through Terminal Services	Not Defined (Use defaults)	Not Defined (Use defaults)	Everyone	Everyone
Enable computer and user accounts to be trusted for delegation	No one	No one	No one	No one
Force shutdown from a remote system	Not Defined (Use defaults)	Not Defined (Use defaults)	Administrators	Administrators
Generate security audits	Not Defined (Use defaults)	Not Defined (Use defaults)	NETWORK SERVICE, LOCAL SERVICE	NETWORK SERVICE, LOCAL SERVICE
Increase scheduling priority	Not Defined (Use defaults)	Not Defined (Use defaults)	Administrators	Administrators
Load and unload device drivers	Not Defined (Use defaults)	Not Defined (Use defaults)	Administrators	Administrators
Log on as a batch job	Not Defined (Use defaults)	Not Defined (Use defaults)	No one	No one
Log on as a service	Not Defined (Use defaults)	Not Defined (Use defaults)	No one	No one
Manage auditing and security log	Not Defined (Use defaults)	Not Defined (Use defaults)	Administrators	Administrators
Modify firmware environment values	Not Defined (Use defaults)	Not Defined (Use defaults)	Administrators	Administrators
Perform volume maintenance tasks	Not Defined (Use defaults)	Not Defined (Use defaults)	Administrators	Administrators

Table 5-14   Best Practice Security Settings for the Four Types of Clients

Security Setting	Enterprise Desktop	Enterprise Laptop	High Security Desktop	High Security Laptop
User Rights				
Profile single process	Not Defined (Use defaults)	Not Defined (Use defaults)	Administrators	Administrators
Profile system performance	Not Defined (Use defaults)	Not Defined (Use defaults)	Administrators	Administrators
Replace a process level token	LOCAL SERVICE, NETWORK SERVICE	LOCAL SERVICE, NETWORK SERVICE	LOCAL SERVICE, NETWORK SERVICE	LOCAL SERVICE, NETWORK SERVICE
Restore files and directories	Not Defined (Use defaults)	Not Defined (Use defaults)	Administrators	Administra- tors, Users
Shut down the system	Not Defined (Use defaults)	Not Defined (Use defaults)	Administrators, Users	Administra- tors, Users
Take ownership of files or other objects	Not Defined (Use defaults)	Not Defined (Use defaults)	Administrators	Administrators
Security Options				
Accounts: Guest account status	Disabled	Disabled	Disabled	Disabled
Accounts: Limit local account use of blank passwords to console logon	Enabled	Enabled	Enabled	Enabled
Accounts: Rename administrator account	Recommended	Recommended	Recommended	Recommended
Accounts: Rename guest account	Recommended	Recommended	Recommended	Recommended
Devices: Allow undock without having to log on	Disabled	Disabled	Disabled	Disabled
Devices: Allowed to format and eject removable media	Administrators, Interactive Users	Administrators, Interactive Users	Administrators	Administrators
Devices: Prevent users from installing printer drivers	Enabled	Disabled	Enabled	Disabled
Devices: Restrict CD-ROM access to locally logged—on user only	Disabled	Disabled	Disabled	Disabled

Table 5-14   Best Practice Security Settings for the Four Types of Clients

Security Setting	Enterprise Desktop	Enterprise Laptop	High Security Desktop	High Security Laptop
Security Options				
Devices: Restrict floppy access to locally logged—on user only	Disabled	Disabled	Disabled	Disabled
Devices: Unsigned driver installation behavior	Warn but allow installation	Warn but allow installation	Do not allow installation	Do not allow installation
Domain member: Digitally encrypt or sign secure channel data (always)	Not Defined (Use defaults)	Not Defined (Use defaults)	Enabled	Enabled
Domain member: Digitally encrypt secure channel data (when possible)	Enabled	Enabled	Enabled	Enabled
Domain member: Digitally sign secure channel data (when possible)	Enabled	Enabled	Enabled	Enabled
Domain member: Disable machine account password changes	Disabled	Disabled	Disabled	Disabled
Domain member: Maximum machine account password age	30 days	30 days	30 days	30 days
Domain member: Require strong (Windows 2000 or later) session key	Enabled	Enabled	Enabled	Enabled
Interactive logon: Do not display last user name	Enabled	Enabled	Enabled	Enabled
Interactive logon: Do not require CTRL+ALT+DEL	Disabled	Disabled	Disabled	Disabled

Table 5-14   Best Practice Security Settings for the Four Types of Clients

Security Setting	Enterprise Desktop	Enterprise Laptop	High Security Desktop	High Security Laptop
Security Options				
Interactive logon: Message text for users attempting to log on	This system is restricted to authorized users. Individuals attempting unauthorized access will be prosecuted. If unauthorized, terminate access now! Clicking on OK indicates your acceptance of the information in the background.	This system is restricted to authorized users. Individuals attempting unauthorized access will be prosecuted. If unauthorized, terminate access now! Clicking on OK indicates your acceptance of the information in the background.	This system is restricted to authorized users. Individuals attempting unauthorized access will be prosecuted. If unauthorized, terminate access now! Clicking on OK indicates your acceptance of the information in the background.	This system is restricted to authorized users. Individuals attempting unauthorized access will be prosecuted. If unauthorized, terminate access now! Clicking on OK indicates your acceptance of the information in the background.
Interactive logon: Message title for users attempting to log on	IT IS AN OFFENSE TO CONTINUE WITHOUT PROPER AUTHORIZA-TION	IT IS AN OFFENSE TO CONTINUE WITHOUT PROPER AUTHORIZA-TION	IT IS AN OFFENSE TO CONTINUE WITHOUT PROPER AUTHORIZA-TION	IT IS AN OFFENSE TO CONTINUE WITHOUT PROPER AUTHORIZA-TION
Interactive logon: Number of previous logons to cache (in case domain controller is not available)	2	2	0	1
Interactive logon: Prompt user to change password before expiration	14 days	14 days	14 days	14 days
Interactive logon: Require Domain Controller authenti-cation to unlock workstation	Disabled	Disabled	Enabled	Disabled
Interactive logon: Smart card removal behavior	Lock Workstation	Lock Workstation	Lock Workstation	Lock Workstation

Table 5-14 Best Practice Security Settings for the Four Types of Clients

Security Setting	Enterprise Desktop	Enterprise Laptop	High Security Desktop	High Security Laptop
Security Options				
Microsoft network client: Digitally sign communications (always)	Not Defined (Use defaults)	Not Defined (Use defaults)	Enabled	Enabled
Microsoft network client: Digitally sign communications (if server agrees)	Enabled	Enabled	Enabled	Enabled
Microsoft network client: Send unencrypted password to third—party SMB servers	Disabled	Disabled	Disabled	Disabled
Microsoft network server: Amount of idle time required before suspending session	15 minutes	15 minutes	15 minutes	15 minutes
Microsoft network server: Digitally sign communications (always)	Enabled	Enabled	Enabled	Enabled
Microsoft network server: Digitally sign communications (if client agrees)	Enabled	Enabled	Enabled	Enabled
Network access: Allow anonymous SID/Name translation	Disabled	Disabled	Disabled	Disabled
Network access: Do not allow anonymous enumeration of SAM accounts	Enabled	Enabled	Enabled	Enabled
Network access: Do not allow anonymous enumeration of SAM accounts and shares	Enabled	Enabled	Enabled	Enabled
Network access: Do not allow storage of credentials or .NET Passports for network authentication	Enabled	Enabled	Enabled	Enabled

Table 5-14 Best Practice Security Settings for the Four Types of Clients

Security Setting	Enterprise Desktop	Enterprise Laptop	High Security Desktop	High Security Laptop
Security Options				
Network access: Let Everyone permissions apply to anonymous users	Disabled	Disabled	Disabled	Disabled
Network access: Shares that can be accessed anonymously	comcfg, dfs$	comcfg, dfs$	comcfg, dfs$	comcfg, dfs$
Network access: Sharing and security model for local accounts	Classic–local users authenticate as themselves	Classic–local users authenticate as themselves	Classic–local users authenticate as themselves	Classic–local users authenticate as themselves
Network security: Do not store LAN Manager hash value on next password change	Enabled	Enabled	Enabled	Enabled
Network security: LAN Manager authentication level	Send NTLMv2 responses only	Send NTLMv2 responses only	Send NTLMv2 response only/refuse LM and NTLM	Send NTLMv2 response only/refuse LM and NTLM
Network security: LDAP client signing requirements	Not defined	Not defined	Require signing	Require signing
Network security: Minimum session security for NTLM SSP based (including secure RPC) clients	Require message confidentiality, Require message integrity, Require NTLMv2 session security, Require 128-bit encryption	Require message confidentiality, Require message integrity, Require NTLMv2 session security, Require 128-bit encryption	Require message confidentiality, Require message integrity, Require NTLMv2 session security, Require 128-bit encryption	Require message confidentiality, Require message integrity, Require NTLMv2 session security, Require 128-bit encryption
Network security: Minimum session security for NTLM SSP based (including secure RPC) servers	Require message confidentiality, Require message integrity, Require NTLMv2 session security, Require 128-bit encryption	Require message confidentiality, Require message integrity, Require NTLMv2 session security, Require 128-bit encryption	Require message confidentiality, Require message integrity, Require NTLMv2 session security, Require 128-bit encryption	Require message confidentiality, Require message integrity, Require NTLMv2 session security, Require 128-bit encryption

Table 5-14   Best Practice Security Settings for the Four Types of Clients

Security Setting	Enterprise Desktop	Enterprise Laptop	High Security Desktop	High Security Laptop
Security Options				
Recovery console: Allow automatic administrative logon	Disabled	Disabled	Disabled	Disabled
Recovery console: Allow floppy copy and access to all drives and all folders	Enabled	Enabled	Disabled	Disabled
Shutdown: Allow system to be shut down without having to log on	Disabled	Disabled	Disabled	Disabled
Shutdown: Clear virtual memory page file	Disabled	Disabled	Enabled	Enabled
System cryptography: Use FIPS compliant algorithms for encryption, hashing, and signing	Disabled	Disabled	Disabled	Disabled
System objects: Default owner for objects created by members of the Administrators group	Object creator	Object creator	Object creator	Object creator
System objects: Require case insensitivity for non-Windows subsystems	Enabled	Enabled	Enabled	Enabled
System objects: Strengthen default permissions of internal system objects (for example, Symbolic Links)	Enabled	Enabled	Enabled	Enabled
Event Log				
Maximum application log size	20480 KB	20480 KB	20480 KB	20480 KB
Maximum security log size	40960 KB	40960 KB	81920 KB	81920 KB
Maximum system log size	20,480 KB	20,480 KB	20,480 KB	20,480 KB

Table 5-14   **Best Practice Security Settings for the Four Types of Clients**

Security Setting	Enterprise Desktop	Enterprise Laptop	High Security Desktop	High Security Laptop
Event Log				
Prevent local guests group from accessing application log	Enabled	Enabled	Enabled	Enabled
Prevent local guests group from accessing security log	Enabled	Enabled	Enabled	Enabled
Prevent local guests group from accessing system log	Enabled	Enabled	Enabled	Enabled
Retention method for application log	As needed	As needed	As needed	As needed
Retention method for security log	As needed	As needed	As needed	As needed
Retention method for system log	As needed	As needed	As needed	As needed
System Services				
Alerter	Disabled	Disabled	Disabled	Disabled
Application Layer Gateway Service	Disabled	Disabled	Disabled	Disabled
Application Management	Disabled	Disabled	Disabled	Disabled
ASP .NET State Service	Disabled	Disabled	Disabled	Disabled
Automatic Updates	Automatic	Automatic	Automatic	Automatic
Background Intelligent Transfer Service	Manual	Manual	Manual	Manual
ClipBook	Disabled	Disabled	Disabled	Disabled
COM+ Event System	Manual	Manual	Manual	Manual
COM+ System Application	Disabled	Disabled	Disabled	Disabled
Computer Browser	Disabled	Disabled	Disabled	Disabled
Cryptographic Services	Automatic	Automatic	Automatic	Automatic
DHCP Client	Automatic	Automatic	Automatic	Automatic
Distributed Link Tracking Client	Disabled	Disabled	Disabled	Disabled
Distributed Link Tracking Server	Disabled	Disabled	Disabled	Disabled

Table 5-14   Best Practice Security Settings for the Four Types of Clients

Security Setting	Enterprise Desktop	Enterprise Laptop	High Security Desktop	High Security Laptop
System Services				
Distribution Transaction Coordinator	Disabled	Disabled	Disabled	Disabled
DNS Client	Automatic	Automatic	Automatic	Automatic
Error Reporting Service	Disabled	Disabled	Disabled	Disabled
Event Log	Automatic	Automatic	Automatic	Automatic
Fax Service	Manual	Manual	Disabled	Disabled
FTP Publishing	Disabled	Disabled	Disabled	Disabled
Help and Support	Disabled	Disabled	Disabled	Disabled
HTTP SSL	Disabled	Disabled	Disabled	Disabled
Human Interface Device Access	Disabled	Disabled	Disabled	Disabled
IIS Admin Service	Disabled	Disabled	Disabled	Disabled
IMAPI CD—Burning COM Service	Disabled	Disabled	Disabled	Disabled
Indexing Service	Disabled	Disabled	Disabled	Disabled
IPSec Services	Automatic	Automatic	Automatic	Automatic
Logical Disk Manager	Manual	Manual	Manual	Manual
Logical Disk Manager Administrative Service	Manual	Manual	Manual	Manual
Messenger	Disabled	Disabled	Disabled	Disabled
MS Software Shadow Copy Provider	Disabled	Disabled	Disabled	Disabled
Netlogon	Automatic	Automatic	Automatic	Automatic
NetMeeting Remote Desktop Sharing	Disabled	Disabled	Disabled	Disabled
Network Connections	Manual	Manual	Manual	Manual
Network DDE	Manual	Manual	Disabled	Disabled
Network DDE DSDM	Manual	Manual	Disabled	Disabled
Network Location Awareness (NLA)	Manual	Manual	Manual	Manual
Network Provisioning Service	Disabled	Disabled	Disabled	Disabled
NTLM Support Provider	Automatic	Automatic	Automatic	Automatic
Performance Logs and Alerts	Manual	Manual	Manual	Manual

Table 5-14   **Best Practice Security Settings for the Four Types of Clients**

Security Setting	Enterprise Desktop	Enterprise Laptop	High Security Desktop	High Security Laptop
System Services				
Plug and Play	Automatic	Automatic	Automatic	Automatic
Portable Media Serial Number	Disabled	Disabled	Disabled	Disabled
Print Spooler	Disabled	Disabled	Disabled	Disabled
Protected Storage	Automatic	Automatic		Automatic
Remote Access Auto Connection Manager	Disabled	Disabled		Disabled
Remote Access Connection Manager	Disabled	Disabled		Disabled
Remote Desktop Helper Session Manager	Disabled	Disabled		Disabled
Remote Procedure Call (RPC)	Disabled	Disabled	Disabled	Disabled
Remote Procedure Call (RPC) Locator	Disabled	Disabled	Disabled	Disabled
Remote Registry Service	Automatic	Automatic	Disabled	Disabled
Removable Storage	Disabled	Disabled	Disabled	Disabled
Routing and Remote Access	Disabled	Disabled	Disabled	Disabled
Secondary Logon	Disabled	Disabled	Disabled	Disabled
Security Accounts Manager	Automatic	Automatic	Automatic	Automatic
Server	Automatic	Automatic	Disabled	Disabled
Shell Hardware Detection	Disabled	Disabled	Disabled	Disabled
Smart Card	Disabled	Disabled	Disabled	Disabled
SSDP Discovery Service	Disabled	Disabled	Disabled	Disabled
System Event Notification	Automatic	Automatic	Automatic	Automatic
System Restore Service	Disabled	Disabled	Disabled	disabled
Task Scheduler	Disabled	Disabled	Disabled	Disabled
TCP/IP NetBIOS Helper Service	Automatic	Automatic	Automatic	Automatic

Table 5-14   **Best Practice Security Settings for the Four Types of Clients**

Security Setting	Enterprise Desktop	Enterprise Laptop	High Security Desktop	High Security Laptop
System Services				
Telephony	Disabled	Disabled	Disabled	Disabled
Telnet	Disabled	Disabled	Disabled	Disabled
Terminal Services	Disabled	disabled	Disabled	Disabled
Themes	Disabled	Disabled	Disabled	Disabled
Uninterruptible Power Supply	Disabled	Disabled	Disabled	Disabled
Volume Shadow Copy	Disabled	Disabled	Disabled	Disabled
WebClient	Disabled	Disabled	Disabled	Disabled
Windows Audio	Disabled	Disabled	Disabled	Disabled
Windows Firewall/ Internet Connection Sharing (ICS)	Disabled	Disabled	Enabled	Enabled
Windows Image Acquisition (WIA)	Disabled	Disabled	Disabled	Disabled
Windows Installer	Automatic	Automatic	automatic	Automatic
Windows Management Instrumentation	Automatic	Automatic	Automatic	Automatic
Windows Management Instrumentation Driver Extensions	Disabled	Disabled	Disabled	Disabled
Windows Time	Automatic	Automatic	automatic	Automatic
Windows User Mode Driver Framework	Disabled	Disabled	Disabled	Disabled
Wireless Zero configuration	Manual	Manual	Manual	Manual
WMI Performance Adapter	Disabled	Disabled		Disabled
Workstation	Automatic	Automatic		Automatic

Ports Required for Clients

Clients must have basic communication on a network to send and receive e-mail and access network resources. Specific ports must be opened to provide this communication, as shown in Table 5-15. Depending on whether your client needs to communicate in some different manner or has an application that requires a different port opened, these ports will allow secure communications.

Table 5-15   Ports Required for Clients

Ports	Description
137 (NetBIOS name service)	Used by the browse master service. This port must be opened for WINS and browse master servers.
138 (NetBIOS datagram service)	Must be open to accept inbound datagrams from NetBIOS applications such as the Messenger service and the Windows Browser.
139 (NetBIOS session service)	Should be closed unless you run applications or operating systems that must support Windows networking (SMB) connections. If you run Windows NT 4.0, Windows Millennium Edition, Windows 98, or Windows 95, this port must be open on your servers.
445 (SMB)	Used by basic Windows networking, including file sharing, printer sharing, and remote administration.
3389 (Remote Desktop Protocol)	Must be open if you are using Terminal Services for application sharing, remote desktop, or remote assistance.

Restricted Groups for Clients

The local groups that exist on client computers should be controlled to ensure that the correct members belong to the administrative groups that exist on each computer. If these groups are not controlled through Group Policy, the local administrator will be able to control who has administrative control over the computer, and this can lead to insecure configurations and vulnerabilities.

Table 5-16 lists best practices for local group and which users or groups should be configured to belong to each group.

Table 5-16   Restricted Group Best Practices for Clients

Local Group	Members
Administrators	Administrator (local)
	Domain Admins
Backup Operators	No one
Network Configuration Operators	No one
Power Users	No one
Remote Desktop Users	No one

Client Computers for IT Staff and Administrators

The standard client computer settings might not work for a computer that is used by someone on the IT staff or an administrator's computer. These users need more privileged access to their own computers, including the ability to install applications, modify their own registries, run Administrative tools, and possibly back up their own computers. These tasks require certain services, ports, and restricted group configurations on the computer. The following sections offer best-practice configurations for computers used by IT staff and administrators to give them the access they need. We will cover only the settings that differ from those for the standard client computer suite described previously.

Security Settings for IT Staff and Administrators

IT staff and administrators need access to key parts of their computers to access files, folders, and registry values. When an application is installed that needs to update these portions of their computers, the security must not prohibit them from doing these tasks. Instead of listing the exact security settings that need to be made (which would be almost impossible to determine without knowing the application or task), we will look at some of key tasks and responsibilities of an administrator and how to loosen security enough to allow these functions.

Local Services and Software

Administrators need to access certain services that might otherwise be disabled. You might need to set the following services to manual or automatic:

- Alerter
- Distributed Link Tracking Client
- Help and Support
- IIS Admin Service
- IMAPI CD-Burning COM Service
- Messenger
- MS Software Shadow Copy Provider
- Remote Procedure Call (RPC)
- Remote Procedure Call (RPC) Locator
- Removable Storage
- Server
- Uninterruptible Power Supply

An administrator might also need to install other software to administer other clients, servers, or Active Directory resources, including the following:

- Administrative Tools (Admnpak.msi)
- Group Policy Management Console (Gpmc.msi)
- Windows Support Tools (\Support\Tools folder on the Windows XP product CD)
- Windows XP Resource Kit Tools, which are on the CD-ROM included in the *Microsoft Windows XP Professional Resource Kit,* Third Edition (Microsoft Press, 2005)

These applications can be installed by Group Policy or by the user of the computer. A user must have administrative privileges to perform the installs.

Local Group Configuration

The recommended local group configuration for a standard client computer does not allow an administrator enough control of her computer to perform her duties. You must consider a different configuration, whether it is deployed using Restricted Groups or manually on each computer. Table 5-17 lists some best-practice configurations for local groups on an IT staff or administrator client machine.

Table 5-17   Restricted Group Best Practices for IT Staff or Administrator Clients

Local Group	Members
Administrators	Administrator (local)
	Domain Admins
	Domain\<*username*> (where <*username*> is the user account for the administrator of the client)
Backup Operators	Administrators (local)
Network Configuration Operators	Administrators (local)

Client Computers for Help Desk Staff

The Help Desk staff also needs more control over their computers than standard users need. However, they should not have as much control as an administrator. Depending on how your Help Desk is structured, you might have different sets of parameters for different Help Desk staff. For example, some Help Desk staff might be allowed to install applications while others are not. Here are some best-practice configurations for computers used by Help Desk staff to give them the access they need. These settings only represent the differences from the standard client computer suite of settings that are described above.

Security Settings for Help Desk Staff

To fulfill their responsibilities and communicate with network servers and resources, the Help Desk staff will need access to certain services on their client computers that might otherwise be disabled. You might need to set the following services to manual or automatic:

- Alerter
- Distributed Link Tracking Client
- Help and Support
- IIS Admin Service
- IMAPI CD-Burning COM Service

- Messenger
- MS Software Shadow Copy Provider
- Remote Procedure Call (RPC)
- Remote Procedure Call (RPC) Locator
- Removable Storage

The Help Desk staff might also need to install additional software to perform administration of the clients, servers, or Active Directory objects. Here is a list of applications that many Help Desk personnel need to use:

- Administrative Tools (Admnpak.msi)
- Group Policy Management Console (Gpmc.msi)
- Windows Support Tools (\Support\Tools folder on the Windows XP product CD)
- Windows XP Resource Kit Tools, which are on the CD-ROM included in the *Microsoft Windows XP Professional Resource Kit,* Third Edition (Microsoft Press, 2005)

Tip   Although these tools provide complete control over all aspects of Active Directory and Group Policy, the Help Desk staff will be delegated privileges within Active Directory and through the GPMC to restrict their control over much of Active Directory.

These applications can be installed using Group Policy, or they can be installed by the user of the computer. To install these tools, the user must have administrative privileges.

Local Group Configuration

The recommended standard local group configuration for a standard client computer will not allow Help Desk staff enough control over their computers to perform their duties. You must consider a different configuration of local groups, whether it is deployed using Restricted Groups or manually on each computer. Table 5-18 lists best-practice configurations for local groups on a Help Desk client.

Table 5-18   Restricted Group Best Practices for Help Desk Clients

Local Group	Members
Administrators	Administrator (local)
	Domain Admins
	Domain*<username>* (where *<username>* is the user account for the administrator of the client. This is needed when the Help Desk employee needs to install software manually on his computer.)
Backup Operators	Administrators (local) or Power Users

Table 5-18   Restricted Group Best Practices for Help Desk Clients

Local Group	Members
Network Configuration Operators	Administrators (local) or Power Users
Power Users	Domain*<username>* (where *<username>* is the user account for the administrator of the client. This is needed when the Help Desk employee needs to modify local resources but not install applications.)

Troubleshooting

When it comes to troubleshooting the security settings that you want to deploy or have deployed to your computers, the avenues for finding where the problem lies are plentiful. The problem might be caused by a service or port that you have inadvertently disabled, or the client might not even be receiving the security template setting via a GPO.

Problems can also range from the user not being able to authenticate on the network to a user not being able to boot successfully. With so many potential problem areas, it is imperative that you have a suite of tools to help you solve the possible issues that can arise. However, let's first quickly go through the different areas of a security template and security policy to investigate where problems might originate.

Security Areas and Potential Problems

Security templates and security policies are the primary ways to configure your clients and servers to be properly secured and hardened. Some of the security areas span both security templates and security policies, while other security areas are configured only in one location. You need to pay particular attention to the following security areas:

- **Account policies**   Account policies are configured in the security templates only. Because account policies determine the restrictions on the password and logon attempts, users might have trouble changing their passwords or logging on if they have forgotten their passwords. It is important to couple user training with any changes that occur within this section of the security template. If password requirements change from simple (or nonexistent) to complex, users must know the parameters for establishing a new password. The error messages are fairly clear here, indicating when the password does not meet complexity requirements, as shown in Figure 5-9, or when the user account has been locked out (instead of just a wrong password), as shown in Figure 5-10.

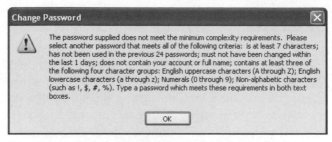

Figure 5-9   Error message that occurs when a user types a password that does not meet the password policy requirements

Figure 5-10   Error message that occurs when a user account is locked out

■ **Audit policies**   Audit policies can be configured in security template or the security policy. An audit policy typically will not cause any visible problems. However, if the object access policy is set for both Success and Failure for many objects on a server, the performance of the server can degrade dramatically. This is especially true if object access has been configured for a domain controller, where auditing of the majority of the Active Directory objects has been configured. If you feel that auditing has caused a performance problem on a server or client, you can quickly disable the auditing and see if performance improves. Another option is to use the System Monitor to determine which application or service is causing the performance degradation.

■ **User rights**   User rights are configured only in security templates. Because user rights control what users can and can't do on a client or server, many problems can originate here. Don't forget that user rights not only affect user and group accounts, but they are also required for service accounts. If user rights are set too restrictively, or a user account is omitted from the policy, many problems with basic functionality of the server or client can occur. Applications can fail, backups can fail, and basic user authentication can fail. Depending on which area of functionality fails, you can use different methods to try and track down the problem. A good place to start is to use the event logs for either object access or privilege use. If you have configured privilege use for both success and failure, you should get good information that will help you track down which user right is incorrectly set so you can add the correct user or group to allow the access and privileges.

■ **Security options**   The security options are mainly set in security templates, but a few security settings can be configured using the Security Configuration Wizard. As we said earlier in this chapter, we cannot cover all of the security options here. However, some of the more common and powerful settings can lead to certain common problems if configured inappropriately for your environment. Be sure to check the SMB signing and anonymous access settings if you are having trouble with accessing resources directly or through an application. If you are having trouble authenticating, you might need to alter the LAN Manager settings to remove any restrictions for basic logon and authentication.

■ **Event logs**   Event log settings can be set only in security templates. If you set the log files too small, you will not be able to track down significant events because the logs will be overwritten so quickly. You should configure the log files to be large enough to store all of the data that is logged between archiving times. It is best to save Event log files periodically so that the log file can be reasonably sized and no data will be lost.

■ **Restricted groups**   Restricted groups can be configured only in security templates. Restricted groups must be thoroughly tested before they are implemented. Because existing groups and users may be removed when the new policy is applied, a number of problems can arise. If you forget to include a user or group in the policy that you implement, applications, services, or resource access might fail. One way to identify the cause of the problem is to configure object access auditing to track down the reason for the failed access.

■ **System services**   Services can be configured in both security templates and using the Security Configuration Wizard. Because the results of deploying a security policy without first testing it can be devastating, you should test your new configuration before you begin disabling services. You must not only be aware of the service you are disabling, but also of any services that depend on the service that you disable. This chain reaction of services is not always obvious. Ideally, you should use the Security Configuration Wizard to modify services. This approach offers two benefits. First, the wizard provides excellent descriptions of how various services depend on each other. Second, the wizard has a rollback feature, which is useful when the settings you deploy cause too many problems.

■ **Registry**   Both the security templates and policies can configure the registry on a target computer. Security templates can configure DACLs for registry keys, while the Security Configuration Wizard can configure important registry settings that govern how Windows computers communicate on your network. The results of an incorrect registry setting might not show up immediately. Problems with registry DACLs or specific settings can mask themselves very well. You can use auditing to help track down where the problem lies, but with thousands of registry settings on a single computer, trying to identify the problem will often be difficult. Your best bet for troubleshooting registry-based configurations is to document your configuration carefully and use the tools listed in the next section to verify that the registry settings and DACLs were set according to your documentation.

- **File system** File system permissions can be configured in security templates. Like registry DACLs, problems with file system DACLs can be difficult to troubleshoot if you have caused the issue through the deployment of a GPO. Your best resource is again to enable auditing for object access. You can configure both success and failure auditing for the file system object to see where a user or group is not being allowed to access it. Documentation and use of the tools described in the next section can also help ensure that your security template settings accomplish your desired goals.

- **Ports** Ports can controlled by both the GPOs and the Security Configuration Wizard. If you are using GPOs to control ports in Windows Firewall, see Chapter 11 for configuration and troubleshooting tips. If you are using the Security Configuration Wizard to control the ports, you must ensure that the ports you want to disable or enable are correctly set. You can manually check the firewall on the affected computer, or you can use the Netstat or Portqry tool (discussed earlier in this chapter).

Tools

When you create and deploy security settings to harden clients and servers, you hope that the settings will be applied properly and that you will not experience any negative repercussions from your design. However, sometimes the results will still not be what you anticipated. If you go through each section of the security template and still find that the settings are correct, you will need to use some tools to track down where the problem lies within your security implementation. The following sections describe some tools that can help you track down errant security configurations on a target computer or associated with GPOs stored in Active Directory.

Secedit

The Secedit tool includes an analysis option that lets you compare the contents of a security template to the current security settings of a computer. More than one security template or GPO can affect a computer that is a member of a domain; this tool lets you to find out which settings comply with the desired security settings in your template.

> **More Info** For more information on how to use the *secedit* command to analyze a computer, type **secedit /?** at a command prompt to get the correct syntax.

Security Configuration and Analysis

The Security Configuration and Analysis snap-in is the GUI version of the *secedit* command. This tool graphically compares the settings in a security template to the existing settings on the computer you are analyzing. To run an analysis on a computer against a security template using the Security Configuration and Analysis snap-in, complete these steps:

1. Click Start, Run.

2. In the Run dialog box, type **mmc** and click OK.

3. From the menu bar, select File, Add-Remove Snap-in.

4. In the Add/Remove Snap-in dialog box, click Add.

5. In the Add Standalone Snap-in dialog box, select Security Configuration And Analysis from the Snap-ins list, and then click Add.

6. Click Close, and then click OK.

7. Right-click the node labeled Security Configuration and Analysis and select Open Database.

8. Type a name for the database and click Open.

9. Select the security template to use for the audit and click Open.

10. Once the database has been created, right-click the Security Configuration and Analysis node and select Analyze Computer Now.

11. Specify a log file path and name and click OK.

12. Once the analysis is complete, scan through the nodes to view the results.

Gpresult

The Gpresult tool has been around for quite some time, but it is still valuable for investigating and troubleshooting GPO settings. The tool is not security-specific, but it can provide you with information about which GPOs apply and the specific settings (including security settings) that exist on a computer.

> **More Info**   For more information on how to use the *Gpresult* command, see Chapter 16.

Resultant Set of Policy

In some instances, you will need to evaluate what the final GPO settings will be for a computer when the computer is not on the network or when you don't have access to the computer. Resultant Set of Policy (RSoP) can help with this, which includes providing details about the security settings that will apply to the computer through GPOs.

> **More Info**   For more information on how to use the RSoP tools, see Chapter 16.

Summary

Hardening clients and servers requires an understanding of the available methods for establishing the security settings in an efficient and consistent manner. Two tools are designed to harden clients and servers: security templates and security policies. Security templates can configure the majority of the security settings to harden any client or server. Security policies are created with the Security Configuration Wizard, which is more intuitive to use and is based on server roles, administrative functions, and other aspects of the servers.

Whether you use a security template, a security policy, or both, you should use Group Policy whenever possible to deploy these settings. As we saw earlier in this book, a key aspect of security hardening is how you design your OUs and link your GPOs in Active Directory. With hundreds of security settings available in a single security template or policy, you must rely on the security best practices detailed in this chapter to get a head start on establishing your security baselines and hardening guidelines. Once you deploy the security settings, you only need to monitor the affected computers for errant behavior or malfunctions to ensure that your security settings don't cause any problems.

Chapter 6

Managing and Maintaining Essential Windows Components

In this chapter:

Configuring Application Compatibility Settings 218

Configuring Attachment Manager Settings 220

Configuring Event Viewer Information Requests. .224

Controlling IIS Installation 225

Configuring Access to and Use of Microsoft Management Console . . .226

Optimizing NetMeeting Security and Features 228

Enabling Security Center for Use in Domains. 230

Managing Access to Scheduled Tasks and Task Scheduler 230

Managing File System, Drive, and Windows Explorer Access Options . . .231

Optimizing the Windows Installer Configuration 236

Optimizing Automatic Updates with Windows Update 243

Summary. 251

Group Policy provides one of the most effective means of managing and maintaining the configuration of systems throughout the enterprise. Not only can you use Group Policy to specify exactly how MicrosoftWindows components and features should be configured, but you can also control access to components and features. This makes it possible for you to optimize system configuration and create custom setups for various office locations and user groups.

More Info Several Windows components are discussed in detail in other chapters. Microsoft Internet Explorer configurations are discussed in Chapter 8. Terminal Services configurations are discussed in Chapter 12.

Related Information

- For more information about customizing user settings and data, see Chapter 7.

- For more information about configuring Internet Explorer, see Chapter 8.

- For more information about customizing systems for various office locations, see Chapter 12.

Configuring Application Compatibility Settings

When 16-bit and MS-DOS programs run on Microsoft Windows XP or Windows Server 2003 systems, they run in a special compatibility mode. Windows creates a virtual machine that mimics the 386-enhanced mode used by Windows 3.1, and the application runs within this context. Like most Windows components, Application Compatibility can be configured through Group Policy. For example, to enhance security and improve system stability, you might want to prevent users from running MS-DOS and 16-bit applications altogether. You can enable the related policy at the domain level. However, if you want computers and users in the DevTest OU to be able to run MS-DOS and 16-bit applications for testing purposes, you can override the policy setting that prevents the DevTest OU from running these programs. We will now look at these and other configuration scenarios for Application Compatibility.

Optimizing Application Compatibility Through Group Policy

When you run multiple 16-bit and MS-DOS programs, they run as separate threads within a single virtual machine, which means they share a common memory space. There are several ways you can prevent problems and force compatibility, including using the Program Compatibility Wizard to adjust the application's settings so that it runs without problems.

> **More Info**   For more information about Application Compatibility, see *Microsoft Windows XP Professional Administrator's Pocket Consultant,* Second Edition (Microsoft Press, 2004).

Policies that affect Application Compatibility are stored in two locations: Computer Configuration\Administrative Templates\Windows Components\Application Compatibility and User Configuration\Administrative Templates\Windows Components\Application Compatibility. This means you can configure some aspects of application compatibility at both the computer level and the user level.

You can prevent the virtual machine (Ntvdm.exe) for the MS-DOS subsystem from running by enabling the Prevent Access To 16-bit Applications policy under Computer Configuration or User Configuration. Once enabled, this policy prevents users from running any 16-bit or MS-DOS program. It also means that any 32-bit applications with 16-bit installers or components will not run.

> **Note**   When a policy appears under both Computer Configuration and User Configuration, the Computer policy settings override those of the User settings by default. However, policy processing preferences can change this effect. For more information, see the section of Chapter 3 titled "Changing Policy Processing Preferences."

> **Tip**   Keep in mind that the requirements of a policy determine which computers the policy's settings apply to. If a policy requires at least Windows Server 2003, the policy applies only to Windows Server 2003 and not to Windows 2000 or Windows XP Professional.

Configuring Additional Application Compatibility Settings

When you work with Application Compatibility, other policies under Computer Configuration\Administrative Templates\Windows Components\Application Compatibility can be useful as well. These policies include:

- **Turn Off Application Compatibility Engine**   This policy disables the application compatibility engine that is used for loading 16-bit and MS-DOS programs and runs them in compatibility mode. Windows will also no longer block the installation of programs with known compatibility problems (which can degrade performance or lead to blue screen lockups). This policy might be useful on Web or application servers that frequently load and run 16-bit and MS-DOS programs, to improve load/run performance. However, you must be sure that the 16-bit and MS-DOS programs you run are fully compatible.

> **Tip**   When you are working with application servers that use Internet Information Services (IIS), you'll want to manage application compatibility a bit closer than with other types of servers. When a Web application starts an external program, the Compatibility Engine runs automatically regardless of whether the .exe is 16-bit or 32-bit. This behavior is designed to ensure that the external program has a compatible environment. Unfortunately, some Web applications might call external programs dozens of times per second, and all the additional calls to the Compatibility Engine can slow down the server performance and reduce responsiveness. If you've thoroughly tested external programs that will be used with your Web application servers, you might want to disable the Compatibility Engine to boost server performance.

- **Turn Off Program Compatibility Wizard**   Prevents users from running the Program Compatibility Wizard, which can automatically adjust a program's compatibility settings. Unless you also disable the Remove Program Compatibility Property Page policy, users can still manually adjust a program's compatibility settings. Previously configured compatibility settings are still applied.

- **Remove Program Compatibility Property Page**   Prevents users from manually adjusting a program's compatibility settings. This policy doesn't affect access to the Program Compatibility Wizard, however, and any previously configured compatibility settings are still applied.

- **Turn On Application Help Log Events**   Enables logging of Application Help events in the application logs. These events are triggered whenever Application Help blocks a user from running a 16-bit or MS-DOS program that is known to be incompatible with the current Windows operating system. If this policy is disabled or not configured, no Application Help events are recorded in the logs. Regardless of the configuration of this policy, the user sees a help prompt whenever Application Help blocks a program from running.

Configuring Attachment Manager Settings

Computers running Windows Server 2003 Service Pack 1 (SP1) or later, or Windows XP Professional Service Pack 2 (SP2) or later, use Attachment Manager to monitor and control access to file attachments. Before you try to configure this Windows component in policy, you should have a strong understanding of how it works.

Working with Attachment Manager

The goal of Attachment Manager is to enhance security by identifying types of files that might represent a security risk and then managing access to these files when they are obtained from network locations. Risk is assessed according to the Internet Security zone from which a file attachment was received. Four Internet Security zones are defined:

- **Restricted Sites**   Web sites that have been specifically designated as restricted due to content or potential to damage computers. Restricted Sites have a higher-than-normal security level by default.

- **Trusted Sites**   Web sites that have been specifically designated as trusted. Trusted Sites are considered to be safe and have a lower-than-normal security level by default.

- **Local Intranet**   All locations on the local network, including intranet sites, sites bypassed by the proxy server, and all network paths. Local intranet sites are considered to be very safe and have a much lower-than-normal security level by default.

- **Internet**   Web sites on the Internet that aren't specifically assigned to another security zone. Internet sites have a moderate security level by default.

Attachment Manager assigns one of three levels of risk to file attachments based on the zone from which they were received:

- **High Risk**   Poses a potential high risk to system security if opened. By default, any file types designated as High Risk are blocked on restricted sites and require that the user be prompted before they can be downloaded from Internet sites. The built-in list of High Risk file types follows: .ade, .adp, .app, .asp, .bas, .bat,

.cer, .chm, .cmd, .com, .cpl, .crt, .csh, .exe, .fxp, .hlp, .hta, .inf, .ins, .isp, .its, .js, .jse, .ksh, .lnk, .mad, .maf, .mag, .mam, .maq, .mar, .mas, .mat, .mau, .mav, .maw, .mda, .mdb, .mde, .mdt, .mdw, .mdz, .msc, .msi, .msp, .mst, .ops, .pcd, .pif, .prf, .prg, .pst, .reg, .scf, .scr, .sct, .shb, .shs, .tmp, .url, .vb, .vbe, .vbs, .vsmacros, .vss, .vst, .vsw, .ws, .wsc, .wsf, and .wsh.

- **Moderate Risk** Poses a potential moderate risk to system security if opened. By default, any file types designated as Moderate Risk require that the user be prompted before they can be downloaded from restricted or Internet sites. Any file types that Attachment Manager does not label as High Risk or Low Risk are automatically labeled as Moderate Risk.

- **Low Risk** Unlikely to pose a risk to system security if opened. By default, any file types designated as Low Risk are opened without prompting from any location. Windows includes a built-in list of file types that are designated as Low Risk. This list applies to two applications—Notepad and Windows Picture And Fax Viewer. When you open a .log, .text, or .txt file on restricted or Internet sites using Notepad, the file is considered to be low risk. When you open a .dib, .emf, .gif, .ico, .jfif, .jpg, .jpe, .jpeg, .png, .tif, .tiff, or .wmf file on restricted or Internet sites using Windows Picture And Fax Viewer, the file is considered to be Low Risk. Note that associating additional file types with Notepad or Windows Picture And Fax Viewer doesn't add that file type to the list of low-risk file types.

> **Tip** Configuring policies related to Attachment Manager is most useful when a computer doesn't have antivirus software or has antivirus software that isn't configured to scan file attachments before opening a file. In either situation, you can use Attachment Manager to monitor access to file attachments and either block access or prompt users before opening files, as appropriate.

Configuring Risk Levels and Trust Logic in Group Policy

In Group Policy, you can configure the way Attachment Manager works through User Configuration. Although there are many ways to configure Attachment Manager settings, you'll usually want to configure them in one of two ways. The first way is to use default risk levels and trust logic to determine how file attachments are handled. The second way is to specifically define the types of files that are High Risk, Moderate Risk, and Low Risk, and by doing so override the built-in list of file types that are designated as having those risk levels—and then set the trust logic. In either case, you might also want to configure antivirus notification.

Trust logic is one aspect of Attachment Manager we haven't yet discussed. Attachment Manager can assess risk for file attachments by file type and also by the application that is attempting to open a file attachment. The default preference is given to the application attempting to open a file attachment, which means a trusted application, such as Word.exe, might be able to open a file attachment that an untrusted application, such as Malware.exe, cannot. You can configure trust logic in two other ways as well. If you want Attachment Manager to look only at the file type, you can determine risk by preferring the file type. If you want Attachment Manager to look at both the application and the file type, you can determine risk by looking at the file handler and the file type. In this configuration, Windows uses the more restrictive of the two conditions, making this the most restrictive (and most secure) option.

To configure Attachment Manager policies, follow these steps:

1. Access the Group Policy object (GPO) you want to work with. Access User Configuration\Administrative Templates\Windows Components\Attachment Manager.

2. The default risk level is Moderate for file attachments received from restricted or Internet locations. With this risk level, users are prompted before they can download files from restricted or Internet locations. To set a different default risk level, double-click Default Risk Level For File Attachments. Select Enabled and then choose a risk level, such as High Risk, as shown in Figure 6-1. Click OK.

> **Note**   To prevent users from downloading files from restricted sites, you can set the default risk level to High Risk. This will block downloading of files from restricted sites while ensuring that users are prompted before they download files from sites in the Internet zone.

Figure 6-1   Enabling and setting the Default Risk Level For File Attachments policy

3. If you want to specifically define the types of files that are High Risk and override the default list, double-click Inclusion List For High Risk File Types. Select Enabled and then enter a semicolon-separated list of file extensions that should be treated as High Risk when file attachments are obtained from restricted or Internet locations (Figure 6-2). Click OK.

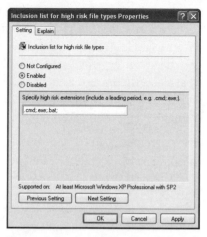

Figure 6-2   Overriding the default list with the file type inclusion list

4. If you want to specifically define the types of files that are Moderate Risk and override the default list, double-click Inclusion List For Moderate Risk File Types. Select Enabled and then enter a semicolon-separated list of file extensions that should be treated as Moderate Risk when file attachments are obtained from restricted or Internet locations. Click OK.

5. If you want to specifically define the types of files that are Low Risk and override the default list, double-click Inclusion List For Low Risk File Types. Select Enabled and then enter a semicolon-separated list of file extensions that should be treated as Low Risk when file attachments are obtained from restricted or Internet locations. Click OK.

6. By default, Windows determines risk by preferring the file handler (the application attempting to open a file attachment). If you want to set a different trust logic, double-click Trust Logic For File Attachments. Select Enabled and then use the Determine Risk By list to set the trust logic, as shown in Figure 6-3. Click OK.

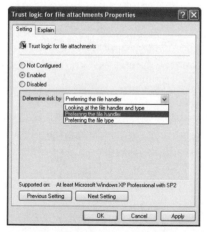

Figure 6-3   Setting the trust logic to override the default preference for file handlers

7. By default, Windows does not call registered antivirus programs before opening file attachments. Most antivirus programs can be configured to scan files automatically before they are opened. However, if the user disables or otherwise overrides this feature, the antivirus program won't scan files before they are opened. To ensure that all registered antivirus programs are notified before a file attachment is opened, double-click Notify Antivirus Programs When Opening Attachments. Select Enabled and then click OK.

> **Note**   Antivirus programs can be configured to scan files received in e-mail messages as they arrive. If the file has already been scanned, the antivirus program might not scan it again.

Configuring Event Viewer Information Requests

Windows computers maintain several types of logs to record important events. Events that are logged include system errors and warnings as well as status information that is important for tracking issues and resolving problems. Some of the details logged with events are customizable through Group Policy. We will discuss these customizable details next.

Using Event Viewer Information Requests

Most events recorded in a computer's log files include a statement in the descriptive text that says the following:

```
For more information, see Help and Support Center at http://go.microsoft.com/fwlink/
events.asp.
```

When you click the URL in this text, the computer does the following:

1. Starts Help and Support Center (%SystemRoot%\PCHealth\HelpCtr\ Binaries\HelpCtr.exe).

2. Passes the command-line option -url hcp://services/centers/support?topic=%s to the Help and Support Center.

3. Accesses the specified URL (*http://go.microsoft.com/fwlink/events.asp*).

If your organization has set up a Web server to handle event information requests or you'd like to use alternate settings, you can use Group Policy to specify the program to launch, the command-line options for this helper program, and the URL that should be accessed. However, the related policies apply only to computers running at least Windows XP Professional with SP2 or Windows Server 2003 with SP1.

Customizing Event Details Through Group Policy

To configure event information request handling through Group Policy, follow these steps:

1. Access the GPO you want to work with. Access Computer Configuration\ Administrative Templates\Windows Components\Event Viewer.

2. To specify the URL to access, double-click Events.asp URL. Select Enabled and, in the Events.asp URL box enter the complete URL path to the Web page, such as *http://CorpIntranet/help/events.asp*. Click OK.

3. To specify the program to launch, double-click Events.asp Program. Select Enabled and, in the Events.asp Program box, type the complete file path to program that should be started, such as %SystemRoot%\system32\custhelp.exe. Click OK.

4. To specify the command-line options to pass to the helper program, double-click Events.asp Program Command-line Parameters. Select Enabled and, in the Events.asp Program Command-Line Parameters box, either type the option to use or to clear the existing options so that command-line parameters are not passed to the helper program. Click OK.

Controlling IIS Installation

Microsoft Internet Information Services (IIS) can pose a security risk when it is installed on a computer that hasn't been specifically designated for use as a Web or application server. To prevent IIS from being installed on a computer running Windows Server 2003, you can enable the Prevent IIS Installation policy. This policy prevents IIS installation for all users, including administrators. Although this in turn might prevent installation of Windows components or programs that require IIS to run, it doesn't have any effect on IIS if IIS is already installed on a computer.

To get a better understanding of how the Prevent IIS Installation policy might be used, consider a scenario in which you want to enhance security by preventing IIS installation throughout the domain. You enable the Prevent IIS Installation policies at the domain level, but you also want computers and users in the Servers OU to be able to install IIS, so you override the policy setting that prevents IIS installation. You do this by disabling the Prevent IIS Installation policy for the Servers OU.

You can prevent IIS installation by completing the following steps:

1. Access the GPO you want to work with and select Computer Configuration\ Administrative Templates\Windows Components\Internet Information Services.

2. Double-click Prevent IIS installation, select Enabled, and then click OK.

> **Note**   If Prevent IIS Installation is enabled and you try to install an application that requires IIS, the installation might fail without you receiving a warning that the failure was due to IIS installation being prevented. When troubleshooting this type of problem, you must review the required components for application installation. If IIS installation is required and IIS cannot be installed, check the computer's Resultant Set of Policy (RSoP), as discussed in the section of Chapter 3 titled "Determining the Effective Group Policy Settings and Last Refresh."

Configuring Access to and Use of Microsoft Management Console

The Microsoft Management Console (MMC) is an administrative framework that provides a unified interface for management applications. As such, MMC is primarily used by administrators but might also be used by those who have been delegated some administrative privileges. Just about every administrative tool on the Administrative Tools menu is an MMC console that includes add-in components, called *snap-ins*, to provide the necessary administrative functionality.

> **Note**   Microsoft Management Console can be customized to include custom menus, command shortcuts, special administration views, and more. Once you've created a custom console, you can distribute it to your administrators and to users to whom you've delegated administration privileges. See *Microsoft Windows Server 2003 Inside Out* (Microsoft Press, 2004) for details.

Group Policy provides several ways to control access to consoles and snap-ins, with the goal of enhancing security by preventing users, delegated administrators, and even other administrators from performing actions they shouldn't. For example, you might not want any member of the Customer Services OU to be able to work with directory trusts or access the Certificate Authority. You can configure the GPO for the Customer Services OU to prevent users (and administrators) whose accounts are in this OU from accessing the Active Directory Domains And Trusts and Certification Authority snap-ins. Any attempt by users or administrators in this OU to access these snap-ins will then fail.

Group Policy settings for MMC are found under User Configuration\Administrative Templates\Windows Components\Microsoft Management Console. Using the policies found here, you can:

- Prevent users in a site, domain, or OU from creating new consoles or adding and removing snap-ins in existing consoles
- Designate specific snap-ins as permitted or prohibited
- Require explicit permission to access any and all snap-ins

The sections that follow examine each of these configuration options.

Blocking Author Mode for MMC

Microsoft Management Consoles can run in either user mode or author mode. In user mode, you can make use of snap-ins already included but you cannot add snap-ins. In author mode, you can create custom consoles or add snap-ins to existing consoles.

To prevent users in a site, domain, or OU from creating new consoles or adding and removing snap-ins in existing consoles, double-click Restrict The User From Entering Author Mode, select Enabled, and then click OK. This policy is found under User Configuration\Administrative Templates\Windows Components\Microsoft Management Console.

> **Note**   Preventing users from creating new consoles also prevents them from opening a new console at the command prompt and in the Run dialog box.

Designating Prohibited and Permitted Snap-ins

In Group Policy, you can designate specific snap-ins as prohibited or permitted for use. When a snap-in is prohibited, it cannot be added to custom consoles and is not displayed in any consoles in which it is included. When a snap-in is explicitly permitted for use, any authorized user can work with the snap-in. As long as you do not block author mode, any authorized user can also add the snap-in to custom consoles.

Every available snap-in has a related policy setting in the Restricted/Permitted Snap-ins folder under User Configuration\Administrative Templates\Windows Components\Microsoft Management Console. To explicitly permit a snap-in, double-click the related policy setting and then select Enabled. To explicitly prohibit a snap-in, double-click the related policy setting and then select Disabled. If you've previously enabled Restrict Users Using Only Explicit Permitted Snap-ins, all snap-ins are prohibited by default, and you must enable the related setting for a snap-in to explicitly permit its use.

> ### Example
> Consider the scenario in which you want to prohibit the use of the Active Directory Domains And Trusts snap-in in the Customer Service OU. You access the GPO for this OU, and double-click Active Directory Domains And Trusts under User Configuration\Administrative Templates\Windows Components\ Microsoft Management Console\Restricted/Permitted Snap-ins. In the Policy Setting dialog box, select Disabled and then click OK.

> Once policy is refreshed, users (and administrators) in the Customer Service OU cannot add the Active Directory Domains And Trusts snap-in to custom consoles or create new consoles that include this snap-in. Further, any existing consoles that include this snap-in will open but will not display the Active Directory Domains And Trusts snap-in. Thus, although a user in this OU might be able to select Active Directory Domains And Trusts from the Administrative Tools menu, the related console would open but would not display the prohibited snap-in.

Requiring Explicit Permission for All Snap-Ins

Another option for configuring snap-in use is to restrict access to *all* snap-ins by default and allow access only to snap-ins that have been explicitly permitted for use. To do this, double-click Restrict Users To The Explicitly Permitted List Of Snap-ins under User Configuration\Administrative Templates\Windows Components\ Microsoft Management Console. In the Policy Setting dialog box, select Enabled and then click OK.

Although the Restrict Users To The Explicitly Permitted List Of Snap-ins policy setting is fairly straightforward to configure, you shouldn't enable it without considerable planning beforehand. Here are some guidelines to follow:

- **Rarely restrict access at domain level.** You should rarely, if ever, restrict access to all snap-ins at the domain level. If you do this without first explicitly permitting snap-ins, you might block yourself and all other administrators from performing essential administration tasks through the built-in administrator tools and any custom consoles your organization uses.

- **Carefully select OUs to restrict.** You should carefully select the OUs for which you want to require explicit permission to use snap-ins. Before you restrict snap-in usage, you should determine which snap-ins will be permitted for use and then explicitly permit their use. Explicitly permitting snap-ins is necessary to ensure that administrators and anyone else authorized to work with snap-ins can perform essential tasks.

Optimizing NetMeeting Security and Features

Many organizations use Microsoft NetMeeting® during video conferences. NetMeeting has many features, including whiteboards, chat, and desktop sharing. Some of these features aren't suitable for all organizations, however, and you might want to fine-tune them. For example, to enhance security, you might want to disable the Remote Desktop Sharing feature of NetMeeting. Or you might want to limit the amount of bandwidth used for conferencing to prevent NetMeeting from using too much of the available network bandwidth. Although you can configure these options on a per-computer basis in NetMeeting itself, you can also configure these and other settings through Group Policy and thus ensure they are applied to all computers and users in a site, domain, or OU.

Configuring NetMeeting Through Group Policy

When it comes to policy settings, NetMeeting is one of several configuration oddballs. Instead of requiring a specific operating system, most policy settings for NetMeeting require a specific version of NetMeeting–typically NetMeeting 3.0 or later. However, this doesn't mean that policy settings will be applied to computers running operating systems that lack support for Active Directory® and Group Policy. Essentially, the requirements mean that policy settings are applicable to computers running Windows 2000 or later when they are configured with NetMeeting 3.0 or later.

Most policy settings for NetMeeting are designed to help enhance security and optimize performance for the available network bandwidth. Under Computer Configuration\Administrative Templates\Windows Components\NetMeeting, you'll find the Disable Remote Desktop Sharing policy setting. If you enable this policy setting, users cannot configure remote desktop sharing or use the remote desktop sharing feature to control their computers remotely.

Under User Configuration\Administrative Templates\Windows Components\NetMeeting, you'll find many other policy settings, including:

- **Enable Automatic Configured**   Defines a URL from which an automatic configuration should be obtained for NetMeeting sessions. For example, if you've set up a NetMeeting configuration page on your organization's intranet, you type this URL (such as *http://CorpIntranet/netmeeting/autoconfig.htm*).

- **Set The Intranet Support Web Page**   Sets the URL that NetMeeting will access when users select the Help Online Support command. For example, if you've set up a NetMeeting help page on your organization's intranet, you type this URL (such as *http://CorpIntranet/help/netmeeting.asp*).

- **Set Call Security Options**   Either disables or requires call security for incoming or outgoing NetMeeting calls. When you enable the policy, you set the Call Security option to either Disabled or Required, as appropriate.

- **Limit The Size Of Sent Files**   Limits the files users can send to others in NetMeeting. Once you enable the policy, you use the Maximum Size In Kbytes option to specify the maximum size, in kilobytes (KB), of files that can be sent. The default value is 500 KB, which means that only files of less than 500 KB can be sent.

- **Limit The Bandwidth Of Audio And Video**   Limits the total bandwidth NetMeeting uses for audio and video transmission. NetMeeting can use this setting to determine the audio and video formats to use as well as the send rate to ensure that the bandwidth limit is not exceeded. This policy setting is in the Audio & Video subfolder under User Configuration\Administrative Templates\Windows Components\NetMeeting. The default value is 621700, which means the total bandwidth usage for audio and video is limited to 621,700 KB per second.

Other policy settings are used to disable or prevent the use of features with the goal of improving security, reducing bandwidth usage, or both. Be sure to check the Application Sharing, Audio & Video, and Options Pages subfolders for additional policy settings that may be useful for your environment.

Enabling Security Center for Use in Domains

Security Center is an additional security feature available on computers running Windows XP Professional with SP2 or later. Security Center monitors the status of a computer's security settings for Automatic Updates, virus protection, and Windows Firewall and warns users if these features aren't configured properly.

Although Security Center is enabled and used automatically in workgroups, by default it is not enabled or configured for Windows XP Professional SP2 computers belonging to domains. To enable Security Center for use in domains, you must enable Turn On Security Center (Domain PCs Only) under Computer Configuration\Administrative Templates\Windows Components\Security Center. Once the affected computers are restarted, all users in the related site, domain, or OU will have the Security Center feature. Once enabled, you can access Security Center from Control Panel or by double-clicking the Security Center icon (the red shield with an x) in the system tray.

> **Note**   When Security Center is enabled, a new icon is added to the notifications area of the Windows taskbar. If there are status issues with monitored areas of security, users are notified with balloon dialog boxes.

Managing Access to Scheduled Tasks and Task Scheduler

The Task Scheduler is used to schedule one-time and recurring tasks that you want to run automatically to perform maintenance or other routine procedures. You can schedule tasks to run on local and remote systems using the Scheduled Tasks Wizard and the Schtasks.exe command-line utility. Once tasks are configured, they can be managed by their creator and anyone with appropriate access permissions, such as domain administrators.

> **More Info**   To learn techniques for creating and managing scheduled tasks across the enterprise, see the *Microsoft Windows Command-Line Administrator's Pocket Consultant* (Microsoft Press, 2004).

In Group Policy, you can manage various aspects of the Tasks Scheduler using either Computer Configuration\Administrative Templates\Windows Components\Task Scheduler policies or User Configuration\Administrative Templates\Windows Components\Task Scheduler policies. These two policies are identical; you can use them to manage the Task Scheduler at the computer level, the user level, or both—and according to the loopback processing preferences, as discussed in Chapter 3. Again, by default, Computer Configuration settings have precedence over those in User Configuration. If there is a conflict between the computer and user settings, the computer settings win.

The key Task Scheduler policies you can use to help enhance security and ensure maintenance tasks run as expected include:

- **Hide Properties Pages**   Prevents all users from viewing or changing the properties of scheduled tasks.

- **Prevent Task Run or End**   Prevents all users from manually starting and stopping scheduled tasks.

- **Prohibit Drag-and Drop**   Prevents all users from moving and copying scheduled tasks. It also prevents users from dragging and dropping scheduled tasks between folders and systems.

- **Prohibit New Task Creation**   Prevents all users from creating new scheduled tasks, whether from the Scheduled Task Wizard or by copying, moving, or dragging. It doesn't, however, prevent administrators from using the command-line At.exe task scheduler.

- **Prohibit Task Deletion**   Prevents all users from deleting existing scheduled tasks. It also prevents users from cutting or dragging a task from the Scheduled Tasks folder.

Note   Administrators whose accounts are affected by the related GPO are also subject to these settings when they are enabled. As a result, these administrators might not be able to modify and work with key aspects of scheduled tasks.

Managing File System, Drive, and Windows Explorer Access Options

Windows Explorer provides access to and views of a computer's files, folders, drives, and network locations. Using Windows Explorer, you can access and configure network drives, folder sharing, file system security, and much more. In some environments, you might want to limit the available features in Windows Explorer and any related views or dialog boxes, such as My Computer and My Network Places, to enhance security and help maintain system integrity. Common scenarios you might want to implement include:

- Hiding specified drives
- Preventing access to drives
- Removing CD-burning features
- Removing the Security tab
- Limiting the maximum allowable size for the Recycle Bin

The sections that follow examine these configuration options. Most of the related policies work with Windows 2000 or later, but there are some specific exceptions. Check the Explain Text to verify specific operating system support for each policy.

Tip   In addition to hiding or blocking access to drives, you can specifically prevent installation from any and all removable media sources. For details, see the "Preventing Installation from Floppy Disk, CD, DVD, and Other Removable Media" section in this chapter.

Hiding Drives in Windows Explorer and Related Views

Hiding a drive removes the corresponding icon from Windows Explorer, My Computer, and other related views. The goal of hiding drives is to make it more difficult for users to get into areas of the computer they shouldn't try to access. Hiding drives doesn't prevent users from running any programs and doesn't affect access to drives using file paths. Users can still run programs and open files on hidden drives, and they can still type file paths that include the hidden drives in the Run dialog box, at the command line, and elsewhere.

To use Group Policy to hide drives in Windows Explorer and related views, follow these steps:

1. Access the GPO you want to work with. Access User Configuration\
   Administrative Templates\Windows Components\Windows Explorer.
2. Double-click Hide These Specified Drives In My Computer.
3. Select Enabled and then select which drives to hide (Figure 6-4). If you want to unhide all drives, select Do Not Restrict Drives.

Tip   Hide These Specified Drives In My Computer is designed with the following in mind: the A and B drives represent removable media drives, the C drive is the main system drive, and the D drive is a CD-ROM or DVD-ROM drive. If computers in the related site, domain, or OU have a different drive configuration, you must carefully select the appropriate drives to hide or specify that all drives should be hidden.

Figure 6-4   Selecting the drives you want to hide

4. After you click OK, consider whether you want to also prevent access to drives. If you do, read the next section.

Preventing Access to Drives in Windows Explorer and Related Views

To improve computer security, the next step beyond hiding drives is to prevent access to the drives in Windows Explorer and related views. Similar to hiding drives, preventing access to drives doesn't affect access to the drives or prevent running of programs. Users can still run programs and open files on restricted drives using applications (such as Microsoft Word). Unlike with hiding drives, however, users cannot type file paths that include the restricted drives in the Run dialog box or the Map Network Drive dialog box. Further, even though users can browse the directory structure of restricted drives, they cannot open folders and access their contents. With this in mind, if you want to ensure that users cannot browse or access a drive, you should both hide and prevent access to a drive.

One of the most common scenarios in which you might want to prevent access to drives is when the A and B drives on computers are used in labs, kiosks, or sensitive areas within your organization. By preventing access to these drives, you block access to one of the easiest ways for users to create copies of files and take the files out of the office on floppy disk or other removable media configured for use with the A and B drives.

To use Group Policy to block access to drives in Windows Explorer and related views, follow these steps:

1. Access the GPO you want to work with. Access User Configuration\
    Administrative Templates\Windows Components\Windows Explorer.

2. Double-click Prevent Access To Drives From My Computer.

3. Select Enabled and then select which drives to block (Figure 6-5). If you want to open access to all drives, select Do Not Restrict Drives.

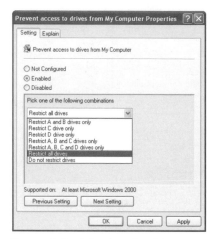

Figure 6-5   Selecting the drives you want to block

4. Click OK.

Removing CD-Burning and DVD-Burning Features in Windows Explorer and Related Views

Both Windows XP Professional and Windows Server 2003 include features that allow you to create and modify rewritable CDs and DVDs. As long as a computer has a CD or DVD writer, the computer can use these built-in features to create and modify rewritable CDs and DVDs. When you consider that most CDs store up to 600 MB of data and most single-layer DVDs store up to 4.7 GB of data, there is great potential for misuse and a high likelihood that CDs and DVDs might be used to store important documents, source code, and so forth if proper safeguards are not in place to protect the data.

To prevent users from using the built-in CD-burning and DVD-burning features, follow these steps:

1. Access the GPO you want to work with. Access User Configuration\ Administrative Templates\Windows Components\Windows Explorer.

2. Double-click Remove CD Burning Features.

3. In the Policy Settings dialog box, select Enabled and then click OK.

Caution   Removing the built-in CD-burning and DVD-burning features doesn't prevent users from installing and using third-party software that performs these tasks. To ensure that users cannot install this type of software, you must also configure software restriction policies. To learn more about software restriction policies, see Chapter 9.

Removing the Security Tab in Windows Explorer and Related Views

When users access the Properties dialog box for files, folders, shortcuts, and drives, the Security tab allows them to view the list of users and groups that have access to those resources (as long as they have some limited permissions on the computer). If users have the appropriate access permissions, they can also use the options of the Security tab to modify the security settings. In some environments, having access to security settings on file system objects is a good thing because it allows users to quickly determine who has access to what and possibly why they can't work with a particular file or folder. In other, more secure environments, being able to access security settings represents a potential security risk. For example, you might not want John to know that Sally can access the secure Finance folder. There might be a reason that she has access and he doesn't, and you probably don't want John asking Sally to give him access to files in that secure folder or asking if he can use Sally's logon to browse the folder.

To prevent users from accessing the Security tab for files, folders, shortcuts, and drives, follow these steps:

1. Access the GPO you want to work with. Access User Configuration\Administrative Templates\Windows Components\Windows Explorer.

2. Double-click Remove Security Tab.

3. In the Policy Settings dialog box, select Enabled and then click OK.

> **Caution**   As with many other security-related policy settings, you should consider carefully whether and where to define the Remove Security Tab policy setting. If you enable this policy setting at the domain level, dire consequences might result because domain administrators cannot access and configure security settings for file system objects. Typically, you should configure this type of policy at the OU or local machine level.

Limiting the Maximum Size of the Recycle Bin

When documents and other types of files are removed from a folder, they aren't normally permanently deleted. Instead, in the standard configuration, deleted files are moved to the Recycle Bin and are permanently deleted only when you empty the Recycle Bin. By default, the maximum allowed size of the Recycle Bin is 10 percent of a volume's disk space. Each volume on a computer has its own Recycle Bin, and you can increase or decrease this maximum allowed size on a per-volume basis. When the Recycle Bin reaches its maximum size, it must be emptied before additional files can be added to it, and when users try to delete files they see a warning prompt telling them to empty the Recycle Bin.

Through Group Policy, you can limit the maximum size of the Recycle Bin to a fixed percentage of a volume's disk space. The value you set in policy cannot be overridden by users, so you can be sure that Recycle Bins have a fixed maximum size. To see how this works, consider the following scenario. All computers in the Shipping OU have a standard configuration that includes a single 60-GB hard drive. The maximum allowed size of the Recycle Bin is therefore 6 GB of deleted files. The standard configuration of the Shipping OU computers uses 52 GB of disk space. As files are added to the system, there is an increased possibility that a full Recycle Bin might cause a drive to run out of space, which would seriously affect system performance. To avoid potential problems with drive space, you configure the maximum allowed size of the Recycle Bin to 2 percent of the disk space, or 1.2 GB in this instance.

To configure a fixed maximum allowed size for the Recycle Bin, follow these steps:

1. Access the GPO you want to work with. Access User Configuration\ Administrative Templates\Windows Components\Windows Explorer.

2. Double-click Maximum Allowed Recycle Bin Size.

3. Select Enabled and then use the Maximum Recycle Bin Size combo box to set the maximum allowed size of the Recycle Bin as a percentage of hard disk space that can be used (Figure 6-6).

4. Click OK.

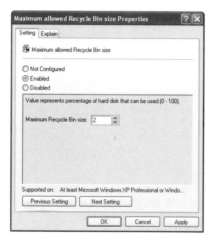

Figure 6-6   Selecting the maximum allowed size of the Recycle Bin

Optimizing the Windows Installer Configuration

The Windows component that handles program installation is Windows Installer. Group Policy includes many policy settings that allow you to modify how Windows Installer works. Windows Installer performs many tasks when programs are installed, including the following:

- Creating a System Restore checkpoint
- Creating or updating the baseline file cache
- Creating rollback copies of files

- Checking user privileges and install mode
- Performing the installation
- Logging the results of the installation

The sections that follow discuss policy settings and configuration options related to these tasks. Most of the related policies work with Windows 2000 or later and any Windows Installer version, but there are some specific exceptions. Check the Explain Text to verify specific support for each policy.

Controlling System Restore Checkpoints for Program Installations

If System Restore is enabled in Windows XP Professional, a System Restore checkpoint is created before the installation begins. This checkpoint helps you recover the computer to the state it was in before the program was installed. The drawback is that each checkpoint uses disk space, and when you have many programs to install or update, you end up with many checkpoints that might not be needed.

In policy, you can configure computers so that System Restore checkpoints aren't created. You do this by enabling Turn Off Creation Of System Restore Checkpoints under Computer Configuration\Administrative Templates\Windows Components\ Windows Installer.

Configuring Baseline File Cache Usage

If a program that uses baselines is being installed or updated, such as Microsoft Office 2003 or any Office 2003 components, Windows Installer version 3.0 or later either creates a baseline file cache or updates the existing baseline file cache to reflect which components have been installed or updated. This baseline is meant to eliminate user prompts for source media when you update programs. Instead of looking for the source media, the Windows Installer uses the baseline file cache to determine the location, version, status, and so forth of installed program components, and then it applies the updates.

By default, the maximum size of the baseline file cache is limited to 10 percent of a volume's disk space. On computers with small drives, the maximum allowed size might not be enough to allow the Windows Installer to create a full baseline file cache. On computers with large drives, the maximum size might allow the baseline file cache to grow too large.

In policy, you can change the way the baseline file cache is used by completing the following steps:

1. Access the GPO you want to work with. Access Computer Configuration\ Administrative Templates\Windows Components\Windows Installer.
2. Double-click Baseline File Cache Maximum Size.

3. Select Enabled and then use the Baseline File Cache Maximum Size combo box to set the maximum allowed size for the baseline file cache as a percentage of hard disk space that can be used (Figure 6-7). Keep the following in mind:

   ❑ A value of 0 disables the baseline file cache so that it cannot be used for future updates. Any existing baseline file cache is not deleted, however. An existing baseline file cache will be removed only if you run Disk Cleanup and elect to delete the files (as with Office baseline files) or uninstall the program for which the files were created.   .

   ❑ A value of 100 allows the Windows Installer to use all available free space on a volume for the baseline file cache.

4. Click OK.

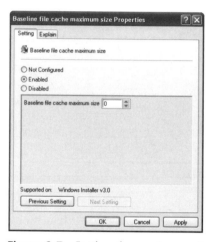

Figure 6-7   Setting the maximum allowed size of the baseline file cache

Controlling Rollback File Creation

Rollback files allow Windows Installer to roll back an incomplete installation and to recover a program or the system to the state it was in before the program or component was updated. When you install programs, including system drivers and service packs, Windows Installer can automatically create rollback files. In some cases, users are prompted to choose whether they want these files to be created. In other cases, rollback files are created automatically. Although rollback files are considered temporary files, they generally remain on the computer until they are manually deleted or until you uninstall the related program.

Caution   The rollback feature can also be used by malicious users. If malicious users can interrupt an installation, they might be able to collection information about the computer and search secure system files.

You can configure Computer Configuration or User Configuration policy to prevent rollback files from being created. Unlike most other types of policy, if you prevent rollback in either location, the policy setting is considered to be enabled even if it is specifically disabled in the other location. For example, if you prevent rollback in User Configuration policy and someone else disables it in Computer Configuration policy, the policy setting is considered to be enabled.

To prevent rollback files from being created, double-click Prohibit Rollback under either Computer Configuration\Administrative Templates\Windows Components\ Windows Installer or User Configuration\Administrative Templates\Windows Components\Windows Installer. In the Policy Settings dialog box, select Enabled and then click OK.

Elevating User Privileges for Installation

The privileges of the user performing an installation and the type of program being installed determine whether and how a program is installed. Programs that have been assigned to the user (offered on the desktop), assigned to the computer (installed automatically), or made available in Add Or Remove Programs in Control Panel have elevated installation privileges and can be installed, upgraded, or patched in directories that the current user might not have permission to view or work with. Other types of programs, however, are installed with normal system privileges and can be installed only in directories for which the current user has the appropriate access permissions.

On systems that have high security or very restrictive settings, you might find that users are prevented from installing needed programs. You can override this behavior in policy using Always Install With Elevated Privileges. This setting allows users who are not administrators to install programs that require access to restricted directories. Keep in mind, however, that this setting applies only to user-installed programs and not to programs distributed or offered by administrators; distributed or offered programs can be installed in restricted directories regardless of the configuration of this policy.

To make the Always Install With Elevated Privileges setting effective, you must enable it under Computer Configuration\Administrative Templates\Windows Components\ Windows Installer and under User Configuration\Administrative Templates\ Windows Components\Windows Installer. This means you enable and configure Always Install With Elevated Privileges as follows:

1. Access the GPO you want to work with. Access Computer Configuration\Administrative Templates\Windows Components\Windows Installer.

2. Double-click Always Install With Elevated Privileges. In the Policy Settings dialog box, select Enabled and then click OK.

3. Access User Configuration\Administrative Templates\Windows Components\ Windows Installer.

   4. Double-click Always Install With Elevated Privileges. In the policy settings
      dialog box, select Enabled and then click OK.

Controlling Per-User Installation and Program Operation

During installation, software programs can be configured for use by all users on a
computer (also referred to as a per-computer configuration) or by the user who is
installing the program (also referred to as a per-user configuration). In a standard
Windows configuration, users can install and run both per-user and per-computer
programs. In some situations, however, this might not be the optimal configuration.
For example, some users might have an incompatible configuration of an application
registered in their user profile, and this can cause problems with normal operations of
both the computer and the application itself.

To prevent problems like this, you might want users to run only per-computer program
installations and not any per-user program installations. This is where Prohibit User
Installs comes in handy. Using this policy, you can specify whether per-user installations
are allowed, hidden (ignored), or prohibited. For example, for computers configured as
kiosks or on a Terminal Server, you might want only per-computer programs to be
installed and available for use.

To configure Prohibit User Installs, follow these steps:

   1. Access the GPO you want to work with. Access Computer Configuration\
      Administrative Templates\Windows Components\Windows Installer.

   2. Double-click Prohibit User Installs.

   3. Select Enabled and then use the User Install Behavior list to select the desired
      user install behavior (Figure 6-8). The options are as follows:

      ❑ **Allow User Installs**   Windows Installer allows and makes use of programs
         that are installed per user, as well as programs that are installed per com-
         puter. If Windows Installer finds a per-user program installation, it hides
         any per-computer installations of that same program. This is the default
         behavior.

      ❑ **Hide User Installs**   Windows Installer ignores per-user applications. Only
         per-computer installations are visible to users, even if those users have
         per-user installations registered in their user profiles.

      ❑ **Prohibit User Installs**   Windows Installer prevents per-user installations of
         programs and ignores any previously installed per-user programs. If users
         try to perform a per-user installation, the Windows Installer displays an
         error message and stops the installation.

   4. Click OK.

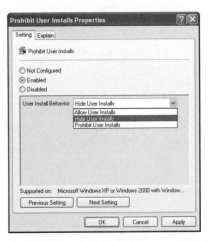

Figure 6-8   Setting the per-user installation behavior

Preventing Installation from Floppy Disk, CD, DVD, and Other Removable Media

In some environments, you might want users to install only programs that have been distributed or offered to them (as discussed in Chapter 11). To prevent users from installing programs from floppy disk, CD, DVD, or other removable media sources, you can enable Prevent Removable Media Source For Any Install under User Configuration\Administrative Templates\Windows Components\Windows Installer.

> **Tip**   In addition to preventing use of removable media sources, you can hide and block access to individual drives. For details, see the "Managing File System, Drive, and Windows Explorer Access Options" section in this chapter.

Configuring Windows Installer Logging

Whenever programs are installed, Windows Installer creates an installation log to record various types of messages and events related to the installation. This log, named Msi.log, is stored in the %SystemDrive%\Temp folder. By default, the log records the following types of messages or events:

- Status messages
- Nonfatal warning messages
- Error messages
- Startup of installation and logging actions

Through policy, you can modify the way logs are created and used. To do so, follow these steps:

1. Access the GPO you want to work with. Access Computer Configuration\ Administrative Templates\Windows Components\Windows Installer.

2. Double-click Logging.

3. Select Enabled and then use the Logging box to specify the desired logging options by using any combination of the following designators (Figure 6-9):

   ❑ **i** To record status messages

   ❑ **w** To record nonfatal warning messages

   ❑ **e** To all record messages

   ❑ **a** To record startup of installation and logging actions

   ❑ **r** To record details on installation and logging actions

   ❑ **u** To record user requests

   ❑ **c** To record the initial user interface parameters

   ❑ **m** To record Out Of Memory errors

   ❑ **p** To record Terminal Services properties

   ❑ **v** To enable verbose logging

   ❑ **o** To record Out Of Disk Space errors

4. Click OK.

Tip   To help with troubleshooting failed installations, you might want to log all messages and events related to installation. To do this, type a value of **iwearucmpvo**.

Figure 6-9   Configuring the installer logging options

Optimizing Automatic Updates with Windows Update

Computers running Windows 2000 or later can use Automatic Updates to maintain the operating system. Automatic Updates is an automatic distribution and installation mechanism for critical updates, security updates, update rollups (which include other updates), and service packs (which provide a comprehensive collection of updates). You can use Automatic Updates in conjunction with Windows Update Service to maintain Office, Microsoft Exchange, Microsoft SQL Server™, and hardware drivers.

Automatic Updates has a client/server architecture. The client component resides on a local computer and is responsible for downloading and installing updates. The server component resides on a remote computer and is the source from which updates are obtained. Many aspects of this client/server process can be configured and optimized for specific environments. You can do the following:

- Optimize the way updates are downloaded and installed
- Immediately install updates or schedule installation
- Block access to Windows Updates
- Designate the server to use for updates

Policy settings for Automatic Updates are found under Computer Configuration\Administrative Templates\Windows Components\Windows Update and under Configuration, Administrative Templates, Windows Components, Windows Update. The sections that follow discuss policy settings and configuration options related to these tasks. Many of the Windows Update policies are designed for either Windows XP Professional SP2 and later or Windows Server 2003 SP1 and later, so be sure to check the compatibility details in the Explain Text.

Enabling and Configuring Automatic Updates

Although you can configure Automatic Updates separately for each computer in your organization, it makes much more sense to manage this feature for groups of computers through Group Policy. Using Group Policy, you can designate a specific Automatic Updates configuration for all computers in a site, domain, or OU. Any time you need to modify the way Automatic Updates is used, you can modify the appropriate policy settings in one location and be sure the new settings will be applied to all computers as appropriate when policy is refreshed.

To specify whether and how computers receive updates, you use Configure Automatic Updates under Computer Configuration\Administrative Templates\Windows

Components\Windows Update. Using the basic Disabled or Enabled settings, you can either prevent or allow the use of Automatic Updates. Here are some guidelines:

- With production servers or other types of critical servers, you might want to disable Configure Automatic Updates to prevent automatic installation of updates and thus allow only updates to be downloaded and installed manually. Requiring manual installation on production servers is often a good idea because you might want to test updates in development servers beforehand.

- With most end-user computers and member servers, you should enable Configure Automatic Updates and then choose a specific update technique that either allows immediate installation or schedules the installation for an appropriate time. Because some installations of some updates require a reboot afterward, you'll often want to schedule installation.

You can disable Automatic Updates by completing the following steps:

1. Access the GPO you want to work with. Access Computer Configuration\ Administrative Templates\Windows Components\Windows Update.

2. Double-click Configure Automatic Updates.

3. Select Disabled and then click OK.

 Note   When automatic updates are disabled, you are not notified about updates. You can, however, download updates manually from the Windows Update Web site (*http://windowsupdate.microsoft.com/*).

You can enable and configure Automatic Updates by completing the following steps:

1. Access the GPO you want to work with. Access Computer Configuration\ Administrative Templates\Windows Components\Windows Update.

2. Double-click Configure Automatic Updates.

3. Select Enabled and then choose one of the following options in the Configure Automatic Updating list (Figure 6-10):

    ❑ **2 - Notify For Download And Notify For Install**   Windows notifies the current user before retrieving any updates. If the user elects to download the update, she still has the opportunity to accept or reject the update. Accepted updates are installed. Rejected updates are not installed, but they remain on the system so they can be installed later.

❑ **3 - Auto Download And Notify For Install**   This is the default option. Windows retrieves all updates at a configurable interval (called the *detection frequency*) and then prompts the user when the updates are ready to be installed. The user can then accept or reject the update. Accepted updates are installed. Rejected updates are not installed, but they remain on the system so they can be installed later.

❑ **4 - Auto Download And Schedule For Install**   Updates are downloaded automatically at a configurable interval (called the *detection frequency*) and then installed according to a specific schedule, which can be once a day at a particular time or once a week on a particular day and at a particular time.

❑ **5 - Allow Local Admin To Choose Setting**   The local administrators can configure Automatic Updates on a per-computer basis through the Automatic Updates tab of the System utility. Local administrators cannot, however, disable Automatic Updates through the System utility.

Figure 6-10   Specifying the automatic update options

4. If you elected to schedule the update installation, select a Scheduled Install Day. Choose 0 to allow updates to be installed on any day of the week. To choose a specific installation day, choose 1 to install updates on Sunday, 2 to install updates on Monday, and so on.

5. If you elected to schedule the update installation, select a Scheduled Install Time. The default value is 03:00 (3 A.M.). Choose 0 to allow updates to be installed on any day of the week. To choose a different installation time, choose an appropriate value. Keep in mind that the time is set using a 24-hour clock, where values from 00:00 to 11:00 are A.M. and values from 12:00 to 23:00 are P.M.

6. When you are ready to continue, click OK.

7. By default, all types of updates are installed only when the system is shut down and restarted. Some updates, however, can be installed immediately without interrupting system services or requiring system restart. To allow immediate installation of updates that do not interrupt system services or require a restart, double-click Allow Automatic Updates Immediate Installation. Select Enabled and then click OK.

8. By default, only computer administrators receive update notification. To allow any user logged on to a computer to receive update notifications as appropriate for the Automatic Updates configuration, double-click Allow Non-Administrators To Receive Update Notifications. Select Enabled and then click OK.

Controlling Auto Download and Notify for Install

When you've configured Automatic Updates for auto download and install, the Automatic Update process works like this:

1. Automatic Updates checks for updates automatically, according to the detection frequency. It then downloads the available updates.

2. With notify user installs, Automatic Updates notifies the user that an update is available. If the computer needs to be restarted, the user is prompted.

3. With scheduled installs, Automatic Updates schedules the install. If the computer needs to be restarted, the computer is restarted automatically by default.

You can control the automatic download and installation process in each of these steps through Group Policy. The sections that follow detail how to do this.

Setting the Automatic Updates Detection Frequency

When you configure Automatic Updates to automatically download updates, it does so according to the interval called the *detection frequency*. By default, this interval is 22 hours, meaning computers will check for updates approximately every 22 hours. To ensure that many computers don't use exactly the same interval, Windows uses an offset of minus zero to minus 20 percent. As a result, computers using the default interval check for updates anywhere between 18 and 22 hours. If you want to use a different interval, you can do so by completing the following steps:

1. Access the GPO you want to work with. Access Computer Configuration\ Administrative Templates\Windows Components\Windows Update.

2. Double-click Automatic Updates Detection Frequency.

3. Select Enabled and then use the combo box provided to set the desired detection frequency interval (Figure 6-11). The range of acceptable values is 1 hour to 22 hours.

4. Click OK.

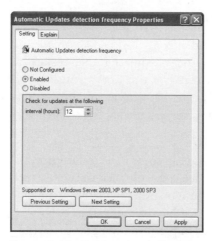

Figure 6-11   Setting the desired detection frequency interval

Optimizing Notify User Installs

With notify user installs, the user is notified that an update is available for installation when update download is complete and is given the option to install the update. If the user elects not to install the update at that time, Windows updates the Shut Down Windows dialog box to include an Install Updates And Shutdown option. This option is selected by default to give users another opportunity to install updates before shutting down their computers.

For user computers and member servers, you typically want the Install Updates And Shutdown option to be selected by default during shutdown of the operating system. On production servers or other critical servers, however, you might not want this behavior to be automatic. For example, you might want updates to be tested prior to installation on development or other test servers. In this case, you might want to do the following:

- **Hide the Install Updates And Shutdown option.**   If you don't want this option to be available in the Shut Down Windows dialog box, enable Do Not Display 'Install Updates And Shutdown' Option under Computer Configuration\ Administrative Templates\Windows Components\Windows Update. The Install Updates And Shutdown option will be hidden from view and users will not be able to select it.

- **Make sure the Install Updates And Shutdown option isn't selected by default.**   If you don't want this option to be the default, enable Do Not Adjust Default Option under Computer Configuration\Administrative Templates\Windows Components\Windows Update. The Install Updates And Shutdown option will not be the automatic default. The default will be the last shutdown option chosen by the user.

Optimizing Scheduled Installs

When a restart is required after a scheduled automatic update, the computer installs the updates according to the schedule and then restarts the computer if necessary after a 5-minute delay. To see how this works, consider the following example. You've scheduled Automatic Updates to install at 5 A.M. every Thursday. The system must be restarted to complete updates installed at 5 A.M. on Thursday. The computer is restarted at 5:05 A.M.

Through Group Policy, you can control the restart process in several ways. If you want to use a different restart delay, double-click Delay Restart For Scheduled Installations under Computer Configuration\Administrative Templates\Windows Components\ Windows Update. Select Enabled, set the restart delay using the combo box provided, and then click OK. For example, if you want to restart the computer after a 15-minute delay, you can set the restart value to 15, as shown in Figure 6-12.

 Note   The acceptable restart delay values are from 1 to 30 minutes. A value of 1 is the closest you can get to an immediate restart after install.

Figure 6-12   Setting an alternative restart interval for scheduled update installs

You can also prevent Auto-Restart after a scheduled install if a user is logged on. To do this, double-click No Auto-Restart For Scheduled Automatic Updates Installations under Computer Configuration\Administrative Templates\Windows Components\ Windows Update. Select Enabled and then click OK. If you enable No Auto-Restart For Scheduled Automatic Updates Installations, the computer does not automatically restart after installing updates that require a restart if a user is currently logged on. Instead, Automatic Updates notifies the user that a restart is needed and waits until the computer is restarted. Restarting the computer enforces the updates.

> **Note**   If you set No Auto-Restart For Scheduled Automatic Updates Installations to Disabled or Not Configured, the computer restarts automatically after a scheduled install. The restart delay in this case is 5 minutes.

Other policy settings you might find useful for controlling restarts are as follows:

- **Re-prompt for Restart With Scheduled Installations**   When Automatic Updates is configured for scheduled installation of updates, this setting ensures that the logged-on user is prompted again after a set interval if a restart was previously postponed. If the setting is disabled or not configured, the default re-prompt interval of 10 minutes is used.

- **Reschedule Automatic Updates Scheduled Installations**   This setting specifies the amount of time that Automatic Updates waits after system startup before proceeding with a scheduled installation that was previously missed.

Blocking Access to Automatic Updates

In rare instances, you might not want users in a domain or OU to be able to use Automatic Updates. For example, if computers are used in a lab or kiosk setting only, you might want to disable Automatic Updates completely; you do this through Group Policy at the domain or OU level.

More typically, however, you disable Automatic Updates for individual local machines rather than at the domain or OU level. For example, if a computer used in a lab or kiosk setting should not be updated, you can disable Automatic Updates completely through the local machine policy (as long as you are configuring a standalone machine or there are no overriding site, domain, or OU policy settings for a machine that is a member of a domain).

You block access to Automatic Updates using Remove Access To Use All Windows Update Features under User Configuration\Administrative Templates\Windows Components\Windows Update. Select Enabled and then click OK. When you enable this setting, all Windows Update features are removed. Users are blocked from accessing Windows Update, and automatic updating is completely disabled.

Designating an Update Server

The Windows Update process is designed so that updates are downloaded over the Internet by default. This process works fine when your organization has a few dozen computers, but when your organization has hundreds or thousands of computers, this process is very inefficient. When you have many computers to maintain, a better way to obtain updates is to use a central update server to host updates from the Microsoft Update Web sites. You can then use this update service to automatically update computers on your network. Thus, rather than having hundreds or thousands of computers downloading the same or similar updates over the Internet, you have a single designated server that downloads updates for the organization. Client computers in the organization then connect to this server to obtain updates. Statistics about the updates are then delivered back to this server or a specifically designated statistics server in the organization. This means you can have a one-server or two-server update configuration.

To configure your site, domain, or OU to use a single update server, complete the following steps:

1. Configure a Windows server as an application server running IIS. The server should be running Windows 2000 Server SP3 or Windows Server 2003 and must have access to the Internet over port 80.

2. DNS must be set up appropriately to allow internal access to the server by its fully qualified domain name.

3. Access the GPO you want to work with. Access Computer Configuration\Administrative Templates\Windows Components\Windows Update.

4. Double-click Specify Intranet Microsoft Update Service Location.

5. Select Enabled and then type the fully qualified domain name of the update server in both boxes, as shown in Figure 6-13.

6. Click OK.

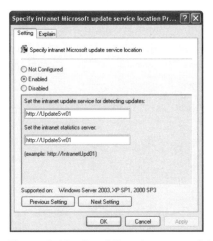

Figure 6-13   Providing the name of the single update server

To configure your site, domain, or OU to use an update server and a statistics server, complete the following steps:

1. Configure two Windows servers as application servers running IIS. The servers should be running Windows 2000 Server SP3 or Windows Server 2003. The update server must have access to the Internet over port 80.

2. DNS must be set up appropriately to allow internal access to the servers by their fully qualified domain name.

3. Access the GPO you want to work with. Access Computer Configuration\Administrative Templates\Windows Components\Windows Update.

4. Double-click Specify Intranet Microsoft Update Service Location.

5. Select Enabled and in the Set The Intranet Update Service box, type the fully qualified domain name of the update server (Figure 6-14).

Figure 6-14 Designating a different server for updates and statistics

6. In the Set The Intranet Statistics Server box, type the fully qualified domain name of the statistics server.

7. Click OK.

Summary

Many component utilities and applications are included with the Windows operating system, including NetMeeting, Windows Explorer, Task Scheduler, Attachment Manager, and Microsoft Management Console. Through Group Policy, you can easily optimize the features and options of these and other Windows components to enable or disable usage, enhance security, improve performance, and much more. In this way, you can standardize the way groups of users access and work with Windows components. You can also configure default settings and options and restrict access to or disable specific component features.

Chapter 7

Managing User Settings and Data

In this chapter:

Understanding User Profiles and Group Policy 254
Configuring Roaming Profiles 257
Optimizing User Profile Configurations. 260
Redirecting User Profile Folders and Data. 271
Managing Computer and User Scripts 281
Summary 287

When it comes to user and computer management, change is the only constant. Change occurs in every organization, large or small. Sally might be using a loaner laptop today instead of her PC. Bob might be logging in from a remote office. Tom might be moving to a new PC. If the environment isn't consistent, Sally, Bob, and Tom might spend more time trying to figure out what's going on than performing work, and they might also have problems accessing their data. This isn't good for them, and it certainly isn't good for the people supporting them.

As an administrator or support staff member, there are many things you can do to reduce and, in many cases, eliminate problems that users experience due to changes in their environment. The most obvious is to use roaming or mandatory profiles for these types of users so that their desktops have a consistent look and feel regardless of the computers they are using. Roaming profiles are only part of the solution, however. To ensure a truly consistent environment, you must consider much more than the user's profile. You must look at the general settings for the desktop, Start menu, taskbar, and Control Panel. You must also consider whether the related folders and data should be redirected to help centralize management and access. For example, you might want to redirect the Start menu, My Documents, and Application Data folders so that users have consistent access to their data across the organization.

Related Information

- For more information about managing Microsoft® Windows® components through Group Policy, see Chapter 6.

- For more information on configuring user profiles and offline files, see Chapter 37 in *Microsoft Windows Server 2003 Inside Out* (Microsoft Press, 2004).

- For more information on configuring Shadow copies, see Chapter 22 in *Microsoft Windows Server 2003 Inside Out*.

Understanding User Profiles and Group Policy

Whenever a user logs on to a computer, a user profile is generated or retrieved. This profile stores important global settings and user data, and it exists physically on disk. The most basic type of profile is a local profile. With a local profile, a user's global settings and data are stored on the local computer and are available only on that computer. You can also configure accounts so that users have roaming or mandatory profiles.

Both roaming and mandatory profiles allow users to access profiles from a designated server and thereby get their global settings and data from anywhere on the network. The difference between roaming and mandatory profiles is in who can make permanent changes to the user's settings. With roaming profiles, individual users can modify their own global settings, and these changes are persistent. With mandatory profiles, administrators define a user's settings and only administrators can change these settings permanently. Users can still change their settings temporarily, however. For example, if Lisa has a mandatory profile, she can log on to a computer and modify the desktop appearance using the Display utility. When Lisa logs off, however, the changes are not saved; the next user of the computer—even if it is Lisa—sees the global settings as set originally in the mandatory profile.

By default, computers running Windows 2000 and later store user profile data locally in a user-specific folder under %SystemDrive%\Documents and Settings\%UserName%. The exception is computers that have been upgraded from Windows NT®, which store local profiles under %SystemRoot%\Profiles\%UserName% because this is the original profile location under Windows NT. However, any data stored under %SystemDrive%\Documents and Settings\%UserName%\Local Settings are specific to a particular local computer and do not roam. Thus, you have two categories of data stored in a local user profile: data that can roam and data that cannot roam.

Data that can roam includes the following folders, which are found under the %UserName% folder:

- Application Data, which is the per-user data store for applications. The folder path is %SystemDrive%\Documents and Settings\%UserName%\Application Data.

- Cookies, which is used to store browser cookies.

- Desktop, which is used to store the desktop configuration and shortcuts.

- Favorites, which is used to store browser favorites.

- My Documents, which is used to store document files.

- My Recent Documents, which is used to store shortcuts to documents opened recently.

- NetHood, which is used to store network connections for My Network Places.

- PrintHood, which is used to store information about network printers.

- SendTo, which is used to store system files that provide the SendTo options.

- Start Menu, which is used to store the Start Menu configuration.

- Templates, which is used to store document template files.

Data that can't roam includes the following folders, which are found under the %UserName%\Local Settings folder:

- The local computer's Application Data folder, which is the per-computer data store for applications. The folder path is %SystemDrive%\Documents and Settings\%UserName%\Local Settings\Application Data.

- History, which is used to store the browser history.

- Temp, which is used to store temporary program files.

- Temporary Internet Files, which is used to store temporary browser files.

The most important aspects of user profiles to understand are where system settings are obtained and how redirection works. User profiles have two key parts:

- **Global settings**   Global settings are loaded from Ntuser.dat (local or roaming profile) or Ntuser.man (mandatory profile) to the HKEY_CURRENT_USER subtree in the registry. These settings define the configuration of the desktop, taskbar, Start menu, Control Panel, and many other aspects of the operating system. You can view the HKEY_CURRENT_USER settings using the Registry Editor, as shown in Figure 7-1. To start the Registry Editor, type **regedit** at a command prompt or click Start, Run, and then type **regedit** in the Open box and click OK.

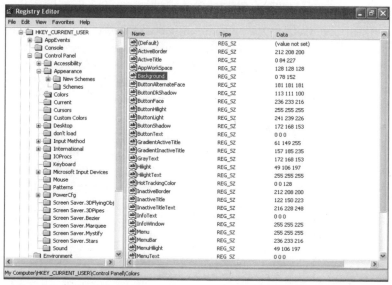

Figure 7-1   Global settings for each user loaded from the profile into the registry

■ **User data**   The user's data is made available through the group of folders within the profile. These folders are accessed by users in a variety of ways and include the Application Data, Cookies, Favorites, Desktop, and My Documents folders discussed previously. The My Documents folder also contains other standard folders such as My Pictures, My Videos, and My Music. Although you can examine a user's data folders, as shown in Figure 7-2, many of the folders are hidden by default. To view them, you must change the configuration of Windows Explorer. Choose Folder Options from the Tools menu. In the dialog box that opens, click the View tab and then select Show Hidden Files And Folders.

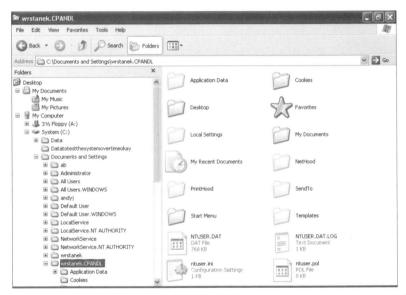

Figure 7-2   User data stored in subfolders within the user's profile

As you can see, many of the visual aspects of a system's configuration come from the global settings in a user's profile. These settings, for example, determine the display mode, the available printers, the desktop shortcuts, and much more. Not so obvious is how user data is obtained in conjunction with the user profile, and this is where redirection enters the picture. As shown in Figure 7-2, the Folders view has nodes for Desktop and My Documents. Within My Documents, you'll find My Music and My Pictures. All of these folders are actually stored in the user profile. Behind the scenes, any time you access the Desktop, My Documents, My Music, or My Pictures folder, Windows seamlessly redirects you to where the related data is actually stored. This is in fact how each user who logs on to a system has a unique desktop, Start menu, and personal folders.

Access to global settings and seamless redirection of personal data folders is what makes it possible to have roaming and mandatory profiles. Group Policy enters the picture by allowing you to take these core user profile features and go a few steps further than would otherwise be possible. Using Group Policy, you can customize the look and feel of Windows to explicitly define available options and settings for the desktop, Start menu, taskbar, Control Panel, and more. These custom settings then override settings in a user's profile and help to ensure a consistent experience. Through Group Policy, you have more control over user data redirection. The many additional options available provide for central management and storage of user data as well as optimization based on group membership. For example, using Group Policy you can specify that the My Documents folders for members of the SeattleSupport group be stored on SeattleSvr08, while the My Documents folders for members of the ChicagoSupport group be stored on ChicagoSvr03.

The added advantage of redirection is that these redirected folders are accessed in much the same way as network shares: The data contained in the redirected folders actually resides on shared folders on the designated server. When a user accesses a redirected folder, the local computer seamlessly connects the user to the shared folder on the designated server. Thus, although it appears that users can log on anywhere and have access to the data in their personal folders, the actual data has been redirected to a fixed location on the network.

The key benefit here is that redirected folders are no longer moved around with the user's roaming profile data. This can speed up logon and logoff dramatically. It also makes backing up user data much easier because you have a centralized location for making backups. The key disadvantage has to do with laptops. In the standard config uration, mobile users have access only to their redirected data when they are connected to the network. The way to avoid this problem is to also configure Offline File caching for the share where the user's data resides.

By default, Windows 2000, Windows XP, and Windows Server 2003 are configured for manual caching of documents for offline use. Users can make files available offline by right-clicking a file in My Documents or another folder and selecting Make Available Offline. A better way to configure Offline Files is to make caching automatic for files that users open from the share. An administrator must make this configuration setting by right-clicking the share and selecting Properties. In the Properties dialog box, you click the Sharing tab and then click Offline Settings. Select All Files And Programs That Users Open From The Share Will Be Automatically Available Offline, and then click OK twice. For more information, see Chapter 37 in *Microsoft Windows Server 2003 Inside Out.*

Configuring Roaming Profiles

Setting up roaming profiles is a multipart process. First you must configure a network share to use for storing the roaming profiles. Then you must configure user accounts to use a roaming profile rather than a standard local profile.

Configuring the Network Share for Roaming Profiles

The network share you use for roaming profiles can be on any server in the organization. However, a bit of planning should go into the rollout. Because profiles can be quite large, you typically don't want users to have to retrieve or update profiles over remote networks. Many other factors go into this consideration, of course, such as whether you will also be redirecting user data folders, but you will typically want the profile server to be in the same geographic location as the users.

> **Caution**   Unlike redirected folders, the network share you use for profiles should not be configured for offline file use or encryption. With this in mind, you should disable offline file caching (as discussed in Microsoft Knowledge Base article 842007) and also turn off the Encrypting File System.

To create the shared folder for the roaming profiles, follow these steps:

1. Log on to the profile server using an account that has administrator privileges.

2. In Windows Explorer, locate the folder you want to share. Right-click it, and then choose Sharing And Security.

3. Select Share This Folder, and then click Permissions.

4. By default, the special group Everyone has Read access to the share. Modify the permissions so the Authenticated Users group has Full Control. This ensures that client computers can access the share and users have appropriate permissions with regard to their profiles.

5. Click OK twice.

Configuring User Accounts to Use Roaming Profiles

Once you create and configure the profile share, you can configure user accounts with roaming profiles to use the share. Typically, you use Active Directory Users And Computers or Server Manager to configure roaming profiles. With these tools, you use the %UserName% environment variable to act as a placeholder in the profile path. The server then creates a subfolder for the user based on the user's account name.

> **Tip**   The %UserName% variable is what tells the server to create subfolders on a per-user basis. For example, if you set the profile path to \\NYServer08\Profiles\ %UserName% and you are configuring the account for ZachM, the profile path will be set as \\NYServer08\Profiles\ZachM. The subfolder, ZachM, is created automatically, and the roaming profile is then stored in this folder. By default, when Windows creates this user-specific folder, NTFS permissions are set so that only the user has access to read and manage its contents. If you want administrators to have access to the profile, you must enable Add The Administrators Security Group To Roaming User Profiles in Group Policy, as discussed in the "Modifying the Way Profile Data Can Be Accessed" section in this chapter.

If you are using Active Directory Users And Computers to configure roaming profiles, follow these steps:

1. Start Active Directory Users And Computers. Click Start, point to Programs or All Programs, Administrative Tools, Active Directory Users And Computers.

2. Double-click the user account you want to work with. Click the Profile tab.

> **Tip**   You can easily edit multiple accounts simultaneously. To do this, hold down Ctrl or Alt so that you can select multiple accounts to work with, right-click, and then select Properties. When you click the Profile tab, any changes you make to the profile path will then be made to all the selected accounts.

3. In the Profile Path box, specify the Uniform Naming Convention (UNC) path to the server, share, and folder to use, in the form \\ServerName\ShareName\ %UserName% (where ServerName is the name of the server, ShareName is the name of the share created for storing roaming profiles, and %UserName% is an environment variable that allows the profile path to be unique for each user).

4. Click OK. The profile folder will be created the next time the user logs on to the network. If a user is currently logged on, she will need to log off and then log back on.

As discussed in Chapter 13 of the *Microsoft Windows Command-Line Administrator's Pocket Consultant* (Microsoft Press, 2004), you can also use the command line to change user profile settings. In fact, you can use a single command line to change the profile setting for every user in a selected site, domain, or OU. Here is an example:

```
dsquery user "OU=Tech,DC=cpandl,DC=com" | dsmod user -profile
"\\NYServer08\profiles\$username$"
```

If you were to type this command on a single line and press Enter, all user accounts in the Tech OU in the Cpandl.com domain would have their profile paths set to \\NYServer08\profiles\%username%. In this example, the quotes and the dollar signs are necessary to ensure proper interpretation of the command.

> **Note**   When users log on to multiple computers or start multiple Terminal Services sessions, changes made to roaming profiles can get lost or overwritten because the profile of the last session is the one reflected on the profile server. To see why this happens, consider the following scenario: You are logged on to two terminal server sessions simultaneously. In session 1, you create a persistent network drive. When you log off session 1, this change is reflected in your profile, but then you log off session 2 and the profile from this session is uploaded, overwriting the changes from session 1. The next time you log on, the network drive will not be mapped as expected. To avoid this situation, you would need to ensure that the last session you log off is the one that contains the profile you want to save.

Optimizing User Profile Configurations

Before looking at specific ways you can optimize Windows settings and handle user data, let's look at the policy settings related to profiles themselves. Policy settings that control the user profile configuration are found under Computer Configuration\Administrative Templates\System\User Profiles and User Configuration\Administrative Templates\System\User Profiles. As you read through this discussion, keep the following in mind:

- A local user profile is created or retrieved each time a user logs on to a computer.

- Changes to global settings and user data are stored in the local user profile and updated in a roaming profile when a user logs off.

- User profile data is only accessible to the user for whom a profile was created.

- Roamable user profile data includes everything under %SystemDrive%\Documents and Settings\%UserName% except for the local computer-specific settings under %SystemDrive%\Documents and Settings\%UserName%\Local Settings.

As you'll see, system and policy settings can modify this behavior in many ways.

Modifying the Way Local and Roaming Profiles Are Used

By default, a local user profile is created or retrieved each time a user logs on to a computer. If the user account is configured to use a local profile, the local profile is created from the Default User Profile or loaded from an existing profile. If the user account is configured to use a roaming or mandatory profile, a locally cached copy of the profile is created from the server-stored user profile. If the profile server is unavailable during logon, the local cached copy of the profile can be used. If no locally cached copy of the profile is available, the Default User Profile is used.

Many policies can change or modify the way local and roaming profiles are used. These policies are stored in Computer Configuration under Administrative Templates\System\User Profiles and include:

- Only Allow Local User Profiles
- Delete Cached Copies Of Roaming Profiles
- Do Not Detect Slow Network Connection
- Log Users Off When Roaming Profile Fails
- Prompt User When Slow Link Is Detected
- Slow Network Connection Timeout For User Profiles
- Timeout For Dialog Boxes
- Wait For Remote User Profile

The sections that follow discuss these policy settings and how they are used.

Only Allow Local User Profiles

The Only Allow Local User Profiles setting prevents users from using a roaming profile. If a user with a roaming profile logs on after this policy is enabled (and computer policy has been refreshed), she will receive a new user profile based on the Default User Profile for the computer. This profile will then be used for all subsequent logons to that computer.

Delete Cached Copies Of Roaming Profiles

When you enable the Delete Cached Copies Of Roaming Profiles settings, any local copies of a user's roaming profile are deleted from the local computer when a user logs off. The roaming profile then exists only on the server on which it is stored. As you might expect, this policy setting is meant to be used in environments where high security is required, and it comes with more than a few caveats. The setting doesn't affect locally cached copies of profiles that were created before this policy setting took effect. Those profiles will remain until a user logs on to the computer where they are stored and logs off (and the log off process proceeds normally—with no unload or update issues at logoff). Because the local cached copy of the profile is deleted when a user logs off, no cached profile is available if the user logs on and the remote server is unavailable. In this case, the user gets a temporary user profile (based on the Default User Profile) that will be removed when he logs off.

You shouldn't enable Delete Cached Copies Of Roaming Profiles on laptops or on computers that might access the network over slow links. When laptop users are disconnected from the network, there is no way to get the roaming profile, and because there is no locally cached profile, they will get a temporary profile. Further, if you enable Delete Cached Copies Of Roaming Profiles and the computer is configured to detect slow links, you'll have similar problems. When users are connected to the network over a slow link, the default system behavior is to use a locally cached profile, but because there is no locally cached profile, they will get a temporary profile instead.

Do Not Detect Slow Network Connection

When you enable Do Not Detect Slow Network Connection, slow-link detection for user profiles is disabled and the computer ignores settings that tell it how to handle slow connections. This setting is useful when you delete locally cached copies of profiles and want to ensure that a roaming profile is available even if a user is connected over a slow link. The downside to this, of course, is that logon and logoff might take a long time (due to profile retrieval or update processing over slow links).

Note   When users connect over remote networks or you use Distributed File System (DFS) shares, you are more likely to see problems with slow links. One way to solve this problem is to disable slow-link detection. You might also want to add a DFS root target to the client site.

Log Users Off When Roaming Profile Fails

When you enable Log Users Off When Roaming Profile Fails, a user is logged off automatically if the computer cannot load her roaming profile. This means she cannot log on if the profile server is down or otherwise unavailable or if the profile contains errors that prevent it from loading correctly.

Log Users Off When Roaming Profile Fails is meant to be used in environments in which you want to be absolutely certain that users load their profiles from a server. For example, in a high-security environment you might not want users to use a temporary local profile. Rather than allowing them to log on with a temporary profile (based on the Default User Profile), you'll want to log them off automatically instead.

Prompt User When Slow Link Is Detected

When you enable Prompt User When Slow Link Is Detected, a user is prompted when a slow link is detected and is asked whether he wants to use a local copy of the profile (if available) or wait for the roaming profile to load. If the setting is disabled or not configured and a slow link is detected, the computer takes one of two actions:

- If you haven't specifically indicated that the computer should wait for a remote user profile, the computer tries to load a locally cached copy of the user's profile (if available).

- If you've specified that the computer should wait for a remote user profile, the computer tries to load the roaming profile (if available).

By default, the system waits 30 seconds for a user to make a selection. If he doesn't make a selection, one of the above actions is taken. You can adjust the wait time using the Timeout For Dialog Boxes setting.

Note   Prompt User When Slow Link Is Detected is ignored if you've enabled Do Not Detect Slow Network Connection and when slow link detection is otherwise disabled. Also keep in mind that if you've enabled Delete Cached Copies Of Roaming Profiles, no locally cached profile will be available. In this case, the computer will use a temporary profile (based on the Default User Profile) as long as you haven't also enabled Log Users Off When Roaming Profile Fails.

Slow Network Connection Timeout For User Profiles

As discussed in Chapter 3 under "Configuring Slow Link Detection," computers use a specific algorithm to determine whether they are connected over a slow link. For computers connected to a network over TCP/IP, the response time to the server is measured using a Ping test and then by sending a message packet, as discussed previously. By default, if the connection speed is determined to be less than 500 kilobits per second (which can also be interpreted as high latency/reduced responsiveness on a fast network), the client computer interprets this as a slow network connection. For computers that aren't using TCP/IP, only the response time to the server is measured. By default, if the server's file system doesn't respond within 120 milliseconds, the client computer interprets this as a slow network connection.

When you are using DHCP for dynamic IP addressing or when clients connect to the network over dial-up, you might want to increase these default values. To change the default values, follow these steps:

1. Access the GPO with which you want to work. Access Computer Configuration\ Administrative Templates\System\User Profiles.

2. Double-click Slow Network Connection Timeout For User Profiles, and then select Enabled, as shown in Figure 7-3.

3. Type the values you want to use for detecting slow links. Use the Connection Speed combo box to configure detection for IP networks. Use the Time combo box to configure detection for non-IP networks.

4. Click OK.

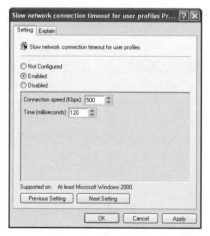

Figure 7-3   Configuring slow link detection for user profiles

Tip   Slow Network Connection Timeout For User Profiles is ignored if you've enabled Do Not Detect Slow Network Connection and when slow link detection is otherwise disabled. Keep in mind that if you've enabled Delete Cached Copies Of Roaming Profiles, no locally cached profile will be available. In this case, the computer will use a temporary profile (based on the Default User Profile) as long as you haven't also enabled Log Users Off When Roaming Profile Fails.

Timeout For Dialog Boxes

When you enable Prompt User When Slow Link Is Detected, the system waits 30 seconds for a user to make a selection. If she doesn't make a selection, a default action is taken, which is to either load the locally cached profile (if allowed) or wait for the roaming profile to load (if this is required). User profile–related prompts are displayed in two other instances as well:

- If the system cannot access the user's server-based profile during logon or logoff, a prompt is displayed. The prompt tells the user that the local profile will be loaded (if one is available).

- If the user's locally cached profile is newer than the server-based profile, a prompt is displayed. The prompt tells the user that the local profile will be loaded (if one is available).

You can adjust the wait time by completing the following steps:

1. Access the GPO with which you want to work. Access Computer Configuration\ Administrative Templates\System\User Profiles.

2. Double-click Timeout For Dialog Boxes and then select Enabled, as shown in Figure 7-4.

Figure 7-4   Configuring the wait time for the slow link prompt

3. Specify the wait time to use, such as 60 seconds.

> **Tip**   You can set any wait time from 0 to 600 seconds. Keep in mind that Timeout For Dialog Boxes is ignored if you've enabled Do Not Detect Slow Network Connection and when slow link detection is otherwise disabled.

4. Click OK.

Wait For Remote User Profile

To force a computer to use a roaming or mandatory profile from a server, you can enable Wait For Remote User Profile. The computer will then wait for the roaming or mandatory profile to load even if the network connection is slow. If you disable this setting or do not configure it and slow link detection is enabled, the user is prompted when a slow link is detected and has the opportunity to use either her local profile or her roaming profile (assuming these are available and no policy restricts their use). If the user doesn't respond to the prompt, the default action is to load the locally cached profile (if allowed) or wait for the roaming profile to load (if this is required).

A typical scenario where you might want to use Wait For Remote User Profile is when users move between computers frequently and the local copy of their profile is not always current. Using the locally cached copy of the profile is best when quick logon is a priority.

> **Note**   Wait For Remote User Profile is ignored if you've enabled Do Not Detect Slow Network Connection and when slow link detection is otherwise disabled. Keep in mind that if Delete Cached Copies Of Roaming Profiles is enabled, there is no local copy of the roaming profile to load.

Modifying the Way Profile Data Is Updated and Changed

Any changes to global settings and user data are stored in the local user profile first. When a user logs off and is using a roaming profile, the changes are written to the roaming profile on the server unless specifically prevented. When Terminal Services is used, areas of the registry (under HKEY_CURRENT_USER) might be locked when a user logs off. For example, this can happen if another program or service is reading or updating the registry; this would prevent the computer from writing the locked registry settings to the profile.

Windows XP and Windows 2003 try to avoid this issue by saving the registry settings after 60 seconds and then updating the roaming profile. Windows 2000 tries to access the registry settings immediately at logoff and then make any necessary updates in the roaming profile. If registry settings are locked, Windows 2000 keeps trying to sync the changes—up to the maximum retry value, which by default is 60. One minute is allotted for these retries, so the retries occur about once every second.

Two key policies change or modify this behavior:

- **Maximum Retries To Unload And Update User Profile**   If you enable this setting, you can specify the number of times the system tries to save registry setting changes to the profile before giving up. The default value is 60. If you disable this setting or do not configure it, the system retries 60 times. If you set the number of retries to 0, the system tries just once to save the registry settings to the profile before giving up. You might want to consider increasing the number of retries specified in this setting if many user profiles are stored in the computer's memory, as might be the case with servers running Terminal Services. Keep in mind that this setting doesn't affect the system's attempts to update the files in the user profile.

- **Prevent Roaming Profile Changes From Propagating To The Server**   When you enable this setting, you prevent users from making permanent changes to their roaming profiles. When the user logs on, she receives the roaming profile as normal. However, any changes she makes to the profile are not saved to her roaming profile when she logs off. Although this setting is similar to using mandatory profiles, there is a fundamental difference between using a mandatory profile and preventing changes to roaming profiles: When you use a mandatory profile, no profile changes are stored when a user logs off, so neither the locally cached copy nor the remote copy of the profile is updated. When you prevent changes to roaming profiles, profile changes made locally are not copied back to the remote copy of the profile. The changes are, however, available the next time the user logs on to that computer. You might want to use this setting in instances in which you don't want the local profile changes and user files to be copied back to a server and saved in the user's roaming profile.

Modifying the Way Profile Data Can Be Accessed

Roaming profiles are stored on designated servers. By default, user profile data can be accessed only by the user for whom the profile was created. Windows 2000 with SP3 or earlier and Windows XP without a service pack also allow the creator/owner of the profile folder to access the profile. For example, a user in the Server Operators or

Account Operators group might pre-create a user's profile folder, and as the creator/ owner, he would be able to access the user's profile data. Windows Server 2003, Windows 2000 with SP4 or later, and Windows XP with SP1 or later close this potential security problem by checking to see if the user is the only one with permissions on the profile folder and then not permitting roaming if the permissions on the user's server-based folder are not those that Windows requires. The requirements are very specific: only the user or the Administrators group can be the owner of the user's profile folder. Thus, if anyone other than the current user or the Administrators group owns the folder, roaming is not allowed and the user is forced to use a local profile. No changes to the local profile are propagated back to the profile server.

When a user with a roaming profile logs on and Windows Server 2003 determines that the roaming profile folder doesn't have the required permissions, the following error message is displayed:

```
Windows did not load your roaming profile and is attempting to log you on with your
local profile. changes to the profile will not be copied to the server when you
logoff. windows did not load your profile because a server copy of the profile folder
already exists that does not have the correct security. Either the current user
or the Administrator's group must be the owner of the folder. Contact your network
administrator.
```

If this is not the desired behavior, you can, through Group Policy, tell Windows Server 2003 not to check the permissions on roaming profile folders. To do this, enable Do Not Check For User Ownership Of Roaming Profile Folders under Computer Configuration\Administrative Templates\System\User Profiles. With this policy setting enabled, Windows Server 2003, Windows 2000 with SP4 or later, and Windows XP with SP1 or later no longer check security permissions before updating data in existing user profile folders.

One of the most common reasons for pre-creating user profile folders is to ensure that a designated administrator can access profile data as necessary. One way to work around this issue is to allow Windows to create profile folders automatically as necessary and then configure security permissions on the profile folders so that administrators can access them. For users who don't already have roaming profile folders, you can tell Windows to set permissions on new profile folders so that both administrators and the user have full control. You do this by enabling Add The Administrators Security Group To Roaming User Profiles under Computer Configuration\Administrative Templates\ System\User Profiles. Keep in mind that this policy setting doesn't affect existing roaming profile folders and must be set on the target client computers rather than the server storing the profile folders.

To allow administrators to access existing profile folders, complete the following steps:

1. Log on to the profile server using an account that has administrator privileges.

2. In Windows Explorer, locate the user's profile folder. Right-click it, and then choose Properties.

3. When you see a warning prompt telling you that you do not have permission to access the profile folder but can take ownership, click OK.

4. In the Properties dialog box, click the Security tab, and then click Advanced.

5. In the Advanced Security Settings dialog box, click the Owner tab.

6. Under Change Owner To, click Administrators, and then select the Replace Owners On Subcontainers And Objects check box.

7. Click OK. When prompted to confirm that you want to take ownership of the folder, click Yes.

8. You are prompted to close and open the folder's Properties dialog box before you can view or change permissions. Click OK three times to close all open dialog boxes.

9. In Windows Explorer, right-click the user's profile folder and then choose Properties.

10. In the Properties dialog box, click the Security tab and then click Advanced.

11. In the Advanced Security Settings For dialog box, click Add.

12. In the Select Users, Computers, Or Groups dialog box, type the user's logon account name and then click Check Names. If the name is shown correctly, click OK.

13. In the Permissions Entry For dialog box, select This Folder, Subfolders And Files under Apply Onto and then select Allow for Full Control. Click OK.

> **Caution**   In the Entry For dialog box, Apply These Permissions To Objects And/Or Containers Within This Container Only is not selected by default. Do not select this option. If you do, permissions will not be set correctly. For example, if this option is selected, a user logging on would see a specific error related to not being able to read the contents of the Application Data\Identities folder. If a user sees such an error during logon, you need to open the Advanced Security Settings For dialog box, select the user name, and click Edit. You then clear Apply These Permissions To Objects And/Or Containers Within This Container Only and click OK.

14. In the Advanced Security Settings For dialog box, select Replace Permission Entries On All Child Objects and then click OK. When prompted to confirm the action, click Yes.

15. Click OK.

> **Note**   If the user sees a prompt indicating that the roaming profile is not available, security permissions have not been configured correctly. Repeat steps 8 through 12 and ensure that you select Replace Permission Entries On All Child Objects.

Limiting Profile Size and Included Folders

User profiles can grow very large, and sometimes when you allow roaming you'll want to limit their size or the folders they include. A key reason for doing this is to save space on the server storing the profiles, but limiting profile size and included folders can also speed up the logon and logoff processes. Don't forget that you can also redirect some of the profile folders, such as My Documents and Application Data, so that they are connected via shares rather than moved around the network in the user's profile. Limiting the profile size in this case might not be necessary.

Limiting Profile Size

If you limit profile size, any user who exceeds the profile limit sees this warning message when she tries to log off: "You have exceeded your profile storage space. Before you can log off, you need to move some items from your profile to network or local storage." The warning dialog box includes a list of files in her profile and provides details on her current profile size and the maximum allowed profile size. The user cannot log off until she deletes files and thereby reduces the size of her profile to within the permitted limits.

To limit the size of user profiles for a site, domain, or OU, follow these steps:

1. Access the GPO with which you want to work. Access User Configuration\
   Administrative Templates\System\User Profiles.

2. Double-click Limit Profile Size, and then select Enabled, as shown in Figure 7-5.

Figure 7-5   Limiting the profile to a specific maximum size and configure notification

3. If a user exceeds the profile limit and tries to log off, she sees the standard warning message. To display a different warning message at logoff, type the text of the message in the Custom Message box.

4. With this policy setting enabled, the default maximum profile size is 30 MB (30,000 KB). If you redirect profile data folders, such as My Documents and Application Data, to network shares, this default value might suffice. If you do not redirect profile data folders, this default value will, in most cases, be much too small. Either way, you should carefully consider what the profile limit should be and then use the Max Profile Size combo box to set the appropriate limit (in kilobytes).

5. By default, global settings are stored in the Ntuser.dat file in a user's profile; the size of the Ntuser.dat file does not count toward the user's profile limit. If you want to include the file size of the Ntuser.dat file in the profile limit, select Include Registry In File List.

6. By default, users see a warning about profile size only at logoff and are then given the opportunity to remove files from their profile. If you want to notify users whenever they exceed their profile storage space, select Notify User When Profile Storage Space Is Exceeded and then use the Remind User Every X Minutes combo box to determine how often the reminder is displayed.

> **Tip** Notifying users that they've exceeded the profile limit can be helpful, but repeatedly reminding them of this can be annoying. Therefore, if you want to notify users, do so infrequently, such as once every 120 minutes.

7. Click OK.

Limiting Folders Included in Profiles

Another way to limit the user's profile size is to exclude folders and prevent them from roaming with the user's profile. As discussed previously, folders under %SystemDrive%\Documents and Settings\%UserName%\Local Settings do not roam. If you want to exclude other folders, you can specify this in policy by completing the following steps:

1. Access the GPO you want to work with. Access User Configuration\Administrative Templates\System\User Profiles.

2. Double-click Exclude Directories In Roaming Profile and then select Enabled, as shown in Figure 7-6.

Figure 7-6   Preventing specific folders from roaming by entering the folder name in a semicolon-separated list

3. Specify the folders that should not roam by entering them in the appropriate box. When you specify multiple folders to exclude, they must be separated by a semicolon. Always type folder names relative to the root of the profile, which is %SystemDrive%\Documents and Settings\%UserName%. For example, if you want to exclude two folders on the desktop called Dailies and Old, type **Desktop\Dailies;Desktop\Old**.

4. Click OK.

Redirecting User Profile Folders and Data

In many organizations, workers use or have access to more than one computer on a daily basis. They might have both a portable computer and a PC in their office. They might have a PC in their office and log on to other computers to do development or test work. They might have to log on to another user's computer while theirs are being repaired, or they might check out a loaner before traveling to a remote office. Whatever the reason, ensuring that users have consistent access to their data is essential, and this is where redirected folders come in handy. Not only do redirected folders make it possible for users to consistently access their data regardless of the computer they use to log on to the network, but redirected folders also make the administrator's job easier by providing a centralized repository for user profile folders and data that can be more consistently managed and more easily backed up. The key reason for this is that with redirected folders, user data resides on a central server or servers rather than on individual user computers.

Understanding Folder Redirection

As discussed previously in "User Profiles and Group Policy," redirected folders allow for seamless redirection of folders and data that would otherwise be a part of a user's profile. In the case of roaming profiles, redirected folders reduce network traffic during logon and logoff because the redirected folders do not need to be retrieved or updated, which also can speed up logon and logoff. So, in a sense, users and administrators get the best of both worlds. Users get better access to their data, experience faster logon and logoff, and have fewer profile-related problems overall. Administrators get centralized management and better control over user data, which in turn makes the data easier to backup and restore.

You can configure folder redirection for domain users at the domain or OU level through User Configuration settings. As Figure 7-7 shows, you can redirect the following user profile folders:

- **Application Data**   The per-user data store for applications under %SystemDrive%\ Documents and Settings\%UserName%\Application Data rather than the per-computer data store for applications under %SystemDrive%\Documents and Settings\%UserName%\Local Settings\Application Data. Many applications have per-user data stores, which can grow very large. With Office, the per-user data store contains the user's custom dictionaries, address book, and more, so it often makes sense to have a single Application Data folder for all the computers a user logs on to.

- **Desktop**   The user's complete desktop including the configuration settings, shortcuts, and any files or folders stored on the desktop. Users often store files and folders on their desktop, so it often makes sense to redirect their desktop data as well as their My Documents data. With a roaming profile, redirecting the desktop also ensures that any desktop shortcuts and setting preferences, such as wallpaper and the quick access toolbar, remain when a user moves from computer to computer. As long as a shortcut points to a valid location, such as a file in a user's profile folder or on a network share, it will work. For example, if the user has a shortcut to a document stored in My Documents, the shortcut will work. On the other hand, a shortcut to a document in a D drive folder, which is only on the user's laptop, will not work.

- **My Documents**   The complete contents of My Documents including all files and folders. By default, all automatically created subfolders are included in this folder. You do have the option of excluding My Pictures, but all other subfolders of My Documents are redirected, including My Data Sources, My Deliveries, My DVDs, My eBooks, My Music, My Received Files, My Videos, My Virtual Machines, and My Web Sites.

■ **Start Menu**   The complete Start menu including the Programs menu and its related menu items, shortcuts pinned to the Start menu, and any applications in the Startup folder. You might want to redirect the Start menu when, for example, users access applications over the network or you have identically configured workstations deployed throughout a department or office. With redirection, you can be certain that users have access to the appropriate applications on their Start menus.

> **Note**   Unlike other types of folder redirection, Start menu redirection does not copy the contents of a user's local Start menu. Instead, users are directed to a standard Start menu that the administrator previously created and stored on a server.

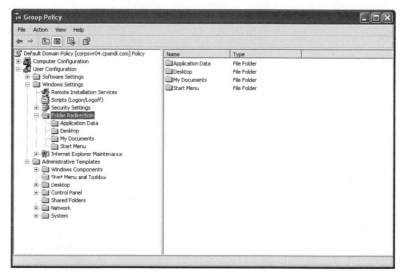

Figure 7-7   Folder redirection

No other user profile folders can be redirected. This means the following user profile folders cannot be redirected:

■ NetHood

■ PrintHood

■ My Recent Documents

■ SendTo

■ Templates

Behind the scenes, redirected folders are connected via network shares. You should consider several other configuration options whenever you redirect folders:

- **Using offline files**   Redirected folders aren't available for offline use by default. Users can make files available offline by right-clicking a file in My Documents or another folder and selecting Make Available Offline. Administrators also can configure offline file usage on the server-stored shared folder. Right-click the share and then select Properties. In the Properties dialog box, click the Sharing tab and then click Caching. Select All Files And Programs That Users Open From The Share Will Be Automatically Available Offline, and then click OK twice. For more information, see Chapter 37 in *Microsoft Windows Server 2003 Inside Out*.

- **Using shadow copies**   Shadow copies of shared folders make it easier to recover previous versions of files and restore accidentally deleted files. If you configure shadow copies on the file shares associated with the redirected folders, users have access to previous versions of all their data files and folders. This allows them to go back and recover files on their own without an administrator's help. For more information, see Chapter 22 in *Microsoft Windows Server 2003 Inside Out*.

Configuring Folder Redirection

Folder redirection is configured under User Configuration\Windows Settings\Folder Redirection. There are separate policy settings for Application Data, Desktop, My Documents, and Start Menu. These can be configured in several ways. If you don't want to redirect a particular folder for the selected site, domain, or OU, you can use the Not Configured setting to disable redirection of the selected folder in the site, domain, or OU whose GPO you are currently working with.

If you want to redirect a particular folder for a designated site, domain, or OU, you can use one of two top-level settings:

- **Basic**   Used to redirect affected users to the same base location
- **Advanced**   Used to redirect affected users according to security group membership

The sections that follow discuss how these top-level settings and their related options can be used in various scenarios.

Using Basic Folder Redirection

The Basic setting is used to redirect all users in a site, domain, or OU to the same base location. Basic redirection is primarily for small organizations or organizations whose OU structure is based on physical location—for example, a small business group or department that is autonomous might want to use basic redirection. An organization in which employees in an OU are in the same physical location might also want to use basic redirection.

To configure basic folder redirection, follow these steps:

1. Access the GPO with which you want to work. Access User Configuration\
    Windows Settings\Folder Redirection.

2. The four folders that can be redirected are listed separately. Right-click the folder
    you want to redirect, and then select Properties.

3. In the Settings list, choose Basic - Redirect Everyone's Folder To The Same
    Location, as shown in Figure 7-8.

Figure 7-8   Configuring basic folder redirection

4. Under Target Folder Location, choose one of the following options:

    ❑   **Redirect To The User's Home Directory**   Applies only to redirection of a
        user's My Documents Folder. If you have configured the user's home
        folder in her account properties, you can use this setting to redirect the My
        Documents folder to the same location as the home folder. For example, if
        the user's home drive is X, the network drive X and the My Documents
        folder will point to the same location (as set in the user's domain account
        properties).

> **Caution**   Use this setting only if the home folder has already been cre-
> ated. If there is no home folder, this option is ignored and the folder is not
> redirected.

    ❑   **Create A Folder For Each User Under The Root Path**   Appends the user's
        name to a designated network share. Individual user folders then become
        subfolders of the designated network share. For example, if you want the
        My Documents folder to be redirected to \\NYServer08\UserData, this

folder will contain subfolders for each user, based on the user's account name (%UserName%), and the user's My Documents data will be stored in the appropriate subfolder. This option is not available with redirection of the Start menu.

❏ **Redirect To The Following Location** Allows you to specify a root path to a file share and folder location for each user. If you do not include a user-specific environment variable, all the users are redirected to the same folder. If you add %UserName% to the path, you can create individual folders for each user, as in the previous option.

> **Note** For classrooms, kiosks, and some office settings, you might want to ensure that all users in an OU or all users who are members of a particular security group have exactly the same folder. In this case, you can redirect to the same folder location. For example, if you want everyone logging on to a classroom computer to have the same Start menu and Desktop even though they use different logon accounts, you can do this by redirecting the Start menu and Desktop to a specific folder. To ensure that only administrators can make changes to the Start menu and Desktop, you can change the security on the redirected folders so that the Administrators groups has Full Control and the Authenticated Users group (or a specific security group) has Read access only.

❏ **Redirect To The Local User Profile Location** Causes the default location of the user's profile to be used as the location for the user data. This is the default configuration if no redirection policies are enabled. If you use this option, the folders are not redirected to a network share and you essentially undo folder redirection.

5. Under Root Path, enter the root path to use, as necessary. If you chose Create A Folder For Each User Under The Root Path, you can enter \\NYServer08\ UserData to redirect the selected folder to a user-specific folder under \\NYServer08\UserData.

6. Any necessary folders and subfolders are created automatically by Windows the next time an affected user logs on. Any currently logged-on user must then log off and log back on. By default, users are granted exclusive access to their redirected data and the contents of the existing folder are moved across the network to the new location the next time they log on. To change these or other configuration behaviors, click the Settings tab and then configure additional settings, as discussed in the "Configuring Setup, Removal, and Preference Settings for Redirection" section in this chapter.

7. Click OK.

Using Advanced Folder Redirection

The Advanced setting is used to redirect user data based on security group membership. If you select this option, you can set an alternative target folder location for each security group you want to configure. For example, you can redirect My Documents separately for the Sales, Engineering, and Customer Service groups. Sales users can have their My Documents redirected to \\NYServer12\Sales. Engineering users can have their My Documents redirected to \\NYServer04\Engineering. Customer Service users can have their My Documents redirected to \\NYServer02\Services. As with basic redirection, the designated folder contains subfolders for each user.

In most cases, the advanced configuration scales better for the large enterprise because it allows you to zero in on security groups within sites, domains, or OUs. Thus rather than assigning a single location for all users within an OU, you can assign each security group within an OU a separate location. However, keep in mind that the group policy you are working with applies only to user accounts that are in the container for which you are configuring Group Policy. So if you set a redirection policy for a group that isn't defined in the site, domain, or OU you are working with, folder redirection is not applied.

To configure advanced redirection of user profiles, follow these steps:

1. Access the GPO with which you want to work. Access User Configuration\Windows Settings\Folder Redirection.

2. The four folders that can be redirected are listed separately. Right-click the folder you want to redirect, and then select Properties.

3. In the Settings list, choose Advanced - Specify Locations For Various User Groups, as shown in Figure 7-9. The Target tab is updated so that you can configure redirection settings by security group membership.

Figure 7-9 Configuring targeting for individual security groups within a site, domain, or OU

4. Click Add to display the Specify Group And Location dialog box (Figure 7-10).

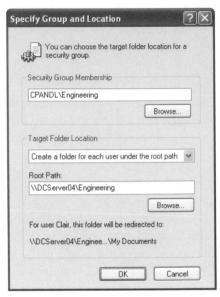

Figure 7-10   Specifying the security group membership and target folder settings

5. Click Browse to display the Select Group dialog box. Type the name of a group account in the selected container, and then click Check Names. When a single match is found, the dialog box is automatically updated as appropriate and the entry is underlined. When you click OK, the group is added to the Security Group Membership list in the Specify Group And Location dialog box.

6. Under Target Folder Location, choose one of the following options:

    ❏ **Redirect To The User's Home Directory**   Applies only to redirection of a user's My Documents Folder. If you have configured the user's home folder in his account properties, you can use this setting to redirect the My Documents folder to the same location as the home folder. For example, if the user's home drive is X, the network drive X and the My Documents folder will point to the same location (as set in the user's domain account properties).

> **Caution**   Use this setting only if the home folder has already been created. If there is no home folder, this option is ignored and the folder is not redirected.

    ❏ **Create A Folder For Each User Under The Root Path**   Appends the user's name to a designated network share. Individual user folders then become subfolders of the designated network share. For example, if you want the My Documents folder to be redirected to \\NYServer08\UserData, this folder will contain subfolders for each user, based on the user's account name (%UserName%), and the user's My Documents data will be stored in the appropriate subfolder. This option is not available with redirection of the Start menu.

❏ **Redirect To The Following Location** Allows you to specify a root path to a file share and folder location for each user. If you do not include a user-specific environment variable, all the users are redirected to the same folder. If you add %UserName% to the path, you can create individual folders for each user as in the previous option.

❏ **Redirect To The Local User Profile Location** Causes the default location of the user's profile to be used as the location for the user data. This is the default configuration if no redirection policies are enabled. If you use this option, the folders are not redirected to a network share and you essentially undo folder redirection.

7. Under Root Path, type the root path to use as necessary. If you chose Create A Folder For Each User Under The Root Path, you can type **\\NYServer08\ UserData** to redirect the selected folder to a user-specific folder under \\NYServer08\UserData.

8. When you are finished configuring these options, click OK. You can then repeat steps 4 through 7 to configure redirection of the selected folder for other groups.

9. Any necessary folders and subfolders are created automatically by Windows the next time an affected user logs on. Any currently logged on user must log off and then log back on. By default, users are granted exclusive access to their redirected data and the contents of the existing folder are moved across the network to the new location the next time they log on. To change these or other configuration behaviors, click the Settings tab and then configure additional settings as discussed in the next section.

10. Click OK.

Configuring Setup, Removal, and Preference Settings for Redirection

When you are configuring folder redirection, the Settings tab (Figure 7-11) provides additional configuration options. In the default configuration shown, several things happen the next time a user logs on to the network:

1. Any necessary folders and subfolders are created automatically.

2. Folder security is set so that only the user has access.

3. The contents of the existing folder are moved across the network to the new location. If you redirected My Documents, My Pictures is copied as well.

4. If you later stop redirecting the folder, the data stays in the shared folder and the user continues to access the data in this location.

Figure 7-11   Specifying additional redirection settings

You can control the redirection behavior by modifying the settings:

■ **Grant The User Exclusive Rights To**   When this option is selected, any necessary folders and subfolders are created automatically the next time a user logs on. The folder security is set so that the user has exclusive access. This means Windows creates the directory and gives the user Full Control to the folder.

When this option is not selected, any necessary folders and subfolders are created automatically the next time a user logs on. The existing security on the folder is not changed. Because of inheritance, the newly created folder has the same permissions as the parent folder.

> **Note**   Through Group Policy, you have two basic configuration options for redirected folder security. You can tell Windows to either give the user exclusive access or accept the inherited security permissions of the parent folder. With exclusive access, all other users (even administrators) are blocked from accessing the redirected folders and their data. One way an administrator can gain access to a redirected folder is to take ownership of it. If you want the user and administrators to have access, you can use a technique described in Microsoft Knowledge Base Article 288991. Basically, you clear Grant The User Exclusive Access and then configure permissions on the redirected folder as follows:
>
> ■ Authenticated Users have Create Folders/Append Data, Read Permissions, Read Attributes and Read Extended Attributes for This folder only
>
> ■ Administrators, System, and Creator Owner have Full Control for This folder, subfolders and files

- **Move The Contents Of**   When this option is selected, the next time the user logs on the contents of the existing folder are moved across the network to the new location. If a user has a local profile on multiple machines, the contents are moved at logon on a per-computer basis.

  When this option is not selected, the existing folder contents are copied across the network rather than moved. This means a local copy of the folder still exists. On a portable computer, this might seem like a good way to ensure that a local copy of data exists, but it is generally better to move the data and then configure offline file caching.

- **Leave The Folder In The New Location When Policy Is Removed**   When this option is selected, if you later stop redirecting the folder or the user account is moved out of the GPO for which redirecting is configured, the data stays in the shared folder. The user continues to access the data in this location.

- **Redirect The Folder Back**   When this option is selected, if you later stop redirecting the folder or the user account is moved out of the GPO for which redirection is configured, a copy of the data is sent to the user's profile location when the user logs off the network. With a roaming profile, this means that a copy is sent to the profile server when the user logs off the network. If the user has a local profile, a copy is sent to the local computer when she logs off (and if she logs on to multiple computers, each will eventually get a copy). If the user account is moved to a GPO where redirection is configured, the data is moved according to the redirection settings.

- **Make My Pictures A Subfolder Of My Documents**   When this option is selected, if you redirected My Documents, My Pictures is copied as a subfolder of My Documents.

- **Do Not Specify Administrative Policy For My Pictures**   When this option is selected, if you redirected My Documents, My Pictures is not copied as a subfolder of My Documents.

Managing Computer and User Scripts

So far in this chapter, we've talked about the many ways you can work with user profiles and data within profiles to optimize the user environment. Now let's look at an additional technique for optimizing user environments that involves scripts. In Windows Server 2003, you can configure two types of scripts to help configure the desktop and user environment:

- Computer scripts, which are run at startup or shutdown
- User scripts, which are run at logon or logoff

Not only can you write these scripts as command-shell batch scripts ending with the .bat or .cmd extension, but you can also write them using the Windows Script Host (WSH). WSH is a feature of Windows Server 2003 that lets you use scripts written in a scripting language, such as Microsoft JScript (.js files) and Microsoft VBScript (.vbs files).

Working with Computer and User Scripts

Computer and user scripts can be used to perform just about any commonly run task. Startup and shutdown scripts can be used to perform any system-wide task, such as maintenance, backups, or virus checking. Logon and logoff scripts can be used to perform user-related tasks, such as launching applications, cleaning up temporary folders, setting up printers, or mapping network drives.

The three basic steps for using scripts with Group Policy are as follows:

1. Create the script, and save it with the appropriate file extension.

2. Copy the script you want to use to an accessible and appropriate folder so that it can be used with Group Policy.

3. Assign the script as a startup, shutdown, logon, or logoff script in Group Policy.

To run a startup or shutdown script, a computer must be in the site, domain, or OU linked to a GPO that contains the script. Similarly, to run a logon or logoff script, a user must be in the site, domain, or OU linked to a GPO that contains the script.

Most scripts are easy to create. For example, with command-shell batch scripts, you can connect users to shared printers and drives with the *NET USE* command. Let's say that at logon you want to connect the user to a printer named CustSvcsPrntr on a print server called PrntSvr03. To do this, you type the following command in a Notepad file:

```
net use \\prntsvr03\custsvcprntr /persistent:yes
```

You then save the script with the .bat extension. Next you copy this file to an accessible folder so that it can be used with Group Policy and you assign it as a logon script. From then on, any user logging on to the affected site, domain, or OU can run the logon script and be connected to the printer.

> **Note**   You don't have to copy a script to a folder within Group Policy. However, scripts are more easily managed if you copy them to the appropriate folder in Group Policy and then assign them as the appropriate type of script.

Configuring Computer Startup and Shutdown Scripts

You can assign startup and shutdown scripts as part of a group policy. In this way, all computers in a site, domain, or OU run the scripts automatically when they're started or shut down.

To configure a script that should be used during computer startup or shutdown, follow these steps:

1. Copy the startup or shutdown script you want to use to a network share or other folder that is easily accessible over the network.

2. Start the Group Policy Object Editor. In the Group Policy Management Console (GPMC), right-click the GPO you want to modify and select Edit.

3. In the Computer Configuration node, double-click the Windows Settings folder, and then click Scripts.

4. To work with startup scripts, right-click Startup, and then select Properties. Or right-click Shutdown, and then select Properties to work with shutdown scripts.

5. Any previously defined startup or shutdown scripts are listed in order of priority, as shown in Figure 7-12. The topmost script has the highest priority. The priority is important because by default startup and shutdown scripts do not all run at the same time. Instead, they run one at a time (synchronously) in order of priority.

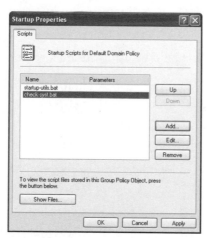

Figure 7-12   A list of current startup or shutdown scripts by order of priority

6. To change the priority of an existing script, select the script in the Script For list, and then click the Up or Down button as appropriate to change the priority order.

7. To change the parameters associated with a script, select the script in the Script For list, and then click Edit. You can then change the script name and the optional parameters to pass to the script.

8. To define an additional startup or shutdown script, click Add. This displays the Add A Script dialog box (Figure 7-13). Click Browse, and in the Browse dialog box, find the script you want to use and then click Open. The script is copied to the Machine\Scripts\Startup or Machine\Scripts\Shutdown folder for the related policy. By default, policies are stored by GUID in the %SystemRoot%\ Sysvol\Domain\Policies folder on domain controllers.

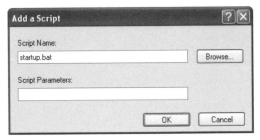

Figure 7-13 Specifying a script and defining optional parameters

9. To delete a script, select the script in the Script For list, and then click Remove.

Configuring User Logon and Logoff Scripts

You can assign logon and logoff scripts as part of a group policy. In this way, all users in a site, domain, or OU run the scripts automatically when they're logging on or logging off.

To configure a script that should be using during logon or logoff, follow these steps:

1. Copy the logon or logoff script you want to use to a network share or other folder that is easily accessible over the network.

2. Start the Group Policy Object Editor. In the GPMC, right-click the Group Policy Object you want to modify, and then select Edit.

3. In the User Configuration node, double-click the Windows Settings folder, and then click Scripts.

4. To work with logon scripts, right-click Logon, and then select Properties. Or right-click Logoff, and then select Properties to work with logoff scripts.

5. Any previously defined logon or logoff scripts are listed in order of priority, as shown in Figure 7-14. The topmost script has the highest priority. The priority is important because logon and logoff scripts are started in order of priority by default. Unlike startup and shutdown scripts, however, logon and logoff scripts are not synchronized and can run simultaneously, so if you've configured multiple logon or logoff scripts, they can all run at the same time.

Figure 7-14 Current logon or logoff scripts are listed in order of priority

6. To change the priority of an existing script, select the script in the Script For list, and then click the Up or Down button as appropriate to change the order.

7. To change the parameters associated with a script, select the script in the Script For list, and then click Edit. You can then change the script name and the optional parameters to pass to the script.

8. To define an additional logon or logoff script, click Add. In the Add A Script dialog box (Figure 7-15), click Browse. In the Browse dialog box, find the script you want to use, and then click Open. The script is copied to the User\Scripts\Logon or User\Scripts\Logoff folder for the related policy. By default, policies are stored by GUID in the %SystemRoot%\Sysvol\Domain\Policies folder on domain controllers.

Figure 7-15 Specifying a script and defining optional parameters

9. To delete a script, select the script in the Script For list, and then click Remove.

Controlling Script Visibility

When you configure and work with computer and user scripts, you should keep several things in mind. Computer and user scripts are not visible to the user when they run. This prevents users from canceling execution of the script and also ensures that the actual tasks performed by the script are hidden.

You can make scripts visible to users when they are running by enabling the following policy settings as appropriate:

- Run Startup Scripts Visible under Computer Configuration\Administrative Templates\System\Scripts.

- Run Shutdown Scripts Visible under Computer Configuration\Administrative Templates\System\Scripts.

- Run Logon Scripts Visible under User Configuration\Administrative Templates\ System\Scripts.

- Run Logoff Scripts Visible under User Configuration\Administrative Templates\ System\Scripts.

Controlling Script Timeout

By default, Windows limits the total time allowed for scripts to run to 10 minutes. If a logon, logoff, startup, or shutdown script has not completed running after 10 minutes (600 seconds), the system stops processing the script and records an error event in the event logs.

You can modify the timeout interval by completing the following steps:

1. Access the GPO with which you want to work. Access Computer Configuration\ Administrative Templates\System\Scripts.

2. Double-click Maximum Wait Time For Group Policy Scripts, and then select Enabled, as shown in Figure 7-16.

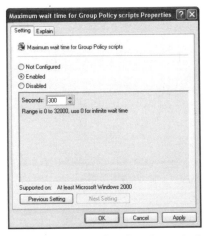

Figure 7-16   Configuring the wait time for computer and user scripts

3. In the Seconds combo box, specify the wait time to use in seconds. In the rare case in which you want Windows to wait indefinitely for scripts to run, use a value of 0.

> **Note**   Think carefully about the wait time. It is extremely important in ensuring that scripts run as expected. If you set the wait time too short, some tasks might not be able to complete, which can cause problems. If you set the wait time too long, the user might have to wait too long to get access to the system.

4. Click OK.

Controlling Script Execution and Run Technique

Computer and user scripts run in slightly different ways. By default, Windows coordinates the running of scripts so that startup scripts run one at a time, in order of priority. This means the system waits for each startup to complete before it runs the next startup script. If you want to allow startup scripts to run simultaneously, which might allow startup to complete faster, you can enable Run Startup Scripts Asynchronously under Computer Configuration\Administrative Templates\System\Scripts.

By default, logon and logoff scripts are not synchronized and can run simultaneously. Thus, if you've configured multiple logon or logoff scripts, they all run at the same time. This setting is designed to ensure that there is little or no delay in displaying the desktop during logon or closing the desktop during logoff. If you'd rather ensure that all logon scripts are complete before allowing users to access the desktop, you can configure logon scripts to run synchronously (one at a time). To do this, enable Run Logon Scripts Asynchronously under Computer Configuration\Administrative Templates\System\Scripts or under User Configuration\Administrative Templates\System\Scripts. By default, the setting in Computer Configuration has precedence over the setting in User Configuration.

Summary

As you've seen in this chapter, you can manage user settings and data in many ways. Through the use of roaming profiles, you can ensure that users have access to their global settings and essential data from anywhere on the network. Not only does this ensure that a user's desktop has a consistent look and feel regardless of the computer he is using, but it also ensures that he can access his My Documents folder, user-specific application data, and desktop settings.

A key drawback of a roaming profile is that a user's data is moved across the network at logon and logoff. You can reduce network traffic during logon and logoff and speed up logon and logoff by using folder redirection. Redirected folders allow for seamless redirection of folders and data that would otherwise be a part of a user's profile, including the Application Data, My Documents, Start Menu, and Desktop folders. Because folders are redirected to a network share, administrators get centralized management and better control over user data, which in turn makes the data easier to back up and restore. Through policy, you can optimize the way profiles are used in many ways.

Windows Server 2003 also allows you to configure two types of scripts to help configure the desktop and user environment: computer scripts, which are run at startup or shutdown, and user scripts, which are run at logon or logoff. Computer and user scripts are also defined in policy.

Chapter 8

Maintaining Internet Explorer Configurations

In this chapter:

Customizing the Internet Explorer Interface. 290
Customizing URLs, Favorites, and Links 295
Configuring Global Default Programs 299
Optimizing Connection and Proxy Settings 301
Enhancing Internet Explorer Security. 306
Configuring Additional Policies for Internet Options 313
Summary. 316

Microsoft® Internet Explorer is a highly configurable browser. Through Group Policy, you can optimize just about every aspect of Internet Explorer configuration to improve the user experience, gain more control over security and privacy, and make your job as an administrator easier. Not only can you customize the general look and feel of the browser for your environment, but you can also dig deep into its internal configuration to specify exactly how to handle connections, proxies, cookies, add-ons, and many other aspects of security.

Related Information

- For more information on Attachment Manager and other Microsoft Windows® components, see Chapter 6.

- For more information on kiosks and other types of custom environments, see Chapter 12.

Customizing the Internet Explorer Interface

The first area of Internet Explorer customization we'll look at is the browser interface. You can add custom titles to the title bar, define custom logos that replace the Internet Explorer logo, and create custom toolbars that replace the existing toolbar.

Customizing the Title Bar Text

Using the Browser Title policy, you can customize the text that appears in the title bar of Internet Explorer. By default, the title bar displays the title of the current page and the name of the browser, such as "Corporate Home Page–Microsoft Internet Explorer." When you add a custom title, you can add "provided by" details that list your organization, as in "Corporate Home Page–Microsoft Internet Explorer provided by City Power & Light."

 Note   Using a custom title is a subtle way to remind employees that they are using a business resource and not a personal resource. The custom title also appears in Microsoft Outlook® Express if this application is installed and used in your organization.

You can add a custom title to Internet Explorer by completing the following steps:

1. Access User Configuration\Windows Settings\Internet Explorer Maintenance\ Browser User Interface in Group Policy, and then double-click Browser Title. This displays the Browser Title dialog box, shown in Figure 8-1.

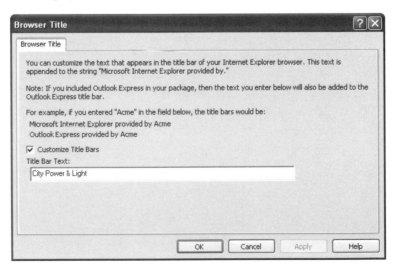

Figure 8-1   Specifying a custom title

2. Select Customize Title Bars, and then type the custom title in the Title Bar Text box.

3. Click OK.

Customizing Logos

Using the Custom Logo policy, you can replace the standard Internet Explorer logos with ones specifically created for your organization. This can serve to brand the browser for your organization as well as subtly remind employees that they are using a business resource and not a personal resource. One of two standard logos is displayed in the upper-right corner in Internet Explorer:

- **Static logo**   Displayed when the browser isn't performing an action
- **Animated logo**   Displayed when the browser is downloading pages or performing other actions

The logos must adhere to exact specifications, so you should ideally work with your organization's art department to create the necessary image files. You need two versions of each logo: one that is 22 × 22 pixels and one that is 38 × 38 pixels. The logos must be saved as bitmap images and use either 256 or 16 colors. Images in 256 colors should be indexed to the Windows halftone palette; 16-color images should be indexed to the 16-color Windows palette. The animated bitmap should consist of numbered bitmaps that are vertically stacked into one bitmap. The first bitmap appears static when no action is taking place, and the remaining bitmaps appear in sequence when the browser is in use, producing the animation effect.

Note   In the Internet Explorer Administration Kit (IEAK), you'll find two tools that can help you with the logos. The first is the Animated Bitmap Creator (Makebmp.exe), which you can use to create the animated logo. The second is the Animated Bitmap Previewer (Animbmp.exe), which you can use to test the animated logo to make sure it is displayed as expected. The IEAK is available for download from *http://www.microsoft.com/windows/ieak/downloads/default.mspx*.

Tip   When you finish creating the image files, you should test the files on your local system before using Group Policy to update computers in a specific site, domain, or organizational unit (OU). Once you tell Group Policy about the logo files, the files become part of Group Policy and are stored within Group Policy. Because the files are imported before use, they don't need to reside on the local computer initially. In fact, it might be best to put the logos on a network drive so that you can test them locally and then incorporate them into Group Policy using the same file paths.

You can add custom logos to Internet Explorer by completing the following steps:

1. Access User Configuration\Windows Settings\Internet Explorer Maintenance\Browser User Interface in Group Policy, and then double-click Custom Logo. This displays the Custom Logo dialog box, shown in Figure 8-2.

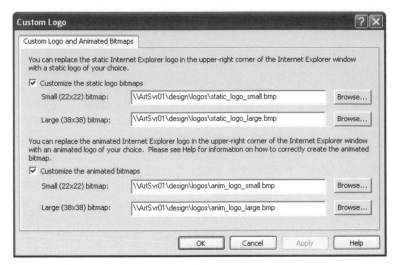

Figure 8-2   The Custom Logo dialog box

2. If you want to set a static logo, select Customize The Static Logo Bitmaps. In the Small (22 × 22) Bitmap box, type the path to the small logo that you want to use or click Browse to find the image you want to use. In the Large (38 × 38) Bitmap box, type the path to the large logo you want to use or click Browse to find the image you want to use.

Note   The images must be exactly sized or they won't be imported into Group Policy. If you see a warning message that says the specified bitmap is too large, you must select a different logo file.

If you want to set an animated logo, select Customize The Animated Bitmaps. In the Small (22 × 22) Bitmap box, type the path to the small animated logo you want to use or click Browse to find the image you want to use. In the Large (38 × 38) Bitmap box, type the path to the large animated logo you want to use or click Browse to find the image you want to use.

3. Click OK. The logo files are imported and stored in Group Policy.

Customizing Buttons and Toolbars

The Internet Explorer toolbar is completely customizable; you can add new buttons to the toolbar to launch applications, run scripts, and perform other tasks. Custom toolbar buttons have four required components:

- **Toolbar caption**   The ToolTip text to display when the pointer is over the button.

- **Toolbar action**   The script file or executable that you want to execute when the button is clicked. Script files can be batch files (.cmd or .bat) or Windows Script Host (WSH) files (.js, .vbs, and so on). With both executables and scripts, you need to know the complete path to the related file.

- **Toolbar color icon file**   A color icon file saved with an .ico extension that contains images for when the toolbar button is active. The icon file should contain three separate bitmaps: one 20 × 20 256-color, one 20 × 20 16-color, and one 16 × 16 16-color. The bitmaps must be indexed to either the 256-color Windows halftone palette or the 16-color Windows palette as appropriate.

- **Toolbar grayscale icon file**   A grayscale icon file saved with an .ico extension that contains images for when the toolbar button is in the default or inactive state. The icon file should contain three separate bitmaps: one 20 × 20 grayscale image using the 256-color Windows halftone palette, one 20 × 20 grayscale image using the 16-color Windows palette, and one 16 × 16 grayscale image using the 16-color Windows palette.

As part of your pre-rollout planning, you should consider how the button will be implemented and who will design the necessary icon files. Because your custom button will be available to many users within a site, domain, or OU, think carefully about placement of any needed scripts or executables. The file path you use should be accessible to all users who will be affected by the policy you are creating. If necessary, you can use environment variables, such as *%SystemDrive%*, to ensure that file paths are consistent for different users. You can also use network file paths, provided they are automatically mapped for users.

You must also work closely with your organization's art department to create the necessary icon files. The different styles of icons are used when Internet Explorer and the button itself are in various states. The large (20 × 20) icons are used when Internet Explorer is in the default state. The small (16 × 16) icons are used when Internet Explorer is in full-screen mode (accessed by pressing F11 with the browser window active). Color icons are used when a button is active. Grayscale icons are used when a button is in the default state.

When you are ready to proceed, you can add a custom button to the Internet Explorer toolbar by completing the following steps:

1. Access User Configuration\Windows Settings\Internet Explorer Maintenance\ Browser User Interface in Group Policy, and then double-click Browser Toolbar Customizations. This displays the Browser Toolbar Customizations dialog box.

2. On the Buttons panel, click Add to display the Browser Toolbar Button Information dialog box (Figure 8-3).

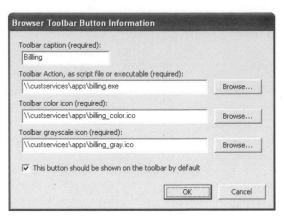

Figure 8-3   Defining the required elements for the custom button

3. In the Toolbar Caption (Required) text box, type the button caption. Keep the caption short—no more than one or two words. The button caption appears as a ToolTip when the mouse pointer is over the button.

4. In the Toolbar Action, As Script File Or Executable (Required) text box, type the path to the script or executable file that you want to run when the button is clicked. If you don't know the file path, click Browse to find the file.

5. In the Toolbar Color Icon (Required) text box, type the path to the color icon file that you created for the button or click Browse to find the file.

6. In the Toolbar Grayscale Icon (Required) text box, type the path to the grayscale icon file that you created for the button or click Browse to find the file.

7. If you want the custom button to be displayed on the toolbar by default, select This Button Should Be Shown On the Toolbar By Default.

> **Note**   If you don't display the button by default, users will have to display the button manually using the Customize Toolbar dialog box. This dialog box is accessed in Internet Explorer by choosing View, Toolbars, Customize.

8. Click OK. Repeat steps 2 through 7 to add other custom buttons.

If you later decide not to use the button, you can remove it by completing the following steps:

1. Access User Configuration\Windows Settings\Internet Explorer Maintenance\ Browser User Interface in Group Policy, and then double-click Browser Toolbar Customizations. This displays the Browser Toolbar Customizations dialog box.

2. On the Buttons panel, click the entry for the button you want to delete, and then click Remove.

3. Click OK.

Customizing URLs, Favorites, and Links

Through policy, you can customize two types of URLs that are available in Internet Explorer:

- **Important URLs**   URLs used for the browser home page, support page, and search page

- **Favorites and links**   Additional URLs made available to users on the Favorites menu

Both types of URLs can help users save time and be more productive. By customizing the important URLs, you can provide quick ways for users to access your organization's home page, get support, and find what they are looking for. By creating custom lists of favorites and links, you can make it easier for users to find internal and external resources that they frequently use.

Customizing Home, Search, and Support URLs

Customizing the Internet Explorer home, search, and support URLs will make users' lives a bit easier. After all, these options put the key resources that users need on a daily basis at their fingertips.

You can configure the Internet Explorer home page, search, and support URLs by completing the following steps:

1. Access Group Policy for the system you want to work with. Then access User Configuration\Windows Settings\Internet Explorer Maintenance\URLs.

2. In the right pane, double-click Important URLs. As shown in Figure 8-4, you can specify a custom home page, a search bar page, and an online support page.

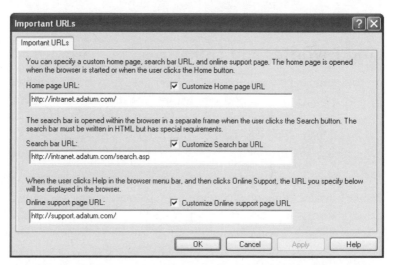

Figure 8-4   Setting custom URLs for a home page, a search bar page, and an online support page

3. To specify a home page URL, select Customize Home Page URL. In the Home Page URL text box, type the URL of the home page you want to use, such as *http://intranet.adatum.com/*. The home page URL is opened whenever the browser is started or the user clicks the Home button on the Internet Explorer toolbar.

> **Tip**   For convenience, you'll probably want to set the home page URL to the home page of your organization's intranet or to the department-level page for the OU you are working with. If your organization doesn't have an intranet, you might want to set this URL to the home page of your company's external Web site.

4. To specify a search page URL, select Customize Search Bar URL. In the Search Bar URL text box, type the URL to the search page you want to use, such as *http://intranet.adatum.com/search.asp*. The search page is opened in a side frame of the Internet Explorer window whenever a user clicks the Search button.

> **Caution**   When developing your search page, you should note two specific requirements: The search page must be formatted as HTML and should include links targeted at the main frame. If your organization already has a search page, you must create a separate version that is modified to work as a side frame.

5. To specify a support page, select Customize Online Support Page URL. In the Online Support Page URL text box, type the URL to the support page you want to use, such as *http://support.adatum.com/*. The support page is opened when a user selects Online Support from the Internet Explorer Help menu.

6. Click OK.

Customizing Favorites and Links

Internet Explorer provides several ways to access commonly used resources. In addition to browser buttons, history lists, and the like, you can use Favorites and Links lists. In Internet Explorer, you access Favorites and Links through the Favorites menu. This menu offers options that allow you to add, organize, and access favorites. Links lists are provided as a subfolder of Favorites that you can customize as well.

Through Group Policy, you can add favorites and links that make it easier for users to access commonly used online resources, such as essential documents, important forms, and corporate phone directories. This saves users time and might also increase use of these important resources. Any favorites and links you add can either replace the existing URL lists or add to them.

You can add URLs individually or you can import an existing folder containing a set of URLs you want to use. These options are discussed in the sections that follow.

Creating Individual Favorites and Links

To create favorites and links one by one, complete the following steps:

1. Access Group Policy for the resource you want to work with. Then access User Configuration\Windows Settings\Internet Explorer Maintenance\URLs.

2. In the right pane, double-click Favorites And Links. This displays the Favorites And Links dialog box (Figure 8-5). Any favorites and links you add are available to all users subject to the current policy.

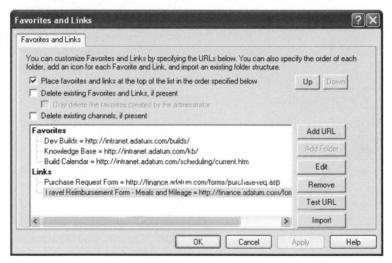

Figure 8-5   Configuring quick access links to important online resources

3. When you plan to add several favorites or links, you can create a folder to hold the options. The folder you create appears as a submenu under the Favorites menu in Internet Explorer. To create a submenu, select Favorites and then click Add Folder. In the Details dialog box, type a name for the submenu in the Name box, and then click OK.

4. To add individual menu options, select Favorites, Links, or a folder entry and then click Add URL. This again displays the Details dialog box. Type the name of the menu option, such as Purchase Request Form, and then type the URL to the resource, such as *http://finance.adatum.com/forms/purchase-req.asp*. Click OK. The entry is added to the menu or submenu you selected.

> **Tip**   To verify that you've typed the URL correctly, select the option and then click Test URL to load the selected item in Internet Explorer. If the related page appears in Internet Explorer, you typed the URL correctly. If it doesn't appear, you probably made a mistake and should edit the URL.

5. After you define the favorites and links you want to use, you can specify additional preferences for adding the items to the Favorites menu. These additional preferences include the following:

    ❑   **Place Favorites And Links At The Top Of The List In The Order Specified Below**   Places the items at the top of the menu and in the order in which you entered them in the list box. If you select this option, you can also use the Up and Down buttons to change the order of submenus and menu items in the list box.

    ❑   **Delete Existing Favorites And Links, If Present**   Removes any existing favorites and links, replacing them with the items you created. Using this option alone removes existing items created by both users and administrators.

    ❑   **Only Delete The Favorites Created By The Administrator**   Removes previous favorites and links created by the administrator but doesn't remove those created by users. This is a good option to use if you previously configured favorites and links and now want to replace those entries with your current items.

6. Click OK.

Importing Favorites and Links Lists

Another way to create Favorites and Links lists is to import an existing folder containing a set of URLs you want to use. This folder becomes a submenu of the Favorites menu in Internet Explorer.

You can create and import a folder by completing the following steps:

1. Create a folder on a network or local drive and then add URL shortcuts that point to the locations you want to be able to access. These shortcuts will become the items in the submenu you are creating. Set the names for the folder and its shortcuts as you want them to appear on the Internet Explorer Favorites menu.

2. Access User Configuration\Windows Settings\Internet Explorer Maintenance\ URLs in Group Policy, and then double-click Favorites And Links in the right pane.

3. In the Favorites And Links dialog box shown earlier in Figure 8-5, select Favorites, Links, or a folder entry, and then click Import. In the Browse For Folder dialog box, select the folder you created in step 1 and then click OK. The folder and its contents are added as a submenu of the selected item.

Caution   The import process can use only properly formatted URL shortcuts. If the folder contains other types of files or shortcuts, the folder doesn't appear as a submenu and the additional items aren't imported.

4.   When you are finished defining the favorites and links you want to use, you can specify additional preferences for these items, including the following:

❑   **Place Favorites And Links At The Top Of The List In The Order Specified Below**   Places these items at the top of the menu and in the order in which you entered them in the list box. If you select this option, you can also use the Up and Down buttons to change the order of submenus and menu items in the list box.

❑   **Delete Existing Favorites And Links, If Present**   Removes any existing favorites and links, replacing them with the items you created. Using this option alone removes existing items created by both users and administrators.

❑   **Only Delete The Favorites Created By The Administrator**   Removes previous favorites and links created by the administrator but doesn't remove those created by users. This is a good option to use if you previously configured favorites and links and now want to replace those entries with your current items.

5.   Click OK.

Configuring Global Default Programs

Windows uses certain default programs for Internet services. These programs are defined in a user's profile and can be modified through Group Policy.

You can set default programs for the following Internet services:

■   **HTML Editor**   The default HTML editor program. On systems with Microsoft Office installed, the standard options are Microsoft Word and Notepad. If Microsoft FrontPage® is installed, FrontPage will also be an option.

■   **E-mail**   The default e-mail program. On systems with Office installed, the standard options are Microsoft Outlook, Outlook Express, and MSN Hotmail®.

■   **Newsgroups**   The default Internet newsreader program. On systems with Office installed, the standard options are Outlook and Outlook Express.

■   **Internet Call**   The default network meeting program. Typically the only standard option is Microsoft NetMeeting®.

■   **Calendar**   The scheduling program used with Internet Explorer. On systems with Office installed, the only standard option is Outlook.

■   **Contact List**   The default address book program. On systems with Office installed, the standard options are Outlook and Address Book.

> **Tip** If other applications are installed on a system, additional options might be available. Also, in some cases (such as with the default HTML editor) you can select a blank value to specify that you don't want to use a default program for this service.

To set default programs through Group Policy, complete the following steps:

1. Access User Configuration\Windows Settings\Internet Explorer Maintenance\ Programs in Group Policy, and then double-click Programs in the right pane. The Programs dialog box is displayed.

2. If you want to stop using custom program settings, select Do Not Customize Program Settings and then click OK. Skip the remaining steps.

3. If you want to start using custom program settings, select Import The Current Program Settings and then click Modify Settings. This displays the Internet Properties dialog box, shown in Figure 8-6.

Figure 8-6   Specify the default programs to use or select a blank value

4. Use the selection lists provided in the Internet Programs panel to set the default Internet programs.

5. When you install additional browser software, the software might be set as the default Internet browser during installation. To have Internet Explorer check to make sure that Internet Explorer is still registered as the default Internet browser when it is started, select Internet Explorer Should Check To See Whether It Is The Default Browser.

6. Click OK twice.

Optimizing Connection and Proxy Settings

When you roll out new computers or make changes to your network, much of your time can be spent configuring connection and proxy settings. Rather than relying on an image build of a machine that might not be up to date or making setting changes manually, you can use Group Policy to roll out changes for you. This saves you time and allows you to focus on more important tasks.

Deploying Connection Settings Through Group Policy

Computers can have network connections for dial-up, broadband, and virtual private network (VPN). You configure network connections manually using the Network Connections utility in Control Panel, and you can use Group Policy to deploy new configurations (to update existing configurations when you need to make changes and to delete existing configurations and replace them with new ones).

Whenever you manage connection settings through Group Policy, you should create the necessary connections on a test system and then check them by dialing in to the network, connecting through broadband, or using VPN as necessary. Once you've verified the settings, you can import the settings into the Connection Settings policy from the test system. Be sure to import settings at the appropriate level in Group Policy. In most cases, you won't want to roll these settings out to the entire domain and instead will want to apply these settings only to the appropriate Active Directory OUs

When you work with connection settings, you should note several important caveats:

- Local area network (LAN) settings for automatic detection and proxy servers are also imported with the connection configuration settings. The address for automatic configuration scripts is not imported, however. These settings are managed with the Automatic Browser Configuration policy.

- Existing connections with the same names as the imported connections are updated with the new settings, so you don't need to delete the existing settings to make these updates. You must delete existing settings only if you think that users or other administrators have created connections that might no longer be valid and you want to make sure they are removed to prevent connectivity problems.

- When you deploy connection settings, you have the option of deleting existing connection settings. When you do this, all previous connections created by both administrators and users are permanently removed.

You can deploy connection settings through Group Policy by completing the following steps:

1. Create the necessary connections on a test system, and then check them by dialing in to the network, connecting through broadband, or using VPN as necessary.

2. Once you've verified the settings, log on to the system where you created the connection settings you want to use.

3. Access User Configuration\Windows Settings\Internet Explorer Maintenance\ Connection in Group Policy. Double-click Connection Settings in the right pane. This displays the Connection Settings dialog box, shown in Figure 8-7.

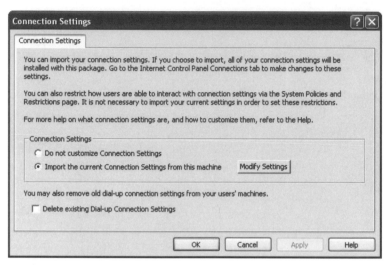

Figure 8-7 Importing connection settings from your test computer

4. Select Import The Current Connection Settings From This Machine. To view or modify the settings that will be imported, click Modify Settings and then use the Connections tab of the Internet Properties dialog box to work with the settings. The options available are the same as those on the Connections tab of the Internet Options utility.

5. If you are replacing previously configured connections, you might want to specify that existing connections should be deleted. To do this, in the Connection Settings dialog box, select Delete Existing Dial-Up Connection Settings.

6. Click OK.

As part of your connection settings rollout, you might also want to restrict the ways users can work with connection settings. You'll find the key policies for controlling access to connections and managing their settings under User Configuration\ Administrative Templates\Network\Network Connections in Group Policy. The available policies include:

- Ability To Rename LAN Connections Or Remote Access Connections Available To All Users

- Ability To Change Properties Of An All User Remote Access Connection

- Ability To Delete All User Remote Access Connections

- Ability To Enable/Disable A LAN Connection
- Ability To Rename All User Remote Access Connections
- Ability To Rename LAN Connections
- Enable Windows 2000 Network Connections Settings For Administrators
- Prohibit Access To Properties Of A LAN Connection
- Prohibit Access To Properties Of Components Of A LAN Connection
- Prohibit Access To Properties Of Components Of A Remote Access Connection
- Prohibit Access To The Advanced Settings Item On The Advanced Menu
- Prohibit Access To The New Connection Wizard
- Prohibit Access To The Remote Access Preferences Item On The Advanced Menu
- Prohibit Adding And Removing Components For A LAN Or Remote Access Connection
- Prohibit Changing Properties Of A Private Remote Access Connection
- Prohibit Connecting And Disconnecting A Remote Access Connection
- Prohibit Deletion Of Remote Access Connections
- Prohibit Enabling/Disabling Components Of A LAN Connection
- Prohibit Renaming Private Remote Access Connections
- Prohibit Tcp/Ip Advanced Configuration
- Prohibit Viewing Of Status For An Active Connection
- Turn Off Notifications When A Connection Has Only Limited Or No Connectivity

Deploying Proxy Settings Through Group Policy

Internet Explorer requests can be directed to a proxy service to determine whether access to a particular protocol is allowed. If the protocol is allowed, the proxy server sends the request on behalf of the client and returns the results to the client securely. Because the proxy server uses network address translation (NAT) or a similar protocol, the actual Internet Protocol (IP) address of the client making the request isn't revealed to the target server. You can configure proxy servers for Hypertext Transfer Protocol (HTTP), Secure Sockets Layer (SSL), File Transfer Protocol (FTP), Gopher, and Socks (the Microsoft proxy service protocol).

You configure proxy settings manually using the Local Area Network (LAN) Settings dialog box. You access this dialog box from the Internet Options utility—on the Connections tab, click LAN Settings, select Use A Proxy Server For Your LAN, and then click the Advanced button. When you want to use Group Policy to deploy new configurations, update existing configurations, or replace existing configurations with new ones, you use Proxy Settings policy. You can configure unique proxy settings for each Web service (HTTP, SSL, FTP, Gopher, and Socks), or you can use one or more proxy servers to handle all types of requests. You can also configure exceptions so that a proxy isn't used for specific services, IP address ranges, or the local network.

You can configure proxy settings through Group Policy by completing the following steps:

1. Access User Configuration\Windows Settings\Internet Explorer Maintenance\ Connection in Group Policy, and then double-click Proxy Settings in the right pane.

2. In the Proxy Settings dialog box, shown in Figure 8-8, select Enable Proxy Settings. On the Proxy Servers panel, you'll find two columns of text boxes:

   ❑ **Address Of Proxy**   Used to set the IP address of the related proxy server or servers. Type the IP address for each service. If multiple proxies are configured for a particular service, type the IP address for each proxy server in the order in which you want the Web client to attempt to use them. The addresses must be separated by a semicolon. If a proxy isn't configured for a service, don't fill in the related box.

   ❑ **Port**   Used to set the port number on which the proxy server responds to requests. Most proxies respond to port 80 for all requests. However, the standard ports are port 80 for HTTP, port 443 for SSL (listed as Secure), port 21 for FTP, port 70 for Gopher, and port 1081 for Socks. Check with your organization's Web administrator for the proper settings.

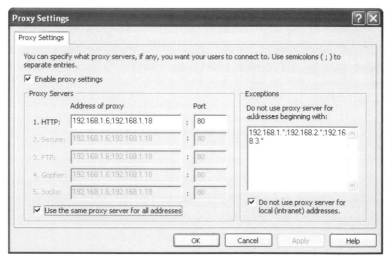

Figure 8-8   Configuring proxy settings for each type of service that should have a proxy

3. The Use The Same Proxy Server For All Addresses check box is selected by default. This setting allows you to use the same IP address and port settings for the HTTP, SSL, FTP, Gopher, and Socks services. You have two options:

    ❑ If your organization has proxy servers that handle all requests, select Use The Same Proxy Server For All Addresses, type the IP address or addresses you want to use, and specify the port number on which the server or servers respond.

    ❑ If you want to use a unique proxy server or servers for each type of service, clear the Use The Same Proxy Server For All Addresses check box and type the necessary IP addresses and port numbers in the text boxes provided.

> **Note** The Do Not Use Proxy Server For Local (Intranet) Addresses check box is selected by default. In most cases, you won't want to use a proxy for requests made to servers on the same network segment, so this is a suitable setting. However, this setting doesn't work well when your internal network uses multiple network segments. In this case, you must specify the IP address range for each network segment on the Exceptions list. An example is shown in Figure 8-8. In this case, you don't want a proxy to be used to access servers on the same network segments as the proxy servers, so you configure the IP addresses on these network segments as exceptions.

4. If your network has multiple segments or if specific address ranges shouldn't be proxied when accessed, specify the appropriate IP addresses or IP address ranges in the Exceptions list. The entries must be separated by a semicolon. You can use the asterisk (*) character as a wildcard to specify an address range of 0 through 255, as in 192.*.*.*, 192.168.*.*, or 192.168.10.*.

5. If your network has specific DNS domain suffixes that shouldn't be proxied, add these DNS domain suffixes to the Exclusion list. As before, separate entries with a semicolon. Use the asterisk as a wildcard to specify all names at a particular level, such as *.*.cpandl.com, *.tech.cpandl.com, or *.cpandl.com.

6. Click OK.

For the next step in the proxy configuration process, you might want to ensure that proxy settings are applied uniformly to all users of a particular computer and also prevent users from changing the proxy settings. You can do this by enabling an additional policy that assigns proxy settings per machine rather than per user and prevents users from overriding the standard proxy settings for the organization.

To set proxy settings per machine, complete the following steps:

1. Access Computer Configuration\Administrative Templates\Windows Components\Internet Explorer in Group Policy, and then double-click Make Proxy Settings Per-Machine (Rather Than Per-User) in the right pane.

2. Select Enabled, and then click OK.

> **Note** The affected computer or computers must be restarted for this policy to be applied. If you disable this policy or do not configure it, users of the same computer can set their own proxy settings. These settings might override those set through Group Policy.

Enhancing Internet Explorer Security

Few areas of security are more important than that of Internet Explorer. When properly configured, Internet Explorer is a secure browser that offers a safe environment for users to navigate the many resources of the Internet and the Web. When you've improperly or poorly configured Internet Explorer, the poor configuration can make your organization's network and computers susceptible to attack and misuse by malicious users.

One of the most important ways you can help protect your network and your computers is to optimize Internet Explorer security, and the most important area of this configuration has to do with Internet Explorer security zones. You use security zones to restrict or permit access to specific types of Web content, including ActiveX® controls, plug-ins, file and font downloads, Java applets, and scripts. You can also use security zones to control the types of actions users can perform while viewing Web content. For example, you can enable launching of programs within an internal browser frame, known as an IFRAME, but disable installation of desktop items.

Working with Security Zones and Settings

You can use Group Policy to manage security zones in several ways. You can set policies that control the user actions with regard to security zones and customize the settings for each security zone. As discussed in Chapter 6, in the section titled "Working with Attachment Manager," four types of security zones are defined:

- **Restricted sites** Sites you don't trust
- **Trusted sites** Sites you trust explicitly
- **Internet sites** Sites on the Internet
- **Intranet sites** Sites on your organization's internal network

Each security zone is assigned a default security level, which can range from low to high. Low security means that most actions are permitted and the security restrictions are very relaxed. High security means that most actions are disabled and the security restrictions are very stringent.

Each security level consists of parameters that typically are enabled, disabled, or set to prompt a user before the related feature can be invoked. You can change the settings by specifying a new security level for a particular security zone or by defining a custom level in which you set the state of each parameter.

You should closely scrutinize several categories of settings, including:

- **ActiveX controls, plug-ins, Java applets, and scripts**   Any time you enable ActiveX controls, plug-ins, Java applets, and scripts, you expose your network and your computers to potential abuse or misuse. You can, in fact, eliminate most problems with malware simply by not allowing the use of ActiveX controls, plug-ins, Java applets, or scripts. Although this is a drastic step, an increasing number of organizations have elected to disable these features to reduce the impact of malware on their networks.

- **Downloads**   With most types of downloads, you should consider prompting the user before the download occurs. Although this can be annoying for users, it makes users more aware of what's being downloaded to their computers and the potential risks. With this in mind, you might want to enable Automatic Prompting For File Downloads and set Font Download to Prompt.

- **User Authentication**   The Logon setting determines whether user name and password information is sent to a trusted or intranet content server when it is requested. The key risk of using this setting is that computers outside the network could gain access to logon names for your network and unauthorized external users could use the logon names to stage attacks on your system.

> **Note**   With Trusted or Intranet zone sites, the current user's logon information can be provided automatically when the client computer receives an NTLM or a NEGOTIATE WWW-Authenticate Challenge. While the risk associated with allowing user authentication is limited to trusted and intranet sites, it is important to remember that the definition of a local intranet site is configurable. The local intranet site can include all local sites not listed in other zones, all sites that bypass the proxy server, and all network paths.

With the Logon setting, all security levels except High present a potential security risk. Keep the following in mind:

- With High security, content servers prompt for a user name and password when a logon is needed, and information is never passed automatically.

- With Medium or Medium-Low security, the current user name and password are returned for logon requests to resources in the Intranet zone, which, as you might recall, can include intranet sites, network paths (UNCs), and sites bypassed by the proxy server. These bypassed sites are easy to forget when you're considering possible security issues.

■ With Low security, logon information is returned for logon requests from content servers in any zone. This is a dangerous setting when used with external content servers.

Restricting Security Zone Configuration

A key way to ensure that security zones are configured exactly as you expect them to be is to implement restrictions on who can change security zone settings and how settings are applied. Several policies control security zone modification and usage:

■ **Disable The Security Page**   If you enable this policy, Windows removes the Security tab in the Internet Properties dialog box. This prevents users from making any changes to security zones. This policy takes precedence over and overrides Security Zones: Do Not Allow Users To Change Policies and Security Zones: Do Not Allow Users To Add/Delete Sites. This policy is located under User Configuration\Administrative Templates\Windows Components\Internet Explorer\Internet Control Panel.

■ **Security Zones: Do Not Allow Users To Add/Delete Sites**   If you enable this policy, Windows disables the Sites button on the Security tab of the Internet Properties dialog box, which then prevents users from modifying the site management settings for the Local Intranet, Trusted Sites, and Restricted Sites zones. This means users cannot add sites, remove sites, or change the Include settings for the Local Intranet zone. This policy is located under Computer Configuration\Administrative Templates\Windows Components\Internet Explorer.

■ **Security Zones: Do Not Allow Users To Change Policies**   If you enable this policy, Windows prevents users from changing security zone settings. When this policy is enabled, the Custom Level and Default Level buttons are disabled on the Security tab of the Internet Properties dialog box. This prevents users from changing the security zone settings established by the administrator. This policy is located under Computer Configuration\Administrative Templates\Windows Components\Internet Explorer.

■ **Security Zones: Use Only Machine Settings**   If you enable this policy, Windows sets security zone settings by machine rather than by user. The policy is intended to ensure that security zones are consistently applied to all users of a computer. If you enable this policy without also preventing users from changing security zones, any user can make changes to security zones that affect all other users of the computer. This policy is located under Computer Configuration\Administrative Templates\Windows Components\Internet Explorer.

You can enable one or more of these policies to enforce restrictions on changing security zone settings. Simply double-click the policy, select Enabled, and then click OK.

Note Windows XP Service Pack 2 and later include policies for locking down the local machine security zone. This special security zone applies only to the security of the local computer and is designed to prevent users from making changes that might materially affect the security of their computers. Any policies set under User Configuration\Administrative Templates\Windows Components\Internet Explorer\ Internet Control Panel\Security Page\Locked-Down Local Machine Zone are locked out in the local machine zone and set according to their policy configuration. Rather than set each policy individually, you can use the Locked-Down Local Machine Zone Template policy under User Configuration\Administrative Templates\Windows Components\Internet Explorer\Internet Control Panel\Security Page to set the local machine zone security so that it is consistent with a specific security level.

Tip For computers running Windows XP Professional with Service Pack 2 or later, you can configure security zones through Administrative Templates. The related policies are found in both Computer Configuration and User Configuration under Administrative Templates\Windows Components\Internet Explorer\Internet Control Panel\Security Page. By administering security zones through the Administrative Templates, you can override imported settings that would otherwise apply. The specific zone settings configured through Administrative Templates will be applied only to computers running Windows XP Professional with Service Pack 2 or later.

Deploying Security Zone Configurations

Through Group Policy, you can implement standard settings for each security zone and deploy these settings to users of one or more computers. Before doing this, you must configure the security settings for each of the four security zones, starting with the Internet security zone. You can then import the settings into policy so that they can be deployed throughout a selected site, domain, or OU. These imported settings then apply to all Windows 2000 or later computers that process the related GPO. The only exception is if you've configured the Internet Control Panel security page for computers running Windows XP Professional Service Pack 2 or later. With these computers, settings in both Computer Configuration and User Configuration under Administrative Templates\Windows Components\Internet Explorer\Internet Control Panel\Security Page override imported security zone settings.

Configuring the Internet Security Zone

The Internet security zone sets Web content permissions for all sites not placed in other zones. Complete the following steps to configure the Internet security zone:

1. Access the Internet Options utility in the Control Panel, and then select the Security tab. Select Internet from the Zone list.

2. To restore the default level if it was changed, click Default Level. Then click OK and skip the remaining steps.

3. To set a different or custom level, click Custom Level. You can use the Security Settings dialog box (Figure 8-9) to set a custom level for individual parameters or reset the zone to a preset security level.

Figure 8-9   Setting custom settings using the Security Settings dialog box

4. If you want to use a custom level, use the buttons provided to set individual parameters, and then click OK.

    If you want to reset the zone to a particular security level, select the level using the Reset To drop-down list, click Reset, and then click OK. The security levels available are Low, Medium-Low, Medium, and High.

Configuring the Local Intranet Zone

The Local Intranet security zone sets Web content permissions on the local network. The default security level is Medium-Low. You can configure this zone by completing the following steps:

1. In the Internet Properties dialog box, click the Security tab, and then select Local Intranet from the Zone list.

2. Set the security level by doing one of the following:

    ❑ To restore the default level if it was changed, click Default Level. Then click OK.

    ❑ To set a different or custom level, click Custom Level. You can then use the Security Settings dialog box to set a custom level for individual parameters or reset the zone to a preset security level. When you are finished configuring settings, click OK.

3. Define which sites are included in the Local Intranet zone by clicking Sites. This displays the Local Intranet dialog box, shown in Figure 8-10.

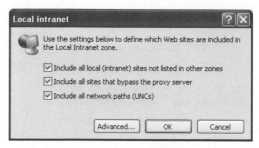

Figure 8-10   Include or exclude sites for the Local Intranet zone

4. You can now include or exclude local (intranet) sites not listed in other zones, sites that bypass the proxy server, and network paths (UNCs). To include a resource, select the related check box. To exclude a resource, clear the related check box.

5. If you want to specify additional sites for the Local Intranet zone or if you require secure verification using Hypertext Transfer Protocol Secure (HTTPS) for all servers in the Local Intranet zone, click Advanced. This displays a new Local Intranet dialog box, in which you can do the following:

    ❑ Add a site by typing its IP address in the Add This Web Site To The Zone text box and then clicking Add.

    ❑ Remove previously defined sites by selecting the site in the Web Sites list box and then clicking Remove.

    ❑ Require secure verification using HTTPS by selecting Require Server Verification (HTTPS:) For All Sites In This Zone.

6. Click OK twice to close the Local Intranet dialog boxes.

Configuring the Trusted Sites Security Zone

The Trusted Sites security zone sets Web content permissions for sites that are explicitly trusted and considered to be free of potentially offensive or unauthorized content and content that might damage or harm the computer. By default, the security level for this zone is set to Low. You can configure this zone by completing the following steps:

1. In the Internet Properties dialog box, click the Security tab, and then select Trusted Sites in the Zone list.

2. Set the security level by doing one of the following:

    ❑ To restore the default level if it was changed, click Default Level. Then click OK.

❑ To set a different or custom level, click Custom Level. You can then use the Security Settings dialog box to set a custom level for individual parameters or reset the zone to a preset security level. When you are finished configuring settings, click OK.

3. Click Sites to define which sites are included in the Trusted Sites zone. This displays the Trusted Sites dialog box, shown in Figure 8-11.

Figure 8-11 Selecting the sites to include in the Trusted Sites zone

4. You can now add and remove trusted sites from this zone. All Web sites in this zone will use the zone's security settings. To add a site, type its IP address in the Add This Web Site To The Zone text box and then click Add. To remove a site, select the site in the Web Sites list box and then click Remove.

5. You can also require secure verification using HTTPS. Select Require Server Verification (HTTPS:) For All Sites In This Zone to enable this feature, or clear the related check box to disable this feature.

6. Click OK.

Configuring the Restricted Sites Security Zone

The Restricted Sites security zone sets permissions for sites with potentially offensive or unauthorized content and content that might damage or harm the computer. Site restrictions don't prevent users from accessing unauthorized sites, however. They merely establish a different security level for these sites. To prevent users from accessing restricted sites, you must configure a proxy server or firewall to block access to the sites.

By default, the security level for Restricted Sites is set to High. You can place sites on the restricted list by completing the following steps:

1. In the Internet Properties dialog box, click the Security tab and then select Restricted Sites in the Zone list.

2. Set the security level by doing one of the following:

    ❑ To restore the default level if it was changed, click Default Level. Then click OK.

    ❑ To set a different or custom level, click Custom Level. You can then use the Security Settings dialog box to set a custom level for individual parameters or reset the zone to a preset security level. When you are finished configuring settings, click OK.

3. Click Sites to define which sites are included in the Restricted Sites zone. This displays the Restricted Sites dialog box, which is similar to the dialog box shown earlier in Figure 8-11.

4. To add a restricted site, type its IP address in the Add This Web Site To The Zone text box and then click Add.

5. To remove a site, select the site in the Web Sites list box and then click Remove.

6. Click OK twice to close the Restricted Sites and Internet Properties dialog boxes.

Importing and Deploying the Security Zone Settings

After you configure the security settings for each of the four security zones, you can import the settings into the Security Zones And Content Ratings policy so that they can be deployed throughout a selected site, domain, or OU. Import the settings by completing these steps:

1. Configure each of the four security zones as discussed earlier. When you are finished, access User Configuration\Windows Settings\Internet Explorer Maintenance\Security in Group Policy and then double-click Security Zones And Content Ratings.

2. Select Import The Current Security Zone Settings And Privacy Settings and then click Modify Settings. You can now check the security zone settings you defined previously.

3. When you are finished, click OK twice to apply the policy.

Configuring Additional Policies for Internet Options

You'll find many policies for managing Internet Options under User Configuration\Administrative Templates\Windows Components\Internet Explorer. You can easily enable one or more of these policies by double-clicking the policy, selecting Enabled, and then clicking OK. In some cases, you'll need to specify additional parameters, such as a file size limit or whether a button is active or inactive.

Table 8-1 describes the key Internet Options policies. As you'll see when you examine the table, many of these policies are useful in preventing users from performing specific actions in Internet Explorer and for controlling Internet Explorer behavior.

Table 8-1   Key Internet Options Policies

Policy Node	Policy Name	Description
User Configuration\ Administrative Templates\ Windows Components\ Internet Explorer\Internet Control Panel\Advanced Page	Allow Active Content From CDs To Run On User Machines	By default, users see a prompt that allows them to continue or cancel the running of the active content from a CD. By enabling this policy, you override the default setting and allow active content from CDs to run without prompting.
User Configuration\ Administrative Templates\ Windows Components\ Internet Explorer\Internet Control Panel\Advanced Page	Allow Software To Run Or Install Even If The Signature Is Invalid	By default, downloaded files and other executables are prevented from running and installing if they have invalid signatures. By enabling this policy, you override the default setting and allow files with invalid signatures to be installed.
User Configuration\ Administrative Templates\ Windows Components\ Internet Explorer\Toolbars	Configure Toolbar Buttons	Specifies which buttons are enabled on the standard toolbar in Internet Explorer. If you enable this policy, you can specify whether a particular button is displayed by default or is hidden.
User Configuration\ Administrative Templates\ Windows Components\ Internet Explorer	Disable Changing Connection Settings	Prevents users from changing dial-up settings.
User Configuration\ Administrative Templates\ Windows Components\ Internet Explorer	Disable Changing Proxy Settings	Prevents users from changing proxy server settings.
User Configuration\ Administrative Templates\ Windows Components\ Internet Explorer	Disable Internet Connection Wizard	Prevents users from running the New Connection Wizard.
User Configuration\ Administrative Templates\ Windows Components\ Internet Explorer\Internet Control Panel	Disable The Advanced Page	Removes the Advanced tab in the Internet Options dialog box, preventing users from enabling advanced features.

Table 8-1   Key Internet Options Policies

Policy Node	Policy Name	Description
User Configuration\ Administrative Templates\ Windows Components\ Internet Explorer\Internet Control Panel	Disable The Connections Page	Removes the Connections tab in the Internet Options dialog box, preventing users from changing connection settings, proxy settings, and automatic configuration settings. Also prevents users from accessing the New Connection Wizard.
User Configuration\ Administrative Templates\ Windows Components\ Internet Explorer\Internet Control Panel	Disable The Programs Page	Removes the Programs tab in the Internet Options dialog box, preventing users from changing the default Internet programs.
User Configuration\ Administrative Templates\ Windows Components\ Internet Explorer\Internet Control Panel	Disable The Security Page	Removes the Security tab in the Internet Options dialog box, preventing users from changing security settings.
User Configuration\ Administrative Templates\ Windows Components\ Internet Explorer	Do Not Allow Users To Enable Or Disable Add-ons	Disables add-on management and prevents users from configuring the related settings. (Add-on management allows users to control whether browser add-ons are enabled or disabled.)
User Configuration\ Administrative Templates\ Windows Components\ Internet Explorer\ Persistence Behavior	File Size Limits For	Allows you to set size limits for cached dynamic files from each of the security zones. You can set per-domain and per-document limits.
User Configuration\ Administrative Templates\ Windows Components\ Internet Explorer\Browser Menus	Hide Favorites Menu	Removes the Favorites menu from Internet Explorer, preventing users from accessing lists for favorites.
User Configuration\ Administrative Templates\ Windows Components\ Internet Explorer	Pop-up Allow List	Allows administrators to specify a list of sites that are permitted to use pop-ups regardless of Internet Explorer settings. Enabling this option and adding internal sites to the list is useful if these sites call the *window.open()* method in JavaScript or use similar methods to open windows.

Table 8-1 **Key Internet Options Policies**

Policy Node	Policy Name	Description
User Configuration\ Administrative Templates\ Windows Components\ Internet Explorer	Turn Off Crash Detection	Turns off crash detection. Crash detection allows the browser to track add-ons that cause problems with browser stability. The user can then elect to disable unstable add-ons.
User Configuration\ Administrative Templates\ Windows Components\ Internet Explorer	Turn Off Pop-Up Management	Prevents a user from configuring pop-up options and hides related dialog boxes. This means pop-up manager controls, notifications, and dialog boxes do not appear when this option is enabled.

Summary

In Group Policy, the key policies for working with Internet Explorer are found under User Configuration\Internet Explorer Maintenance. These policies are organized into five broad categories: browser user interface, URLs, programs, connections, and security. These policies have the broadest impact on Internet Explorer configuration and security, so they are the policies you'll work with the most. Under User Configuration\Administrative Templates\Windows Components\Internet Explorer, you'll find many additional policies, which are primarily for fine-tuning Internet Explorer menus, toolbars, and related options. For computers running Windows XP Professional SP2 or later, the policies under User Configuration\Administrative Templates\Windows Components\Internet Explorer\Internet Control Panel can be used to configure security settings and lock down Internet security zones.

Chapter 9
Deploying and Maintaining Software Through Group Policy

In this chapter:

Understanding Group Policy Software Installation 318

Planning the Software Deployment 322

Deploying Software Through Group Policy. 326

Configuring Advanced and Global Software Installation Options. 334

Deploying Microsoft Office and Service Packs 349

Maintaining Deployed Applications. 354

Summary 368

Software installation and maintenance is both time consuming and labor intensive, whether you are working to roll out new applications, implement service packs, or install patches. Of the many products and tools available to help ease the software installation and maintenance burden, few are as powerful and easy to use as Software Installation policy. Using Software Installation policy, you can efficiently and centrally manage the full life cycle of your software deployments, from software installation to repair, patches, updates, and removal. Efficient, central management significantly reduces the effort required to deploy and maintain software, which can also represent a significant cost savings for your organization.

Related Information

- For more information about deploying Group Policy, see Chapter 4.

- For more information about the Windows Installer, see *http://msdn .microsoft.com/library/default.asp?url=/library/en-us/msi/setup/windows_ installer_start_page.asp*.

- For more information about deploying Microsoft Office 2003 using Group Policy, see the Office 2003 Resource Kit or *http://www.microsoft.com/resources/ documentation/office/2003/all/reskit/en-us/depc04.mspx*.

Understanding Group Policy Software Installation

Software Installation policy isn't meant to replace enterprise solutions such as Microsoft Systems Management Server (SMS). Instead, it is designed as a versatile and easy-to-use departmental solution for deploying and maintaining software. Before diving into actual deployment, let's look at:

- How software installation works
- What you need to know to prepare for installation
- How to set up the install location
- What limitations apply

How Software Installation Works

Software Installation through Group Policy works like this: You define one or more applications within a Group Policy object (GPO) in your Active Directory domain. When a user or computer processes that GPO, any applications that have been defined in Software Installation policy are installed. For example, if a GPO is linked to the Finance OU and you deploy Office using Software Installation policy, all users or computers in the Finance OU will get Office installed when that GPO is processed. Some qualifying conditions apply, and we'll discuss them in this chapter, but essentially that is how it works.

Software deployed through Group Policy is referred to as *managed software*. Within the Group Policy, Software Installation policy is found under both Computer Configuration\Software Settings\Software Installation and User Configuration\Software Settings\Software Installation (Figure 9-1), which means you can deploy software on either a per-computer or a per-user basis.

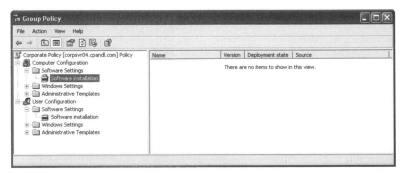

Figure 9-1   Viewing the location of Software Installation policy

Generally speaking, per-computer applications are available to all users of a computer and per-user applications are available to individual users. The actual computers and users who have access to an application depend on the GPO you are working with.

The access permissions on the application installer package and related installation files also can affect the deployment. If you are deploying software on a per-computer basis, the appropriate computer accounts must have Read access. If you are deploying software on a per-user basis, the appropriate user accounts must have Read access.

> **Note** Unlike most policies, Software Installation policies are only applied during foreground processing of policy and are not applied during background refresh of policy. Per-computer deployments are processed at startup and per-user deployments are processed at logon.

What You Need to Know to Prepare

Before you deploy your software, you first need to have an installation package for the application you want to deploy. As discussed later in this chapter under "Deploying Software Through Group Policy," the installation package includes an installer file, which can be a Windows Installer package with an .msi extension or an application setup package with a .zap extension, and the application files that are needed to install the software.

The basic installation package can be customized in several ways. Typically, you'll use transform files. These files, ending with the .mst extension, are used to modify the installation process so you can optimize the installation for various users or user groups. Transforms give you the ability to customize almost every aspect of a Windows Installer package for deployment. For applications that include a standard installer package, you might be able to obtain a utility for creating transform files. For most custom packages that you've created, however, you will likely have to rely on a third-party packaging tool to create transform files for those packages.

> **Note** Installation packages must be authored using the Windows Installer packaging format to take full advantage of policy-based installation and management. However, it is possible to deploy non–Windows Installer packages using Software Installation policy. The catch it that you don't get any of the life-cycle management features using this method. See the "Deploying Software with Non–Windows Installer Packages" section in this chapter for more information.

> **Tip** Transform files are such a common method for customizing deployments of Office that Microsoft provides a customization utility in the Microsoft Office Resource Kit called the Custom Installation Wizard. You'll learn more about this utility in the "Using Transforms to Customize a Microsoft Office Deployment" section in this chapter.

In addition to the installation package itself, you need a distribution point on your network for making the package available to users and computers. This install location should be a network share that is available to the users and computers for which you are deploying the software. These users and computers must have at least Read permission on the share and the file system where the package and the related files reside. You should also consider the geographic location of the server hosting the share relative to the users and computers.

> **Tip**   Plan the install location carefully. Once assigned, the install location cannot be changed in the GPO without redeploying the application.

Due to network latency or bandwidth issues, installation packages might need to be on a server in the same physical location or site as the users and computers. In some instances, you might want to consider using the Windows Distributed File System (DFS) service to geographically distribute these files across multiple server shares. Using DFS, you can create a logical directory structure that is independent of the location where the files are actually stored on the network.

Because DFS provides a virtual, rather than physical, file storage location, you never have to change the path to the package within the GPO. If you need to make a change, you can do so in DFS. For example, you might create a DFS root named \\AppSvr\ deployedapps and then create application-specific subdirectories under this share point. You can then locate the subdirectories on multiple servers and configure multiple physical links to the same logical directories. If one of these servers goes down or you have some other program, you can simply replace the link replica reference to point to a different server without ever having to change the package within the GPO.

Further, if you use Active Directory-integrated DFS, you gain several additional benefits:

- You can configure automatic replication of application folder contents. This feature allows you to copy new installation packages to a folder and have them automatically copied to the other servers that need these files.

- Because DFS is a site-aware technology, client computers will always connect to a copy of a DFS folder in their own site. This means that a client will always try to download the package from a server that is close to it from a network perspective and also minimizes latency.

How to Set Up the Installation Location

Placing an installation package on a share is often a simple matter of copying the installer file and all of the necessary application files to your chosen install location. However, for some applications, especially Microsoft applications, a better solution is to perform an *administrative installation* to the share that you will be using to deploy the package.

> **Tip**   For most Microsoft applications, you can initiate an administrative installation by passing the */a* parameter to the *setup.exe* command.

The main reason for performing an administrative install rather than a straight file copy of an application's setup files from the distribution CD-ROM is that you can directly patch an administrative install as future updates to the application become available. Once the administrative install is patched, you can use the Redeploy feature of Software Installation to have the updates applied to all target clients the next time policy is refreshed. This makes it much easier to keep an application package and the clients that have installed it up-to-date. The alternative—copying and executing the patch outside of Group Policy on each machine that requires it—is time consuming and labor intensive, so an administrative install usually makes much more sense.

What Limitations Apply

Although Software Installation policy provides a versatile framework for deploying and maintaining software, the technology is better suited to department-level deployments than to enterprise-wide deployments. Why? Because some limitations apply to the technology that might affect your decision to use it for large scale deployments.

One key limitation is that policy can be used to distribute software only to computers running Windows 2000 or Windows XP Professional. While server versions of the Windows operating system might have the Windows Installer service, they cannot receive applications deployed through policy. Computers running Windows 95, Windows 98, or Windows NT Workstation also can't receive applications deployed through policy. If your organization has client computers running any of these unsupported operating systems, you must deploy software using an alternative technology or technique. Microsoft Systems Management Server (SMS) and Intel LANDesk provide possible solutions.

The way in which deployed applications are sent over the network can be a limitation as well. With an enterprise solution such as SMS, you can schedule the application deployment and use multicasting. Scheduling the deployment allows you to install the application whenever you'd like, such as in the middle of the night when no one is on the network. Multicasting allows you to send one copy of the software over the network and have it be received simultaneously by multiple clients. This means you can potentially send an application once over the network and have it be received by all client computers on the network.

In contrast, with Group Policy, there is no scheduling or multicasting capability. Generally, client computers receive the deployed application when a specific, configurable event occurs, such as computer startup, user logon, or user activation, and you cannot otherwise control when the application is installed. Further, each client receives a separate copy of the deployed application that is sent over the network.

Another important limitation has to do with control over who receives a software package. Enterprise solutions such as SMS and Intel LANDesk feature built-in capabilities to limit which client computers get a particular software installation based on their configuration. You can, in fact, limit the deployment to computers that have a specific operating system or hardware configuration, as well as by previous versions of installed applications.

The key way to control who receives an application through policy is through the assignment of the GPO or through filtering. You can, for example, create a GPO, configure Software Installation policy, and then link the GPO to the Sales OU to have the GPO apply to all users in the Sales GPO. As discussed in Chapter 3 under "Filtering By Security Group, User, or Computer," you can apply a security filter so the GPO applies only to specific security groups within a site, domain, or OU. For more granular control, you can modify the security on the installer file itself, as discussed in the "Controlling Deployment by Security Group" section in this chapter.

You can also create a WMI filter to filter the application deployment based on operating system or hardware configuration, or based on existing applications that are installed. Although WMI filters can help you implement very advanced deployment scenarios, they can be tricky to use and they must be thoroughly tested before use. See the "Creating Software Deployment GPOs" section in this chapter for more details on using WMI filters.

Planning the Software Deployment

We've already discussed what you need to do to prepare for deployment and set up the install location. Now let's look at deployment planning. With any type of software deployment, you must spend some time planning the rollout. It is no different with Software Installation through Group Policy. The key factors to consider are:

- Whether to use special software deployment GPOs
- Whether to advertise the software to users or computers

Creating Software Deployment GPOs

As part of your planning, you should think carefully about the policy objects you will use to deploy software. Although you might be tempted to use existing site, domain, or OU GPOs, doing so limits your flexibility in terms of how you can deploy software.

To see why, consider the follow example: You need to deploy Office 2003 in the Sales OU. You edit the GPO for the Sales OU and configure Software Installation policy. Later you find out that you need to deploy the software to the rest of the organization. At this point, you can edit the GPO for each additional OU or change the way you are deploying software; changing the way you deploy software is probably the better option.

Rather than editing individual site, domain, and OU GPOs to deploy software, you can create GPOs just for software deployment. Then, when you need to deploy software to a site, domain, or OU, you simply link the software deployment GPO to the site, domain, or OU. With this technique, it is usually best to create one GPO for each software application or category of application you want to deploy. For example, if you need to deploy Microsoft Visio, you can create a GPO called Visio Deployment Policy, configure the GPO to deploy Visio, and then link the GPO to the appropriate sites, domains, or OUs in your organization.

When you create and configure the software deployment GPO, you must consider who will receive the software. By default, the policy will apply to all users or computers within the site, domain, or OU to which you've linked the GPO. Sometimes this isn't the behavior you want. For example, say you want all developers in the organization to have a copy of Visio but that developers are spread throughout the organization. The dilemma becomes: how do you deploy Visio only to developers without having to do individual installations on each developer system. One way to do this is to use your organization's security groups to filter the policy application. If you configure security filtering on your software deployment GPO so that only members of the Developers security group have the policy applied, Visio will be deployed only to developers.

Some situations are more complex, however. For example, you might want to deploy Visio only to computers with a certain configuration, such as only the Dell Dimension 8300 computers in your organization. In this situation (and any other time you want to limit policy application based on system configuration, operating system assignment, or hardware), you must use a WMI filter. You create a WMI filter that detects the computer manufacturer and model, and then you link the WMI filter to the software deployment GPO so that only computers with this configuration have the policy applied. The WMI filter would look like this:

```
Root\cimV2;Select * FROM Win32_ComputerSystem WHERE Manufacturer="Dell Computer
Corporation" and Model="Dimension 8300"
```

In this example, you use WMI to examine the *Win32_ComputerSystem* object and select all computers that have the manufacturer set to Dell Computer Corporation and the model set to Dimension 8300. Be sure to test this type of filter in your environment before rolling out into production.

> **Tip**   When you use WMI filters, two key objects you'll work with are *Win32_ ComputerSystem* and *Win32_OperatingSystem*. A handy tool for digging into these objects and examining all the related values is Netsh Diag. With Netsh Diag, you don't need to know any thing about WMI to access properties and determine the values you can use for filtering. The *Microsoft Windows Command-Line Pocket Consultant* (Microsoft Press, 2004) provides techniques for working with Netsh Diag, *Win32_ComputerSystem*, and *Win32_OperatingSystem*.

Configuring the Software Deployment

Software Installation policies are only applied during foreground processing of policy and are not applied during background refresh of policy. You can deploy applications in several ways:

- Assign the software to client computers so it is installed when a client computer starts.

- Advertise the software so a computer can install the software when it is first used.

- Assign the software to users so it is installed when a user logs on.

- Publish the application so users can install it manually through Add Or Remove Programs.

When you want to completely automate a software installation, you can use assignment as your deployment option. You can assign the software on either a per-computer or per-user basis. Assigning software per-computer means the software is completely installed the next time the affected computer is restarted. Because the software is installed on a per-computer basis, it is available to all users who log on to the computer.

When you assign an application to a user, the default installation mode when that user logs on is to advertise the application rather than fully install it. Advertisement, also known as *install-on-first-use*, is a Windows Installer capability that can be leveraged by Group Policy. Advertisement essentially lets you provide install-on-demand software for users, and when used in conjunction with Software Installation policy, it provides a means to distribute software to only those who need it. This can reduce the need to maintain software where it's not required, and you also do not have to explicitly perform an action to distribute an application when the user finally needs it.

Advertisements work on the basic principle that an application isn't installed unless the user requests something that requires the application—whether it's a document or a bit of functionality. To take advantage of advertisements, a Windows Installer package must be authored to present aspects of the application as advertisements rather than as a full local installation.

An application can advertise itself in three ways:

- **Shortcuts** A package can install shortcuts to the user's desktop or Start menu. When the user clicks on a shortcut to launch the application, the full application is installed.

- **File associations** A package can register file extension associations in the registry to indicate that the deployed application is associated with a particular file extension (for example, .doc for Word or .vsd for Visio®) When the user opens a file with the advertised file association, the application is installed.

- **COM components** For applications that contain shared COM components, a package can advertise those components in the registry for install-on-first-use. For example, if Word is not yet installed but Microsoft Outlook is, and if the user decides to use Word as an e-mail editor, the moment she calls that component out of Outlook, Word is installed.

Another option for user assignment is to install the application when a user logs on. The logon process takes longer because the application must be installed.

The final deployment option is to publish an application and make it available on a per-user basis. When you publish an application to a user, the application is advertised the next time the user logs on. Unlike the previously described advertisement approach, this technique is limited. The application is advertised in Add Or Remove Programs and is also available for install-on-first-use. This means a user can install the application manually using Add Or Remove Programs or activate the installation by trying to open a file associated with the application.

You can see evidence of an advertisement by looking at the properties on a shortcut for an application that has been advertised. For example, in Figure 9-2, we assigned Visio 2003 to a user via policy. Note the value of the Target Type on the properties of the shortcut that was installed for Visio. It indicates that when the user clicks on this shortcut, Visio will be installed.

Figure 9-2 Viewing an advertised Visio shortcut

Regardless of the targeting method you use, the steps for actually deploying software via policy are essentially the same. To help you decide whether to target your software deployment to a computer or to a user, see Table 9-1, which summarizes the advantages and disadvantages of computer assignment, user assignment, and user publishing.

Table 9-1   Overview of Software Deployment Methods

Capability	Computer Assignment	User Assignment	User Publishing
Activation	Requires restart to install software	Requires user logon to install or advertise software	Requires user to explicitly install software or activate install
Availability	Available to all users on a computer	Software associated with user only—follows users wherever they log on	Software associated with user only when software is installed
Intervention Requirement	Install on startup; no user intervention required	Install on logon or first use; no user intervention required	User intervention required

Deploying Software Through Group Policy

Most software deployments using Group Policy rely on the Windows Installer technology to facilitate software deployment and life-cycle management. However, it is also possible to deploy an application setup package that has not been packaged using the Windows Installer technology. This means there are two general approaches for deploying and maintaining software:

■ Software deployments using Windows Installer packages

■ Software deployments using non-Windows Installer packages

Each of these techniques is discussed in the sections that follow.

Deploying Software with Windows Installer Packages

Windows Installer packages are designed to simplify software installation. The Windows Installer technology relies on two key components:

■ A software installation package file

■ A software installer service

The software installation package file contains a database of information detailing how the software should be installed and removed. This machine-readable file ends with the .msi extension and is used by the Windows Installer service (Msiexec.exe).

The Windows Installer service is a standard component on all Windows-based computers. The service uses a dynamic-link library (Msi.dll) to read .msi package files.

During installation, the contents of the package file tell the Windows Installer service exactly what application files should be copied to the local computer, the shortcuts to create, the registry entries to modify, and so on. This same information can be used when you uninstall an application to completely remove the software.

There are many benefits to using Windows Installer packages, not the least of which is that any application using a Windows Installer package can be self-repairing. How does this work? Well, the Windows Installer package contains all the details needed to install and uninstall the related application. Because it lists all the files and the system configuration required to properly run the software, the installer file can also be used to repair an application that has failed. Here's how this works: Say that a critical file needed to run the application was deleted or became corrupt. Because of this, the application failed to start for the next user, but because the application was installed using Windows Installer, the file can be used to repair the application by reinstalling the missing or corrupted file.

Other advantages of deploying software with Windows Installer packages include:

- **Privilege escalation**   When you use policy to install managed applications assigned or published to users, the processing runs in an elevated security context so users who belong to neither the local Administrators group nor the Power Users group on their workstations can successfully install the applications. Essentially, during the application installation, the package is in the context of a privileged user, with full rights to install applications on the system.

- **Transforms**   Using Software Installation policy, you can automatically apply one or more Windows Installer transform files during application deployment. Transforms allow you to customize an application's default Windows Installer package at install time to modify the elements of the application that are installed on the user's computer.

- **Advertisement**   This feature, also known as *install-on-first-use*, is a Windows Installer capability that can be leveraged by Software Installation policy. Specifically, when you assign an application to a user, the default installation mode when that user logs on is to advertise the application rather than fully install it. Advertisements are a set of associations that use an "activator"—such as a shortcut, document extension (for example, .doc files for Microsoft Word), or COM object registration. If the user launches one of these activators, the application package is installed.

- **Upgrades**   Using Software Installation policy, you can establish upgrade relationships between old and new versions of applications. For example, if you previously deployed Office XP via policy, you can deploy Office 2003 and create an upgrade relationship between it and the previous version. All computers or users who previously deployed Office XP will be upgraded to Office 2003 when the Software Installation policy is processed.

■ **Automatic removal**   Using Software Installation policy, you can automatically remove, or uninstall, an application when the user or computer is no longer subject to the GPO that originally installed the application. For example, if a user gets Microsoft Excel installed on his machine by virtue of being located within the Finance OU within an Active Directory domain, you can specify that if his job changes and he moves into the Marketing OU, Excel will automatically be removed during the next foreground Group Policy processing cycle.

Getting the Necessary Windows Installer File

You'll find that just about every new software application has a .msi package file that can be used to install and uninstall the application. When a .msi package file is included with an application, it is referred to as a *native Windows Installer file*. Using a native Windows Installer file to deploy software through Group Policy is the easiest deployment technique to use, but you can also create your own installer file.

To create a Windows Installer file, you first need a third-party Windows Installer packaging tool, such as WISE for Windows Installer from Wise Solutions, Inc. The steps you follow to create a .msi package differ depending on the tool you use, but the basic steps are as follows:

1. Start with a clean installation of each operating system to which you plan to deploy the software. For example, if you plan to deploy the software to Windows XP Professional, start a new installation of Windows XP Professional on a computer and do not install any other application software.

2. After the operating system is installed, use a software packaging tool to create a snapshot of the computer. You must take this snapshot before you install the application software.

3. Install the application software on the computer. In most cases, you will perform a standard installation of the software. Be sure to select the install options that will offer the best support and configuration for your users.

4. After the application is installed, optimize the application configuration. You can create or remove application shortcuts, customize toolbars, set default options, and so on. Run the application at least once in case there are components that install only after startup.

5. Use your chosen software packaging tool to create a second snapshot of the computer. During this process, you will create the Windows Installer file.

6. Repeat this procedure for each operating system to which you plan to deploy the software. If you want to install to both Windows 2000 and Windows XP Professional, you will usually need two separate Windows Installer files.

Once you have the necessary installer files, you can use policy to distribute the software throughout your organization.

Deploying the Software Using a Windows Installer File

Once you have your Windows Installer file and have copied all the necessary files to a network share, you can configure software installation through Group Policy. As discussed in "Creating Software Deployment GPOs," in most cases you should create a new GPO, configure Software Installation policy, and then link the GPO to the appropriate sites, domains, or OUs to deploy the software.

To configure Software Installation policy to deploy your software, complete the following steps:

1. Access Software Installation in Group Policy. For a per-computer software deployment, access Computer Configuration\Software Settings\Software Installation. For a per-user software deployment, access User Configuration\ Software Settings\Software Installation.

2. Right-click Software Installation and choose New, Package.

3. In the Open dialog box, type the path to the network share where your package is located or use the options provided to navigate to the package and select it.

> **Caution**   If you are delivering the package from a network share, you must always enter the UNC path to that share when defining the package in policy. Generally speaking don't use local paths. For example, if you enter the path *c:\packages\office2003\pro.msi* in policy because the package is on the server's C drive, the client that is processing that policy will look for the package on its own C drive rather than on the server.

4. Click Open. If for some reason the network path cannot be verified, you'll see a warning message asking you whether you want to continue. If you click Yes, the path you entered will be used. If you click No, you will exit the Software Installation deployment process and will have to start over.

> **Caution**   Once you click Open, there is no way to change the installation path for the software package. This means if you select the wrong path or need to modify the path later, you must delete and re-create the software package.

5. In the Deploy Software dialog box (Figure 9-3), you'll see the Published, Assigned, and Advanced options. Select Published to publish the application without modifications; select Assigned to assign it without modifications. Select Advanced to deploy the application using advanced configuration options, as discussed in the "Configuring Advanced and Global Software Installation Options" section in this chapter.

> **Note**   Global defaults can affect whether the Deploy Software dialog box is
> displayed. If the dialog box isn't displayed, a default deployment option is set.
> For more information, see "Setting Global Deployment Defaults" later in this
> chapter.

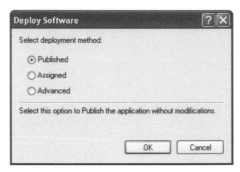

Figure 9-3   Selecting the basic deployment option

Once the policy is configured, the application will be deployed to all computers or
users as appropriate. By default, per-computer software packages are made available
when a computer starts up and per-user software packages are made available when a
user logs on. As discussed in Chapter 3 under "Refreshing Group Policy Manually,"
you can also use the Gpupdate command-line utility to force restart and logoff.

Deploying Software with Non–Windows Installer Packages

To deploy software using a non–Windows Installer package file, you must create a
special text-based file called a Zero Administration Package (ZAP) file. Once you have
the necessary ZAP file, you can configure the software for deployment through Group
Policy. However, this approach is limited and does not provide any of the benefits of a
managed application—such as privilege escalation, life-cycle management, and automatic removal. Specifically, you can perform only user-based publishing, which means
the program will be listed as an available application in the Add Or Remove Programs
utility and user's will be able to select the application for installation from there. If you
include information about an application's file extensions, you also get a limited
install-on-first-use capability.

Other than that, that's the extent of what you can do with non–Windows Installer
package files. The installation of the application runs in the normal installation file
and with the user's normal permissions. This means that although you can pass the
installation file optional parameters, you cannot customize the installation. You cannot, for example, perform an installation with elevated permissions, so a user might
need local Administrator privileges to install the application. In addition, the self-
repair, upgrade, and patching benefits available with Windows Installer files are no
longer available.

Note   Because of the limitations of ZAP files, these files are best used for deploying applications that you will not need to upgrade or patch. The only way to upgrade or patch software deployed using ZAP is to remove the existing software through policy and then use policy to redeploy a completely new version of the software.

Creating the ZAP File

A ZAP file takes the form of a standard Windows initialization file, with a section header and a set of *key, value* pairs. The file can be created in a standard text editor, such as Notepad, and must be saved with the .zap extension so Software Installation policy can recognize it.

ZAP files must contain the following sections and keys, at minimum, to be valid:

```
[Application]
FriendlyName="ApplicationName"
SetupCommand="\\Servername\Sharename\Applicationinstaller.exe" /Parameter
```

where *ApplicationName* is the name that will be displayed in Add Or Remove Programs, *\\Servername\Sharename\Applicationinstall.exe* is the complete path to the application's installation file on a network share, and *Parameter* is a setup parameter you want to pass to the application's installation file.

To see how this would look with an actual application, consider the following example:

```
[Application]
FriendlyName="Microsoft Visio 2003"
SetupCommand="\\cpandl.com\dfsroot\packages\Visio 2003\setup.exe" /unattend
```

This example calls Setup.exe from a domain DFS root share called *packages*. We also pass an */unattend* switch to allow the application to be deployed in an unattended fashion. Note that this switch is setup-package independent. Your application packages might support different switches to provide an unattended setup.

Note   You should consider several caveats when setting the installation path. If the path to the setup command contains spaces or long filenames, it must be enclosed in quotation marks. Also note that referencing drive letters within the *SetupCommand* path causes the application deployment to fail.

The *FriendlyName* and *SetupCommand* values represent the minimum information needed in a ZAP file to properly deploy an application. A set of optional *key, value* pairs can provide additional information within Add Or Remove Programs. Specifically, the following three keys can provide additional information about the application:

```
DisplayVersion = VersionNumberToDisplay
Publisher = SoftwarePublisher
URL = SoftwarePublishersURL
```

where *VersionNumberToDisplay* is a software revision or version number you want to display in Add Or Remove Programs, *SoftwarePublisher* is the software manufacturer, and *SoftwarePublishersURL* is the URL for the software manufacturer's Web site. Here is an example:

```
DisplayVersion = 11.0
Publisher = Microsoft Corporation
URL = http://www.microsoft.com/office
```

The following additional section and *key, value* pair let give you some limited install-on-first-use capability by associating a file extension with the application being published:

```
[ext]
ext=
```

where ext is the extension you want to associate with the application being published. In the following example, the file extension .vsd is referenced within the section called *[ext]*:

```
[ext]
vsd=
```

If a user who has had this application published via a ZAP file opens a .vsd file, the application is installed from the path specified in the *SetupCommand* key. However, because ZAP file–based deployment provides no privilege escalation, the user must have sufficient rights on her machine to be able to successfully run the application setup.

Listing 9-1 shows a complete listing of a ZAP file based on the previous examples.

Listing 9-1   Sample ZAP File Including Required and Optional Values

```
[Application]
FriendlyName="Microsoft Visio 2003"
SetupCommand="\\cpandl.com\dfsroot\packages\Visio 2003\setup.exe" /unattend

DisplayVersion = 11.0
Publisher = Microsoft Corporation
URL = http://www.microsoft.com/office

[ext]
vsd=
```

Deploying the Software Using a ZAP File

Once you have your ZAP file and have copied all the necessary files to a network share, you can configure software installation through Group Policy. As discussed previously in "Creating Software Deployment GPOs," in most cases you should create a new GPO, configure Software Installation policy, and then link the GPO to the appro-priate sites, domains, or OUs to deploy the software.

To configure Software Installation policy to deploy your software, complete the follow-ing steps:

1. Non–Windows Installer files can be installed only on a per-user basis. Access Software Installation under User Configuration\Software Settings\Software Installation.

2. Right-click Software Installation and choose New, Package.

3. In the Open dialog box, type the path to the network share where your package is located or use the options provided to navigate to the package and select it.

> **Caution**   If you are delivering the package from a network share, you must always type the UNC path to that share when defining the package in policy. Generally speaking, don't use local paths. For example, if you enter the path *c:\packages\visio\viso.zap* in policy because the package is on the server's C drive, the client that is processing that policy will look for the package on its own C drive rather than on the server.

4. In the Files of Type list, select ZAW Down-Level Applications Packages (*.zap) as the file type.

5. Click Open. If, for some reason, the network path cannot be verified, you'll see a warning message asking you whether you want to continue. If you click Yes, the path you entered will be used. If you click No, you will exit the Software Installation deployment process and will have to start over.

> **Caution**   Once you click Open, there is no way to change the path to the .zap file. This means if you select the wrong path or need to modify the path later, you must re-create the software package.

6. In the Deploy Software dialog box, select Published to publish the application without modifications. Select Advanced to deploy the application using advanced configuration options, as discussed in the next section.

> **Note**   Global defaults can affect whether the Deploy Software dialog box is dis-played. If the dialog box isn't displayed, a default deployment option is set. For more information, see the "Setting Global Deployment Defaults" section in this chapter.

Once the GPO is configured, the application will be advertised to all users as appropriate. By default, Software Installation policy published to users is applied only when a user logs on. As discussed in Chapter 3 under "Refreshing Group Policy Manually," you can use the Gpupdate command-line utility to force logoff.

Configuring Advanced and Global Software Installation Options

After you create an assigned or published software package, you can modify the package properties using the advanced software installation options. These options are also available if you choose Advanced as the package option in the Deploy Software dialog box. You can use these options to:

- View or set the general deployment properties
- Change the deployment type and installation options
- Define application categories for easier management when you have many deployed applications
- Specify that the package represent an upgrade of a previously deployed application
- Define the transform files that you want to use to customize the installation
- Control deployment of an application by security group

Another set of related options are the global software installation options, which you can use to set global options for Software Installation policy.

Viewing and Setting General Deployment Properties

A software package's general deployment properties are primarily for information purposes only and include:

- **Name** The name of the package as it appears to the user (within Add/Remove Programs). This name comes from the *ProductName* property in a .msi file or the *FriendlyName* property in a .zap file. The name can be modified using the general options.

- **Product Information** The version, publisher, language, and platform details from the package file. In a .zap file, version and publisher are set with the *DisplayVersion* and *Publisher* properties, respectively. Once the product information is set, it cannot be modified.

- **Support Information** The contact name, phone number, and URL of the software manufacturer. In a .zap file, the URL is set with the *URL* property. The URL can be modified using the general options.

You can view and set the general options for a software package by completing the following steps:

1. Access Software Installation under Computer Configuration\Software Settings\ Software Installation or User Configuration\Software Settings\Software Installation as appropriate for the type of package you want to work with.

2. A list of defined packages should be listed in the right pane. Right-click the package you want to work with, and select Properties.

3. Name, product information, and support information details are provided on the General tab, as shown in Figure 9-4.

Figure 9-4   Viewing and setting general software package options

Changing the Deployment Type and Installation Options

During the package creation process, you can set only the basic options that control whether an application should be published or assigned. Because you'll often need to fine-tune the configuration, you should always review the deployment type and installation options in the software package's Properties dialog box and make any necessary changes. To do this, follow these steps:

1. Access Software Installation under Computer Configuration\Software Settings\ Software Installation or User Configuration\Software Settings\Software Installation as appropriate for the type of package you want to work with.

2. Right-click the package you want to work with, and select Properties. Select the Deployment tab, as shown in Figure 9-5.

Figure 9-5 Reviewing and modifying deployment type and installation options

3. On the Deployment tab, you can choose whether to publish or assign the application. Based on that choice, other options become available or unavailable. The Deployment options you can choose from are:

    ❏ **Auto-Install This Application By File Extension Activation**   Advertises any file extensions associated with this package for install-on-first-use deployment. This option is selected by default and is not modifiable when you assign a package to a user. With a published application that normally requires the user to explicitly install the application through Add/Remove Programs, enabling this option provides assignment features for file extensions associated with the application.

    ❏ **Uninstall This Application When It Falls Out Of The Scope Of Management**   Removes the application if it no longer applies to the user. An application falls out of scope when the GPO that has deployed it is no longer processed by the user or computer. If an application falls out of scope and this option is selected, the application is uninstalled during the next foreground (user logon or computer restart) processing cycle.

> **Note**   An application can fall out of scope for three general reasons: a user or computer object moves to a new location within the Active Directory hierarchy where the GPO no longer applies, a GPO is disabled or deleted from the current scope of management, or the GPO's security filtering is changed such that the user or computer no longer process that GPO.

❑ **Do Not Display This Package In The Add/Remove Programs Control Panel**   Prevents the application from appearing in Add/Remove Programs. This option can be useful if you want to prevent a user who has administrative access over his own machine from manually removing the policy-deployed application.

❑ **Install This Application At Logon**   Configures full installation, rather than advertisement, of an application at user logon. This option is cleared by default and is not modifiable when you publish a package for users.

> **Note**   With large applications, full install at logon will slow down the user logon process considerably. The application setup will need to be completed before the desktop is presented to the user.

4. Installation User Interface Options settings let you define whether the user sees all messages during the application installation. With the default setting, Maximum, the user sees all setup screens and messages. With the Basic option, the user sees only error and completion messages. Some applications require you to choose the Basic option when the user initiates the installation because the user has insufficient privileges to make setup choices during the installation.

5. If you click Advanced, you get the Advanced Deployment Options dialog box (Figure 9-6), which has the following options:

   ❑ **Ignore Language When Deploying This Package**   Applies when the user is running one language version of Windows and is trying to install a different language version of an application. Normally this fails, but if you select this option, the application is installed anyway.

   ❑ **Make This 32-Bit X86 Application Available To IA64 Machines**   Allows you to deploy 32-bit x86 applications on 64-bit Windows versions using Intel IA-64 chip architecture. This option applies to applications installed with either .msi or .zap installer files.

   ❑ **Include OLE Class And Product Information**   Allows you to include COM registration information within Active Directory. If you choose this option, COM advertisements that are part of the application package are stored within the Active Directory Class Store, which is part of the GPC related to Software Installation policy. Because the number of advertised COM components within a large package can be significant, choose this option only if you absolutely need to use COM advertisements with your deployment. See Chapter 12 for more information on the Class Store.

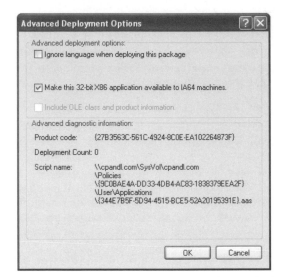

Figure 9-6   Configuring advanced software deployment options

Tip   The Advanced Software Deployment Options dialog box also provides some useful diagnostic information for the package. The first value provided is the Windows Installer product code, which Software Installation policy uses as a key to determine whether an application has already been installed on a computer. The next value is the deployment count, which is the number of times the application has been redeployed. Finally, the path to the application assignment script is shown. This file is stored within the GPT portion of the GPO and holds information related to the package path and any advertisements that have been made.

Defining Application Categories

In a large enterprise, when you use Software Installation policy to deploy many applications, you might want to define application categories to help organize the list of available applications in the Add Or Remove Programs utility. If you don't create categories and dozens of applications are available, users see the entire list of available applications, and this long list can be confusing. To help reduce confusion, you might want to define application categories, such as Sales Applications, Engineering Applications, Marketing Applications, Administrative Applications, and General Use Applications.

Once you define the categories, they are listed in the Add Or Remove Programs dialog box (Figure 9-7). Creating and defining categories is a fairly straightforward process. First you define your application categories using the global software installation defaults, which we discuss in "Setting Global Deployment Defaults." Then you add an application to a category using Categories tab options in the related Properties dialog box.

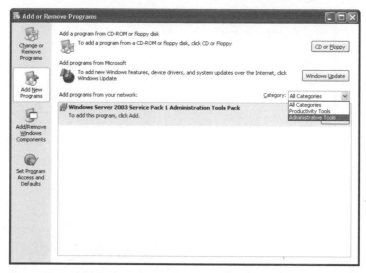

Figure 9-7   Displaying application categories in Add Or Remove Programs

Adding, Modifying, and Removing Application Categories

Application categories are defined using the global Software Installation defaults. To define application categories, follow these steps:

1. Access Software Installation under Computer Configuration\Software Settings\ Software Installation.

> **Note**   For application categories, the same global defaults are used for both per-computer and per-user Software Installation policy.

2. Right-click Software Installation and choose Properties.

3. Select the Categories tab in the Software Installation Properties dialog box, as shown in Figure 9-8.

4. To define a new application category, click Add, type the name of the application category, and then click OK.

   To modify an existing application category, select the category to modify and then click Modify. After you change the category name, click OK.

   To remove an application category, select the category and then click Remove.

Figure 9-8   Creating and managing application categories

Adding an Application to a Category

Once you've defined the categories you want to use in global defaults, you can add applications to these categories. To add an application to a category, follow these steps:

1. Access Software Installation under Computer Configuration\Software Settings\ Software Installation or User Configuration\Software Settings\Software Installation as appropriate for the type of package you want to work with.

2. Right-click the package you want to work with, and select Properties. Select the Categories tab.

3. Select a category under Available Categories and then click Select to select and list the application. If the application should be listed under additional categories, repeat this step.

4. Click OK.

Performing Upgrades

As discussed previously, Software Installation policy provides upgrade paths for applications when you use Windows Installer packages. There are two general types of upgrades:

■ Upgrades to perform a patch or install a service pack

■ Upgrades to deploy a new version of an application

The sections that follow discuss both types of upgrades. Keep in mind that you should thoroughly test any upgrade before deploying it. You should check to make sure the upgrade doesn't cause conflicts or other problems with existing applications that are deployed. You should also test the upgrade process to make sure it works as expected. If you don't test, you might, for example, find that you have compatibility problems or that you haven't included all the necessary files for the upgrade.

Patching or Installing an Application Service Pack

To patch or apply a service pack on a previously deployed application, you complete the following steps:

1. Obtain a .msi file or .msp (patch) file for the application. The software manufacturer should provide this. If not, you must create your own, as discussed in the "Getting the Necessary Windows Installer File" section in this chapter.

2. Copy the .msi or .msp file and any new installation files to the folder containing the original .msi file. Overwrite any duplicate files if necessary.

3. Access Software Installation under Computer Configuration\Software Settings\ Software Installation or User Configuration\Software Settings\Software Installation as appropriate for the type of package you want to work with.

4. Redeploy the application. Right-click the related package and then select All Tasks, Redeploy Application.

The application is redeployed to all users and computers as appropriate for the GPO you are working with. For more information on how redeployment works, see the "Redeploying Applications" section in this chapter. Keep in mind that only applications that have Windows Installer files can be upgraded in this way. If your application uses a .zap file instead, you need to complete the following steps:

1. Remove the existing application (as described in the "Removing Deployed Applications" section in this chapter).

2. Create a completely new package for the application (as described in the "Creating the ZAP File" section in this chapter).

3. Deploy the new package (as described in the "Deploying the Software Using a ZAP File" section in this chapter).

Deploying a New Version of an Application

In a software package's Properties dialog box, you can establish or verify upgrade relationships between the application you are deploying and previously deployed applications. This feature allows you to perform enforced upgrades of previously installed applications. For example, if you previously published Office XP, you can deploy Office 2003 and create an upgrade relationship between the Office XP deployment and the Office 2003 deployment. Any users or computers with

Office XP automatically get Office 2003 installed during the next foreground policy processing cycle.

> **Tip** If you deploy two applications within a single GPO that have identical Windows Installer product code SKU numbers (the third and fourth digits in the product code), the second application deployed is automatically deployed with an upgrade relationship to the first. For example, if you deploy Office XP and then Office 2003, Office 2003 is deployed automatically as an upgrade to Office XP.

To upgrade a previously deployed application to a new version, you complete the following steps:

1. Create a new software package to deploy the new version of the application (as discussed in the "Deploying the Software Using a Windows Installer File" section in this chapter).

2. Access Software Installation under Computer Configuration\Software Settings\ Software Installation or User Configuration\Software Settings\Software Installation as appropriate for the type of package you want to work with.

3. Right-click the related package, and then select Properties. If the package is already configured to upgrade an existing package, the package will be listed under Packages That This Package Will Upgrade, as shown in Figure 9-9. Select the package, and click Remove to remove this relationship.

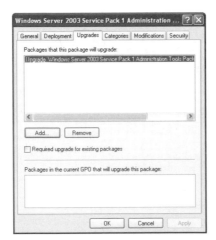

Figure 9-9 Configuring upgrade relationships

4. To establish an upgrade relationship between the application you are deploying and the previously deployed application, click Add on the Upgrades tab. This opens the Add Upgrade Package dialog box (Figure 9-10).

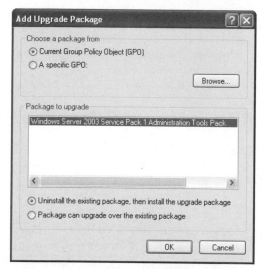

Figure 9-10   Adding a package to upgrade

5. You can establish an upgrade relationship between applications that are deployed within the same GPO by selecting Current Group Policy Object. If you want to establish a relationship between a package in a different GPO, select A Specific GPO, click Browse, and then use the Browse For A Group Policy Object dialog box to select the GPO.

6. Under Package To Upgrade, select the package to upgrade. You can then choose an upgrade option:

    ❑ **Uninstall The Existing Package, Then Install The Upgrade Package**   Recommended if you want to completely reinstall the application with the new version

    ❑ **Package Can Upgrade Over The Existing Package**   Recommended if you want to perform an in-place upgrade over the existing installation.

7. Click OK to close the Add Upgrade Package dialog box.

8. If you want to make this a required upgrade, select Required Upgrade For Existing Packages. The application you're deploying will automatically upgrade any existing packages the next time the computer restarts or when a user logs on. The user won't have a choice in the matter. If you do not make this a required upgrade, the user can choose when to install the upgrade through Add Or Remove Programs or by activating the application.

After you create an upgrade relationship, the package doing the upgrading will have an icon depicting a green, up arrow to indicate that it is an upgrade.

> **Note**   If you deploy two applications and one upgrades the other, new clients that come on the network and don't have either application installed will first install the earlier version of the application and then, during the next foreground processing cycle, install the upgraded version.

Customizing the Installation Package with Transforms

When an application uses a Windows Installer package, you can customize the installation using transforms. Transforms are special instruction files that modify the instructions embedded in the default package during application installation. Transform files have an .mst extension.

You can manage the transforms associated with an application using the related software package's Properties dialog box. Access Software Installation under Computer Configuration\Software Settings\Software Installation or User Configuration\Software Settings\Software Installation as appropriate for the type of package you want to work with. Right-click the related package, select Properties, and then select the Modifications tab.

You can add multiple transform files to an application; they are processed in the order listed on the Modifications tab, from the top of the list to the bottom, which means that transforms lower in the list take precedence over higher ones. For more information about creating transforms for Office, see the "Deploying Microsoft Office and Service Packs" section in this chapter.

> **Caution**   Once you add transforms to a published or assigned application and click OK to deploy the application, you can no longer add to or modify the list of transforms for that application. To change the applied transforms, you must remove the current application from the GPO, let all clients that have installed the application successfully uninstall it, and then re-create the package within the GPO, specifying the new transforms.

Controlling Deployment by Security Group

As discussed previously, you can manage which users and computers install deployed software in several ways: You can apply a security filter so the GPO applies only to specific security groups within a site, domain, or OU. You can create a WMI filter to filter the application deployment based on operating system or hardware configuration. You can also modify the security on the installer file itself, which is the technique discussed in this section.

Modifying the security on the installer file itself provides a more granular way to control which users or computers will process the Software Installation policy than if you use GPO-based security filtering. For example, even though a GPO might be linked to an OU and have security filtering that specifies that all users in that GPO will process it, you can use this Security tab to control which users within that OU will receive a particular deployed application package. Because you can have multiple applications deployed within a given GPO, you have a lot of flexibility in targeting application deployment.

To manage the security on an installer file, and thereby manage which computers and users can make use of it, you use the software package's Properties dialog box. Access Software Installation under Computer Configuration\Software Settings\Software Installation or User Configuration\Software Settings\Software Installation as appropriate for the type of package you want to work with. Right-click the related package, select Properties, and then select the Security tab, as shown in Figure 9-11.

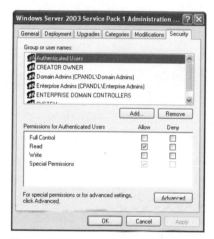

Figure 9-11   Viewing the Security permissions on an application package

The options on the Security tab allow you to define delegation for the selected installer file within a GPO. The default security provides:

- Read access to Authenticated Users, which allows all users and computers to which the GPO applies to process the file as appropriate

- Read, Write, Special Permissions to Creator Owner and Enterprise Admins, which allows the creator and Enterprise Admins to work with the installer file

- Read and Special Permissions to Enterprise Domain Controllers, which allows Enterprise Domain Controllers to work with the installer file

- Full Control to System and Domain Admins, which allows the operating system and Domain Admins to fully manage the installer file and the installation process

To allow a user or computer to install a deployed application package, you simply grant that user or computer (or user or computer group) Read permission on the application. A deployed application package grants the Authenticated Users group read access by default—which means that all users and computers have access to the application package by default. To target an application package to a specific group, you must first remove the Authenticated Users access from that application and then add Read access for the appropriate users, computers, or groups. However, because permissions are inherited from the application package object itself, you must remove inheritance before you can modify the permissions. Follow these steps to perform this operation:

1. Access Software Installation under Computer Configuration\Software Settings\ Software Installation or User Configuration\Software Settings\Software Installation as appropriate for the type of package you want to work with.

2. Right-click the related package, and select Properties. On the Security tab, click Advanced.

3. Clear the check box labeled "Inherit From Parent The Permission Entries That Apply To Child Objects."

4. A dialog box appears, asking you whether you want to copy or remove the inherited permissions or cancel the operation completely. Choose Copy. Click OK to return to the basic security dialog box.

5. Select the Authenticated Users group in the Group Or User Names list, and then click Remove.

6. Click Add, and then use the Select Users, Computers, Or Groups dialog box to select the user, computer, or group for which you want to add permissions. Click OK.

7. Select the newly added user, computer, or group in the Group Or Users Names list. Under Permissions For, select Read in the Allow column.

8. Repeat steps 6 and 7 to add permissions for other users, computers, or groups.

9. Click OK.

The newly added users, computers, or groups can now install the application. Other users, computers, or groups cannot install the application (unless they are a member of one of the default groups, such as Domain Admins).

Setting Global Deployment Defaults

If you always use certain installation options for Software Installation policy, you might want to configure global defaults. For example, if you want applications to be uninstalled by default when they fall out of focus, you can use global defaults to do this.

> **Note**   For Software Installation Categories, the same global defaults are used for both per-computer and per-user options on a per-GPO basis. Otherwise, the global defaults are set separately for Software Installation policy under Computer Configuration and User Configuration.

You can view current global defaults and define others by completing the following steps:

1. Access Software Installation under Computer Configuration\Software Settings\Software Installation.

2. Right-click the Software Installation node, and choose Properties. This opens the Software Installation Properties dialog box (Figure 9-12).

   You can view and set global defaults for Software Installation policy for both users and computers.

Figure 9-12   The Software Installation Properties dialog box

Table 9-2 provides an overview of the global defaults you can configure and lists that tab that each option is located on.

Table 9-2   Global Software Installation Defaults

Tab	Option	Description
General	Default Package Location	Sets a default path to packages within this GPO. When you select New, Package, this path appears in the Open File dialog box.
	New Packages	Determines whether the Deploy Software dialog box is displayed or a default pack deployment option is chosen automatically. By default, the Deploy Software dialog box lets you choose the deployment option. You can specify that the GPO should always choose one of these options right away.

Table 9-2   **Global Software Installation Defaults**

Tab	Option	Description
	Installation User Interface Options	Sets the default user interface option: Basic or Maximum. With the default setting, Maximum, users see all setup screens and messages. With the Basic option, users see only error and completion messages.
Advanced	Uninstall The Applications When They Fall Out Of The Scope Of Management	An application falls out of scope when the GPO that has deployed it is no longer processed by the user or computer. If an application falls out of scope and this option is selected, the application is uninstalled during the next foreground (user logon or computer restart) processing cycle.
	Include OLE Information When Deploying Applications	If you choose this option, COM advertisements that are part of the application package are stored within the Active Directory Class Store. See Chapter 13 for more information on the Class Store.
	Make 32-Bit X86 Windows Installer Applications Available To IA64 Machines	Allows you to use .msi files to deploy 32-bit x86 applications on 64-bit Windows versions using Intel IA-64 chip architecture.
	Make 32-Bit X86 Down-Level Applications Available To IA64 Machines	Allows you to use .zap files to deploy 32-bit x86 applications on 64-bit Windows versions using Intel IA-64 chip architecture.
File Extensions	Application Precedence	Within a GPO, if you have multiple applications that register the same file extension, you can use this option to control which application is installed when the user opens a document with the advertised extension.
Categories	Categories For The Domain	Lets you specify global defaults for application categories. The categories appear in Add Or Remove Programs.

Deploying Microsoft Office and Service Packs

Software Installation policy is useful for a wide variety of application deployment scenarios, but the two most common scenarios are for Office and operating system service packs. In this section, we'll discuss best practices for the both scenarios, as well as design and deployment considerations for each.

Deploying Office Through Policy

Office is probably the application most frequently deployed through policy. Because the distribution files are so large (500 MB or more), Office provides a good example of the special considerations you need to make when deploying large applications through policy.

With Office or any large application deployment, you should consider several issues prior to deployment, including:

- What package distribution technique to use
- Whether you should use transforms to customize the installation
- What deployment mode to use
- How to keep Office updated

 Note   You will often need to customize Office after the initial installation. The Office 2003 Resource Kit includes a set of Administrative Template files that you can use to customize Office configurations. Chapter 10 covers this customization in detail.

Choosing a Package Distribution Technique

The first consideration is the placement of the package itself. You essentially have two choices for getting the package to the client: an administrative installation or a nonadministrative installation.

You can perform an administrative installation of Office to a network share by using the *setup /a* option. As mentioned earlier, you should use a DFS share to deploy any applications in policy because it is impossible to change the path to an application once it's been deployed. The advantage of an administrative installation is that you can patch the installation directly and then perform a redeployment to force all clients to reinstall the application with the new, patched version.

You can perform a nonadministrative installation of Office to a network share. That is, you can simply copy the contents of the Office CD to the network share and reference the Windows Installer package in policy. The advantage of this approach is that if you are deploying Office 2003, you can use the Local Install Source feature to cache the

Office setup files on the local workstation during installation. The downside of a non-administrative install is that when you do have to patch or update Office, you must distribute and run the patch on each computer where the application is installed.

> **Note**   If you perform an administrative installation of Office 2003, you can use the new Local Install Source feature in Office. This feature allows you to cache all Office cabinet (.cab) files needed for repairs, updates, or patches on the local computer in a hidden folder called MSOCache. In this way, the user doesn't have to have the CD available during an update. You can specify that you want to create an LIS cache on the workstation during the installation of Office 2003 by creating a transform on the package prior to deployment. Of course, caching all of these .cab files takes nearly 200 MB of disk space on the workstation, in addition to using network bandwidth to copy the files to the client.

These two network-based options are best for deploying Office to computers with high-speed, low-latency network links to the servers where the packages reside. In some cases, however, you might have clients that are connected across intermittent, slow, or even dial-up links. When Group Policy detects a slow link, Software Installation policy is not processed by default, even during foreground policy processing. Even if it were, an application setup the size of Office would likely never complete, given how long it would take to run the install over a slow network link.

Even on fast networks, having many computers downloading 600 MB of Office at nearly the same time would likely saturate the network, causing intermittent failures as computers attempted to retry their communications. Therefore, a third and better approach for deploying Office or any large application is to deploy the setup package locally to each computer before deploying the application through policy. This pre-staging of the Office setup package offers two advantages:

- You can take as long as you need to get the package to the computer before deploying the policy.

- Roaming users can download the package at the office, or you can send them a CD with an automated copy process that copies the files to the local computer.

You can use to get the files to the client using different mechanisms. You can use everything from the low-tech approach—such as the CD approach we just mentioned or simply running a series of *xcopy* commands to copy the files to each client—to high-tech approaches such as creating a scheduled task or a startup script to have the computer copy the files on its own time from the server. You can even use a robust file copy utility such as Robocopy (from the Windows Server 2003 Resource Kit) to get the files out to your clients.

The challenge in getting the files to the client is that, for a large package such as Office, copying the entire setup to every client on a large network can be extremely bandwidth intensive. In these cases, you should consider networking technology such as IP Multicast because as it can significantly minimize the repetitive data that flows over your network to remote sites. Another solution for these remotes sites is to first stage the Office setup files on a server at the remote location and then create a startup script or other job to pull those files from the server. In this way, you distribute the load of deploying the package and ensure that the file copying occurs only on local area networks (LANs).

Once you've deployed the package to every computer that will install it, you can set up policy to point to the local path where you've copied the setup files on each machine. This is a case where you do not use a path to a UNC share, but rather an absolute path to a folder somewhere on the computer's local hard drive (for example, c:\packages\ office2003\pro11.msi).

> **Tip**   Sometimes when you copy the setup files to clients to stage the package to remote clients connected over slow links still might not be able to install the software. This can occur because the slow-link detection process does not consider the location of the package—only the fact that the computer is connected over a slow link. To get around this issue and ensure that Software Installation policy is always processed, you can enable Allow Processing Across A Slow Network Connection under Computer Configuration\Administrative Templates\System\Group Policy\Software Installation Policy Processing on all of the computers to which you will be distributing applications. By enabling this policy, you ensure that computers where you've locally staged the setup package will always run the installation, even when the computer is connected over a slow link.

Using Transforms to Customize an Office Deployment

Using transforms is a common method of customizing deployments of Office. Transforms give you the ability to customize almost every aspect of a Windows Installer package for deployment. In the case of Office, you can use a transform to control, for example, which Office applications are installed, what the default document locations are for each application, and settings for the user's default Outlook profile.

To create a transform for Office 2003, you must download the free Office 2003 Editions Resource Kit Tools from *http://www.microsoft.com/downloads/ details.aspx?FamilyID=4bb7cb10-a6e5-4334-8925-3bcf308cfbaf&DisplayLang=en*.

After installing the tools on your administrative workstation, you can run the Custom Installation Wizard to create transform files. Figure 9-13 shows how you can specify that certain applications—in this case, Microsoft Access—won't be installed, while others that are not installed by default, such as New And Open Office Document Shortcuts, are added back into the installation.

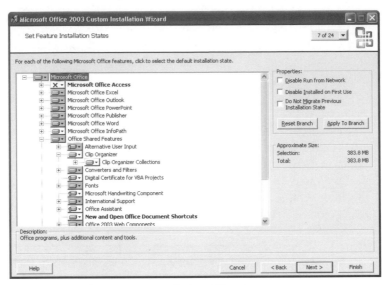

Figure 9-13 The Custom Installation Wizard

When you complete the wizard, you are asked where to save the .mst transform file. If you copied the Office installation files to a network share in preparation for deployment, place a copy of the transform file within that share location. If you plan to copy the installation files to each local computer, you should copy the transform file along with the installation files to ensure that it's available during installation. You'll also need to configure policy so the transforms are used. See the "Customizing the Installation Package with Transforms" section in this chapter for details.

Selecting a Deployment Mode

Software Installation policy provides a number of ways to deploy applications—including user assignment and user publishing—but the preferred method for deploying a large application such as Office is through computer assignment. Computer assignment provides for an unattended installation, with no user interaction required. All user-based deployment mechanisms require that the user be unable to use her workstation until the application installation completes. For an application such as Office, this could mean tens of minutes if the network is busy—or, even in the best case, 5 to 10 minutes.

Because computer assignment runs at restart, it offers the added benefit that no users will be logged on to the computer during deployment. The only challenge with computer assignment is that you must trigger a restart of the computer to kick off the installation. You can do this using a variety of methods, such as by using remote WMI script or by using the Shutdown.exe utility in conjunction with a Task Scheduler job.

The key here is that if you use a network-based share for the Office installation files, you should stagger the restarts to ensure that your network is not saturated by many machines requesting files from the share at once.

Keeping Office Updated

When Microsoft issues new service packs or patches for Office, you should also use policy to deploy them. The deployment process is relatively straightforward if you use an administrative installation of Office to deploy the application via policy. The first thing to note is that if the update is a service pack, you should download the full file version rather than the client version. Then you should extract the service pack files to a working directory rather than run the installation as is. This last step also applies to patches. Always extract the files in the service pack or patch to a working directory first rather than run the service pack or patch directly from your administrative work-station. You can do this by using the /t and /c options on a service pack or patch as follows:

```
officexpSp3-kb832671-fullfile-enu.exe /t:C:\downloads\officexp-sp3 /c
```

You will notice that many of the downloaded files have an .msp extension; this extension indicates a Windows Installer patch file, which must be applied to your administrative installation. To apply the updates to your administrative installation, you use the built-in Msiexec.exe command-line utility to patch the main .msi file on your administrative installation share. The command for this patching is as follows:

```
msiexec /p PathToMSPFile /a PathToMSIFile SHORTFILENAMES=TRUE /qb /L* PathToLogFile
```

You provide the path to the .msp file, the path on your administrative share to the main Office .msi file (usually pro*.msi for Office Professional), and a path to a log file that logs the success or failure of the patching process.

Once you've patched all of your administrative installation points, you must redeploy Office through policy. During the next foreground processing cycle, these computers or users will perform a reinstallation of the updated version of Office.

If you have deployed the Office setup files to your computers directly, the process of applying a service pack or update is different:

1. Copy the service pack or patch setup files to the local computer.

2. Run the *msiexec.exe* command on each of these clients to update their local installation sources.

3. Redeploy Office in policy to trigger a reinstallation from the updated local source.

Note If you are using the Local Install Source feature with Office 2003, you don't need to perform this manual *msiexec* operation. You simply execute the client version of the patch or service pack on the local computer and the Local Install Source cache is updated.

Deploying Windows Service Packs Through Policy

Another common scenario is deploying Windows service packs to your computers through policy. Windows service packs present many of the same challenges as Office because service packs are generally large in size. However, service packs also present a unique challenge because a failure in the middle of a service pack installation can render a computer unable to restart. For that reason, service packs have some unique requirements.

You should avoid installing service packs from an administrative network share. Network latencies and network outages can have disastrous consequences if they occur in the middle of an update. If you have remote computers for which no physical systems administration resources are available in the event of a failure, it's best to copy the service pack files to your computers before performing the update.

You still use the same approach to deploy a service pack through policy:

1. Download the full service pack installation files from Microsoft. Within that full set of files is a file called Update.msi, which is the main update Windows Installer package for the service pack.

2. You use the Update.msi file when you define your software package. As with Office, you must create this package as a computer assignment to ensure that the package is deployed at computer restart with no users present.

> **Tip**   It's a good idea to create the software package for a Windows service pack within its own GPO. This allows you to easily link the GPO to whatever container you want to apply the service pack to.

3. After you create the computer assignment, any computers that process the policy at their next restart will apply the service pack. They will reboot once more before presenting the logon dialog box. You can verify that the patch was applied by executing the *winver* command on the target workstation.

> **Tip**   In most cases, if a computer has already successfully applied a Windows service pack through policy, it will not attempt to do so again on subsequent foreground processing cycles. However, you can make sure this problem doesn't arise by creating a WMI filter linked to the GPO to check for the service pack version on the system prior to processing.

Maintaining Deployed Applications

Software Installation policy is designed to manage the complete life cycle of deployed applications. After you deploy applications using Software Installation policy, you might need to make changes to the deployment or even remove a deployment. By right-clicking on a deployed application within a GPO, you get a series of options for managing the application. For example, you can switch a user-deployed application from published to assigned simply by choosing the appropriate menu item. If you previously chose to autoinstall the application by file extension activation, you can disable this by clearing the Auto-Install option.

In the "Configuring Advanced and Global Software Installation Options" section, we discussed performing upgrades, customizing installation packages with transforms, and other routine maintenance tasks that can be performed using installation options. Additional tasks that you might also need to perform include:

- Removing deployed applications
- Redeploying applications
- Configuring Software Restriction policy
- Troubleshooting

Removing Deployed Applications

You can use Software Installation policy to install applications and to uninstall previously deployed applications. You can manually trigger an uninstall by removing the software package that deployed the application in policy. An uninstall can also be triggered automatically. Automatic uninstalls occur if an application falls out of scope and you've configured Uninstall This Application When It Falls Out Of The Scope Of Management.

To trigger removal of a previously deployed application, follow these steps:

1. Access Software Installation under Computer Configuration\Software Settings\ Software Installation or User Configuration\Software Settings\Software Installation as appropriate for the type of package you want to work with.

2. Right-click the related package, and select All Tasks, Remove.

3. In the Remove Software dialog box that appears, you have two removal options:

   ❑ **Immediately Uninstall The Software From Users And Computers**   Immediately removes the application from all clients that are using it

   ❑ **Allow Users To Continue To Use The Software, But Prevent New Installations**   Stops future deployments but allows the application to remain on systems where it has already been installed

> **Note**   If you choose immediate removal, the removal isn't truly immediate—it means that during the user or computer's next foreground policy processing cycle, the application will be uninstalled.

4. Click OK.

> **Tip**   When you remove an application, even though it is no longer visible within policy, the application itself still resides within the Group Policy Container (GPC) in Active Directory and the Group Policy Template (GPT) in SYSVOL until it's manually removed. To indicate that the package has been removed, the *msiScriptName* attribute on the *packageRegistration* object within Active Directory takes the value *R*. For more information about the storage of policy settings, see Chapter 13.

Redeploying Applications

As discussed previously in "Patching or Installing a Service Pack," the need to redeploy an application can arise for a number of reasons. If you patch an administrative installation of an application that was previously deployed, you can use the redeploy feature to have all targeted users or computers reinstall the application with the updated file. When you redeploy, the application is reinstalled wherever it was already installed, and on the next foreground processing cycle, all targeted users and computers perform a reinstall. What they actually do is call the Windows Installer engine to perform a repair using the options *o*, *m*, *u*, *s*, and *v*. These options provide the following behavior:

- Reinstalls the application if a file is missing or an older version of the file is present.
- Rewrites all computer-specific registry entries associated with the package.
- Rewrites all user-specific registry entries associated with the package.
- Overwrites all shortcuts associated with the package.
- Runs the repair from the source Windows Installer package file and recaches the .msi file locally. (Windows Installer .msi files are always cached on the local computer during an installation—and stored in the %windir%\installer folder.)

> **Note**   When a package is redeployed, any user settings and data that were created since the application was first installed should be retained. However, this depends on how the application setup was written and where the settings and data were stored. For applications such as Office, user settings and data are retained through a redeployment.

Configuring Software Restriction Policies

After you deploy your software, you might want to ensure that only the correct software and software versions are executed on your user's systems. You can use Software Restriction Policies for this purpose. These policies are found in the Computer Configuration area or User Configuration area within Windows Settings\Security Settings\Software Restrictions Policies.

Note   Within the local GPO, Software Restriction Policy is available only per computer, not per user.

Software Restriction Policies provide a powerful mechanism for blocking software execution. You can restrict known software types that cause problems on your network, such as games or peer-to-peer file sharing applications, as well as unknown types of software that can perform malicious activities.

Getting Started with Software Restriction Policies

Software Restriction Policies are configured on a per-GPO basis. Software Restriction Policies under Computer Configuration are used to set restrictions for all users of a computer. Software Restriction Policies under User Configuration are used to set restrictions for individual users or user groups.

When you access the Software Restriction Policies node under either configuration area for the first time within a GPO, you see a message stating that no software restriction policies have been defined. You begin the process of using Software Restriction Policies by right-clicking the Software Restriction Policies node and choosing Create New Policies. You then see a set of nodes in the results pane:

- **Enforcement policy**   Determines how software restriction is applied to software files and to whom software restriction applies.

- **Designated File Types policy**   Determines what file types and extensions are considered to be executable code.

- **Trusted Publishers policy**   Sets trusted software publishers.

- **Security Levels node**   Contains policies that specify whether and how restricted software runs.

- **Additional Rules node**   Contains policies that control software execution. Rules can be established based on publisher certificates, the Internet zone from which the software is obtained, file path, and a secure hash of a file.

Together, these policies allow you to set global behaviors for software restriction as well as specific custom rules and behaviors for restricting or allowing specific software execution. Once you've used these settings to define the rules for your Software Restriction Policies, you can deploy them to your users and computers.

Whether you deploy Software Restriction Policies per computer or per user depends on whether you need to control software execution for all users on a computer or just particular users, regardless of where they are logged on. You can merge Software Restriction Policies from multiple GPOs if you need different levels of control based on the user or computer's location in Active Directory.

Configuring Enforcement Policy

Enforcement policy settings determine how software restriction is applied to software files and to whom software restriction applies. To view or set enforcement policy settings, follow these steps:

1. Access Software Restriction Policies under Computer Configuration\Windows Settings\Security Settings\Software Restrictions Policies or User Configuration\ Windows Settings\Security Settings\Software Restrictions Policies as appropriate.

2. If software restriction has not been set up yet, right-click the Software Restriction Policies node and choose Create New Policies.

3. In the right pane, right-click Enforcement and select Properties.

4. You can apply software restriction policies to all types of executable code except DLLs or to all software (Figure 9-14). The default is to exclude DLLs, which is a safe place to start.

Figure 9-14   Working with enforcement options in Software Restriction Policy

5. You can you control who will process the software restriction policies. By default, all users are subject to the policy, but to be safe you can choose to exclude members of the computer's local Administrators group. This lets administrators undo any overly restrictive policies.

6. Click OK.

Caution   Because Software Restriction Policies can prevent execution of code, you should carefully plan how to use this policy. It is easy to paint yourself into a corner by being overly restrictive.

Viewing and Configuring Designated File Types

Designated File Types policy determines what file types and extensions are considered to be executable code. To view or set designated file types, follow these steps:

1. Access Software Restriction Policies under Computer Configuration\Windows Settings\Security Settings\Software Restrictions Policies or User Configuration\ Windows Settings\Security Settings\Software Restrictions Policies as appropriate.

2. If software restriction has not been set up yet, right-click the Software Restriction Policies node and choose Create New Policies.

3. In the right pane, right-click Designated File Types and select Properties.

4. In the Designated File Types Properties dialog box (Figure 9-15), common extensions are listed by default, such as .exe, .bat, and .vbs.

Figure 9-15   Working with designated file types in Software Restriction Policy

5. You can add to the list if you have executable types that you want to include in the policy. Type the file extension of a file type that has already been registered on the system in the File Extension box and then click Add.

6. You can remove executable types from the list as well. Select the file type to remove, and then click Delete.

7. Click OK.

Configuring Trust Publishers Policy

Using Trusted Publishers policy, you can allow software execution based on public-key signing of the executable code. You can specify whether regular users can add to the list of trusted publishers maintained on their computer or whether this action can be performed only by administrators. For example, when you download a file from Microsoft, you have the option at download time to add Microsoft to the list of publishers whose content you trust.

Using Trusted Publishers policy, you can prevent your users from ever adding a trusted publisher to their computer. This can be a good thing if you suspect your users are downloading software that, while signed by a legitimate publisher, is not appropriate for use on your computers. You can also use this policy to configure whether certificates that a publisher has used to sign their software are still valid. This is done by checking their certificate authority to see if the certificate has been revoked—either because the publisher or the certificate's timestamp is no longer valid. This is a good idea, but it can result in latency for the user because Windows must contact the signing authority each time a certificate is used to ensure that it is still valid.

To view or configure trusted publisher options, follow these steps:

1. Access Software Restriction Policies under Computer Configuration\Windows Settings\Security Settings\Software Restrictions Policies or User Configuration\Windows Settings\Security Settings\Software Restrictions Policies as appropriate.

2. If software restriction has not been set up, right-click the Software Restriction Policies node and choose Create New Policies.

3. In the right pane, right-click Trusted Publishers and select Properties. The Trusted Publishers dialog box opens.

4. Specify who can select trusted publishers. The options are:

   ❑ **End Users**   All users can select trusted publishers

   ❑ **Local Computer Administrator**   Only local computer administrators can select trusted publishers (and any domain or enterprise administrators).

   ❑ **Enterprise Administrators**   Only members of Domain Admins or Enterprise Admins can select trusted publishers.

5. Specify whether to check if a certificate has been revoked—either because the publisher revoked the certificate, the certificate's timestamp is no longer valid, or both.

6. Click OK.

Configuring Disallowed and Unrestricted Applications

Security Levels policy specifies that restricted software is either disallowed or unrestricted. The Disallowed and Unrestricted modes are mutually exclusive.

By default, the Unrestricted mode is active. This means that any computer or user processing these Software Restriction Policies can run any code except those explicitly restricted by additional rules that you specify. When Disallowed mode is active, any computers or users processing these Software Restriction Policies cannot run any code except those explicitly allowed through additional rules.

Thus, your choice with Security Levels is to either lock down everything and allow for known exceptions or to allow everything and lock down code you know to be unsafe. The best choice depends on your security requirements, but using Disallowed as the default means a lot more work for your administrators to respond to user needs as new legitimate applications are required. However, if you have a tightly controlled and fairly static environment, it can be an excellent choice for preventing unknown, potentially malicious code from executing.

To set the security level, follow these steps:

1. Access Software Restriction Policies under Computer Configuration\Windows Settings\Security Settings\Software Restrictions Policies or User Configuration\ Windows Settings\Security Settings\Software Restrictions Policies as appropriate.

2. If software restriction has not been set up yet, right-click the Software Restriction Policies node and choose Create New Policies.

3. Select the Security Levels node. The currently selected default is shown with a green circle and a check mark on its icon.

   ❑ To set Disallowed as the default security level, right-click Disallowed and select Set As Default.

   ❑ To set Unrestricted as the default security level, right-click Unrestricted and select Set As Default.

Configuring Security Rules

You can use Additional Rules policy to configure the actual rules that specify what software is restricted or allowed to run. If you right-click the Additional Rules node, you have four rule types to choose from:

- Certificate Rules
- Hash Rules
- Internet Zone Rules
- Path Rules

The sections that follow discuss how to use each rule in your Software Restriction Policies.

Using Certificate Rules   Certificate rules enable you to allow or disallow code execution based on who has digitally signed the code. For example, if our in-house development team signs all applications that are developed and deployed to our users, we can create a certificate rule to always allow these applications to run, as shown in Figure 9-16.

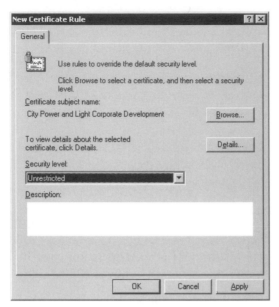

Figure 9-16   Creating a certificate rule in Software Restriction Policy

To create a certificate rule, follow these steps:

1. Access Software Restriction Policies under Computer Configuration\Windows Settings\Security Settings\Software Restrictions Policies or User Configuration\ Windows Settings\Security Settings\Software Restrictions Policies as appropriate.

2. Right-click Additional Rules, and select New Certificate Rule.

3. In the New Certificate Rule dialog box, click Browse to browse to a certificate file on your local computer or network.

4. Use the Security Level list to specify whether applications signed by this certificate are unrestricted or disallowed.

5. Click OK.

Using Hash Rules   File hashes are unique, nonreproducible values that are computed on a file based on its content. By creating a hash rule, you can restrict or allow execution of very specific file versions.

To create a hash rule, follow these steps:

1. Access Software Restriction Policies under Computer Configuration\Windows Settings\Security Settings\Software Restrictions Policies or User Configuration\ Windows Settings\Security Settings\Software Restrictions Policies as appropriate.

2. Right-click Additional Rules, and select New Hash Rule.

3. In the New Hash Rule dialog box, click Browse to browse to the executable file you want to control and select it. As shown in Figure 9-17, the file hash is then automatically computed.

4. Use the Security Level list to specify whether applications signed by this certificate are unrestricted or disallowed.

5. Click OK.

> **Note** For Figure 9-17, we created a hash rule to prevent execution of Solitaire. Because the rule is based on the file hash rather than the name or other data that can be easily changed, the user can rename Sol.exe to anything else and it will still be restricted from running.

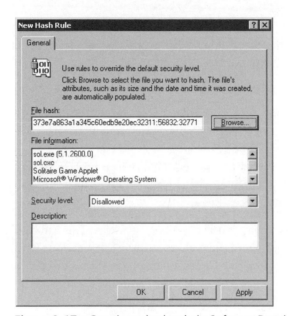

Figure 9-17 Creating a hash rule in Software Restriction Policy

Using Internet Zone Rules The Trusted Zones rule lets you control code execution based on where the code is running from. This rule augments the controls that Microsoft Internet Explorer provides, letting you control code that is installed by Windows Installer. That is, this rule applies only to applications that are installed via a Windows installer package from a particular location on the network. For example, if a user attempts to run an application installation using a Windows Installer package downloaded from the Internet, this rule can prevent that installation.

You can essentially use Internet Zone rules to control what software a user can install from where. Unfortunately, however, these rules do not affect software that is packaged using a format other than Windows Installer.

To create an Internet Zone rule, follow these steps:

1. Access Software Restriction Policies under Computer Configuration\Windows Settings\Security Settings\Software Restrictions Policies or User Configuration\Windows Settings\Security Settings\Software Restrictions Policies as appropriate.

2. Right-click Additional Rules and select New Internet Zone Rule.

3. Use the Internet Zone list to specify the zone you want to configure. The zones are:

   ❑ Local Computer

   ❑ Local Intranet

   ❑ Restricted Sites

   ❑ Trusted Sites

   ❑ Internet

4. Use the Security Level list to specify whether applications from this zone are unrestricted or disallowed.

5. Click OK.

Using Path Rules   Path rules are probably the most flexible in terms of allowing or denying code execution. You simply enter a file system path—to a file or a folder—and any code that falls under the Designated File Types is controlled by the rule. Note that the path you enter is recursed. That is, if you type *c:\program files*, all files and folders under this parent folder are controlled. Because of this, use caution when disallowing access to large folder hierarchies.

You can also create path rules to registry keys. This can be useful if you want to control what can run out of the various autostartup locations within the registry, such as the *RunOnce* key. The trickiest part of a registry path configuration is that you can't browse to registry paths from the Path Rule dialog box. Instead, you must manually type the path to the registry key or copy/paste it from the Registry Editor to the Path box. You must also enclose the registry path in % symbols, as shown here:

```
%HKEY_LOCAL_MACHINE\SOFTWARE\Microsoft\Windows\CurrentVersion\RunOnce%
```

By restricting common registry paths that perform autostartup tasks, you can control malicious code that tries to install itself in the user's workstation.

To create a Path rule, follow these steps:

1. Access Software Restriction Policies under Computer Configuration\Windows Settings\Security Settings\Software Restrictions Policies or User Configuration\Windows Settings\Security Settings\Software Restrictions Policies as appropriate.

2. Right-click Additional Rules, and select New Path Rule.

3. Type the path you want to use. You can click Browse to browse to the file or folder you want to control and select it. With registry paths, you must type the path or copy/paste it from the Registry Editor to the Path box.

> **Note**   Don't forget to enclose the registry path in % symbols, as shown previously.

4. Use the Security Level list to specify whether applications from this zone are unrestricted or disallowed.

5. Click OK.

Troubleshooting Software Installation Policy

Many tools and techniques are available for ensuring that Software Installation policy functions properly. The main tools are the various log files that you can enable to gain insight into what is or isn't happening during Software Installation policy processing. The primary log files for troubleshooting include:

- **Application event log**   The Application event log on the target computer generates messages related to general Group Policy processing as well as Software Installation–specific messages. Software Installation messages have an event source of Application Management or AppMgmt. Windows Installer–related messages have an event source of MsiInstaller. These messages tell you whether an application installation was successful, and if not, it will often provide some basic explanation.

- **%windir%\debug\usermode\userenv.log**   Provides insight into problems with Group Policy core processing and specifically high-level error codes for Software Installation processing. It can also point to why a GPO wasn't processed during a given cycle.

- **%windir%\Debug\UserMode\appmgmt.log**   Provides detailed logging of the Software Installation processing steps, including which GPOs are being processed for Software Installation policy and what applications are being installed.

- **%temp%\msi*.log**   The Windows Installer engine can create detailed logs that enumerate every step of the package installation. This log file is useful for troubleshooting problems with the package when you know that Software Installation policy is functioning properly but the application is failing on installation. For per-computer deployments, these log files are created with a unique name, beginning with *msi*.*log*, within the %windir%\temp folder. For per-user installations, the log files are created within the user's %temp% folder.

These log files are stored on the client computers that are processing Software Installation policy, not on the domain controller. To learn how to enable and use these log files, see Chapter 16.

In addition to log files, you can use the Group Policy Management Console's Group Policy Results Wizard to remotely collect Software Installation policy information on a particular computer and verify that the application was installed as expected. Figure 9-18 shows an example of a settings report generated by the wizard. The wizard also shows a filtered view of the application event log on the client computer—showing only Group Policy–related events from the Policy Events tab.

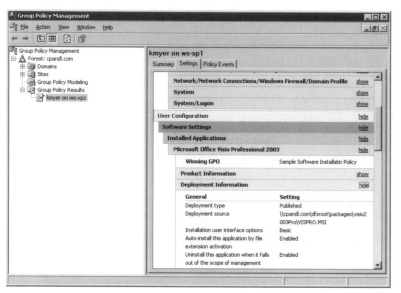

Figure 9-18   Viewing Software Installation information in a Group Policy Results report

Troubleshooting Steps

The first thing you can do to ensure that you understand what's happening during Software Installation policy processing is to enable verbose Group Policy status messages. You can do this easily by enabling Verbose Vs. Normal Status Messages under Computer Configuration\Administrative Templates\System.

Enabling this policy gives you visual clues about what's happening during foreground Group Policy processing, including when managed applications are being installed and what application installation is currently running.

Using the tools and logs described above, the following general approach to troubleshooting Software Installation processing works well:

1. If an application fails to install correctly for the target user or computer, use the GPMC Group Policy Results Wizard to ensure that the user or computer is actually processing the GPO containing the application package. If not, see Chapter 17 for possible solutions.

2. If you've confirmed that the GPO is being processed but the application is not being installed, the next step is to enable logging to determine where the failure is occurring. Start by enabling the Appmgmt.log file to determine whether the application installation is being attempted and, if so, whether any errors have occurred. This file generally shows error codes related to the installation or provides a reason why the installation can't be completed.

3. If Appmgmt.log indicates that the installation is being attempted but is failing, the next step is to enable verbose Windows Installer logging. The log file generated during a Windows Installer installation steps through each action the package takes and can provide insight into where the failure is occurring and why.

Common Software Installation Policy Problems

A number of issues that arise during Software Installation policy processing can be resolved relatively easily. The most common of these issues are explained here:

- **It takes two or three reboots or user logons to trigger a installation via policy.** If your clients are running Windows XP, they probably have Fast Logon Optimization enabled. This causes some Group Policy processing, such as Software Installation policy, to require multiple restarts for logon. You can disable this feature by enabling Always Wait For The Network At Computer Startup And Logon under Computer Configuration\Administrative Templates\System\ Logon.

- **Software Installation policy is not being processed even though other policy is being processed correctly.** As mentioned earlier, Software Installation policy is not processed by default if a slow link is detected between the computer and the domain controller. To verify whether a slow link was detected, run the GPMC's Group Policy Results Wizard against the client. This will tell you whether a slow link was detected at the last foreground policy processing cycle.

- **Users or computers are unable to run an application setup, and the error is "Access Denied."** To run the setup, the user or computer must have Read permission to the share and the files where the Windows Installer package resides. Make sure the users or computers that will process the policy have sufficient permissions to access the packages.

- **Software Installation policy uninstalls a version of the software that already exists on your computers before installing the managed copy.** This happens by design. If Software Installation policy finds an application that was installed manually outside of the Software Installation policy process and that application has the same Windows Installer product code as the managed application that is to be installed, the unmanaged application is automatically uninstalled first. This ensures that only managed applications are installed on your systems.

■ **An administrator manually uninstalled an application that was previously deployed via Software Installation policy. When that computer processes the policy again, the application is not reinstalled.**   Managed applications deployed via Software Installation policy should never be manually uninstalled. Even though the application is gone, registry-based information is left behind that causes Software Installation policy to think the application is already installed. If needed, you can manually delete this information to force a reinstall. From the Registry Editor, open HKEY_CURRENT_USER\Software\Microsoft\Windows\CurrentVersion\Group Policy\AppMgmt (or HKEY_LOCAL_MACHINE if the application was deployed per computer). Each managed application has a subkey under this key that contains information about the deployment. Locate the subkey that lists the uninstalled application, and delete that subkey.

Summary

Software Installation policy allows you to easily deploy software to users and computers in departmental settings. You can publish or assign applications to users or computers. When you use Software Installation policy with the Windows Installer technology, you can manage the full life cycle of applications in your environment—providing for installation, repair, updating and patching, and removal. When you add Software Restriction policy, you can manage not only what software is installed on your user's desktops, but you can also ensure that only approved software is executed in your environment. These two policies together provide a powerful one-two punch for providing a secure, managed environment in which your users can be productive.

Chapter 10

Managing Microsoft Office Configurations

In this chapter:

Introducing Office Configuration Management .370

Customizing Office Configurations 371

Managing Office-Related Policy 383

Summary 396

Microsoft Office is an application suite composed of multiple applications. Each application contains dozens of configuration settings. In just about any-sized environment, you'll want to roll out Office with some of those settings already customized to meet the needs of your users. You can do this with transforms and a special set of policy settings for Office.

Transforms allow you to tailor what applications are installed and how those applications are configured for first use. The special set of Administrative Templates for Office allow you to control and configure Office features through Group Policy in much the same way as you control Windows features. If you configure Office-related policy before you deploy Office, you can be sure that required configuration settings are already in place when users start up the new Office programs. Once you've deployed Office, you can use Office-related policy to manage the installation as well. You can also modify the setup of previously deployed applications using custom maintenance files, which are similar to transforms.

Related Information

- For more information about deploying Office through Group Policy, see Chapter 9.

- For more information about maintaining Office installations, see *http://office.microsoft.com/en-us/assistance/HA011402391033.aspx*.

- For more information about the Custom Maintenance Wizard, see *http://office.microsoft.com/en-us/assistance/HA011513681033.aspx*.

Introducing Office Configuration Management

Office is a large software application suite. Deploying and managing Office is more complex than managing Windows itself or related Windows components. You can manage your Office installations using:

- Custom Installation Wizard, which allows you to create .mst transform files for customizing Office installations. You can use the wizard to choose the folder location to install Microsoft Office; specify whether to remove previous versions of Office applications; configure whether and how various Office applications are installed; create a profile with default application settings, registry entries, and shortcuts; and set security and other options for Office.

- Custom Maintenance Wizard, which allows you to update an existing Office deployment using .cmw files. You can use the wizard to change your organization name in the Office installation, reconfigure the installation options of the Office applications, modify default application settings, registry entries, and shortcuts, and modify security and other options for Office.

- Office-related policy which allows you to configure options and manage the available features of Office as a whole as well as individual Office applications. Each GPO to which you've deployed Office-related policy is updated to include the Administrative Templates you selected for installation. The Office 2003 Administrative Templates contain over 2500 policy settings.

These tools can be used together. Prior to deployment, you use the Custom Installation Wizard and Office-related policy to optimize the configuration of Office. The wizard creates a transform file that is deployed along with Office. The transform file provides the initial settings for Office and determines the components that are installed. Policy settings provide default settings for options as well as enforced settings that control available features. For example, you can use Office-related policy to disable menu options or to hide entire menus.

After deployment, you use Office-related policy and the Custom Maintenance Wizard to manage your Office installations. With Office-related policy, you make the necessary changes in policy and then, when policy is refreshed, the changes are applied. With the Custom Maintenance Wizard, you create a .cmw file that is used like a transform and then deploy the .cmw file as a modification to the Office deployment. The .cmw file is used to reconfigure the Office installation. For example, you could remove an application or change other installed components, such as tools or templates.

Customizing Office Configurations

The Custom Installation Wizard, the Custom Maintenance Wizard and the Administrative Templates for Office are provided in the Office Resource Kit. Each version of Office has a separate resource kit that contains tools and administrative template files. You'll find there is a resource kit for Office 2000, Office XP, and Office 2003. If you install multiple resource kits, you'll have separate tools and policy files for each.

Downloading and Installing the Tools

The best place to look for Office tools and information is the Office Web site (*http://office.microsoft.com*). You'll find several important resource pages including:

- *http://office.microsoft.com/en-us/FX011511491033.aspx* covering the Office 2000 Resource Kit

- *http://office.microsoft.com/en-us/FX011511511033.aspx* covering the Office XP Resource Kit

- *http://office.microsoft.com/en-us/FX011511471033.aspx* covering the Office 2003 Resource Kit

- *http://office.microsoft.com/en-us/FX011511561033.aspx* covering Office updates administrators might be interested in

Because the Office Web site is continually updated, it is sometimes hard to locate the resources you need. At the time of this writing, *http://www.microsoft.com/downloads/details.aspx?FamilyID=4bb7cb10-a6e5-4334-8925-3bcf308cfbaf&DisplayLang=en* is the best download location for the Office 2003 Resource Kit tools. While you are online you might want to download the additional updates for Office 2003 service packs from *http://www.microsoft.com/downloads/details.aspx?FamilyID=ba8bc720-edc2-479b-b115-5abb70b3f490&DisplayLang=en*. Additional resource tools and files for Visio 2003 and for Project 2003 can be obtained from *http://www.microsoft.com/office/ork/2003/tools/BoxA19.htm*.

After you download the necessary files, you should run the associated installers on a computer that is part of the domain with which you want to work or a development machine if you want to test prior to deploying the tools. With the Office 2003 Resource Kit tools, you will want to perform a Complete Install. A complete install uses 30 MB of disk space. The default local path for the install is %SystemDrive%\Program Files\ORKTOOLS. Once the install is complete, you'll find a new tools menu under Start, Programs or All Programs, Microsoft Office, Microsoft Office Tools, Microsoft Office 2003 Resource Kit. Table 10-1 provides an overview of the standard tools.

Table 10-1   Overview of Office 2003 Resource Kit Tools

Tool Name	Description
CMW File Viewer	Allows you to view the contents of Custom Maintenance Wizard (.cmw) files.
Custom Installation Wizard	Allows you to create .mst transform files for customizing Office installations.
Custom Maintenance Wizard	Allows you to update an existing Office deployment using .cmw files.
Customizable Alerts	Provides detailed information for handling custom error messages.
International Information	Provides detailed information on configuring and using multiple language versions of Office.
MST File Viewer	Allows you to view the contents of .mst files.
Office Information	Provides detailed information on Office files, registry entries and migration.
OPS File Viewer	Allows you to view the contents of .ops files.
Package Definition Files	Provide templates for deploying Office with Systems Management Server (SMS).
Profile Wizard	Allows you to capture a user's Office settings into a .ops file which can be included in an Office deployment.
Removal Wizard	Allows you to selectively remove previous versions of Office applications.

The Office 2003 Service Pack updates to the resource kit include additions and corrections to policies for administrative support of Office 2003 as well as several spreadsheets that describe available policies. These updated template files will be stored in the folder you designate when installing the updates. With updates to the Office 2003 Resource Kit, like a service pack, you'll need to roll out two types of updates. First, you'll roll out the actual update or service pack for Office 2003 through policy as discussed in Chapter 9 under "Deploying Microsoft Office Through Policy." You'll then need to check for Administrative Templates or other types of policy updates, such as the ones from *http://www.microsoft.com/downloads/details.aspx?FamilyID=ba8bc720-edc2-479b-b115-5abb70b3f490&DisplayLang=en*, and deploy any updated policy files as appropriate to the GPOs that use Office-related Administrative Templates. The steps you'll need to follow are discussed in the next section.

Working with the Custom Installation Wizard

You configure new installations of Office using the Custom Installation Wizard. When you run this wizard, it creates transform files you can distribute through policy when you deploy Office. You can use the wizard to:

- Choose the folder location to install Microsoft Office
- Specify whether to remove previous versions of Office applications

- Configure whether and how various Office applications are installed
- Create a profile with default application settings, registry entries and shortcuts
- Set security and other options for Office

Because there are several prerequisites, working with the Custom Installation Wizard isn't as straightforward as you'd expect. Before you get started, you'll need to create an administrative install of the Office .msi file. You'll then need to use the Custom Installation Wizard to create the require .mst file. Once you have the transform file, you can deploy the Office configuration through policy. Keep in mind that you can add .mst files only when you are initially Assigning or Publishing an installer package.

Step 1: Create the Administrative Install of Office's .msi File

Before you can use the Custom Installation Wizard, you will need an administrative install of Office's .msi file. To perform an administrative install, complete the following steps:

1. Log on to a computer where you've installed the Office version you want to work with and where you have administrator privileges.

2. Perform an administrative installation of Office's main .msi file by typing the following command at the command prompt:

   ```
   setup /a MSIFileName
   ```

   where *MSIFileName* is the name of the main .msi file for the version of Office you are configuring, for example:

   ```
   setup /a pro11.msi
   ```

> **Note**   The .msi file must be in the same folder as Setup.exe.

3. This starts the Office Installation Wizard. Use the wizard to prepare the Office's .msi file for deployment. You will need to specify your organization name and a valid product key. You will also need to accept the End User License Agreement.

4. Copy the administrative install of the .msi file to the network share from which it will later be deployed through policy.

> **Note**   Although it might seem like it, Office is not being installed on the computer you are working with. The Office installation is being configured for deployment, data is being written to the local disk, but Office is not actually being installed at this point.

Step 2: Use the Custom Installation Wizard for Office Configuration

When you have an administrative install of Office's .msi file, you can use the Custom Installation Wizard to configure the Office installation. To do this, complete the following steps:

1. Click Start, point to Programs or All Programs, Microsoft Office, Microsoft Office Tools, Microsoft Office 2003 Resource Kit, and click Custom Installation Wizard.

2. When the Custom Installation Wizards starts, click Next.

3. On the Open The MSI File page, click Browse and then browse to the location of the administrative install of Office's .msi file. Click Next.

4. Set a name for the .mst transform file that will be used to customize the Office installation. Click Next.

5. You can now configure the Office installation. On the final wizard page, click Finish and then specify a save location for the .mst transform file. Generally, you will want to copy the .mst file to the same location as the administrative install of the .msi file.

Step 3: Deploy the Transformed Office Configuration

When the Custom Installation Wizard finishes, configure policy to deploy the Office configuration using the transform file. Follow these steps:

1. Access Software Installation in Group Policy. For a per-computer Office deployment, access Computer Configuration\Software Settings\Software Installation. For a per-user Office deployment, access User Configuration\Software Settings\Software Installation.

2. Right-click on the Software Installation and choose New, Package.

3. In the Open dialog box, type the UNC path to the network share where your .msi package is located or use the options provided to navigate to the package and select it.

4. Click Open. Select Published or Assigned to publish or assign the application without modifications.

5. Wait for the package to be created. When you can see the package in the right pane, right-click it and select Properties.

6. On the Modifications tab, click Add. Specify the path to the .mst file and then click OK. The selected transform file will then be deployed with Office.

Working with the Custom Maintenance Wizard

You can modify existing installations of Office using the Custom Maintenance Wizard. When you run this wizard, it creates .cmw files, which you can distribute through policy to update an Office Installation. You can use the wizard to:

- Change your organization name
- Reconfigure the installation options various Office applications
- Modify default application settings, registry entries and shortcuts
- Modify security and other options for Office

You work with the Custom Maintenance Wizard in much the same way as you work with the Custom Installation Wizard. Before you get started, you'll need to know the location of the administrative install of Office's .msi file. You'll then need to use the Custom Maintenance Wizard to create the require .cmw file. Once you have the .cmw file, you can deploy Office configuration change through policy.

Step 1: Update the Microsoft Office Configuration

To update the configuration of a previously deployed Office installation, complete the following steps:

1. Click Start, point to Programs or All Programs, Microsoft Office, Microsoft Office Tools, Microsoft Office 2003 Resource Kit, and click Custom Maintenance Wizard.

2. When the Custom Maintenance Wizards starts, click Next.

3. On the Open The MSI File page, click Browse and then browse to the location of the administrative install of Office's .msi file. Click Next.

4. Set a name for the .cmw file that will be used to modify the Office configuration. Click Next.

5. You can now reconfigure the Office installation. On the final wizard page, click Finish and then specify a save location for the .cmw file. Generally, you will want to copy the .cmw file to the same location as the administrative install of the .msi file.

Step 2: Deploy the New Configuration of Office

After you create the .cmw file, copy the .cmw file and Maintwiz.exe to the administrative installation point. One way to apply the updates is to run the Custom Maintenance Wizard on your users' computers. You can do this using a logon script, as an example. In the script, enter the following line:

```
UNCpath\maintwiz.exe /c "ConfigFile"
```

where *UNCPath* is the complete UNC path to the administrative share and *ConfigFile* is the name of the .cmw file, such as:

```
\\CorpSvr08\apps\Office\updates\maintwiz.exe /c "EngOfficeUpdate.cmw"
```

The Custom Maintenance Wizard calls Windows Installer to apply the changes in the .cmw file to the user's computer. By default, the wizard runs with a minimal user interface, displaying only progress indicators and error messages. To run the wizard silently, add the /q option to the command line, such as:

```
\\CorpSvr08\apps\Office\updates\maintwiz.exe /c "EngOfficeUpdate.cmw" /q
```

When working with the Custom Maintenance Wizard keep the following in mind:

- If Office 2003 was installed per-computer, the updates are applied per-computer and affect all users on the computer. However, if Office 2003 was installed per-user, Windows Installer makes the changes only for the user who runs the wizard and applies the .cmw file.

- The Office Source Engine checks only the source from which the user originally installed Office and passes that information to the Custom Maintenance Wizard. If you installed Office from an administrative installation point, Windows Installer searches for a valid source from which to apply the .cmw file. If you installed Office from a local installation source, you must store the .cmw file on the original compressed image source.

- Only administrators can apply .cmw files from any location to a user's computer. To allow non-administrator users to apply the updates to their computers, you must store Maintwiz.exe and the .cmw file together on the administrative installation point (as recommended previously). You can work around this requirement by enabling Always Install With Elevated Privileges under Computer Configuration\Administrative Templates\Windows Components\Windows Installer.

You can also deploy .cmw files through policy. To do this, complete these steps:

1. Access Software Installation in Group Policy. For a per-computer Office deployment, access Computer Configuration\Software Settings\Software Installation. For a per-user Office deployment, access User Configuration\Software Settings\Software Installation.

2. Right-click the Office software package and select Properties.

3. On the Modifications tab, click Add. Specify the path to the .cmw file and then click OK. The selected .cmw file will then be deployed and used to reconfigure Office.

Preparing the Policy Environment

The Office 2003 Resource Kit includes a set of Administrative Templates, which we'll refer to as the Office 2003 Administrative Templates. These templates include policies settings for customizing the configuration of Office applications. Keep in mind that the Office 2003 Administrative Template files do not expose every user interface element in each Office application for configuration. Rather, they expose the most commonly used elements to allow you maximum control while minimizing the complexity of managing Office installations.

During installation of the Office 2003 Resource Kit, the Office 2003 Administrative Templates are copied to the %SystemRoot%\Inf folder on the local computer. This location is the default location for policy templates. At this point, the policy templates are not available for use in your organization. If you examine the %SystemRoot%\Inf folder, you will find a set of .adm files; each related to an individual Office application. Table 10-2 lists each file and the application to which it relates. If you downloaded the tools and files for Project and Visio, you'll find two additional .adm files. These files are listed in the table as well.

Table 10-2   Office System 2003 Administrative Template Files

Filename	Office Application
Access11.adm	Microsoft Access 2003
Excel11.adm	Microsoft Excel 2003
Fp11.adm	Microsoft FrontPage 2003
Gal11.adm	Microsoft Clip Organizer
Inf11.adm	Microsoft InfoPath 2003
Office11.adm	Microsoft Office 2003, which controls global Office configuration settings
Onent11.adm	Microsoft OneNote 2003
Outlk11.adm	Microsoft Outlook 2003
Ppt11.adm	Microsoft PowerPoint 2003
Proj11.adm	Microsoft Project 2003; only available if you install the Project policy file
Pub11.adm	Microsoft Publisher 2003
Visio11.adm	Microsoft Visio 2003; only available if you install the Visio policy file
Word11.adm	Microsoft Word 2003

Deploying Office Administrative Template Files

You can deploy one or all of the Office 2003 Administrative Template files, depending on your configuration needs. To deploy a template within your Group Policy environment, you must first add the template file to the Group Policy Object (GPO) in which it will be used. There are two different recommended techniques, depending on whether you are deploying Office Administrative Templates files for the first time in your organization or updating Office-related policy due to availability of new files from an Office Service Pack or other Office update.

> **Note**   Office 2003 Administrative Templates are deployed on a per-GPO basis. This deployment technique is different from the technique used for new operating system versions and operating system service packs. With new operating system versions and operating system service packs, you can update the entire Group Policy environment, meaning the updates will be applied to all GPOs.

Deploying Office Administrative Template Files for the First Time

To deploy Office-related policy templates for the first time to a GPO in your organization, follow these steps:

1. If you are deploying Office policy settings for the first time, and have updated policy files, such as those for Office 2003 Service Pack 1, you should copy the updated files to the %SystemRoot%\Inf folder on the local computer before you continue.

2. Open the GPO you want to work with. Right-click Administrative Templates under User Configuration and choose Add/Remove Templates to view the currently loaded .adm files as shown in Figure 10-1.

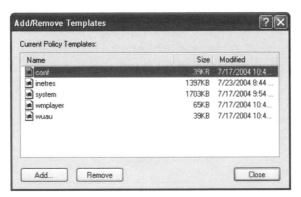

Figure 10-1   Viewing the Add/Remove Templates dialog box within the Group Policy Object Editor

3. Click Add to open the Policy Templates dialog box. The default folder location opened is %SystemRoot%\Inf.

4. Choose the template file or files to load. To select multiple files at once, hold the Shift or Ctrl keys as appropriate.

5. Click Open and then click Close. The Administrative Templates namespace changes to include new nodes representing the policy settings you've just added as shown in Figure 10-2.

6. Repeat this procedure for each GPO that should use Office-related policy.

> **Note** The files you've added are copied to the SYSVOL portion of that GPO and are replicated to all domain controllers in the domain. (See Chapter 13, "Group Policy Structure and Processing," for more information about Group Policy storage.)

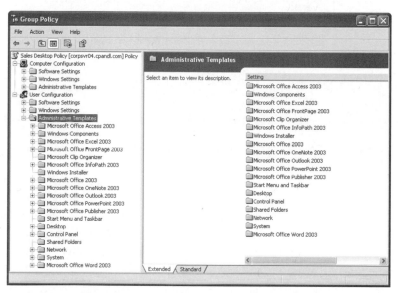

Figure 10-2 Viewing the Group Policy namespace after the adding Office 2003 Administrative Template files

Updating Previously Deployed Office-Related Policy Templates

Updates to Office-related policy are provided as service packs or general updates to an Office Resource Kit. Office 2003 is the first version of Office to use Group Policy as the recommended method for setting and maintaining policies throughout an organization. Several service packs for the Office 2003 Resource Kit have been released; each containing updates to the Office 2003 Administrative Templates. For more information about Office 2003 template updates, see *http://office.microsoft.com/en-us/assistance/ HA011513711033.aspx*.

After you download the service pack, create a new folder on your computer's local drive and then double-click the file you downloaded to begin the extraction process. When prompted to provide the extraction location, specify the path to the new folder you created. The updates tools and files will then be copied to this location.

To update previously deployed Office-related policy templates, follow these steps:

1. Access the GPO you want to work with. Right-click Administrative Templates under User Configuration and choose Add/Remove Templates to view the currently loaded .adm files.

2. Click Add to open the Policy Templates dialog box. Use the Look In list to select the folder in which you installed the policy updates from the Office Service Pack.

3. Choose the template file or files to load. To select multiple files at once, hold the Shift or Ctrl keys as appropriate.

4. When you click Open, you'll see the Confirm File Replace dialog box. Click Yes To All if you've selected multiple templates. Otherwise, click Yes.

5. Click Close. The files you've added are copied to the SYSVOL portion of that GPO. Once the updates are replicated to all domain controllers in the domain, you'll be able to use any new policies. You should check previously configured policies for material changes as well, which can sometimes occur.

6. Repeat this procedure for each GPO that should use Office-related policy.

Creating Office Configuration GPOs

To save yourself a lot of work, you should carefully plan your Office configuration roll out. You might be tempted to add Office policy to existing site, domain or OU GPOs. However, you will probably want to use separate Office configuration GPOs and then link them to the appropriate sites, domains or OUs in your organization. This approach will give you increased flexibility and make it easier to manage your Office installations.

To see why, consider the following deployment scenarios:

- **Scenario A:**   You've deployed Microsoft Office 2003 to the Marketing, Sales, Technology and Customer Service OUs. You want to manage the Office configuration in each of the environments so you add Office 2003 Administrative Templates to the OU GPOs for the Marketing, Sales, Technology and Customer Service OUs. You then set about configuring Office in each of these GPOs. You have separate configurations but had to configuration each option in multiple GPOs.

- **Scenario B:**   You've deployed Microsoft Office 2003 to the NE Sales, NW Sales, SE Sales, SW Sales and Midwest Sales OUs. You want to manage the Office configuration in each of the environments in the same way. You create an Office configuration GPO and add the Office 2003 Administrative Templates to it. You then configure Office in this GPO and can then link the GPO to the NE Sales, NW Sales, SE Sales, SW Sales and Midwest Sales OUs. You have a single configuration deployed to multiple GPOs.

- **Scenario C:**   You've deployed Microsoft Office 2003 to the Engineering, IT, Accounting, and Sales OUs. You want to manage the Office configuration in each of the environments separately. You create an Office configuration GPO and add the Office 2003 Administrative Templates to it. You then configuring Office in this GPO. This GPO establishes your Office configuration baseline. You then create 4 copies of the GPO and name the GPOs Engineering Office Policy, IT Office Policy, Accounting Office Policy and Sales Office Policy. You make adjustments to the baseline configuration as necessary in each GPO and then link the GPOs as appropriate to the OUs. You use a baseline configuration to minimize the work required to create separate custom configurations of Office.

As you can see, the way you deploy Office configurations can have a significant impact on the amount of work you have to do. In creating your Office configuration GPOs, you also consider who will receive a particular configuration. By default, the policy will apply to all users or computers within the site, domain or OU to which you've linked the GPO. As this might not be the ideal behavior, you might need to filter the policy application. For example, if you configure security filtering on an Office configuration GPO so that only members of the Temp Sales security group have the policy applied, only members of the Temp Sales group will have this Office configuration.

Managing Multiple Office Configuration Versions

The choice to deploy a particular version of Office isn't an all or nothing decision. You'll often find that you have different groups of users running different versions of Office. For example, the Sales and Accounting departments might be running Office XP while the rest of the company is using Office 2003. This mixed environment is okay and you can manage both installations of Office through policy.

As discussed previously, the policy files for Office are distributed with the Office Resource Kit. If you have users running both Office 2003 and Office XP, you will need to install the Office 2003 Resource Kit and the Office XP Resource Kit. In the Office 2003 Resource Kit, you'll find the policy files you'll use to manage Office 2003 configurations. In the Office XP Resource Kit, you'll find the policy files you'll use to manage Office XP configurations.

As of this writing, the Office XP Resource Kit Tools can be downloaded from *http://www.microsoft.com/downloads/details.aspx?FamilyID=25b30c79-b248-4eb9-8057-be0043f5b881&DisplayLang=en*. the Office XP Resource Kit includes an Administrative Template file for each Office XP application. You install and work with these administrative templates using the techniques discussed previously. As shown in Table 10-3, the Office XP policy files are named different than other Office versions. Not only does this ensure that you won't accidentally overwriting existing Office policy configurations, it also is used to manage various Office policy versions separately from each other. You will, in fact, have separate policy nodes for each Office version and their associated applications.

Table 10-3   **Office XP Administrative Template Files**

Filename	Office Application
Access10.adm	Microsoft Access 2002
Excel10.adm	Microsoft Excel 2002
Fp10.adm	Microsoft FrontPage 2002
Gal10.adm	Microsoft Clip Organizer
Office10.adm	Microsoft Office 2002, which controls global Office configuration settings
Outlk10.adm	Microsoft Outlook 2002
Ppt10.adm	Microsoft PowerPoint 2002
Pub10.adm	Microsoft Publisher 2002
Word10.adm	Microsoft Word 2002

As of this writing, the Administrative Template files for managing Office 2000 installations are part of the Office 2000 Resource Kit, available at *http://www.microsoft .com/downloads/details.aspx?FamilyID=982348b3-0005-4792-a15c-34f738b3c328 &DisplayLang=en*. As with Office XP, Office 2000 Administrative Template settings can coexist with settings for other Office versions in a single GPO.

It is important to point out that because different versions of Office have different features, each version of the Office Administrative Template files supports a slightly different set of policies. This means you will not be able to have a complete one-to-one mapping of policy settings as you move from version to version. But in general, the settings are similar from version to version.

It is also important to point out that different Office versions are managed separately in the Windows Registry. For example, Office XP Administrative Template policies make changes to the HKEY_CURRENT_USER\Software\Policies\Microsoft\Office\ 10.0\ key, while the Office 2003 policies make changes to the HKEY_CURRENT_ USER\Software\Policies\Microsoft\Office\11.0 key. This means that the Office XP and Office 2003 policy settings can coexist for a given user. It also means that you can have a GPO that contains both Office XP and Office 2003 Administrative Template files if you choose.

An example of when you might want both Office XP and Office 2003 Administrative Template settings in a single GPO is when that GPO is linked to an OU where users are running both versions of Office. In this case, having all of your Office configuration settings in a single GPO would make it easier to keep track of which settings you are using and let you quickly compare Office XP settings and their counterpart settings in Office 2003.

You could also implement each version of Office Administrative Template files within separate GPOs. You might want to do this to prevent groups of users from processing one or the other set of policies. In this case, you could split the Office policy settings into separate GPOs by version and then using security filtering to control which group of users receives which policy. Within the Marketing OU, for example, members of the Marketing Support security group might use Office XP and the Marketing Main security group might use Office 2003. If so, you could create Office XP Users and Office 2003 Users GPOs and use security group filtering to ensure policy is only applied to users who are using the respective version of Office.

An alternative that is easier to implement in some cases is to use a WMI filter to detect which version of Office is installed on a given computer. For example, a simple WMI filter, linked to a GPO, that detects the presence of Office 2003 looks like this:

```
Root\cimV2;Select * FROM Win32_Product WHERE Caption="Microsoft Office
Professional Edition 2003"
```

Similarly, you can have a WMI filter linked to the Office XP GPO that searches for the Office XP string within the caption property of the *Win32_Product* class. Keep in mind, however, that if a computer has a large number of applications installed on it, this WMI query might take some time to execute, slowing Group Policy processing. Be sure to test this in your environment before rolling out into production.

Managing Office-Related Policy

Each GPO to which you've deployed Office-related policy is updated to include the Administrative Templates you selected for installation. The Office 2003 Administrative Templates contain over 2500 policy settings.

> **Note**   Appendix D highlights some of the more commonly used settings in each template file. The updated Administrative Templates for Office 2003 Service Pack 1 also include an Excel spreadsheet called "Office 2003 Group Policies.xls." This spreadsheet describes all of the settings available.

Working with Office-Related Policy

Most of Office-related policies are configured under User Configuration\Administrative Templates as shown in Figure 10-3. Only a select few are configured under Computer Configuration\Administrative Templates.

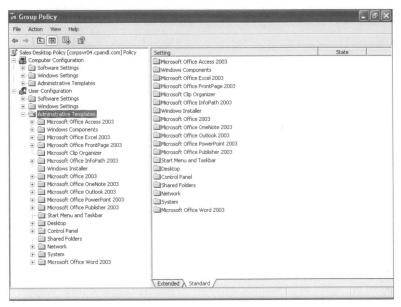

Figure 10-3   Viewing the Office-related policies

Each policy represents an option or feature of an Office application. When working with these policies keep the following in mind:

■ The Office-related policies configured under User Configuration are used to set per-user policies. Per-user policies affect individual users, typically for users within a particular OU.

■ The Office-related policies configured under Computer Configuration are used to set per-computer policies. Per-computer policies affect all users of computers for which a GPO applies.

Because there are so few per-computer policy settings for Office, you'll primarily work with per-user policy settings.

Examining Global and Application-Specific Settings

The Office-related policies in both configuration areas are divided into two broad categories:

■ Global settings for all Office applications, configured under Microsoft Office 2003.

■ Application-specific settings, configured through a policy folder named after the application to which the policy settings apply.

For general management of Office and its configuration, the global settings should be the first you examine and modify. Global settings are used to configure the standard options, tool bars and menus, language settings, messaging and collaboration features, and security settings that will be used in all Office applications. For example, you can use User Templates Path policy under User Configuration\Administrative Templates\ Microsoft Office 2003\Shared Paths to set a standard folder location for template files. If you specify a network share as the folder location, all users for which the current GPO applies would, use this location as the default path for template files.

When you want to fine-tune the configuration of a specific application, you'll use the application-specific settings. Every Office application has a separate policy folder. Most also have Disable Items In User Interface policy as well, which you can use to disable specific command bar buttons and menu items.

> **Tip**   Don't overlook the power of Disable Items In User Interface to help you optimize your Office configurations and restrict use of features that might compromise security or cause problems in your environment. You can use Disable Items In User Interface policy to disable a predefined set of options and create your own custom sets of disabled options as well. For details, see "Preventing Users from Changing Office Configurations."

Configuring Office-Related Policy Settings

Unlike other administrative template files that you might encounter, the Office-related policy templates have a feature that can be confusing at first. Specifically, some policy items require you to select the state of the policy (Not Configured, Enabled, or Disabled) and then select an additional check box to enable the policy. Figure 10-4 shows one such policy.

Figure 10-4   Viewing an Office policy that requires confirmation to be enabled

To enable this policy, you need to select the Enabled state *and* the Check To Enforce Setting On; Uncheck To Enforce Setting Off" check box. If you do not select this check box, the policy will revert to a Disabled state when you apply it. Keep this in mind when you configure Office policies because this is different behavior than what you will find for normal Windows administrative templates.

When working with Office policy settings keep the following in mind as well:

- Clearing an Enabled policy setting doesn't reverse the policy. It only changes the behavior set through the policy. To reverse the policy, you should set it to Not Configured.

- Setting a previously enforced policy to Not Configured removes enforcement and restores the setting or option to either the standard default or the last setting specified by a user.

- Setting a policy to Disabled is generally the same as setting the policy to Not Configured. That is to say, in most cases, the policy settings return to their default behavior, and users will be able to manage the related settings as they could before a restriction or change was applied.

Note   This behavior is specific to Office-related policy. For other policy settings, the behavior for the Enabled, Disabled, and Not Configured states is as described elsewhere in this book. See "Understanding Group Policy Settings and Options" in Chapter 1 for an overview.

Preventing Users from Changing Office Configurations

If you deploy Office-related policies, you might notice that the policy settings you've specified are delivered as expected but it appears that the user can still change the settings to some other value. In other areas of policy, an option is usually dimmed when the user can't change it. This is not the case with Office-related policies.

Understanding How to Prevent Office Configuration Changes

With Office-related policy, restricted options are not dimmed. Any changes users make to restricted options are temporary. When a user exits and restarts the application, the application uses the value from policy.

It is possible, however, to completely prevent users from accessing a given menu option within an Office application. Every Office administrative template, with the exception of those for OneNote, Project, and Publisher, includes Disable Items In The User Interface policy. You can use this policy to control what menu options a user actually sees.

For example, say that we want to disable the Startup Task Pane in Word 2003. This option is set under Tools, Options, View. However, we don't want users to even be able to see this option. What we can do is use the Word 2003 policies to disable parts of the Word 2003 user interface to prevent the Options command from appearing on the Tools menu.

Now, when users open the Tools menu, Options is dimmed and unavailable. This approach allows you to tightly control what your users can and can't do with their Office configurations. This in turn, can reduce unwanted help desk calls when they accidentally change a setting that they shouldn't have touched and if used correctly, it can also help increase the security of your environment.

If you want to inform your users why certain options are grayed out (to prevent them from having to call the help desk to determine the reason), you can attach a custom ToolTip to disabled menu items. The custom message will appear to the user when her mouse hovers over any menu item that has been disabled by policy. See "Configuring Notification for Disabled Menu Items and Options" for details.

Disabling Office Menu Items and Options Using Predefined Options

Disable Items In The User Interface policy controls what menu options a user actually sees. You can use this policy to prevent configuration changes in all Office applications, except OneNote, Project, and Publisher. To do so, complete the following steps:

1. Access User Configuration\Administrative Templates and then expand the node for the Office application for which you want to disable menu options.

2. Double-click Disable Command Bar Buttons And Menu Items under Disable Items In User Interface\Predefined.

3. In the Properties dialog box, select Enabled. As shown in Figure 10-5, you will then see a list of menu options you can disable.

4. Select the checkboxes for the menu options you want to disable.

> **Note**   The menu items and options listed are only the ones that you might commonly want to disable. If you don't see the menu option you want to disable, it doesn't mean you can't disable that option. See "Disabling Office Menu Items and Options Using Custom Options."

5. Click OK.

Figure 10-5   Disabling menu options through policy

Disabling Office Menu Items and Options Using Custom Options

The previous section discussed how to disable menu items using a predefined set of options. As you might have already seen, these predefined options are rather limited. To extend this list, you can create a custom option to disable a menu item and in this way, you can disable menu items and options that aren't included in the predefined list. Doing so is a multiple part process.

Step 1: Determining the Menu Item ID   The custom policy expects a unique ID for the menu item you want to disable. Every menu item and button bar in Office applications has a unique ID. To determine that unique ID, you need to run some VBA code within the Office application you're trying to control. Follow these steps:

1.   Start the Office application for which you are trying to determine a menu ID. Press Alt+F11 or select Tools, Macro, Visual Basic Editor to start the Visual Basic Editor.

2.   In the Visual Basic Editor, select View, Immediate Window. When the immediate window appears in the bottom portion of the screen, paste the following command into it:

```
? CommandBars("menu bar").controls("MenuName").controls("MenuItem").id
```

where *controls("MenuName")* and *controls("MenuItem")* represent the menu item whose ID you want to return. For example, if you wanted the control ID for Tools | Options you would use the following command:

```
? CommandBars("menu bar").controls("Tools").controls("Options...").id
```

3.   Press Enter and the value is returned just below the command in the Immediate window. In this case, the value returned is 522.

If you are familiar with Visual Basic, you can extend this approach by running a macro that enumerates the top-level options on a toolbar. Listing 10-1 provides the code you would use to do this. In this example, you examine the Tools menu, but you can easily change the name of the menu you are enumerating by modifying the Controls value assigned.

Listing 10-1   Sample Code to Enumerate Items on a Menu

```
Sub EnumerateControls()
 Dim icbc As Integer
 Dim cbcs As CommandBarControls
 Set cbcs = Application.CommandBars("Menu Bar").Controls("Tools").Controls
 For icbc = 1 To cbcs.Count
  MsgBox cbcs(icbc).Caption & " = " & cbcs(icbc).ID
 Next icbc
End Sub
```

Step 2: Using a Custom Disable Policy   Once you get the menu bar ID, you can enter use it to configure a custom disable policy. When the policy is deployed, the designated menu item will be grayed out for the user.

To create or modify custom disable policy, follow these steps:

1.   Access User Configuration\Administrative Templates and then expand the node for the Office application for which you want to disable menu options.

2.   Double-click Disable Command Bar Buttons And Menu Items under Disable Items In User Interface\Custom.

3.   In the Properties dialog box, select Enabled and then click Show.

4.   The Show Contents dialog box provides a list of any menu IDs that are currently disabled as shown in Figure 10-6.

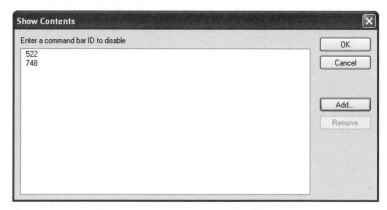

Figure 10-6   Using a custom menu ID to disable menu items

5. To disable an additional menu item for the selected application, click Add. In the Add Item dialog box, enter the menu item ID and then click OK.

6. To enable a menu item that was previously disabled, select the menu item in the Command Bar ID list and then click Remove.

Configuring Notification for Disabled Menu Items and Options

When you disable menu items and options through policy, you might also want to notify users about this. One way to do this is to set a global ToolTip which is displayed when users try to access a disabled menu item or option. While the ToolTip can be something as simple as "This feature has been restricted due to security or compatibility concerns," it can help to ease users frustration over not being to select a menu item or option.

To configure a global tool tip for disabled menu items and options:

1. Access User Configuration\Administrative Templates\Microsoft Office 2003\Disable Items In User Interface.

2. Double-click ToolTip For Disabled Toolbar Buttons And Menu Items under Predefined.

> **Note**   ToolTip For Disabled Toolbar Buttons And Menu Items is provided in the Administrative Templates update for Office 2003 Service Pack 1.

3. In the Properties dialog box, select Enabled and then enter the descriptive text for the ToolTip as shown in Figure 10-7. This text can be up to 69 characters in length.

4. Click OK.

Figure 10-7   Setting ToolTip text for disabled menu items and options

Controlling Default File and Folder Locations

You'll often want to control where users open and save Office documents. For example, in Terminal Server environments where Office is installed you might want not want users to store files on the Terminal Server itself. While this scenario is ultimately controlled using NTFS file system and share permissions, you can use Office Administrative Template policy to steer the user in the right direction. Each Office 2003 policy template includes options for specifying the default document location.

Say you want to ensure Excel 2003 workbooks are always opened and saved from a shared Excel folder on your network that is backed up nightly. You can configure the default file open and save location for Excel 2003 and then specify a path to the location where you want files to be stored. The default path is the user's My Documents folder. You can also specify a drive letter mapped to a server share or a UNC path. The paths you provide can use environment variables as. For example, if you have defined home directories for your Active Directory user objects and you want to ensure that Excel files are always stored in a subfolder of the user's home directory called Excel, you can enter a path such as this:

```
%homeshare%\excel
```

This variable—*%homeshare%*—is resolved to the UNC path where the user's home directory resides when you open or save a file in Excel. If you want to prevent user from changing that path, such as might be the case in Terminal Server environments, you might want to disable the related option in policy. In this case, you would disable the Tools, Options, General option in Excel, as described in the "Preventing Users from Changing Office Configurations" section in this chapter.

Setting the Default Database Folder Location for Access 2003

To set the default database folder location for Access 2003, follow these steps:

1. Double-click Default Database Folder under User Configuration\Administrative Templates\Microsoft Office Access 2003\Tools | Options...\General.

2. As shown in Figure 10-8, select Enabled and then enter the default path to use in the Default Database Folder field.

3. Click OK.

Figure 10-8   Setting the default database folder location for Access 2003

Setting the Default File Location for Excel 2003

To set the default file location for Excel 2003, follow these steps:

1. Double-click Default File Location policy under User Configuration\Administrative Templates\Microsoft Office Excel 2003\Tools | Options...\General.

2. Select Enabled and then enter the default path to use in the Default File Location field.

3. Click OK.

Setting Default Folder Locations for OneNote 2003

To set the default My Notebook folder location for OneNote 2003, follow these steps:

1. Double-click Location Of The My Notebook Folder under User Configuration\Administrative Templates\Microsoft Office OneNote 2003\Tools | Options\Open And Save.

2. Select Enabled and then enter the default path to use in the Location Of The My Notebook Folder field.

3. Click OK.

> **Note**   You can also set default locations for e-mailed Notes, side notes, and backup folders. The related policies are in the User Configuration\Administrative Templates\Microsoft Office OneNote 2003\Tools | Options\Open And Save policy folder.

Setting Default Folder Locations for Publisher 2003

To set the default publication or picture location for Publisher 2003, follow these steps:

1. Double-click Publication Location or Picture Location under User Configuration\ Administrative Templates\Microsoft Office Publisher 2003\Default File Locations.

2. Select Enabled and then enter the default publication path in the Publication Location field.

3. Click OK.

Setting Default Folder Locations for Word 2003

To set the default document location for Word 2003, follow these steps:

1. Double-click Documents under User Configuration\Administrative Templates\ Microsoft Office Word 2003\Tools | Options...\File Locations.

2. Select Enabled and then enter the default publication path in the Documents field.

3. Click OK.

 Note   You can also set default locations for clipart and AutoRecover file saves. The related policies are in the User Configuration\Administrative Templates\Microsoft Office Word 2003\Tools | Options...\File Locations. policy folder.

Configuring Outlook Security Options

Because e-mail is prone to containing content that might be harmful to your environment, it's important that the e-mail applications your users run are secured from the most common types of problems. The first and most important step you can take is to prevent your users from modifying Outlook attachment security, which controls which attachments types are visible. You can enforce this setting by enabling Prevent Users From Customizing Attachment Security Settings under User Configuration\ Administrative Templates\Microsoft Office Outlook 2003\Tools | Options\Security. In addition, you can prevent users from creating exceptions to the list of extensions that are covered by Outlook attachment security by disabling Allow Access To E-mail Attachments under User Configuration\Administrative Templates\Microsoft Office Outlook 2003\Tools | Options...\Security.

You might also want to disable access to Tools, Options\Security in the Outlook interface. To do this, you will need to create a custom disable policy as shown here:

1. Access User Configuration\Administrative Templates\Microsoft Office Outlook 2003\Disable Items In User Interface\Custom.

2. Double-click Disable Command Bar Buttons And Menu Items. In the Properties dialog box, select Enabled and then click Show.

3. Click Add. In the Add Item dialog box, enter the menu item ID for the Tools, Options menu, which is 522.

4. Click OK twice.

Controlling Office Language Settings

If you support a worldwide environment with users running many different language versions of Windows and Office, it might be useful to be able to control which language Office applications start in, depending on where the user is located. For example, you could create a site-linked GPO that sets one language when the user is in the United States and another when she is visiting France. Assuming the user has the appropriate language packs for Office installed on her computer, she will get the appropriate language version as she moves around.

You can set global language settings for Office by completing the following steps:

1. In the site-linked GPO access User Configuration\Administrative Templates\ Microsoft Office 2003\Language Settings\User Interface.

2. Double-click Display Menus And Dialog Boxes In. In the Properties dialog box, select Enabled, use the list provided to choose the language to use, and then click OK. The default (same as the system) is to use whatever language Windows is currently running.

3. Double-click Display Help In. In the Properties dialog box, select Enabled, use the list provided to choose the language to use, and then click OK.

Troubleshooting Office Administrative Template Policy

In most cases, if you've configured Office-related policy in a GPO and linked the GPO appropriately, the settings usually are delivered to and process by clients as expected. If you find that Office isn't configured as expected, you can troubleshoot to try to determine where the breakdown is occurring.

Follow these general troubleshooting steps:

1. Start by running the Group Policy Results Wizard against the user and computer that is having problems. See "Determine the Effective Group Policy Settings and Last Refresh" in Chapter 3 for details.

2. As shown in Figure 10-9, under User Configurations\Administrative Templates, you'll see results that you whether Office policy is being applied.

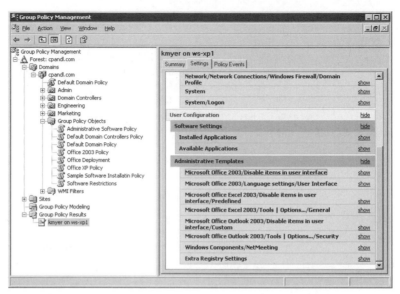

Figure 10-9   Using the Group Policy Results Wizard to determine whether Office Policy is being delivered

3. If you discover that the policy is not being applied, check the following:

    ❑   Make sure the GPO is properly linked

    ❑   Make sure the GPO doesn't have security or WMI filtering that is preventing the user or computer from processing it

    ❑   Make sure the GPO isn't being blocked by a conflicting policy setting with higher precedence

4. If the wizard shows that the policy is being applied, but Office isn't configured as expected there might be a problem with how the application is reading the related policy. Check to ensure the policy is set as expected for the specific version of Office being used. For example, you might have configured a policy for Office XP but not for Office 2003 which is being used.

> **Note**   Certain policy options that appear in the Office 2003 Administrative Template files don't always work as expected. This is primarily due to changes in the way features are implemented in Office applications from version to version and the Administrative Template files not keeping up with those changes. For example, there is an Outlook policy to prevent a user's signature from being included in new messages as well as replies and forwards. This policy is found under User Configuration\Administrative Templates\Microsoft Office Outlook 2003\Tools | Options...\Mail Format\ Signature. However, in Office 2003 signatures are stored per e-mail account, and if you set this policy, Outlook simply ignores it because the value is now stored in a different location in the registry. These kinds of issues are often found in the Microsoft Knowledge Base (*http://support.microsoft.com*). You can save yourself a lot of time by searching there first if you discover a situation like this.

> **Tip**   If everything seems to be configured correctly, you can check the Registry to
> confirm that the related registry value is set as expected. If it's a per-user policy,
> changes are made to the HKEY_CURRENT_USER hive of the registry; otherwise, com-
> puter policies are made to HKEY_LOCAL_MACHINE. One way you can find out which
> key and value a particular policy is setting by looking at the Office 2003 Group Policies
> spreadsheet included in the Office 2003 Resource Kit Service Pack 1. If a value is not
> being set, there might be problems with registry permissions. Or if it's in a user's pro-
> file (HKEY_CURRENT_USER), corruption issues might be preventing proper writing of
> those values. In this case, creating a new temporary profile for the user can confirm
> whether this is the problem.

Summary

As you've seen in this chapter, there are many ways to work with and manage
Microsoft Office through Group Policy, and deploying Office through policy is only
the beginning. Not only can you use policy to deploy Office, but you can also use
transforms to customize the installation so that individual users and groups get custom configurations that are tailored to the way they use Office. Using a special set
of Administrative Templates, which are available for Office 2000, Office XP, and
Office 2003, you can control and configure Office features in much the same way as
you control Windows features. You can also modify the setup of previously deployed
applications using custom maintenance files.

Chapter 11

Maintaining Secure Network Communications

In this chapter:

Understanding IPSec Policy 398

Managing and Maintaining IPSec Policy 401

Deploying Public Key Policies 415

Understanding Windows Firewall Policy 420

Managing Windows Firewall Policy 424

Summary 438

Proper configuration of Network Communications security is essential for protecting your organization's computers and your network as a whole. Without proper security precautions, your computer resources are vulnerable to attack and misuse. Through Group Policy, you can ensure secure network communications in three broad ways:

- IP Security, also known as IPSec, which allows for secure, authenticated, and encrypted communications on TCP/IP networks

- Public key encryption, which lets you control the use of public key certificates and enables related public key technologies

- Windows Firewall, formerly Internet Connection Firewall, which provides stateful host-based TCP and UDP port filtering to protect computers against unauthorized access

Policy settings related to these features provide many options that allow for full customization and offer a great deal of flexibility. However, you need a strong understanding of the underlying technologies and a solid implementation plan before you modify any network communications security policies.

Related Information
- For more information on Microsoft Windows authentication mechanisms and techniques, see "Design Considerations for Active Directory Authentications and Trusts," in Chapter 33 of *Microsoft Windows Server 2003 Inside Out* (Microsoft Press, 2004).

- For more information about IPSec in the Windows Server 2003 operating system, see *http://www.microsoft.com/ipsec/*.

- For more information about Public Key Infrastructure (PKI) and certificate security, see *Microsoft Windows Server 2003 PKI and Certificate Security* (Microsoft Press, 2004).

- For more information about PKI technologies, see *http://www.microsoft.com/pki/*.

Understanding IPSec Policy

The sections that follow discuss how you can use IPSec and IPSec policy. As you'll see, you can use IPSec with or without an Active Directory environment, but the management and distribution of IPSec policies is much easier if you have an Active Directory and Group Policy infrastructure in place.

How IPSec Works

Internet Protocol security (IPSec) is an Internet Engineering Task Force (IETF) standard (RFCs 2401-2409) for providing secure network communications over TCP/IP. IPSec provides protection against common types of attacks, such as:

- Data modification, where an attacker modifies the data as it travels between the source and destination devices

- Identity spoofing, where an attacker impersonates the source or destination device's identity in order to initiate or "take over" communications

- Man-in-the-middle attacks, where the attacker intercepts traffic between source and destination devices with the intent of changing the communication or otherwise interrupting traffic

- Denial of Service, where an attacker tries to cause a service to fail by flooding it with network packets that are either invalid or too numerous to be handled

- Data capture, where an attacker captures network traffic to obtain sensitive information

IPSec provides protection against these common types of attacks by implementing two protocols:

- Authentication Header (AH) protocol, which specifies an authentication mechanism for IP traffic that prevents data modification, man in the middle attacks, and identity spoofing

- Encapsulating Security Payload (ESP) protocol, which provides authentication and encryption to help with all of the above types of attacks

Because IPSec is implemented at the IP layer, upper-layer protocols are not affected by it, which makes IPSec a good solution for implementing network security without requiring applications to explicitly support it.

How IPSec Policy Is Deployed

The Microsoft implementation of IPSec can be used with or without an Active Directory environment, but the management and distribution of IPSec policies is much easier if you have an Active Directory and Group Policy infrastructure in place. With Active Directory and Group Policy in place, you can store IPSec policies centrally and distribute them across your enterprise network. You can also take advantage of Active Directory's built-in support for Kerberos authentication. Without Kerberos authentication in place, you would need to rely on X.509 public key certificates to provide authentication services when implementing IPSec policy.

IPSec policy is most often implemented when you need to secure network communications on an internal network. For example, if you have servers that contain very sensitive data, you might want to control which computers can talk to those servers and whether the traffic to and from those servers is authenticated, encrypted, or both. The technique used to secure network traffic in this case is port filtering. IPSec can also be used in conjunction with the Layer 2 Tunneling Protocol (L2TP) to provide secure Virtual Private Network (VPN) access across external networks.

For Active Directory–based Group Policy, IPSec policies are stored under Computer Configuration\Windows Settings\Security Settings\IP Security Settings On Active Directory. If you configure one of these IPSec policies in a particular GPO, the policy is processed by computers that process that GPO.

For Local Group Policy, IPSec policies are stored under Computer Configuration\Windows Settings\Security Settings\IP Security Settings On Local Computer. If you want to implement IPSec policy for computers that are not part of an Active Directory domain, define policy on the local computer.

Note   With local policy, any IPSec policies that you define are stored on that local computer but can be exported to a file for import into another machine or even to an Active Directory–based IPSec policy store. IPSec policy can be managed on the local computer using either the Local Security Policy MMC snap-in or via command line using the Netsh.exe utility built into Windows Server 2003 and Windows XP. On Windows XP, you can also use the Ipseccmd.exe tool.

When to Use IPSec and IPSec Policy

IPSec can be used in a variety of scenarios where you need to protect network communications on your internal network. The most common of these are:

- Server-to-server communications, where the traffic between servers needs to be private and you want to prevent unauthorized access to or interception of network packets

- Server-to-client communications, where you want to control access to a server or its services or to a particular set of authorized client machines

> **Note**   In certain scenarios, IPSec policy requires defining of a static IP address, a subnet address, or all possible addresses on machines at each end of the communication path. This requirement makes it difficult to implement IPSec policies on dynamically addressed client machines if you want the policy to affect just those machines.

- Server-to-server communications across a perimeter network (also known as a demilitarized zone, or DMZ), where you need to protect and filter network traffic based on certain applications

> **Note**   Perimeter networks are essentially subnets between your internal network and the Internet. In this environment, the security services that IPSec can provide, such as authentication and encryption of network traffic, and filtering of TCP or UDP traffic based on port numbers, can add an extra layer of protection on top of any firewall solutions you might have in place.

The scenarios in which IPSec is not well suited include:

- Secure communications across your entire internal network. For large networks, using IPSec everywhere can make management of the myriad of policies you are likely to need too difficult.

- Secure communications for computers using dynamic IP addressing. Using IPSec for dynamically addressed systems can present a problem if you want to use the port filtering features of the policy as these filtering rules rely on static IP addresses.

- Secure communications between remote systems in which some of the remote systems are not running Windows. Using IPSec and its tunneling feature as a replacement for a VPN is recommended only when connecting to a third-party VPN server or router that does not support L2TP/IPSec.

> **Tip**   Before the release of Windows Firewall in Windows XP Service Pack 2 and Windows Server 2003 SP1, IPSec-based port filtering was the best way to implement a centrally manageable set of firewall policies within your network. Now the port filtering capabilities in IPSec policy are less compelling and less manageable than what is available through Windows Firewall. For more information about managing Windows Firewall through Group Policy, see the "Managing Windows Firewall Policy" section in this chapter.

Managing and Maintaining IPSec Policy

IPSec policies are stored and available for domain-wide access. When you create an IPSec policy in one GPO, you can edit other GPOs in a site, domain, or OU and assign the IPSec policy within those GPOs as well.

Activating and Deactivating IPSec Policies

Within Active Directory domains and on local computers, there are three default IPSec policies:

- **Server (Request Security)**   Any server processing this policy will request secure communications from all clients. Secure communications will not be required, however, if a client does not support it. For example, Windows NT 4.0 clients are not IPSec-aware and cannot support IPSec.

- **Client (Respond Only)**   Any client processing this policy will communicate unsecured normally but will respond to server requests for secure communication.

- **Secure Server (Require Security)**   Any server processing this policy will communicate only with clients that either initiate or can respond to secure communication requests. Servers will not respond to clients that cannot use secure IPSec communications.

These predefined policies provide a starting point for you to implement the various services IPSec offers. You can assign and enforce these and other policies by completing the following steps:

1. Access Computer Configuration\Windows Settings\Security Settings\IP Security Settings On Active Directory in Group Policy.

2. Under the Policy Assigned column in the right pane, you'll see the current state of the default IPSec polices and any additional IPSec policies that you've created (Figure 11-1). A status of No indicates that a policy is not assigned and therefore is not applied.

3. To assign an IPSec policy and therefore apply it, right-click the policy and select Assign. The status under Policy Assigned should change to Yes.

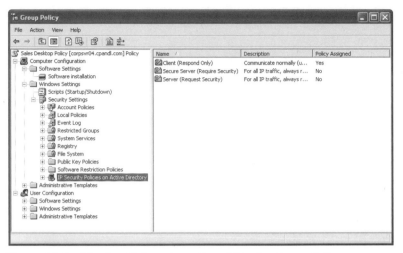

Figure 11-1   Viewing IP Security policy within the Group Policy namespace

If you later want to deactivate an IPSec policy, you can do so by right-clicking it and selecting Un-assign. The status under Policy Assigned should change to No.

Create Additional IPSec Policies

You can create your own IPSec policies as well. An IPSec policy is composed of the following:

- General settings, which apply regardless of which rules are configured. These settings determine the name of the policy, its description for administrative purposes, key exchange settings, and key exchange methods.

- One or more IPSec rules that determine which types of traffic IPSec must examine, how traffic is treated, how to authenticate an IPSec peer, and other settings such as the type of network connection to which the rule applies and whether to use IPSec tunneling.

The steps you need to follow when creating a new IPSec policy are pretty straightforward. First you create the policy, then you create the rules within the policy that are composed of filters, filter actions, and other required settings. Finally, you assign one IPSec policy to each GPO that requires an IPSec policy.

Creating and Assigning the IPSec Policy

You can create an IPSec policy by completing the following steps:

1. Access Computer Configuration\Windows Settings\Security Settings.

2. Right-click IP Security Settings On Active Directory, and choose Create IP Security Policy. This starts the IP Security Policy Wizard. Click Next.

3. On the IP Security Policy Name page, enter a policy name and description, as shown in Figure 11-2. Click Next.

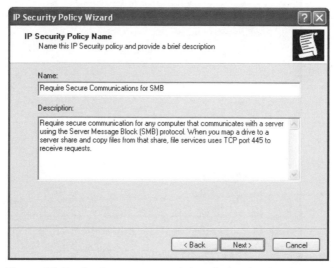

Figure 11-2   Setting a name and description for the IPSec policy

4. In the absence of any other defined rules on this policy, a Default Response Rule is created by default. The Default Response Rule guarantees that the machines that process this policy will respond with secure communications when requested to do so. It's generally a good practice to keep this enabled for GPOs being applied to client computers. Click Next.

5. On the Default Response Rule Authentication Method page (Figure 11-3), choose an authentication mechanism for the Default Response Rule. The authentication options are:

    ❑ **Active Directory Default (Kerberos V5 Protocol)**   Uses Kerberos authentication. Kerberos is the default authentication method for all domain computers running Windows 2000 or later. If you are managing systems that are all members of an Active Directory domain, this is the best choice.

    ❑ **Use A Certificate From This Certification Authority (CA)**   Uses a public key encryption technology for authentication. This requires a certificate from a designated Certification Authority (CA) in your organization. If your systems are not part of Active Directory, this option is best.

    ❑ **Use This String To Protect The Key Exchange**   Uses a preshared key for authentication. You must type (or copy and paste) the text of the preshared key into the text box provided. Preshared keys don't provide the same level of security as the other two approaches and recommended only for use in test environments or for third-party IPSec peer interoperability.

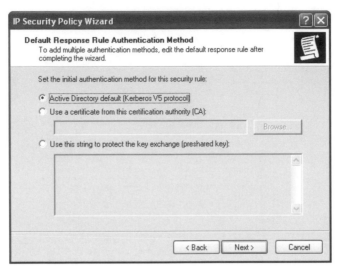

Figure 11-3 Setting the IP Security authentication method

6. Click Next, and then click Finish. The Edit Properties box is selected by default so you can further customize the policy with rules and actions (as detailed in the next section).

Once the new policy has been created, you must activate the IPSec policy so it will be processed. If you want to activate the IPSec policy for the currently selected GPO, right-click the policy and choose Assign. The IPSec policy is assigned in the GPO being edited. Any computer that processes that GPO will receive the policy.

> **Tip** IPSec policies are stored and available for domain-wide access, so you can edit other GPOs in the site, domain, or OU and assign the IPSec policy to these GPOs as well. Simply access Computer Configuration\Windows Settings\Security Settings\IP Security Policies On Active Directory, right-click the IPSec policy, and then select Assign.

Defining Security Rules and Actions

After you create an IPSec policy, the next step is to define the rules that govern how network communications should be secured and what actions should be taken by those rules. To do this, follow these steps:

1. Display the Properties dialog box for the IPSec policy you are configuring. If necessary, Access Computer Configuration\Windows Settings\Security Settings\ IP Security Settings On Active Directory, right-click the policy, and select Properties.

2. As shown in Figure 11-4, any current IP security rules, such as the Default Response Rule, are listed under IP Security Rules.

Figure 11-4   Viewing current IP security rules

3. To define a new security rule, click Add. This starts the Security Rule Wizard.

4. Specify whether to use an IP tunnel for this rule, as shown in Figure 11-5, and then click Next. You have two choices:

    ❑ **This Rule Does Not Specify A Tunnel**   Allows for secure communications between computers without the use of IPSec tunnel mode. Choose this option to allow for secure communications when you do not have a requirement for direct, private connections, such as when communicating on a private network. Keep in mind that you do not need to tunnel traffic to ensure that it is encrypted. Other encryption options can be set within a rule.

    ❑ **The Tunnel Endpoint Is Specified By This IP Address**   Creates an encrypted communications tunnel over a private or public network between two computers that are communicating. When you choose this option, you must also enter the IP address of the tunnel endpoint. This option allows direct, private connections between two computers, such as may be needed when communicating over a public network such as the Internet.

5. Choose the network type that you want the rule to cover, and then click Next:

    ❑ **All Network Connections**   Applies the rule to all network connections on the computers to which the policy is assigned, including both LAN and remote access interfaces

    ❑ **Local area network (LAN)**   Limits the rule application to LAN connections on the computers to which the policy is assigned

    ❑ **Remote Access**   Limits the rule application to Remote Access connections on the computers to which the policy is assigned

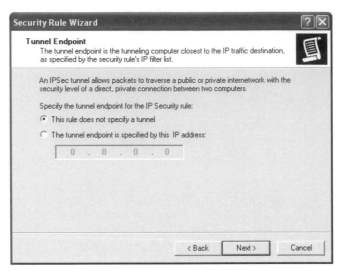

Figure 11-5   Choosing a tunneling or no-tunneling option

Note   Typically, you will apply security rules to LAN interfaces because these are the most commonly used types of interfaces on internal networks. If your organization has users with portable computers and must connect remotely with third-party VPN servers that do not support L2TP/IPSec, you should also consider how policy will be applied to users who access the internal network from remote connections. To handle local and remote connections separately, you need two rules, one that specifies how to handle IP security for local connections and one that specifies how to handle IP security for remote connections.

6. The IP Filter List page, shown in Figure 11-6, allows you to specify the type of traffic to which the rule should apply as well as the source and destination IP addresses to which the rule applies. By default, two filter lists are provided:

   ❑ **All ICMP Traffic**   Specifies all ICMP traffic from any source to any destination

   ❑ **All IP Traffic**   Specifies all IP traffic from any source to any destination

7. Select one of the default filter lists if you want to specify a particular action for all ICMP or all IP traffic. If neither of these filter lists works for you, click Add and then create a new filter list (as discussed under "Creating and Managing IP Filter Lists"). Click Next.

8. On the Filter Action page, shown in Figure 11-7, you set the action that should be taken with network traffic that meets the filter requirements. By default, three filter actions are specified:

   ❑ **Permit**   Permits unsecured packets to be sent and received.

❑ **Request Security (Optional)** Allows unsecured communications but asks clients to establish trust and use secure communications. Allows communication with unsecure clients if they do not respond successfully to the request to use security.

❑ **Require Security** Allows unsecured communications but always requires clients to establish trust and use secure communications. No communications with unsecure clients are allowed.

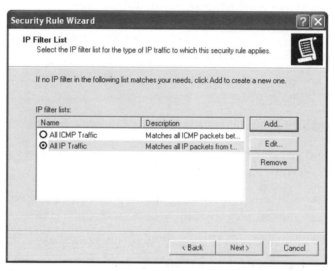

Figure 11-6 Choosing a filter option

9. Select a default filter action or create a new filter action by clicking Add (as detailed in the upcoming section titled "Creating and Managing Filter Actions." Click Next.

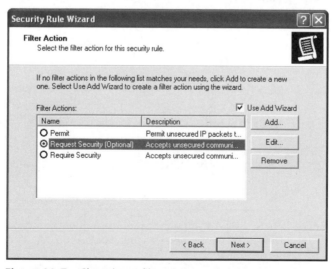

Figure 11-7 Choosing a filter action

10. Click Finish. The Edit Properties box is selected by default so you can further customize the security rule.

Now you assign the policy so that it will be applied to computers that process the current GPO. To do this, simply right-click the new IPSec policy and choose Assign. The policy is actively linked to this GPO, and any computer that processes the GPO will receive and apply the policy.

Creating and Managing IP Filter Lists

IP filter lists allow you to specify the type of traffic to which an IP filter action will apply. Two default filter lists are provided:

- All ICMP Traffic, which specifies all ICMP traffic from any source to any destination

- All IP Traffic, which specifies all IP traffic from any source to any destination

You can create additional filter lists for IP Security rules as well. To see how filter lists work, consider the following example:

- You want to filter Server Message Block (SMB) traffic between clients on your subnet and a specific file server with the IP address 192.168.1.50.

- You create an IP security rule and then add an IP filter list to this rule.

- You set the source IP address for the filter to any IP address that originates on your IP subnet, 192.168.1.0 with a subnet mask of 255.255.255.0.

- You set the destination IP address for the filter to the IP address of the file server, 192.168.1.50.

- You mirror the filter because you want SMB traffic both from and to the server to be secured.

To create new IP filter lists or manage existing filter lists assigned to a rule, follow these steps:

1. Display the Properties dialog box for the IPSec policy you are configuring. If necessary, access Computer Configuration\Windows Settings\Security Settings\ IP Security Settings On Active Directory, right-click the policy, and then select Properties.

2. Select a previously defined IP Security rule, and then click Edit. This opens the Edit Rule Properties dialog box.

> **Note**   Unless you want to set the authentication method, do not edit the Default Response rule. This rule handles the default response to requests to secure traffic.

3. The IP Filter List tab shows the currently defined IP filter lists. You can now edit or remove existing IP filter lists or create a new IP filter list. The selected IP filter list specifies which network traffic will be in affect for the current rule. Only one filter list can be selected for each rule.

4. To create a new filter list, click Add. In the IP Filter List dialog box, type a name for the filter list and then add a description (Figure 11-8). For example, if you are creating an SMB filter list, you might use the name SMB Filter List and a description such as This filter list covers all SMB traffic between servers and their clients.

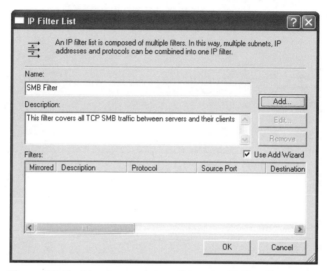

Figure 11-8   Naming and describing the IP filter list

5. Click Add. When the IP Filter Wizard starts, click Next.

> **Note**   The Use Add Wizard check box must be selected before you click Add. If it isn't, clicking Add displays the Filter Properties dialog box, which is best used by administrators with a solid understanding of IP security filtering.

6. On the IP Traffic Source page, specify the source address of the IP traffic that you want to filter (Figure 11-9). Select one of the following options, provide any necessary information, and then click Next:

   ❑ **My IP Address**   Sets the filter source to the IP address of the computer on which the IPSec policy is applied

   ❑ **Any IP Address**   Sets the filter source to any IP address

   ❑ **A Specific DNS Name**   Sets the filter source to the IP address resolved from the DNS host name you specify

   ❑ **A Specific IP Address**   Sets the filter source to the specific IP address with a given subnet mask

❑ **A Specific IP Subnet**   Sets the filter source to a specific IP subnet using a given subnet address and subnet mask

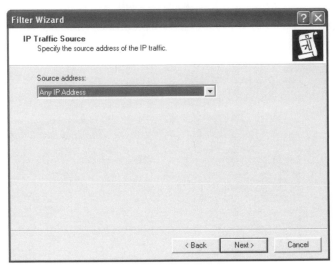

Figure 11-9   Setting the source for the filter

7. On the IP Traffic Destination page, specify the destination address of the IP traffic that you want to filter. After selecting one of the following options, provide any necessary information and then click Next.

❑ **My IP Address**   Sets the filter destination to the IP address of the computer on which you are configuring IP security

❑ **Any IP Address**   Sets the filter destination to any IP address on the network

❑ **A Specific DNS Name**   Sets the filter destination to the specific DNS host name you specify

❑ **A Specific IP Address**   Sets the filter destination to the specific IP address with a given subnet mask

❑ **A Specific IP Subnet**   Sets the filter destination to a specific IP subnet using a given subnet address and subnet mask

8. On the IP Protocol Type page, set the protocol type to filter. Select Any to filter packets sent and received on any IP protocol. Select Other to manually configure the protocol type. Click Next.

9. If you chose TCP or UDP as the protocol type, you can now specify the source and destination ports. For example, if you want to filter SMB traffic, which can originate on any port but connects to TCP port 445 on file serves, select From Any Port and To This Port with 445 entered, as shown in Figure 11-10. Click Next.

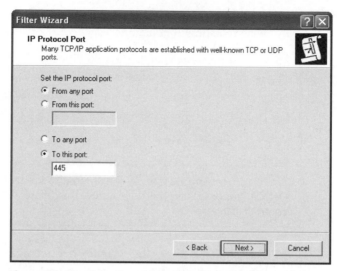

Figure 11-10   Selecting the protocol port to use in the filter

10.   Select Edit Properties, and then click Finish.

11.   On the Addressing tab of the Filter Properties dialog box, confirm that the mirroring option is the one you want to use. When a filter is mirrored, the same filter is applied to both source and destination computers. Thus if you want the rule to apply only one way—from clients to servers or from servers to clients, depending on the filter configuration—you clear the Mirrored check box.

12.   Click OK.

Creating and Managing Filter Actions

The filter action lets you tell computers that process the IPSec policy what to do with network traffic that meets the filter list you just created. By default, three filter actions are specified:

- **Permit**   Permits unsecured packets.

- **Request Security (Optional)**   Allows unsecured communications but requests that client establish trust and use secure communications. Allows communications with unsecured clients if they do not respond successfully to the request to use security.

- **Require Security**   Allows unsecured communications but always requires that clients establish trust and use secure communications. No communications with unsecured clients are allowed.

You can create additional filter actions for IPSec rules as well. To create new IP filter actions or manage existing filter actions assigned to a rule, follow these steps:

1. Display the properties dialog box for the IPSec policy you are configuring. If necessary, access Computer Configuration\Windows Settings\Security Settings\IP Security Settings On Active Directory, right-click the policy, and select Properties.

2. Select a previously defined IP Security rule, and then click Edit. This opens the Edit Rule Properties dialog box.

> **Note**   Unless you want to set the authentication method, do not edit the Default Response rule. This rule handles the default response to network communications.

3. The Filter Action tab shows the currently defined filter actions. You can now edit or remove existing filter actions or create a new filter action. The selected filter action specifies how traffic that meets the filter list selected on the Filter List tab is handled. Only one filter action can be selected for each rule.

4. To create a new filter action, click Add. When the IP Security Filter Action Wizard starts, click Next.

> **Note**   The Use Add Wizard check box must be selected before you click Add. If it isn't selected, clicking Add displays the New Filter Action Properties dialog box, which is best used by administrators with a solid understanding of IP security filtering.

5. On the Filter Action Name page, type a name for the filter action and then add a description. For example, if you are creating a filter action for an SMB filter list, you might use the name Require Security for SMB and a description such as This filter actions is used to require secure communications for SMB traffic between severs and their clients.

6. Click Next. On the Filter Action General Options page, you can now set the filter action behavior (Figure 11-11). Choose one of the following options:

   ❑ **Permit**   All traffic that meets the filter is permitted.

   ❑ **Block**   All traffic that meets the filter is blocked.

> **Note**   You can use blocking to provide basic port filtering via IPSec policy. By choosing particular types of traffic and particular ports and then specifying the block option, you can control which types of traffic are processed by your computers and which are dropped. However, Windows Firewall is a better approach because it is more versatile and easier to manage.

❑ **Negotiate Security**   Allows you to specify additional requirements for secure communication.

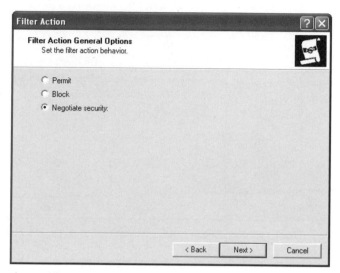

Figure 11-11   Selecting the general filter action

7. If you chose Permit or Block, click Next and then click Finish, and skip the remaining steps.

8. If you chose Negotiate Security, click Next and then specify whether you want this filter action to allow communication with computers that do not support IPSec:

   ❑ If you want to ensure that only IPSec-capable computers can communicate according to the filter rule, choose Do Not Communicate With Computers That Do Not Support IPSec.

   ❑ If you want to allow unsecured communications with clients that don't support IPSec-based secure communications, choose Fall Back To Unsecured Communications.

9. Click Next. Choose the security method you want to use for this filter (Figure 11-12).

   ❑ **Encryption And Integrity**   Data is encrypted, authenticated and unmodified. The default encryption algorithm is 3DES. The default integrity algorithm is SHA1.

   ❑ **Integrity Only**   Data is authenticated and unmodified. Integrity is checked using the SHA1 integrity-checking algorithm.

   ❑ **Custom**   Allows you to specify the encryption and integrity techniques and algorithms to use. You can also specify that you want to generate session keys and configure session key handling.

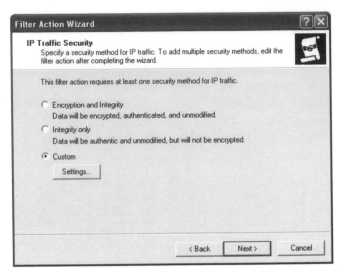

Figure 11-12   Choosing the security method for the filter action

> **Note**   In most cases, you should use integrity and encryption to completely protect network traffic. However, encryption requires additional processing cycles and thus might not be ideal on a heavily loaded server, especially if you are requiring that all communications with that server be protected.

10. Click Next, and then click Finish.

Monitoring IPSec Policy

After you deploy IPSec policy, you should check individual machines to make sure they are receiving the correct policy and that the policy is being used. Windows Server 2003 provides the IP Security Policy Management snap-in for this purpose. You can start and use this snap-in by following these steps:

1. To open a new Microsoft Management Console, click Start, Run. In the Run dialog box, type mmc and then click OK.

2. Choose File, Add/Remove Snap-in.

3. In the Add/Remove Snap-in dialog box, click Add.

4. In the Add Standalone Snap-in dialog box, select IP Security Monitor and then click Add.

5. Click Close, and then click OK.

6. By default, the IP Security Monitor snap-in opens with its focus on the computer where it's being run. However, you can right-click the IP Security Policy Monitor node and choose Add Computer to select a different computer.

As shown in Figure 11-13, the IP Security Monitor snap-in shows details about the active IPSec policies on a given computer. You can thus see at a glance if IPSec is being used, how it is being used, and which policy is in effect.

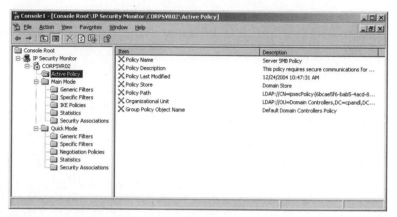

Figure 11-13   Viewing active policy details within the IP Security monitor snap-in

The IP Security Monitor snap-in also lets you view details of:

- Main Mode, which represents the key exchange negotiation phase of an IPSec communication

- Quick Mode, which is the data protection negotiation phase.

> **Note**   You can also use the Resultant Set of Policy (RSoP) features built into the Group Policy Management Console (GPMC) to view effective IPSec policies on a given computer. An RSoP walkthrough is provided in Chapter 2. Chapter 3 details how to use RSoP to model Group Policy for planning.

Deploying Public Key Policies

Kerberos authentication is the most commonly used computer to computer authentication mechanism for Windows computers. Kerberos is in fact, the default authentication mechanism in Active Directory domains. In addition to Kerberos authentication, Windows computers can use public key certificates for authentication.

How Public Key Certificates Work

Public key certificates provide a standard way of identifying users and computers securely. A certificate is like a unique signature that can be associated only with a particular identity. Public key certificates have a wide variety of uses for users and computers alike. They can be used for enabling IPSec communications between computers, for signing code to ensure the code comes from a trusted publisher, for encrypting e-mail, and for enabling the Microsoft Encrypting File System (EFS). Public key technologies are sometimes referred to as the public key infrastructure, or PKI.

Public key policy within Group Policy lets you control which certificates your computers and users use and how they are used. Public key policy provides for autoenrollment of certificates that you specify so your computers and users don't have to manually add certificates to use services such as encrypted e-mail. You can also ensure that your users use certificates only from reputable certificate authorities (CAs). A CA can be a trusted external organization or an internal CA that you create. You establish your own internal CA by installing Microsoft Certificate Services on a Windows Server 2003 computer within your Active Directory forest.

The CA is responsible for creating and distributing public key certificates to users and computers for a variety of purposes. The CA also provides certificate revocation lists (CRLs) that let users and computers know when previously issued certificates are no longer valid, even if they have not expired.

> **More Info**   A good starter reference about the essentials of establishing and working with a CA is Chapter 8 of the *IIS 6.0 Administrator's Pocket Consultant* (Microsoft Press, 2003). It shows how to set up a CA, issue certificates, revoke certificates, and manage Certificate Services in general.

How Public Key Policies Are Used

Public key policies are available as both per-computer and per-user policy within the Group Policy namespace under Windows Settings\Security Settings\Public Key Policies, as shown in Figure 11-14. The per-user Public Key Policies folder, however, includes only a subset of the capabilities found in the per-computer settings. Specifically, you can use per-user settings only to manage enterprise trust lists and autoenrollment settings.

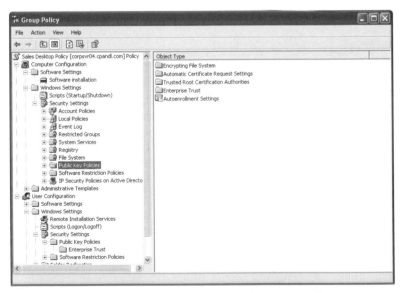

Figure 11-14   Viewing public key policies in the Group Policy namespace

Public key policies allow for a variety of public key deployment scenarios and enforcement rules. The four general policy areas are:

- **Encrypting File System** Used to establish key recovery agents for data that is encrypted using EFS. EFS policies allow you to unencrypt data encrypted by users who are no longer around or whose user accounts have been removed. By default, within an Active Directory environment the domain Administrator account is automatically made a key recovery agent for all computers in the domain. These policies apply to computers only.

- **Automatic Certificate Request Settings** Used to specify the types of certificates that a computer can request automatically. These policies apply only to certificate usage that is computer specific, and you must have one or more existing certificate templates. These policies apply to computers only.

> **Note** Each type of template has a specific use—for example, for computers, domain controllers, enrollment agents, or IP security. You can install certificate templates using Certtmpl.msc. When a computer processes the related policy, it autoenrolls with the enterprise CA for that type of certificate.

- **Trusted Root Certification Authorities** Used to configure the types of trusted root CAs allowed. By default, both third-party root CAs and enterprise root CAs are trusted. You can change this configuration and add new trusted root CAs. Keep mind that Active Directory–based CA root certificates are automatically installed on domain based computers without the use of public key policies. These policies apply to computers only.

- **Enterprise Trust** Used to specify certificate trust lists (the certificates issued by third-party CAs that you trust). Trusted certificates are listed according to the CA that issued them, the effective date, and the intended purpose. These policies apply to both users and computers.

In addition to these four general policy areas, you can configure autoenrollment behavior for computers and users. By default, users and computers are configured to enroll certificates automatically. You can view or change the autoenrollment settings by completing the following steps:

1. Select the Public Key Policies under Computer Configuration\Windows Settings\Security Settings or User Configuration\Windows Settings\Security Settings as appropriate.

2. Double-click Autoenrollment Settings in the right pane. This displays the dialog box, shown in Figure 11-15.

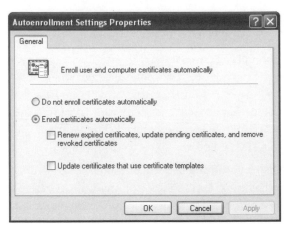

Figure 11-15   Specifying global autoenrollment options within public key policy

3. To disable autoenrollment, select Do Not Enroll Certificates Automatically. To allow autoenrollment, select Enroll Certificates Automatically.

   If you choose autoenrollment, two additional options are available:

   ❑ **Renew Expired Certificates, Update Pending Certificates, And Remove Revoked Certificates**   Choose this option to ensure that, beyond simple autoenrollment, certificates installed to your users and computers are managed if they expire, are pending, or are revoked.

   ❑ **Update Certificates That Use Certificate Templates**   Choose this option to use certificate templates to control what kinds of certificates are autoenrolled and to allow certificates to be updated.

4. Click OK.

Managing Public Key Policy

Public key certificates are most commonly used in certain scenarios. For example, if you have an enterprise CA root installed, you can automatically enroll your user accounts with a certificate for e-mail signing and encryption. This doesn't require the use of public key policies, however, because autoenrollment is enabled by default within an Active Directory environment with a CA installed.

One area that requires configuration in policy is the implementation of EFS within an Active Directory environment. By default, when a user encrypts a file using EFS, that user and the domain administrator account (if the computer is in an Active Directory) are made the key recovery agents for that file. This means that either the user or the domain administrator can unencrypt that file. However, you might want to create additional key recovery agents to ensure that the right people within your organization can recover encrypted files before you allow your users to use EFS.

To add a new key recovery agent for EFS, complete the following steps:

1. Select the Public Key Policies under Computer Configuration\Windows Settings\Security Settings.

2. Right-click Encrypting File System and choose Add Data Recovery Agent. This starts the Add Recovery Agent Wizard. Click Next.

> **Note**   The shortcut menu that appears when you right-click Encrypting File System also has a Create Data Recovery Agent option. If you select this option, the domain administrator account is automatically added to the GPO as the default key recovery agent. This is necessary only if you want to have the domain administrator account included as a key recovery agent for the computers that process that GPO. You can also select All Tasks followed by Delete Policy to remove all recovery agents specified within that GPO so far.

3. On the Select Recovery Agent page, shown in Figure 11-16, you can choose to browse Active Directory or a file folder to locate the user certificate that will be used to establish the key recovery agent. The user whose certificate you selected is then added to the Recovery Agents list. Repeat this process to designate additional recovery agents.

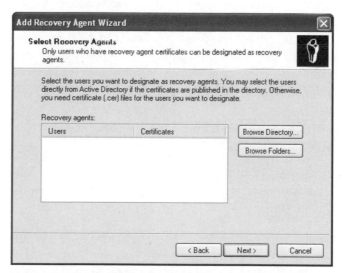

Figure 11-16   Specifying a new EFS key recovery agent

> **Note**   Certificates can be exported to files and then imported using the Browse Folders option. In this way, you can import the certificate file when the certificate itself is not stored with the user object in Active Directory.

> **Tip**   You can view the certificates installed for your user account or for a particular computer account by loading the Certificates MMC snap-in from a blank MMC console. The Certificates snap-in provides details about currently enrolled certificates and allows you to manually enroll certificates. It also lists the currently trusted CAs for the user or computer.

4. Click Next, and then Click Finish. When this GPO is next processed by computer objects, the policy you configured will add the designated user or users as a valid recovery agent to any encrypted files.

Understanding Windows Firewall Policy

Most organizations have firewall and proxies in place to help protect the internal network from intruders. When users or computers connect indirectly to the Internet through these firewalls and proxies, you can be reasonably sure the computers are protected from attacks and malicious users. When users or computers connect directly to the Internet, however, these protections might not apply. For example, if a user takes a portable computer to an offsite meeting or uses a portable computer on a coffee shop wireless network while at lunch, the computer isn't automatically protected from attack or intrusion. If the infected computer is reconnected to the internal network, it can infect other computers, bypassing the protection of the firewall or proxy. To help prevent these infection scenarios, you must run a firewall on each computer—not just rely on the firewall or proxy that separates the internal network from the Internet. This is where Windows Firewall and Windows Firewall Group Policy settings enter the picture.

How Windows Firewall Works

Windows Firewall, the successor to the Internet Connection Firewall (ICF), was released with Windows XP SP2 and Windows Server 2003 SP1. Like ICF, Windows Firewall provides stateful IP port filtering on a per-host basis to protect computers that are running Windows from unauthorized access.

Stateful port filtering means that Windows Firewall keeps track of connections coming into and going out of your Windows computers and lets you dynamically control the flow of traffic. Windows Firewall also allows for exception-based firewall protection. When traffic that does not pass the firewall rules arrives at a Windows Firewall–protected computer, the user has the option to allow or deny that traffic through a pop-up dialog box called a Security Alert.

Windows Firewall differs from ICF in that it is completely manageable and configurable via Group Policy. The default configuration is different for Windows workstations and servers as well. The default configuration of Windows Firewall is more secure, for example, because Windows Firewall is enabled for all network connections by default. Keep the following in mind:

- On computers running Windows XP SP2 or later, Windows Firewall is installed and enabled by default. The Windows Firewall/Internet Connection Sharing (ICS) service, which provides the underlying firewall protection service, is configured to start automatically with the operating system. Enabling or disabling Windows Firewall doesn't change the state of the underlying firewall service.

- On computers running Windows Server 2003 SP1 or later, Windows Firewall is installed but disabled by default. The Windows Firewall/Internet Connection Sharing (ICS) service does not start automatically with the operating system and is disabled by default.

You start, stop, and configure Windows Firewall by using the Windows Firewall utility in Control Panel. When you access the utility and the Windows Firewall/Internet Connection Sharing (ICS) service is not running, you are given the opportunity to start the service (Figure 11-17). Click Yes to start the service. Keep in mind that if you later configure exceptions for applications or services that were running before the service was started, you should restart the computer to ensure that these applications and services run properly.

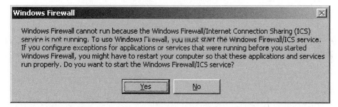

Figure 11-17   Start the Windows Firewall/Internet Connection Sharing (ICS) service if you plan to use Windows Firewall.

When Windows Firewall is enabled, it is also enabled by default on all network connections on a computer. This means that all LAN, wireless, and remote access connections are protected by the firewall when it is enabled. You can, of course, disable Windows Firewall on specific network connections.

How Windows Firewall Policy Is Used

Windows Firewall policies are found under Computer Configuration\Administrative Templates\Network\Network Connections\Windows Firewall. Windows Firewall policy has two modes of operation. The *Domain Profile* lets you configure Windows Firewall behavior when a computer is connected to the corporate network. The *Standard Profile* lets you configure firewall settings that apply when the user is disconnected from the corporate network, such as when a laptop user takes his computer home. The standard profile is useful to ensure that even when your computers are not connected to the corporate network, they are protected.

To determine whether a computer is connected to the corporate network, Windows first compares the DNS suffix of the currently active network connection or connections to the DNS suffix that was found during the last Group Policy processing cycle. Specifically, it looks at the following registry value to determine the DNS suffix the last time Group Policy was processed:

```
HKEY_LOCAL_MACHINE\SOFTWARE\Microsoft\Windows\CurrentVersion\Group Policy\
History\NetworkName
```

If the DNS suffix listed in this registry value is the same as the current active network connection (a network connection that has an IP address assigned to it and is enabled), the computer is assumed to be on the corporate network and the Domain Profile policy is applied. Looking at the DNS suffix of the computer is only one part of the detection algorithm, however.

A computer is assumed to be off the corporate network and the Standard Profile policy is applied when any of the following conditions are true:

- If the DNS suffix of the computer's current active network connection(s) does not match the DNS suffix of the *NetworkName* registry value, the computer is considered off the corporate network and the Standard profile applies.

- If the computer is not part of an Active Directory domain, it is considered to be off the corporate network and the Standard Profile applies.

- If the only active network connection for a computer is a dial-up or VPN connection, the computer is considered off the corporate network and the Standard profile applies.

Windows checks for these conditions at computer startup or when a network connection changes (such as when a new connection becomes active or a change is made to an existing connection).

> **Note**   Technically, computers process both the Domain Profile and Standard Profile policy settings and set those policy values in the registry, but they apply the settings (based on the current profile) only at computer startup or a network configuration change. This makes sense: if computers are no longer on the corporate network, they cannot process Group Policy to receive the Standard Profile policy settings. By processing both profiles, computers ensure that the settings are available and are applied whenever and wherever the computer's network state changes.

To view the current profile that is being applied to a computer, follow these steps:

1. Access the Windows Firewall utility by double-clicking Windows Firewall in Control Panel or right-clicking a currently active network connection icon in the system notification area and choosing Change Windows Firewall Settings.

2. If the Windows Firewall/Internet Connection Sharing (ICS) service is turned off or disabled, you are given the opportunity to start the service:

   ❑ Click Yes to start the service if you want to run Windows Firewall on this computer. The service is started and configured for automatic startup. Windows Firewall is enabled in its default state: off for servers and on for workstations.

   ❑ Click No to exit the Windows Firewall utility. The status of the Windows Firewall/Internet Connection Sharing (ICS) service will not change and Windows Firewall will not be available for use on this computer.

3. The options on the General tab specify the state of Windows Firewall and the profile being used (Figure 11-18). In the lower left corner you'll see one of the following statements:

   ❑ **Windows Firewall Is Using Your Domain Settings**   Indicates that the Domain Profile is currently in effect

   ❑ **Windows Firewall Is Using Your Non-Domain Settings**   Indicates that the Standard Profile is currently in effect

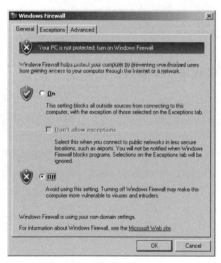

Figure 11-18   The state of Windows Firewall

One limitation of the profile determination process is that it assumes that DNS suffixes are assigned dynamically as network connections change. For example, if you are using DHCP to assign IP configurations to your corporate computers, you might also specify a DNS suffix option. Similarly, when your users roam to external networks, those networks will mostly likely provide their own DNS suffix.

However, if you have computers whose DNS suffix is hard-coded within the DNS properties for a connection, as shown in Figure 11-19, this can short-circuit the profile determination process. Why? Because if that connection is in use on both the corporate and noncorporate networks, it will have the same DNS suffix for each area and will always use the Domain Profile. For this reason, if you plan to implement a different Domain Profile and Standard Profile, you must ensure that DNS suffixes are provided dynamically via DHCP and are not hard-coded.

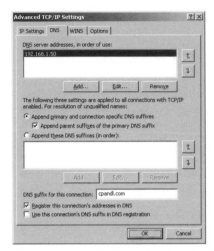

Figure 11-19   Viewing a hard-coded DNS suffix on a network connection

Managing Windows Firewall Policy

When you access Computer Configuration\Administrative Templates\Network\ Network Connections\Windows Firewall in Group Policy, you'll find separate policy sections for the Domain Profile and the Standard Profile. Both policy sections contain the same policies and settings. The only difference is that one set of policies is used to configure Windows Firewall on the corporate network while the other is used to configured Windows Firewall off the corporate network. There is one global policy setting as well, which is found at the same level as these two profile nodes. This global policy setting controls the way Windows Firewall works with IPSec.

When you work with Windows Firewall policy, you should generally determine whether IPSec bypass should be allowed, and if so, configure the computers that should be allowed to use IPSec bypass, and then you should determine whether Windows Firewall should be enabled or disabled in the Domain Profile and the Standard Profile. You should then configure permitted exceptions, notification, and logging for when Windows Firewall is enabled in a profile.

Configuring IPSec Bypass

You can use the Windows Firewall: Allow Authenticated IPSec Bypass policy to configure Windows Firewall to allow IPSec-secured communications to bypass the firewall. If you enable this policy, computers using IPSec to communicate with a computer processing this policy will not be subject to firewall restrictions. If you disable or do not configure this policy, no exceptions will be granted for computers using IPSec and they will be subject to the same firewall restrictions as other computers.

To allow IPSec-secured communications to bypass the Windows Firewall, follow these steps:

1. Access Computer Configuration\Administrative Templates\Network\Network Connections\Windows Firewall.

2. In the rightmost pane, double-click Windows Firewall: Allow Authenticated IPSec Bypass.

3. Select Enabled, and then specify the IPSec computers to be exempted from the firewall policy by entering a Security Descriptor Definition Language (SDDL) string in the box provided. For more information on SDDL, see Chapter 15.

> **Note**   The SDDL string provides the Security Identifiers (SIDs) of the computers in your organization that should be able to bypass the firewall when using IPSec-secured communications. Typically, you enter the security descriptors for your domain's Domain Computers and Domain Controllers global security groups. If you have created other domain or OU-specific groups for computers, you enter these instead if you want to limit bypass of IPSec-secured communications to computers within the domain or OU.

4. Click OK.

Enabling and Disabling Windows Firewall with Group Policy

Through Group Policy, you can enforce whether Windows Firewall is turned on or turned off across your servers and workstations. For example, you might want servers to have Windows Firewall turned on for the Standard Profile and turned off for the Domain Profile. If you have specific groups of computers that should use Windows Firewall when connected to the corporate network, you might want to create a separate Windows Firewall GPO and apply this GPO selectively using security filtering or WMI filters.

> **Tip**   In some environments, such as a small office with limited hardware firewall protection, you might want Windows Firewall to be enabled in the Domain Profile. In this case, you should also consider configuring the firewall so that computers can be remotely managed. For details, see "Allowing Remote Desktop Exceptions" in this chapter.

In policy, you can control whether Windows Firewall is enabled or disabled by using the Windows Firewall: Protect All Network Connections. Keep the following in mind when working with this policy:

- If this policy is enabled, Windows Firewall will be enabled for all network connections on all computers that process the GPO containing this policy setting (according to the profile in which it is enabled).

- If this policy is disabled, Windows Firewall will be disabled for all network connections on all computers that process the GPO containing this policy setting (according to the profile in which it is enabled).

- Whether this policy is set as Enabled or Disabled, a user on the computer where the policy has been applied will be unable to change the setting. The option to change it will be grayed out.

Note Although you can use the Advanced tab of the Windows Firewall dialog box on the local computer to specify per-network connection firewall protection, this functionality is not exposed through Group Policy. With Group Policy, you can only enable or disable Windows Firewall for *all* network connections on a given computer. Group Policy also does not allow you to configure the advanced per-connection settings for services and ICMP configuration.

Managing Firewall Exceptions with Group Policy

Another option related to enabling and disabling of Windows Firewall functionality is the allowing of exceptions. You can use exceptions to allow programs to access certain well-known ports on the computer even when Windows Firewall is enabled. By default, a user who is working on a computer that has Windows Firewall enabled receives security alerts when an application attempts to open a port for listening on the computer. Through Group Policy, you can control which applications and ports are allowed to pass through the firewall so the user does not have to make those decisions.

On servers, which typically have no logged on users, the ability to predefine exceptions through Group Policy can be valuable. A number of predefined policies are available for allowing exceptions to known applications. You can also define your own exceptions, based on the application or port that is needed. For most exceptions, you can set the scope of allowed communications by entering any combination of the following identifiers in a comma-separated list:

- **IPAddress** An actual IP address, such as 192.168.1.10. Allows file and print traffic from this IP address to be accepted by computers that process this GPO.

- **SubnetAddress** An actual IP subnet address, such as 192.168.1.0/24. Allows file and print traffic from any computers on this IP subnet to be accepted by computers that process this GPO.

- **localsubnet** Allows file and print traffic from any computers on the local subnet to be accepted by computers that process this GPO.

For example, to allow exceptions for the local subnet, a computer with an IP address of 192.168.1.10, and the subnet 192.168.1.0/24, you would type:

```
localsubnet, 192.168.1.10, 192.168.1.0/24
```

> **Tip** You can also use a asterisk (*) to specify that all networks can communicate with a particular application. A good resource for learning about IP subnets and how to specify them is *Windows Server 2003 Inside Out.*

Disabling the Use of Exceptions

You can completely control the use of exceptions by using the Windows Firewall: Do Not Allow Exceptions policy. Keep the following in mind:

- If you enable this policy, no exceptions will be allowed and any exceptions defined in the Windows Firewall configuration will be ignored. Further, in the Windows Firewall dialog box, the Don't Allow Exceptions check box will be selected and both users and local administrators will be unable to clear this setting.

- If you disable this policy, exceptions defined in policy will be allowed and any exceptions defined in the local Windows Firewall configuration will also be accepted. Further, in the Windows Firewall dialog box, the Don't Allow Exceptions check box will be cleared and both users and local administrators will be unable to change this setting.

Administrators who log on locally can work around this policy setting by turning off Windows Firewall.

Allowing File and Printer Sharing Exceptions

You can use file and printer sharing exceptions to accept or block file and print traffic to and from specific computers. File and printer sharing exceptions manage traffic on these ports:

- TCP 139
- TCP 445

- UDP 137

- UDP 138

These ports are used during file and printer sharing. You can manage their use by enabling or disabling the Windows Firewall: Allow File And Printer Sharing Exceptions policy. When working with this policy, keep the following in mind:

- If you need to be able to map server shares and printers to a computer (usually a server), you can enable this policy. In the Windows Firewall dialog box, the File And Printer Sharing check box will be selected and both users and local administrators will be unable to clear this setting.

- If you want to prevent computers from mapping server shares and printers, you can disable this policy. In the Windows Firewall dialog box, the File And Printer Sharing check box will be cleared and both users and local administrators will be unable to change this setting.

To enable and configure file and printer sharing exceptions, complete the following steps:

1. Access Computer Configuration\Administrative Templates\Network\Network Connections\Windows Firewall.

2. Access Domain Profile or Standard Profile as appropriate, and then double-click Windows Firewall: Allow File And Printer Sharing Exceptions.

3. Select Enabled.

4. Use the Allow Unsolicited Incoming Message From text box to specify the scope of allowed communications. As shown in Figure 11-20, you can type any combination of the following identifiers in a comma-separated list:

   - **IPAddress**   An actual IP address, such as 192.168.1.10. Allows file and print traffic from this IP address to be accepted by computers that process this GPO.

   - **SubnetAddress**   An actual IP subnet address, such as 192.168.1.0/24. Allows file and print traffic from any computers on this IP subnet to be accepted by computers that process this GPO.

   - **localsubnet**   Allows file and print traffic from any computers on the local subnet to be accepted by computers that process this GPO.

5. Click OK.

Figure 11-20   Configuring the scope of the exception

Allowing Remote Administration Exceptions

Remote administration exceptions open a set of ports that allow remote administrative operations to be performed on computers that allow these exceptions. A good example of a remote administrative function that will fail if this exception is not enabled is the Group Policy Results Wizard. You cannot perform remote RSoP logging on a system that does not have the remote administration exceptions enabled.

You control remote administration exceptions using Windows Firewall: Allow Remote Administration Exception. When you enable this policy, TCP ports 135 (for the RPC port mapper) and 445 (for SMB) are enabled for listening, which allows use of remote procedure calls (RPCs) and Distributed Component Object Model (DCOM). This policy setting also allows Svchost.exe and Lsass.exe to receive incoming messages and allows hosted services to open TCP ports in the 1024 to 1034 range to facilitate RPC communications. If you have any administrative applications that require RPC or SMB, you should enable this exception. If this policy is disabled or not configured, the following MMC snap-in tools cannot remotely access a computer protected by Windows Firewall:

- Certificates
- Computer Management
- Device Management
- Disk Management
- Event Viewer
- Group Policy

- Indexing Service
- IPSec Monitor
- Local Users and Groups
- Removable Storage Management
- Resultant Set of Policy
- Services
- Shared Folders
- WMI Control

> **Note** Because malicious users often try to attack computers through RCP and DCOM, you should enable remote administration exceptions only when you are certain they are needed. Also, note that if you allow remote administration exceptions, Windows Firewall allows incoming ICMP echo request (ping) messages on TCP port 445 even if Windows Firewall: Allow ICMP Exceptions policy would otherwise block them.

To enable and configure remote administration exceptions, complete the following steps:

1. Access Computer Configuration\Administrative Templates\Network\Network Connections\Windows Firewall.

2. Access Domain Profile or Standard Profile as appropriate, and then double-click Windows Firewall: Allow Remote Administration Exceptions.

3. Select Enabled, and then use the Allow Unsolicited Incoming Message From text box to specify the scope of allowed communications, as described previously.

4. Click OK.

Allowing Remote Desktop Exceptions

Remote Desktop exceptions allow users to connect to a remote computer using the Remote Desktop feature. This means TCP port 3389 is excepted, which is the default port that Terminal Services listens on. Keep the following in mind:

- If you enable this policy, computers that process this policy can receive Remote Desktop requests from specifically allowed computers. In the Windows Firewall dialog box, the Remote Desktop check box will be selected and both users and administrators will be unable to clear this setting.

- If you disable this policy, Windows Firewall will block Remote Desktop requests for all computers that process this policy. In the Windows Firewall dialog box, the Remote Desktop check box will be cleared and both users and administrators will be unable to change this setting.

To enable and configure Remote Desktop exceptions, complete the following steps:

1. Access Computer Configuration\Administrative Templates\Network\Network Connections\Windows Firewall.

2. Access Domain Profile or Standard Profile as appropriate, and then double-click Windows Firewall: Allow Remote Desktop Exceptions.

3. Select Enabled, and then use the Allow Unsolicited Incoming Message From text box to specify the scope of allowed communications, as described previously.

4. Click OK.

Allowing UPnP Framework Exceptions

UPnP Framework exceptions permit Universal Plug and Play (UPnP) messages to be received by a computer. UPnP messages are used by services such as built-in firewall software to communicate with a Windows computer. When you permit UPnP Framework exceptions, TCP port 2869 and UDP port 1900 are allowed for use by the UPnP Framework services. Keep the following in mind:

- If you enable this policy, computers that process this policy can receive UPnP Framework requests from specifically allowed computers. In the Windows Firewall dialog box, the UPnP Framework check box will be selected and both users and administrators will be unable to clear this setting.

- If you disable this policy, UPnP Framework requests will be blocked by Windows firewall for all computers that process this policy. In the Windows Firewall dialog box, the UPnP Framework check box will be cleared and both users and administrators will be unable to change this setting.

To enable and configure UPnP Framework exceptions, complete the following steps:

1. Access Computer Configuration\Administrative Templates\Network\Network Connections\Windows Firewall.

2. Access Domain Profile or Standard Profile as appropriate, and then double-click Windows Firewall: Allow UPnP Framework Exceptions.

3. Select Enabled, and then use the Allow Unsolicited Incoming Message From text box to specify the scope of allowed communications, as described previously.

4. Click OK.

Defining Program Exceptions

In addition to configuring various exceptions for services, you can define exceptions for programs, ICMP messages, and specific ports. When you configure program exceptions, you specify applications for which you want to allow communications rather than services.

Program exceptions are useful if you don't know the particular port that an application requires. You can simply select the executable name and Windows Firewall will detect the port that the application needs to communicate on. Keep in mind that program exceptions imply that the application is running on the computers for which that you are defining the exception. If the application is not running, the ports are not excepted.

Windows Firewall allows you to define program exception lists in Group Policy and through the Windows Firewall utility in Control Panel. To define program exceptions in Group Policy, you enable and configure the Windows Firewall: Define Program Exceptions policy.

Program exceptions take the form of a free text string that contains a set of parameters in the following format:

```
PathToProgram:Scope:Status:Name
```

These parameters are used as follows:

- **PathToProgram** The path to the executable for which you want to allow exceptions.

- **Scope** A comma-separated list of IP addresses or IP subnets, or the entire local subnet for which you are configuring the exception. Any computers that process the related GPO are either allowed to communicate or blocked from communicating with the defined program on the designated IP addresses.

- **Status** Specifies whether communications are allowed or blocked (*enabled* or *disabled*).

- **Name** Sets the name of the exception as displayed on the Exceptions tab in the Windows Firewall dialog box.

To see how this works, consider the following example: Suppose we have a server application that provides stock quotes to client computers on the network. It is located at C:\Program files\Quotes\Quotes.exe. We want to allow all clients on the subnet at 192.168.3.0/24 to be able to communicate with this application on this server, and we also want to allow another server at IP address 192.168.1.5, which provides the quotes from the Internet, to be able to able to communicate with this application. In this case, the program exception looks like this:

```
%ProgramFiles%\quotes\quotes.exe:192.168.3.0/24,192.168.1.5:enabled:Progam
Exception for the Quotes Application
```

We use the environment variable *%ProgramFiles%* because this policy might need to run on multiple computers and we don't necessarily know which disk volume the program files folder are on. The scope of 192.168.3.0/24 indicates that we want this exception to apply to all devices on the 192.168.3.0 subnet—/24 indicates a 24-bit subnet mask. If we want to allow all computers on the local subnet to talk with this application, we can use the *localsubnet* string within the scope portion in addition to any IP subnet or IP addresses that are specified:

```
192.168.3.0/24,localsubnet,192.168.1.5
```

Tip   You can also use an asterisk (*) to specify that all networks can communicate with a particular application.

To enable and configure program exceptions, complete the following steps:

1. Access Computer Configuration\Administrative Templates\Network\Network Connections\Windows Firewall.

2. Access Domain Profile or Standard Profile as appropriate, and then double-click Windows Firewall: Define Program Exceptions.

3. Select Enabled, and then click Show. The Show Contents dialog box lists any currently defined program exceptions (Figure 11-21).

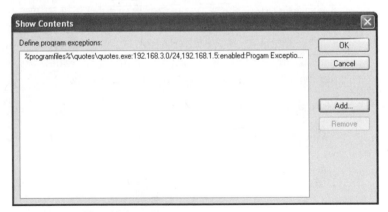

Figure 11-21   Viewing and managing program exceptions

4. To add a new program exception, click Add. In the Add Item dialog box, type the exception string. Exception strings take the form of a free text string that contains a set of parameters in the following format:

```
PathToProgram:Scope:Status:Name
```

> **Note**   Do not use quotation marks when specifying any elements of the program exception, including the *localsubnet* string within the scope option. Even the name string should be entered without quotation marks.

5. To remove an existing program exception, select the exception and then click Remove.

6. Click OK twice.

Once a program exception is applied to the target computer, it appears on the Exceptions tab of the Windows Firewall configuration but is grayed out so that it cannot be changed. You will also notice that the Group Policy column shows Yes, indicating that the exception is being delivered via Group Policy.

If you define a program exception via Group Policy, users cannot manually define other program exceptions. If you want to allow users to define additional program exceptions, you must also enable Windows Firewall: Allow Local Program Exceptions. If you have not defined any program exceptions through policy, you can disable Windows Firewall: Allow Local Program Exceptions to prevent users from defining any program exceptions themselves.

Defining ICMP Exceptions

ICMP exceptions allow you to specify whether the computer will respond to ICMP messages. ICMP is used most commonly by the *ping* command but can be used by other applications as well to determine whether a computer is available. ICMP is normally completely disabled when Windows Firewall is active, but you can enable certain types of responses that might be needed by your applications.

To enable and configure ICMP exceptions, complete the following steps:

1. Access Computer Configuration\Administrative Templates\Network\Network Connections\Windows Firewall.

2. Access Domain Profile or Standard Profile as appropriate, and then double-click Windows Firewall: Allow ICMP Exceptions.

3. Select Enabled, and then use the options provided to allow specific types of ICMP communications (Figure 11-22). For example, if you want to enable a computer to respond to ping requests, you select the Allow Inbound Echo Request check box.

4. Click OK.

Figure 11-22 Configuring ICMP exceptions using Group Policy

> **Tip** You can set this policy for outgoing ICMP messages as well as incoming ones. This allows you to allow or block a computer from sending ICMP messages as well as receiving them.

If you disable Windows Firewall: Allow ICMP Exceptions, no ICMP communications are allowed and an administrator cannot set any exceptions. However, if you enabled remote administrative exceptions or the file and printer sharing exceptions as described previously, Allow Inbound Echo Request is allowed for the related ports regardless.

Defining Port Exceptions

Port exceptions policy works much like program exceptions policy, except that you specify a particular port to allow communications to instead of an application. If you enable this policy, you can add a series of exceptions using the following format:

```
Port:Transport:Scope:Status:Name
```

These parameters are used as follows:

- **Port** Specifies a particular port number.
- **Transport** Specifies whether the port is UDP or TCP.
- **Scope** A comma-separated list of IP addresses or IP subnets or the entire local subnet for which you are configuring the exception. Any computers that process the related GPO are either allowed to communicate or blocked from communicating with the defined program on the designated IP addresses.

- **Status**   Specifies whether communications are allowed or blocked (*enabled* or *disabled*).
- **Name**   Text that can describe anything about the exception.

To see how this works, consider the following example: Suppose we want to allow TCP port 80 (HTTP) access to a server from the 192.168.1.0/24 subnet. We define the port exception as follows:

```
80:TCP:192.168.1.0/24:enabled:Allow HTTP Access
```

To enable and configure port exceptions, complete the following steps:

1. Access Computer Configuration\Administrative Templates\Network\Network Connections\Windows Firewall.

2. Access Domain Profile or Standard Profile as appropriate, and then double-click Windows Firewall: Define Port Exceptions.

3. Select Enabled, and then click Show.

4. The Show Contents dialog box lists any currently defined port exceptions.

5. To add a new port exception, click Add. In the Add Item dialog box, type the exception string. Exception strings take the form of a free text string that contains a set of parameters in the following format:

```
Port:Transport:Scope:Status:Name
```

> **Note**   Do not use quotation marks when specifying any elements of the port exception, including the *localsubnet* string within the scope option. Even the name string should be entered without quotation marks.

6. To remove an existing port exception, select the exception and then click Remove.

7. Click OK twice.

Once a port exception is applied to the target computer, it appears on the Exceptions tab of the Windows Firewall configuration but is grayed out so it cannot be changed. You will also notice that the Group Policy column shows Yes, indicating that the exception is being delivered via Group Policy.

If you define a port exception via Group Policy, users cannot manually define other port exceptions. If you want to allow users to define additional port exceptions, you must also enable Windows Firewall: Allow Local Port Exceptions. If you have not defined any program exceptions through policy, you can disable Windows Firewall: Allow Local Port Exceptions to prevent users from defining any program exceptions themselves.

Configuring Firewall Notification, Logging, and Response Requests

Group Policy also allows you to configure some other settings related to Windows Firewall, as described in the following sections.

Prohibiting Notifications

The Windows Firewall: Prohibit Notifications policy allows you to prevent the security alert messages that appear when an remote computer is trying to talk to an application on a computer that is blocking communications to that application. This policy is most often enabled on servers because there are typically no users logged on to see these messages.

Allowing Logging

The Windows Firewall: Allow Logging policy allows to you enforce logging of Windows Firewall activity. You'll typically want to enable Windows Firewall logging only when you need to troubleshoot a problem. If you disable this policy, users and administrator cannot configure logging locally on computers that process the policy.

To enable and configure logging, complete the following steps:

1. Access Computer Configuration\Administrative Templates\Network\Network Connections\Windows Firewall.

2. Access Domain Profile or Standard Profile as appropriate, and then double-click Windows Firewall: Allow Logging.

3. Select Enabled, and then use the following options to configure logging:

    ❑ **Log Dropped Packets**   Configures logging of any incoming packets that are blocked due to the firewall. You can use this information to troubleshoot applications that are unable to communicate with a computer.

    ❑ **Log Successful Connections**   Configures logging on all incoming and outgoing connections that succeed. This can obviously result in a lot of data, but you can see all traffic going to and from the computer.

    ❑ **Log File Path And Name**   Select this option to specify the folder path and filename for the Windows firewall log. The default location for logging is %SystemRoot%\pfirewall.log.

> **Tip**   You can specify a different path and filename, including a remote UNC path (as long as the computer logging the data has permissions to that remote path). If you log on to a UNC path, you should include the *%ComputerName%* environment variable in the filename or path to create a unique log for each computer. Keep in mind, however, that this can generate a lot of network traffic on the remote computer.

❑   **Size Limit**   Select this option to specify the maximum log file size in kilo-bytes. When a log file reaches this maximum size, it overwrites older records as needed. Therefore, you must judge the size based on how busy your computers are and what information you are logging. A log file set too small can be overwritten before you have a chance to view the entries, especially on a busy server.

4.   Click OK.

Prohibiting Unicast Responses to Multicast or Broadcast Requests

Windows Firewall: Prohibit Unicast Response To Multicast Or Broadcast Requests prevents certain types of network attacks when an infected computer sends a broadcast or multicast message and looks to receive unicast responses from target computers. If this policy is enabled on the infected computer, the unicast responses to broadcasts or multicasts are simply dropped. If this policy is disabled, the computer accepts all uni-cast responses for the first 3 seconds and then blocks subsequent responses.

Note   If you enable Windows Firewall: Prohibit Unicast Response To Multicast Or Broadcast Requests, DHCP requests from the computer, which typically take the form of a broadcast request followed by a unicast response from the DHCP server, will not be affected.

Summary

Using Group Policy, you can manage network communications security for IP secu-rity, public key encryption, and Windows Firewall. IP Security allows for secure, authenticated, and encrypted communications on TCP/IP networks. IPSec is ideally suited for special-purpose servers that require extra network-layer protection. It also provides rudimentary port filtering, although with the advent of Windows Firewall, using IPSec is probably not the best approach for this task. Public key encryption lets you control the use of public key certificates and enables such useful end-user features as Encrypting File System (EFS) and e-mail encryption. Windows Firewall provides stateful TCP/IP filtering to protect computers against unauthorized access. Through Group Policy, you can configure Windows Firewall exceptions and prevent users and local administrators from modifying Windows Firewall configurations locally.

Chapter 12

Creating Custom Environments

In this chapter:

Loopback Processing. 440
Terminal Services 444
Group Policy over Slow Links. 461
Summary 469

This chapter focuses mainly on modifying the default behavior of Group Policy objects (GPOs) in custom environments, such as when a user's computer is connecting to the network in a unique manner or needs special configurations. We will investigate the GPO settings that allow you to control, secure, and configure these environments to ensure a functional but secure environment.

The scenarios we will examine here may include the use of loopback processing, and this is reviewed first. Loopback processing is a unique and flexible option that allows for control of user settings through computer configurations. You can thus have control over the settings for all users who use a particular computer. We will next discuss Terminal Services sessions, which require special security and functionality control. Finally, we will look at slow link detection and how to control the GPO settings for slow link clients differently from those GPOs that typically affect all computers.

Active Directory Design and Normal GPO Processing

To design and implement custom environments, you need a good understanding of the basics of Group Policy, including how to design Active Directory® to facilitate deploying GPOs. Here are some basic and important concepts to remember with regard to designing Active Directory and deploying GPOs:

- You must design GPOs with consideration of delegation of administration in mind.

- Group Policy applies only to user and computer accounts, not group accounts.

- GPOs affect the container at which they are applied, as well as all subordinate containers through inheritance.

- GPOs affect all objects at the container at which they are deployed, including domain controllers, administrative groups, and administrative user accounts.

- An administrator can limit a GPO's scope of influence by configuring inheritance blocking, security filtering, and WMI filters.

- Keep your (organizational unit) OU structure to a maximum of 10 levels deep.

To design and implement custom environments, you also need a good understanding of how Group Policy is applied. Here is a quick summary of the order and precedence rules for how GPOs are normally processed.

1. When the computer starts, network connectivity also starts.

2. The computer account communicates with DNS and Active Directory.

3. The computer obtains an ordered list of GPOs that apply to the *computer*.

4. Computer policies under Computer Configuration are applied.

5. Computer-based startup scripts run.

6. The user is validated against Active Directory.

7. The user's profile loads.

8. The computer obtains an ordered list of GPOs that apply to the *user*.

9. User policies under User Configuration are applied.

10. User-based logon scripts run.

11. The user is presented with her desktop interface, as configured by Group Policy.

For more information on designing Active Directory and deploying GPOs, see Chapter 4. For more information on how Group Policy is applied, see Chapter 2 and Chapter 13.

Loopback Processing

User Group Policy loopback processing mode is a policy setting you can use to maintain a computer's configuration regardless of who logs on. Loopback processing mode configures the user policy settings based on the computer rather than on the user. When this policy setting is enabled, one set of user settings applies to all users who log on to the computer. Because this policy setting targets computer accounts, it is a powerful tool and ideally suited for closely managed environments such as servers, terminal servers, classrooms, public kiosks, and reception areas.

> **Note**   When you enable the policy setting for loopback processing mode, you must ensure that both the computer and user portions of the GPO are enabled.

The loopback policy is set in the Group Policy Object Editor snap-in by using the following policy setting:

Computer Settings\Administrative Templates\System\Group Policy\User Group Policy loopback processing mode

As shown in Figure 12-1, when you enable this policy you can select one of two loopback processing modes: Replace or Merge.

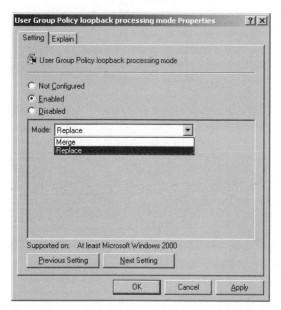

Figure 12-1   The Replace and Merge loopback processing modes

Replace Mode

In Replace mode, the list of GPOs and their settings for the user account is not used. Instead, the GPO list for the user is entirely replaced by the GPO list that was obtained for the computer at startup, and the User Configuration settings from the GPO that has the loopback setting configured are applied to the user account instead. This means that when loopback processing in Replace mode is enabled, policy is processed as follows:

1.   The computer settings in the GPOs for the computer account are applied.

2.   The user settings in the GPOs for the user account are ignored.

3.   The user settings in the GPOs for the computer account are applied.

As a best practice, you might use Replace mode when you have computers that are exposed to the public—for example, if you have a computer that is located in the reception area of your company's corporate office or a public kiosk that you provide somewhere within your office or company. When the public has access to the computer, you want to lock down the interface completely to ensure that the user cannot run operating system tools or other potentially dangerous applications on the computer.

Here are some best practices when using loopback processing in Replace mode:

- Create Software Restriction Policies that limit available applications to what the public user needs.
- Remove the entire shell except for Microsoft® Internet Explorer.
- Remove the user's ability to gain access to features and functions by pressing Ctrl+Alt+Del.
- Disable the ability to right-click and access shortcut menus.
- Remove the Shutdown menu option and button.

Merge Mode

In Merge mode, the list of GPOs and settings for the user is gathered during the logon process. Then the list of GPOs and settings for the computer is gathered. Next, the list of GPO settings for the user account that are contained within the GPO with the loopback setting enabled is added to the end of the GPO settings originally compiled for the user account. As a result of this appending of the user settings, the GPO settings that were obtained from the GPO with the loopback setting configured will have higher precedence. Therefore, when loopback processing in Merge mode is enabled, policy is processed as follows:

1. Computer settings in the GPOs for the computer account are applied.
2. User settings in the GPOs for the user account are applied.
3. User settings in the GPOs for the computer account are applied, taking precedence over user settings in the GPOs for the user account.

Although Merge mode offers great control, it still allows many of the individual user GPO settings to affect the logon environment. Merge mode is appropriate for settings such as student labs, Terminal Services sessions, and classrooms. With Merge mode, you can control many of the environment features that are security risks while still providing users with their desktops, applications, and other features that allow them to perform their job functions.

Here are some best practices when using loopback processing in Merge mode:

- Access to Control Panel items

- Access to Add/Remove Programs
- Access to Network Configuration
- Controlling user profiles
- Controlling offline files

Troubleshooting Loopback

When you are testing and validating the use of the loopback feature, it will usually be obvious whether the correct settings are being applied. The difficulty arises when the correct settings are not being applied. Remember that when you are using Replace mode, none of the user settings from the GPOs affecting the user are applied, only user settings in the GPOs affecting the computer. Therefore, if you see any of the user settings coming through that you specifically did not configure in the GPO in which loopback processing has been enabled, the GPO in which loopback processing is enabled is most likely not being applied at all. Here are some possible reasons for this:

- The computer account is not in the correct OU to receive the GPO settings.
- The user or computer (or both) settings have been disabled for the GPO that has the loopback policy configured.
- The GPOs have not replicated properly to all of the domain controllers.
- The GPO containing the loopback policy has been filtered to not include the computer account you are targeting.

Another option for troubleshooting the application of loopback policy is to use the Group Policy Modeling Wizard or the Group Policy Results Wizard in the Group Policy Management Console (GPMC). The Group Policy Modeling Wizard allows you to evaluate a scenario for a particular computer account and user account based on specific GPO settings and criteria. This includes the ability to model the effects of loopback processing, as shown in Figure 12-2.

> **More Info**   For more information on how to use the Group Policy Modeling Wizard, see Chapter 3.

The Group Policy Results Wizard offers real-time evaluation of an existing user and computer account. After you run the wizard, you are presented with a summary of the settings that should be applied to both accounts. These results will indicate which policies were applied, the policy setting configuration, and which GPO the policy came from. If you run the wizard and learn that the loopback policy should be applied to the computer but hasn't been, you must evaluate the list of potential problems that are listed above. If the wizard indicates that no loopback setting is configured, you must determine where the GPO is linked and where the computer account is located.

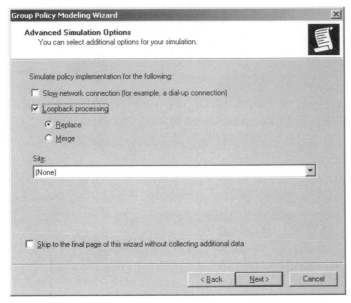

Figure 12-2   Evaluating a scenario by using the Group Policy Modeling Wizard

Terminal Services

If your company relies on Terminal Services for clients to access applications, the network, or resources, you know how important and powerful this technology is. Terminal Services allows a company to provide high-end solutions for legacy operating systems and limited hardware. Without Terminal Services, many companies would be far less productive.

Controlling and limiting Terminal Services sessions can be a full-time job. Terminal server sessions must be protected, along with the servers that run Terminal Services. This is why Microsoft has provided more than 50 Group Policy settings that help control Terminal Services. Many of these settings can be configured to help lock down terminal servers and client sessions.

You can use Group Policy to configure Terminal Services connection settings, set user policies, configure terminal server clusters, and manage Terminal Services sessions. You can enable Group Policy for users of a computer, for individual computers, or for groups of computers belonging to an OU of a domain. To set policies for users of a particular computer, you must be an administrator for that computer. To set policies for an OU in a domain, you must be an administrator for that domain.

Controlling Terminal Services Through Group Policy on an Individual Computer

Sometimes you might need to control the Terminal Services settings for an individual computer. The computer might be a shared computer for which you want to configure the settings that apply to the computer object. You might also need to configure the Terminal Services settings for the user or users who will use the computer, and in this case you would want to configure the settings that apply to the user object.

You can access Terminal Services settings on a standalone computer by using local Group Policy. The Group Policy Object Editor snap-in allows you to access the Local Group Policy Object (LGPO) on that particular computer. Once you are in the Group Policy Editor, you can view and configure Terminal Services settings under both the Computer Configuration and User Configuration nodes, as shown in Figures 12-3 and 12-4.

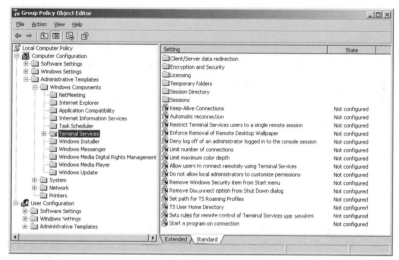

Figure 12-3   Terminal Services GPO settings under Computer Configuration

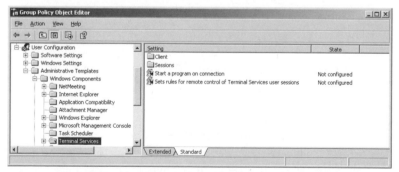

Figure 12-4   Terminal Services GPO settings under User Configuration

Controlling Terminal Services Through Group Policy in a Domain

In Active Directory environments, you may need to lock down several Terminal servers. The policy settings for locking down terminal servers in a domain are similar to those for standalone terminal servers, as shown above. The significant difference is in how you implement Group Policy for terminal servers in a domain.

To configure Terminal Services for multiple computers using Active Directory, you must organize the user and computer accounts into OUs. Then you can configure GPOs that contain the specific Terminal Services settings for those objects.

> **More Info**   For more information on how to design and deploy GPOs and Active Directory, see Chapter 4.

> **Important**   The Terminal Services Group Policies are geared toward computers running Microsoft Windows® XP and Windows Server™ 2003. If you are running Windows 2000 servers and clients, you cannot use Group Policy settings to control Terminal Services on these computers.

Configuring Order of Precedence

It is possible to make Terminal Services configurations at both the local and Active Directory levels using Group Policy. You can also make configurations within different GPOs at various levels within Active Directory. This is an issue because there is an order of precedence in which the Terminal Services configurations apply. The following is a list of highest to lowest precedence of the locations where Terminal Services settings can be set.

- Computer-level Group Policies (if set)
- User-level Group Policies (if set)
- Local computer configuration set with Terminal Services Configuration tool
- User-level policies set with Local Users and Groups
- Local client settings

Configuring Terminal Services User Properties

When Terminal Services is used in your environment, it is important to configure and control the user environment and properties. If you don't, the user might have too much access or too much flexibility for the sessions that are created on the Terminal Server. This section focuses on some best practices for the general settings related to user properties associated with Terminal Services. It also discusses the GPO settings that can be configured in this area.

Best Practices

Here are some general best practices for establishing user properties for Terminal Services. Your environment might differ slightly, but these suggestions will point you in the right direction for establishing a secure, stable, and functional Terminal Services environment.

- **Use Terminal Services–specific groups.**   Create user groups that are specifically for Terminal Services users. Windows Server 2003 family operating systems contain a default user group called Remote Desktop Users, which is specifically for managing Terminal Services users.

- **Use Terminal Services–specific profiles.**   Assign a separate profile for logging on to Terminal Services. Many common options stored in profiles, such as screen savers and animated menu effects, are not needed when users connect through Terminal Services. Assigning a specific profile allows users to get the most out of the system they are working with without requiring additional server resources.

- **Use mandatory profiles.**   Use a mandatory Terminal Services profile that was created to suit the needs of all of types of clients and that provides the best server performance. Be aware that 16-bit computers and Windows-based terminals might not support some screen resolutions.

- **Set time limits.**   Setting limits on the duration of client connections can improve server performance. You can limit how long a session lasts, how long a disconnected session is allowed to remain active on the server, and how long a session can remain connected yet idle.

- **Use the Starting Program option.**   If you have users who need to access only one application on the terminal server, use the Starting Program option. You can do this for all users by using Terminal Services Configuration or you can do it on a per-user basis by using either the Terminal Services Extension to Local Users and Groups or Active Directory Users and Computers.

- **Create preconfigured connection files for users or groups of users.**   To make connecting to Terminal Services easier, you can supply users with preconfigured connection files. Collections of connection files can also be made for different departments within your organization or for different job titles. Preconfigured connection files are created using Remote Desktop Connection.

Configuring License Server Using Group Policy Settings

Several GPO settings help you control the terminal server licensing. If you use these settings, you can centrally control and configure license servers and maintain consistency in the environment. You should configure two specific settings to help control the licensing. Both are located under the following path in a default GPO:

Computer Configuration\Administrative Templates\Windows Components\Terminal Services\Licensing

License Server Security Group

This setting is used to control the Terminal Servers that are issued licenses. In a default configuration, the Terminal Services License Server will issue a license to all computers that request one. When this setting is enabled, the license server responds only to requests from terminal servers that are located in the Terminal Services Computers local group. This is an excellent way to prevent rogue terminal servers from requesting licenses. If you have more than one license server, you can add all of the license servers to the group; this allows the license servers to request licenses on behalf of the terminal servers.

Prevent License Upgrade

A license server attempts to provide the most appropriate client access license (CAL) for a connection. Windows 2000 Terminal Services CAL tokens are provided for Windows 2000 clients. A Windows Server 2003 family Terminal Services CAL is provided when a connection is made to a terminal server running Windows Server 2003. The default behavior is that a Windows 2000 terminal server requests a token, and if the license server does not have any Windows 2000 CALs, it issues a Windows Server 2003 Per-Device token. The Prevent License Upgrade setting can stop this behavior by giving a temporary license to clients connecting to Windows 2000 terminal servers. When the temporary token expires, the connection is refused.

Configuring Terminal Services Connections

Many aspects of the Terminal Services connection can and should be controlled using Group Policy. If these settings are left to individual settings on the Terminal Server or the client, inconsistencies will be introduced throughout the enterprise that waste time, increase help desk calls, and make troubleshooting Terminal Services connection problems more difficult. The following GPO settings can establish a security baseline for the sessions that are running through Terminal Services:

Limit Number Of Connections

The Limit Number Of Connections setting specifies whether Terminal Services limits the number of simultaneous connections to the server. You can use this setting to restrict the number of remote sessions that can be active on a server. If this number is exceeded, additional users who try to connect receive an error message telling them that the server is busy and to try again later. Restricting the number of sessions improves performance because fewer sessions are demanding system resources. By default, terminal servers allow an unlimited number of remote sessions, and Remote Desktop for Administration allows two remote sessions. To use this setting, specify the number of connections you want as the maximum for the server, as shown in Figure 12-5. To specify an unlimited number of connections, type **999999**.

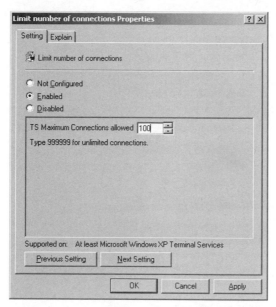

Figure 12-5   The Terminal Services GPO setting that controls the maximum number of connections for a server

To access this GPO setting, follow this path:

Computer Configuration\Administrative Templates\Windows Components\Terminal Services\Limit number of connections

When this setting is enabled, you can specify the number of connections in the TS Maximum Connections Allowed box.

Set Client Connection Encryption Level

For Terminal Services connections, using data encryption helps to protect your information on the communications link between the client and the server by preventing unauthorized transmission interception.

The Set Client Connection Encryption Level setting allows you to enforce an encryption level for all data sent between the client and the remote computer during a Terminal Services session, as shown in Figure 12-6.

To access this GPO setting, follow this path:

Computer Configuration\Administrative Templates\Windows Components\Terminal Services\Encryption and Security\Set client connection encryption level

When this setting is enabled, you can set the encryption level to one of four levels, as described in Table 12-1. By default, Terminal Services connections are encrypted at the highest level of security available (128-bit). However, some earlier versions of the

Terminal Services client do not support this high level of encryption. If your network contains such legacy clients, you can set the encryption level of the connection to send and receive data at the highest encryption level supported by the client.

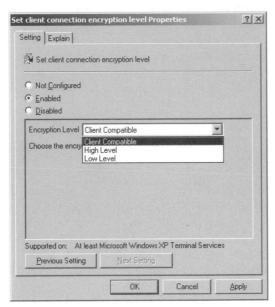

Figure 12-6   The Terminal Services GPO setting that controls client encryption levels

Table 12-1   Client Connection Encryption Levels

Level of Encryption	Description
FIPS Compliant	Encrypts data sent from client to server and from server to client to meet the Federal Information Processing Standard 140-1 (FIPS 140-1), a security implementation designed for certifying cryptographic software. Use this level when Terminal Services connections require the highest degree of encryption. FIPS 140-1–validated software is required by the U.S. government and requested by other prominent institutions.
	Important: If FIPS compliance has already been enabled by the System Cryptography: Use FIPS Compliant Algorithms For Encryption, Hashing, And Signing Group Policy, administrators cannot change the encryption level for Terminal Services connections by changing the Terminal Services Set Client Connection Encryption Level Group Policy setting or by using Terminal Services Configuration.
High	Encrypts data sent from client to server and from server to client by using strong 128-bit encryption. Use this level when the remote computer is running in an environment containing only 128-bit clients (such as Remote Desktop Connection clients). Clients that do not support this level of encryption cannot connect.

Table 12-1   Client Connection Encryption Levels

Level of Encryption	Description
Client Compatible	Encrypts data sent from client to server and from server to client at the maximum key strength supported by the client. Use this level when the remote computer is running in an environment containing mixed or legacy clients.
Low	Encrypts data sent from the client to the server using 56-bit encryption. **Caution:** Data sent from the server to the client is not encrypted.

Secure Server (Require Security)

The Secure Server (Require Security) setting specifies whether a Terminal Server requires secure RPC communication with all clients or allows unsecured communication. When this setting is enabled, all RPC communication with clients is more secure because only authenticated and encrypted requests are allowed. The Terminal Server will allow communication only with secure requests and will deny unsecured communication with untrusted clients.

To access this GPO setting, follow this path:

Computer Configuration\Administrative Templates\Windows Components\Terminal Services\Encryption and Security\RPC Security Policy\Secure Server (Require Security)

Start A Program On Connection

You can use the Start A Program On Connection setting to specify a program to run automatically when a user logs on to a remote computer. By default, Terminal Services sessions provide access to the full Windows desktop unless otherwise specified with this setting. Enabling this setting overrides the Start Program settings set by the server administrator on the Terminal Server or set by the user from the Terminal Services client. When this setting is configured, the Start menu and Windows desktop are not displayed, and when the user exits the program the session is automatically logged off.

To use this setting, you must provide the fully qualified path and file name of the executable file to be run when the user logs on. If necessary, you can also provide the working directory by typing the fully qualified path to the starting directory for the program.

> **Note**   If the specified program path, file name, or working directory is not the name of a valid directory, the terminal server connection fails with an error message.

> **Note**   The Start A Program On Connection setting appears in both Computer Configuration and User Configuration. If this setting is configured in both places, the Computer Configuration setting takes precedence.

To access this GPO setting, follow this path:

Computer Configuration\Administrative Templates\Windows Components\Terminal Services\Start a program on connection

When this setting is enabled, you can configure the Program Path And File Name box as well as the Working Directory box, as shown in Figure 12-7.

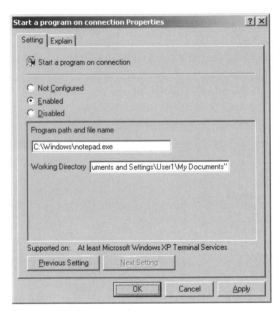

Figure 12-7   Terminal Services GPO settings to start a program on connection

> **Important**   These policies affect every client that connects to the terminal server. To specify a program to start on a per-user basis, use the corresponding policy under User Configuration.

Set Rules For Remote Control To Terminal Services User Sessions

You can monitor the actions of a client logged on to a terminal server by remotely controlling the user's session from another session. Remote control allows you to observe or actively control another session. If you choose to actively control a session, you can input keyboard and mouse actions to the session. A message can be displayed on the client session asking permission to view or take part in the session before the session is remotely controlled. You can use Terminal Services Group Policies to configure remote control settings for a connection and Terminal Services Manager to initiate remote control on a client session.

Tip   Windows Server 2003 family operating systems also support Remote Assistance, which allows greater versatility for controlling another user's session. Remote Assistance also provides the ability to chat with the other user.

To access the Set Rules For Remote Control To Terminal Services User Sessions GPO setting, follow this path:

Computer Configuration\Administrative Templates\Windows Components\Terminal Services\Set rules for remote control of Terminal Services user sessions

When this GPO setting is enabled, you can configure the Options setting, which sets the desired remote control permissions. Five permission levels are available, as shown in Figure 12-8.

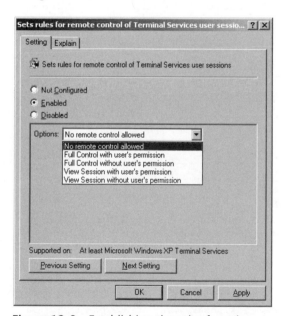

Figure 12-8   Establishing the rules for using remote control over a Terminal Services session

Important   These settings affect every client that connects to the Terminal Server. To configure Remote Control on a per-user basis, use the corresponding policy under User Configuration.

Set Time Limit For Disconnected Sessions

For a Terminal Services connection, you can limit the amount of time that active, disconnected, and idle (without client activity) sessions remain on the server. This is useful because sessions that run indefinitely on the server consume valuable system resources. When a session limit is reached for active or idle sessions, you can opt to disconnect the user from the session or end the session. A user who is disconnected from a session can reconnect to the same session later. When a session ends, it is permanently deleted from the server and any running applications are forced to shut down, which can result in loss of data at the client. When a session limit is reached for a disconnected session, the session ends, which permanently deletes it from the server. Sessions can also be allowed to continue indefinitely.

You can use the Set Time Limit For Disconnected Sessions setting to specify the maximum amount of time that a disconnected session is kept active on the server. By default, Terminal Services allows users to disconnect from a remote session without logging off and ending the session.

When a session is in a disconnected state, running programs are kept active even though the user is no longer actively connected. By default, these disconnected sessions are maintained for an unlimited time on the server.

To access the Set Time Limit For Disconnected Sessions setting, follow this path:

Computer Configuration\Administrative Templates\Windows Components\Terminal Services\Sessions\Set time limit for disconnected sessions

When this GPO setting is enabled, you can configure the End A Disconnected Session setting, which specifies when a disconnected session will be ended.

Note   The Set Time Limit For Disconnected Sessions setting affects every client that connects to the terminal server. To define Session settings on a per-user basis, use the Sessions policies under User Configuration.

Important   The setting does not apply to console sessions such as Remote Desktop sessions with computers running Windows XP Professional. Also note that this setting appears in both Computer Configuration and User Configuration. If both settings are configured, the Computer Configuration setting takes precedence.

Set Time Limit For Active Terminal Services Sessions

You can use the Set Time Limit For Active Terminal Services Sessions setting to specify the maximum amount of time a Terminal Services session can be active before it is disconnected. By default, Terminal Services allows sessions to remain active for an unlimited time.

To access this GPO setting, follow this path:

Computer Configuration\Administrative Templates\Windows Components\Terminal Services\Sessions\Set time limit for active Terminal Services sessions

When this setting is enabled, you can configure the Active Session Limit setting to set the time limit for any Terminal Services session.

> **Note**   The Set Time Limit For Active Terminal Services Sessions setting affects every client that connects to the terminal server. To define Session settings on a per-user basis, use the Sessions policies under User Configuration.
>
> This setting appears in both Computer Configuration and User Configuration. If it is configured in both places, the Computer Configuration setting has precedence. Active session limits do not apply to the console session. To specify that user sessions terminate at timeout, enable the Terminate Session When Time Limits Are Reached setting.

Terminate Session When Time Limits Are Reached

You can use the Terminate Session When Time Limits Are Reached setting to direct Terminal Services to terminate a session (that is, the user is logged off and his session is disconnected from the server) after time limits for active or idle sessions are reached. By default, Terminal Services disconnects sessions that reach their time limit.

To access this GPO setting, follow this path:

Computer Configuration\Administrative Templates\Windows Components\Terminal Services\Sessions\Terminate session when time limits are reached

When this setting is enabled, Terminal Services terminates any session that reaches its timeout limit. This setting exists under both the Computer Configuration and User Configuration. The policy under the Computer Configuration has precedence.

Allow Reconnection From Original Client Only

You can use the Allow Reconnection From Original Client Only setting to configure settings for reconnecting disconnected Citrix ICA sessions. You can prevent Terminal Services users from reconnecting to the disconnected session using a computer other than the client computer from which they originally created the session. By default, Terminal Services allows users to reconnect to disconnected sessions from any client computer.

To access this GPO setting, follow this path:

Computer Configuration\Administrative Templates\Windows Components\Terminal Services\Sessions\Allow reconnection from original client only

When this setting is enabled, users can reconnect to disconnected sessions only from the original client computer. If a user attempts to connect to the disconnected session from another computer, a new session is created instead.

> **Tip**   The Allow Reconnection From Original Client Only setting affects every client that connects to the terminal server. To define Session settings on a per-user basis, use the Sessions policies under User Configuration.

> **Note**   The Allow Reconnection From Original Client Only setting is supported only for Citrix ICA clients that provide a serial number when connecting; it is ignored if the user is connecting with a Windows client. Also note that this setting appears in both Computer Configuration and User Configuration. If both settings are configured, the Computer Configuration setting has precedence.

Managing Drive, Printer, and Device Mappings for Clients

Because client sessions can establish multiple data channels between client and server, users can map to local devices, such as drives and printers. By default, drive and printer mappings that a user sets in a client session are temporary and are not available the next time the user logs on to the server. However, using Terminal Services Configuration, you can specify that client mappings be restored when the user logs on. In addition, you can disable specific client devices so that a user cannot map the device. Users can map the following devices:

- Drives
- Windows printers
- LPT ports
- COM ports
- Smart cards
- Clipboard
- Audio

Whenever possible, use Terminal Services Group Policies to configure the settings described in the following sections.

Allow Audio Redirection

The Allow Audio Redirection setting specifies whether users can choose where to play the remote computer's audio output during a Terminal Services session (audio redirection). Users can use the Remote Computer Sound option on the Local Resources tab of Remote Desktop Connection to specify whether to play the remote audio on the remote computer or on the local computer. Users can also choose to disable the audio.

By default, users cannot apply audio redirection when connecting via Terminal Services to a server running Windows Server 2003. Users connecting to a computer running Windows XP Professional can apply audio redirection by default.

To access this GPO setting, follow this path:

Computer Configuration\Administrative Templates\Windows Components\Terminal Services\Client/Server data redirection\Allow audio redirection

Do Not Allow COM Port Redirection

The Do Not Allow COM Port Redirection setting specifies whether to prevent the redirection of data to client COM ports from the remote computer in a Terminal Services session. You can use this setting to prevent users from redirecting data to COM port peripherals or mapping local COM ports while they are logged on to a Terminal Services session. By default, Terminal Services allows this COM port redirection.

To access this GPO setting, follow this path:

Computer Configuration\Administrative Templates\Windows Components\Terminal Services\Client/Server data redirection\Do not allow COM port redirection

Do Not Allow Client Printer Redirection

You can use the Do Not Allow Client Printer Redirection setting to prevent users from redirecting print jobs from the remote computer to a printer attached to their local (client) computer. By default, Terminal Services allows this client printer mapping.

To access this GPO setting, follow this path:

Computer Configuration\Administrative Templates\Windows Components\Terminal Services\Client/Server data redirection\Do not allow client printer redirection

When this setting is enabled, users cannot redirect print jobs from the remote computer to a local client printer in Terminal Services sessions.

Do Not Allow LPT Port Redirection

The Do Not Allow LPT Port Redirection setting specifies whether to prevent the redirection of data to client LPT ports during a Terminal Services session. You can use this setting to prevent users from mapping local LPT ports and redirecting data from the remote computer to local LPT port peripherals. By default, Terminal Services allows this LPT port redirection.

To access this GPO setting, follow this path:

Computer Configuration\Administrative Templates\Windows Components\Terminal Services\Client/Server data redirection\Do not allow LPT port redirection

When this setting is enabled, users in a Terminal Services session cannot redirect server data to the local LPT port.

Do Not Allow Drive Redirection

The Do Not Allow Drive Redirection setting specifies whether to prevent the mapping of client drives in a Terminal Services session (drive redirection). By default, Terminal Services maps client drives automatically upon connection. Mapped drives appear in the session folder tree in Windows Explorer or My Computer in the format *<driveletter>* on *<computername>*. You can use this setting to override this behavior.

To access this GPO setting, follow this path:

Computer Configuration\Administrative Templates\Windows Components\Terminal Services\Client/Server data redirection\Do not allow drive redirection

When this setting is enabled, client drive redirection is not allowed in Terminal Services sessions.

Do Not Set Default Client Printer To Be Default Printer In A Session

The Do Not Set Default Client Printer To Be Default Printer In A Session setting specifies whether the client default printer is automatically set as the default printer in a Terminal Services session. By default, Terminal Services automatically designates the client default printer as the default printer in a Terminal Services session. You can use this setting to override this behavior.

To access this GPO setting, follow this path:

Computer Configuration\Administrative Templates\Windows Components\Terminal Services\Client/Server data redirection\Do not set default client printer to be default printer in a session

When this setting is enabled, the default printer is the printer specified on the remote computer.

Controlling Terminal Services Profiles

Each session that is created on a terminal server requires a user profile. As we discussed earlier, you can control this profile if you want it to roam. This option is handy for users who move from computer to computer but want a consistent desktop.

In some cases, you might not want users to download profiles or have profiles stored on certain terminal servers. The following sections offer some suggested settings for controlling these behaviors.

Set Path For TS Roaming Profiles

You can use the Set Path For TS Roaming Profiles setting to specify a network share where the profiles are stored, allowing users to access the same profile for sessions on all terminal servers in the same OU. By default, Terminal Services stores all user profiles locally on the terminal server. This setting allows you to override the setting in the user account on a per-server basis. It also provides an excellent method for specifying a different Terminal Server profile server for groups of terminal servers. If you have server farms that are spread over different locations, you can use this setting to allow users to roam between the servers in the server farms seamlessly.

To access this GPO setting, follow this path:

Computer Configuration\Administrative Templates\Windows Components\Terminal Services\Set path for TS Roaming Profiles

When this setting is enabled, you type the path to the network share in the form *\\Computername\Sharename* in the Profile Path box, as shown in Figure 12-9.

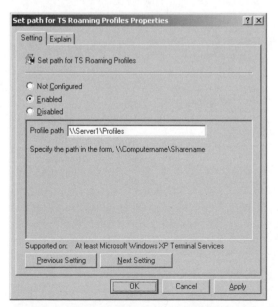

Figure 12-9   The Terminal Services GPO setting that controls the profile path

Caution Do not specify a placeholder for the user alias because Terminal Services automatically appends this at logon. Make sure the specified network share exists; otherwise, Terminal Services will display an error message on the server and will store the user profile locally.

TS User Home Directory

You can use the TS User Home Directory setting to select the location for the home directory for the Terminal Services session. The options are a network share or a local directory. For a network share path, you must type the path in the form *Computername**Sharename*. For local directories, you can type the drive letter, followed by the path to the home directory root, such as *C:\users\homedir*. Like the roaming profiles setting, this setting provides an excellent way to configure users' home directories for when they roam between Terminal Server farms throughout the organization.

To access this GPO setting, follow this path:

Computer Configuration\Administrative Templates\Windows Components\Terminal Services\TS User Home Directory

When this setting is enabled, you use the Location drop-down list to specify whether the path will be local or on the network, as shown in Figure 12-10. You then type the path to the home directory based on the syntax we discussed earlier. Finally, you specify a drive letter for the home directory, which the user will use to access the home directory on her computer.

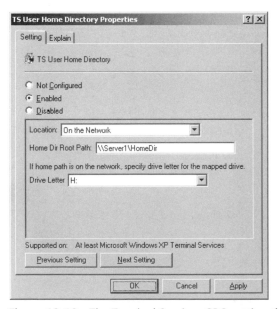

Figure 12-10 The Terminal Services GPO setting that controls the user's home directory

Restrict Terminal Services Users To A Single Remove Session

To control Terminal Services licenses as well as how many Terminal Services sessions a user can start, you can restrict users to a single remote session. The Restrict Terminal Services Users To A Single Remove Session setting restricts users who log on remotely via Terminal Services to a single session on that server. This includes both active and disconnected sessions. This means that if a user disconnects from a session, any attempt to start a new session will fail and will send the user to the disconnected session.

To access this GPO setting, follow this path:

Computer Configuration\Administrative Templates\Windows Components\Terminal Services\Restrict Terminal Services users to a single remove session

Only Allow Local User Profiles

The Only Allow Local User Profiles setting is not designed for Terminal Services, but it can be used with a Terminal Services session. This setting prevents the roaming user profile from being downloaded, even if the user's account specifies a roaming profile path. This setting is useful if you have terminal servers at different sites and you don't want to maintain profile servers at each site.

To access this GPO setting, follow this path:

Computer Configuration\Administrative Templates\System\User Profiles\Only allow local user profiles

Delete Cached Copies Of Roaming Profiles

Sometimes you will need to free up disk space on terminal servers but also need the users to use their roaming profiles. In this case, you cannot force the user to use a local profile. However, you can use the Delete Cached Copies Of Roaming Profiles setting to configure a different GPO that removes the roaming profile from the server when the user ends the session.

To access this GPO setting, follow this path:

Computer Configuration\Administrative Templates\System\User Profiles\Delete cached copies of roaming profiles

Group Policy over Slow Links

The availability of network bandwidth can affect how Group Policy settings are applied. By default, some policies are not processed across a slow network connection. If the network link speed between a client and the authenticating domain controller falls below the default slow link threshold of 500 kilobits per second (Kbps), only the administrative template (registry-based) settings and security settings are applied. When the available bandwidth between the client and the domain controller falls below this preset threshold, the client is said to be on a slow link.

If necessary, you can modify the default slow link behavior by using a policy setting that appears under both Computer Configuration and User Configuration in a GPO. You can also adjust the Group Policy extensions that are processed below the slow link threshold. However, depending on your situation, it might be more appropriate to place a local domain controller at a remote location to serve your management requirements.

It is important to have sufficient network bandwidth available between servers and workstations when you deploy roaming user profiles, Offline Files, and Folder Redirection. It is also recommended that the servers to which workstations connect for this data be on a fast network link. Check your network configuration for ways to minimize network routing hops when accessing frequently needed data. Keeping the needed data and the user on the same subnet improves performance.

Default Policy Application over Slow Links

When you want Group Policy to be applied but the network is congested, when you are connecting over slow links, or when you are using a remote access to connect to your network, you might be apprehensive about which portions of the Group Policy to apply because applying many potentially large policies can hurt performance. The behavior of Group Policy application over these slow links is straightforward.

What does Group Policy consider to be a slow link by default? Microsoft has established that a slow link is less than 500 Kbps. Therefore, if you are connecting over your LAN and network congestion slows down your communication with the domain controllers to below 500 Kbps, Group Policy considers this connection to be slow.

In this example, you might not want to have Group Policy consider your connection to be slow. However, in other situations you will want the connection to be considered slow to allow control over which policies are processed. For example, you might want a connection from a branch office that connects over a slow frame-relay link to be considered slow so that you can control whether Microsoft Office will be installed over this small connection. Other situations in which slow link speeds might be a factor include:

- Virtual Private Network (VPN) connections
- Dial-up connections
- Branch offices
- Remote Terminal Services connections
- Wireless connections

Policies That Apply over Slow Links

Let's look at which settings apply over slow links by default. Even if a link is slow, you still want some settings to apply to ensure a secure and functional environment.

Microsoft has thus configured two sections of Group Policy to apply over any link speed: Security and Administrative Templates. Other sections are enabled to apply over slow links but can be turned off. Table 12-2 shows all the GPO sections and their behaviors during slow link application.

Table 12-2   Default Settings for Processing Group Policy over Slow Links

Setting	Default
Security Settings	ON (cannot be turned off)
IP Security	ON
EFS	ON
Software Restriction Policies	ON
Wireless	ON
Administrative Templates	ON (cannot be turned off)
Software Installation	OFF
Scripts	OFF
Folder Redirection	OFF
IE Maintenance	ON

Slow Link Behavior for RAS Connections

A user has two ways to log on to her computer when is she plans to use RAS to connect to Active Directory during her session. The choice affects how GPOs are applied for remote access users.

The first option is to select the Logon Using Dial-Up Connection check box, which in essence tells the computer to communicate directly to the RAS server to authenticate the user, bypassing local authentication. This option allows the GPOs (Security Settings and Administrative Templates) to be applied at logon. However, computer-based software installation settings are not processed, nor are computer-based startup scripts executed, because computer policy is normally processed before the logon screen appears.

The second option is to log on locally or with cached credentials. With this option, the domain-based GPOs are not applied, except for what is in the cached profile. When the user connects to the RAS server, she is authenticated to the domain and has access to the remote network resources. However, the GPOs are not applied immediately in this situation—only at the GPO refresh interval.

Slow Link Detection Group Policy Settings

You can configure numerous settings to control how GPO settings react when they are applied over slow links. Not all of the settings are in one location, so it can be confusing to figure out what the settings do, where they are located, and how they are all related.

The following slow link settings are at the core of the slow link detection and Group Policy implementation. You typically begin with these settings as you start to alter the default behavior of how GPOs apply over slow links.

Group Policy Slow Link Detection

The Group Policy Slow Link Detection setting defines a slow connection for purposes of applying and updating Group Policy. If the rate at which data is transferred from the domain controller providing a policy update to the computers in this group is slower than the rate specified by this setting, the system considers the connection to be slow. The default value for this setting is 500 Kbps, which is also what the computer will use if this policy is disabled.

To access this GPO setting, follow this path:

Computer Configuration\Administrative Templates\System\Group Policy\Group Policy slow link detection

When this setting is enabled, as shown in Figure 12-11, you must enter a decimal number between 0 and 4,294,967,200 in the Connection Speed box. The units for this entry are kilobits per second.

Note   The User Configuration node in a GPO also has a Group Policy Slow Link Detection setting.

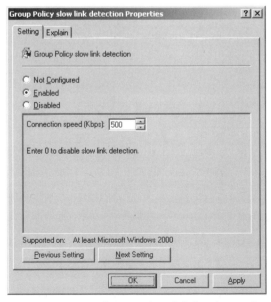

Figure 12-11   Defining a slow link for the application of GPOs over slow network connections

Slow Network Connection Timeout for User Profiles

The Slow Network Connection Timeout for User Profiles setting controls how a slow connection is defined for application of roaming user profiles. If the server on which the user's roaming profile resides takes longer to respond than the thresholds set by this setting, the system considers the connection to the profile to be slow.

To access this GPO setting, follow this path:

Computer Configuration\Administrative Templates\System\User Profiles\Slow network connection timeout for user profiles

When this GPO setting is enabled, as shown in Figure 12-12, you must enter a decimal number between 0 and 4,294,967,200 in the Connection Speed box. The units for this entry are kilobits per second. For non-IP computers, the system measures the responsiveness of the remote server's file system. To set a threshold for this test, in the Time box type a decimal number between 0 and 20,000. The units for this entry are milliseconds.

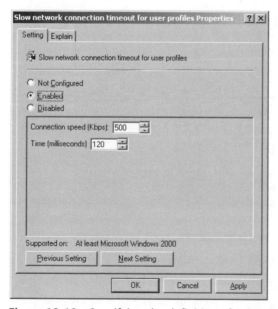

Figure 12-12   Specifying the definition of a slow link

Do Not Detect Slow Network Connections

The Do Not Detect Slow Network Connections setting controls whether user profiles are controlled by the speed of the link. Slow link detection measures the speed of the connection between a user's computer and the remote server that stores the roaming user profile. When the system detects a slow link, the related settings in this folder tell the system how to respond. When this policy is enabled, the roaming user profile ignores any slow link connection policy settings.

To access this GPO setting, follow this path:

Computer Configuration\Administrative Templates\System\User Profiles\Do not detect slow network connections

> **Note**   If the Do Not Detect Slow Network Connections setting is enabled, the Slow Network Connection Timeout For User Profiles setting is ignored.

Prompt User When Slow Link Is Detected

The Prompt User When Slow Link Is Detected setting allows the user to be notified when his roaming profile is slow to load. This gives the user the ability to decide whether to use the local cached copy of his profile or to wait for the roaming user profile.

To access this GPO setting, follow this path:

Computer Configuration\Administrative Templates\System\User Profiles\Prompt user when slow link is detected

> **Note**   If the Do Not Detect Slow Network Connections setting is enabled, the Prompt User When Slow Link Is Detected setting is ignored.

> **More Info**   For more information on user profiles, see Chapter 7.

Configure Slow Link Speed

When a user uses offline files, it can take a long time to synch the files—with a slow link, it might take hours. When a user is connected over a slow link, you might want to use the Configure Slow Link Speed setting and other settings that control Offline Files behavior.

The Configure Slow Link Speed setting configures the threshold value at which offline files considers a network connection to be slow. If the connection is considered to be slow, the offline files feature adjusts itself to avoid excessive synchronization traffic.

To access this GPO setting, follow this path:

Computer Configuration\Administrative Templates\Network\Offline Files\Configure Slow link speed

When this setting is enabled, as shown in Figure 12-13, you must enter a value in the Value box that defines what offline files will consider to be a slow link. The units for this entry are bits per second divided by 100.

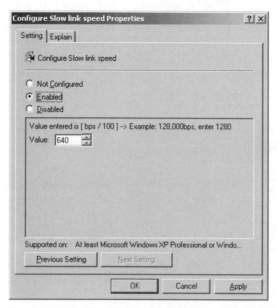

Figure 12-13   Specifying the definition of a slow link for the synchronization of offline files

Additional Slow Link Detection Settings for Client-Side Extensions

Each section of a GPO is controlled by a client-side extension (CSE). Security, administrative templates, and folder redirection are examples of these sections. Most of these CSEs can be controlled when a slow link is detected, to make the connection faster and to reduce the settings that are applied over the slow network connection.

The CSEs that can be controlled when a slow link is detected include:

- Internet Explorer Maintenance policy
- Software Installation policy
- Folder Redirection policy
- Scripts policy
- Security policy
- IP Security policy
- EFS recovery policy
- Wireless policy
- Disk Quota policy

These settings are all in the same location in the GPO and are named accordingly. For example, the policy setting for the Scripts CSE is named Scripts Policy Processing. You can find them at the following path in a GPO:

Computer Configuration\Administrative Templates\System\Group Policy

Once you access the policy you want to control, you will find a specific setting that controls slow network connections, as shown in Figure 12-14. The Allow Processing Across A Slow Network Connection setting controls whether the client-side extension is applied when a slow network connection is detected.

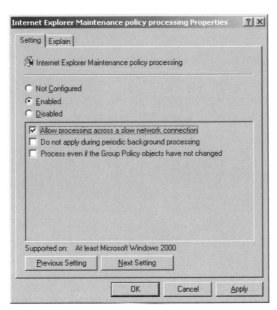

Figure 12-14   The Allow Processing Across A Slow Network Connection setting

The setting specifies whether the client-side extension adheres to slow links. When this setting is enabled for the client-side extension, the policy settings related to this portion of the GPO will apply over a slow link. This is the opposite of the default behavior, which is to not apply policy settings over slow links (except for the few client-side extensions that apply by default over slow links, which were described earlier in this chapter).

More Info   For more information on client-side extensions and applying GPOs, see Chapter 13.

Summary

Group Policy can be extended to accommodate almost any network environment. These networks include remote access connections, slow network connections, special security requirements, Terminal Services sessions, and more. When custom scenarios arise, you have great flexibility within Group Policy to meet your needs. Settings such as loopback processing, slow link detection, and Terminal Services settings allow you to easily control almost any environment. These settings should be used only for unique situations, to allow the default Group Policy behavior to work to your advantage when you need to customize a user's environment.

Part III
Group Policy Customization

In this part:

Chapter 13: Group Policy Structure and Processing 473

Chapter 14: Customizing Administrative Templates 515

Chapter 15: Security Templates. 553

Group Policy Structure and Processing

In this chapter:

Navigating Group Policy Logical Structure 474

Navigating Group Policy Physical Structure 483

Navigating Group Policy Link Structure. 488

Understanding Group Policy Processing 492

Navigating Local GPO Structure 511

Summary 514

To understand the structure of Group Policy, you first need to understand the structure of Active Directory®. Active Directory has both physical and logical components. The heart of Active Directory's physical architecture is an extensible storage engine (ESE) for reading and writing information to the Active Directory data store. The ESE uses an object-based hierarchy to represent information in the data store. The data store is essentially a database with a primary data file, working files for maintaining the state of the data file, and transaction logs for recording changes. Within Group Policy, there is a logical and physical representation of every Group Policy object (GPO) as well. The logical component of a GPO is a Group Policy container (GPC), which is stored in Active Directory. The physical component is a Group Policy template (GPT), which is stored on the file systems of domain controllers. The way these logical and physical components are handled depends largely on the Group Policy processing configuration.

Related Information

- For essential background on Group Policy, see Chapters 1 and 2.

- For more information on the Active Directory architecture, see "Active Directory Physical Architecture" and "Active Directory Logical Architecture" in Chapter 32 of *Windows Server 2003 Inside Out* (Microsoft Press, 2003).

- For more information about Group Policy inheritance and processing, see "Managing Group Policy Inheritance" and "Managing Group Policy Processing and Refresh" in Chapter 3.

Navigating Group Policy Logical Structure

Logically, GPOs are represented in Active Directory as container objects, which are stored in the Active Directory data store and are referred to as Group Policy containers (GPCs). The GPC contains attributes that relate to the basic information about a GPO—such as its display name, the path to the GPT, its version number, and its access control list (ACL). It also contains references to which CSEs will be invoked in order to process the GPO.

> **Caution**   Keep in mind that you never need to interact with GPCs and GPTs directly. In fact, it is easy to create problems with a GPO if you attempt to make changes directly to the GPC or GPT. Your primary interface for managing Group Policy is the Group Policy Management Console (GPMC) and the Group Policy Object Editor. However, on the rare occasion when, for troubleshooting purposes, you need to view the GPC and GPT directly, it is useful to understand GPC and GPT structure and what kinds of information they store.

Working with Group Policy Containers

When you create a GPO, Active Directory creates a GPC for that GPO. This GPC is created as a container object with the *groupPolicyContainer* object class and is named with a globally unique identifier (GUID). The GPC is then stored under the *CN=Policies,CN=System* container within the currently selected domain. Active Directory and related tools find the container according to its distinguished name (DN). A DN, as you might recall from Chapter 2, is the exact path to an object in the Active Directory data store.

To see how this works, consider the following example:

1. You create a GPO called Sales Policy to handle policy settings for the Sales OU in the cpandl.com domain.

2. Active Directory creates a container object with a GUID of {0BF0F7D6-0245-4133-BC78-B98AFBA21F48}} and stores it in the CN=Policies,CN=System container within the cpandl.com domain.

3. The DN of the Sales Policy GPO is then CN={0BF0F7D6-0245-4133-BC78-B98AFBA21F48},CN=Policies,CN=System,DC=Cpandl,DC=COM, and the full LDAP path is LDAP://CN={0BF0F7D6-0245-4133-BC78-B98AFBA21F48}, CN=Policies,CN=System,DC=Cpandl,DC=COM.

Objects in the directory store also have a *canonical name*, which is specified more like a path. The canonical name for the Sales Policy GPO is:

cpandl.com/System/Policies/{0BF0F7D6-0245-4133-BC78-B98AFBA21F48}

You could access and view the container object for the Sales Policy GPO in many ways, but one way is to use the Advanced view in Active Directory Users And Computers. Follow these steps:

1. Start Active Directory Users And Computers. Click Start, Programs or All Programs, Administrative Tools, Active Directory Users And Computers.

2. On the View menu, make sure Advanced Features is selected. If it isn't, select it.

3. After expanding the domain entry, expand System and then Policies.

As Figure 13-1 shows, each folder entry under System, Policies represents a GPC container. The name of the folder is the GUID of the related container object. As the Active Directory User And Computer's folder representation shows, within each GPC there are Machine and User subcontainers that represent the Computer Configuration and User Configuration portions of a GPO, respectively. Depending on which policy areas are configured within a GPO, there might also be additional subcontainers under the Machine and User containers. We'll explore these additional subcontainers when we talk about how Group Policy settings are processed later.

> **Note**   Each GPC container represents one GPO, and the GUID name of the container is the GUID of the GPO. Naming a GPC using a GUID guarantees that the GPO is always uniquely named within Active Directory even if two GPOs have the same "friendly name" (the descriptive name you enter when you create the GPO). The only exceptions are the Default Domain Policy and Default Domain Controllers Policy GPOs which have the same GUID regardless of in which domain in the forest they reside.

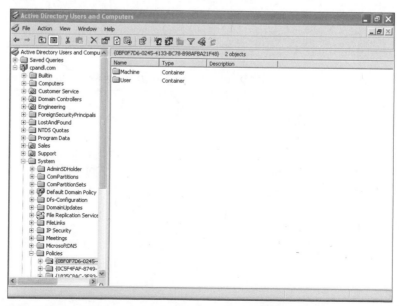

Figure 13-1   Viewing the policy containers in a domain

Examining Attributes of *groupPolicyContainer* Objects

You can learn more about GPCs by examining the class definition of the *groupPolicyContainer* object itself. One way to view object attributes is to use the Active Directory Schema snap-in for the Microsoft Management Console (MMC). When you start this snap-in, it makes a direct connection to the schema master for the current Active Directory forest.

> **Note**   The Active Directory Schema snap-in is not available by default. You must install the Administration Tools (Adminpak.msi) from the Microsoft Windows Server 2003 CD-ROM. Or, if you are working with a server, you can simply double-click Adminpak.msi in the %SystemRoot%\System32 folder.

Once you install the Administrative Tools, you can add the Active Directory Schema snap-in to a custom console by following these steps:

1. Click Start, select Run, type **mmc** in the Open box, and then click OK.

2. Choose Add/Remove Snap-In from the File menu in the main window. Choose Add, which displays the Add Standalone Snap-in dialog box.

3. Click Active Directory Schema, and then choose Add. The Active Directory Schema snap-in is added to the list of snap-ins in the Add/Remove Snap-In dialog box. Click Close, and then click OK.

After you add the snap-in to a custom console, you can view the class definition of the *groupPolicyContainer* object. In Active Directory Schema, expand the Active Directory Schema node, and then expand the Classes node. When you select groupPolicyContainer, you'll see a list of the attributes for this object in the right pane. Table 13-1 describes some of the more interesting attributes.

Table 13-1   **Key Attributes of the *groupPolicyContainer* Object**

Attribute	Description
createTimeStamp	Stores the date and time that the GPC object was created.
displayName	Stores the friendly name of the GPO that you entered when you created it.
DistinguishedName	Stores the full DN of GPC object.
Flags	Stores the state of the GPO.
	Flags=0;GPO is enabled
	Flags=1;User Configuration portion of the GPO is disabled
	Flags=2;Computer Configuration portion of GPO is disabled
	Flags=3;GPO is disabled

Table 13-1   Key Attributes of the *groupPolicyContainer* Object

Attribute	Description
gPCFileSysPath	Stores the SYSVOL path to the corresponding GPT for the GPO.
gPCMachineExtensionNames	Stores a list of GUIDs that correspond to the computer-specific client-side extensions (CSEs) that have been implemented in the GPO.
gPCUserExtensionNames	Stores a list of GUIDs that correspond to the user-specific CSEs that have been implemented in this GPO.
versionNumber	Stores the current version number for the GPC portion of a GPO. Versioning is used to determine how many changes have been made to the GPO and whether those changes in are in sync between the GPC and GPT.

Examining the Security of *groupPolicyContainer* Objects

Like any objects in Active Directory, GPOs have a set of permissions that control who has access for editing and processing. You can view the security settings on a GPO, just as you can on any other object in Active Directory. To do this, follow these steps:

1. Start Active Directory Users And Computers. Click Start, Programs or All Programs, Administrative Tools, Active Directory Users And Computers.

2. On the View menu, make sure Advanced Features is selected. If it isn't, select it.

3. After expanding the domain entry, expand System and then Policies.

4. Right-click the folder that represents the GPO you want to work with, and choose Properties.

5. In the Properties dialog box, select the Security tab, as shown in Figure 13-2.

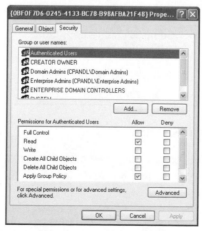

Figure 13-2   Viewing a GPO's security settings

Viewing a GPO's security settings in Active Directory Users And Computers is much like viewing a GPO's advanced security settings from the GPMC's Delegation tab—the settings are one and the same. The Delegation tab itself provides a "cleaned-up" view of the security settings. While the GPMC differentiates between managing the delegation of a GPO and the security filtering on a GPO, Active Directory Users And Computers does not. Thus, in Active Directory Users And Computers, you have a slightly different view of a GPO's security settings.

Table 13-2 lists the permissions associated with each delegation and security filtering task. Delegation determines who can read, edit, delete, or modify security on a GPO. Security filtering determines which user or computer can process the GPO.

Caution   Don't edit security settings from within Active Directory Users And Computers. If you do, you are modifying only the permissions of the corresponding GPC and not the complete set of permissions for the GPO. Remember that each GPO has a logical and physical representation, so if you edit the permissions on the GPC, the permissions on the GPT are not changed. Always use the GPMC, Group Policy Object Editor, or GPMC scripting interfaces to correctly modify GPO security.

Table 13-2   Active Directory Permissions on GPCs

GPMC Task	Corresponding GPC Permissions
Delegation: Read	■ Allow: List Contents ■ Allow: Read All Properties ■ Allow: Read Permissions
Delegation: Edit Settings	Same as Read plus: ■ Allow: Write All Properties ■ Allow: Create All Child Objects ■ Allow: Delete All Child Objects
Delegation: Edit Settings; Delete, Modify Security	Same as Edit Settings plus: ■ Allow: Delete ■ Allow: Modify Permissions ■ Allow Modify Owner

Examining GPO Creation Permissions

In addition to permissions on the GPO object itself, you can delegate who can create a GPO within a domain. You do this on the Delegation tab in the GPMC with a focus on the Group Policy Objects container, as discussed in Chapter 2.

Underlying GPO creation delegation is a set of permissions in Active Directory. These permissions are for creation of new GPOs rather than delegation of existing ones, so the permissions are set on the Policies container (*CN=Policies,CN=System*). This makes sense because the Policies container is the parent container of all GPCs that are created in a domain.

The permission that is granted on the Policies container is Allow: Create groupPolicy-Container Objects. If you grant this permission to a user or group, the user or group can create new GPC objects under that container and can thus create new GPOs in the designated domain.

You can view the security permissions on the Policy container by following these steps:

1. Start Active Directory Users And Computers. Click Start, Programs or All Programs, Administrative Tools, Active Directory Users And Computers.

2. On the View menu, make sure Advanced Features is selected. If it isn't, select it.

3. After expanding the domain entry, expand System. Right-click Policies, and choose Properties.

4. In the Properties dialog box, select the Security tab and then click Advanced.

5. Select the user or group whose permissions you want to view, and then click Edit.

6. If the selected user or group has been granted the Create groupPolicyContainer Objects permission, that user or group can create GPOs in the domain. Certain restrictions and rules apply, of course, for determining the scope of these creation rights.

Caution   Again, don't edit security settings from within Active Directory Users And Computers. Always use the GPMC, Group Policy Object Editor, or GPMC scripting interfaces to correctly modify GPO security.

Viewing and Setting Default Security for New GPOs

To round out the discussion of security on the GPC, we should also discuss how the default security is set on a GPO. When you use the GPMC to create a new GPO on Windows Server 2003, a new GPC is created in the Policies container with a set of default permissions. These default permissions include the following Access Control Entries (ACEs):

- **Authenticated Users**   Read and apply Group Policy
- **Domain Admins**   Edit settings, delete and modify security settings
- **Enterprise Admins**   Edit settings, delete and modify security settings
- **Enterprise Domain Controllers**   Read

- **System**   Edit settings, delete and modify security settings
- **Group Policy Creator Owner**   Edit settings, delete and modify security settings

This list is controlled via the *defaultSecurityDescriptor* attribute on the instance of the *groupPolicyContainer* schema class object within your Active Directory domain. You can modify this attribute to include other security principals so that when a new GPO is created, those principals have permissions on the GPO. The *defaultSecurityDescriptor* attribute on the *groupPolicyContainer* takes the form of a Security Descriptor Definition Language (SDDL) string. For more information on creating SDDL strings, see Chapter 15.

Let's walk through the steps for viewing and modifying the *defaultSecurityDescriptor* on the *groupPolicyContainer* class in order to add a new group to the default security settings on newly created GPOs. Our example includes a domain global security group called GPO Admins that contains administrative users who need to be able to edit any newly created GPOs within a domain. In this case, we want to ensure that this group always has permissions on new GPOs. To add the security group to the default security settings of newly created GPOs, you use the ADSI Edit snap-in for the MMC.

Note   The ADSI Edit snap-in is not installed by default—it is instead included in the Windows Server 2003 Support Tools. Once you install the Support Tools, you can use and work with ADSI Edit as you can other MMC snap-ins.

Viewing the *defaultSecurityDescriptor* Attribute

You can use ADSI Edit to view the *defaultSecurityDescriptor* on the *groupPolicyContainer* class by following these steps:

1. Click Start, select Run, type **adsiedit.msc** in the Open box, and then click OK.

Note   You should be automatically connected to the Domain, Configuration, and Schema naming contexts for your logon domain. If this isn't the domain you want to work with, right-click ADSI Edit and then select Connect To. You can then connect to another domain.

2. Double-click the Schema node, and then double-click CN=Schema,CN=Configuration to access the schema naming context for the domain.

3. Find the CN=Group-Policy-Container class in the right-hand results pane, and double-click it to access its properties (Figure 13-3).

4. In the CN=Group-Policy-Container Properties dialog box, scroll down to the defaultSecurityDescriptor attribute and double-click it to show the current contents.

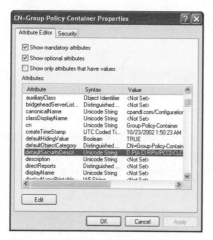

Figure 13-3   Viewing the contents of the *defaultSecurityDescriptor* attribute within ADSI Edit

The *defaultSecurityDescriptor* attribute value will look similar to the following:

```
D:P(A;CI;RPWPCCDCLCLOLORCWOWDSDDTSW;;;DA)(A;CI;RPWPCCDCLCLOLORCWOWDSDDTSW;;;EA)
(A;CI;RPWPCCDCLCLOLORCWOWDSDDTSW;;;CO)(A;CI;RPWPCCDCLCLORCWOWDSDDTSW;;;SY)
(A;CI;RPLCLORC;;;AU)(A;CI;LCRPLORC;;;ED)
```

The SDDL strings stored within the *defaultSecurityDescriptor* attribute are separated by parentheses (). This means the value shown previously contains the following SDDL strings:

```
(A;CI;RPWPCCDCLCLOLORCWOWDSDDTSW;;;DA)
(A;CI;RPWPCCDCLCLOLORCWOWDSDDTSW;;;EA)
(A;CI;RPWPCCDCLCLOLORCWOWDSDDTSW;;;CO)
(A;CI;RPWPCCDCLCLORCWOWDSDDTSW;;;SY)
(A;CI;RPLCLORC;;;AU)
(A;CI;LCRPLORC;;;ED)
```

Each SDDL string is used to assign security permissions to a particular group. The settings for the security groups discussed earlier are:

- **Authenticated Users**   (A;CI;RPLCLORC;;;AU)
- **Domain Admins**   (A;CI;RPWPCCDCLCLOLORCWOWDSDDTSW;;;DA)
- **Enterprise Admins**   (A;CI;RPWPCCDCLCLOLORCWOWDSDDTSW;;;EA)
- **Enterprise Domain Controllers**   (A;CI;LCRPLORC;;;ED)

- **System**   (A;CI;RPWPCCDCLCLORCWOWDSDDTSW;;;SY)
- **Group Policy Creator Owner**   (A;CI;RPWPCCDCLCLOLORCWOWDSDDTSW;;;CO)

Modifying the *defaultSecurityDescriptor* Attribute

If you want to add a new group to the default security settings on a newly created GPO, you add an SDDL string for this group to the *defaultSecurityDescriptor* attribute. The easiest way to do this is to place your mouse pointer at the end of the existing set of strings and add it from there.

If you want to give a group called GPO Admins the same rights on newly created GPOs as the Domain Admins group gets automatically, you can use the SDDL string for Domain Admins as a template and modify it for the GPO Admins group. The Domain Admins string looks like this:

`(A;CI;RPWPCCDCLCLOLORCWOWDSDDTSW;;;DA)`

This string results in Domain Admins having Edit Settings, Delete, and Modify security permissions on all newly created GPOs. To grant this same set of permissions to the GPO Admins group, you simply add this SDDL string to the end of the *defaultSecurity-Descriptor* attribute and change the *DA* to the SID of the GPO Admins group. For example, if the SID for that group is S-1-5-21-817735531-4269160403-1409475253-1123, the new SDDL string is as follows:

`(A;CI;RPWPCCDCLCLOLORCWOWDSDDTSW;;;S-1-5-21-817735531-4269160403-1409475253-1123)`

After this new SDDL string is appended to the end of the *defaultSecurityDescriptor* attribute, you simply click OK in the String Attribute Editor dialog box to commit the change. Newly created GPOs will have the new GPO Admins ACE associated with them. You can verify this by creating a test GPO and checking the security on the GPO's Delegation tab in the GPMC (Figure 13-4).

Caution   Be careful when editing the *defaultSecurityDescriptor* attribute. Removing or changing existing SDDL strings can cause incorrect security to be applied to new GPOs when they are created.

Tip   After you make the change to the *defaultSecurityDescriptor* attribute, it might not be applied right away to newly created GPOs. You can make sure the change is committed to the schema by starting the Active Directory Schema MMC snap-in tool, right-clicking the Active Directory Schema node, and choosing Reload The Schema. The change must then be replicated to the rest of the domain controllers.

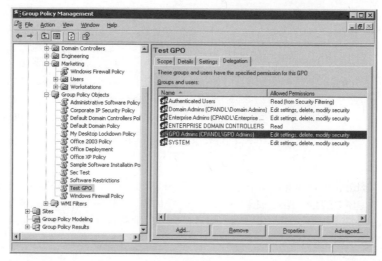

Figure 13-4   Viewing a newly created GPO with a modified *defaultSecurityDescriptor*

Navigating Group Policy Physical Structure

Physically, GPOs are represented through a series of template files that are stored on disk. These templates files contain information about the many thousands of policy settings and the state of these policy settings. Each GPO has a master template folder associated with it. This template folder is physically stored in the %SystemRoot%\SYSVOL folder on domain controllers and is referred to as a Group Policy template (GPT).

> **Caution**   Keep in mind that you never need to interact with GPCs and GPTs directly. In fact, it is easy to create problems with a GPO if you attempt to make changes directly to the GPC or GPT. Your primary interface for managing Group Policy is the GPMC and the Group Policy Object Editor. However, on the rare occasions when, for troubleshooting purposes, you need to view the GPC and GPT directly, it is useful to understand GPC and GPT structure and what kinds of things they store.

Working with Group Policy Templates

When a new GPO is created, Active Directory creates the associated GPT for that GPO. This GPT is created as a folder and is named with the GUID for the GPO. This GUID is identical to the GUID used to name the related GPC. Within the GPT folder are a set of files and subfolders that contain the actual policy settings that have been made within a GPO.

> **Note**   For new GPOs, the GPTs are stored in the %SystemRoot%\SYSVOL folder on the domain controller where you are currently focused (which by default is the PDC emulator domain controller) and is later replicated to all domain controllers in the domain by the File Replication Service (FRS). The %SystemRoot%\SYSVOL\SYSVOL folder is shared as SYSVOL and is often referred to as the SYSVOL share.

To see how this works, let's continue the example from the previous section:

1. You create a GPO called Sales Policy to handle policy settings for the Sales OU in the cpandl.com domain.

2. Active Directory creates a Group Policy Container (GPC) object with a GUID of {0BF0F7D6-0245-4133-BC78-B98AFBA21F48} and stores it in the CN=Policies,CN=System container within the cpandl.com domain.

3. Active Directory also create a master template file with this same GUID in the %SystemRoot%\SYSVOL folder.

The full local file path to the GPT is %SystemRoot%\SYSVOL\domain\Policies\ {0BF0F7D6-0245-4133-BC78-B98AFBA21F48}. With regard to the SYSVOL share, the path to the GPT is SYSVOL\CPANDL.COM\Policies\{0BF0F7D6-0245-4133-BC78-B98AFBA21F48}.

 Note   Two copies of each GPT are created. One is stored under %SystemRoot%\ SYSVOL\domain\Policies*GPOGUID*. The other is in the SYSVOL share under SYSVOL\ *DomainName*\Policies*GPOGUID*.

You can access and view the GPT using Windows Explorer. Simply navigate to the local file path or the SYSVOL share path on a domain controller, as shown in Figure 13-5.

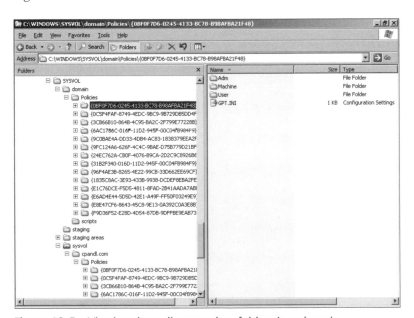

Figure 13-5   Viewing the policy template folders in a domain

Within each GPT, you'll find Adm, Machine, and User subfolders as well as a file called Gpt.ini. These resources are used as follows:

- **Adm** Contains the Administrative Template .adm files that the GPO is using. The .adm files are copied to the GPT by the Group Policy Object Editor when you open that GPO for editing for the first time. In addition to the .adm files themselves, there is a file stored in this folder called Admfiles.ini that lists which .adm files are used within the GPO and their version numbers.

> **Note** By default, the Administrative Templates are copied from the %SystemRoot%\inf folder on the machine that was used to create the policy. From then on, the .adm files are loaded from that GPO into the Group Policy Object Editor. This enables you to use the same version of the .adm files that were used to create the GPO while editing a GPO. You can change this behavior by enabling Always Use Local ADM Files For Group Policy Object Editor under Computer Configurations\Administrative Templates\System\Group Policy. If you enable this setting, Group Policy Object Editor always uses the local .adm files in your %SystemRoot%\inf folder when editing GPOs. This is useful in multilanguage environments where you might want to edit the GPO in the local system language. Keep in mind, however that if the Administrative Templates that you require are not all available locally, you might not be able to see all the settings that have been configured in the GPO that you are editing.

- **Machine** Stores the Computer Configuration policy settings for the GPO and related configuration information, including Security Settings from the Computer Configuration, computer scripts, and per-computer deployed software.

- **User** Stores the User Configuration policy setting for the GPO and related configuration information, including Security Settings from the User Configuration, user scripts, and per-user deployed software. You'll also find data from folder redirection and Microsoft Internet Explorer maintenance if these settings have been configured.

- **Gpt.ini** Contains information concerning the version number of the GPT and the display name of the related GPO.

While we'll explore the contents of the Adm, Machine, and User subfolders in more detail in "Examining Server-Side Extension Processing," the Gpt.ini file deserves a bit more discussion now. A typical Gpt.ini file contains the following information:

```
[General]
Version=0
displayName=Sales Policy
```

The *displayName* key-value pair is the friendly name of the GPO. The *Version* key-value pair relates to the number of changes that have been made to the GPO; it is equivalent to the *versionNumber* attribute found on the corresponding GPC. A version value of 0 indicates that this is a new GPO and that no policy changes have yet been applied. As policy changes are made, the version value increases.

Understanding Group Policy Versioning

Versioning isn't an exact science. The version number in the GPC and the GPT can be different. This can happen for a variety of reasons. For example, changes might have been recorded in the GPC but not yet written to the GPT on disk, such as when the GPC has been replicated but the GPT has not yet been replicated. Windows 2000, Windows Server 2003, and Windows XP Professional handle version discrepancies in different ways:

- In Windows 2000, if the version number of the GPT and GPC are not identical on a given domain controller, any computers or users accessing that GPO on that domain controller will not process that GPO until the versions are identical. This guarantees that all changes between the AD and SYSVOL portions of a GPO are replicated identically.

- In Windows Server 2003 and Windows XP Professional, synchronization of version numbers is not required for proper Group Policy processing. If the GPT and GPC version numbers are not in sync on a given domain controller, that GPO is processed if possible and if not, it is processed during the next processing cycle.

The version number of a GPO is incremented differently for computer-specific and user-specific changes:

- For each change made to the Computer Configuration, the version number is incremented by 1 in most cases. For example, if we enable three Administrative Template policies within the Group Policy Object Editor, the version number within the GPC and GPT will be incremented by 3 when those changes are committed.

- For each change made to the User Configuration, the version number is incremented by 65536. This means that if we change three user-specific Administrative Template policy settings within a GPO, the version number will be incremented by 196608 (65536 x 3).

Note   The version increment is meant to represent each incremental change required. As some Computer Configuration changes must be written more than once, a change to a related policy setting can result in the version number incrementing by 2 or more. Some changes might also require the enabling and configuration of related policies, such as with Account Policies. In this case, the version number would be incremented accordingly.

By making a logical XOR comparison of the current version number, Windows can determine the exact number of separate revisions made to User Configuration and Computer Configuration. You can view this version information by completing the following steps:

1. In the GPMC, expand the entry for the forest you want to work with, expand the related Domains node, and then expand the related Group Policy Objects node.

2. Select the GPO for which you want to determine version information, and in the right pane select the Details tab.

    As Figure 13-6 shows, the User Version and Computer Version fields provide details on the number of versions made. Active Directory revisions, indicated with *(AD)*, are revisions made to the GPC. SYSVOL revisions, indicated with *(sysvol)*, are revisions made to the GPT.

Figure 13-6   Viewing the revisions made to a GPO based on its version number

Each time you edit a GPO, the related changes are made in the GPC and the GPT. For the GPT, this means that the version number in the Gpt.ini file is incremented and client CSE files are updated as appropriate. In the standard configuration with domain controllers running Windows Server 2003 SP 1, there is a 3-second window before the FRS replicates the changes to the GPT. Only the changed files are replicated. On a LAN, that means if you made multiple successive changes to a GPO, FRS replicates the GPT changes as they occur in 3-second intervals. On a WAN, the site replication process consolidates these changes so the changes are replicated according to the configured replication interval. Keep in mind that FRS configuration and other factors can affect or lengthen the replication interval. For example, a future service pack might change the FRS implementation of replication and the interval with which it performs batch updates.

Understanding Group Policy Template Security

From a security perspective, the NTFS permissions on a GPT for a given GPO should be very similar to the Active Directory permissions on the related GPC. Because permissions that apply to Active Directory objects are different from those that apply to NTFS file system objects, however, there is no one-to-one correspondence. Table 13-3 summarizes how GPO permissions in Active Directory correspond to GPT permissions on NTFS.

Table 13-3   How GPO Permissions Correspond to GPT Permissions

GPO Permission	Corresponding GPT Permission
Read	If a group has Read permission on a GPO, there will be an ACE for that group on the GPT folder that allows Read and Execute permissions on that folder and its contents.
Edit Settings	If a group has Edit Settings permission on a GPO, there will be an ACE for that group on the GPT folder that allows Read and Write permissions on that folder and its contents.
Edit Settings, Delete, Modify Security	If a group has Edit Settings, Delete, Modify Security permissions on a GPO, there will be an ACE for that group on the GPT folder that allows Full Control over the folder and its contents.

Navigating Group Policy Link Structure

Creating a new GPO is a separate process from linking that GPO to an Active Directory site, domain, or OU. When you choose to create a new GPO with the Create And Link A GPO Here option in the GPMC, a new GPO (with its component GPC and GPT parts) is created and the GPO is linked to the currently focused container object. As with the GPC and GPT, a lot happens behind the scenes during GPO link creation.

Examining Group Policy Linking

Like the GPC for a GPO, sites, domains, and OUs are represented in the directory as a type of container object. When you link a GPO to a site, domain, or OU, a link reference is inserted into the *gPLink* attribute on that container object. The link reference includes the full LDAP path for the GPC portion of the GPO as well as a status flag. Here is an example:

```
LDAP://cn={E6AD4E44-5D5D-42E1-A49F-
FF50F03249E9},cn=policies,cn=system,DC=cpandl,DC=com;0
```

If more than one GPO is linked to a particular container object, the *gPLink* attribute contains a bracket-delimited ([]) list of the LDAP DNs for all GPOs linked to that container. Each LDAP DN has its own status flag, as shown in the following example:

```
[LDAP://cn={E6AD4E44-5D5D-42E1-A49F-FF50F03249E9},cn=policies,cn=system,
DC=cpandl,DC=com;0][LDAP://cn={E8E47CF6-8643-45C8-9E13-0A392C0A3E8B},
cn=policies,cn=system,DC=cpandl,DC=com;0][LDAP://cn={F9D36F52-E28D-4D54-87DB-
9DFFBE9EAB73},cn=policies,cn=system,DC=cpandl,DC=com;0]
```

As you can see, three GPOs are linked to this container object. Each bracketed DN points to the GPC for a particular GPO, and within each reference is a numeric flag value at the end, delimited by a semicolon from the DN. The flag lists the current state of the link; it can have different values, depending on the options you've chosen for the link. Link states are controlled by the administrator from the GPMC, on the Scope tab for a GPO, as shown in Figure 13-7.

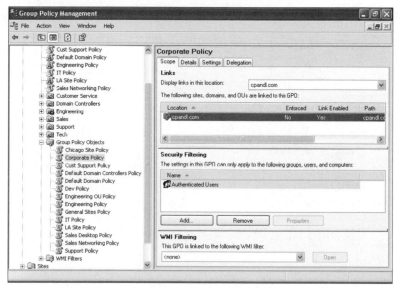

Figure 13-7   Viewing the state of a GPO link from the GPMC

The *gpLink* flag tracks the enabled and enforced state of the link, as described in Chapter 3. The combination of enforced and enabled states on a link controls the flag value that appears within the *gPLink* list. Table 13-4 shows the possible values of this flag.

Table 13-4   Possible Values for the *gPLink* Flag

Flag Value	Enabled?	Enforced?
0	Yes	No
1	No	No
2	Yes	Yes
3	No	Yes

> **Note** When you disable a link, an enforcement setting of Yes is simply ignored until the link is enabled again. Also, disabling a link on an active GPO can have the same effect as moving the computers or users to a different scope of management from that GPO. That is, when the link is disabled, the GPO no longer applies to computers and users that were processing it, and any settings provided by that GPO are undone, if supported. See Chapter 3 for details.

The order of the link entries is also important because it reflects the rank order of the links. Lower-ranking policy objects are processed before higher-ranking policy objects. With the *gPLink* attribute, the lower-priority links go at the beginning of the list of DNs and the higher-priority links go at the end of the list of DNs. The link order reflected in the previous example is as follows:

Link Order 3: [LDAP://cn={E6AD4E44-5D5D-42E1-A49F-FF50F03249E9},cn=policies, cn=system,DC=cpandl,DC=com;0]

Link Order 2: [LDAP://cn={E8E47CF6-8643-45C8-9E13-0A392C0A3E8B},cn=policies, cn=system,DC=cpandl,DC=com;0]

Link Order 1: [LDAP://cn={F9D36F52-E28D-4D54-87DB-9DFFBE9EAB73},cn=policies, cn=system,DC=cpandl,DC=com;0]

Here the GPO with the first link reference (and a link order of 3) is processed first, giving it the lowest link order and the lowest precedence. The GPO with the second link reference (and a link order of 2) is processed next. The GPO with the third link reference (and a link order of 1) is processed last, giving it the highest link order and the highest precedence.

Viewing the *gPLink* Attribute

You should not edit the *gPLink* attribute directly. You should always use the GPMC to change the state of a GPO link. That said, you can use ADSI Edit to view the *gPLink* attribute for a domain or OU container object by following these steps:

1. Click Start, select Run, type **adsiedit.msc** in the Open box, and then click OK.

> **Note** You should be automatically connected to the Domain, Configuration, and Schema naming contexts for your logon domain. If this isn't the domain you want to work with, right-click ADSI Edit and then select Connect To. You can then connect to another domain.

2. Double-click the Domain naming context and then double-click the node for the domain you want to work with, such as DC=Cpandl,DC=Com.

3. Right-click the container object for the domain or OU you want to work with, and then select Properties.

4. In the Properties dialog box, scroll down to the gPLink attribute and double-click it to show the current contents.

Site objects are not stored in the Domain naming context. They are stored in the Configuration naming context within a forest. Therefore, you must connect to the Configuration naming context to view site objects and their *gPLink* properties. Follow these steps:

1. In ADSI Edit, double-click the Configuration naming context and then double-click the configuration node for the domain you want to work with, such as CN=Configuration,DC=Cpandl,DC=Com.

2. Double-click CN=Sites. Right-click the container object for the site you want to work with, and then select Properties.

3. In the Properties dialog box, scroll down to the gPLink attribute and double-click it to show the current contents.

Examining Inheritance Blocking on Links

In addition to the gPLink attribute, there is one other attribute of interest on container objects when it comes to Group Policy Processing: the *gPOptions* attribute. The *gPOptions* attribute is a flag that gets set whenever block inheritance is enabled for that container.

In addition to the *gPLink* attribute, another important attribute of container objects that concerns Group Policy Processing is *gPOptions*. The *gPOptions* attribute is a flag that is set whenever block inheritance is enabled for that container.

Block inheritance lets you control which upstream GPOs are processed by essentially specifying that any GPOs linked to containers upstream of the blocked container will not apply. When block inheritance is set on a container object, the value of the *gPOptions* attribute on that container is set to 1. If block inheritance is not set, the attribute is either 0 or *<Not Set>*.

Understanding Group Policy Security and Links

It might be obvious, but it's important to note that security filtering and delegation of a GPO is set on the GPO object itself—or, more precisely, on its component GPC and GPT objects, as described earlier in the chapter. Security does not reside within the GPO link. As a result, you might have a single GPO linked to multiple containers but the security filtering applied to that GPO will apply equally across all containers to which it is linked. This can cause some confusion if you are reusing a GPO for multiple containers but need different security filtering or delegation for each one. You essentially need to set all of the security filtering or delegation you need across all links on the GPO and ensure that no group memberships have overlapping scopes of management that materially alter the desired behavior.

Understanding Group Policy Processing

Like Active Directory itself, Group Policy also has a client-server architecture. Group Policy clients use client-side extensions (CSEs) for Group Policy to process policy settings. Group Policy servers use server-side extensions to manage policy.

Examining Client-Side Extension Processing

Client-side extensions (CSEs) are implemented as DLLs that are installed with the operating system. The Group Policy Engine running on a client triggers foreground policy processing when a computer is started or a user logs on. The architecture of Group Policy processing is shown in Figure 13-8.

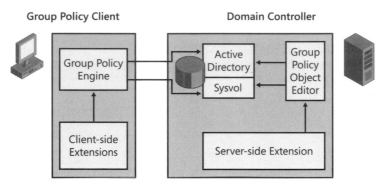

Figure 13-8   Group Policy processing architecture

CSEs are called by the Group Policy Engine, and they in turn read each GPC and GPT of a GPO that applies to determine what policy settings to apply to a given computer or user. The CSE makes the actual changes (for example, registry changes, security changes, software installation) that are specified within the GPOs that are processed by the user or computer.

The CSE DLLs are installed with Windows in the %Windir%\System32 folder on a standard Windows Server 2003 installation. Third parties can also write custom CSEs that provide additional Group Policy functionality. The installed CSEs for a given Windows computer are registered under the following registry key:

`HKEY_LOCAL_MACHINE\Software\Microsoft\Windows NT\CurrentVersion\Winlogon\GPExtensions`

Each CSE is stored under a GUID-named key within this registry key. The GUID refers to the particular CSE. This GUID is the same across all Windows–based systems. For example, the CSE for Software Installation has the same GUID regardless of which system it is installed on. If you look at the contents of one of these keys using the Registry Editor (regedit.exe), you will see a set of values that describes the policy capability that the CSE is implementing and the name of the DLL that is implementing that policy, as shown in Figure 13-9.

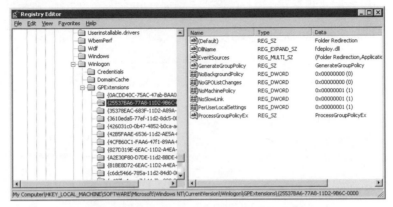

Figure 13-9   Viewing the contents of a CSE registry key

As you can see in the figure, a number of values relate to how this CSE processes policy, such as *NoSlowLink* and *NoBackgroundPolicy* (as discussed later in this chapter). Table 13-5 lists the CSEs that are installed with Windows Server 2003 Service Pack 1 along with the DLL that implements that functionality.

Table 13-5   Client-Side Extensions Installed with Windows Server 2003 SP1

CSE GUID	DLL Name of CSE	Policy Functionality
{0ACDD40C-75AC-47ab-BAA0-BF6DE7E7FE63}	Gptext.dll	Wireless Networking policy
25537BA6-77A8-11D2-9B6C-0000F8080861}	Fdeploy.dll	Folder Redirection policy
{35378EAC-683F-11D2-A89A-00C04FBBCFA2}	Userenv.dll	Administrative Templates policy
3610eda5-77ef-11d2-8dc5-00c04fa31a66}	Dskquota.dll	Disk Quota policy (found within Administrative Templates policy)
{426031c0-0b47-4852-b0ca-ac3d37bfcb39}	Gptext.dll	QoS Packet Scheduler policy (found within Administrative Templates policy)
{42B5FAAE-6536-11d2-AE5A-0000F87571E3}	Gptext.dll	Scripts policy (both computer and user scripts)
{4CFB60C1-FAA6-47f1-89AA-0B18730C9FD3}	Iedkcs32.dll	Internet Explorer zone-mapping policy (part of Administrative Templates policy)
{827D319E-6EAC-11D2-A4EA-00C04F79F83A}	Scecli.dll	Security policy
{A2E30F80-D7DE-11d2-BBDE-00C04F86AE3B}	Iedkcs32.dll	Internet Explorer Maintenance policy

Table 13-5 Client-Side Extensions Installed with Windows Server 2003 SP1

CSE GUID	DLL Name of CSE	Policy Functionality
{B1BE8D72-6EAC-11D2-A4EA-00C04F79F83A}	Scecli.dll	EFS Recovery policy (part of Public Key policy)
{c6dc5466-785a-11d2-84d0-00c04fb169f7}	Appmgmts.dll	Software Installation policy
{e437bc1c-aa7d-11d2-a382-00c04f991e27}	Gptext.dll	IP Security policy

You will notice in the table that several policy areas share the same CSE, while others implement a separate CSE even though they are part of another CSE's policy namespace. For example, QoS Packet Scheduler policy uses its own CSE even though this policy appears within Administrative Templates policy (for exampl, QoS Packet Scheduler policy is under the Computer Configuration\Administrative Templates\Network\QoS Packet Scheduler namespace). Also note that Administrative Templates policy does not have its own standalone CSE DLL, but instead is implemented as part of the core Group Policy Engine (Userenv.dll).

Examining Server-Side Extension Processing

Server-side extensions to Group Policy are used to manage policy implementation and enforce policy rules. When you configure policy settings, you primarily work with the management interfaces to these server-side extensions. Each server-side extensions is managed via a set of MMC snap-ins that provide a policy editing user interface and a mechanism for storing Group Policy settings.

Table 13-6 lists the complete set of MMC snap-ins used for Group Policy editing and their associated DLLs. The snap-ins available in Windows Server 2003 SP1 and the name of the DLL that implements the snap-in can be found in the Windows registry under:

```
HKEY_LOCAL_MACHINE\Software\Microsoft\MMC\Snap-ins
```

Table 13-6 MMC Snap-Ins Used for Group Policy Editing

Policy Editing Functionality	MMC Snap-in DLL Name
Administrative Templates and Scripts (computer and user)	Gptext.dll
Software Installation	Appmgr.dll
Wireless Network Policy	Wlsnp.dll
Public Key Policy	Certmgr.dll
Security Policy	Wsecedit.dll
Folder Redirection Policy	Fde.dll
Software Restriction Policy	Certmgr.dll
Internet Explorer Maintenance Policy	Ieaksie.dll
IP Security Policy	Ipsecsnp.dll

Note   Generally speaking, the policy editing snap-ins are registered when you install Windows and run the Group Policy Object Editor the first time. Not all the snap-ins listed are always available either. For example, many security settings don't appear when editing local policy. Others may be intentionally not included in the policy set at various times.

Tip   On rare occasions, a particular policy area might be missing from the editor namespace. In that case, you can reregister the DLL that implements that policy area, and it should re-appear the next time you load the Group Policy Object Editor. To reregister a snap-in, type **regsvr32 <snap-in DLL name>** at a command prompt. You will receive a message either confirming that the registration succeeded or telling you that it failed.

Note   Strictly speaking, however, reregistration is rarely needed. The Group Policy Object Editor handles the reregistration if it is necessary the next time you run the editor after policy has been fully refreshed.

When you use the Group Policy Object Editor to modify a GPO, these MMC snap-ins are doing the actual work. While most policy data is stored within the GPT, some policy data is stored within the GPC. Additionally, some extensions, such as IPSec, store their policy information completely outside both structures.

The sections that follow take an in-depth look at how each policy area stores its policy settings within either the GPC or GPT (or, in some cases, both).

Note   Wondering why most but not all policy data is stored within the GPT? The GPT is provided as a location for Group Policy extensions to store and write their data, but there is no requirement for them to do so. As such, the developers of Group Policy extensions might decide to write their data external to the GPT, such as in Active Directory.

Setting Storage for Wireless Network Policy

Wireless Network policy stores its settings within the GPC for a given GPO. Specifically, a new container structure is created under the GPC container in Active Directory with the path of CN=Wireless,CN=Windows,CN=Microsoft. Within the CN=Wireless container, a new object of class *msieee80211-Policy* is created that holds the Wireless Network policy settings that you specify.

Setting Storage for Folder Redirection Policy

Folder Redirection policy is stored in the GPT for a given GPO and specified within a file called Fdeploy.ini. The Fdeploy.ini file contains the policy details. For example, if you configure redirection for the My Documents folder so that it points to the user's home directory, the Fdeploy.ini file is created or updated to include the related settings, as shown here:

```
[FolderStatus]
My Documents=11
My Pictures=2
[My Documents]
s-1-1-0=\\%HOMESHARE%%HOMEPATH%
[My Pictures]
```

In this example, the [FolderStatus] section tells the CSE what to do with the My Documents folder if redirection no longer applies. It also tells the CSE what to do about the My Pictures folder underneath My Documents. The values of these keys change as you choose different options within the Folder Redirection policy. The [My Documents] section lists the redirection that is taking place. Because we are specifying basic redirection, it specifies that the SID S-1-1-0, which indicates the Everyone group, should be redirected to the user environment variables that point to the user's specified home directory when they log on.

When the Folder Redirection CSE is processed, the contents of Fdeploy.ini are cached on the workstation within the user's profile, along with another file containing information about the redirected folders prior to redirection. These files are found in %UserProfile%\Local Settings\Application Data\Microsoft\Windows\File Deployment. Typically, this folder contains two .ini files—one called {0E35E0EC-FD6D-4CEF-9267-6EDB00694026}.ini, which contains the cached folder redirection instructions from Fdeploy.ini, and one called {25537BA6-77A8-11D2-9B6C-0000F8080861}.ini, which contains information about all possible redirected folders (such as Desktop, Start Menu, and so on), including the GUID of the GPO that is currently responsible for any redirection that is taking place.

Setting Storage for Administrative Templates Policy

Administrative Templates policy is stored within the GPT in a file called registry.pol. When both per-computer and per-user Administrative Templates policy is specified within a GPO, there will be a registry.pol file under both the Machine and User folders within the GPT. Registry.pol files are text files, but you cannot edit them manually because they contain some special characters and follow a precise format.

Setting Storage for Disk Quota Policy

Because Disk Quota policy is a subset of Administrative Templates policy, the settings for this policy area are stored within the registry.pol file, just as with Administrative

Templates policy. Because Disk Quota policy is available only per computer, the registry.pol file containing these policy settings is found only under the Machine folder within the GPT.

Setting Storage for QoS Packet Scheduler Policy

As with Disk Quota policy, QoS Packet Scheduler policy has its own CSE to process policy settings, but QoS Packet Scheduler policy is a subset of Administrative Template policy. The settings for this policy area are stored within the registry.pol file, just as with Administrative Templates policy.

Setting Storage for Scripts

Scripts policy encompasses both startup/shutdown and logon/logoff scripts. Both are stored within the GPT. Shutdown and startup scripts are found within the Machine subfolder of the GPT (in a scripts\shutdown or scripts\startup folder, respectively). Logon and logoff scripts are found within the User subfolder of the GPT (in a scripts\logon or scripts\logoff folder, respectively).

When you configure scripts, you specify where they are located and any parameters that should be passed to the scripts when they are run. References to the scripts that you specify are stored in a file called Scripts.ini within the GPT. This file is located within the machine\scripts or user\scripts folder, depending on whether the policy describes per-computer or per-user scripts. The file contains references to the defined scripts and any parameters that are passed to them. When the Scripts CSE runs, information about which scripts need to be executed is stored within the registry. For per-computer scripts, the registry location is:

```
HKEY_LOCAL_MACHINE\Software\Policies\Windows\System\Scripts
```

For per-user scripts, the registry location is:

```
HKEY_CURRENT_USER\Software\Policies\Windows\System\Scripts
```

When it comes time to actually execute the script, the path to the script is read from one of these two registry locations.

Setting Storage for Internet Explorer Maintenance Policy

Internet Explorer Maintenance policy is stored within the GPT in the \User\Microsoft\ IEAK folder. The actual settings are stored in a file called install.ins. In addition, there might be a Branding folder within the IEAK folder that holds any custom bitmaps, icons, or other files that are specified within the Internet Explorer Maintenance policy.

When the Internet Explorer Maintenance CSE processes this policy, the install.ins file and any related folders and files under the Branding folder are downloaded and cached within the user's profile under %UserProfile%\Application Data\Microsoft\Internet

Explorer\Custom Settings. From here, they are processed and applied to the Internet Explorer configuration.

Table 13-7 shows where each of the Internet Explorer Maintenance policy areas stores its settings within the GPT.

Table 13-7   Internet Explorer Maintenance Policy File Locations

Setting	Policy File Location
Browser Title	Install.ins
Custom Bitmaps	Install.ins
	Branding\Logo\<<*small logo file name*>>
	Branding\Logo\<<*big logo file name*>>
	Branding\Animbmp (empty folder created)
Toolbar Customization	Install.ins
	Branding\Btoolbar\<<*color logo file name*>>
	Branding\Btoolbar\<<*grayscale logo file name*>>
	Branding\Toolbmp\<<*toolbar bmp file name* >>
Connection Settings	Install.ins
	Branding\cs\connect.set
	Branding\cs\cs.dat
Automatic Browser Configuration	Install.ins
Proxy Settings	Install.ins
User Agent String	Install.ins
Favorites and Links	Install.ins
Important URLs	Install.ins
Security Zones	Install.ins
	Branding\Zones\seczones.inf
	Branding\Zones\seczrsop.inf
Content Ratings	Install.ins
	Branding\Ratings\ratings.inf
	Branding\Ratings\ratrsop.inf
Authenticode Settings	Install.ins
	Branding\Authcode\authcode.inf
Programs	Install.ins
	Branding\Programs\programs.inf
Corporate Settings (in Preference mode only)	Branding\Adm\inetcorp.adm
	Branding\Adm\inetcorp.inf
Internet Settings (in Preference mode only)	Branding\Adm\inetset.adm
	Branding\Adm\inetset.inf

Setting Storage for Security Policy

Security policy is stored within the GPT in the Machine\Microsoft\Windows NT\ SecEdit folder. Within this folder, a file called GptTmpl.inf is created to store policy settings. Not all security policy is stored within this file, however. Specifically, policies found within Computer Configuration\Windows Settings\Security Settings and including Local Policies, Event Log, Restricted Groups, System Services, Registry and File System are stored in GptTmpl.inf. The settings in Account Policies are stored in the LSA database. Software Restriction settings are written to Registry.pol. IP Security policies are written to Active Directory.

If you open GptTmpl.inf in Notepad, you will see that the file has the same format as the Security Configuration and Analysis templates that you can create and apply outside of Group Policy. This is because Group Policy uses the same SecEdit engine to process Security policy as it does to process Security Configuration and Analysis templates.

When the Security Policy client CSE, Scecli.dll, processes security policy, it copies the GptTmpl.inf file to the computer's local hard drive and processes the policy from there. The standard location to which GptTmpl.inf is copied is the %Windir%\ security\templates\policies folder.

Because a computer can have multiple security policies from multiple GPOs, a series of temporary files is created within the %Windir%\security\templates\policies folder. These temporary files represent each GPO's security policy settings and are numbered sequentially starting with Gpt00000.dom. Further, because some security policies, such as Account and Kerberos policy, can be applied only to the domain when found in a domain-linked GPO, these policies are downloaded to a special file with a .dom extension. This ensures that all domain controllers process only this domain-linked policy for these special policy settings.

Setting Storage for Software Installation Policy

Software Installation policy is a policy area that uses both the GPC and GPT to store its settings. Within the GPT under the Machine (or User) folder, an Applications folder is created with an Application Assignment Script file (.aas file). The .aas file is specific to the application, its MSI file, and the network path that it has been deployed from. The GPC portion of Software Installation policy is stored within the corresponding Machine (or User) container in the CN=Packages,CN=Class Store container within the GPC. For each application deployed within the GPO, there is *packageRegistration* object within the Packages container.

Each *packageRegistration* object contains information about the application that has been deployed. Some of the more interesting attributes on this object are:

- **msiFileList** Stores the paths to the MSI file that this application uses, as well as the path to any files that modify this installation, such as .mst transform files.

- **msiScriptName** Stores the deployment state of the application—P for Published, A for Assigned, or R for Removed. Note that the *packagRegistration* object for a removed application does not get deleted, but instead remains within the GPC indefinitely.

- **msiScriptPath** Stores the file path to the .aas file associated with this application—as it is stored in the SYSVOL.

- **packageName** Stores the friendly name of the application being deployed.

> **Note** Because the path to the MSI file is embedded in both the GPC and GPT portions of a Software Installation policy, you cannot change the path of an application once it has been deployed without redeploy the application. As discussed in Chapter 9, it's best to use DFS paths when deploying application packages for this very reason.

Setting Storage for IP Security Policy

Unlike other areas of policy, details about IP Security policy are stored in a different part of Active Directory than the GPC. You'll find IP Security Policy in the CN=IP Security,CN=System container within the domain naming context. This means you access it in ADSI Edit by connecting to the domain naming context, double-clicking the domain node, such as DC=cpandl,DC=com, expanding CN=System, and then selecting CN=IP Security (Figure 13-10).

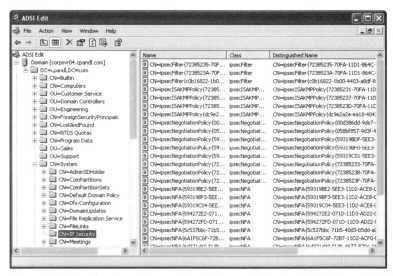

Figure 13-10   Viewing IPSec policy objects within the CN=IP Security, CN=System container

When an IPSec policy that has been created in a domain and stored in Active Directory is assigned to a GPO, a container is created within the GPC to hold that association.

Specifically, within the CN=Windows,CN=Microsoft,CN=Machine container under the GPC, an object of class *ipsecPolicy* is created to hold the reference to the IPSec policy that is associated with that GPO. The reference to the IP Security policy itself is stored within the *ipsecOwnersReference* attribute on this *ipsecPolicy* object, and it contains the DN of the IP Security Policy object within the CN=IP Security container.

Understanding Policy Processing Events

Two types of policy processing can occur: foreground processing and background processing. Foreground processing occurs at computer startup and at user logon. Foreground processing is unique because it typically occurs before the user is able to interact with his desktop, so it is well suited for certain kinds of policy processing that need a "user-free" environment.

Background processing occurs periodically and by definition asynchronously with any other processes for both the computer and user. Background processing is useful for policy that might need to be reapplied periodically, such as Security Settings policy or Administrative Templates policy. Background processing for member servers and workstations occurs every 90 minutes, plus a random amount up to a 30 minute skew factor. Background processing for domain controllers occurs every 5 minutes.

The background processing interval, and the skew factor, can be modified. To do this, you use the following policies:

- Group Policy Refresh Interval For Computers under Computer Configuration\ Administrative Templates\System\Group Policy

- Group Policy Refresh Interval For Domain Controllers under Computer Configuration\Administrative Templates\System\Group Policy

- Group Policy Refresh Interval For Users under User Configuration\Administrative Templates\System\Group Policy

You can set both the update interval and the skew factor for each of these, as discussed in Chapter 3. As we mentioned, foreground processing allows Group Policy to perform system changes without the user involvement. In Windows 2000, foreground processing of Group Policy always happened synchronously—that is, policy for a computer was processed before the logon screen appeared for the user, and policy for a user was processed before the desktop was presented to the user. Windows XP Professional introduced the possibility of asynchronous foreground processing, which is supported using the "fast logon optimization" mechanism.

Fast logon optimization essentially means that Windows does not wait for the network stack to initialize before starting up and letting the user log on. Thus, with fast logon optimization enabled, foreground processing of Group Policy need not wait until the network is available. You can disable fast logon optimization by enabling

Always Wait For The Network At Computer Startup And Logon under Computer Configuration\Administrative Templates\System\Logon.

Windows Server 2003 does not support fast logon optimization, so foreground processing always runs synchronously.

> **Note**   You can also trigger a background refresh of Group Policy manually using the gpupdate utility. Gpupdate essentially mimics the processes that happen during a normal background refresh of Group Policy. See "Refreshing Group Policy Manually" in Chapter 3 for details.

Asynchronous vs. Synchronous Policy Processing

Its important to understand how policy processing differs during foreground and background processing cycles and how asynchronous and synchronous processing can affect that. For instance, Software Installation and Folder Redirection policy can be applied only during a foreground, synchronous policy processing event. This means that, for example, if fast logon optimization is enabled on a computer running Windows XP Professional, it will take two user logons for Software Installation and Folder Redirection policy changes to be processed completely. Similarly, certain policy areas aren't processed at all during background refresh, while others are processed but don't necessarily run.

Table 13-8 lists when each CSE will run during policy processing. Note that with Scripts policy, synchronous and asynchronous behavior can be modified. See "Controlling Script Execution and Run Technique" in Chapter 7 for details.

Table 13-8   CSE Foreground and Background Processing Support

CSE	Runs During Foreground Synchronous	Runs During Foreground Asynchronous	Runs During Background (Asynchronous)
Wireless Networking	Yes	Yes	Yes
Folder Redirection	Yes	No	No
Administrative Template	Yes	Yes	Yes
Disk Quota	Yes	Yes	Yes
QoS Packet Scheduler	Yes	Yes	Yes
Scripts	*	*	*
Internet Explorer Maintenance	Yes	Yes	Yes
Security	Yes	Yes	Yes*
EFS Recovery	Yes	Yes	Yes
Software Installation	Yes	No	No
IP Security	Yes	Yes	Yes

> **Note**   Security policy can be applied to a machine during background refresh. However, some security policy settings may not take effect without a reboot. Additionally, some of the CSEs listed in Table 13-8 apply only to the user or to the computer, so background asynchronous processing might mean something different for each. For example, if no user is logged on to a computer, no user-specific background processing occurs.

Tracking Policy Application

Now let's look at the actual Group Policy processing process. We'll look at the flow of two different scenarios. In the first scenario, we'll look at what happens during each step of foreground policy processing during computer startup and when a user logs on. During startup, the following events take place:

1. The computer finds a domain controller and authenticates itself in Active Directory. (The same process occurs when a user logs on to Active Directory because a computer is just a special instance of a user account.) To perform this authentication, a series of protocols must be successfully passed over the network, including UDP port 53 (DNS), UDP and TCP port 389 (LDAP), TCP port 135 (RPC Portmapper), and UDP port 88 (Kerberos).

2. The computer performs an ICMP ping to the domain controller to determine whether it is connected via a slow link to the domain controller.

3. The computer queries Active Directory using LDAP to determine which GPOs are linked to the OU(s), domain, and site to which the computer belongs. From these queries, it builds a list of distinguished names for all of the GPOs that apply to the computer.

4. The computer queries Active Directory using LDAP. It sends as the query filter the list of all GPOs found in step 3 and requests a number of attributes for them, including the path to the GPT, the version number of the GPC, and the *gpCMachineExtensionNames* and *gpCUserExtensionnames* attributes. These attributes contain a list of CSE GUIDs that are implemented within the GPO.

> **Note**   The Windows operating system uses the results of this query to determine which CSEs need to be called and which ones don't when it comes time to process a particular GPO. This optimizes Group Policy processing performance.

5. The Windows operating system uses TCP Port 445 (SMB) to connect to the SYSVOL share and reads the Gpt.ini file out of each GPO found in step 3. The core Group Policy engine then hands off processing of policy to the CSEs that need to be called (found in step 4).

6. As Group Policy processing begins, each CSE compares the version number of the GPOs that it needs to process with those stored on the computer in its Group Policy history and state keys. (More on these later, in the "Understanding Group Policy History and State" section.)

7. If a GPO's version number has not changed since the last time it was processed in either foreground or background processing, it is skipped. In addition, if one or more GPOs have been deleted from the list of GPOs to process since the last time Group Policy processing occurred, that is considered a change and the CSE will remove any related policy settings.

> **Note** The rule about GPOs not being processed unless their version number has changed is always true unless you modify the behavior of a CSE using Administrative Templates policy (described in the "Modifying CSE Behavior" section in this chapter) or you use the *gpupdate /force* option.

8. The CSE checks to make sure it has sufficient permissions to all of the GPOs it is supposed to process. Any GPOs to which it does not have access are dropped from the list. In addition, if you have specified anything that would modify the behavior of Group Policy processing, such as setting a GPO link to Enforced, this is taken into consideration at this time.

> **Note** When a GPO link is set to Enforced, it is moved to the end of the list of GPOs to process. In that way, it is processed last and always "wins" over conflicting GPOs.

9. As each CSE runs, it performs the checks described in step 6 and then processes the GPOs by reading the contents of the GPT (or GPC, if needed) using SMB. If the Administrative Templates Policy CSE needs to run, the CSE actually removes all registry values within the predesignated policy keys. The Administrative Templates policy then reapplies any registry policy from the list of GPOs that are processed. Then the next CSE in the list is run. The CSEs run in the order they are registered in the GPExtensions key within the registry, and of course they are called only if the gpCMachineExtensionNames and gpCUserExtensionnames attributes indicate that they need to run.

10. As each CSE completes its job, it logs RSoP data to WMI in the CIMOM database on the computer where policy is being processed.

11. When a user logs on, this process is repeated to obtain and process the GPOs that apply to the currently logged on user.

In the second scenario, we'll look at what happens during each step of background policy processing—when a manual refresh of policy is done using Gpupdate.exe. During a manual refresh, the following events take place:

1. The Group Policy processing cycle starts with the slow-link detection process. This is repeated, just as in the previous example, for computer startup. If a user is logged on, the slow link detection process is repeated according to the User Configuration settings.

2. If a user is logged on when gpupdate is run, user processing begins first. The Group Policy client running on the user's computer queries Active Directory to retrieve the list of GPOs that apply. The same process is completed for the computer account.

3. Active Directory is queried for information about the GPOs, as discussed previously.

4. The CSEs process their GPO lists, contacting Active Directory and SYSVOL as needed. Only GPOs that have settings changed since last cached on the client will be processed by default. If a user is logged on, user and computer processing can happen in parallel, and you might have computer processing going on at the same time as user processing.

5. Each CSE writes RSoP data to WMI on the computer as it completes its processing.

As you can see, the processing of Group Policy in the background is not that different from the steps taken during foreground processing—the same protocols are used, and the same decisions are made along the way, based on whether the user or computer has access to the GPOs, whether the GPOs have changed since the last processing cycle, and so on.

> **Tip**   To get an inside look at Group Policy processing, you can enable verbose userenv logging on your Windows computers. Other logging is also available to look at specific CSE processing as well. Logging is examined in detail in Chapter 16.

Tracking Slow Link Detection

Because certain CSEs will not process policy if a slow link is detected, troubleshooting policy problems can be difficult. Table 13-9 lists the default behavior of CSEs when a slow link is detected.

Table 13-9   CSE Slow Link Processing Behavior

CSE	Processes on Slow Link?
Security	Yes (and can't be disabled)
IP Security	Yes
EFS Recovery	Yes
Wireless Network	Yes

Table 13-9   CSE Slow Link Processing Behavior

CSE	Processes on Slow Link?
Administrative Templates	Yes (and can't be disabled)
Scripts	No
Folder Redirection	No
Software Installation	No
IE Maintenance	Yes

Using Administrative Templates policy, you can modify the behavior of these CSEs with respect to slow link detection as discussed in Chapter 3. One challenge of slow link detection is that it primarily relies on ICMP network traffic to be available between the computer processing Group Policy and the domain controller from which it receives Group Policy. If ICMP is blocked or restricted, slow link detection will fail. However, perhaps more catastrophically, if ICMP traffic is blocked or restricted, Group Policy processing itself will fail.

Process failure occurs because when the Group Policy client finds that it cannot successfully ping the domain controller that it has been authenticated to, it simply gives up and stops Group Policy processing. If you work in a network that has disabled or restricted ICMP, you must take steps to work around this reliance on ICMP. Specifically, you might want to disable slow link detection altogether, in both Computer Configuration and User Configuration. As discussed in Chapter 3, you disable slow link detection entirely by enabling Group Policy Slow Link Detection under Computer Configuration\Administrative Templates\System\Group Policy and User Configuration\Administrative Templates\System\Group Policy and then specifying a Connection Speed of 0 Kbps.

Note   Restrictions that affect slow link detection include restricting the packet size of ICMP traffic. Because slow link detection requires sending a data-filled packet of 2048 bytes, if only smaller ICMP packet sizes are allowed on the network, slow link detection and Group Policy processing will still fail.

Of course, if you have already disabled ICMP on your network, you cannot deliver these two policies using Group Policy. In that case, you must manually distribute the corresponding registry changes for these two policies. The following registry values must be delivered to both policies to completely disable slow link detection:

```
HKEY_LOCAL_MACHINE\Software\Policies\Microsoft\Windows\System\
GroupPolicyMinTransferRate = REG_DWORD 0
HKEY_CURRENT_USER\Software\Policies\Microsoft\Windows\System\
GroupPolicyMinTransferRate = REG_DWORD 0
```

Once this is done, Group Policy processing will no longer perform slow-link detection. All links will be assumed to be fast.

Modifying Security Policy Processing

CSE behavior can vary based on several factors. In general, CSEs will not process a GPO that has not changed since the last time Group Policy was processed. Certain CSEs will not process a GPO if a slow link has been detected. Some CSEs will not process a GPO if the processing event is a background refresh. As discussed in Chapter 3, you can optimize slow link detection and background refresh using policies in the Computer Configuration\Administrative Templates\System\Group Policy folder.

One CSE behavior modification you can make that is not available in the Administrative Templates policy is related to security policy processing. By default, the Security Policy CSE processes the related security settings every 16 hours on non-domain controllers and ever 5 minutes on domain controllers, even if these settings have not changed. This mechanism ensures that the important security configuration aspects of Group Policy are reinforced even if no GPO changes have been made. You can reduce or increase this interval as needed by making a registry change. Specifically, the value that controls the processing interval is:

```
HKEY_LOCAL_MACHINE\SOFTWARE\Microsoft\Windows NT\CurrentVersion\Winlogon\GPExtensions\
{827D319E-6EAC-11D2-A4EA-00C04F79F83A}\MaxNoGPOListChangesInterval
```

This value is set to 960 (hex 0x3C0) by default, which is the number of minutes between refreshes. You can adjust this value up or down to modify the interval. To deliver this change to your computers, you can create a custom .adm file that lets you manage this change centrally. For more information on creating custom .adm files, see Chapter 14.

Don't modify the Security Policy processing interval without careful thought to the impact the change will have on your network. Generally speaking, you should modify the interval only if there is a valid business reason or concern. For example, if you are in a high-security environment with 24/7 operations, you might want Security Policy to be refreshed more often than normal, such as every 12 hours. In this case, you set the Security Policy refresh interval to 720 minutes and set the *MaxNoGPOListChangesInterval* value in the registry to 0x2D0 (which is the hex value for 720).

Group Policy History and State Data

On each computer that receives Group Policy, history and state information about the GPOs that were processed is stored in the registry. As part of policy processing, group membership information is also stored. The related registry keys that store this information include:

- **HKEY_LOCAL_MACHINE\SOFTWARE\Microsoft\Windows\CurrentVersion\Group Policy\History** Used to store Group Policy history data

- **HKEY_CURRENT_USER\SOFTWARE\Microsoft\Windows\CurrentVersion\Group Policy\State** Used to store Group Policy state data

- **HKEY_LOCAL_MACHINE\SOFTWARE\Microsoft\Windows\CurrentVersion\Group Policy\GroupMembership**   Used to store group membership information for the computer for which policy was processed

- **HKEY_CURRENT_USER\SOFTWARE\Microsoft\Windows\CurrentVersion\Group Policy\GroupMembership**   Used to store group membership information for users for which policy was processed

These keys and their values are discussed in the sections that follow.

Group Policy History Data

Group Policy history data is stored in the registry under *HKEY_LOCAL_MACHINE\ SOFTWARE\Microsoft\Windows\CurrentVersion\Group Policy\History*. One primary use for maintaining history information is to determine whether a GPO being processed has changed since the last time it was processed. For this reason, version information and other details about processed GPOs are stored for later retrieval. Each key under the History key represents the CSE being processed and is named with the GUID of the related CSE. Following this, history data from processing the Administrative Templates CSE is stored in the *HKEY_LOCAL_MACHINE\SOFTWARE\Microsoft\Windows\CurrentVersion\ Group Policy\History\{35378EAC-683F-11D2-A89A-00C04FBBCFA2}* key.

Organizing the history keys according to the GUID of the related CSE makes it easy to compare the previously processed GPOs. A numerically indexed (0, 1, 2, and so on) list of keys under the CSE keys is used to store information related to the actual GPOs that have been processed during the last processing cycle by that CSE (Figure 13-11). The values stored in these keys include the GPO's friendly name, its GUID, the path to the GPC and GPT, and most important, the version number of the GPO when it was last processed.

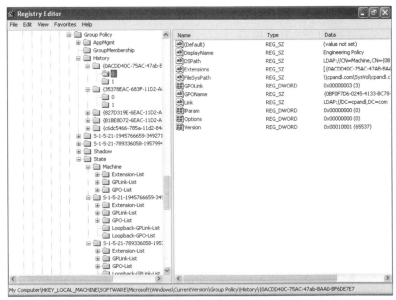

Figure 13-11   Viewing a GPO's history within the registry CSE key

The version information is used to compare the GPO currently being processed to the previously processed one. If the GPO being processed has a version number greater than the one held in the registry, the CSE continues processing the GPO. If the version number is equal to that held in the registry, the CSE stops processing the GPO unless you've overridden the default processing behavior for that CSE.

> **Note** The version number of the GPO about to be processed should never be less than that held in the history key. If it is, that indicates some kind of problem with your Group Policy infrastructure. If a GPO's version number is 0, it is not processed because it is assumed that there are no policies set on it.

The history information is also important in one other aspect of Group Policy processing that we haven't covered yet—the notion of the deleted list. Here's how the deleted list works:

1. A Windows computer must be able to determine when a GPO that used to apply no longer applies. To do this, it compares the history information in the registry to the current list of GPOs to process.

2. If some GPOs no longer apply, Windows knows that it might need to undo those policy settings (if the CSE supports such an undo). The GPOs that no longer apply are added to the deleted GPO list.

3. The CSEs that have responsibility for the deleted GPOs remove the related policy settings. If multiple GPOs for a given CSE no longer apply, the settings are removed in reverse precedence order to preserve the original processing hierarchy.

As an example of how the deleted GPO list is used, consider the following: Folder Redirection policy provides an option that lets you redirect folders back to their original location when the GPO no longer applies. To know that a GPO no longer applies, the Folder Redirection CSE has to build a deleted GPO list before processing policy. If it didn't do this, folders would never be redirected back to their original location.

Group Policy State Data

Group Policy state data is stored in the registry under *HKEY_CURRENT_USER\SOFTWARE\Microsoft\Windows\CurrentVersion\Group Policy\State*. State information is used primarily by RSoP logging to report on certain aspects of the last policy processing cycle. Some of these include whether a slow link was detected during the last processing cycle, the time at which policy processing was last performed, the state of each GPO link, and the state of each GPO that was processed. If you examine the contents of the state keys, you will see that they are arranged in per-computer (under the Machine key) and per-user (under SID-named keys) fashion.

The per-machine and per-user SID keys have three subkeys in common:

- *Extension-List*
- *GPLink-List*
- *GPO-List*

The *Extension-List* key usually contains a sub-key called {00000000-0000-0000-0000-000000000000}. This all-zero GUID stands for the core Group Policy Engine. Within this key, you will see values that list when the last computer-specific Group Policy processing cycle started and ended (such as, *StartTimeLo, StartTimeHi, EndTimeLo, EndTimeHi*). Other extension keys typically contain RSoP logging information. The *DiagnosticNamespace* value lists which namespace was processed for logging, such as *ENGPC07\ROOT\Rsop\Computer*.

> **Tip**   The Gptime.exe utility on the companion CD uses this start and stop state information to report the times and duration of the last Group Policy processing cycle.

All linked GPOs that were processed by this machine are listed in the *GPLink-List* key along with their link status—such as Enabled or Enforced (a.k.a. No Override). The *DsPath* value provides the DN of the linked GPO, such as *cn={9FC124A6-626F-4C4C-9BAE-D75B779D21BF},cn=policies,cn=system,DC=cpandl,DC=com*. The SOM value provides the scope of the linked GPO (which level the GPO applies to, such as *DC=cpandl,DC=com* for a GPO that applies to the domain scope). For the local machine GPO, the *DsPath* and *SOM* values are set to *LocalGPO* and *Local*, respectively.

Within the *GPO-List* key, information about each GPO that was processed is stored. The *AccessDenied* value indicates whether the GPO was skipped because security filtering prevented it from being processed. The *GPO-Disabled* value indicates whether the GPO was disabled. The *Options* value details any options that were set on the GPO (for example, whether the Computer Configuration or User Configuration portions of the GPO were disabled). The *GPOID* value contains the GPO GUID. The *GPO-List* information is used when reporting on RSoP using a tool such as Gpresult.exe or the GPMC Group Policy Results Wizard.

The per-user SID-named key has two additional sub-keys: *Loopback-GPLink-List* and *Loopback-GPO-List*. These subkeys are used when you change the default loopback processing mode. *Loopback-GPLink-List* contains information on all linked GPOs that were loopback processed, and *Loopback-GPO-List* contains information on the loopback processed GPOs themselves.

Group Membership Data

Group Policy caches group membership information to track the specific security groups that the computer and the currently logged on user belong to. The membership information is used determine whether and how security filtering will affect the list of GPOs that need to be processed, and because it is so critical, the information is updated each time policy is processed. The membership information is also used to provide output details for Gpresult.exe and the GPMC Group Policy Results Wizard when tracking security or examining security filtering details.

The SIDs for all security groups a computer belongs to are stored under the *HKEY_ LOCAL_MACHINE\SOFTWARE\Microsoft\Windows\CurrentVersion\Group Policy\ GroupMembership* key. For any users who have logged on to a computer, a list of the groups they belong to is stored according to their SID under the *HKEY_LOCAL_ MACHINE\SOFTWARE\Microsoft\Windows\CurrentVersion\Group Policy\<SID of user>\ GroupMembership* key.

If you examine the *GroupMembership* key, you'll find key values named *Group0*, *Group1*, *Group2*, and so on that contain the SID of the security group to which they relate. You'll also find a *Count* value, which provides a count of all the security groups that apply. For example, if four security groups apply, *Count* has a value of 4 and there are key values named *Group0*, *Group1*, *Group2*, and *Group3*.

Navigating Local GPO Structure

Local Group Policy objects (LGPOs) cannot be managed using GPMC. They are visible only in the GPMC as the result of RSoP logging reports that include LGPO settings that have been applied as part of normal policy processing. You can, however, access your computer's LGPO at any time by simply typing *gpedit.msc* at a command line. You can access a remote computer's LGPO by following the steps discussed in Chapter 2 under "Accessing Local Group Policy on a Remote Machine."

Understanding LGPO Creation and Application

When you perform a clean install of a new machine running Windows XP Professional or Windows Server 2003, there is initially no LGPO. The LGPO is created the first time you try to put settings in the LGPO. For example, if you try to view the LGPO by running Gpedit.msc, the LGPO is instantiated and a special Group Policy folder (%Windir%\System32\GroupPolicy) is created as well . Further, on machines without an LGPO, the LGPO is not processed during foreground or background policy processing. Policy application from LGPO only happens when there are some settings in the LGPO (indicated by Gpt.ini having a nonzero version number).

While editing the LGPO settings on a computer running Windows XP or later, you might find that some settings are dimmed. This can occur because policy settings enabled or disabled through domain-based policy cannot be overridden by LGPO settings. In Windows 2000, you were allowed to configure the LGPO settings that would be overridden by site, domain, or OU policy. In Windows XP Professional and later, those settings are dimmed in the interface because no policy setting change you can make locally will override site, domain, or OU policy.

The LGPO is not affected in any way by settings in other GPOs. If you enable or disable a setting anywhere in the domain, it will not impact what you see in the LGPO. The settings you see in the LGPO are simply whatever settings that administrator set in the LGPO.

Understanding LGPO Structure

Local GPOs are structured a bit differently than Active Directory–based GPOs. The LGPO is stored on the local file system of your Windows computer—specifically, within the %Windir%\System32\GroupPolicy folder. If you examine the LGPO on a given Windows computer, you will notice that its file structure is similar to that found within the GPT for an Active Directory–based GPO. There are the familiar ADM, Machine, and User folders as well as the Gpt.ini file that holds version information for the LGPO.

The *gPCMachineExtensionNames* and *gPCMachineUserNames* attributes, which are unique to the Gpt.ini file on the LGPO, are stored within this file because there is no GPC available to store them. These attributes serve the same purpose as their Active Directory counterparts. They tell Group Policy processing which CSEs should be run on the local GPO based on which policy areas have been set.

If you drill into the Machine or User folders under the GroupPolicy folder, you will find a Registry.pol file that contains Administrative Templates policy settings. Also, if you've defined machine or user scripts, you will see a scripts directory that contains subfolders for startup, shutdown, logon, and logoff scripts. However, if you define security policy on the local GPO, the changes are made directly to the local machine's security database rather than stored in a file within the GroupPolicy folder or elsewhere. The security database is stored in the Secedit.sdb file in the %Windor\Security\Database folder.

Managing and Maintaining LGPOs

Because the LGPO cannot be managed by the GPMC, you cannot perform many of the management tasks that are supported by the GPMC. Chief among these tasks is the ability to back up and copy the LGPO between computers. While there is no supported mechanism for copying the LGPO, most LGPO settings are merely files on a computer's local file system, so you can usually copy them between computers without too much trouble.

Specifically, if you have made some changes to a LGPO on one computer and you need to propagate those changes to other computers but you don't have the ability to deploy Active Directory—the preferred mechanism for Group Policy deployment—you can copy the contents of %Windir%\System32\GroupPolicy between computers using a simple copy command, where *NewComputer* is the name of the computer to which you want to copy the local policy settings:

```
xcopy %windir%\system32\GroupPolicy \\NewComputer\admin$\system32\GroupPolicy /e
```

You don't need to copy the entire set of policy between computers. You can copy only part of the policy settings. For example, if you want to copy the local Administrative Templates settings between computers, you can do this by copying the Registry.pol file. Similarly, if you defined a startup script in the LGPO on Computer A and want to propagate that startup script to other computers in your environment, you can simply copy the contents of %Windir%\System32\GroupPolicy\User\Scripts\Logon (including the Scripts.ini file) to the remote machines and the script will be deployed. You would also need to modify the Gpt.ini on the target machine to list the proper CSEs in the extensions list.

If you need to copy security policy between local computers, you can do this by copying the security database (Secedit.sdb), located in %windir%\security\database. Because not all security-related changes are in the security database, however, you might want to create a security template file that represents your local security policy and then use the Secedit.exe utility to apply that template to all of your computers instead. See Chapter 15 for more details about customizing security templates.

> **Tip** Any time you work with the LGPO, you must ensure that the related Gpt.ini has a version number greater than 0. For example, if you copy a Registry.pol file from one computer's LGPO to another computer that has not had any Local Group Policy defined, the version number on that LGPO will be 0. If this number isn't changed, the LGPO will be skipped during Group Policy processing. Therefore, it's a good idea to increment the version number within the Gpt.ini file so it is greater than 0 and greater than it was during the last processing cycle. Otherwise, your new policy settings will never be processed.

Controlling Access to the LGPO

Restricting computer access to the LGPO has no meaning because, by definition, only one computer can process the LGPO. On the other hand, you might need to control which users will process a local GPO. Unfortunately, there isn't a Group Policy editing tool for managing the delegation and security filtering on LGPOs.

A limited way to manage security on LGPOs is to modify the NTFS permissions on the files that make up the LGPO. For example, if you don't want desktop restrictions to apply to local administrators, you can prevent administrative users from processing Administrative Templates policy—the Registry.pol file.

The Registry.pol file is found in the %Windir%\System32\GroupPolicy\User folders. By default, this file grants Administrators Full Control rights over the file. By removing Read permissions for Administrators, you effectively prevent local administrators from being able to read, and thus process, the Registry.pol file. By allowing Write permission, you ensure that Administrators still have access to Administrative Templates policy for editing purposes.

Note Controlling access to the LGPO is relevant only for users who log on to a computer using local credentials. If a domain user logs on to a computer, you can, of course, use domain-based GPOs to manage that user.

Tip You can modify NTFS permissions on other policy files (including scripts and Internet Explorer maintenance policy) just as easily. Keep in mind, however, that this approach is not very manageable. It is always risky to modify the default permissions, and if you make a mistake, you might prevent critical policy settings from being applied. For this reason, always thoroughly test any changes you make before deploying them in production.

Summary

Within Group Policy, there is a logical and physical representation of every Group Policy object (GPO). The logical component of a GPO is a Group Policy container (GPC), which is stored in Active Directory. The physical component is a Group Policy template (GPT), which is stored on the file systems of domain controllers. If you understand this structure and how it is processed, you will be better equipped to troubleshoot advanced Group Policy issues. While LGPOs don't have a corresponding GPC or GPT, most policy settings are stored on a computer's local disk. You can manage file-based LGPO settings in a limited way. Primarily, you do this using the copy command and configuring file system permissions.

Chapter 14
Customizing Administrative Templates

In this chapter:

What Is an Administrative Template?............................516
Creating Custom .adm Files....................................525
A Simple .adm File...526
Using .adm File Language 527
Best Practices 550
Summary 552

Microsoft® Windows Server™ 2003 uses administrative templates within Group Policy for configuring registry settings. With the release of Windows Server 2003 SP1, more than 1300 default settings are specified by the administrative templates in a new Group Policy object (GPO). Even so, you will want to customize numerous settings through your own administrative templates.

In this chapter, we will look closely at administrative templates. We will describe how administrative templates are used to create the interface within a GPO, and we will explain how the administrative template is structured to modify the registry values and data. Administrative templates are unquestionably an integral part of Group Policy. Microsoft has used them since Microsoft Windows® 95 and Windows NT®, when system policies were the method of controlling security and the computing environment.

Related Information

- For information on using administrative templates to configure desktops, see Chapter 6.

- For information on Microsoft Office administrative templates, download the Office Resource Kit Tools at *http://office.microsoft.com/en-us/FX011511471033.aspx*.

What Is an Administrative Template?

Administrative template files describe where registry-based policy settings are stored in the registry. Administrative template files, typically referred to as .adm files, do not affect the actual policy processing by the administrative templates client-side extension (CSE). The .adm files affect only the display of the policy settings in the Group Policy Object Editor snap-in. If the .adm file is removed from a Group Policy object (GPO), the settings corresponding to the .adm file will not appear in the Group Policy Object Editor.

The .adm files are Unicode text files that enable a user interface to allow you to modify registry-based policy settings using the Group Policy Object Editor. After a setting that is established using the .adm files is configured within the Group Policy Object Editor, the setting information is stored in the Registry.pol file located in the Group Policy Template (GPT) for the GPO. The actual policy settings are stored in the Registry.pol file, so the .adm file can be removed from the GPO, but the setting remains in the Registry.pol file and continues to apply to the appropriate target computer or user.

More than 1300 administrative template settings are available, and administrators can add hundreds more custom settings.

Default .adm Files

Every Windows 2000, Windows XP, and Windows Server 2003 computer comes with some default .adm files. These files are used to create the default interface under the Administrative Templates portions of a GPO. The standard .adm files are listed in Table 14-1.

Table 14-1   Standard .adm Files

.adm Template	Features
Common.adm	Policy settings for the user interface common to Windows NT 4.0 and Windows 9x. Designed to be used with System Policy Editor (Poledit.exe).
Conf.adm	Policy settings for configuring Microsoft NetMeeting®. Conf.adm is loaded by default in Windows 2000 Server, Windows XP, and Windows Server 2003. (It is not available on Windows XP 64-Bit Edition and the 64-bit versions of the Windows Server 2003 family.)
Inetcorp.adm	Policy settings for dial-up, language, and control over Temporary Internet Files settings.
Inetres.adm	Policy settings for configuring Microsoft Internet Explorer. Inetres .adm is loaded by default in Windows 2000 Server, Windows XP, and Windows Server 2003.

Table 14-1   Standard .adm Files

.adm Template	Features
Inetset.adm	Policy settings for additional Internet properties: autocomplete, display settings, and some advanced settings.
System.adm	Policy settings for configuring the operating system. System.adm is loaded by default in Windows Server 2000, Windows XP, and Windows Server 2003.
Windows.adm	Policy settings for the user interface options specific to Windows 9x. Designed to be used with System Policy Editor (Poledit.exe).
Winnt.adm	Policy settings for the user interface options specific to Windows NT 4.0. Designed to be used with System Policy Editor (Poledit.exe).
Wmplayer.adm	Policy settings for configuring Microsoft Windows Media® Player. Wmplayer.adm is loaded by default in Windows XP and Windows Server 2003. It is not available on Windows XP 64-Bit Edition and the 64-bit versions of the Windows Server 2003 family.
Wuau.adm	Policy settings for configuring Windows Update. Wuau.adm is loaded by default in Windows 2000 Service Pack 3 (SP3), Windows XP Service Pack 1 (SP1), and Windows Server 2003.

The .adm files that ship with Windows Server 2003, Windows XP Professional, and Windows 2000 Server are located in the %windir%\inf folder.

Additional .adm files are available for security settings, Internet Explorer, Microsoft Office, and more. Some applications also come with their own .adm files to help centralize administration and customization of the application. Table 14-2 lists the current Office 2003 and Internet Explorer .adm files that you can obtain from the Office Administration Kit and the Windows Server 2003 Resource Kit.

Table 14-2   Office 2003 and Internet Explorer .adm Files

Office Template	Features
Aer_1033.adm	Microsoft Office 2003 Application Error Reporting client configuration.
Access11.adm	Microsoft Access 2003 settings.
Dw20.adm	Old Office Application Reporting configuration file, replaced with Aer_1033.adm.
Excel11.adm	Microsoft Excel 2003 settings.
Fp11.adm	Microsoft FrontPage® 2003 settings.
Gal11.adm	Microsoft Clip Organizer settings.
Inf11.adm	Microsoft InfoPath™ 2003 settings.
Instlr11.adm	Microsoft Windows Installer settings.
Office11.adm	Common Office 2003 settings.
Onent11.adm	Microsoft OneNote® 2003 settings.

Table 14-2   Office 2003 and Internet Explorer .adm Files

Office Template	Features
Outlk11.adm	Microsoft Outlook® 2003 settings.
Ppt11.adm	Microsoft PowerPoint® 2003 settings.
Pub11.adm	Microsoft Publisher 2003 settings.
Word11.adm	Microsoft Word 2003 settings.
Internet Explorer Template	**Features**
Aaxa.adm	Data Binding settings.
Chat.adm	Microsoft Chat settings.
Inetesc.adm	Microsoft Internet Explorer Enhanced Security Configuration settings.
Oe.adm	Microsoft Outlook Express Identity Manager settings. Use this to prevent users from changing or configuring identities.
Sp1shell.adm	Active Desktop settings.
Subs.adm	Offline Pages settings.
Wmp.adm	Windows Media Player, Radio Toolbar, and Network Settings customizations.

Working with .adm Files

Acquiring an .adm file is only the first step in the process of updating the registry on a target computer or user account. You must then properly insert it into the GPO structure. You do this by importing the .adm file into the GPO that will target the computer or user accounts. The settings that are established in the .adm file will show up when the GPO is edited in the Group Policy Object Editor, allowing the policy to be configured. Several default .adm files are imported into every standard GPO, however, which creates the default administrative template section under both Computer Configuration and User Configuration.

Default Installed .adm Files

Every new GPO has default Administrative Template sections. These sections are created by three or more .adm files, depending on the operating system you are working with. The following is a list of the default .adm files associated with each operating system:

- Windows 2000: Conf.adm, Inetres.adm, System.adm. (Wuau.adm is also installed on computers running Windows 2000 SP3 or later.)

- Windows XP Professional: Conf.adm, Inetres.adm, System.adm, Wmplayer.adm. (Wuau.adm is also installed on computers running Windows XP Professional SP1 or later.)

- Windows Server 2003: Conf.adm, Inetres.adm, System.adm, Wmplayer.adm, Wuau.adm.

Each successive version of an operating system has more features that need to be controlled. Windows XP includes an .adm file to control Windows Media Player. Windows Server 2003 added a new .adm file for controlling the Windows Update and Software Update Service (SUS) features. From version to version, the standard .adm files have changed slightly.

Before you add or remove any .adm files, you can view a list of the default .adm files used with all new GPOs created on a Windows Server 2003 computer (Figure 14-1).

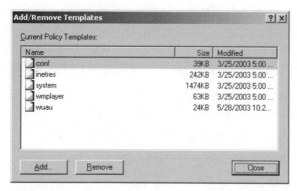

Figure 14-1   Default .adm files for Windows Server 2003 GPOs

Tips for Importing .adm Files

If you want to use a particular .adm file to configure some policy settings in a GPO, you must import it into the GPO. The following tips will help the import process go smoothly:

- Make sure that the syntax of the .adm file is correct. If it is incorrect, you will receive an error message during the import process indicating that an error was recognized within the .adm file.

- A single .adm file can contain both computer and user registry–based settings. The Group Policy Object Editor handles the separation of the two sections when it displays the GPO with the new .adm template inserted.

- You can store the .adm file anywhere you want before you import it into the GPO. During the import procedure, you can browse for the file on the local computer or on the network.

- After you import an .adm file into a GPO, it is available to be configured in that GPO only. If you want the .adm file settings to be available for a different GPOs, you must import the .adm file into each GPO.

■ The importing of the .adm file makes a copy of the file in the GPO structure stored in the SYSVOL of the domain controllers. The .adm file is copied into the Adm subfolder under the correct GPO folder represented by the GPO GUID.

 More Info   For more information on the GPO structure and the SYSVOL share, see Chapter 13.

Adding .adm Files

Let's look at an example in which you need to add the Visio11.adm template to a GPO named OFFICE11. The Visio11.adm template is currently located on the desktop of the computer from which you are editing the GPO. To add the template, complete these steps after opening the OFFICE11 GPO in the Group Policy Object Editor:

1. Right-click the Administrative Templates node under the Computer Configuration section of the GPO and then choose Add/Remove Templates.

2. In the Add/Remove Templates dialog box, click Add.

3. In the Policy Templates dialog box, select Desktop in the left pane.

4. Select the Visio11.adm file in the list. Click Open. You will see the Add/Remove Templates dialog box with the Visio11.adm file listed, as shown in Figure 14-2.

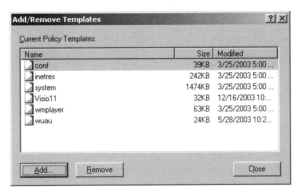

Figure 14-2   Visio11.adm template added to a GPO

5. Click Close.

6. After the .adm file has been imported to the GPO, you can see the Microsoft Visio node and policy settings in the GPO, as shown in Figure 14-3.

Figure 14-3   Visio® 2003 policy settings after the Visio11.adm file is added to the GPO

Note   By default, newly created GPOs that have not been edited will create a new GPT, but without any associated .adm files. Once the GPO is edited with the Group Policy Object Editor, the .adm files from the %windir%\Inf folder of the computer performing the administration are copied to the GPT.

Removing .adm Files

Sometimes you might need to remove an .adm file from a GPO. This removes any settings from the Group Policy Object Editor that were created by the .adm file.

Note   If a policy was configured using the settings in the .adm file before the .adm file was removed from the GPO, the policy setting will still be active in the GPO. The policy settings are stored not in the .adm file but in the Registry.pol file. You should modify all settings made using the .adm files as needed before you remove the .adm files from the GPO. For more information about the Registry.pol file, see Chapter 13.

Much like our example of adding an .adm file to a GPO, we will now walk through an example of removing an .adm file. To remove the Visio11.adm file from the OFFICE11 GPO, complete these steps:

1. Right-click the Administrative Templates node under the Computer Configuration section of the GPO and then choose Add/Remove Templates.

2. In the Add/Remove Templates dialog box, select the Visio11.adm template in the list of templates and then click Remove. The template is removed from the list.

3. Click Close.

Managing .adm Files

Over time you will make changes to the custom .adm files that you have implemented within your GPOs. Built-in controls are available that help update new versions of the .adm files. To make this process easier, it is best to have a dedicated workstation for creating and modifying GPOs.

Controlling Updated Versions of .adm Files

The default behavior of controlling updated .adm files ensures that the latest version of the files are located in the GPT for the GPO. There are two aspects to how .adm files are updated and referenced. First, the .adm file timestamp is referenced. The timestamp of the local .adm file in the %windir%\Inf folder is compared to the .adm file in the GPT. If the local .adm file is newer than the GPT version, the local .adm file is copied to the GPT, replacing the current .adm file in the GPT. Second, the Group Policy Object Editor uses the .adm file from the GPT to create the interface within the Administrative Templates nodes within the GPO.

Two GPO settings control this behavior:

■ Turn Off Automatic Updates Of ADM Files

■ Always Use Local ADM Files For The Group Policy Editor

Turn Off Automatic Updates Of ADM Files   This GPO setting can be found at the following location: User Configuration\Administrative Templates\System\Group Policy. This policy controls whether the timestamps of the two .adm files are compared and the latest one placed in the GPT. By default, the timestamp is compared and the newer .adm file is placed in the GPT.

When this policy is set to Enabled, the .adm file timestamps are not checked for newer versions, so the GPT is not updated. When this policy is set to Disabled, the .adm files are checked, and if the .adm file from the local computer performing the administration has a newer timestamp, the .adm file stored in the GPT of the GPO is updated.

Always Use Local ADM Files For Group Policy Editor   This GPO setting can be found at the following location: Computer Configuration\Administrative Templates\System\Group Policy. This policy controls which .adm file is used to create the interface of the GPO when edited. By default, the .adm file that is stored in the GPT is used.

When this policy is set to Enabled, the .adm files from the local computer are used. The results can be undesirable if the local .adm files are updated without your knowledge.

When this policy is set to Disabled, the .adm files from the GPT of the GPO are used. This creates a safer environment for version control and ensures that all policies can be viewed consistently from any computer.

Tips for Working with .adm Files

Here are some tips for working with .adm files.

- If the saved GPO contains registry settings for which there is no corresponding .adm file, these settings will not appear in the Group Policy Object Editor. They will still be active, however, and will be applied to users or computers targeted by the GPO.

- Because of the importance of timestamps to .adm file management, you should not edit the standard .adm files. If a new policy setting is required, create a custom .adm file.

- The GPMC controls the .adm files in a much different manner when it creates HTLM reports, uses Group Policy Modeling, and generates Group Policy Results.

> **More Info**   For more information on the GPMC and how it handles .adm files, see Chapter 3.

- Windows XP Professional does not support the Always Use Local ADM Files For Group Policy Editor policy setting. Therefore, if your GPO administrative computer is a Windows XP Professional computer, you must use the .adm files stored in the GPT.

> **More Info**   For more information on the structure of the GPO structure and the GPT, see Chapter 13.

Operating System and Service Pack Release Issues

Each operating system or service pack release includes a superset of the .adm files provided by earlier releases, including policy settings specific to earlier versions of the operating system. For example, the .adm files provided with Windows Server 2003 include all policy settings for all earlier versions of Windows, including settings relevant only to Windows 2000 or Windows XP Professional. This means that merely viewing a GPO from a computer with the new release of an operating system or service pack effectively upgrades the .adm files for that GPO. Because later releases are a superset of previous .adm files, this typically does not create problems (as long as the .adm files being used have not been edited).

In some situations, an operating system or service pack release includes a subset of the .adm files that were provided with earlier releases, potentially resulting in policy settings no longer being visible to administrators when they use Group Policy Object Editor. However, the policy settings remain active in the GPO. Any active (either **Enabled** or **Disabled**) policy settings are not visible in Group Policy Object Editor. Because the settings are not visible, an administrator cannot easily view or edit them. To work around this issue, you must become familiar with the .adm files included with each operating system or service pack release *before* using Group Policy Object Editor on that operating system. You must also keep in mind that the act of viewing a GPO is enough to update the .adm files in the GPT when the timestamp comparison determines that an update is appropriate.

To plan for such potential issues in your environment, it is recommended that you do one of the following:

- Define a standard operating system/service pack for all viewing and editing of GPOs, making sure that the .adm files being used include the policy settings for all platforms in your enterprise.

- Use the Turn Off Automatic Updates Of ADM policy setting for all Group Policy administrators to make sure that .adm files are not overwritten in the SYSVOL by any Group Policy Object Editor session, and make sure that you are using the latest .adm files from Microsoft.

Policies vs. Preferences

Policies are registry-based settings that can be fully managed by administrators and Group Policy. They are also referred to as *true policies*. In contrast, registry-based settings that are configured by users or are set as a default state by the operating system at installation are referred to as *preferences*.

True policies are stored under approved registry keys. These keys are not accessible by users, so they are protected from being changed or disabled. The four approved registry keys are shown in Table 14-3.

Table 14-3   Approved Registry Key Locations for Group Policy Settings

Computer-Based Policy Settings	User-Based Policy Settings
HKLM\Software\Policies	HKCU\Software\Policies
HKLM\Software\Microsoft\Windows\CurrentVersion\Policies	HKCU\Software\Microsoft\Windows\CurrentVersion\Policies

Preferences are registry-based settings that are located in registry keys other than the approved registry keys listed in Table 14-3. Users can typically change their preferences at any time. For example, users can decide to set their wallpaper to a different bitmap. Most users are familiar with setting preferences through the operating system or application user interface.

You can create custom .adm files that set registry values outside of the approved registry keys. When you do create these preferences, you only ensure that a given registry key or value is set in a particular way. These preferences are not secured as true policies are; users can access these settings and modify them. Another issue with preferences is that the settings persist in the registry. The only way to alter preferences is to configure them using the .adm file or to manually update the registry.

In contrast, true policy settings have access control list (ACL) restrictions to prevent users from changing them, and the policy values are removed when the GPO that set them goes out of scope (when the GPO is unlinked, disabled, or deleted). For this reason, true policies are considered to be policy settings that can be fully managed. By default, the Group Policy Object Editor shows only true policy settings that can be fully managed. To view preferences in the Group Policy Object Editor, you click the Administrative Templates node, click View, click Filtering, and then clear Only Show Policy Settings That Can Be Fully Managed.

 Note To learn more about controlling policies and preferences using the Group Policy Object Editor, see Chapter 3.

True policy settings take priority over preferences, but they do not overwrite or modify the registry keys used by the preferences. If a policy setting is deployed that conflicts with a preference, the policy setting takes precedence over the preference setting. If a conflicting policy setting is removed, the original user preference setting remains intact and configures the computer.

Creating Custom .adm Files

In addition to the hundreds of default settings in the standard .adm files, you will undoubtedly want more registry-based policy settings for applications and components installed on computers within your organization. To create and implement custom .adm files, complete the following steps:

1. Determine the specific registry path, value, and data. This step might not be as easy at it seems, considering the complexity of the registry and some of the registry value names. A good way to track down this information is to reference the standard .adm files to find the correct registry path for similar settings.

> **Tip**   You can also use tools to help you track down registry values as they are changed from within the operating system or application. An excellent tool for this task is REGMON, which can be found at *http://www.sysinternals.com/ntw2k/source/regmon.shtml*.

2. Develop the .adm file, including the information gathered in step 1. Custom .adm files are created as Unicode text files that describe policy settings. A framework language is provided for .adm files, as described in the "Language Reference for .adm Files" section in this chapter.

3. Import the .adm file into a GPO. Each GPO can have a unique set of .adm files, so you must do this for each GPO that will distribute the custom registry settings configured within the .adm file.

4. Use Group Policy Object Editor to view and configure the custom entries under the Administrative Templates nodes, which were created by the .adm file. This is where you establish the settings that will configure the user accounts or computers in the domain.

> **Note**   Keep in mind that the .adm file does not actually apply any settings to the computer or user account. The policy within the GPO must be configured first, then the target user or computer must have a corresponding component or application that responds to the registry value affected by the policy setting.

A Simple .adm File

To get an idea of what an .adm file looks like, we will look at a simple example, which is a snippet from the System.adm file. You can look at the larger System.adm file to see what the code looks like within a larger .adm file.

```
CLASS USER
CATEGORY !!DesktopLockDown
    POLICY !!DisableTaskMgr
        EXPLAIN !!DisableTaskMgr_Explain
        VALUENAME "DisableTaskMgr"
        VALUEON NUMERIC 1
        VALUEOFF NUMERIC 0
        KEYNAME "Software\Policies\System"
    END POLICY
END CATEGORY
[strings]
DisableTaskMgr="Disable Task Manager"
DisableTaskMgr_Explain="Prevents users from starting Task Manager"
DesktopLockDown="Desktop Settings"
```

This policy setting defines the following behavior:

- When enabled, this policy setting creates a registry key called *DisableTaskMgr* and sets its value to 1. The **VALUEON** tag implements this behavior. After this policy is implemented, users cannot start Task Manager.

- When disabled, this policy setting creates a registry key called *DisableTaskMgr* and sets its value to 0. The **VALUEOFF** tag implements this behavior. After this policy is implemented, users can start Task Manager.

- In both cases, the *DisableTaskMgr* registry key is created below **HKCU\ Software\Policies\System** in the registry. Note that the key is created under **CLASS USER** and not under **CLASS MACHINE** because this is a user policy setting. You will find this policy under the User Configuration node within Group Policy Object Editor.

- When set to Not Configured, this policy setting deletes the registry key called *DisableTaskMgr*.

Using .adm File Language

If you have a custom registry value that you need to distribute and configure to all computers in the organization or just a select few computers in the organization, you should use custom .adm files. To create these files, you must use and understand the .adm file language. Don't fret—the language is simple and easy to pick up. This section will give you all of the information you need to create your own .adm files for importing into a GPO.

Structure of an .adm File

An .adm file is designed for two functions. The first function is to create the interface within the Group Policy Object Editor for the registry values that you want configured on users or machines targeted by a GPO. This formatting is the same for all .adm files, so you can use existing .adm files as a guide. The second function of the .adm file is to format the registry path, value, and data that will be updated in the target computer's registry. Again, this syntax is the same for all .adm files and is easy to follow.

> **Note** Although the syntax is easy to follow for the registry path in the .adm file, the path must be accurate or you could potentially corrupt the registry on the target computer.

Take a look at the following .adm file example. It enables the computer to log on without any user input by using a predetermined user name and password.

```
CLASS MACHINE
CATEGORY "Microsoft Custom ADM Entries"
   POLICY "Automatic Logon"
```

```
KEYNAME "SOFTWARE\Microsoft\WindowsNT\CurrentVersion\Winlogon"
    PART "What is the name of the user?" EDITTEXT
    VALUENAME "autoadminlogon"
    END PART
    PART "What is the user's password?" EDITTEXT
    VALUENAME "defaultpassword"
    END PART
    END POLICY
END CATEGORY
```

You can see that the structure of the .adm file is very methodical. If you look closely at the example, you can see that there are some rules that must be adhered to. One such rule is the need to include an END syntax for PART, POLICY, and CATEGORY entries.

Take a look at the structure of the example to evaluate the key components that you need to fully understand:

- **CLASS MACHINE**   Specifies that the registry HKEY that we are modifying is under HKEY_Local_Machine.

- **CATEGORY**   Specifies the name that will be given to the folder that will appear in the Group Policy Object Editor. In our example, it is Microsoft Custom ADM Entries.

- **POLICY**   Specifies the name we are giving to the policy that will show up in the Group Policy Object Editor. In our example, it will show up as Automatic Logon.

- **KEYNAME**   Specifies the path in the registry where the value that will be modified exists. Notice that KEYNAME does not include the HKEY name or the name of the value.

- **PART**   Specifies to the Group Policy Object Editor that input will be required from the administrator of the GPO.

- **EDITTEXT**   Specifies that a text box will be presented to allow the administrator to type text for the data of the registry value.

- **VALUENAME**   Specifies the exact registry value that is being modified. Notice that VALUENAME is not the specified data for the registry value (the string or setting associated with the registry value); rather, it is the name of the Registry value. The data for the registry value will be input through the Group Policy Editor.

- **END PART**   Indicates to the Group Policy Object Editor that the syntax related to this PART is done.

- **END POLICY**   Indicates to the Group Policy Object Editor that the syntax related to this POLICY is done.

■ **END CATEGORY** Indicates to the Group Policy Object Editor that the syntax related to this CATEGORY is done.

If you were to create a shell of what a standard administrative template structure should look like, it would look something like this:

```
CLASS (Group Policy Editor and Registry)
CATEGORY (Group Policy Editor)
KEYNAME (Registry)
POLICY (Group Policy Editor)
PART (Group Policy Editor)
VALUENAME (Registry)
```

To create your own .adm files, you must build on this structure and understand all of the syntax that can be placed in the .adm files. We will do this by breaking down the syntax into two categories: the interface for the Group Policy Object Editor and the registry path and value inputs.

#if version

Instead of creating an .adm file for each set of operating system settings, you can use the *#if version* syntax within one .adm file to break up the settings. The *#if version* syntax breaks up the .adm file into zones, with each zone targeting a specific operating system range. The standard .adm files use this method to create these zones, providing settings for older operating systems and newer operating systems in a single .adm file.

Each operating system matches up with a specific version number within the .adm file. Table 14-4 specifies each operating system and the .adm file *#if syntax* version number associated with it.

Table 14-4   #if Syntax Version Number by Operating System

Operating System	Version	Type
Windows Server 2003 SP1	5.0	Group Policy
Windows XP SP2	5.0	Group Policy
Windows Server 2003 and Windows XP	4.0	Group Policy
Windows Server 2000	3.0	Group Policy
Windows NT 3.x and 4.x	2.0	Group Policy
Windows 95	1.0	System Policy

In some instances, the *#if version* syntax can be omitted and the .adm code can span multiple operating system generations. This is possible because the registry value and location of the setting is the same for the different operating systems.

You can control the *#if version* syntax by adding operators to control ranges of operating systems that the .adm syntax should affect. Here are the operators that can be used with the *#if version* syntax.

>	Greater than
<	Less than
==	Equal to
!=	Not equal to
>=	Greater than or equal to
<=	Less than or equal to

Syntax for Updating the Registry

You know that the .adm file generates the interface for the Group Policy Object Editor and specifies the registry path, value, and data. Specific syntax is used within the .adm file to handle all of these variables.

The syntax that builds the Group Policy Object Editor interface is essential within the .adm file. If any syntax for one of these components is missing, the file will fail to work properly. The syntax used to build the registry path, value, and data includes: CLASS, KEYNAME, VALUENAME, VALUEON/VALUEOFF, and PART.

CLASS

There are two CLASS options: MACHINE and USER. The CLASS syntax indicates which portion of the registry will be modified. If the MACHINE option is specified, the GPO will modify the HKEY_Local_Machine handle in the registry. If the USER option is specified, the GPO will modify the HKEY_Current_User handle in the registry.

> **Note**   There are only two primary handles within the registry: HKEY_Local_Machine and HKEY_Users. The other three handles are subsets of these two primary handles. The HKEY_Current_User handle is a subset of the HKEY_Users handle. The HKEY_Current_User handle is the current user's profile that is placed in the registry when the user logs on.

You need to use the CLASS syntax only once for each of the MACHINE and USER options. All of the registry settings that fall under the HKEY_Local_Machine handle will be grouped together, after the CLASS MACHINE syntax is listed. The same goes for the registry settings that fall under the HKEY_Current_User handle and the CLASS USER syntax.

Note   If there are multiple CLASS MACHINE or CLASS USER sections in the same .adm file, they will be merged together when the Group Policy Object Editor interface is created.

If the .adm file you are creating will refer to only one of the registry handles, you list only that CLASS syntax in the .adm file.

The CLASS syntax also places the interface changes under Computer Configuration or User Configuration, based on MACHINE or USER, respectively. When the Group Policy Object Editor accesses the .adm file, it places the interface settings under the proper node.

Note   There is no END CLASS statement associated with the CLASS syntax.

KEYNAME

The KEYNAME syntax is not optional within the .adm file. KEYNAME specifies the path from the HKEY to the registry value. KEYNAME comes after the CATEGORY syntax and either before or after the POLICY syntax, depending on how you choose to structure the .adm file. However, KEYNAME must come after the CLASS syntax and before the PART or VALUENAME syntax.

Note   If you want to group multiple policy settings together that reside under the same path in the registry, you can place the KEYNAME entry after the CATEGORY syntax. This results in a grouping of all the entries following the CATEGORY syntax under the same folder in the Group Policy Object Editor.

The KEYNAME syntax indicates the path to the registry value. Do not include HKEY_Local_Machine or HKEY_Current_User in the registry path—this is handled by the CLASS syntax. You also don't need to use an introductory slash (/) to start the path within the KEYNAME text. For our example, the KEYNAME entry is as follows:

```
KEYNAME SOFTWARE\Microsoft\WindowsNT\CurrentVersion\Winlogon
```

If there is a space within the path following the KEYNAME syntax, you must put quotation marks (") around the entire path string, but don't include the KEYNAME word in the quotes. Here is an example of an entry that requires quotes:

```
KEYNAME "SOFTWARE\Microsoft\Windows NT\CurrentVersion\Winlogon"
```

Note   There is no END KEYNAME statement associated with the KEYNAME syntax.

VALUENAME

VALUENAME references the registry value that will be updated. You must find the approved registry value name—you are not allowed to make up registry values. If the computer registry is updated with an incorrect registry value, the computer might experience a stop error. Values in the registry are typically cryptic words that are not found in a dictionary.

You can use two methods to modify the values specified with the VALUENAME syntax. These methods are controlled by the values that the registry can handle.

- Many registry values support only two numeric values: 0 and 1. If the numeric value is 0, the registry value is off. If the numeric value is 1, the registry value is on. When the registry value is controlled in this fashion, you use the VALUEOFF/VALUEON syntax.

- The other registry values require text or more than just 0 or 1 numeric values. These registry values are controlled using the PART syntax.

When you use the VALUEOFF/VALUEON syntax, you are directly affecting the behavior of the registry value. When you use the PART syntax, you are modifying the Group Policy Object Editor, which allows for a more complex entry to be set for the registry value.

 Note   There is no END VALUENAME statement associated with the VALUENAME syntax.

VALUEOFF/VALUEON

The VALUEOFF/VALUEON syntax works like a switch. The registry value is either off or on. This goes back to the simple use of binary values of 0s and 1s. When you look at many of the registry entries in the Registry Editor, you will see that they actually support the string data type, which is denoted at REG_SZ. This does not alter the behavior or the limited values that the registry value supports.

Here is an example of a standard .adm entry that uses VALUEON and VALUEOFF:

```
KEYNAME "Software\Microsoft\Windows\CurrentVersion\Policies\System"
VALUENAME "HideStartupScripts"
VALUEON NUMERIC 0
VALUEOFF NUMERIC 1
```

For this .adm entry, no input is required once you are in the Group Policy Object Editor. You have only the ability to enable or disable the policy to toggle between the VALUEOFF and VALUEON numeric values. The Group Policy Object Editor shows this policy with the standard interface, as shown in Figure 14-4.

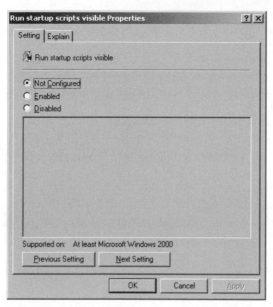

Figure 14-4   A registry value determined by the VALUEON/VALUEOFF syntax
in the .adm file

There are three options: Not Configured, Enabled, and Disabled.

- **Not Configured**   Does not set any entry for the registry value; instead, it leaves the registry value as it is set on the computer.

- **Enabled**   Sets the registry value to the VALUEON specified numeric value.

- **Disabled**   Sets the registry value to the VALUEOFF specified numeric value.

You can use a second method that is indirectly associated with the VALUEOFF/ VALUEON syntax; you use this method when you don't explicitly use the VALUEOFF and VALUEON statements. Here is a sample of what that might look like:

```
POLICY!!EnableSlowLinkDetect
   EXPLAIN !!EnableSlowLinkDetect_Help
   KEYNAME "Software\Policies\Microsoft\Windows\System"
   VALUENAME "SlowLinkDetectEnabled"
END POLICY
```

Notice that there is no explicit use of VALUEON/VALUEOFF, but the behavior is similar. In this example, the three settings of the GPO policy behave in the following manner:

- **Not Configured**   Nothing is changed in the registry.

- **Enabled**   Sets the registry value to a numeric value of 1.

- **Disabled**   Deletes the registry value.

Note the policy-disabled state. The value is not written to the registry with the value of 0; instead, it is explicitly deleted. This means that a component reading the policy will not find the value in the registry and will fall back to using the default in the code.

> **Note**   There is no END VALUEON/VALUEOFF statement associated with the VALUEON/VALUEOFF syntax.

Syntax for Updating the Group Policy Object Editor Interface

The .adm files do more than just indicate the registry path, value, and data that need to be updated. They also configure the interface of the Group Policy Object Editor. The interface configurations are essential because the Group Policy Object Editor interface is where the actual configurations are made.

Four main areas of syntax create the interface within Group Policy Object Editor:

- STRINGS
- CATEGORY
- POLICY
- PART

The CATEGORY and POLICY syntax are the only required entries in the .adm file, but the other two variables are important. The STRINGS syntax is used extensively in the standard .adm files, but it is seldom used in custom .adm files. The PART syntax is used when the registry value or values being referenced require more than an ON or OFF configuration.

STRINGS

The STRINGS syntax is used to help organize and logically format the string variables used within the .adm file. The STRINGS syntax is not mandatory, but it can help reduce the code within the main body of the .adm file. The STRINGS syntax allows for variables to be used for lengthy strings. Strings are used to create the interface within the Group Policy Object Editor. The following example uses the STRINGS syntax whenever there is a string variable to create the interface.

```
CLASS MACHINE
CATEGORY !!CUSTOMADM
    POLICY !!Autologon
    KEYNAME "SOFTWARE\Microsoft\WindowsNT\CurrentVersion\Winlogon"
        PART !!Username
        EDITTEXT
        VALUENAME "autoadminlogon"
        END PART
```

```
        PART !!Password
        EDITTEXT
        VALUENAME "defaultpassword"
        END PART
    END POLICY
END CATEGORY
[STRINGS]
CUSTOMADM = "Microsoft Custom ADM Entries"
AutoLogon = "Automatic Logon"
Username = "What is the name of the user?"
Password = "What is the user's password? "
```

As you can see, the STRINGS syntax cleans up the main part of the .adm file. It also allows for easy administration of all of the string variables because they are all located under the [STRINGS] section at the bottom of the .adm file. If a string variable is used more than once in the .adm file, you can just use the STRINGS syntax and the string variable name at each instance, which will point to the single instance of the actual string at the end of the .adm file. Within the main body of the .adm file, the strings are referenced by using the double exclamation point (!!) followed by the string variable name.

For smaller .adm files, you might not need to use the STRINGS syntax. However, in larger .adm files, the STRINGS syntax can help reduce the complexity of the main body of the .adm file. The STRINGS syntax is especially useful in conjunction with the EXPLAIN syntax. The EXPLAIN text is generally very lengthy and can clog up the main body of the .adm file. By using the STRINGS syntax within the main body of the .adm file, you can leave the longer strings to the STRINGS section at the bottom of the .adm file.

> **Tip** If you need to convert .adm files to different languages, you should place all interface strings in the STRINGS section. You then only need to convert the STRINGS section to the different languages.

The STRINGS syntax can be used with the CATEGORY, POLICY, PART, and EXPLAIN statements.

CATEGORY

The CATEGORY syntax produces that folders that you see in the Group Policy Object Editor. Both the Computer Configuration and User Configuration display these folders, so you use the CATEGORY syntax under both the CLASS MACHINE and CLASS USER entries. The CATEGORY syntax can be nested in a hierarchy to generate subfolders. Each CATEGORY statement that you list produces a folder or subfolder in the Group Policy Object Editor.

The following structure creates three folders in a hierarchy:

```
CATEGORY "First level"
   CATEGORY "Second level"
         CATEGORY "Third level"
         END CATEGORY
   END CATEGORY
END CATEGORY
```

If you want to display multiple policies under a single folder (CATEGORY statement), you can just list the policies after the CATEGORY syntax and before the END CATEGORY syntax.

> **Note**   The CATEGORY syntax must be combined with an END CATEGORY statement. This is required so that the Group Policy Object Editor knows where to stop nesting folders as well as where to stop placing policies within the folder.
>
> Additional syntax that you can use in conjunction with CATEGORY includes KEYNAME, CATEGORY, END, SUPPORTED, and POLICY.

POLICY

The POLICY syntax is used to identify a policy setting that the user can modify within the Group Policy Object Editor. The POLICY syntax generates the "policy settings displayed" in the details pane of the Group Policy Object Editor, under the folders that are created by the CATEGORY syntax.

If you want to have different registry paths and values show up under a single policy within the Group Policy Object Editor, you need the POLICY syntax followed by the KEYNAME syntax. However, if multiple registry paths and values that fall under the same KEYNAME need to be placed under the same policy, you must have the KEYNAME syntax precede the POLICY syntax.

An example of having the KEYNAME statement followed by the POLICY statement containing multiple registry values is shown here:

```
CLASS USER
CATEGORY "Microsoft Custom ADM Entries"
   POLICY "Controls hidden files."
   KEYNAME "SOFTWARE\Microsoft\Windows\CurrentVersion\Explorer\Advanced"
         PART "Do you want to see hidden files?" TEXT
         END PART
         PART "Hidden Files and Folders:" DROPDOWNLIST
         VALUENAME Hidden
               ITEMLIST
               NAME "Yes" VALUE Numeric 1
               NAME "No" VALUE Numeric 2
               END ITEMLIST
```

```
        END PART
        PART "Do you want to see Super Hidden files?" TEXT
        END PART
        PART "Super Hidden" DROPDOWNLIST
        VALUENAME Showsuperhidden
            ITEMLIST
            NAME "Yes" VALUE Numeric 1
            NAME "No" VALUE Numeric 0
            END ITEMLIST
        END PART
    END POLICY
END CATEGORY
```

This .adm snippet generates the interface in the Group Policy Object Editor, as shown in Figure 14-5.

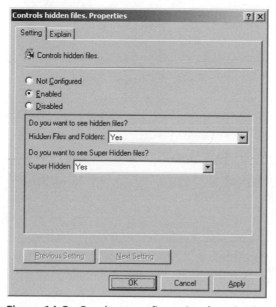

Figure 14-5   Resultant configuration from having multiple registry values in the same .adm file

The POLICY syntax requires an END POLICY to tell the Group Policy Editor when to stop grouping the settings together. Additional syntax that you can use in conjunction with POLICY includes KEYNAME, VALUENAME, VALUEON, VALUEOFF, POLICY, PART, END, ACTIONLISTON, ACTIONLISTOFF, and CLIENTTEXT.

PART

The PART syntax is used to specify options such as drop-down list boxes, text boxes, and text in the lower pane of a policy in the Group Policy Object Editor. The previous example, which illustrates the use of the PART syntax, shows the PART syntax used in the .adm file and the resulting Group Policy Object Editor interface from Figure 14-5.

You can also use the PART syntax to create an introduction or information about the policy in the lower pane of the policy. This PART syntax would simply introduce a clarifying sentence, without associating it with a registry value:

```
PART "Do you want to see Super Hidden files?" TEXT
END PART
```

Associating a PART within a "policy" to a registry value would look like this:

```
PART "Super Hidden" DROPDOWNLIST
VALUENAME Showsuperhidden
   ITEMLIST
   NAME "Yes" VALUE Numeric 1
   NAME "No" VALUE Numeric 0
   END ITEMLIST
END PART
```

The PART syntax can handle the various types of registry values that you include in your custom .adm files. Each type of registry value requires use of additional syntax to handle the input for the registry value. The previous example uses ITEMLIST, but other syntax options are available that you will need to use. We will go over ITEMLIST and other syntax options later in this chapter.

> **Note**   The PART syntax requires an END PART to tell the Group Policy Object Editor when to stop the configuration of the registry value within the interface. Additional syntax that you can use in conjunction with PART includes CHECKBOX, CLIENTTEXT, COMBOBOX, DROPDOWNLIST, EDITTEXT, LISTBOX, NUMERIC, PART, and TEXT.

To create the environment that allows the user to modify the registry values, you must include additional syntax after the PART syntax. Table 14-5 lists the valid syntax options that are used in conjunction with the PART syntax.

Table 14-5   Syntax That Can Be Used with the PART Syntax

Type	Description
CHECKBOX	Displays a check box. The value is set in the registry with the *REG_DWORD* type. The value is other than zero if the check box is selected and zero if it is not selected.
CLIENTTEXT	Specifies which client-side extension to use for the specific policy setting.
COMBOBOX	Displays a combo box.
DROPDOWNLIST	Displays a combo box with a drop-down list style. The user can choose only one of the entries supplied.

Table 14-5 Syntax That Can Be Used with the PART Syntax

Type	Description
EDITTEXT	Displays a text box that accepts alphanumeric text. The text is set in the registry with the REG_SZ or the REG_EXPAND_SZ type.
LISTBOX	Displays a list box with Add and Remove buttons. This is the only PART type that can be used to manage multiple values under one key.
NUMERIC	Displays a text box with an optional spin control that accepts a numeric value. The value is set in the registry with the REG_DWORD type.
TEXT	Displays a line of static text. No registry value is associated with this PART type.

CHECKBOX   When you are combining multiple registry values under one policy, you use the CHECKBOX syntax to function like the VALUEON/VALUEOFF syntax. If the check box is selected, the registry value associated with the CHECKBOX syntax has a value of 1 written to the registry. A value of 0 is written to the registry value if the check box is not selected.

You can also combine the CHECKBOX syntax with the VALUEON/VALUEOFF syntax to clearly specify what the registry values should be when the check box is selected and not selected. Here is a snippet of the System.adm file, which uses the CHECKBOX syntax:

```
PART !!StdCheckT CHECKBOX
VALUENAME "DisableRollback"
VALUEON NUMERIC 1
VALUEOFF NUMERIC 0
END PART
```

> **Note**   Additional syntax that you can use in conjunction with CHECKBOX includes KEYNAME, VALUENAME, ACTIONLISTON, ACTIONLISTOFF, DEFCHECKED, VALUEON, VALUEOFF, DEFCHECKED, CLIENTTEXT, and END.

CLIENTTEXT   The **CLIENTTEXT** keyword is used to specify which client-side extension to the Group Policy Object Editor needs to process the particular settings on the client computer. By default, the registry extension processes all settings configured under the Administrative Templates node. The **CLIENTTEXT** keyword changes the default behavior and causes the specified extension to process these settings after the registry extension has placed them in the registry.

The **CLIENTTEXT** syntax must be used within the **POLICY** scope or the **PART** scope and should follow the **VALUENAME** statement.

CLIENTTEXT alters the default behavior of typical GPOs. Typical GPOs process all settings under the Administrative Templates node. The CLIENTTEXT syntax specifies the specific extension to process a GPO setting once it has been placed in the registry.

The following is an example from the System.adm file. It configures the disk quotas within the GPO. As you can see, Disk Quotas has a separate client-side extension (CSE), which is referenced within the example code.

```
POLICY !!DQ_Enforce
KEYNAME "Software\Policies\Microsoft\Windows NT\DiskQuota"
    VALUENAME "Enforce"
    VALUEON  NUMERIC 1
    VALUEOFF NUMERIC 0
    CLIENTEXT {3610eda5-77ef-11d2-8dc5-00c04fa31a66}
END POLICY
```

> **Note** To learn more about CSEs, see Chapter 13.

COMBOBOX This **PART** type displays a combo box. It accepts the same options as **EDITTEXT**, as well as the **SUGGESTIONS** option, which begins a list of suggestions to be placed in the drop-down list. The **suggestions** are separated by spaces and must be enclosed in quotation marks (") when a value includes spaces. If a suggestion name includes white space, it must be enclosed in quotation marks. The list ends with **END SUGGESTIONS**.

For example, you can establish a list of screensaver names so the administrator doesn't have to know the names of the screensavers. Here is snippet of the original administrative template code for the screensaver file name and the modified syntax using the COMBOBOX syntax:

```
POLICY !!ScreenSaverFilename
KEYNAME "Software\Policies\Microsoft\Windows\Control Panel\Desktop"
    PART !!ScreenSaverFilename EDITTEXT
    VALUENAME "SCRNSAVE.EXE"
    END PART
END POLICY
```

Here's an updated version of the screensaver option with a COMBOBOX:

```
POLICY !!ScreenSaverFilename
KEYNAME "Software\Policies\Microsoft\Windows\Control Panel\Desktop"
    PART !!Screensaverpicker COMBOBOX
    VALUENAME "SCRNSAVE.EXE"
        SUGGESTIONS
          C:\WINNT\System32\ssstars.scr
          C:\WINNT\System32\ssbezier.scr
          C:\WINNT\System32\ssflwbox.scr
        END SUGGESTIONS
    END PART
END POLICY
```

The resulting Group Policy Editor for this new syntax looks like Figure 14-6.

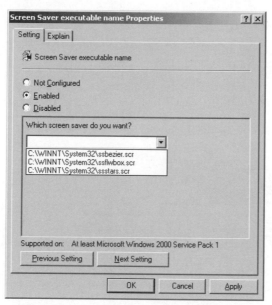

Figure 14-6 COMBOBOX syntax results

> **Tip** If you use the STRINGS syntax for the name of the COMBOBOX, the entry can have just a single word, where the variable is an entire sentence. This approach is useful because if you have more than one word in the quotes, you will receive an error when you attempt to import the administrative template into the GPO. Additional syntax that you can use in conjunction with COMBOBOX includes KEYNAME, VALUENAME, DEFAULT, SUGGESTIONS, REQUIRED, MAXLENGTH, OEMCONVERT, END, EXPANDABLETEXT, NOSORT, and CLIENTTEXT.

DROPDOWNLIST The DROPDOWNLIST syntax provides a combo box with a drop-down list style. It is similar to the COMBOBOX syntax, except that the actual registry value is converted to simple language text. The user can choose only one of the entries from the drop-down list. The DROPDOWNLIST syntax is preferable to the COMBOBOX syntax when the registry value does not indicate clearly what setting the policy will accomplish. To better illustrate this, let's take a look at the COMBOBOX example with a DROPDOWNLIST solution:

```
POLICY !!ScreenSaverFilename
KEYNAME "Software\Policies\Microsoft\Windows\Control Panel\Desktop"
    PART "what screen saver do you want? " DROPDOWNLIST
    VALUENAME "SCRNSAVE.EXE"
        ITEMLIST
        NAME "Starfield"
        VALUE C:\WINNT\System32\ssstars.scr
        NAME "Bezier"
```

```
                VALUE C:\WINNT\System32\ssbezier.scr
                NAME "Flowerbox"
                VALUE C:\WINNT\System32\ssflwbox.scr
                END ITEMLIST
        END PART
END POLICY
```

The resulting Group Policy Editor text for this syntax and administrative template is shown in Figure 14-7.

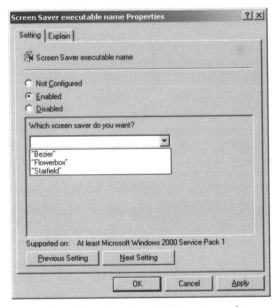

Figure 14-7   DROPDOWNLIST syntax results

Tip   If any item in the drop-down list requires more than one word, you must use the STRINGS syntax for the entries; otherwise, the .adm file will generate an error during importing. The STRINGS syntax allows you to use a single word for each entry, but the Group Policy Object Editor converts the string variable to the actual string for the list.

Note   Additional syntax that you can use in conjunction with DROPDOWNLIST includes KEYNAME, VALUENAME, DEFAULT, REQUIRED, ITEMLIST, END, NOSORT, and CLIENTTEXT.

EDITTEXT   The EDITTEXT syntax allows the user to input alphanumeric text into an edit field. We have already seen an example of editing text in the screensaver file name example. Here is that example again:

```
POLICY !!ScreenSaverFilename
KEYNAME "Software\Policies\Microsoft\Windows\Control Panel\Desktop"
```

```
    PART !!ScreenSaverFilename EDITTEXT
    VALUENAME "SCRNSAVE.EXE"
    END PART
END POLICY
```

By default, the EDITTEXT syntax provides an empty box for editing the policy. If you want to display an initial value in the edit box, you can use the DEFAULT syntax along with the EDITTEXT syntax. The options you can use with EDITTEXT syntax include:

- **DEFAULT value**   Specifies the initial string to place in the edit field. If this option is not specified, the field is initially empty.

- **EXPANDABLETEXT**   Specifies that the text is set in the registry with the REG_EXPAND_SZ type. By default, the text is set in the registry with the REG_SZ type.

- **MAXLEN value**   Specifies the maximum length of a string. The string in the edit field is limited to this length.

- **REQUIRED**   Specifies that the Group Policy Object Editor does not allow a policy containing this PART to be enabled unless a value has been entered for this PART.

- **OEMCONVERT**   Sets the ES_OEMCONVERT style in the edit field so typed text is mapped from ASCII to OEM and back. ES_OEMCONVERT converts text entered in the edit control. The text is converted from the Windows character set (ASCII) to the OEM character set and then back to the Windows set. This ensures proper character conversion when the application calls the *CharToOem <JavaScript:hhobj_1.Click()>* function to convert an ASCII string in the edit control to OEM characters. This style is most useful for edit controls that contain file names.

> **Note**   Additional syntax that you can use in conjunction with EDITTEXT includes KEYNAME, VALUENAME, DEFAULT, REQUIRED, MAXLENGTH, OEMCONVERT, END, EXPANDABLETEXT, and CLIENTTEXT.

LISTBOX   The LISTBOX **PART** component specifies various options such as dropdown list boxes, text boxes, and text in the lower pane of the Group Policy Object Editor. The LISTBOX is a simple syntax, as you can see from this snippet from the System.adm template.

```
PART !!RestrictAppsList LISTBOX
    KEYNAME "Software\Microsoft\Windows\CurrentVersion\Policies\Explorer\RestrictRun"
    VALUEPREFIX ""
END PART
```

The resulting Group Policy Editor interface is shown in Figure 14-8.

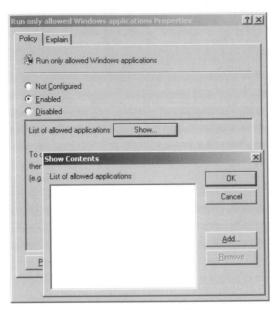

Figure 14-8   LISTBOX syntax results

In addition to the standard LISTBOX syntax, you can also add more options to the administrative template. The following are additional options you can add to the LISTBOX syntax:

- **ADDITIVE**   By default, the content of list boxes overrides any values set in the target registry. This means that a control value is inserted in the policy file that causes existing values to be deleted before the values set in the policy file are merged. If this option is specified, existing values are not deleted and the values set in the list box are in addition to whatever values exist in the target registry. If a GPO that uses this syntax is disabled, the disabled settings are not applied and are thus removed from the registry.

> **Caution**   The ability to display a policy setting that uses the LISTBOX ADDITIVE syntax was not supported prior to Service Pack 2 for Windows XP. If you attempt to administer a GPO that uses the LISTBOX ADDITIVE syntax on a computer that does not run Windows XP Professional SP2 or Windows Server 2003 SP1, you will receive an error message: "The following entry in the [strings] section is too long and has been truncated." For more information, see article 842933 in the Microsoft Knowledge Base at *http://support.microsoft.com/kb/842933*.

- **EXPLICITVALUE**   This option makes the user specify the value data and the value name. The list box shows two columns, one for the name and one for the data. This option cannot be used with the VALUEPREFIX option.

- **VALUEPREFIX prefix** The prefix you specify is used in determining value names. If you specify a prefix, the prefix and an incremented integer are used instead of the default value naming scheme described previously. For example, a prefix of *SampleName* generates the value names *SampleName1*, *SampleName2*, and so on. The prefix can be empty (""), which causes the value names to be *1, 2,* and so on.

> **Note** Additional syntax that you can use in conjunction with LISTBOX includes KEYNAME, VALUEPREFIX, END, VALUE-PREFIX, ADDITIVE, EXPLICITVALUE, EXPANDABLETEXT, NOSORT, and CLIENTTEXT.

NUMERIC Displays an edit field with an optional spinner control (an up-down control) that accepts a numeric value. It is best to use the MIN and MAX syntax in conjunction with the NUMERIC syntax to ensure that the registry does not become corrupted with invalid data. The following is a snippet from the System.adm template using the NUMERIC syntax.

```
PART !!ProfileSize
   NUMERIC REQUIRED SPIN 100
   VALUENAME "MaxProfileSize"
   DEFAULT 30000
   MAX     30000
   MIN     300
END PART
```

The SPIN syntax allows for a spin control to set the range of values that can be set. This adds to the MIN and MAX controls to provide a boundary for the data of the registry value. Other syntax that you can use along with the NUMERIC syntax include:

- **DEFAULT value** Specifies the initial numeric value for the edit field. If this option is not specified, the field is initially empty.

- **MAX value** Specifies the maximum value for the number. The default value is 9999.

- **MIN value** Specifies the minimum value for the number. The default value is 0.

- **REQUIRED** Specifies that the Group Policy Object Editor does not allow a policy containing this PART to be enabled unless a value has been entered for this PART.

- **SPIN value** Specifies increments to use for the spinner control. The default is SPIN 1.

- **SPIN 0** Removes the SPIN control from the "policy" settings.

- **TXTCONVERT** Writes values as REG_SZ strings ("*1*", "*2*", or "*128*") rather than as binary values.

> **Note**   Additional syntax that you can use in conjunction with NUMERIC includes KEYNAME, VALUENAME, END, MIN, MAX, SPIN, SPIN, END, TXTCONVERT, REQUIRED, DEFAULT, and CLIENTTEXT.

TEXT   The TEXT syntax can be used to display text on the property page of a policy setting. The following is a snippet from the System.adm template that uses the TEXT syntax:

```
PART !!GPRefreshRate_C_Desc1  TEXT
END PART
PART !!GPRefreshRate_C_Desc2  TEXT
END PART
```

This creates two lines of static text in the dialog box when you edit the policy setting.

ACTIONLIST

You can use the ACTIONLIST syntax to specify a set of arbitrary registry changes to make in response to a control being set to a particular state. Here is a snippet of code for the ACTIONLIST syntax:

```
POLICY  "Deny connections requests"
    EXPLAIN "If enabled, TS will stop accepting connections"
    ACTIONLISTON
    VALUENAME "fDenyTSConnections"    VALUE NUMERIC 1
    END ACTIONLISTON
    ACTIONLISTOFF
    VALUENAME "fDenyTSConnections"    VALUE NUMERIC 0
    END ACTIONLISTOFF
END POLICY
```

ACTIONLIST has two variants that you can use with the POLICY and CHECKBOX syntax. Table 14-6 describes these variants.

Table 14-6   Variants That Can Be Used with the CHECKBOX Syntax

Variant	Description
ACTIONLISTON	Specifies an optional action list to be used if the check box is selected
ACTIONLISTOFF	Specifies an optional action list to be used if the check box is not selected

Additional Statements in the .adm Template

You have now seen all of the essential syntax to add to your .adm files to handle the array of registry values you need to offer. However, other syntax is important for development and troubleshooting purposes. These statements are not required in the .adm file, but they provide additional control over the registry values you insert into the .adm file.

Comments

Although comments are not often used in standard .adm files, using them in your custom .adm files can benefit you and everyone else who needs to reference them. The comments don't alter the registry or the Group Policy Object Editor interface—they are there to help you understand the syntax and code in the .adm file.

You can use two methods to add comments to an .adm file. You can precede the comment with a semicolon or two forward slashes, or you can add comments at the end of any valid line or on a line by themselves. Here is a small example that uses the comments syntax:

```
PART !!ProfileSize    //this is the user profile
   NUMERIC REQUIRED SPIN 100
         ; The spin control will increment by 100's,
         ; starting at 300, then 400, 500, 600, etc.
   VALUENAME "MaxProfileSize"
   DEFAULT 30000
   MAX     30000
   MIN     300
END PART
```

REQUIRED

The REQUIRED syntax is straightforward. When you use it in conjunction with another statement in the .adm file, the registry value must be configured for the policy to be enabled.

MAXLEN

This syntax controls the maximum length of the text within a "policy" entry. This is useful when a single digit value must be maintained for a "policy" entry.

EXPLAIN

The **EXPLAIN** syntax is used to provide online Help text for a specific GPO setting. Starting with Windows 2000, the **Properties** page for each policy setting includes an **Explain** tab, which provides the details about the policy settings.

Each custom GPO setting that you create should include one **EXPLAIN** keyword, followed by at least one space, and then the **EXPLAIN** string in quotation marks (") or a reference to the Help string. Here is an example snippet from the System.adm template that uses the EXPLAIN syntax. The resulting interface is shown in Figure 14-9.

```
POLICY !!Run_Startup_Script_Sync
EXPLAIN !!Run_Startup_Script_Sync_Help
   KEYNAME     "Software\Microsoft\Windows\CurrentVersion\Policies\System"
   VALUENAME "RunStartupScriptSync"
   VALUEON  NUMERIC 0
   VALUEOFF NUMERIC 1
END POLICY
```

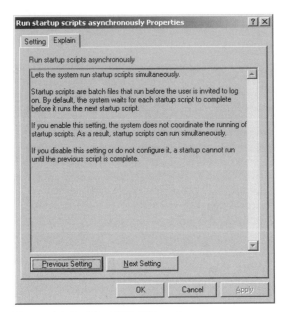

Figure 14-9   The EXPLAIN syntax

If you want to create a hard return within the Help text, just use the /*n* syntax. If you want to create a line break, you can use the /*n*/*n* syntax. You can use up to 4096 characters in any single EXPLAIN syntax entry—more than enough for a good description of the policy.

SUPPORTED

The Group Policy Object Editor uses the **SUPPORTED** tag to populate the **REQUIREMENT** field. This tag informs the Group Policy administrator about the platforms or applications for which the policy setting is supported. For example, many of the policy settings included in the System.adm file use a **SUPPORTED** tag that specifies a specific service pack release. The string used for the SUPPORTED tag often refers to multiple operating systems or service packs.

While operating system components generally use an operating system or service pack reference in this field, applications (which can be updated outside the release of a service pack) can refer to a specific version of an application. The **SUPPORTED** tag is essential for ensuring that Group Policy administrators have the information to make informed decisions about the use of the policy setting.

Your .adm file might also be localized, and you should use the *!!Stringname* construct in the **SUPPORTED** tag because it allows the referenced string to be localized easily. In addition, the **SUPPORTED** tag is supported only in Windows XP and later operating systems, so it should be enclosed within the *if version* construct, as follows. (This ensures that the Windows 2000 version of the Group Policy Object Editor does not attempt to interpret the **SUPPORTED** tag.)

```
POLICY !!ScreenSaverFilename
   #if version >= 4
   SUPPORTED !!SUPPORTED_Windows2003
   #endif
KEYNAME "Software\Policies\Microsoft\Windows\Control Panel\Desktop"
   PART !!ScreenSaverFilename EXPANDABLETEXT
   VALUENAME "SCRNSAVE.EXE"
   END PART
END POLICY
```

The SUPPORTED syntax and the operating system description accomplish two things in the Group Policy Object Editor. First, they list the operating system version under the requirements label in the Extended view of the Group Policy Editor, as shown in Figure 14-10. Second, they provide a way for the Filtering option to select the correct operating system versions to be displayed.

Figure 14-10   Extended view of the Group Policy Object Editor

.adm File String and Tab Limits

The .adm files cannot contain unlimited amounts of information. Restrictions are bound to each .adm file (although the chances of reaching these limits for custom .adm entries are small). Table 14-7 lists these restrictions.

Table 14-7   .adm File String and Tab Limits

File String	Tab Limit
Maximum string length for Explain text	4096
Maximum string length for Category Explain text	255
Maximum string length for EDITTEXT string	1023

Best Practices

In general, if a policy setting can be configured using a simple user interface and configuration input can be stored in the registry as plain text, consider using an .adm file to configure the setting. Specifically, .adm files are an appropriate solution for the following scenarios:

- Creating on/off or yes/no functionality. You can use .adm file settings to act as a switch to turn functionality on or off. It is common for desktop features and functions to be controlled in this manner.

- Defining a set of static modes. For example, you can set the language used on a computer. You can set up a static list of language selections, and when the policy setting is enabled, the administrator can select a language from that list. This action is typically shown in the user interface as a drop-down list.

- Creating a policy setting that requires simple input that can be stored in the registry as plain text. For example, you can create a policy setting to define the screensaver or bitmap that is displayed on the user's desktop. With this policy setting enabled, Group Policy administrators see a text dialog box into which they can type the name and path of the bitmap file to be used. This information is then stored in the registry as plain text.

 Note   Binary values that are stored in the registry can't be placed in an .adm file because they are non-ASCII format. You can place binary registry values in customized security templates, which are discussed in Chapter 15.

Consider using an administrative template to distribute registry-based policy settings for the following purposes:

- To help manage and increase security of desktop computers.

- To hide or disable a user interface option that can lead users into a situation that requires Help Desk support.

- To hide or disable new behavior that might confuse users. This allows the Help Desk to gradually introduce these new features until all users can be trained properly.

■ To hide settings and options that tend to distract users or are too complex for them to configure without assistance from the Help Desk.

There are also times when you should consider *not* using .adm files to configure settings on all computers through GPOs. Here are some instances where you should avoid using .adm files:

■ Implementing the entire list of settings and options for a large application. Large applications can contain hundreds or thousands of settings, which can slow down GPO processing and restrict users' ability to configure the application to their own needs. Be selective about the features you enable or disable. You should implement only a subset of the available options, based on whether an administrator would want this kind of management over the application.

■ Implementing unsupported policy settings. You should only implement .adm file settings that will be fully tested, validated, and supported.

As you design your custom .adm file settings, consider the end state, administration of the settings, support for distribution of the setting, and troubleshooting when settings fail to take effect as expected. You should consider the following guidelines when you design your policy settings:

■ Do not alter the standard .adm files. This includes removing settings within the standard .adm files or adding new settings to them. Subsequent versions of the .adm files (released through updates or service packs) will add the settings back and overwrite any new custom settings.

■ Remember that computer policy settings always override user policy settings when they conflict.

■ Consider making the enabled behavior of all .adm file settings the opposite of what the default behavior exhibits. This will keep the configurations within the policy setting consistent with the default behavior of Windows.

> **Note**   This design might make some settings work as a "double negative," but it keeps the consistency of the default behavior and Enabled state in tact. The Explain text that you include with your setting will help clarify what the Enabled and Disabled configurations produce.

■ Provide a thorough and detailed Explain tab. Well-written Explain text can help reduce support calls and troubleshooting for custom .adm file settings.

Summary

The standard .adm files provide a wide variety of settings that control almost every aspect of the registry. With the standard .adm files adding over 1300 policy settings to a default GPO, you have many options. If these .adm files don't provide enough options, you can import additional .adm files into a GPO to provide control over security, Word, Excel, PowerPoint, and more.

If these .adm files don't give you all of the settings that you need, you can easily create custom .adm files and import them into existing GPOs. With the flexibility of targeting specific computers and users, the custom .adm files can be very granular in their application. The key to configuring a new .adm file is understanding the language. The administrative template language is not very complex, and you can generate and implement new .adm files in minutes.

Chapter 15
Security Templates

In this chapter:

Understanding the Security Template Structure 554

Where Security Template Settings Overlap with GPO Settings 561

Working with Security Templates 562

Customizing Security Templates 563

Customizing Security Options 564

Customizing Services in the Security Templates. 572

Microsoft Solutions for Security Settings 574

Summary 577

In this chapter, we will unravel the complexity of security templates. Security templates provide an excellent way to help lock down security on servers and clients. We will look in detail at the structure of security templates so you are fully aware of the standard settings as well as areas that you can expand with custom settings.

Security templates are administered using the Security Templates snap-in. This snap-in allows you access to the standard security templates and helps you to create your own custom templates. We will look in detail at the syntax and methods required to create your own custom security settings. We will top off the chapter by listing some of the more common custom security settings that you might want to include, as well as some best practices with regard to security templates.

Related Information

- For information on hardening servers and clients within your domain using security templates, see Chapter 5.

- For more information about configuring security templates, see *Microsoft Windows Security Resource Kit, Second Edition* (Microsoft Press, 2005).

- For more information about auditing security events, see *Microsoft Windows Security Resource Kit, Second Edition* (Microsoft Press, 2005).

- For more information about the registry, see *Microsoft Windows Registry Guide, Second Edition* (Microsoft Press, 2005).

Understanding the Security Template Structure

To fully understand the options for customizing security templates, we must first review what a standard security template provides, as well as the structure of the template. You will then have a much better understanding of what you can add to security templates.

The standard security templates provided with the operating system are stored in the C:\Windows\Security\Templates folder by default. Every security template has the same structure and the same configurable security attributes. To access and modify these security templates, you use the Security Templates snap-in. Figure 15-1 shows the Security Templates snap-in, as well as the security template structure.

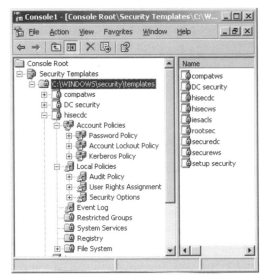

Figure 15-1   Security Templates snap-in and structure

More Info   For more information about the standard security templates and how to access the Security Templates snap-in, see Chapter 5.

Account Policies

The account policies settings affect how user accounts can interact with the computer or domain with regard to authentication and passwords. Each domain account can have only one account policy. The account policy must be defined in the Default Domain policy (or in another GPO linked to the domain level), and it is enforced by the domain controllers that manage the domain. Domain controllers always obtain the account policy from the Default Domain Policy Group Policy object (GPO), even if a different account policy has been applied to the organizational unit (OU) that contains the domain controller computer accounts. By default, clients and servers that are joined to the domain also receive the same account policy for their local user accounts. However, you can configure the account policy for the client and server local SAM to be different from the domain account policy by defining an account policy that is linked to an OU containing the client and server accounts.

Account policies have three subsets: Password Policy, Account Lockout Policy, and Kerberos Policy, as shown in Figure 15-2.

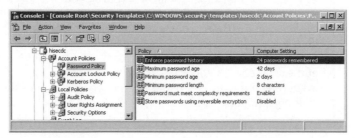

Figure 15-2   The three subsets of account policy

- **Password Policy**   These settings are for passwords, such as password length, maximum password age, and password complexity. These settings are applied to domain accounts and local user accounts. They can't be extended with custom password policy categories added to the security template.

- **Account Lockout Policy**   These settings determine the circumstances and length of time that an account can be locked out of the system. They apply to domain accounts and local user accounts. These settings can't be extended with custom account lockout policy categories added to the security template.

- **Kerberos Policy**   These are Kerberos-related settings such as ticket lifetimes and enforcement. Kerberos policies do not exist in Local Computer Policy. They are used for domain user accounts and even though they are available to configure in a GPO linked to an OU, they are only valid at the domain level. These settings can't be extended with custom Kerberos policy categories.

More Info   For more information about password policies, account lockout policies, and kerberos policies, see Chapter 5.

Local Policies

Local policies include various security settings that apply to computers. There are three categories of settings under local policies: Audit Policy, User Rights Assignment, and Security Options.

More Info   For information about audit policy categories, user rights, and security options, see Chapter 5.

- **Audit Policy**   These settings determine whether security events are logged in the Security log in Event Viewer on the computer. For example, they determine whether a logon or attempt to access a resource has been successful or has failed. These settings can't be extended with custom audit policy categories.

> **Tip**   Before you implement an audit policy, you must decide which event categories you want to audit. The audit settings that you choose for the different event categories define your auditing policy. On member servers and workstations that are joined to a domain, audit settings for all of the event categories are undefined by default. On domain controllers, auditing is turned on for most of the audit policy settings by default. By defining audit settings for specific event categories, you can create an audit policy that suits the security needs of your organization.

- **User Rights Assignment**   These settings determine which users or groups have logon rights or privileges on the computer. These settings can't be extended with custom user rights.

- **Security Options**   These options enable or disable various security settings for the computer, such as digital signing of data, Administrator and Guest account names, floppy drive and CD-ROM access, driver installation, and logon prompts. These settings can be expanded with custom security options.

> **Note**   See the "Customizing Security Options" section in this chapter for more information on how to customize your own settings within the security templates.

Event Log

The Event Log settings define attributes related to the application, security, and system logs. You can configure maximum log size, access rights to the logs, and the retention method of the logs. These settings can't be expanded with custom event log categories in a security template.

The application and system logs track events on every computer by default. The security log on member servers and clients does not track any events by default, but Windows Server 2003 domain controllers do. To start tracking security events on member servers and clients, you must first enable auditing, as described in the "Local Policies" section. You must also enable auditing on the appropriate resource (file, folder, registry key, printer, or Active Directory object) to begin tracking object access events. All event logs are accessed and reviewed from the Event Viewer.

> **More Info**   For information about event logs, see Chapter 5.

Restricted Groups

The Restricted Groups settings allow the administrator to control two properties for security groups on both local computers and in Active Directory. The first property that can be controlled is the list of members of the group. The Members setting within the restricted groups interface controls this behavior, as shown in Figure 15-3.

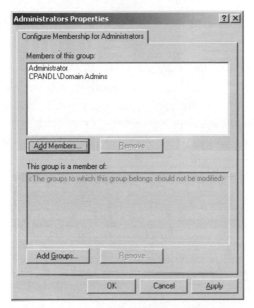

Figure 15-3   Restricted Groups within the security templates

Tip   An empty Members list means that the restricted group has no members.

The Members Of setting controls the groups to which the configured group belongs. This, too, can be seen in Figure 15-3.

Tip   An empty Member Of list means that the groups to which the restricted group belongs are not specified within the policy.

You can use Restricted Groups policy to control group membership. Using the policy, you can specify which members can be part of a group. Any members that are not specified in the policy are removed during Group Policy refresh. In addition, the second membership configuration option ensures that each Restricted Group is a member of only those groups that are specified in the Member Of column.

For example, you can create a Restricted Groups policy to allow only specified users (for example, Alice and John) to be members of the Administrators group. When policy is refreshed, only Alice and John will remain as members of the Administrators group.

> **Note** Restricted Groups should be used primarily to configure membership of local groups on workstation or member servers.

> **More Info** For information about restricted groups, see Chapter 5.

System Services

The System Services area of the security templates allows an administrator to centrally control services on clients, servers, and domain controllers. System Services can define the startup mode for any service on any computer in the domain. The startup mode options include Manual, Automatic, and Disabled. System Services also defines the access permissions for services on the target computer. Permissions can be set to allow any combination of starting, stopping, or pausing a service on the computer. This greatly improves control over the services running on computers in the domain. Figure 15-4 shows the interface for a standard service that you can specify within the security templates.

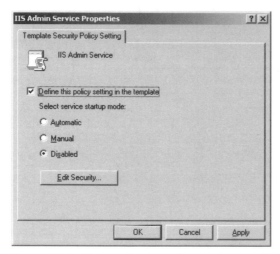

Figure 15-4 System Services allows you to configure the startup type of the service

> **Tip** For performance optimization, set unnecessary or unused services to Manual.

The System Services area of the security templates is dynamic in that the list of services corresponds to the computer performing the administration of the security template or GPO. Therefore, the service you need to configure for a workstation or server might not be listed as you attempt to configure the services. This behavior can be controlled and in some ways customized. See the "Customizing Services in the Security Templates" section in this chapter for more information on customizing system services within a security template.

> **More Info**   For information about system services, see Chapter 5.

Registry

The Registry section within the security template allows an administrator to define access permissions on registry keys on the target computer. When you configure a registry key within the security template, you see a list with HKEY_CLASSES_ROOT, HKEY_LOCAL_MACHINE, and HKEY_USERS that let's you find the key that you want to control. This interface can be seen in Figure 15-5.

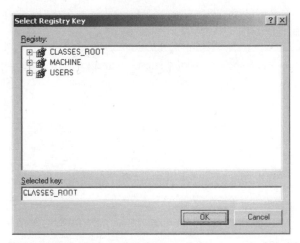

Figure 15-5   Using security templates to control registry keys

After selecting the registry key, you will have the option to configure all aspects of the security permissions for the object. This includes the following, which can be seen in Figure 15-6:

- **Discretionary access control list (DACL)**   The part of the security descriptor that grants or denies specific users and groups permission to access the object.

- **System access control list (SACL)**   The part of the security descriptor that triggers the auditing of events to be logged in the security log.

- **Ownership**   The part of the security descriptor that controls which user or group has ultimate control over the object, including the ability to change any permission, modify the contents, and delete the object.

> **More Info**   For more information about the accessing and editing the registry, search for "registry", "registry editing tools", and "overview of the windows registry" in TechNet at *http://www.microsoft.com/technet*. For information about the registry settings in the security templates, see Chapter 5.

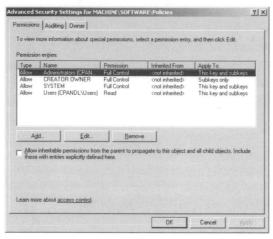

Figure 15-6   Configuring permissions, auditing, and ownership for registry keys

File System

The File System section within the security template is similar to the registry section. It allows an administrator to define access permissions on files and folders on the target computer. When you configure a file or folder within the security template, you are shown a list of all files and folders on the local computer, as shown in Figure 15-7.

Figure 15-7   Controlling files and folders using security templates

Again, like the registry keys, the file and folder permissions can be finely controlled. You can control the DACL, SACL, and ownership using security templates.

> **More Info**   For more information about file and folder permissions, permission inheritance, auditing, and ownership, search for "dacl", "sacl", "ownership", "security descriptors", and "ACL inheritance" in TechNet at *http://www.microsoft.com/technet*.

Where Security Template Settings Overlap with GPO Settings

Security templates are powerful and important for ensuring that clients, servers, and domain controllers are secured properly within the domain. Security templates cover a lot of security areas. However, it is also important to understand how security templates overlap with GPOs so you know which custom settings are possible and where they will show up in the GPOs.

A typical security template covers more than 10 security-related areas, with hundreds of potential policy settings. A standard GPO contains well over 100 areas that can be configured, and more than 1000 individual policy settings. The big question is, where do security templates and GPOs overlap?

Security templates only affect computer accounts, so you can start by ruling out all of the policy settings that affect user accounts, which are all located under the User Configuration node in a GPO. You saw in Chapter 14 that the Administrative Templates nodes for both computer and user accounts are created using .adm files. Therefore, you can also rule out these policy settings. It is rather obvious that security templates are not related to software settings or scripts, so these areas can be ruled out, too.

After ruling out what the security templates don't configure within a GPO, you are left with the Security Settings node under the Computer Configuration\Windows Settings path in a standard GPO, as shown in Figure 15-8.

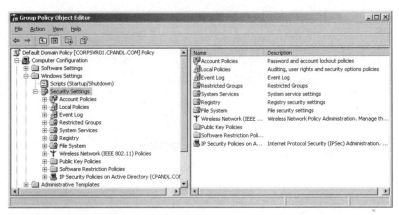

Figure 15-8   The Security Settings node in a GPO

When you compare this structure to that shown in Figure 15-1, you can quickly see the similarities. However, some security areas included in the GPO are not supported by the security template. These areas include the following:

- Wireless Network (IEEE 802.11) Policies
- Public Key Policies

- Software Restriction Policies
- IP Security Policies on Active Directory

These areas also fall outside the scope of security templates, but they are located in the Security Settings section of a GPO where security templates take effect.

Working with Security Templates

When you consider customizing security templates, you need to know how to access them to make the changes and adjustments. Although security templates are simple text files, it is common to use a tool—the Security Templates snap-in—to access and configure them. However, you need to use a text editor like Notepad if you want to edit these text files to make custom changes to the security templates.

Security Templates Snap-In

The most common method of accessing, configuring, and modifying the security templates is to use the Security Templates snap-in. This snap-in is accessed through the Microsoft Management Console (MMC).

> **More Info**   For information about how to use the MMC and import the Security Templates snap-in, see Chapter 5.

The Security Templates snap-in automatically sends you to the default storage location of the built-in security templates, the C:\Windows\Security\Templates folder, which can be seen in Figure 15-9.

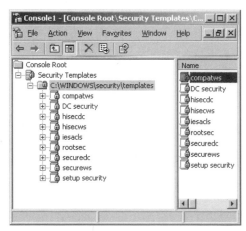

Figure 15-9   The Security Templates snap-in default location for built-in security templates

From here, you can modify existing templates, copy templates, or create new templates. We will cover how to do all of these custom tasks later in this chapter.

Raw Security Template INF Files

You might need to access the raw security template files while you customize the settings; for example when you are adding custom settings for services, files, and folders. These template files have an .inf extension, which makes them easy to pick out of a list of files. The files are simple text files, and you can use Notepad to edit them. You can use a different editor, but the additional formatting used in other applications might cause problems when the system accesses the templates.

 Caution   Entries do not show up in the security template files until the setting has been established using the Security Templates snap-in. You can add text directly to these files, but you must use the exact syntax that would be used if you were using the snap-in.

Customizing Security Templates

When you start to customize security templates, you must first determine whether you can work with an existing default or standard template as a foundation. (To get a better idea of what is included and targeted in the default security templates, see Chapter 5.) You have two options for working with security templates to create your own customized version: You can copy a default template, making changes to what is included in the original template, or you can create your own template from scratch.

Copying Templates

An excellent option that allows you to take advantage of existing configurations in a security template is to copy one of the default templates. This approach can save you a lot of effort and time.

First, be sure to pick the template that has the majority of the settings that you want to configure. (See Chapter 5 for a list of what each default security template covers.) Next, make a copy of the template using the Security Templates snap-in. To copy an existing template, follow these steps:

1. Click Start, Run. In the Run dialog box, type **mmc**, and then click OK.

2. Choose Add/Remove Snap-In from the File menu.

3. In the Add/Remove Snap-In dialog box, click Add.

4. Scroll down and select Security Templates from the list of available snap-ins, click Add, and then click Close.

5. In the Add/Remove Snap-In dialog box, click OK.

6. Find the security template that you want to copy in the Security Template snap-in list of templates, right-click the template, and click Save As.

7. Type a new name for the security template, and click Save.

This procedure generates a new security template with the same settings as the original template you copied. Now you can make additional configuration changes within the newly copied template.

Creating New Security Templates

If the default security templates don't include the settings you want, you can create a new security template from scratch instead of copying an existing template.

To create a new security template, follow these steps:

1. In the Security Templates snap-in, right-click the C:\Windows\Security\Templates node, and select New Template.

2. Type a template name and a description for the security template.

3. Click OK.

This generates a new security template that has no settings configured. Although this creates more work for you because you have to configure all of the settings, it is a straightforward way to ensure that you know which settings are configured within the template. After you make all of the required custom modifications in the template, it will be ready for deployment.

Customizing Security Options

There is more to the customization of security templates than modifying configurations in the standard templates that come with the operating system. You can also create new settings to control authentication and other security-related areas of the computer. You can't customize every section of a security template, but you can add hundreds of new settings. To get these new custom settings into your security templates, you must first make some modifications to the Sceregvl.inf file.

Structure of the Sceregvl.inf File

The Sceregvl.inf file is responsible for creating the Security Options policy settings within the security template. These policy settings can be found under the Local Policies\Security Options node in the security template. The Sceregvl.inf file creates the interface and associated control points in the computer's registry that control security. The default settings in the Sceregvl.inf file create the following categories of security settings within the security template:

- Accounts
- Audit
- Devices

- Domain controller

- Domain member

- Interactive logon

- Microsoft network client

- Microsoft network server

- Network access

- Network security

- Recovery console

- Shutdown

- System cryptography

- System objects

- System settings

Figure 15-10 shows these categories listed in the Security Options node.

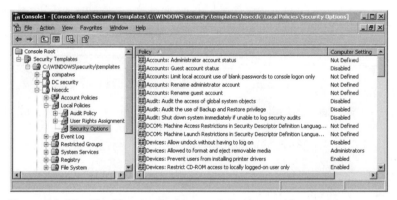

Figure 15-10   The Security Options node in the security template

The Sceregvl.inf file is a simple text file, located in the %windir%/inf folder, that you can edit if necessary. You can alter the existing settings with new descriptions or you can append entries to the file by adding your own custom entries. All of the custom entries you add to the Sceregvl.inf file will update the registry on the computer targeted by the GPO, which was configured using the custom entries.

The default Sceregvl.inf file does more than add registry entries that can be configured. The file is also designed to delete settings from a select group of registry keys and values in cases where the Windows NT 4.0 Security Configuration Editor (SCE) had been used previously and had updated these registry keys and values.

Although the syntax might not seem easy to follow, the file structure is simple, as shown in Figure 15-11. The structure of the file helps you figure out how to input the new custom entries.

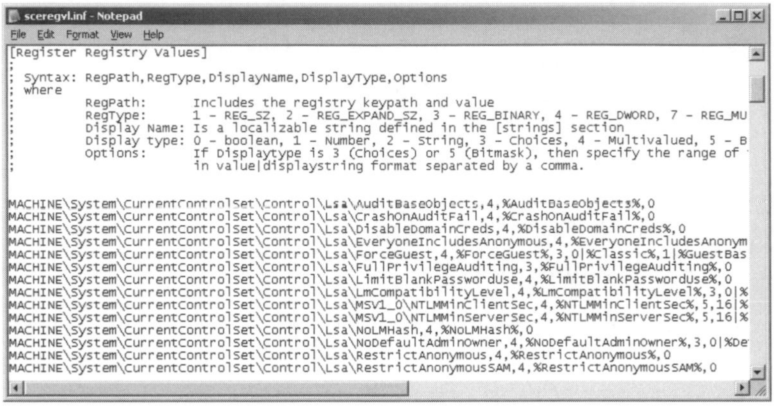

Figure 15-11 The Sceregvl.inf file structure

Each entry in the Sceregvl.inf file has the same format, with five fields. Not all entries need to contain all five fields, but the first four fields are required for each entry. An entry has the following structure:

```
RegistryPath,RegistryType,DisplayName,DisplayType,Options
```

Here is a description of what each field represents:

- **RegistryPath** Defines the full path of the registry key and value that you want to expose in the interface. Only values that exist in the HKEY_LOCAL_MACHINE hive can be configured, and this hive is referenced by the keyword MACHINE.

- **RegistryType** A number that defines the type of the registry value, as follows:

  1 - REG_SZ
  2 - REG_EXPAND_SZ
  3 - REG_BINARY
  4 - REG_DWORD
  5 - REG_MULTI_SZ

- **DisplayName** The string that ultimately appears when you access and configure the security setting. This is usually a replaceable parameter that refers to an entry in the [strings] section of the Sceregvl.inf file, thus making localization easier.

- **DisplayType** Specifies the type of dialog box the security options interface should render to allow the user to define the setting for the registry value. Supported display types include:

  - **0 – Boolean** Causes the interface to render Enable and Disable options for the registry value. If Enabled is selected, the registry value is set to 1. If Disabled is selected, the registry value is set to 0.

Here is an example of an entry that uses the Boolean DisplayType:

```
MACHINE\System\CurrentControlSet\Control\Lsa\CrashOnAuditFail,4,
%CrashOnAuditFail%,0
```

> **Note**   The *%variablename%* entries are variables taken care of in the [Strings] section, similar to the ADM templates we discussed earlier.

This entry generates a simple entry form in the security template policy, which can be seen in Figure 15-12.

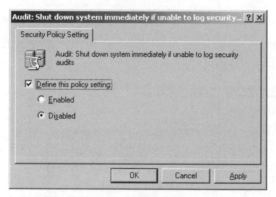

Figure 15-12   A security template entry that uses a DisplayType of 0

❑ **1 – Numeric**   Causes the interface to render a numeric spin control that allows the user to type or select a numeric value in the range 0 through 99999. Numeric display types can specify "unit" strings such as minutes and seconds that appear next to the spin control in the interface. These unit strings are defined in the Options field described below. The registry value is set to the number entered by the administrator.

Here is an example of an entry that uses the numeric *DisplayType*:

```
MACHINE\Software\Microsoft\Windows NT\CurrentVersion\Winlogon\
CachedLogonsCount,1,%CachedLogonsCount%,1,%Unit-Logons%
```

This entry generates a spinner for a numeric input in the security template policy, which can be seen in Figure 15-13.

❑ **2 – String**   Causes the interface to render a text box. The registry value is set to the string entered by the administrator.

Here is an example of an entry that uses the string *DisplayType*:

```
MACHINE\Software\Microsoft\Windows\CurrentVersion\Policies\
System\LegalNoticeCaption,1,%LegalNoticeCaption%,2
```

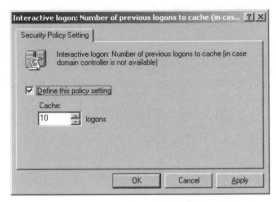

Figure 15-13   A security template entry that uses a DisplayType of 1

This entry generates a text entry form in the security template policy, which can be seen in Figure 15-14.

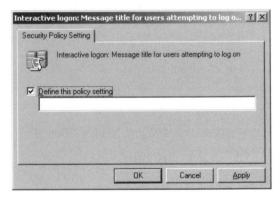

Figure 15-14   A security template entry that uses a DisplayType of 2

❑   **3 – List**   Causes the interface to render a list box from which the administrator can select one of several options. The registry value is set to the numeric value associated with the option chosen by the administrator. The options presented to the administrator are defined in the Options field described below.

Here is an example of an entry that uses the list *DisplayType*:

```
MACHINE\Software\Microsoft\Driver Signing\Policy,3,%DriverSigning%,3,0|
%DriverSigning0%,1|%DriverSigning1%,2|%DriverSigning2%
```

This entry generates a drop-down list entry form in the security template policy, which can be seen in Figure 15-15.

❑   **4 - Multivalued (available on Windows XP only)**   Causes the interface to render a multi-line edit control that allows the administrator to enter multiple lines of text. This display type should be used to define values for

MULTI_SZ types. The registry value is set to the strings entered by the user where each line is separated by a NULL byte.

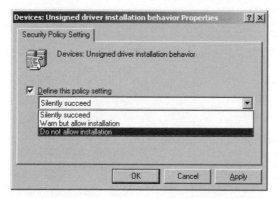

Figure 15-15   A security template entry that uses a DisplayType of 3

Here is an example of an entry that uses the multivalued *DisplayType*:

```
MACHINE\System\CurrentControlSet\Services\LanManServer\Parameters\
NullSessionShares,7,%NullShares%,4
```

This entry generates a multiple text entry form in the security template policy, which can be seen in Figure 15-16.

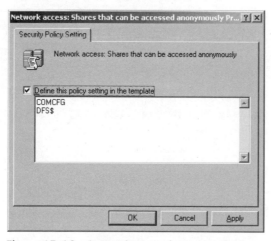

Figure 15-16   A security template entry that uses a DisplayType of 4

❑ **5 - Bitmask (available on Windows XP only)**   Causes the interface to render a series of check boxes where each check box corresponds to a numeric value defined in the Options field described below. The registry value is set to the bitwise OR of the selected values.

Here is an example of an entry that uses the bitmask *DisplayType*:

```
MACHINE\System\CurrentControlSet\Control\Lsa\MSV1_0\NTLMMinClientSec,4,
%NTLMMinClientSec%,5,16|%NTLMIntegrity%,32|$NTLMConfidentiality%,524288|
%NTLMv2Session%,536870912|%NTLM128%
```

This entry generates a multiple check box entry form in the security template policy, which can be seen in Figure 15-17.

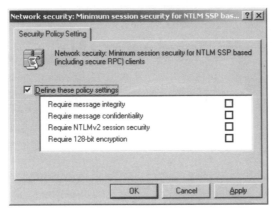

Figure 15-17   A security template entry that uses a DisplayType of 5

- **Options**   Qualifies the different display types within the same entry.

  - **If DisplayType=1 (Numeric)**   The entry can contain a string that defines the units for the numeric value. The unit string is displayed next to the spin control in the interface. The unit string has no effect on the value set in the registry.

  - **If DisplayType=3 (List)**   The entry defines the list of options that are available to the user. Each option consists of a numeric value separated by the pipe character (|) followed by the text for the choice. The registry value is set to the numeric value associated with the choice made by the administrator.

  - **If DisplayType=5 (Bitmask)**   The entry defines the list of choices available to the user. Each choice consists of a numeric value separated by the pipe character (|) followed by the text for the choice. The registry value is set to the bitwise OR of the choices selected by the administrator.

Customizing the Sceregvl.inf File

You can include almost any registry value you want in the Sceregvl.inf file, but you should focus only on the security-related settings because other registry settings can be configured using the .adm files as discussed in Chapter 14. Once you pick out your registry value, you use the structure we just discussed to update the existing Sceregvl.inf file.

Warning   Unlike .adm files, where you create new .adm files for custom entries, the security templates require that you update the existing Sceregvl.inf file to make custom entries.

Here is an example of a custom entry to the Sceregvl.inf file:

```
MACHINE\System\CurrentControlSet\Services\Tcpip\Parameters\SynAttackProtect,4, "Syn
Attack Protection against DoS",3,0|"No additional protection",1|"Time out sooner if
Syn Attack is detected"
```

This security entry updates the *SynAttackProtect* registry value with an entry of 0 or 1, depending on whether you want to keep the default setting (don't protect against a Syn attack) or 1 (have connections time out sooner if a Syn attack is detected).

This entry uses the List *DisplayType*, which as noted has a value of 3. This custom entry shows up in the security template as shown in Figure 15-18.

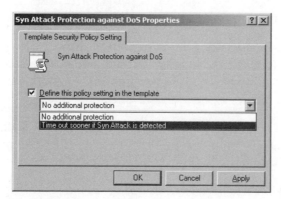

Figure 15-18   A custom entry for a Syn attack in a security template

Getting the Custom Entry to Show Up

After you update the Sceregvl.inf file with your custom entry, the new policy will not show up automatically. This is good behavior–if an attacker could modify the Sceregvl.inf file and have the new input take immediate affect, he could change registry values without your knowledge.

You are required to register the new Sceregvl.inf file with the computer that is performing the administration of the security template. To get the changes to show up in the security template interface, you must register the DLL that controls the Sceregvl.inf file. This DLL is named Scecli.dll. To register it, follow these steps on the computer performing the administration of the security templates:

1.   On the Start menu, choose Command Prompt.

2. Type **regsvr32 C:\Windows\system32\scecli.dll** and press Enter.

You will get a confirmation dialog box titled "RegSvr32," which indicates that the registration of the DLL succeeded.

Each time you modify a security template or a GPO on this computer, the new security policy setting will be available.

Customizing Services in the Security Templates

Earlier we described a pitfall with the System Services portion of the security template: the list of services that shows up in the security templates interface is driven by the computer that performs the administration. Because many of the computers used for administering security templates and GPOs are workstations, some server-related services will not be available when you attempt to edit them in the Security Templates snap-in.

Getting the Correct Service to Automatically Display

One workaround for not having the correct service display when you edit the security templates is to administer the security templates from a computer that has the appropriate services already installed. However, this can be a problem, depending on the physical location of the server and the privileges that you have on that computer.

Another solution is to install as many services as possible on your workstation that you use for administration purposes. Of course, this will work only for a subset of all of the services that can run on a server.

Yet another solution is to install a dedicated server for administering security templates and GPOs. You can install all of the services on this computer, giving you access to all of the services you need for creating and modifying the security templates and GPOs with regard to services.

Another solution to consider is to manually control the services using the raw security template files. This approach requires you to get a listing of all of the services and the correct syntax stored in the security template file.

Acquiring the Service Syntax for the Security Template File

You will not always have a computer available to you that has every service required to make changes to the security templates or GPOs. In this case, you can manually update the security template files with the syntax that is associated with your service. To do this, you must have a list of all services your company uses and the syntax associated with each service as it is stored in the security template.

To get this list of service syntax, you must go at least once to a computer that has each service installed on it. This will allow you to get the syntax from the saved security template after configuring the service. Because the syntax used to modify the service is stored in the .inf files on the local computer, you can quickly acquire this list of services. You can then quickly compile the list into a single file that can be referenced from any computer and manually inserted into any security template file as needed.

Here is a list of some common services and the syntax used when they are configured in a security template.

DHCP	`"DHCPServer",X,""`
DNS	`"DNS",X,""`
HTTP SSL	`"HTTPFilter",X,""`
IIS Admin	`"IISADMIN",X,""`
Certificate Services	`"CertSvc",X,""`
World Wide Web Publishing Service	`"W3SVC",X,""`

The *X* in each syntax listing is a numeric variable that depends on the startup mode that you configure for the service. There are three startup modes: Automatic, Manual, and Disabled. Each has a numeric value associated with it, which you must insert in place of the *X* for each service and startup type. The numeric values for the startup types are as follows:

Startup Mode	Numeric Value
Automatic	2
Manual	3
Disabled	4

The double quotes (`""`) following the numeric value will include any permissions that you establish from within the security template for the service. This syntax is complex and can take a long time to configure. In most cases, the service permissions are not set.

Manually Updating Services in the Security Template File

Once you know the service syntax and you know which security template it needs to be added to, your work is almost finished. All you need to do is open up the security template file using Notepad and insert the correct code for the service you want to control.

When you open up the security template in Notepad, you must find the [Service General Setting] section. If this section does not exist, you can just add it to the bottom of the current file text. If you want to ensure that the DNS, DHCP, and Certificate

Services start automatically but you wanted the IIS Admin Service to start disabled, you can add the following code to the appropriate security template file:

```
[Service General Setting]
"DNS",2,""
"DHCPServer",2,""
"CertSvc",2,""
"IISADMIN",4,""
```

Microsoft Solutions for Security Settings

Microsoft has developed a list of custom registry entries that extend the list of security policy settings dramatically. The list, provided here for your convenience, can be quickly implemented by including the following code in your Sceregvl.inf file and registering the Scecli.dll file, as described earlier.

```
MACHINE\System\CurrentControlSet\Services\Tcpip\Parameters\
EnableICMPRedirect,4,%EnableICMPRedirect%,0
MACHINE\System\CurrentControlSet\Services\Tcpip\Parameters\
SynAttackProtect,4,%SynAttackProtect%,3,0|%SynAttackProtect0%,1|
%SynAttackProtect1%
MACHINE\System\CurrentControlSet\Services\Tcpip\Parameters\
EnableDeadGWDetect,4,%EnableDeadGWDetect%,0
MACHINE\System\CurrentControlSet\Services\Tcpip\Parameters\
EnablePMTUDiscovery,4,%EnablePMTUDiscovery%,0
MACHINE\System\CurrentControlSet\Services\Tcpip\Parameters\
KeepAliveTime,4,%KeepAliveTime%,3,150000|%KeepAliveTime0%,300000|
%KeepAliveTime1%,600000|%KeepAliveTime2%,1200000|%KeepAliveTime3%,
2400000|%KeepAliveTime4%,3600000|%KeepAliveTime5%,7200000|
%KeepAliveTime6%
MACHINE\System\CurrentControlSet\Services\Tcpip\Parameters\
DisableIPSourceRouting,4,%DisableIPSourceRouting%,3,0|
%DisableIPSourceRouting0%,1|%DisableIPSourceRouting1%,2|
%DisableIPSourceRouting2%
MACHINE\System\CurrentControlSet\Services\Tcpip\Parameters\
TcpMaxConnectResponseRetransmissions,4,
%TcpMaxConnectResponseRetransmissions%,3,0|
%TcpMaxConnectResponseRetransmissions0%,1|
%TcpMaxConnectResponseRetransmissions1%,2|
%TcpMaxConnectResponseRetransmissions2%,3|
%TcpMaxConnectResponseRetransmissions3%
MACHINE\System\CurrentControlSet\Services\Tcpip\Parameters\
TcpMaxDataRetransmissions,4,%TcpMaxDataRetransmissions%,1
MACHINE\System\CurrentControlSet\Services\Tcpip\Parameters\
PerformRouterDiscovery,4,%PerformRouterDiscovery%,0
MACHINE\System\CurrentControlSet\Services\Tcpip\Parameters\
TCPMaxPortsExhausted,4,%TCPMaxPortsExhausted%,1
MACHINE\System\CurrentControlSet\Services\Netbt\Parameters\
NoNameReleaseOnDemand,4,%NoNameReleaseOnDemand%,0
MACHINE\System\CurrentControlSet\Control\FileSystem\
NtfsDisable8dot3NameCreation,4,%NtfsDisable8dot3NameCreation%,0
```

```
MACHINE\SOFTWARE\Microsoft\Windows\CurrentVersion\Policies\
Explorer\NoDriveTypeAutoRun,4,%NoDriveTypeAutoRun%,3,0|
%NoDriveTypeAutoRun0%,255|%NoDriveTypeAutoRun1%
MACHINE\SYSTEM\CurrentControlSet\Services\Eventlog\Security\
WarningLevel,4,%WarningLevel%,3,50|%WarningLevel0%,60|
%WarningLevel1%,70|%WarningLevel2%,80|%WarningLevel3%,90|
%WarningLevel4%
MACHINE\SYSTEM\Software\Microsoft\Windows NT\CurrentVersion\Winlogon\
ScreenSaverGracePeriod,4,%ScreenSaverGracePeriod%,1
MACHINE\System\CurrentControlSet\Services\AFD\Parameters\
DynamicBacklogGrowthDelta,4,%DynamicBacklogGrowthDelta%,1
MACHINE\System\CurrentControlSet\Services\AFD\Parameters\
EnableDynamicBacklog,4,%EnableDynamicBacklog%,0
MACHINE\System\CurrentControlSet\Services\AFD\Parameters\
MinimumDynamicBacklog,4,%MinimumDynamicBacklog%,1
MACHINE\System\CurrentControlSet\Services\AFD\Parameters\
MaximumDynamicBacklog,4,%MaximumDynamicBacklog%,3,10000|
%MaximumDynamicBacklog0%,15000|%MaximumDynamicBacklog1%,20000|
%MaximumDynamicBacklog2%,40000|%MaximumDynamicBacklog3%,80000|
%MaximumDynamicBacklog4%,160000|%MaximumDynamicBacklog5%
MACHINE\SYSTEM\CurrentControlSet\Control\
Session Manager\SafeDllSearchMode,4,%SafeDllSearchMode%,0
[Strings} section
EnableICMPRedirect = "MSS: (EnableICMPRedirect) Allow ICMP redirects
to override OSPF generated routes"
SynAttackProtect = "MSS: (SynAttackProtect) Syn attack protection
level (protects against DoS)"
SynAttackProtect0 = "No additional protection, use default settings"
SynAttackProtect1 = "Connections time out sooner if a SYN attack is detected"
EnableDeadGWDetect = "MSS: (EnableDeadGWDetect) Allow automatic
detection of dead network gateways (could lead to DoS)"
EnablePMTUDiscovery = "MSS: (EnablePMTUDiscovery ) Allow automatic
detection of MTU size (possible DoS by an attacker using a small MTU)"
KeepAliveTime = "MSS: How often keep-alive packets are
sent in milliseconds"
KeepAliveTime0 ="150000 or 2.5 minutes"
KeepAliveTime1 ="300000 or 5 minutes (recommended)"
KeepAliveTime2 ="600000 or 10 minutes"
KeepAliveTime3 ="1200000 or 20 minutes"
KeepAliveTime4 ="2400000 or 40 minutes"
KeepAliveTime5 ="3600000 or 1 hour"
KeepAliveTime6 ="7200000 or 2 hours (default value)"
DisableIPSourceRouting = "MSS: (DisableIPSourceRouting) IP source
routing protection level (protects against packet spoofing)"
DisableIPSourceRouting0 = "No additional protection, source routed
packets are allowed"
DisableIPSourceRouting1 = "Medium, source routed packets ignored
when IP forwarding is enabled"
DisableIPSourceRouting2 = "Highest protection, source routing is
completely disabled"
TcpMaxConnectResponseRetransmissions = "MSS:
(TcpMaxConnectResponseRetransmissions) SYN-ACK retransmissions when
a connection request is not acknowledged"
TcpMaxConnectResponseRetransmissions0 = "No retransmission,
```

```
half-open connections dropped after 3 seconds"
TcpMaxConnectResponseRetransmissions1 = "3 seconds, half-open
connections dropped after 9 seconds"
TcpMaxConnectResponseRetransmissions2 = "3 & 6 seconds, half-open
connections dropped after 21 seconds"
TcpMaxConnectResponseRetransmissions3 = "3, 6, & 9 seconds,
half-open connections dropped after 45 seconds"
TcpMaxDataRetransmissions = "MSS: (TcpMaxDataRetransmissions) How
many times unacknowledged data is retransmitted (3 recommended, 5 is default)"
PerformRouterDiscovery = "MSS: (PerformRouterDiscovery) Allow IRDP
to detect and configure Default Gateway addresses (could lead to DoS)"
TCPMaxPortsExhausted = "MSS: (TCPMaxPortsExhausted) How many dropped
connect requests to initiate SYN attack protection (5 is recommended)"
NoNameReleaseOnDemand = "MSS: (NoNameReleaseOnDemand) Allow the
computer to ignore NetBIOS name release requests except from WINS servers"
NtfsDisable8dot3NameCreation = "MSS: Enable the computer to stop
generating 8.3 style filenames"
NoDriveTypeAutoRun = "MSS: Disable Autorun for all drives"
NoDriveTypeAutoRun0 = "Null, allow Autorun"
NoDriveTypeAutoRun1 = "255, disable Autorun for all drives"
WarningLevel = "MSS: Percentage threshold for the security event log
at which the system will generate a warning"
WarningLevel0 = "50%"
WarningLevel1 = "60%"
WarningLevel2 = "70%"
WarningLevel3 = "80%"
WarningLevel4 = "90%"
ScreenSaverGracePeriod = "MSS: The time in seconds before the screen
saver grace period expires (0 recommended)"
DynamicBacklogGrowthDelta = "MSS: (AFD DynamicBacklogGrowthDelta)
Number of connections to create when additional connections are
necessary for Winsock applications (10 recommended)"
EnableDynamicBacklog = "MSS: (AFD EnableDynamicBacklog) Enable
dynamic backlog for Winsock applications (recommended)"
MinimumDynamicBacklog = "MSS: (AFD MinimumDynamicBacklog) Minimum
number of free connections for Winsock applications (20 recommended
for systems under attack, 10 otherwise)"
MaximumDynamicBacklog = "MSS: (AFD MaximumDynamicBacklog) Maximum
number of 'quasi-free' connections for Winsock applications"
MaximumDynamicBacklog0 = "10000"
MaximumDynamicBacklog1 = "15000"
MaximumDynamicBacklog2 = "20000 (recommended)"
MaximumDynamicBacklog3 = "40000"
MaximumDynamicBacklog4 = "80000"
MaximumDynamicBacklog5 = "160000"
SafeDllSearchMode = "MSS: Enable Safe DLL search mode (recommended)"
```

Note   You can copy and paste this code from the file to the Sceregvl.inf file. To access the Microsoft document that this code originated from, go to *http://www.microsoft.com/technet/security/guidance/secmod57.mspx.*

After you have included the custom changes from the list above into your Sceregvl.inf file, you will have a large list of new policy settings in the security templates, as shown in Figure 15-19.

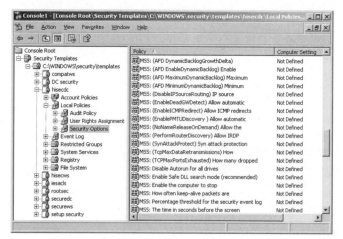

Figure 15-19 Microsoft-supplied custom security policies in the security template interface

Warning The customizations listed above use features available only on Windows XP Professional with Service Pack 1 or later and Windows Server 2003. Do not try to install them on earlier versions of the Windows operating system.

Summary

Security is a top priority for every IT administrator, so it is important to know which options are available. The default security templates and GPOs provide an extensive list of security settings. You can use the standard security templates or you can customize them with tailor-made security settings for all computers in the domain.

If you need settings that are not available in the standard security templates, you can customize the settings to meet your needs. Any registry value that you need to control on target computers can be included in a security template and therefore a GPO. You simply modify the Sceregvl.inf file and register the Scecli.dll file to make the new custom security policies available within the security templates and GPOs.

Part IV
Group Policy Troubleshooting

In this part:

Chapter 16: Troubleshooting Group Policy. 581

Chapter 17: Resolving Common Group Policy Problems 625

Chapter 16

Troubleshooting Group Policy

In this chapter:

Group Policy Troubleshooting Essentials............................582

Essential Troubleshooting Tools 593

Group Policy Logging 609

Summary...623

Group Policy, like any other area of administration, has to be managed carefully. When things aren't working as expected or you suspect there's a problem, you have to roll up your sleeves and start troubleshooting. The problem is where to begin. Group Policy has many infrastructure dependencies. For things to go exactly right, the infrastructure must be set up appropriately and there must be no failure of essential services such as Domain Name System (DNS), Distributed File System (DFS), or even Active Directory® itself. Because of this, Group Policy troubleshooting should always begin with an examination of the supporting infrastructure. Once you confirm that the problem isn't within the underlying infrastructure, you can work to troubleshoot Group Policy.

Related Information

- For more information about DNS architecture, see Chapters 26 and 27 in *Microsoft® Windows Server™ 2003 Inside Out* (Microsoft Press, 2004).

- For more information about Active Directory architecture, see Chapter 32 in *Microsoft Windows Server 2003 Inside Out.*

- For more information about Group Policy structure, see Chapter 13.

- For more information about common Group Policy problems, see Chapter 17.

Group Policy Troubleshooting Essentials

When you discover problems with Group Policy processing, you can take a number of avenues to track down the problem. Because Group Policy processing has many moving parts, with many interdependent pieces of infrastructure, it is important to take a methodical approach to troubleshooting. By using the information about Group Policy processing presented in Chapter 13, we can create a high-level list of items to check when Group Policy processing fails on a workstation or server. Here are the steps:

1. Check the required infrastructure. Make sure required services and components are running and configured as expected.

2. Check the core configuration. Verify that the computer is connected to the network, joined to the domain, and has the correct system time. Check the startup state of services and other basics.

3. Check the scope of management (SOM). Verify that items such as security filtering, WMI filters, block inheritance, enforcement, loopback processing, and slow-link settings aren't affecting normal GPO processing.

4. Use tools such as GPResult.exe, GPOTool.exe, and the Group Policy Management Console (GPMC) to ensure that Group Policy settings are being delivered as expected and that Group Policy objects (GPOs) on domain controllers are consistent and available.

5. Use event logs and Group Policy core and client-side extension (CSE) logs to drill into the problem and find the solution.

In this chapter, we will look closely at each of these steps and at the tools and techniques for solving many Group Policy problems. Chapter 17 also provides details on resolving common problems with Group Policy.

Verifying the Core Configuration

Administrators frequently jump into in-depth troubleshooting of Group Policy without checking the essentials. Before you get too deep into troubleshooting, you should always perform some essential checks:

- Verify the network connection and configuration.
- Verify the computer account and domain trust.
- Validate the computer and network time.
- Verify the computer and user account configuration.

Verifying the Network Connection and Configuration

To receive and process policy, a computer must be connected to the network and have a properly configured connection. You can verify this by typing the following command at the command prompt:

```
netsh interface ip show config
```

If a computer's network connection is disabled or corrupted, you'll see an error message such as this one:

```
No more data is available.
```

In this case, you must access Network Connections and solve the problem by enabling or repairing the connection. To enable the connection, right-click the connection and select Enable. To attempt to repair the connection, right-click the connection and select Repair.

If the network connection is enabled, you should see network configuration details similar to the following:

```
Configuration for interface "Local Area Connection"
    DHCP enabled:                         No
    IP Address:                           192.168.1.28
    SubnetMask:                           255.255.255.0
    Default Gateway:                      192.168.1.50
    GatewayMetric:                        0
    InterfaceMetric:                      0
    Statically Configured DNS Servers:    192.168.1.50
    Statically Configured WINS Servers:   None
    Register with which suffix:           Primary only
```

 Note Netsh is a built-in utility. Chapter 15 in the *Microsoft Windows® Command-Line Administrator's Pocket Consultant* (Microsoft Press, 2004) covers Netsh in detail.

This list of settings shows that there is an active network connection and provides the settings of this connection. As part of troubleshooting, check the network settings closely to ensure that they are configured as expected.

Verifying the Computer Account and Trust

To receive and process policy, a computer must be joined to the domain, and the trust between the computer and the domain must be properly established. You can verify the computer account and computer trust in the domain by typing the following command at the command prompt:

```
nltest /sc_query:DomainName
```

where *DomainName* is the name of the domain to which the computer is joined, such as:

```
nltest /sc_query:cpandl.com
```

If the computer is properly joined to the domain and the trust is valid, you should see a query response similar to the following:

```
Flags: 30 HAS_IP  HAS_TIMESERV
Trusted DC Name \\corpsvr04.cpandl.com
Trusted DC Connection Status Status = 0 0x0 NERR_Success
The command completed successfully
```

Note   Nltest is included in the Windows Server 2003 Support Tools. The output of the test doesn't validate the current state of a computer's network connection—only the status of the computer account and the related trust.

Verifying Time Synchronization

Kerberos validation and authentication will fail if the time difference between a client computer and its logon domain controller is greater than 5 minutes. This failure can in turn cause problems with DNS registration, Group Policy processing, and other essential computer processes.

To check a computer's current system time and date, type the following command exactly as shown at a command prompt:

```
net time \\%ComputerName%
```

The output is the current time and date on the local computer, such as:

```
Current time at \\ENGPC07 is 2/7/2005 2:02 PM
```

To check the system time on the logon domain controller, type the following command at a command prompt:

```
net time
```

The output is the current time and date on the logon domain controller, such as:

```
Current time at \\CORPSVR04 is 2/7/2005 2:02 PM
```

Note   You can type **net time /set** to synchronize the local computer time with the time on the logon domain controller. To automatically synchronize time for all computers in a domain, you can use the W32Time Service.

Verifying the Computer and User Account Configuration

Sometimes we assume that computers and users are in a particular container or that they are members of a particular security group. When you are troubleshooting Group Policy, you can no longer make this assumption, and you should verify both the Active Directory container in which computer and user accounts are placed and the security groups they belong to.

The fastest way to determine the container in which a computer is placed is to type the following command:

```
dsquery computer -name ComputerName
```

where *ComputerName* is the name of the computer, such as:

```
dsquery computer -name engpc07
```

The output of this command specifies the current container location of the related computer object, such as:

```
"CN=engpc07,OU=Engineering,DC=cpandl,DC=com"
```

> **Note** If a computer or user was recently moved to this container, the computer or user might not be processing the applicable GPOs for this container. This occurs because Active Directory clients cache their location within the directory. To solve this problem you must either reboot the machine or wait for the location cache to be refreshed (which occurs in approximately 30 minutes). You can verify which GPOs are being processed by using Resultant Set of Policy (RSoP) logging, as discussed later in the chapter. Chapters 11 through 13 in the *Microsoft Windows Command-Line Administrator's Pocket Consultant* provide in-depth details on *dsquery*, *dsget*, and related directory services commands.

The fastest way to determine the container in which a user is placed is to type the following command:

```
dsquery user -samid LogonAccountName
```

where *LogonAccountName* is the logon name of the user, such as:

```
dsquery user -samid wrstanek
```

The output of this command specifies the current container location of the related user object, such as:

```
"CN=William R. Stanek,CN=Users,DC=cpandl,DC=com"
```

When security filtering is used, you might also want to know the security groups a user belongs to. You can determine this by typing the following command:

```
dsquery user -samid LogonAccountName | dsget user -memberof
```

where *LogonAccountName* is the logon name of the user, such as:

```
dsquery user -samid wrstanek | dsget user -memberof
```

The output of this command specifies the group membership for the specified user, such as:

```
"CN=Domain Admins,CN=Users,DC=cpandl,DC=com"
"CN=Administrators,CN=Builtin,DC=cpandl,DC=com"
"CN=Domain Users,CN=Users,DC=cpandl,DC=com"
```

Verifying Key Infrastructure Components

For Group Policy to work properly, a number of key infrastructure components must be functioning properly. These include:

- **Active Directory Replication**   Domain controllers use Active Directory to replicate changes to the GPC to other domain controllers. If Active Directory replication isn't working properly, changes to files in the GPC won't be distributed properly. Active Directory makes extensive use of a storage engine and has a data store referred to as the *Active Directory data store*. The data store and related files are stored in the %SystemRoot%\Ntds folder on domain controllers.

- **DNS**   Computers processing Group Policy must be able to find the Windows domain controllers that are acting as LDAP servers. They do this via DNS. If DNS isn't available or SRV records are not registered for available domain controllers, computers cannot correctly query a domain controller for the GPOs that apply to them.

- **ICMP (Ping)**   Computers processing Group Policy rely on ICMP pings to determine whether the domain controller that is servicing them is available over a slow or fast network link. If ICMP is blocked or domain controllers are unable to respond to ICMP pings, Group Policy processing will fail.

- **TCP/IP NetBIOS Helper Service**   After a Windows computer obtains its list of GPOs to process from Active Directory, it contacts the Distributed File System (DFS) SYSVOL share to get the contents of the GPT for each GPO. Windows then requests the contents of the GPT in the SYSVOL. Because SYSVOL is a fault-tolerant DFS root, it is referred to using the DNS name of the domain in which it resides (for example, \\cpandl.com\SYSVOL). If the TCP/IP NetBIOS Helper service is not running on the computer processing Group Policy, the conversion of the DNS domain name within the UNC request into a valid server name will fail. The TCP/IP NetBIOS Helper service must be running for any computer that is processing Group Policy.

- **Distributed File System (DFS)**   Domain controllers use DFS and its related services to share the SYSVOL. If DFS isn't working, computers in the domain cannot read the contents of the GPT in SYSVOL. DFS depends on the DfsDriver and Mup components as well as the Security Accounts Manager, Server, and Workstation services.

- **File Replication Service (FRS)**   Domain controllers use FRS to replicate changes to the GPT to other domain controllers. If FRS isn't working properly, changes to files in the GPT won't be distributed properly. Like Active Directory, FRS makes extensive use of a storage engine and has a data store referred to as the *replication store*. The replication store uses the Microsoft Jet database technology, and the related files are stored in the %SystemRoot%\Ntfrs\Jet folder on domain controllers.

Your Group Policy troubleshooting should always start with an examination of these infrastructure components. Once you've eliminated the underlying infrastructure as a possible source of the problem, start troubleshooting Group Policy by verifying the scope of management. For more information on troubleshooting required infrastructure, see Chapter 17.

Verifying the Scope of Management

Sometimes the problem with Group Policy processing is a simple but not obvious one: a particular policy is not being applied because it should not apply. To verify whether a policy should or should not apply, you can use a number of techniques.

Checking the GPO Status and Version

A GPO can have a variety of status states that can affect processing. A GPO can be disabled, or just the user or computer sides of the GPO can be disabled. To rule out GPO status as a potential source of a problem, you can examine the GPO in the GPMC by completing these steps:

1. In the GPMC, expand the entry for the forest you want to work with, expand the related Domains node, and then expand the related Group Policy Objects node.

2. Select the GPO you are troubleshooting, and in the right pane, click the Details tab.

3. The GPO Status field reflects the current state of the GPO (Figure 16-1). Generally speaking, the GPO should have a status of Enabled. Any other status means that the GPO is either partially or fully disabled. Before you change the status of the GPO, you should check with other administrators to see if there is a reason why the GPO state has been reset.

4. The User Version and Computer Version fields provide details on the current version of the GPO, as reflected in Active Directory (the GPC) and the SYSVOL (the GPT). Changes to the user and computer configuration are tracked separately, but the version number for each should be the same in the GPC and GPT. If they aren't, there might be a problem with Active Directory replication or FRS.

Figure 16-1 Viewing the GPO status and version

Checking the GPO on the Logon Domain Controller

When you work with the GPMC, remember that you are connected by default to the PDC Emulator for the domain and are therefore seeing the general state of the GPO in question. In most cases, though, the problem will be with another domain controller or will be in another area of the network. As a result, you'll often want to log on to a computer that is experiencing problems with Group Policy and determine to which domain controller you are connected. You can then either identify or rule out this domain controller as a source of the problem.

Complete the following steps to troubleshoot a specific domain controller:

1. If a particular user is experiencing a problem with Group Policy, access a command prompt on his computer and type **set**. Otherwise, log on to a computer in the area or network segment that is having problems with Group Policy, access a command prompt, and then type **set**.

2. Scroll back through the results to determine the value of the *LOGONSERVER* environment variable. This is the domain controller to which you are (or the current user is) connected.

> **Note**   Because logon information can be cached, the computer might be disconnected from the network or have a disabled local area connection and still have a setting for the *LOGONSERVER* environment variable. Check the status of Local Area Connection under Network Connections or try to connect over the LAN to a network resource to confirm the network status.

3. In the GPMC, right-click the domain node and then select Change Domain Controller. Under Change To, select This Domain Controller and then select the logon server you located previously. Click OK.

> **Note**   You don't have to start the GPMC on the computer for which you are troubleshooting Group Policy. You can start the GPMC on your computer or another computer located on the same network segment as that computer.

4. Expand the Group Policy Objects node for the domain in question. Select the GPO you are troubleshooting, and in the right pane, click the Details tab.

   You will see the status and version of the GPO as seen by the selected domain controller.

> **Note**   There are, of course, other ways to check the logon server and the status of GPOs with regard to a particular user or computer. You can, for example, use RSoP logging to determine this information (as covered in the "Essential Troubleshooting Tools" section in this chapter). Keep in mind that Windows Firewall on computers running Windows XP Professional Service Pack 2 may block you from remotely accessing the problem machine. See Chapter 11 to learn how to configure Windows Firewall exceptions.

Checking the GPO Link Status and Order

A Group Policy link can have different states that affect whether that GPO applies to a user or computer. For example, a Group Policy link might be disabled or enforced. If a link is disabled, the GPO will not apply to users or computers within the container to which that GPO is linked. If a link is enforced, the GPO will actually apply over any conflicting settings that are subsequently processed. For example, an enforced GPO linked to the domain will overwrite any conflicting settings from a GPO linked to an organizational unit (OU) in that domain.

Link order also affects how policy is applied. When multiple policy objects are linked to a particular level, the link order determines the order in which policy settings are applied. Generally speaking, the order of inheritance goes from the site level to the domain level and then to each nested OU level.

To check link status and link order for a specific GPO, complete these steps:

1. In the GPMC, expand the entry for the forest you want to work with, expand the related Domains node, and then expand the related Group Policy Objects node.

2. Select the GPO you are troubleshooting, and in the right pane, click the Scope tab.

   On the right side, you will see the containers to which that GPO is linked and their status, as shown in Figure 16-2.

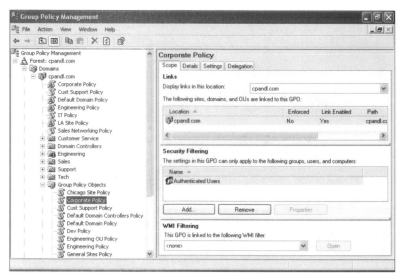

Figure 16-2 Viewing link status on a GPO within the GPMC

To check the order and status of GPOs linked to a specific container, complete these steps:

1. In the GPMC, expand the entry for the forest you want to work with.

2. Do one of the following:

   ❏ If you are troubleshooting domain policy, select the domain node.

   ❏ If you are troubleshooting OU policy, select the OU node.

   ❏ If you are troubleshooting site policy, expand Sites and then select the site node.

   The Linked Group Policy Objects tab shows the link order and the status of each GPO linked to the selected container (Figure 16-3). Linked policy objects are always applied in link ranking order. Lower-ranking policy objects are processed first and then higher-ranking policy objects are processed.

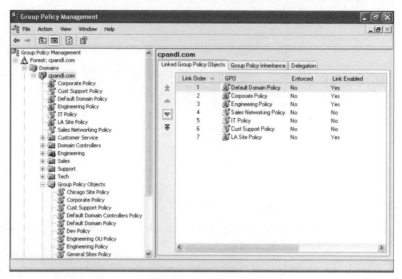

Figure 16-3   Viewing link status on a container object within the GPMC

Checking the GPO Permissions

As discussed in Chapter 3, you must set Read and Apply Group Policy permissions to ensure that a GPO is processed. By default, members of the Authenticated Users group are granted these permissions on all GPOs, which means the policy will be applied to all users and computers in the container to which a particular GPO is linked. If the default security filtering is changed, this will also affect how users and computers process a particular GPO. An additional type of filter that can be applied to GPOs is a WMI filter. The specific criteria of the WMI filter must be met in order for the GPO to be processed.

A security group, user, or computer must have both Read and Apply Group Policy permissions for a policy to be applied. By default, all users and computers have these permissions for all new GPOs. These permissions are inherited from their membership in the implicit group Authenticated Users. An authenticated user is any user (or computer) that has logged on to the domain and been authenticated.

To examine the filtering that has been applied to a GPO, complete these steps:

1. In the GPMC, expand the entry for the forest you want to work with, expand the related Domains node, and then expand the related Group Policy Objects node.

2. Select the GPO you are troubleshooting, and in the right pane, click the Scope tab. The Security Filtering and WMI Filtering panels show the current filtering configuration.

3. To see the exact set of permissions for users, groups, and computers, click the Delegation tab and then click Advanced. Select the security group, user, or computer you want to review. Keep the following in mind:

   ❑ If the policy object should be applied to the security group, user, or computer, the minimum permissions should be set to allow Read and Apply Group Policy.

   ❑ If the policy object should not be applied to the security group, user, or computer, the permissions should be set to allow Read and deny Apply Group Policy.

Checking the Loopback Processing Status of the GPO

You can manage loopback processing by enabling User Group Policy Loopback Processing Mode under Computer Configuration\Administrative Templates\System\ Group Policy and then setting the loopback processing mode to either replace or merge settings:

■ When you use the Replace option, user settings from the computer's GPOs are processed and the user settings in the user's GPOs are not processed. This means the user settings from the computer's GPOs replace the user settings normally applied to the user.

■ When you use the Merge option, user settings in the computer's GPOs are processed first, then user settings in the user's GPOs are processed, and then user settings in the computer's GPOs are processed again. This processing technique serves to combine the user settings in both the computer and user GPOs. If there are any conflicts, the user settings in the computer's GPOs take precedence and overwrite the user settings in the user's GPOs.

Because loopback processing changes the way policy is applied, you must know whether the computer that a user is logging on to has loopback processing enabled. Otherwise, you cannot troubleshoot properly. One way to determine whether loopback processing is enabled is to use the Group Policy Results Wizard in the GPMC to view which policies are in effect on a machine. To learn more about loopback processing and how to disable it, see "Changing Policy Processing Preferences" in Chapter 3, or see Chapter 12, which provides additional scenarios for configuring and working with loopback processing.

Checking for Slow Links

Slow links can also affect policy processing. By default, the client computer considers any connection speed less than 500 kilobits per second as slow. As a result, only Security Settings and Administrative Templates in the applicable policy objects are sent by the domain controller during policy refresh (by default). See "Configuring Slow Link Detection" in Chapter 3 for more information.

Essential Troubleshooting Tools

After you have verified that the core configuration and infrastructure required for proper Group Policy processing are functional and available, the next step is to use the Group Policy troubleshooting tools to try to further isolate the problem. The best place to start is with tools that report on RSoP for a given computer and user. The two main tools for doing this are the Group Policy Results Wizard and the Gpresult command-line utility. Other useful tools include Gpotool, which can help you verify the health of the GPC and GPT, and Group Policy Monitor, which allows you to centralize and automate collection of Group Policy Results reports.

Working with Resultant Set Of Policy

Chapters 2 and 3 introduced RSoP and the Group Policy Results Wizard. The Group Policy Results Wizard (which you access by right-clicking the Group Policy Results node within the GPMC console) allows you to connect to a remote Windows computer to determine what Group Policy processing occurred for a given user on that computer during the last Group Policy processing cycle. This mechanism is known as *RSoP logging mode.*

> **Note** RSoP logging uses the WMI-based RSoP infrastructure available in Windows XP and Windows Server 2003 to remotely obtain this RSoP logging data. Group Policy processing, running under the Winlogon process, calls CSEs to perform policy processing. These CSEs send their RSoP data to the WMI CIMOM database. The GPMC then requests the RSoP data from the CIMOM database for reporting in HTML format.

To use the Group Policy Results Wizard to obtain RSoP logging data from a remote user and computer, complete these steps:

1. In the GPMC, right-click the Group Policy Results node, and then select Group Policy Results Wizard.

2. When the Group Policy Results Wizard starts, click Next. On the Computer Selection page, select Local Computer to view information for the local computer. If you want to view information for a remote computer, select Another Computer and then click Browse. In the Select Computer dialog box, type the name of the computer, and then click Check Names. Once the correct computer account is selected, click OK.

> **Tip** If you are unable to connect to the remote computer to run the Group Policy Results Wizard, Windows Firewall running on the remote computer might be preventing the appropriate network traffic from being passed. You can allow this kind of administrative traffic using Remote Administration Exception policy. See "Allowing Remote Administration Exceptions" in Chapter 11 for details.

3. By default, both user and computer policy settings are logged. If you want to see results only for user policy settings, select Do Not Display Policy Settings For The Selected Computer.

4. In the wizard, click Next. On the User Selection page, select the user whose policy information you want to view. You can view policy information for any user who has logged on to the computer.

5. If you want to see results only for computer policy settings, select Do Not Display User Policy Settings.

6. To complete the modeling, click Next twice, and then click Finish. The wizard generates a report and displays it in the Details pane.

7. Right-click the report in the left pane to perform additional management of the report. The options include:

   ❑ **Advanced View**   Provides a modified view of the policy settings that have been applied in a separate window

   ❑ **Rerun Query**   Allows you to rerun your original query, which can update the report to reflect the most current policy processing for a remote user and computer

   ❑ **Save Report**   Allows you to save the report for later reference

The information provided by the Group Policy Results Wizard can be very useful for troubleshooting Group Policy processing issues. Every results report has three tabs (Summary, Settings, and Policy Events) as well as an advanced view.

Navigating the Summary Tab

The Summary tab provides information about core Group Policy processing on the target system. Similar information is provided for both computer-specific and user-specific policies. You can click the Show All link to view all of the aspects of this tab.

As Figure 16-4 shows, the summary information is organized into five subcategories:

   ❑ **General**   Provides information about the computer that is being queried for RSoP information, the domain the computer resides in, the site the computer was found in (for site-linked Group Policy), and the date and time of the last Group Policy processing cycle (foreground or background).

   ❑ **Group Policy Objects**   Provides information as to the computer-specific GPOs that have been applied to this computer or denied. The list of applied GPOs shows the name of the GPO, where it was linked when it was applied, and the number of revisions in both the GPC (referred to as *AD*) and GPT (referred to as *SYSVOL*) portions of the GPO. If the GPC and GPT version numbers are different for a given GPO, this might indicate Active Directory or FRS replication problems.

The list of GPOs that have been denied includes the reason for the denial. A GPO might be denied because it's empty (for example, no policy settings have been made within it), because security group filtering prevents the computer (or user) from processing it, or because of a WMI filter that blocks processing.

❑ **Security Group Membership When Group Policy Was Applied**   Lists the members of all groups the computer (or user) was a member of when Group Policy processing last occurred. You can use this information to determine why security group filtering might or might not be working for a particular GPO.

❑ **WMI Filters**   Shows any WMI filters linked to GPOs that are processed by the computer and the result of the filter as it was evaluated for that computer (or user). WMI filters can affect whether a particular GPO is being processed. If a WMI returns a false value, the GPO that it is linked to will not be processed.

❑ **Component Status**   Shows whether core Group Policy processing succeeded and whether each CSE that was processed succeeded. It also shows the date and time that core processing and each CSE processing cycle last ran.

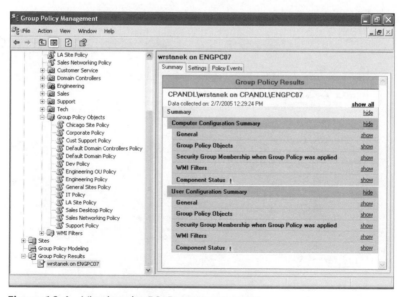

Figure 16-4   Viewing the RSoP summary report

Note The reported run times in the Component Status section will not always be the same, and that is OK. For example, core GP processing runs during every background and foreground processing cycle, but some CSEs might not process any GPOs if none of the GPOs containing those settings has changed since the last processing cycle. Therefore, if each CSE listed in this section has a different time, this does not necessarily indicate a problem.

Tip What you are looking for in the Component Status section is a failure status on one or more elements of policy processing. For example, if core policy processing fails, this usually indicates a failure of some part of the policy infrastructure or related components. Failure of a particular CSE can mean any number of things, including corrupted policy data for that CSE or a problem reading a GPO containing those policy settings. The next step for drilling into CSE problems is to look at the various logs that are available for that CSE. We'll examine this in the "Group Policy Logging" section later in this chapter.

Navigating the Settings Tab

The Settings tab provides detailed information about which policy settings have been made on a given computer or for a given user. You can drill down through each section by clicking the Show link, or you can click the Show All link to expand all the sections. Within the subsections, each policy setting that has been applied is listed by name, along with its status (Enabled or Disabled) and the "winning" GPO that delivered that setting (Figure 16-5).

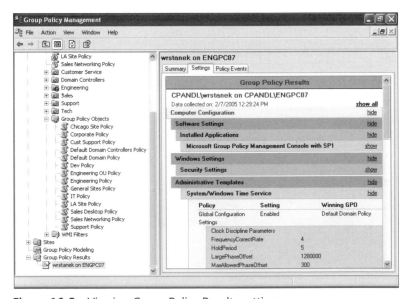

Figure 16-5 Viewing Group Policy Results settings

The Settings details are valuable for confirming that a particular policy setting is indeed being made, and also for letting you know whether the right GPO is being applied or whether some issue is preventing the correct GPO from winning for a particular setting. You can use this information in conjunction with the information on the Summary tab to determine why a particular setting is not being applied as expected.

Navigating the Policy Events Tab

The Policy Events tab lists events retrieved from the computer against which the Group Policy Results Wizard was run. These events are retrieved from the application event log on the remote machine and are specific to Group Policy processing. Figure 16-6 shows an example.

What makes the Policy Events tab so useful is that the events shown represent a filtered view of the remote computer's application event log—only Group Policy–related events are shown. We'll look in more detail at application event logs related to Group Policy shortly, but this tab can give you a quick indication of any problems related to both core and CSE-specific Group Policy processing. A quick glance at this tab after running the wizard can point out obvious errors that need to be addressed before policy processing can succeed.

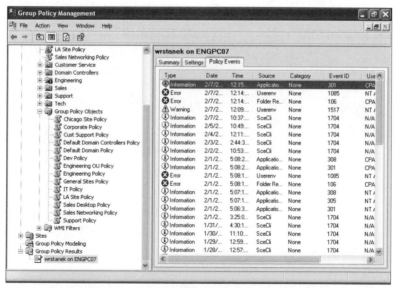

Figure 16-6   Viewing policy-related events

Navigating the Advanced View

If you right-click a particular Group Policy Results report in the left-hand pane and select Advanced View, you can access a modified view of the policy settings that have been applied in a separate Microsoft Management Console (MMC) window. As Figure 16-7 shows, the advanced view is similar to the view provided in the Group Policy Object Editor. The key difference is that the advanced view shows only the policy settings that have been delivered to the computer and user. The source or origin GPO is also listed for every policy setting.

Tip You can see the advanced view on a local computer by typing **rsop.msc** at a command prompt. When run on the local computer, RSoP logging is performed automatically against the local computer and the currently logged-on user. This means you don't need to generate a report manually for a local computer—the report is generated automatically when you start Rsop.msc. Rsop.msc is only available on computers running Windows XP Professional and later.

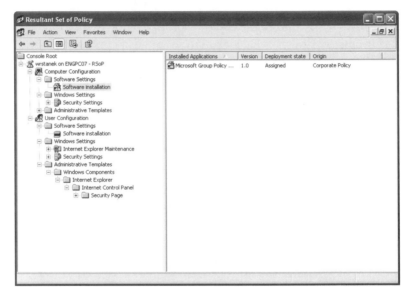

Figure 16-7 Accessing the advanced view

If, after running the Group Policy Results Wizard, you want to see whether the next Group Policy processing cycle might fix the problem, you can force a background refresh of Group Policy using Gpupdate. Type the following command:

```
gpupdate /force
```

This command reapplies all Group Policy to the user and computer, regardless of whether the GPO has changed since the last processing cycle. After you refresh policy, you can right-click the Group Policy Results report in the GPMC and select the Rerun option. The GPMC will recollect RSoP logging data from the computer and user in question.

Note Gpupdate /force can be used on computers running Windows XP Professional and later versions of the Windows operating system. For Windows 2000, you must use Secedit /refreshpolicy instead.

Viewing RSoP from the Command Line

Gpresult is essentially identical to the GPMC-based Group Policy Results Wizard. The significant difference is that Gpresult is a command-line tool, which means you can easily incorporate it into automation scripts that perform periodic queries against computers and users to determine Group Policy status. Gpresult.exe is a standard part of Windows XP and Windows Server 2003 and provides a number of command-line options.

Gpresult is pretty straightforward to use. The basic syntax is as follows:

```
gpresult /s ComputerName /user Domain\UserName
```

ComputerName is the name of the remote computer for which you want to log policy results and *Domain\UserName* indicates the remote user. For example, if you want to perform RSoP logging against a remote computer called engpc07 and return RSoP logging information for the user wrstanek in the CPANDL domain, you can type the following command:

```
gpresult /s engpc07 /user cpandl\wrstanek
```

You will see only the summary information about which GPOs were applied or denied and group membership information. You won't see the equivalent of the Group Policy Results Wizard Settings tab. To get the same level of detail as the GPMC's Group Policy Results Wizard, you must use the /v or /z option. The difference between these two verbose options is that if a policy setting has conflicting settings from multiple GPOs, the /v option shows only the setting delivered by the winning GPO and the /z option shows the setting of the winning GPO and any other GPOs that have set that policy.

> **Tip**   If you need to run Gpresult within the context of another user, such as when you use an administrative account, you can use the */u* and */p* options to provide the account and password for the alternate user context. If you use the */scope user* or */scope computer* option, you can specify that you want to report on only user or computer policy settings.

As with the Group Policy Results Wizard, Gpresult.exe is useful for viewing the results of Group Policy processing to determine whether certain policies have been applied and if not, why not. In verbose mode, Gpresult provides just about the same information that the Group Policy Results Wizard does, with a few exceptions. Specifically, Gpresult provides some additional useful configuration information about the computer you are querying, such as the computer's operating system version and whether the computer and user policies were processed over a slow link. As an example, the following listing shows a snippet of the first part of a Gpresult listing with this additional information:

```
OS Type:              Microsoft(R) Windows(R) Server 2003, Standard Edition
OS Configuration:     Primary Domain Controller
OS Version:           5.2.3790
```

```
Terminal Server Mode:        Remote Administration
Site Name:                   Default-First-Site-Name
Roaming Profile:
Local Profile:               C:\Documents and Settings\Administrator
Connected over a slow link?: No
```

Since calling Gpresult using one of the verbose modes can result in a large amount of data, especially in environments with many GPOs, it is easier to redirect the output of this command to a text file, using the syntax shown here:

```
gpresult /s engpc07 /user cpandl\wrstanek /z > gplogging.txt
```

Verifying Server-Side GPO Health

When you want to examine the health of Group Policy on your domain controllers, the Group Policy verification tool, Gpotool, is particularly useful. This command-line utility is included in the Windows Server 2003 Resource Kit and is useful for troubleshooting problems with the server-side aspects of Group Policy. It's a good idea to run this tool early in your troubleshooting process to verify that there are no problems with the GPOs themselves.

You can use Gpotool in two key ways: to scan all GPOs in your domain across all domain controllers or to query specific GPOs on specific domain controllers. The first technique is useful if you are trying to determine whether there is a problem with the server-side health of Group Policy. The second technique is useful if you believe that there are problems with GPOs on specific domain controllers. Gpotool looks at both the GPC and GPT to verify consistency and version numbers between the GPC and GPT. It also reports on any options that have been enabled on a given GPO (for example, disabled or user disabled only).

Checking the GPC and GPT for Errors

Using Gpotool to check all GPOs in the current (logon) domain is fairly straightforward. You simply type **gpotool** at a command prompt. Gpotool then verifies the consistency of the GPC and GPT, checks permissions on the GPT, and checks the GPC and GPT version numbers to ensure that there are no problems. If there are no problems with the GPOs, the report looks similar to the following:

```
Validating DCs...
Available DCs:
corpsvr04.cpandl.com
...
corpsvr25.cpandl.com
Searching for policies...
Found 14 policies
```

```
==========================================================
Policy {0BF0F7D6-0245-4133-BC78-B98AFBA21F48}
Friendly name: Engineering Policy
Policy OK
==========================================================
Policy {0C5F4FAF-8749-4EDC-9BC9-9B729DB5DD4F}
Friendly name: General Sites Policy
Policy OK
==========================================================

...


==========================================================
Policy {F9D36F52-E28D-4D54-87DB-9DFFBE9EAB73}
Friendly name: Support Policy
Policy OK
==========================================================

Policies OK
```

If consistency problems are found, a verbose listing of the GPO in question is provided, along with the specific issues and errors. In the following example, the Engineering Policy GPO has a version discrepancy between the GPT and GPC:

```
Validating DCs...
Available DCs:
corpsvr04.cpandl.com
Searching for policies...
Found 14 policies
==========================================================
Policy {0BF0F7D6-0245-4133-BC78-B98AFBA21F48}
Error: Version mismatch on corpsvr04.cpandl.com, DS=1, sysvol=889
Friendly name: Engineering Policy
Details:
----------------------------------------------------------
DC: corpsvr04.cpandl.com
Friendly name: Engineering Policy
Created: 12/10/2004 8:08:46 PM
Changed: 12/10/2004 8:18:11 PM
DS version:      16384000(user) 720(machine)
Sysvol version: 16384000 (user) 889(machine)
Flags: 0 (user side enabled; machine side enabled)
User extensions: not found
Machine extensions: [{0ACDD40C-75AC-47AB-BAA0-BF6DE7E7FE63}{2DA6AA7F-8C88-4194-A558-
0D36E7FD3E64}]
Functionality version: 2
----------------------------------------------------------
==========================================================
Policy {0C5F4FAF-8749-4EDC-9BC9-9B729DB5DD4F}
Friendly name: General Sites Policy
Policy OK
==========================================================

...
```

```
==============================================================
Policy {F9D36F52-E28D-4D54-87DB-9DFFBE9EAB73}
Friendly name: Support Policy
Policy OK
==============================================================

Errors found
```

The version discrepancy tells you there is something wrong and that you should dig deeper to find out what it is. It might indicate a problem with replicating GPT changes or a problem with the file system itself. Because SYSVOL changes are replicated using the File Replication Service (FRS), the FRS is a likely suspect. However, your troubleshooting should start with a look at the GPT itself and the required services. For example, permissions on the GPT might be incorrect, the disk might be full, or there might be corruption on the disk. The File Replication Service or the Distributed File System service might also have stopped.

Checking the SYSVOL Permissions

By default, Gpotool doesn't check the permissions on the SYSVOL. You can check permissions on the SYSVOL by adding the /*CHECKACL* option, as shown here:

```
gpotool /checkacl
```

Unfortunately, Gpotool checks permissions only on the SYSVOL. The permissions on subfolders within the SYSVOL are not checked. Still, if SYSVOL permissions were accidentally changed, this check would reveal the problem.

Verifying Specific GPOs

You can also use Gpotool to check the state of a specific GPO with regard to specific domain controllers. For example, say you want to check the Default Domain Policy GPO on the domain controllers corpsvr01 and corpsvr02. You can use the following syntax with Gpotool to get the desired results:

```
gpotool /gpo:"Default Domain Policy" /domain:cpandl.com /dc:corpsvr01,corpsvr02
/verbose
```

When the tool runs, it returns an OK status if the GPO is found with no problems and returns an error if problems are found.

Navigating the GPO Details

While the verbose information is provided automatically if there is a problem with a GPO, you can specify that you want verbose output for all GPOs by using the /*verbose* option. Some of the most important additional details you'll find in the verbose output relate to which user and machine extensions have settings configured for a particular GPO. Each CSE that has configured settings is listed according to its GUID.

To see how this works, consider the following sample output:

```
==============================================================
Policy {31B2F340-016D-11D2-945F-00C04FB984F9}
Friendly name: Sales Policy
Policy OK
Details:
--------------------------------------------------------------
DC: corpsvr04.cpandl.com
Friendly name: Sales Policy
Created: 5/11/2004 11:05:05 PM
Changed: 1/14/2005 1:37:13 AM
DS version:     71(user) 128(machine)
Sysvol version: 71(user) 128(machine)
Flags: 0 (user side enabled; machine side enabled)
User extensions: [{25537BA6-77A8-11D2-9B6C-0000F8080861}{88E729D6-BDC1-11D1-BD2A-
00C04FB9603F}][{3060E8D0-7020-11D2-842D-00C04FA372D4}{3060E8CE-7020-11D2-842D-
00C04FA372D4}][{35378EAC-683F-11D2-A89A-00C04FBBCFA2}{0F6B957E-509E-11D1-A7CC-
0000F87571E3}][{C6DC5466-785A-11D2-84D0-00C04FB169F7}{BACF5C8A-A3C7-11D1-A760-
00C04FB9603F}]
Machine extensions: [{0ACDD40C-75AC-47AB-BAA0-BF6DE7E7FE63}{2DA6AA7F-8C88-4194-A558-
0D36E7FD3E64}][{35378EAC-683F-11D2-A89A-00C04FBBCFA2}{0F6B957D-509E-11D1-A7CC-
0000F87571E3}{53D6AB1B-2488-11D1-A28C-00C04FB94F17}][{827D319E-6EAC-11D2-A4EA-
00C04F79F83A}{803E14A0-B4FB-11D0-A0D0-00A0C90F574B}][{B1BE8D72-6EAC-11D2-A4EA-
00C04F79F83A}{53D6AB1B-2488-11D1-A28C-00C04FB94F17}][{C6DC5466-785A-11D2-84D0-
00C04FB169F7}{942A8E4F-A261-11D1-A760-00C04FB9603F}]
Functionality version: 2
--------------------------------------------------------------
==============================================================
```

From this output, you know that quite a few CSEs are active in this GPO. The extensions are identified by their GUID. So, for example, {25537BA6-77A8-11D2-9B6C-0000F8080861} is the GUID for the Folder Redirection CSE. Chapter 13 includes a list of the GUIDs of all of the CSEs that are installed by default on Windows Server 2003.

Both the standard and verbose details offer a lot of helpful information. Here are the pieces of information the tool provides:

- **GPO GUID**   The unique identifier that each GPO is known by.

- **Friendly Name**   The name you entered for the GPO when you created it. This need not be unique.

- **Policy OK**   If Gpotool.exe finds no problems with the GPO, it lists the status as OK.

- **Created and Changed**   The date and time that the GPO was created and when it was last changed. This information can be useful if you are trying to determine whether a change you made to a GPO has propagated to the domain controller that the tool is focused on.

- **DS Version and SYSVOL Version**   The number of revisions made to the GPC and GPT portions of the GPO. The numbers should be identical if the GPO has fully replicated to the domain controller that the tool is focused on.

- **Flags**   Indicates the state of the GPO—whether it is disabled, whether the user side only is disabled, or whether the computer side only is disabled.

- **User Extensions and Machine Extensions**   The GUIDs of the CSEs that have been implemented within this GPO.

- **Functionality Version**   The functional version, which is always listed as 2.

Managing RSoP Logs Centrally

Group Policy Monitor (GPMonitor.exe) is another Windows Server 2003 Resource Kit tool that can help with troubleshooting. Group Policy Monitor allows you to centrally manage and automate the collection of Group Policy Results reports. You can use Group Policy Monitor to closely track GPO processing for troubleshooting.

Getting Started with Group Policy Monitor

Group Policy Monitor has three main components:

- **Group Policy Monitor service**   A service that runs on each computer from which you want to collect RSoP data

- **Group Policy Monitor console**   A UI that provides the administrator with a way of viewing the collected RSoP logs from multiple machines

- **Group Policy Monitor Administrative Template**   A file that lets you configure the server share used for logging data sent from the Group Policy Monitor service

When Group Policy Monitor is configured, a log report can be generated each time a GPO is refreshed or at a specific interval that is configurable through the Administrative Templates of GPOs you are monitoring.

Preparing the Group Policy Monitor Installation

Before you can use Group Policy Monitor, you must prepare the installation by extracting the monitoring components from the Gpmonitor.exe file in the Windows Server 2003 Resource Kit Tools. To prepare the installation, complete the following steps:

1. Create a folder to store the extracted Group Policy Monitor components.

2. Type **gpmonitor** at a command prompt.

3. When prompted for a location to place the extracted files, click Browse and then browse to the folder you previously created.

4. The following files are extracted to the specified location:

- ❏ **GPMonitor.adm**   An administrative template file
- ❏ **GPMonitor.chm**   A help file
- ❏ **GPMonitor.msi**   A Windows Installer package that can be deployed via Group Policy
- ❏ **GPMon.cab**   A .cab file containing the executables for the Group Policy Monitor service and the Group Policy Monitor console

Deploying and Configuring Group Policy Monitor

Group Policy Monitor is provided as an .msi file so that you can install this tool and its components on target computers using the Group Policy Software Installation feature. When you deploy the GPMonitor.msi file via Group Policy, you must also include the Gpmon.cab file in the installation folder because it is used by the .msi file to complete the installation. The installation process configures and starts the Group Policy Monitor service. It also installs the Group Policy Monitor console.

You can, of course, install Group Policy Monitor by completing the following steps:

1. Copy the Group Policy Monitor files to the domain controller(s) you want to configure.

2. Start the installation process by double-clicking Gpmonitor.msi.

3. When the installation wizard starts, click Next, accept the license agreement, and then click Next again.

4. Provide your customer information, and then click Next.

5. Click Complete Installation, and then click Finish. The Group Policy Monitor service is installed and started. The Group Policy Monitor console is also installed and is available on the Administrative Tools menu.

Once the service is installed on target machines, you must create a new GPO or edit an existing GPO, add the Gpmonitor.adm file, and then configure the monitoring options. You can perform these procedures by completing the following steps:

1. Access the GPO you want to work with. Right-click Administrative Templates under User Configuration, and then choose Add/Remove Templates to view the currently loaded .adm files.

2. Click Add to open the Policy Templates dialog box. The default folder location opened is %SystemRoot%\Inf, which is where any installed template files are normally located.

3. Navigate to the location where you extracted the Group Policy Monitor setup files, and then choose the Gpmonitor.adm template file.

> **Note** The Gpmonitor.adm file is copied to the SYSVOL portion of that GPO and is replicated to all domain controllers in the domain. (See Chapter 13 for more information about Group Policy storage.)

4. Click Open, and then click Close. The Administrative Templates namespace changes to include a new node for Group Policy Monitor, as shown in Figure 16-8.

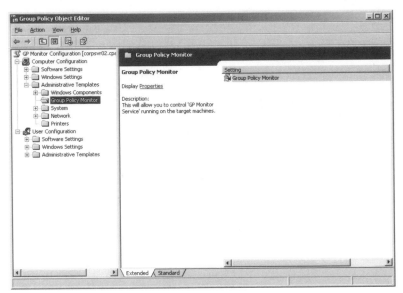

Figure 16-8 Viewing the Group Policy Monitor node in the GPMC

5. Expand Computer Configuration, Administrative Templates, Group Policy Monitor node, and then double-click Group Policy Monitor.

6. To enable monitoring, select Enabled (as shown in Figure 16-9) and then set the share point where you want the domain controllers running the monitoring service to copy the RSoP log file.

7. Configure the interval of Group Policy refresh for sending a new report to the server share. By default, the service sends a new report every eighth Group Policy refresh (foreground or background), but you can increase or decrease this interval.

8. Click OK.

> **Note** The amount of disk space used for RSoP logging depends on the number of domain controllers you are monitoring and the report interval. Keep in mind that sending more frequent reports will affect network bandwidth as well as server storage.

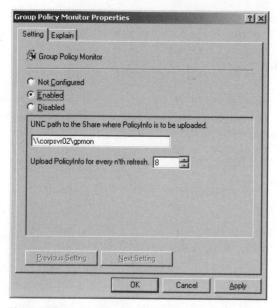

Figure 16-9   Configuring monitoring and logging

Viewing Group Policy Monitor Reports

Once Group Policy Monitor is installed and configured, computers running the service will send RSoP data to the designated logging share. The data will be organized into folders based on the computer name of the system sending the report. You can then use the Group Policy Monitor console to view the reports collected from each machine. Complete these steps to view report data from the Group Policy Monitor console:

1. Start Group Policy Monitor by clicking Start, Programs or All Programs, Administrative Tools, Group Policy Monitor.

2. Choose New Query from the File menu.

3. In the Query dialog box, type the UNC path to the server share where you are storing your Group Policy Monitor logs.

4. Type the names of the machines you want to report on. Machine names should be separated by a comma (for example, corpsvr01,corpsvr02,corpsvr03). You can also specify * to return all machines that have reported to the share.

5. Choose the number of refreshes to report on. The default is 4. The more refreshes you return, the more the query returns.

6. When you click OK, a new node is created in the Group Policy Monitor console for each computer that returns data.

Under the computer node, you will see nodes for ComputerPolicyRefreshes and UserPolicyRefreshes. Under each of these nodes will be a series of date/time stamps that indicate individual Group Policy refresh events on these computers, as shown in Figure 16-10.

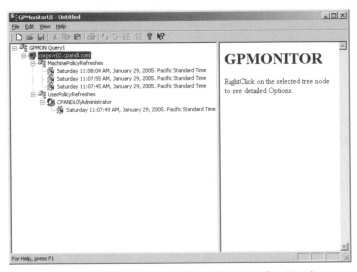

Figure 16-10   Displaying reports from Group Policy Monitor

To get RSoP details from a given refresh interval, you can right-click that interval and choose from one of two options: Choose Generate RSOP Report to create the familiar HTML-based RSoP report that GPMC provides, or choose Generate Detailed RSOP View to get the equivalent of the Group Policy Results advanced view.

Examining Differences Between Refresh Intervals

Another interesting Group Policy Monitor feature is its ability to show differences between two refresh intervals. You can use this to compare how Group Policy results might have changed from one interval to the next. To use this feature, complete the following steps:

1. Select an entry within any node under any query, hold down the Ctrl key, and select a select a second entry.

2. Right-click the two selected refreshes, and then choose Show XML Diff.

3. An instance of the WinDiff utility is launched, showing where the results files differ.

Figure 16-11 shows that one file contains a setting that the other does not. This indicates that a policy that was once enabled or disabled was set to Not Configured during the second interval.

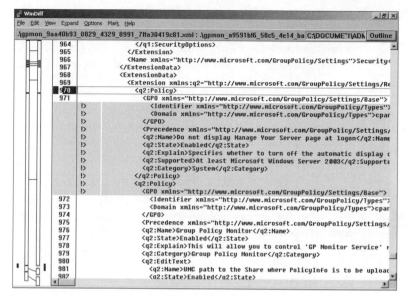

Figure 16-11   Displaying differences in RSoP reports through WinDiff

Managing Report Log Deletion

If you want to manage deletion of the files stored on the Group Policy Monitor share that you've specified, you can use the Delete Refresh Info From GPMON Share option on the File menu. This option lets you choose the share, computer names, and number of the last refreshes to keep. For example, if you choose to keep the last four refreshes, any refresh reports stored before that for the chosen computers will be deleted from the designated share.

Group Policy Logging

We've examined some tools for looking at what policies have been processed for a given computer or user, but what if this RSoP data doesn't provide enough information to solve the problem? Sometimes problems related to Group Policy core processing or CSE processing don't reveal themselves easily. In that case, the next step is to turn to the detailed Group Policy log files.

Basically, you can use two classes of logs for in-depth Group Policy troubleshooting:

- The Application event log on a given computer. This is where any Group Policy related events are reported.

- Text file logs that are generated by various parts of the Group Policy infrastructure.

Group Policy events are record automatically in the Application logs, but some of the Group Policy text logs have to be explicitly enabled before they become available.

Application event logs can be a good starting point in the log troubleshooting process—when verbose logging is enabled, they can provide high-level, step-by-step feedback on what is and isn't working within the processing cycle. However, when the application event log does not return enough data or does not lead to a solution, the next step is to examine the more detailed text file logs.

On the CD   You can find a file called Gpolog.adm on the companion CD. Use this file to enable all of the logging discussed in this chapter.

Tip   A good strategy that applies to all the logging we've talked about in this chapter is to enable verbose logging only when troubleshooting a problem. When you are finished troubleshooting, you should disable verbose logging.

Navigating the Application Event Logs

By default, when you install Windows Server 2003, a variety of events are written to the application event log during Group Policy processing. These events consist of both core Group Policy processing and CSE processing operations. Each type of Group Policy–related event has a different event source, depending on whether it's reporting on Group Policy core processing or CSE processing.

Configuring the Level of Application Logging

The information logged with Group Policy events is fairly terse. If you want more detail, there are several registry keys you can modify:

- To enable verbose logging, set RunDiagnosticLoggingGroupPolicy registry value under HKEY_LOCAL_MACHINE\SOFTWARE\Microsoft\Windows NT\CurrentVersion\Diagnostics to 0x00000001. Verbose logging will start after you restart the computer.

- To turn on verbose logging for Software Installation policy and application deployments, set RunDiagnosticLoggingApplicationDeployment under HKEY_ LOCAL_MACHINE\Software\Microsoft\Windows NT\CurrentVersion\ Diagnostics to 0x00000001.

- To turn on verbose logging for all GPO processing events, including diagnostics and application deployment, set RunDiagnosticLoggingGlobal under HKEY_ LOCAL_MACHINE\Software\Microsoft\Windows NT\CurrentVersion\ Diagnostics to 0x00000001.

Use the Registry Editor to add one or more of these values or modify the values if they already exist. By making these changes to the registry, you enable full logging for

Group Policy and you can get more detail during the Group Policy processing cycle. However, full logging results in a much larger number of events being sent to the Application event log, so you should enable it only during periods when you need to troubleshoot core Group Policy processing.

When you enable full logging, each step of the Group Policy processing cycle is sent to the application event log, including details of what happens along the way. There will be events marking the beginning and ending of Group Policy processing. In between, you can view what is happening as each GPO that must be processed for a given computer and user is enumerated and then the CSEs are called to process policy.

Understanding Group Policy Events

You access event logs on a local or remote machine by completing the following steps:

1. Start the Computer Management console by selecting it on the Administrative Tools menu.

2. Connect to the computer whose event logs you want to view by right-clicking the Computer Management node and selecting Connect To Another Computer.

3. Expand Systems Tools, Event Viewer, and then select Application.

Table 16-1 lists the main event sources reported by Group Policy. Within each event source are common event IDs that refer to problems with that particular area of Group Policy processing.

Table 16-1   Event Sources Related to Group Policy Events

Event Source	Description
Userenv	Events related to Core Group Policy processing (includes Administrative Templates policy)
SceCli	Events related to Security CSE processing
Appmgmt or Application Manager	Events related to Software Installation CSE processing
Userinit	Events related to Scripts CSE processing
Folder Redirection	Events related to Folder Redirection CSE processing
DiskQuota	Events related to Disk Quota CSE processing

Table 16-2 lists the most common event IDs for each event source. These event IDs are taken from the Group Policy Management Pack for Microsoft Operations Manager. These event IDs typically indicate some kind of problem related to that Group Policy processing area. However, in some cases they simply indicate that Group Policy processing was completed successfully.

Table 16-2   Viewing Group Policy–Related Event IDs

Event Source	Event IDs	Description
Userenv	1003, 1036, 1037, 1038, 1040, 1041, 1085	Core GP Processing indicates that at least one CSE was processed with an error and policy could not be fully applied.
Userenv	1002, 1035, 1063, 1075, 1078, 1081, 1082, 1094, 1107	Group Policy processing has failed because of a low-memory or low-disk condition on the computer.
Userenv	1099, 1100, 1101	Group Policy processing did not have access to an object required within Active Directory.
Userenv	1001, 1066, 1083, 1084, 1108	Group Policy processing failed because the client file system or the client registry is corrupted. A necessary DLL file required to process Group Policy is unregistered or has been deleted.
Userenv	1057, 1058, 1059, 1060, 1064, 1072, or 1077	Group Policy processing failed because the GPO has been corrupted in some way.
Userenv	1065, 1104, 1106	Group Policy processing was unable to query WMI to apply a WMI filter or was unable to find a WMI filter that was linked to a GPO.
Userenv	1052, 1097	Group Policy processing failed because the machine account for the computer is missing or corrupt in the domain.
Userenv	1088	Group Policy Processing failed because too many GPOs were applied to a computer or user. The maximum number of GPOs that can be applied to computer or user is 1000.
Userenv	1089, 1090, 1091, 1095	Group Policy processing might have succeeded, but RSoP information could not be logged. This might indicate a problem with WMI.
Userenv	1005, 1006, 1008, 1053, 1054, 1055, 1056, 1079, 1080, 1105, 1110	Group Policy processing failed because of a network connectivity or network configuration problem.
DiskQuota	1, 2, 3, 4, 5, 6, 7, 8	The Disk Quota CSE failed to apply the quota to a disk volume.
Folder Redirection	401	The Folder Redirection CSE was processed successfully.
Folder Redirection	101, 102, 103, 104, 106, 107, 108, 109, 110, 111, 112	The Folder Redirection CSE was not processed successfully, and folders were not redirected as expected.

Table 16-2   Viewing Group Policy–Related Event IDs

Event Source	Event IDs	Description
Folder Redirection	301	The Folder Redirection CSE delayed redirecting user folders until the next logon because Windows XP Fast Logon Optimization is enabled.
Userenv	1019, 1020, 1022, 1043, 1096	The Administrative Templates (Registry) CSE was unable to apply registry policy because the Registry.pol file was corrupt, missing, or inaccessible or because the computer was unable to write to the registry.
Userinit	1000, 1001	The Scripts CSE was unable to execute a script. This might have been caused by the script being inaccessible or invalid.
Scecli	1704, 1705	The Security CSE successfully processed policy.
Scecli	1202	The Security CSE might have failed as a result of being unable to resolve a security account specified in security policy to the SID of the account in the domain.
Scecli	1001, 1005	The Security CSE failed to apply security policy successfully. This usually occurs when the computer cannot read the security-related policy files from the GPT in the GPO.
Application Management	201, 202, 203	The Software Installation CSE succeeded in processing policy, but there were some warnings that might require attention.
Application Management	204	The Software Installation CSE succeeded, but RSoP information was not logged for it.
Application Management	101, 102, 103, 104, 105, 106, 107, 108, 109, 110, 150	The Software Installation CSE failed to apply policy successfully. Some aspect of the installation, uninstallation, upgrade, or reinstallation failed.
Application Management	301, 302, 303, 304, 305, 306, 307, 308	The Software Installation CSE successfully applied policy.

Managing Userenv Logging

Perhaps the most detailed general Group Policy log file available is the Userenv.log file. This log file is enabled by default and is found in the %Windir%\debug\usermode folder. Using the Userenv.log, you can often find where policy processing has broken down. However, sometimes you will need to drill deeper into a specific CSE to find the cause of a problem. Some, but not all, of the CSEs provide deeper logging for this purpose.

Configuring the Level of Userenv Logging

As with the application logs, the Userenv information logged is fairly terse. If you want more detail, you can increase the verbosity of the logging to see all Group Policy–related events. To do so, you must modify the *UserEnvDebugLevel* registry value under HKEY_LOCAL_MACHINE\SOFTWARE\Microsoft\Windows NT\CurrentVersion\Winlogon.

You use the Registry Editor to add the *UserEnvDebugLevel* registry value or to modify it if the value already exists. *UserEnvDebugLevel* can have the following values:

- 0x00000000 for no logging
- 0x00000001 for normal logging
- 0x00000002 for verbose logging
- 0x00010000 for log file usage
- 0x00020000 for debugger mode

You can disable all Userenv logging by setting the value to 0x00000000. The default logging mode is normal with log filing, so the value is 0x00010001. If you want verbose logging with a log file, you can combine the verbose value (0x00000002) with the log file value (0x00010000) to get 0x00010002.

> **Note**   Userenv logging provides both detailed Group Policy and user profile logging, so you must be prepared to parse through events that aren't relevant to Group Policy to get real value out of the log.

Examining the Userenv Logs

You must have some understanding of the structure and format of Userenv.log to benefit from it. Each line of the file represents an event within the Group Policy processing cycle. For example, the following line is usually the first event you see when Group Policy processing begins. (In this case, it's a background refresh of Group Policy.)

```
USERENV(2c0.13c) 21:07:48:573 ProcessGPOs: Starting user Group Policy (Background)
processing...
```

You will notice that every line in the file begins with *USERENV*. The number in parentheses, in this case 2c0.13c, indicates the process and thread IDs that are running that step of the processing cycle. Most often, the process ID corresponds to the Winlogon process, under which Group Policy processing runs. The number *21:07:48:573* indicates the time of day when that event was logged. The *ProcessGPOs* tag of the event usually indicates the name of the API being called. This is usually followed by a description of the event; in this case, it indicates that user-specific background processing is occurring.

> **Tip** A date stamp is not included in Userenv.log file events, but newer events are appended to the end of the file. During a background processing event, especially one triggered by *gpupdate*, user and computer processing happens in parallel, and you might see the same starting message shown above for background computer processing, right after the user processing message appears. You can identify which subsequent processing step belongs to computer or user processing by viewing the thread ID—user and computer processing will have different thread IDs for the same process.

Normally, the first reported events, after the message indicating the beginning of Group Policy processing, constitute a slow-link test. During the test, three pairs of pings are sent to determine the speed of the link between the computer processing Group Policy and its domain controller. This test, as it appears in Userenv.log, will look similar to the following:

```
USERENV(4c0.378) 16:23:50:792 PingComputer: Adapter speed 11000000 bps
USERENV(4c0.378) 16:23:50:962 PingComputer:  First time:  129
USERENV(4c0.378) 16:23:51:122 PingComputer:  Second time:  141
USERENV(4c0.378) 16:23:51:302 PingComputer:  First time:  175
USERENV(4c0.378) 16:23:51:443 PingComputer:  Second time:  131
USERENV(4c0.378) 16:23:51:443 PingComputer:  Second time less than first time.
USERENV(4c0.378) 16:23:51:543 PingComputer:  First time:  96
USERENV(4c0.378) 16:23:51:683 PingComputer:  Second time:  135
USERENV(4c0.378) 16:23:51:683 PingComputer:  Transfer rate:  1280 Kbps
Loop count:  2
```

The transfer rate shown here is the calculated link speed, which is compared to the slow-link threshold. If a slow link is found, this changes the behavior of certain CSEs.

After the slow-link test, the next task is to locate the GPOs that apply to this user or computer, by querying Active Directory. These events typically appear as follows:

```
USERENV(2c0.13c) 21:07:52:372 SearchDSObject:  Searching <DC=cpand1,DC=com>
USERENV(2c0.13c) 21:07:52:372 SearchDSObject:  Found GPO(s):  <[LDAP://CN={31B2F340-
016D-11D2-945F-00C04FB984F9},CN=Policies,CN=System,DC=cpand1,DC=com;0]>
```

The first event in this listing shows that the domain (as opposed to a site or an OU) is being searched. The next event shows that a link to a GPO has been located on the domain—and the path to the GPC is returned.

Once all linked GPOs have been found, Group Policy processing determines whether the computer and user have access to the GPO (for example, whether the GPO is filtered using security groups to prevent processing). This step typically looks like the following:

```
USERENV(2c0.13c) 21:07:52:452 ProcessGPO:  Searching <CN={31B2F340-016D-11D2-945F-
00C04FB984F9},CN=Policies,CN=System,DC=cpand1,DC=com>
USERENV(2c0.13c) 21:07:52:452 ProcessGPO:  User has access to this GPO.
USERENV(2c0.13c) 21:07:52:452 ProcessGPO:  GPO passes the filter check.
```

When all GPOs are searched like this, the GPC for each GPO is examined to determine the GPO's friendly name, its version number, any flags that might be set (for example, the GPO is disabled or part of the GPO is disabled), and what CSEs have been implemented for that GPO. This is shown in the following lines:

```
USERENV(2c0.13c) 21:07:52:622 ProcessGPO:  Found common name of:
<{31B2F340-016D-11D2-945F-00C04FB984F9}>
USERENV(2c0.13c) 21:07:52:622 ProcessGPO:  Found display name of:
<Default Domain Policy>
USERENV(2c0.13c) 21:07:52:622 ProcessGPO:  Found user version of:
GPC is 7, GPT is 7
USERENV(2c0.13c) 21:07:52:622 ProcessGPO:  Found flags of:  0
USERENV(2c0.13c) 21:07:52:622 ProcessGPO:  Found extensions:  [{3060E8D0-7020-11D2-
842D-00C04FA372D4}{3060E8CE-7020-11D2-842D-00C04FA372D4}][{C6DC5466-785A-11D2-84D0-
00C04FB169F7}{BACF5C8A-A3C7-11D1-A760-00C04FB9603F}]
```

The *Found extensions* statement lists the GUIDs of the CSEs that are used within this GPO. This information is used to tell Group Policy processing which CSEs need to be called during this processing cycle. Next, each CSE runs and processes its policies. The following line shows the Administrative Templates (Registry) CSE running:

```
USERENV(2c0.13c) 21:07:52:783 ProcessGPOs: Processing extension Registry
```

The first thing the registry CSE does after starting up is to delete any existing policy values so that it can reapply them from scratch. This delete operation is captured in the following lines:

```
USERENV(2c0.13c) 21:07:52:813 DeleteRegistryValue: Deleted Software\Policies\
Microsoft\Conferencing\Use AutoConfig
USERENV(2c0.13c) 21:07:52:823 DeleteRegistryValue: Deleted Software\Policies\
Microsoft\Conferencing\ConfigFile
```

In this case, only two policies have been set for this user, so only two need to be deleted. After the existing policies are deleted, any registry policy from any GPOs that apply are processed, as shown in the following lines:

```
USERENV(2c0.13c) 21:07:52:823 ParseRegistryFile: Entering with <C:\WINDOWS\System32\
GroupPolicy\User\registry.pol>.
USERENV(2c0.13c) 21:07:52:823 SetRegistryValue: Use AutoConfig => 1  [OK]
USERENV(2c0.13c) 21:07:52:823 SetRegistryValue: ConfigFile =>   [OK]
USERENV(2c0.13c) 21:07:52:823 ParseRegistryFile: Leaving.
```

The first line indicates that the registry CSE is reading from the local GPO's Registry.pol file to obtain registry policy settings. The two *SetRegistryValue* lines show the registry values that are being applied from the Registry.pol, although they don't indicate the full path to the registry setting being applied. The final line indicates that registry policy processing has been completed. After the registry CSE does its work, each subsequent CSE is processed in turn and shows events in the Userenv.log file. When a CSE runs, if it finds that the GPO it is processing hasn't changed since the last processing cycle and if no GPOs have been deleted, it simply passes on to the next CSE, as shown in the following lines:

```
SERENV(2c0.13c) 21:07:52:953 ProcessGPOs: Processing extension Scripts
USERENV(2c0.13c) 21:07:52:953 CompareGPOLists:  The lists are the same.
USERENV(2c0.13c) 21:07:52:953 CheckGPOs: No GPO changes but couldn't read extension
Scripts's status or policy time.
USERENV(2c0.13c) 21:07:52:953 ProcessGPOs: Extension Scripts skipped because both
deleted and changed GPO lists are empty.
```

In this listing, the Scripts CSE has run, but as the last line shows, no changed or deleted GPOs have been found, so Scripts processing is skipped.

Each CSE lists what it is doing in detail, although some CSEs are more detailed than others in terms of how much useful information they write to the Userenv.log. In the next section, we'll look at how to enable some CSE-specific logging when the information found in Userenv.log is not sufficient. When Group Policy processing has completed, the following lines appear:

```
USERENV(2c0.13c) 21:07:53:053 ProcessGPOs: User Group Policy has been applied.
USERENV(2c0.13c) 21:07:53:053 ProcessGPOs: Leaving with 1.
USERENV(2c0.13c) 21:07:53:053 GPOThread:  Next refresh will happen in 107 minutes
```

This listing shows that the user Group Policy processing cycle has completed and that the next background refresh will happen in 107 minutes.

Managing Logging for Specific CSEs

You can enable CSE-specific logsto get more detailed troubleshooting information. These logs track application management and software installation logging.

Enabling Debug Logging for Windows Installer Policy

You can enable detailed debugging logging for Windows Installer policy by modifying the *AppmgmtDebugLevel* registry value under HKEY_LOCAL_MACHINE\SOFTWARE\ Microsoft\Windows NT\CurrentVersion\Diagnostics. Use the Registry Editor to add the *AppmgmtDebugLevel* registry value or modify it if the value already exists. Set the value to *0x0000004b*.

After you add this registry value, a new log file is created under %windir%\debug\ usermode called Appmgmt.log. This log file captures all events related to software installation policy. For example, the following lines capture errors related to the attempted deployment of Microsoft Visio® Professional 2003:

```
Assigning application Microsoft Office Visio Professional 2003 from policy Visio
Deployment.
Application Microsoft Office Visio Professional 2003 from policy Visio Deployment is
  configured to remove any unmanaged install before being assigned.
Calling the Windows Installer to advertise application Microsoft Office Visio
```

```
Professional 2003 from script C:\WINDOWS\system32\appmgmt\S-1-5-21-817735531-
4269160403-1409475253-1107\{32cb86da-f34c-4074-9855-d86a2c689d64}.aas with flags 61.
The assignment of application Microsoft Office Visio Professional 2003 from policy
Visio Deployment succeeded. Calling the Windows Installer to install application
Microsoft Office Visio Professional 2003 from policy Visio Deployment.
The install of application Microsoft Office Visio Professional 2003 from policy
Visio Deployment failed.  The error was : %1612

Removing application Microsoft Office Visio Professional 2003 from the software
installation database.
Calling Windows Installer to remove application advertisement for application
Microsoft Office Visio Professional 2003 from script C:\WINDOWS\system32\appmgmt\
S-1-5-21-817735531-4269160403-1409475253-1107\{32cb86da-f34c-4074-9855-d86a2c689d64}.aas.
The removal of the assignment of application Microsoft Office Visio Professional
2003 from policy Visio Deployment succeeded.

Policy Logging for Software Management is attempting to log application Microsoft
Office Visio Professional 2003 from policy Visio Deployment.
Failed to apply changes to software installation settings.  Software changes could
not be applied.  A previous log entry with details should exist.  The error was :
%1612

Software installation extension returning with final error code 1612.
```

As this listing shows, Windows Installer attempts to deploy Visio via assignment, but it first checks to make sure that no unmanaged versions of Visio need to be uninstalled. Windows Installer then calls the Application Assignment Script (.aas file) that was cached in the folder C:\WINDOWS\system32\appmgmt\S-1-5-21-817735531-4269160403-1409475253-1107. The SID name at the end of this folder indicates that this is a per-user installation.

The application assignment script execution succeeds, but when Windows Installer runs the actual installation of Visio, the installation fails with an error 1612. This Windows Installer error indicates that the source .msi file is either not available or not accessible (for example, the user might not have permission to read the file from the share where it's stored). Windows Installer then removes the application assignments that it made using the .aas file and then returns the final 1612 error code.

The Appmgmt.log file can be useful in pointing out obvious errors, such as the error just mentioned, where the user might not have appropriate permission to view the package. In other cases, you might not get enough detail from the Appmgmt.log file to successfully troubleshoot the problem. In that case, the best approach is to use Windows Installer logging to view the steps that Windows Installer took during the attempted installation.

Windows Installer logging is enabled by default, but you can increase the verbosity of logging by modifying the Logging policy under Computer Configuration\Administrative Templates\Windows Components\Windows Installer. You can choose from a number of logging levels. To enable full logging, specify **iweaprucmvo** as the logging option (Figure 16-12).

Figure 16-12 Enabling verbose Windows Installer logging through Administrative Template policy

When Windows Installer logging is enabled, log files are written to the temporary folder on the computer. By default, this folder is located at %Windir%\temp. The log file that is created is named with a sequential file name starting with *MSI* (for example, MSI1a77f.log). The following listing shows an example of the kind of verbosity you get from the Windows Installer log. Every step of the installation process is logged, as shown here:

```
=== Verbose logging started: 1/30/2005  8:40:05
Build type: SHIP UNICODE 3.00.3790.2180  Calling process:
\??\C:\WINDOWS\system32\winlogon.exe ===
MSI (c) (BC:74) [08:40:05:338]: User policy value 'DisableRollback' is 0
MSI (c) (BC:74) [08:40:05:338]: Machine policy value 'DisableRollback' is 0
MSI (c) (BC:74) [08:40:05:348]: Executing op: Header(Signature=1397708873,
Version=301,Timestamp=842940553,LangId=1033,Platform=0,ScriptType=3,
ScriptMajorVersion=21,ScriptMinorVersion=4,ScriptAttributes=0)
MSI (c) (BC:74) [08:40:05:348]: Executing op: ProductInfo(ProductKey={90510409-6000-
11D3-8CFE-0150048383C9},
ProductName=Microsoft Office Visio Professional 2003,PackageName=VISPRO.MSI,
Language=1033,Version=184552592,Assignment=1,ObsoleteArg=0,ProductIcon=misc.exe,6,
PackageMediaPath=\ENGLISH\OFFICE_SYSTEM\VISIO2003\,PackageCode={0C7A8254-2463-495B-
BA6A-AD74E3A5FEF1},,,InstanceType=0,LUASetting=0)
MSI (c) (BC:74) [08:40:05:348]: SHELL32::SHGetFolderPath returned: C:\Documents and
Settings\debbiec\Application Data
MSI (c) (BC:74) [08:40:05:348]: Executing op: DialogInfo(Type=0,Argument=1033)
MSI (c) (BC:74) [08:40:05:348]: Executing op: DialogInfo(Type=1,Argument=Microsoft
Office Visio Professional 2003)
MSI (c) (BC:74) [08:40:05:348]: Executing op: RollbackInfo(,RollbackAction=Rollback,
RollbackDescription=Rolling back installation,RollbackTemplate=[1],CleanupAction=
RollbackCleanup,CleanupDescription=Removing backup files,CleanupTemplate=File: [1])
MSI (c) (BC:74) [08:40:05:358]: Executing op: ActionStart(Name=MsiPublishAssemblies,
Description=Publishing assembly information,Template=Application Context:[1],
Assembly Name:[2])
MSI (c) (BC:74) [08:40:05:358]: Executing op: AssemblyPublish(Feature=Forms_PIA,
```

```
Component={835AC3CE-E36B-4D65-B50F-
2863A682ABEE},AssemblyType=1,,AssemblyName=Microsoft.Vbe.Interop.Forms,Version="11.0
.0.0000",Culture="neutral",PublicKeyToken="71e9bce111e9429c",FileVersion="11.0.5530.
0",)
```

If you are familiar with the installation package and you can follow the log, this level of detail can be useful in troubleshooting installation problems. To prevent too much detail from being generated, you can modify the Administrative Templates policy for Windows Installer logging.

Enabling Debug Logging for Folder Redirection Policy

You can enable detailed debugging logging for Folder Redirection policy by modifying the *FdeployDebugLevel* registry value under HKEY_LOCAL_MACHINE\SOFTWARE\ Microsoft\Windows NT\CurrentVersion\Diagnostics. Use the Registry Editor to add the *FdeployDebugLevel* registry value or modify it if the value already exists. Set the value to *0x0000000F* to enable logging. To disable logging, set the value to *0x00000000*.

When the *FdeployDebugLevel* registry value is set for logging, log events related to Folder Redirection policy are written to the file %windir%\Debug\UserMode\ fdeploy.log whenever Folder Redirection policy is subsequently processed. You get a log file that looks similar to the listing here:

```
09:25:21:984 Entering folder redirection extension
09:25:21:984 Flags = 0x0
09:25:22:024 Group Policy Object name = {0E35E0EC-FD6D-4CEF-9267-6EDB00694026}
09:25:22:024 File system path = \\cpandl.com\SysVol\cpandl.com\Policies\{0E35E0EC-
FD6D-4CEF-9267-6EDB00694026}\User
09:25:22:024 Directory path = LDAP://CN=User,cn={0E35E0EC-FD6D-4CEF-9267-
6EDB00694026},cn=policies,cn=system,DC=cpandl,DC=com
09:25:22:024 Display name = Marketing Folder Redirection Policy
09:25:22:044 Found folder redirection settings for policy Marketing Folder
Redirection Policy.
09:25:22:084 The user was found to be a member of the group s-1-1-0.
The corresponding path was \\%HOMESHARE%%HOMEPATH%.
09:25:22:084 Successfully obtained redirection data for My Documents, (Flags: 0x31).
09:25:22:084 Successfully obtained redirection data for My Pictures, (Flags: 0x2).
09:25:22:084 Querying the DS for user debbiec's home directory.
09:25:22:334 Obtained home directory : \\corpsvr01\home\debbiec.
09:25:22:344 Homedir redirection path %HOMESHARE%%HOMEPATH% expanded to \\corpsvr01\
home\debbiec.
09:25:22:344 Successfully gathered folder redirection settings for policy Marketing
Folder Redirection Policy.
09:25:22:344 Homedir redirection path %HOMESHARE%%HOMEPATH% expanded to \\corpsvr01\
home\debbiec.
09:25:22:344 Redirecting folder My Documents to \\%HOMESHARE%%HOMEPATH%.
09:25:42:453 Previous folder path C:\Documents and Settings\debbiec\My Documents
expanded to C:\Documents and Settings\debbiec\My Documents.
09:25:42:453 New folder path \\%HOMESHARE%%HOMEPATH% expanded to \\corpsvr01\home\
debbiec.
```

```
09:25:42:513 Contents of redirected folder My Documents will be copied to the new
location.
09:25:43:304 Homedir redirection path %HOMESHARE%%HOMEPATH%\My Pictures expanded to
\\corpsvr01\home\debbiec\My Pictures.
09:25:43:304 Redirecting folder My Pictures to \\%HOMESHARE%%HOMEPATH%\My Pictures.
09:25:43:415 Previous folder path C:\Documents and Settings\debbiec\My Documents\My
Pictures expanded to C:\Documents and Settings\debbiec\My Documents\My Pictures.
09:25:43:415 New folder path \\%HOMESHARE%%HOMEPATH%\My Pictures expanded to
\\corpsvr01\home\debbiec\My Pictures.
09:25:43:595 Contents of redirected folder My Pictures will be copied to the new
location.
09:25:44:025 Previous contents of folder My Pictures at C:\Documents and Settings\
debbiec\My Documents\My Pictures will be deleted.
09:25:44:086 Successfully redirected folder My Pictures.
The folder was redirected from <C:\Documents and Settings\debbiec\My Documents\
My Pictures> to <\\corpsvr01\home\debbiec\My Pictures>.

09:25:44:086 Previous contents of folder My Documents at C:\Documents and Settings\
debbiec\My Documents will be deleted.
09:25:44:236 Successfully redirected folder My Documents.
The folder was redirected from <C:\Documents and Settings\debbiec\My Documents> to
<\\corpsvr01\home\debbiec>.

09:25:44:236 Disabling permission for user redirection of My Documents.
09:25:44:336 Successfully updated the shortcut to My Pictures in <\\corpsvr01\home\
debbiec>.
```

As the listing shows, Folder Redirection policy processing is tracked from beginning
to end. In this example, the user debbiec has logged on to her computer for the first
time and is getting her My Documents and My Pictures folder redirected to her home
share. The Folder Redirection CSE starts off by enumerating the GPC and GPT paths
for the GPO that will provide the policy. It then determines that the user is a member
of the Everyone group (SID S-1-1-0) and needs to be redirected to %HOMESHARE%
%HOMEPATH%. It then queries Active Directory for the user's home path location
and then redirects the user's My Documents and My Pictures folders from the local
user profile to the server share.

In another example of failed Folder Redirection policy, you can use the Fdeploy.log
file to track down the cause. The following listing shows a failed redirection for the
user joew.

```
09:38:44:609 Entering folder redirection extension
09:38:44:609 Flags = 0x0
09:38:44:649 Group Policy Object name = {0E35E0EC-FD6D-4CEF-9267-6EDB00694026}
09:38:44:659 File system path = \\cpandl.com\SysVol\cpandl.com\Policies\{0E35E0EC-
FD6D-4CEF-9267-6EDB00694026}\User
09:38:44:659 Directory path = LDAP://CN=User,cn={0E35E0EC-FD6D-4CEF-9267-
6EDB00694026},cn=policies,cn=system,DC=cpandl,DC=com
09:38:44:659 Display name = Marketing Folder Redirection Policy
09:38:44:679 Found folder redirection settings for policy Marketing Folder
Redirection Policy.
```

```
09:38:44:769 The user was found to be a member of the group s-1-1-0. The
corresponding path was \\%HOMESHARE%%HOMEPATH%.
09:38:44:769 Successfully obtained redirection data for My Documents, (Flags: 0x31).
09:38:44:769 Successfully obtained redirection data for My Pictures, (Flags: 0x2).
09:38:44:769 Querying the DS for user joew's home directory.
09:38:45:019 Obtained home directory : .
09:38:45:019 Homedir redirection path %HOMESHARE%%HOMEPATH% expanded to .
09:38:45:019 Successfully gathered folder redirection settings for policy Marketing
Folder Redirection Policy.
09:38:45:029 Homedir redirection path %HOMESHARE%%HOMEPATH% expanded to .
09:38:45:029 Redirecting folder My Documents to \\%HOMESHARE%%HOMEPATH%.
09:38:45:039 Failed to perform redirection of folder My Documents.
The full source path was <C:\Documents and Settings\joew\My Documents>.
The full destination path was <>.
At least one of the shares on which these paths is currently offline.
```

As you can see, this listing indicates that Folder Redirection policy is unable to properly redirect his My Documents folder. This is a relatively straightforward problem, but without this log file or the application event log, you would not get any outward evidence of what caused the problem.

Enabling Debug Logging for Security Policy

The Security Policy CSE plays an important role in the management of your Windows-based computers—it's responsible for ensuring that critical security configurations are always applied as expected. When security policy processing fails, you need to know about it. The Application event log is the first place to look to help locate the problem, but when you need more detailed logging, you can enable an additional log file for Security policy called Winlogon.log.

You do this by modifying the *ExtensionDebugLevel* registry value under HKEY_LOCAL_MACHINE\SOFTWARE\Microsoft\Windows NT\CurrentVersion\Winlogon\GPExtensions\{827D319E-6EAC-11D2-A4EA-00C04F79F83A}. Use the Registry Editor to add the *ExtensionDebugLevel* registry value or modify it if the value already exists. Set the value to *0x00000002*. To disable security logging, set this value to *0x00000000*.

When this value is enabled, Winlogon.log is created under %Windir%\security\logs. This log tracks security policy processing events, as shown in the following listing:

```
Process GP template gpt00001.inf.
-------------------------------------------
Sunday, January 30, 2005 10:05:20 AM
   Administrative privileged user logged on.
   Parsing template C:\WINDOWS\security\templates\policies\gpt00001.inf.
----Configuration engine was initialized successfully.----
```

```
----Reading Configuration Template info...
----Configure Group Membership...
   Configure CPANDL\Desktop Admins.
   Group Membership configuration was completed successfully.
----Configure Security Policy...
        Start processing undo values for 7 settings.
        There is already an undo value for group policy setting <MinimumPasswordLength>.
        There is already an undo value for group policy setting <PasswordHistorySize>.
        There is already an undo value for group policy setting <MaximumPasswordAge>.
        There is already an undo value for group policy setting <MinimumPasswordAge>.
        There is already an undo value for group policy setting <PasswordComplexity>.
        There is already an undo value for group policy setting <RequireLogonTo-
ChangePassword>.
        There is already an undo value for group policy setting <ClearTextPassword>.
   Configure password information.
        Start processing undo values for 3 settings.
        There is already an undo value for group policy setting <LockoutBadCount>.
        There is already an undo value for group policy setting
<ForceLogoffWhenHourExpire>.
   Configure account force logoff information.
   System Access configuration was completed successfully.
   Audit/Log configuration was completed successfully.
   Configure machine\system\currentcontrolset\services\lanmanserver\parameters\
autodisconnect.
        There is already an undo value for group policy setting <machine\system\
currentcontrolset\services\lanmanserver\parameters\autodisconnect>.
   Configuration of Registry Values was completed successfully.
----Configure available attachment engines...
   Configuration of attachment engines was completed successfully.
----Un-initialize configuration engine...
this is the last GPO.
```

In this example, security policy processing is working from the cached copy of the security template file that it received from the GPO. This file is called Gpt00001.inf and it is stored in the %SystemRoot%\security\templates\policies folder. The first task it performs is to configure group membership, also known as Restricted Group policy, to add a group called Desktop Admins to another group. It then processes the rest of security policy, including account policy information (which, in this case, needs to be removed) and any other security-related policy that has been set. Any problems with security policy processing will appear in this log file, so you can often use the file to determine the nature of the problem.

Summary

When you discover problems with Group Policy processing, you can use a number of techniques to track down the problem. You should first check the most obvious points of possible failure, which primarily have to do with the general configuration of Group Policy and the configuration of systems that are processing policy. If you are unable to locate the problem in the policy or system configuration, you can dig deeper by checking the Resultant Set of Policy (RSoP) from both a client and server perspective. You can often track down policy problems in the RSoP logs, but if you don't find the answers you are looking for, you can use the Group Policy logs to further investigate the problem. Many types of Group Policy logs are available. Some must be enabled or configured for detailed logging. When you are finished troubleshooting using the logs, you should disable any detailed logging modes you've enabled to restore normal policy processing and logging.

Chapter 17
Resolving Common Group Policy Problems

In this chapter:

Solving GPO Administration Problems 626

Group Policy Settings Are Not Being Applied Due
to Infrastructure Problems 638

Solving Implementation Problems 647

Summary 657

This chapter presents some common GPO application problems and suggests strategies for solving them. Fixing problems related to Group Policy objects (GPOs) is not a hard science. Rather, you have to use the knowledge you have gained throughout this book to logically interpret the situation at hand and determine the origin of the problem.

Problems with GPO deployment are typically related to problems with initial replication of the GPO settings, errant administration of the GPOs and GPO settings, incorrect delegation of administration for GPO management, IP configuration mistakes, or other administrative errors and misconfigurations. It is sometimes difficult to predetermine what the user or administrator will experience when a GPO setting or configuration is incorrectly set. Users might not be able to access resources, or an administrator might be unable to administer any GPOs. Tools are available for tracking down GPO problems, and this chapter discusses these tools where appropriate. Chapter 16 also covered some of these tools in detail, and here we put them to use working through some of the problems that can arise from a GPO implementation.

Related Information

- For information on tools and procedures for troubleshooting Group Policy, see Chapter 16.

- For more information on troubleshooting GPOs, go to *http://go.microsoft.com/ fwlink/?linkid=14949*.

Solving GPO Administration Problems

From the initial creation of GPOs to the editing of GPOs and the management of all aspects of Group Policy, many areas of the operating system and Active Directory are involved. If any of these areas becomes corrupt, unavailable, misconfigured, or inaccessible, your access to GPOs and GPO settings can be affected.

Many aspects of administering GPOs can be affected. In essence, they fall into five general areas:

- Creating GPOs
- Linking GPOs
- Editing GPO settings
- Managing GPOs
- Viewing GPO settings

Let's look at some root problems that can prohibit you from accessing GPOs or from performing GPO administration tasks as desired.

Domain Controller Running the PDC Emulator Is Not Available

The creation, editing, and management of GPOs takes place on a single domain controller by default. If your environment contains multiple domain controllers, it only makes sense that there is a preselected domain controller on which all Group Policy changes occur by default. The preselected domain controller is the one within the domain that also is responsible for the PDC Emulator.

If you attempt to control GPOs and the PDC Emulator is not available, you will receive an error message, as shown in Figure 17-1.

Figure 17-1   Error message indicating that the PDC Emulator is not available

At this point, you have to decide how to proceed. You still have the option of modifying your GPOs, but it will need to be on a different domain controller than the one that contains the PDC Emulator. To make the best decision, you must understand that the PDC Emulator does not have any special features that make it a better choice than any other domain controller for managing GPOs. The PDC Emulator was selected by Microsoft as the default domain controller for managing GPOs because it is a domain controller that must always exist within an Active Directory environment.

If you choose a different domain controller, you must understand how that decision will affect application of the GPO. The main concern is where the domain controller that holds the PDC Emulator role resides physically, compared to the domain controller that you choose for updating GPOs. This affects which accounts receive the GPOs immediately and which accounts receive the GPO updates after all the domain controllers replicate and converge.

It is best to always use the same domain controller for updating GPOs. This might not be the same domain controller for each administrator, especially if the administrators work in different physical locations (which typically means different Active Directory sites). If the domain controller that you typically use for updating GPOs is not available, you should first determine why it is unavailable. Then you can decide whether the GPO changes that you need to make can wait until that domain controller comes back online or whether the changes must occur immediately on any domain controller that remains online.

If you do choose to use a different domain controller, the worse thing that can happen is that the GPO settings might not apply as quickly as you want. This lag is dictated by the replication structure and schedule that you create between the Active Directory sites.

Not All Settings Show Up in the Group Policy Editor

In some cases, you will be able to access the GPO and open it in the Group Policy Editor, but not all of the settings will be visible within the editor. This might happen when you are viewing a GPO that has only the default settings, or it might happen when you have customized some Administrative Template or Security Template settings.

No matter the situation, something is causing some or all of the settings within the GPO to be unavailable for editing. Focusing on what is missing and what you expected to see will help you determine the cause of the problem. The following sections describe situations you might encounter, what you will see within the Group Policy Editor, and how to fix the problem.

Custom Administrative Template Settings Are Not Visible

As you saw in Chapter 14, you can create custom administrative templates to add new settings to the default GPOs. These custom settings you add to an administrative template modify registry paths and values. To ensure that you have followed the correct steps to get the settings to show up in the GPO, here is a brief summary:

1. Create a new administrative template with the file extension .adm.

2. In the Group Policy Editor, open the GPO that will include the custom registry settings and .adm template.

3. Open the GPO to the Administrative Templates node (under Computer Configuration or User Configuration).

4. Right-click the Administrative Templates node, and select Add/Remove Templates.

5. Select the .adm template you created to add it to the GPO.

If you did not complete these steps, or if you selected to view GPOs with a domain controller different than the one that you used to add the .adm template initially, verify all of the steps and the replication convergence of the GPO files to all domain controllers.

If you completed all of these steps, you still might not see your custom settings within the Group Policy Object Editor. The most likely cause of this behavior is that the Only Show Policy Settings That Can Be Fully Managed check box is selected (in the Group Policy Editor under View, Filtering), as shown in Figure 17-2.

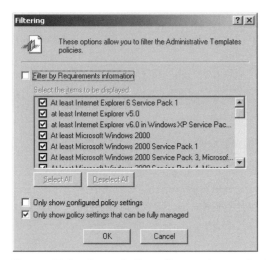

Figure 17-2   Group Policy Editor setting to display only policy settings that can be fully managed

When this setting is selected, only the GPO settings that fall under one of the four Policies registry subkeys will be displayed in the Group Policy Object Editor. Settings that don't fall under these registry subkeys will be hidden from view. They are actually still available, but you see them only if this setting is not selected.

One key indicator that this is the solution to the problem is that the policy structure for the GPO setting will be shown but the policy setting will not (Figure 17-3).

More Info   For more information on policies that can be managed, the Policies registry subkeys, and the syntax to configure these settings in an administrative template, see Chapter 14.

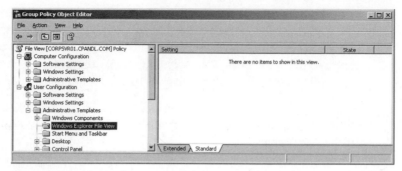

Figure 17-3 The policy structure for a new policy setting without showing the policy setting

Administrative Templates and Settings Depend on the Operating System Version

There are many variations of .adm templates, based on which operating system you are using for both your domain controllers and to administer GPOs. With different service packs, operating system releases, and security updates, these .adm files have gone through considerable changes since Windows 2000 was first released. If you have a mismatch between the operating system version that is running Active Directory and the operating system version that is used to administer GPOs, you might see more strange behavior than if you use the same operating system version for both tasks. This strange behavior will include missing GPO settings when editing GPOs, overwriting of administrative templates during editing of GPOs, and errors when editing GPOs from one operating system version to another.

For this discussion, the following products are considered the same version:

- Windows 2000 Server and Windows 2000 Professional
- Windows Server 2003 and Windows XP Professional
- Windows Server 2003 SP1 and Windows XP Professional SP2

These combinations are based on the major changes made to the Administrative Templates settings. You can accommodate the differences between these GPO settings by using the latest .adm templates when you are modifying the GPOs. The Group Policy Editor displays only what the .adm file tells it to display.

Two other settings are important with regard to the .adm templates. First, you can control whether the computer you are using to administer the GPOs will use the local .adm templates or those stored on the domain controller. This setting is located under the Computer Configuration\Administrative Templates\System\Group Policy node. The setting is named Always Use Local .adm Files For Group Policy Object Editor. When this setting is enabled, the Group Policy Editor uses the local copy of the .adm templates; when it is disabled, the Group Policy Editor relies on the version stored on the domain controller.

Second, you can control whether the .adm template versions stored on the domain controller and local computer are compared when the GPO is being edited. By default, this comparison results in the newest .adm template being used to edit the GPO. This setting can be controlled under the User Configuration\Administrative Templates\System\ Group Policy node. The setting is named Turn Off Automatic Update Of .adm Files.

> **Note**   For more information about the two GPO settings that control .adm templates, see Chapter 14.

Security Template Settings Are Not Taking Effect

You can use the security templates to establish baseline security settings for computers. One of the most common methods of producing these security templates is to use the Security Templates snap-in through the Microsoft Management Console (MMC), as shown in Figure 17-4.

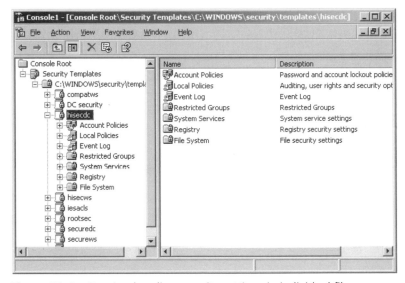

Figure 17-4   Creating baseline security settings in individual files

If you have used the snap-in to create the security templates, you must ensure that you deploy the security templates to the computers in some way. Multiple methods are available, but using GPOs is the best and most efficient method. To deploy the security settings that you configure in a security template using Group Policy, you must import the security template into the GPO by following these steps:

1. Edit the GPO that will receive the security template settings.

2. Expand the Administrative Templates\Windows Settings\Security Settings node.

3. Right-click the Security Settings node, and select Import Template.

4. Select the correct security template file, and click OK.

This procedure imports the security template and all of its related configurations into the GPO and thereby deploys the settings to all computer accounts that the GPO affects.

> **More Info**   For more information on security templates and methods for deploying them, see Chapter 4.

New Custom Security Settings Are Not Displayed

Much like customizing the .adm templates, you can also customize the security settings that reside in a standard GPO. This can be done by modifying the Sceregvl.inf file, as previously explained in Chapter 15. There are many reasons that you might want to customize the security settings. Regardless of the reason, you might find that those custom settings are not showing up in the Group Policy Object Editor.

The one big difference between customizing .adm templates and security settings is in how the settings are updated so the Group Policy Object Editor can read them. As we just saw, .adm templates are imported into the GPO. When you modify the Sceregvl.inf file however, you can't import this file into a GPO. Instead, you must reregister the DLL that is associated with this file to get the new settings to show up in the Group Policy Object Editor. To reregister the DLL, you type the following command on the computer that has the new copy of the Sceregvl.ing file and will be used to administer the GPO:

```
regsvr32 C:\Windows\system32\scecli.dll
```

Unless you perform this registration, the new custom security settings will not show up in the Group Policy Object Editor.

> **More Info**   For more information on customizing security settings within a GPO, see Chapter 15.

Delegation Restrictions Within the GPMC

When you need to administer GPOs within the Group Policy Management Console (GPMC), you might find that some of the administration options do not appear, depending on what permissions your user account has been assigned. The GPMC is a perfect environment for controlling what each administrator of GPOs is responsible for. Five different administrative tasks can be delegated to one or more administrators within the GPMC. What appears to be a problem might simply be the result of another administrator restricting your access to the GPOs within the GPMC.

Because establishing delegation restrictions within the GPMC can be tricky, we'll look at where you can modify these delegations within the GPMC for the five administrative tasks.

Creating GPOs

You can create GPOs within the GPMC in two ways. First, you can go to the node where the GPO will be linked, right-click the node, and select Create And Link A GPO Here, as shown in Figure 17-5.

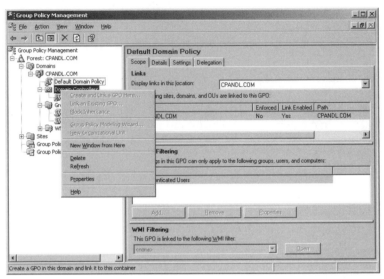

Figure 17-5   Creating and linking a GPO to an Active Directory node using the GPMC

The second way to create a GPO using the GPMC is to right-click the Group Policy Objects node and select New, as shown in Figure 17-6.

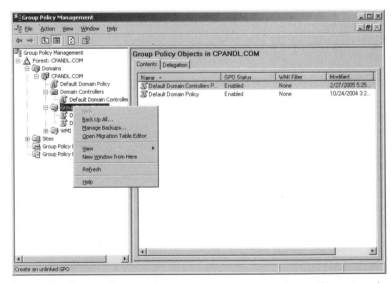

Figure 17-6   Creating a new GPO using the Group Policy Objects node within the GPMC

In both figures, the option to create a new GPO is unavailable. This is because the user who is administering Group Policy using the GPMC has not been delegated the ability to create GPOs in the domain.

You configure this delegation by accessing the Delegation tab, after highlighting the Group Policy Objects node in the GPMC. On the Delegation tab, you will see the list of administrators who have permission to create a new GPO, as shown in Figure 17-7. The menu options for creating GPOs are available to those administrators only.

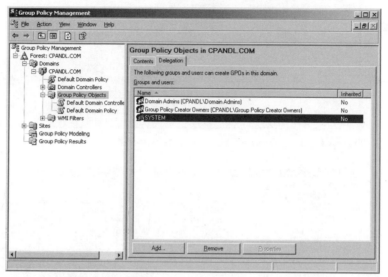

Figure 17-7   Granting administrators the ability to create GPOs

Linking GPOs

Linking GPOs to nodes within Active Directory is an important administrative task—certainly one that should not be taken lightly. Therefore, if you go to a domain, an organizational unit (OU), or a site only to find that the option to link a GPO to the node is grayed out, don't be alarmed. It is at the domain, OU, or site where you can link a GPO to one of these nodes. By right-clicking one of these nodes, you should see the Link An Existing GPO menu item, as shown in Figure 17-8.

If, as shown in Figure 17-8, the Link A GPO option is unavailable, you don't have the permission to link a GPO to this node. Remember that the creation of GPOs is domain wide, while linking GPOs to containers is container-specific. Therefore, if you go to any container (domain, OU, or site), you will have a Delegation tab. On that tab, you can specify which administrators can link GPOs to this portion of Active Directory, as shown in Figure 17-9.

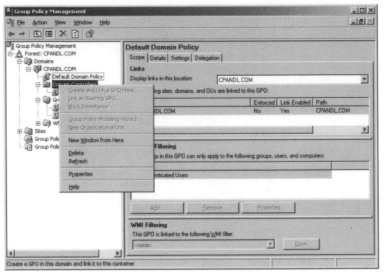

Figure 17-8   Linking a GPO to a node within Active Directory

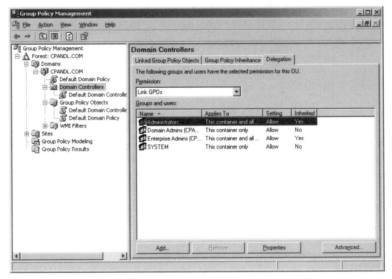

Figure 17-9   Granting administrators the permission to link GPOs to a node within Active Directory

Managing GPOs

Management of GPOs includes editing the GPO settings, setting the security of the GPO, and deleting the GPO. If you need to accomplish one of these tasks but the task is unavailable (like the ACL settings shown in Figure 17-10), you have most likely not been delegated the permissions to manage that GPO.

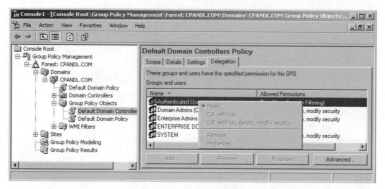

Figure 17-10   The option to modify the GPOs from within the GPMC is unavailable

The permissions to manage a GPO are configured on a GPO-by-GPO basis. To see the list of administrators who have permission to manage a GPO, follow these steps:

1. Open the list of GPOs under the Group Policy Objects node in the GPMC.

2. Click the GPO you want to investigate.

3. Select the Delegation tab.

4. Right-click the user or group to which you want to grant the ability to manage GPOs.

5. From here, you can assign the Edit Settings, Delete, Modify Security permissions as shown in Figure 17-11.

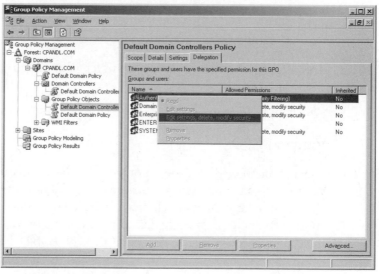

Figure 17-11   Granting administrators the ability to manage a GPO

Editing GPOs

The ability to edit a GPO is in some ways more powerful than the ability to create or link a GPO. If a GPO is already created and linked, an administrator can go into the GPO and do any configuration she has the privilege to do. However, if you are trying to edit a GPO but do not have the privilege to do so, the option to edit the GPO will be unavailable, as shown in Figure 17-12.

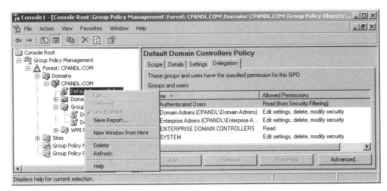

Figure 17-12   Option to edit a GPO from within the GPMC is unavailable

The ability to edit a GPO is similar to the ability to manage a GPO, in that it is set on a GPO-by-GPO basis. To set the permissions for editing a GPO from within the GPMC, complete these steps:

1. Open the list of GPOs under the Group Policy Objects node in the GPMC.

2. Click the GPO you want to investigate.

3. Select the Delegation tab.

4. Right-click the user or group to which you want to grant the permission to edit the GPO.

5. From here, you can set the Edit Settings, option, as shown in Figure 17-13.

Viewing GPOs

Viewing the GPO settings does not have a lot of security implications, but granting this permission unnecessarily can have vulnerabilities associated with it. For example, if a user has the ability to track down which GPO settings are affecting a server or another computer, they might discover or exploit a known vulnerability based on how the computer is configured. Of course, this vulnerability was already present, but the ability to view the settings makes the vulnerability apparent.

For this reason, you might not have access to view the GPO settings when you are in the GPMC. If you have not been granted the ability to view a GPO on the Delegation tab, you cannot see the GPO listed under the Group Policy Objects node (as shown in Figure 17-14, where Default Domain Controllers Policy is no longer visible).

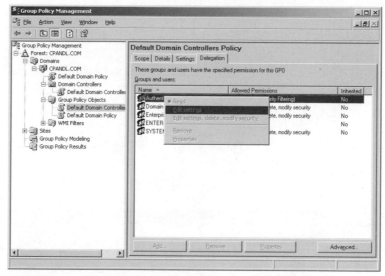

Figure 17-13   Granting administrators the ability to edit a GPO

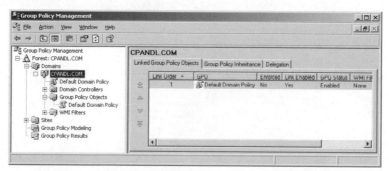

Figure 17-14   GPO under the Group Policy Objects node in the GPMC is unavailable

The GPO itself will also show up as Inaccessible under the Active Directory container where it is linked, as shown in Figure 17-15.

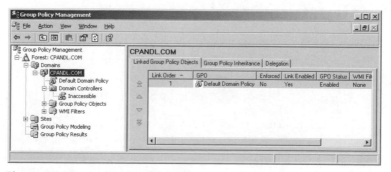

Figure 17-15   An inaccessible GPO

The ability to view a GPO is similar to the ability to manage and edit a GPO in that it is set on a GPO-by-GPO basis. The steps to access the configuration for viewing a GPO from within the GPMC are as follows:

1. Open the list of GPOs under the Group Policy Objects node in the GPMC.

2. Click the GPO you want to investigate.

3. Select the Delegation tab.

4. Right-click the user or group to which you want to grant the ability to view the GPO.

5. From here, you can assign Read permission, as shown in Figure 17-16.

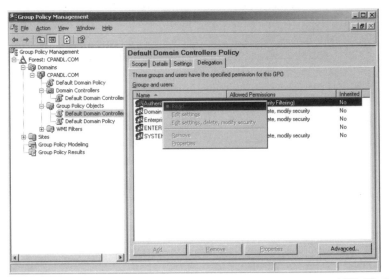

Figure 17-16   Granting administrators the ability to view the settings of a GPO

Group Policy Settings Are Not Being Applied Due to Infrastructure Problems

Because the final application of Group Policy settings depends heavily on the domain controllers replicating the GPOs, there are many areas where the process can fail. This is not to say that Active Directory is unstable; rather, there are many areas that can be configured incorrectly, which can break the application of Group Policy settings.

This section focuses on the many aspects of configuration that are on the server side or for which the server is responsible. Smaller problems will arise due to the server, but we will look only at the most common problems that make Group Policy fail to apply to clients.

Domain Controllers Are Not Available

It is common for Group Policy settings to fail to apply to computers and users in branch offices where the WAN link is not reliable. If the WAN link is unavailable, a user who has never logged on to the computer before will be unable to logon if there is no local domain controller to authenticate him. However, if the user has logged on successfully before, he will be able to log on using his cached credentials even if the WAN link is down and a domain controller is available, but there are several policy settings that can restrict this kind of behavior. If you find that certain Group Policy settings are not being applied to certain users, it might be because those users have logged on using cached credentials.

The first option you can configure using policy is to limit the number of logons that can be cached on the client in case the domain controller becomes unavailable. This setting can be found under the Computer Configuration\Windows Settings\Security Settings\Local Policies\Security Options node. The policy setting is named Interactive Logon: Number Of Previous Logons To Cache (In Case Domain Controller Is Not Available), as shown in Figure 17-17. If this policy is set to 0, no cached logons are allowed, which will make the logon attempt fail should the WAN link go down and no domain controller be available.

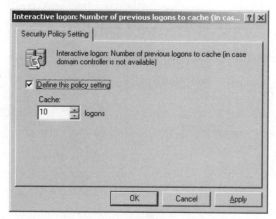

Figure 17-17   GPO setting that can limit the number of cached logons for a client or server

The other option configurable by policy is for use with roaming profiles. This setting is located under the Computer Configuration\Administrative Templates\System\ User Profiles node. The setting is named Wait For Remote User Profile, as shown in Figure 17-18. It forces the user to wait for his roaming user profile to log on to the network. The roaming user profile is determined by the domain controller that authenticates the user. If no domain controller can authenticate the user, the roaming profile will not be found. Ideally, this setting should also be configured with Delete Cached Copies Of Roaming Profiles, which is located under the same path, to ensure that the user cannot log on with any cached credentials (because there won't be any).

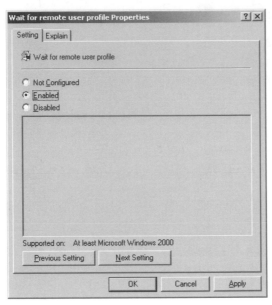

Figure 17-18   Enabling the GPO setting that forces the user to wait for his roaming user profile

If the user successfully logs on with cached credentials, the GPO settings that applied the last logon will still be cached in his user profile. However, any new GPO settings that were configured since the last logon will not be applied to the user. This can result in a security vulnerability, depending on which security settings were configured using Group Policy since the last logon. This is why many companies do not allow logons using cached credentials.

Active Directory Database Is Corrupt

If the Active Directory database becomes corrupt, Group Policy settings are almost guaranteed to fail to apply. If the Active Directory database references the wrong GUID, DNS server, or SRV record, Group Policy might fail to apply to user and computer accounts. In many cases, the computer or user account might fail to log on altogether, presenting an error that the domain the account is trying to authenticate to is no longer available.

In such a case, you must track down the root problem. If the problem is that a domain controller has failed, you can replace either the Active Directory database on this domain controller or the entire domain controller. If the problem is bigger and the entire Active Directory database is corrupt, you must restore a valid copy of the Active Directory database using your backup application and/or use the authoritative restore procedure.

> **More Info**   For more information about nonauthoritative and authoritative restores of the Active Directory database, see "The Active Directory Operations Guide" at *www.microsoft.com/technet*.

Local Logon vs. Active Directory Logon

If the computer-based GPO settings are being applied properly but the user-based GPO settings are not, the problem might relate to where the user is being authenticated. If all of the computer, network, and DNS settings are configured properly, it is difficult to bypass the computer-based GPO settings. However, if a user logs on to the local computer and be authenticated by the local Security Accounts Manager (SAM), the user-based GPO settings that reside at the Active Directory level will not apply.

Users log on locally for many reasons. Some administrators use local accounts to bypass GPO security settings. Some users have a local account for reasons that typically yield little benefit. In all cases, if a user is allowed to log on locally, the GPO settings that exist within GPOs linked to Active Directory containers will not apply to the user account.

One solution is to not allow local user accounts in the local SAM of clients and servers. These accounts are seldom needed. Considering the security vulnerabilities that these accounts can lead to, the case for eliminating these accounts and not allowing users to use the local SAM to authenticate is a strong one.

You can even remove the use of the Administrator account in the local SAM by disabling this account. To disable it, you configure a policy setting located at this path: Computer Configuration\Windows Settings\Security Settings\Local Policies\Security Options. Under this node, you configure the Accounts: Administrator Account Status policy to be disabled, as shown in Figure 17-19. This completely disables the account—no one can use it for local logons or any other resource access, except for Safe Mode recovery.

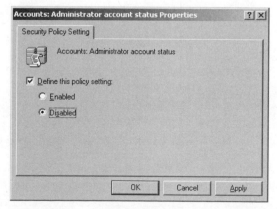

Figure 17-19   Disabling the Administrator account for clients and servers

SYSVOL Files Are Causing GPO Application Failure

The SYSVOL folder contains the configurable files that are associated with GPOs. Here you will find the .adm templates, Registry.pol files, scripts, and more. These files can be manipulated manually, but it is best not to do so. However, manual configuration is not the only way that the SYSVOL files can be misconfigured or corrupted.

Because the application of GPOs depends on the contents of the SYSVOL, incorrect settings within the SYSVOL structure can cause some or all of the settings to fail to apply. The failures might be as small as one setting not applying or as large as no setting from any GPO applying to any object, including domain controllers. Therefore, it is best to avoid going into the SYSVOL structure and modifying ACLs, files, folders, or settings.

The remainder of this section describes some of the ways in which the SYSVOL can be misconfigured or corrupted.

GPO Files Manually Modified Incorrectly

There are many files within the Policies subfolder under the SYSVOL structure. These GPO files are named by GUID, as shown in Figure 17-20. Under each GUID, you will find a collection of files and folders that are logically arranged so the GPO settings can be updated, backed up, and applied correctly. However, if the contents of the files, folders, or text within the files are misconfigured, the GPO settings will most likely fail to apply.

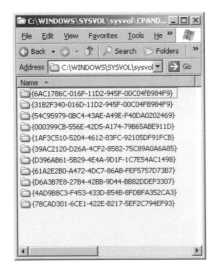

Figure 17-20   GPO files under the Policies subfolder and categorized by GUID

One example of an update to these files is an update to the Registry.pol file. This file contains the updates that are made to the Administrative Templates settings within the GPO. The file contains some text that can be read, plus some text that can't be updated manually. Even though you can read some of this text, you should not update these files manually. Should an administrator attempt to make a change to the value of a setting within the Registry.pol file, but the value was set incorrectly, as was the syntax after the value. This caused the entire suite of settings within the Registry.pol file to fail to apply. The problem did not end there. Because the file was updated and had a new timestamp, the update replicated to all domain controllers and caused this failure on every computer that was supposed to have the settings within this GPO apply.

SYSVOL Share Removed

The SYSVOL share is essential for Active Directory to function. Included in Active Directory is the application of GPOs. It is easy to go in and remove the SYSVOL share from any domain controller—this breaks all replication to and from that domain controller. If the domain controller that has the SYSVOL broken is used as a replication bridge between two other domain controllers, replication can fail for more than just the one domain controller.

If the SYSVOL share is removed, you will have numerous entries in the Event Viewer logs indicating that much of the Active Directory replication and GPO application is failing. To fix this problem, you must restore the SYSVOL share and ensure that the domain controller is joined back to the replica set. For more information on how to accomplish this, see article 257338 in the Microsoft Knowledge Base.

Incorrect Date and Time of GPO Files

When you install and configure domain controllers, you might sometimes need to change the system time or time zone. You must be cautious about doing this so files don't get out of synch when it comes to replication. If the system time on a computer is is changed to a time in the future, all files created after this time will receive the time stamp of that time zone. However, if the time is reset back to an earlier time zone soon thereafter, due to a mistake of some sort, the files that were created in the interim period will have a "future" timestamp. Future time-stamped files do not replicate and cause severe issues for Active Directory and GPO functionality.

To ensure that this does not happen, make sure the time zone and server system time are set properly before any files are changed. Otherwise, you might need to restore Active Directory files or GPO files from a tape backup.

Problems with Replication and Convergence of Active Directory and SYSVOL

When a GPO is created or modified, those changes must be updated on all of the domain controllers in the domain. If the replication fails or does not finish before the GPOs need to be refreshed, target accounts might not receive the proper GPO settings. There are many reasons that replication and convergence might take a long time or fail. We will go over some of the main reasons that GPOs don't apply due to replication or convergence issues.

Syncing Group Policy GPC and GPT

We have seen that there are two parts of a GPO. One part is stored in Active Directory and is referred to as the Group Policy container (GPC). The other part is stored in the SYSVOL and is referred to as the Group Policy template (GPT). When a GPO is created or modified, both parts are updated on the domain controller that performs the update. These changes must then be replicated to other domain controllers before the changes take affect in all accounts in the domain.

The main issue with having two parts of a GPO is that each part relies on a different replication service. The GPC relies on Active Directory replication, which is driven by the Knowledge Consistency Checker (KCC) and Intersite Topology Generator (ISTG) for replicating between Active Directory sites. The GPT relies on the File Replication Service (FRS), which takes care of replicating the SYSVOL contents between domain controllers.

These two replication services do not communicate or rely on each other in any way. Therefore, they replicate on different intervals and at different times. This can cause a difference in GPC and GPT version on any one domain controller before the replication of the two parts synchronizes. During this time, you might find that GPO settings that are applied to accounts are not the latest configured settings.

If this problem occurs with the GPC and GPT being out of sync, you can verify the version number of each portion using the GPMC, as shown in Figure 17-21. This will help you figure out which portion of the GPO is not synchronized on each domain controller. Then you can track down whether Active Directory replication or FRS is just not finished replicating or if there is a bigger problem with replication.

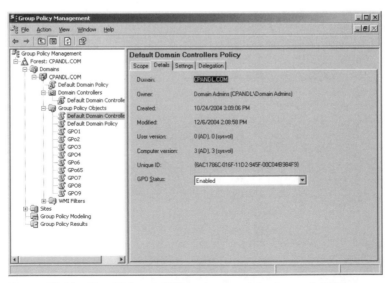

Figure 17-21 The GPC and GPT version numbers for each GPO

> **More Info**   For more information on GPO replication, see Chapter 13.

Intrasite Replication

When a GPO is modified on a domain controller that is located in a specific site, it should only take a maximum of 15 minutes to replicate to all of the other domain controllers in that site. So if you are waiting for a GPO setting to show up on a computer, you might need to be patient. If, after 15 minutes or more, the GPO settings are not applying properly, you should confirm that the changes have replicated to all domain controllers within the site. If the changes have not replicated to all of the domain controllers in the site, you should investigate the Active Directory replication and FRS replication services. If the GPO changes have replicated to all domain controllers, you must investigate other possible problems.

Intersite Replication

Intersite replication adds more complexity to the concept of standard GPO replication. Not only do GPOs need to replicate between domain controllers in the same site, but they must replicate to domain controllers in different sites. Because one of the main reasons for site creation is to control replication, GPO application from site to site can vary over time after a GPO has been updated.

It can be difficult to track down GPO replication problems across sites. You can take the same philosophy for verifying the GPC and GPT versions on domain controllers in the different sites, to see if they have been synchronized. If the versions are not in synch, your first task is to see whether the replication should have occurred already. With replication across sites, the replication interval is set by the administrator when the sites are created. The default site replication interval is 180 minutes, but it can be set as low as 15 minutes and as high as many hours. Therefore, it is a good idea to first check the intersite replication interval to ensure that replication should have occurred.

If replication should have occurred, you must verify that Active Directory replication and FRS replication are working properly. If so, you might have another issue that is causing the intersite replication to fail. Checking the event logs can help you track down these possible problems.

DNS Problems Causing GPO Application Problems

DNS is integral to Active Directory. Without DNS, Active Directory features, functions, and communications will fail. Thus, GPOs rely on DNS to ensure that the client can find the correct domain controller to apply settings. The configurations for DNS with regard to the servers and clients are not complex, but in certain areas the configurations can become incorrect, causing GPOs to fail to apply.

DHCP Servers Allocating Incorrect DNS Information

On most networks, clients are configured to receive their IP configurations from the DHCP server. One of the IP configurations they receive is the IP addresses of the primary and secondary DNS servers. This information is manually input into the DHCP server and can be misconfigured or can become incorrect if the DNS server is changed.

If the client receives the wrong DNS server IP address, the client can still authenticate the user. However, in almost every case the GPOs will not apply from the domain controller. No error message will appear, so the problem can be difficult to track down.

Manual Client Configuration Is Incorrect

Even though a client computer is configured to receive its IP address from the DHCP server, the IP configuration might allow for a manual configuration for the DNS server. If a client is manually configured with the incorrect DNS IP address, GPOs will fail to apply.

This scenario can happen in several ways. For example, users of laptop computers might manually configure their DNS server IP address when they go to a branch office or use their home network. For example, they might configure the IP address of an Internet-based DNS server so they can browse the Web while off the corporate network. Another example is when the local user of the computer does not want GPOs to apply to her. Although this is a breach of corporate security policy, users sometimes misconfigure DNS to bypass GPOs but still gain access to Web resources. To prevent this behavior, you need to enforce the corporate security policy or remove the ability for users to make these modifications on their local computer.

SRV Records Have Been Deleted

Domain controllers are found by domain computers through DNS. Depending on what the domain computer needs from the domain controller, they might go to DNS to find the domain controller that is running that service. These services are stored in DNS as SRV records. There are SRV records for domain controller services, DFS, Kerberos, and more.

If these SRV records fail to get inserted into DNS for the domain controllers, the application of GPOs to some clients might fail. The SRV records might also be deleted accidentally or by an attacker. If the SRV records are missing for a domain controller, you can stop and start the NETLOGON service for the domain controller to update the SRV records within the DNS server.

Warning   You should stop and start the NETLOGON service when no clients are attempting to authenticate to the domain controller. If the domain controller is not communicating with any network computers, you must toggle the NETLOGON service regardless of the network traffic attempting to communicate with it.

Solving Implementation Problems

With more than 1600 GPO settings in a typical GPO and potentially hundreds of GPOs within your Active Directory infrastructure, and with WMI filters, security filtering, blocking GPOs, enforcing GPOs, and so much more, the implementation of GPOs is bound to fail sometimes. Even with the best GPO testing and integrity checks, certain settings and configurations will cause problems on the production network. This section explores some of the most common errors that can be made in GPOs during implementation.

Tracking Down Incorrect GPO Settings

With so many GPO settings to choose from, settings can easily become misconfigured. The ability to quickly track down the incorrect setting and in which GPO it resides is extremely important. Here are some common situations where a GPO setting might be set incorrectly and some possible solutions.

GPO Settings That Can Be Set to Enabled or Disabled

Most of the Administrative Template GPO settings have three options when you configure them: Not Configured, Enabled, and Disabled. When you select Enabled or Disabled, you must pay close attention to the wording associated with the policy setting. In some cases, Enabled removes a feature, and in other cases it adds the feature. The same concern applies to the Disabled option. Figures 17-22 and 17-23 show how Enabled removes a feature and adds a feature, respectively.

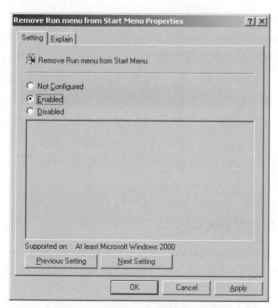

Figure 17-22   Enabling a GPO policy setting to remove a feature

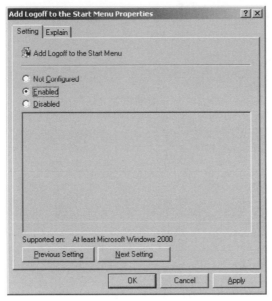

Figure 17-23   Enabling a GPO policy setting to add a feature

When you configure these policy settings, read the descriptions of the settings carefully. Be aware of double negatives as well as the double positives. To help you understand what each policy setting does, read the Explain tab for the setting; it typically explains the result of the policy for both the Enabled and Disabled configurations.

Tools that can help you determine what the settings are for the policy configurations include:

- **Resultant Set of Policy (RSoP)**   Runs on the client and indicates what the final setting configured on the client

- **GPRESULT**   Similar to RSoP but runs from the command line of the client

- **Group Policy Modeling**   Runs using the GPMC and helps determine what the final policy settings would be as well as which GPO would make the settings

More Info   For more information on how to use these troubleshooting tools, see Chapter 16.

Incorrect Setting Selected

Once you open up a GPO in the editor, you are faced with many decisions and policies. If you set a policy accidentally or select the incorrect check box, option button, or spin box, the result can be problems with network connectivity, resource access, Internet access, and more. These incorrect settings are hard to track down because the result is simply that the computer does not work in some fashion. You will not see any error message indicating that a GPO setting was set to make the computer fail.

In a situation like this, you must find out which GPO has the errant setting and which setting is causing the problem. This can take some time. However, plenty of tools are available that can help you locate the problem. These tools include:

- **Resultant Set of Policy (RSoP)**   Runs on the client and indicates what the final setting configured on the client

- **GPRESULT**   Similar to RSoP but runs from the command line of the client

- **Group Policy Modeling**   Runs using the GPMC and helps determine what the final policy settings would be as well as which GPO would make the settings

The best way to eliminate these problems is to first test and verify all GPO settings in a nonproduction environment. This is time consuming with so many GPO settings, but with good documentation, testing, and a testing lab, you can reduce errors dramatically.

More Info   For more information on how to use these troubleshooting tools, see Chapter 16.

Computer Configuration vs. User Configuration Settings

Administrators often get confused about which settings in a GPO apply to computer accounts and which apply to user accounts. A GPO separates these settings clearly, as shown in Figure 17-24, but some settings appear to be for user accounts when in reality they affect computer accounts. A good example of this is the Account Policies settings, which configure user password restrictions. Because these policies relate to user passwords, administrators tend to assume that these settings apply to user accounts. However, these settings control user passwords by controlling the directory database on the computer where the accounts reside, which is why they are found under Computer Configuration instead of User Configuration.

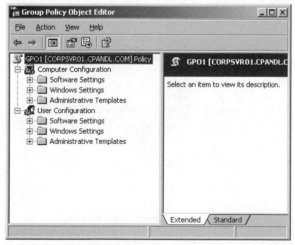

Figure 17-24   Typical GPO separates the computer settings from the user settings

There are limited tools for tracking down a computer-based setting that is intended to affect a user account. When a specific GPO setting is not applying as expected, you need to determine first whether the setting is a computer-based or user-based setting. Then locate the corresponding accounts within Active Directory and its OU structure. It is common for accounts to be located in the wrong OU, which prevents GPO settings from applying to them as expected.

GPO Links Causing GPO Application Problems

When a GPO is created, it must be linked to an Active Directory container to apply to accounts. As we saw in Chapter 4, the design and implementation of Active Directory and the GPOs is the foundation for where these GPOs should be linked. If the design philosophy is changed or an administrator decides to start changing GPO links without understanding the ramifications, problems can occur. This section explores some common problems that can occur with regard to linking GPOs.

Linking GPOs to Multiple Containers

It is not a bad practice to create a GPO that will be linked to multiple containers within Active Directory. In fact, this is commonly done to reduce the number of GPOs that need to be created, managed, and tracked. However, sometimes administrators decide to link a GPO to a container that was not designed to be linked to that GPO causing problems with clients and servers on the network. The administrator might not be experienced enough about GPOs or Active Directory design to know the ramifications.

Errant GPO links can cause loss of data, loss of production time, and loss of money due to simple GPO settings that affect the accounts that reside in the OU where the errant GPO link is made. Without documentation, finding these errant GPO links can be difficult. The following tools can help track down all GPOs that affect an account, but unless a clear GPO naming strategy or clear documentation has been used, the tools might not be enough.

- **Resultant Set of Policy (RSoP)**   Runs on the client and indicates what the final setting configured on the client

- **GPRESULT**   Similar to RSoP but runs from the command line of the client

- **Group Policy Modeling**   Runs using the GPMC and helps determine what the final policy settings would be as well as which GPO would make the settings

 More Info   For more information on how to use these troubleshooting tools, see Chapter 16.

Administering GPOs that are Linked to Multiple Containers

When you administer GPOs from within the GPMC, it is a good idea to determine where the GPO is linked before you modify any policies in the GPO. You know that modifications in a GPO will affect a subset of accounts within Active Directory, but the change might also affect other accounts located in other areas of Active Directory where the GPO is also linked.

You should follow two best practices when updating GPO settings within GPOs that are linked to more than one Active Directory container. First, work with the GPO from under the Group Policy Objects node within the GPMC. This ensures that you do not narrow your focus to just one GPO link—instead, you have to think about the entire Active Directory structure and the fact that the GPO might be linked to more than one container. Second, before making any changes to the GPO, you should investigate all of the containers where the GPO is linked. You can do this by viewing the Scope tab when you click on the GPO in the GPMC, as shown in Figure 17-25. You can see a list of all of the containers that have a link to this GPO.

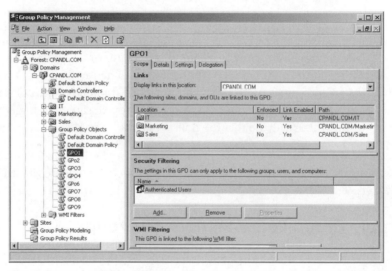

Figure 17-25   GPMC allows you to see a list of all containers that have links to each GPO

Accounts Are Not Located in the Correct OU

OUs are designed to house computer and user accounts. If an account is not placed in the proper OU, the appropriate GPOs won't apply to it. We'll look next at common scenarios in which accounts are in the incorrect OU to receive GPO settings.

Reasons That Accounts Are Placed in the Incorrect OU

If an account is placed in the incorrect OU, the GPO settings will not apply to the account. By following proper change management procedures, you can generally avoid such simple oversights. However, even with the most sophisticated change management procedures, accounts can still sometimes be misplaced in the Active Directory structure. Here are some common reasons that accounts get misplaced in wrong OUs:

- The newly created computer or user account was not moved to the correct OU.

- The computer or user account was not moved from the Computers or Users container after the OU structure was implemented.

- The OU design was modified, but accounts were not relocated.

- The Active Directory object representing the employee or his computer was not moved to the new OU after the computer or employee changed departments.

- A new OU structure was implemented, but some computer or user accounts were not moved into the proper OU.

Wrong Account in OU

GPO settings can apply to a computer account or a user account. As we mentioned earlier, it can sometimes be confusing as to whether a particular GPO setting is targeting a computer or user. If the administrator thinks that a GPO setting is designed to target a computer account when in reality it is designed to target a user account, the result will usually be that the policy will not be applied as expected.

To resolve such problems, you should verify whether the GPO settings you want to apply are computer-based or user-based, and then ensure that the correct account type is located in the OU where the GPO is linked.

Trying to Apply Group Policy Settings to Groups

Since the days of Windows NT 4.0 System Policy, administrators have sometimes been confused about how to apply GPOs to group accounts. System Policies could target computer and user accounts based on group membership, so some administrators have tried this within an Active Directory environment, but to no avail. Here are some tips to help you avoid trying to apply GPOs to groups.

Linking GPOs to OUs That Contain Only Groups

A common error is to link GPOs to OUs that contain only group accounts. The assumption is that the user accounts with membership in these groups will receive the GPO settings, but this procedure fails because GPOs apply only to computer and user accounts, not to groups.

All of the tools that help you track the GPOs that are applied to a computer or user account will confirm this foundational GPO application concept. Tools such as RSoP, GPRESULT, and Group Policy Modeling all omit the GPOs that are attempting to affect computer and user accounts via group membership.

This restriction still baffles some administrators, but there is a simple way to remind yourself that GPOs affect only computer and user accounts: when you open up a GPO in the editor, you see only two sections: Computer Configuration and User Configuration. There is no section named Group Configuration! In this way, you can remind yourself that GPOs do not affect groups or their members.

Setting GPO Security Filtering to Apply GPO Settings to Groups

Sometimes administrators try to modify a GPO's ACL so the GPO settings affect the members of a group. This will, of course, fall short of the desired outcome. If we look at the default configuration of the GPO ACL, we can see why this approach cannot work.

All computer and user accounts receive GPO settings by default through the Authenticated Users group, via permissions of the ACL. All computer and user accounts have membership in this group once they authenticate to Active Directory. When an administrator attempts to add another group to the ACL, in hopes of having the GPO settings apply to the members of this group, this action duplicates the permissions already in place.

The bottom line is that the computer or user account *must* be located in the OU where the GPO is linked. (The account can be located in a child OU, below where the GPO is linked to receive the GPO settings.)

 More Info   For more information on using GPO security filtering, see Chapter 3.

Conflicting Settings in Two GPOs

Most Group Policy implementations include more than a single GPO affecting the target accounts. In some cases, you might have numerous GPOs that affect a single target account. When the final GPO settings are applied to the account, it can be difficult to track down where one setting conflicts with another one.

Having conflicting settings in different GPOs is not a problem. But if the conflicting setting does not resolve itself correctly to properly apply to the account, the computer or user will not have a particular feature, security setting, application, network configuration, etc. This will cause down time and force you to track down where the conflicting setting resides.

Many tools can help you in this situation. The following tools from Microsoft are geared toward finding and fixing these problems. They require that you know which settings are causing the problem, but once you know, the tools can help you track down where the setting conflicts exist.

- **Resultant Set of Policy (RSoP)**   Runs on the client and indicates what the final setting configured on the client

- **GPRESULT**   Similar to RSoP but runs from the command line of the client

- **Group Policy Modeling**   Runs using the GPMC and helps determine what the final policy settings would be as well as which GPO would make the settings

 More Info   For more information on how to use these troubleshooting tools, see Chapter 16.

Modifying Default GPO Inheritance

The default GPO inheritance takes the GPOs from the local computer down through sites, the domain, and OUs to determine the resultant set of policy. As a best practice, you should leverage this default inheritance and GPO application wherever possible throughout the Active Directory implementation and avoid modifying default GPO processing unless necessary. If you maintain the default inheritance, the only potential problems are those described in earlier sections. However, altering the default inheritance can cause problems if you are not careful. The next section describes the most common ways to alter GPO inheritance and how to investigate problems that might arise.

Enforcing GPOs

Enforcement of GPOs pushes the settings in a GPO down through the Active Directory structure. Nothing can stop a GPO setting that is set to Enforced. Chapter 4 explains that in some instances setting a GPO to Enforced is a best practice. However, if you overuse this setting, the end result can be undesirable.

If you think that your GPO settings are not working properly due to other GPOs that are set to Enforced, you can use a couple of tools to track down the setting:

- **Resultant Set of Policy (RSoP)**   Runs on the client and indicates what the final setting configured on the client

- **GPRESULT**   Similar to RSoP but runs from the command line of the client

- **Group Policy Modeling**   Runs using the GPMC and helps determine what the final policy settings would be as well as which GPO would make the settings

- **GPMC interface**   Lets you see whether a GPO linked to a container is set to Enforced by the icon on the GPO link. When the setting is Enforced, the icon has a lock symbol attached to it, as shown in Figure 17-26.

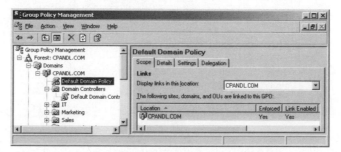

Figure 17-26   GPO links set to Enforced are identified by using a special icon

More Info   For more information on how to use these troubleshooting tools, see Chapter 16.

Block Policy Inheritance

GPO settings are appended to one another as the operating system processes them from the local computer, sites, the domain, and OUs. In some special instances, you might not want all of the GPO settings from the sites, the domain, and some OUs to apply to some accounts. You can use the Block Policy Inheritance configuration on the domain or at an OU to negate the GPO settings that have lower priority. You should use this setting only rarely because of the complexity of implementing the policies and troubleshooting the problems that can occur from using this configuration.

Block Policy Inheritance is configured at the domain or OU level, so you can go to these containers within the GPMC to see if the configuration is set. This is similar to the Enforced setting, described previously. When a container is set to Block Policy Inheritance, the icon changes to include a blue exclamation point on the container, as shown in Figure 17-27. Other tools that can also help you track down where Block Policy Inheritance is configured include:

- **Resultant Set of Policy (RSoP)**   Runs on the client and indicates the final setting configured on the client

- **GPRESULT**   Similar to RSoP but runs from the command line of the client
- **Group Policy Modeling**   Runs using the GPMC and helps determine what the final policy settings would be as well as which GPO would make the settings

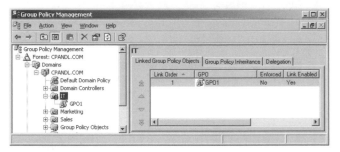

Figure 17-27   Container that is set to Block Policy Inheritance

More Info   For more information on how to use these troubleshooting tools, see Chapter 16.

Security Filtering

When you have computer and user accounts located in a single OU for administration purposes, not all of the accounts will necessarily need to receive the same GPOs. In this instance, using security filtering is a good solution (although a good Active Directory and OU design will also solve most of these kinds of problems).

When security filtering is used, it can cause problems with application of GPOs to all of the desired accounts. You must then track down where the security filtering is being used and fix the configuration of the ACL to correct the application of the GPO settings.

The same tools we just looked at for the enforcement and blocking of GPO inheritance can also be used for tracking down security filtering issues. They include:

- **Resultant Set of Policy (RSoP)**   Runs on the client and indicates the final setting configured on the client
- **GPRESULT**   Similar to RSoP but runs from the command line of the client
- **Group Policy Modeling**   Runs using the GPMC and helps determine what the final policy settings would be as well as which GPO would make the settings
- **GPMC interface**   Lets you see the ACL of the GPO, which is located on the Security tab, as shown in Figure 17-28.

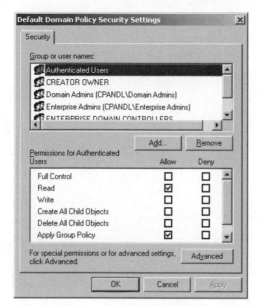

Figure 17-28   Accessing the list of users and groups that have been given the permission to apply GPOs

More Info   For more information on how to use these troubleshooting tools, see Chapter 16.

Summary

You are bound to run into problems as you design, implement, and modify GPOs in your enterprise. Working with GPOs seems complex at first, but excellent tools are available that can help you track down problems, find incorrect configurations, and fix the policies that apply to the target accounts.

Part V
Appendixes

In this part:

Appendix A: Group Policy Reference 661

Appendix B: New Features in Windows Server 2003
Service Pack 1. 669

Appendix C: GPMC Scripting 687

Appendix D: Office 2003 Administrative Template Highlights. . 705

Appendix A
Group Policy Reference

In this appendix:
Computer Configuration Reference 661
User Configuration Reference 664

Computer Configuration Reference

This appendix offers a Group Policy quick reference that cites chapters in the book or additional resources that cover each given area of policy. It includes two tables: Table A-1 lists the areas of Computer Configuration and where in the text or on the companion CD they are discussed. Table A-2 does the same for areas of User Configuration.

Table A-1   Computer Configuration Reference

Group Policy Area	Discussed in...
Software Settings\Software Installation	Chapter 9, "Deploying and Maintaining Software Through Group Policy"
Windows Settings\Scripts	Chapter 7, "Managing User Settings and Data"
■ Windows Settings\Security Settings	Chapter 5, "Hardening Clients and Servers"
■ Windows Settings\Security Settings\Account Policies	
■ Windows Settings\Security Settings\Local Policies	
■ Windows Settings\Security Settings\Event Log	
■ Windows Settings\Security Settings\Restricted Groups	
■ Windows Settings\Security Settings\System Services	
■ Windows Settings\Security Settings\Registry	
■ Windows Settings\Security Settings\File System	
Windows Settings\Security Settings\Wireless Network Policies	Group Policy spreadsheet available for download at *http://www.microsoft.com/downloads /details.aspx?FamilyId=7821C32F-DA15- 438D-8E48-45915CD2BC14&displaylang=en*

Table A-1   **Computer Configuration Reference**

Group Policy Area	Discussed in...
Windows Settings\Security Settings\Public Key Policies	Chapter 11, "Maintaining Secure Network Communications"
Windows Settings\Security Settings\Software Restriction Policies	Chapter 9, "Deploying and Maintaining Software Through Group Policy"
Windows Settings\Security Settings\IP Security Policies on Active Directory	Chapter 11, "Maintaining Secure Network Communications"
Administrative Templates\Windows Components\NetMeeting	Group Policy spreadsheet available for download at *http://www.microsoft.com/downloads* */details.aspx?FamilyId=7821C32F-DA15-* *438D-8E48-45915CD2BC14&displaylang=en*
Administrative Templates\Windows Components\Internet Explorer	Chapter 8, "Maintaining Internet Explorer Configurations"
Administrative Templates\ Windows Components\Application Compatibility	Chapter 6, "Managing and Maintaining Essential Windows Components"
Administrative Templates\Windows Components\Event Viewer	Chapter 6, "Managing and Maintaining Essential Windows Components"
Administrative Templates\Windows Components\Internet Information Services	Chapter 6, "Managing and Maintaining Essential Windows Components"
Administrative Templates\Windows Components\Security Center	Chapter 6, "Managing and Maintaining Essential Windows Components"
Administrative Templates\Windows Components\Task Scheduler	Chapter 6, "Managing and Maintaining Essential Windows Components"
Administrative Templates\Windows Components\Terminal Services	Chapter 12, "Creating Custom Environments"
Administrative Templates\Windows Components\Windows Explorer	Chapter 6, "Managing and Maintaining Essential Windows Components"
Administrative Templates\Windows Components\Windows Installer	Chapter 6, "Managing and Maintaining Essential Windows Components"
■ Administrative Templates\ Windows Components\ Windows Messenger ■ Administrative Templates\ Windows Components\ Windows Media Digital Rights Management ■ Administrative Templates\ Windows Components\ Windows Movie Maker	Group Policy spreadsheet available for download at *http://www.microsoft.com/downloads* */details.aspx?FamilyId=7821C32F-DA15-* *438D-8E48-45915CD2BC14&displaylang=en*

Table A-1   Computer Configuration Reference

Group Policy Area	Discussed in...
Administrative Templates\ Windows Components\Windows Update	Chapter 6, "Managing and Maintaining Essential Windows Components"
Administrative Templates\Windows Components\Windows Media Player	Group Policy spreadsheet available for download at *http://www.microsoft.com/downloads /details.aspx?FamilyId=7821C32F-DA15- 438D-8E48-45915CD2BC14&displaylang=en*
■ Administrative Templates\ System ■ Administrative Templates\ System\User Profiles ■ Administrative Templates\ System\Scripts	Chapter 7, "Managing User Settings and Data"
Administrative Templates\ System\Logon	Chapter 6, "Managing and Maintaining Essential Windows Components"
Administrative Templates\ System\Disk Quotas	Group Policy spreadsheet available for download at *http://www.microsoft.com/downloads /details.aspx?FamilyId=7821C32F-DA15- 438D-8E48-45915CD2BC14&displaylang=en*
Administrative Templates\ System\Net Logon	Chapter 6, "Managing and Maintaining Essential Windows Components"
Administrative Templates\ System\Group Policy	Group Policy spreadsheet available for download at *http://www.microsoft.com/downloads /details.aspx?FamilyId=7821C32F-DA15- 438D-8E48-45915CD2BC14&displaylang=en*
■ Administrative Templates\ System\Remote Assistance ■ Administrative Templates\ System\System Restore ■ Administrative Templates\ System\Error Reporting	Chapter 6, "Managing and Maintaining Essential Windows Components"
Administrative Templates\System\ Windows File Protection	Chapter 5, "Hardening Clients and Servers"
Administrative Templates\System\ Remote Procedure Call	Chapter 6, "Managing and Maintaining Essential Windows Components"
Administrative Templates\System\ Windows Time Service	Group Policy spreadsheet available for download at *http://www.microsoft.com/downloads /details.aspx?FamilyId=7821C32F-DA15- 438D-8E48-45915CD2BC14&displaylang=en*

Table A-1   Computer Configuration Reference

Group Policy Area	Discussed in...
Administrative Templates\Internet Communication Management	Chapter 8, "Maintaining Internet Explorer Configurations"
Administrative Templates\ System\Distributed COM	Group Policy spreadsheet available for download at *http://www.microsoft.com/downloads /details.aspx?FamilyId=7821C32F-DA15- 438D-8E48-45915CD2BC14&displaylang=en*
Administrative Templates\Network	Chapter 11, "Maintaining Secure Network Communications"
■ Administrative Templates\ Network\Microsoft Peer-to-Peer ■ Administrative Templates\ Network\DNS Client ■ Administrative Templates\ Network\Offline Files	Group Policy spreadsheet available for download at *http://www.microsoft.com/downloads /details.aspx?FamilyId=7821C32F-DA15- 438D-8E48-45915CD2BC14&displaylang=en*
Administrative Templates\ Network\Network Connections	Chapter 11, "Maintaining Secure Network Communications"
■ Administrative Templates\ Network\QoS Packet Scheduler ■ Administrative Templates\ Network\SNMP ■ Administrative Templates\ Network\Background Intelligent Transfer Service ■ Administrative Templates\ Printers	Group Policy spreadsheet available for download at *http://www.microsoft.com/downloads /details.aspx?FamilyId=7821C32F-DA15- 438D-8E48-45915CD2BC14&displaylang=en*

User Configuration Reference

Table A-2   User Configuration Reference

Group Policy Area	Discussed in...
■ Software Settings\Software Installation ■ Windows Settings\Remote Installation Services	Chapter 9, "Deploying and Maintaining Software Through Group Policy"
Windows Settings\Scripts	Chapter 7, "Managing User Settings and Data"
Windows Settings\Security Settings	--
Windows Settings\Security Settings\ Public Key Policies	Chapter 11, "Maintaining Secure Network Communications"

Table A-2   User Configuration Reference

Group Policy Area	Discussed in...
Windows Settings\Security Settings\Software Restriction Policies	Chapter 9, "Deploying and Maintaining Software Through Group Policy"
Windows Settings\Folder Redirection	Chapter 7, "Managing User Settings and Data"
Windows Settings\Internet Explorer Maintenance	Chapter 8, "Maintaining Internet Explorer Configurations"
Administrative Templates\Windows Components\NetMeeting	Group Policy spreadsheet available for download at *http://www.microsoft.com/downloads /details.aspx?FamilyId=7821C32F-DA15-438D-8E48-45915CD2BC14&displaylang=en*
Administrative Templates\Windows Components\Internet Explorer	Chapter 8, "Maintaining Internet Explorer Configurations"
■ Administrative Templates\Windows Components\Application Compatibility ■ Administrative Templates\Windows Components\Attachment Manager ■ Administrative Templates\Windows Components\Windows Explorer ■ Administrative Templates\Windows Components\Microsoft Management Console ■ Administrative Templates\Windows Components\Task Scheduler	Chapter 6, "Managing and Maintaining Essential Windows Components"
Administrative Templates\Windows Components\Terminal Services	Chapter 12, "Creating Custom Environments"
Administrative Templates\Windows Components\Windows Installer	Chapter 6, "Managing and Maintaining Essential Windows Components"
Administrative Templates\Windows Components\Windows Messenger	Group Policy spreadsheet available for download at *http://www.microsoft.com/downloads /details.aspx?FamilyId=7821C32F-DA15-438D-8E48-45915CD2BC14&displaylang=en*
Administrative Templates\Windows Components\Windows Update	Chapter 6, "Managing and Maintaining Essential Windows Components"

Table A-2   **User Configuration Reference**

Group Policy Area	Discussed in...
■ Administrative Templates\ Windows Components\ Windows Movie Maker ■ Administrative Templates\ Windows Components\ Windows Media Player ■ Administrative Templates\ Start Menu and Taskbar ■ Administrative Templates\ Desktop ■ Administrative Templates\ Control Panel ■ Administrative Templates\ Control Panel\Add or Remove Programs ■ Administrative Templates\ Control Panel\Display ■ Administrative Templates\ Control Panel\Printers ■ Administrative Templates\ Control Panel\Regional and Language Options ■ Administrative Templates\ Control Panel\Shared Folders	Group Policy spreadsheet available for download at *http://www.microsoft.com/downloads /details.aspx?FamilyId=7821C32F-DA15- 438D-8E48-45915CD2BC14&displaylang=en*
Administrative Templates\Network	Chapter 11, "Maintaining Secure Network Communications"
Administrative Templates\Network\ Offline Files	Group Policy spreadsheet available for download at *http://www.microsoft.com/downloads /details.aspx?FamilyId=7821C32F-DA15- 438D-8E48-45915CD2BC14&displaylang=en*
Administrative Templates\ Network\Network Connections	Chapter 11, "Maintaining Secure Network Communications"
Administrative Templates\System	--
■ Administrative Templates\ System\User Profiles ■ Administrative Templates\ System\Scripts	Chapter 7, "Managing User Settings and Data"

Table A-2   **User Configuration Reference**

Group Policy Area	Discussed in...
■ Administrative Templates\ System\Ctrl + Alt + Del Options ■ Administrative Templates\ System\Logon ■ Administrative Templates\ System\Disk Quotas ■ Administrative Templates\ System\Net Logon ■ Administrative Templates\ System\Group Policy ■ Administrative Templates\ System\Power Management	Group Policy spreadsheet available for download at *http://www.microsoft.com/downloads /details.aspx?FamilyId=7821C32F-DA15- 438D-8E48-45915CD2BC14&displaylang=en*
Administrative Templates\Internet Communication Management	Chapter 8, "Maintaining Internet Explorer Configurations"

Appendix B

New Features in Windows Server 2003 Service Pack 1

In this appendix:

Adprep. 670

Administrative Tools 671

Internet Explorer Feature Control Settings 672

Internet Explorer URL Action Security Settings .674

Resultant Set of Policy. 676

Post-Setup Security Updates 678

Security Configuration Wizard 679

Windows Firewall. 681

Microsoft Windows Server 2003 Service Pack 1 offers a set of security technologies that can help reduce the attack surface of Windows Server systems and ease the administrative tasks associated with configuring server security. Windows XP SP2 introduced many of these technologies. Others are specific to the Windows Server family of operating systems. The implementation of a particular feature on the server operating system might differ from the implementation on the desktop operating system.

The security technologies provide enhancements in the following areas:

- Management, security, and performance

- File, print, and collaboration services

- Internet, application, and networking services

> **Note** With the combined enhancements to these technologies, it is more difficult to attack systems running Windows Server 2003—even if the latest updates are not applied.

This appendix focuses primarily changes in Windows Server 2003 SP1 that affect Group Policy. It doesn't cover changes that update the registry but don't affect

Group Policy (although those values might be included in a Group Policy through custom administrative templates or security templates, as discussed in Chapters 14 and 15).

Related Information

- For information on all of the changes included in Windows Server 2003 SP1, see "Changes to Functionality in Microsoft Windows Server 2003 Service Pack 1," which can be obtained from the Microsoft Download Center at *http://www.microsoft.com/downloads/details.aspx?familyid=C3C26254-8CE3-46E2-B1B6-3659B92B2CDE&displaylang=en.*

- To download the reference spreadsheet, "Group Policy Settings Reference for .adm Files and Security Settings Included with Windows XP Professional Service Pack 2," from the Microsoft Download Center at *http://go.microsoft.com/fwlink/?LinkId=15165.*

Adprep

Adprep.exe is a command-line tool used to prepare a Windows 2000 forest or a Windows 2000 domain for the installation of Windows 2003 domain controllers. In earlier versions of Windows Server 2003, running *adprep /domainprep* added an inheritable access control entry (ACE) to all Group Policy objects (GPOs) in the SYSVOL folder. This ACE gives enterprise domain controllers read access to the GPOs to support Resultant Set of Policy (RSoP) functionality for site based policy. The File Replication Service (FRS) detects the addition of the ACE and initiates an FRS synchronization of all GPOs in the SYSVOL folder.

In Windows Server 2003 SP1, the ACE is not added to the GPOs in the SYSVOL folder while *adprep /domainprep* is running. A new switch (*/gpprep*) for *adprep* adds the inheritable ACE to the GPO folders in the SYSVOL directory. This allows administrators to update the ACE of the GPO objects at their convenience.

Letting the administrators determine when to update the ACE of the GPOs makes it possible for this operation to be planned and scheduled as part of the deployment. Otherwise, if an organization has a large number of files contained in the GPOs or slow links to replication servers, the FRS synchronization triggered by the */domainprep* operation can adversely affect the deployment schedule for Windows Server 2003.

 Tip The deployment of a Windows Server 2003 domain controller can occur after you run *adprep /forestprep* and *adprep /domainprep*. RSoP functionality will be operational only after you run *adprep /gpprep*.

Administrative Tools

The administrative tools in Windows Server 2003 SP1 are a set of Microsoft Management Console (MMC) snap-ins that you can use to administer users, computers, services, and other system components on local and remote computers.

If Windows Firewall is enabled on a computer, these snap-ins use two system-generated dialog boxes for management: Select Users, Computers, Or Groups and Find Users, Contacts, And Groups. These dialog boxes are commonly used to perform tasks such as the following:

- Setting access control lists (ACLs) on a shared folder
- Specifying a remote computer for retargeting a snap-in
- Managing local users and groups.

Find Users, Contacts, And Groups is used for tasks such as the following:

- Searching Active Directory in My Network Places
- Finding a printer using the Add A Printer Wizard
- Finding objects in the directory within the Active Directory Users and Computers snap-in.

Both dialog boxes are used to find and select objects such as users, computers, printers, and other security principals from the local computer or Active Directory. Although other applications can use these dialog boxes, we'll discuss only the changes that affect the administrative tools that are listed below.

For the administrative tools that are listed below to connect to a remote computer, that remote computer must allow incoming network traffic on TCP port 445. However, if Windows Firewall is enabled, it might block incoming network traffic on TCP port 445 and you might therefore receive one or more of the following error messages:

- `Failed to open Group Policy object on Computer_Name. You might not have appropriate rights.`
- `Details: The network path was not found.`

These errors can occur when one of the following MMC snap-ins is used for remote administration:

- Group Policy
- IP Security Policy
- Resultant Set of Policy

To use these tools to remotely connect a computer with Windows Firewall enabled, you must open TCP port 445 in the firewall on the remote computer. To do this, complete the following steps:

1. Click **Start**, point to **All Programs**, point to **Accessories**, and click **Command Prompt.**

2. At the command prompt, type **netsh firewall set portopening TCP 445 ENABLE** and then press Enter.

> **Caution**   Open firewall ports can be a security vulnerability. You should carefully plan and test any such configuration change before implementing it.

Internet Explorer Feature Control Settings

Windows XP SP2 introduces new registry keys and values for Microsoft Internet Explorer security features. These security features, called *Feature Control*, have been incorporated in Windows Server 2003 SP1. This section explains the behavior of the Feature Control registry settings with each security feature.

A modified Inetres.adm file contains the Feature Control settings as policies. Administrators can manage the Feature Control policies by using GPOs. When Internet Explorer is installed, the default Feature Control settings are registered on the computer in HKEY_LOCAL_MACHINE. In Group Policy, the Administrator can set them in either HKEY_LOCAL_MACHINE (Computer Configuration) or HKEY_CURRENT_USER (User Configuration).

The new Feature Control policies are:

- Binary Behavior Security Restriction
- MK Protocol Security Restriction
- Local Machine Zone Lockdown Security
- Consistent Mime Handling
- Mime Sniffing Safety Feature
- Object Caching Protection
- Scripted Window Security Restrictions
- Protection From Zone Elevation
- Information Bar
- Restrict ActiveX Install
- Restrict FileDownload

- Add-on Management
- Network Protocol Lockdown

Managing Feature Control Settings

The Feature Control policies can be found in the Group Policy Management Console (GPMC). To locate the local computer policies, follow this path:

\Computer Configuration\Administrative Templates\Windows Components\Internet Explorer\Security Features

To locate the current user policies, follow this path:

\User Configuration\Administrative Templates\Windows Components\Internet Explorer\Security Features

The policy for the feature must be enabled for the process—for example, IExplore.exe—before the zones' individual security setting policies or preferences are applied.

Administrators of Group Policy can manage these new policies in the Administrative Templates extension to the GPMC. When configuring these policies, the administrator can enable or disable the security feature for explorer processes (Internet Explorer and Windows Explorer), for executable processes he has defined, or for all processes that host the WebOC.

Users cannot see any of the Feature Control policies or preference settings in Internet Explorer except Local Machine Zone Lockdown Security. Feature Control policies can be set only by using the GPMC, and Feature Control preference settings can be changed only programmatically or by editing the registry.

Configuring Policies and Preferences

Group Policy is the recommended tool for managing Internet Explorer for client computers on a corporate network. Internet Explorer supports Group Policy management for the Internet Explorer feature controls included in Windows XP SP2 and Windows Server 2003 SP1 as well as for Security page settings or URL Actions. Administrators of Group Policy can manage these policy settings in the Administrative Templates extension of the GPMC.

When you implement policy settings, you should configure template policy settings in one GPO and configure any related individual policy settings in a separate GPO. You can then use Group Policy management features (such as precedence, inheritance, or enforce) to apply individual settings to specific client computers.

Policies can be read by users but can be changed only by Group Policy management or by an administrator. You can change preference settings programmatically by editing the registry or, in the case of URL Actions, by using Internet Explorer.

> **Note**   Settings associated with policies take precedence over settings specified using Internet Explorer preferences.

Internet Explorer Administration Kit/Internet Explorer Maintenance

For operating systems earlier than Windows XP SP2 and Windows Server 2003 SP1 and for previous Internet Explorer versions, Internet Explorer Kit/Internet Explorer Maintenance (IEAK) 6.0 SP1 is the recommended tool for solution providers and application developers to customize Internet Explorer for users. IEAK support and the IEAK/IEM process does not change for Internet Explorer versions before Windows XP SP2. The process also has not changed for using IEAK/IEM to set user setting preferences in Internet Explorer versions before and including Windows Server 2003 SP1. This includes the new Internet Explorer 6.0 in Windows XP SP2 and Windows Server 2003 SP1 preference settings. However, the true policy settings incorporated by this feature can be managed only within Group Policy.

> **More Info**   For more information about IEAK, see "Microsoft Internet Explorer 6 Administration Kit Service Pack 1" on the Microsoft Web site at *http://go.microsoft.com/ fwlink/?LinkId=26002*.

Internet Explorer URL Action Security Settings

Windows XP SP2 introduced true policies for the configurable actions in the Internet Explorer Security tab settings. These policies are incorporated into Internet Explorer in Windows Server 2003 SP1. You can set these actions to allow less secure behavior within a security zone. In this release, these security settings are managed using the GPMC and, if set, can be changed only by a GPO or by an administrator.

Administrators can manage the new Feature Control policies by using GPOs. An updated Inetres.adm file contains the same list of URL Action settings as policies that are found in Internet Explorer as preferences. When Internet Explorer is installed, the default HKEY_CURRENT_USER preference settings for these URL Action settings are registered on the computer, as they were in previous versions.

> **Note**   The administrator must use the GPMC snap-in to add URL Actions as policies. Group Policy administrators can uniformly configure the new Internet Explorer URL Action security setting policies for the computers and users that they manage. If the administrator chooses to set selected URL Actions and not all URL Actions, it is important to tell users which actions are controlled by policy because these actions will not respond to user preference settings.

By adding the new Internet Explorer URL Action security setting policies to Group Policy, administrators can manage these true policies to establish standard security settings for all the computers they configure. The administrator can control these settings in such a way that they cannot be changed except through Group Policy or by a user with administrator privileges, thus ensuring that users cannot set URL Action settings that override a Feature Control policy or preference setting.

Changes to Internet Explorer URL Action Security Settings

The following definitions apply to Internet Explorer settings for Windows Server 2003 with SP1:

- Security zones: Internet, Intranet, and Local Machine. There are also special zone settings: Locked-Down Local Machine Zone, Trusted Sites, and Restricted Sites.

- Templates: Standard settings for all URL Actions in a security zone. Templates can be applied in any zone, and settings provide a range of choices from low security to medium-low, medium, and up to high security for the zone.

- URL Actions: Security settings in the registry that identify the action to take for that feature in the security zone where the URL resides. URL Action settings include enable, disable, prompt, and others as appropriate.

- URL Action policies: You can add these policies individually by enabling the desired URL Action policy and then selecting the setting for the policy registry key value. They can also be set by zone template.

Internet Explorer looks for a policy in the following order:

- HKEY_LOCAL_MACHINE policy hive
- HKEY_CURRENT_USER policy hive
- HKEY_CURRENT_USER preference hive
- HKEY_LOCAL_MACHINE preference hive

If Internet Explorer finds a policy in the HKEY_LOCAL_MACHINE policy hive, it stops. If it does not find a policy in theHKEY_LOCAL_MACHINE policy hive, it looks in the HKEY_CURRENT_USER policy hive, and so on. The administrator can set a policy for one or more URL Actions in one or more zones and allow the user to manage preferences for URL Actions that do not require policy-level security management.

More Info   For details about using URL Action flags, see "URL Action Flags" on the MSDN Web site at *http://go.microsoft.com/fwlink/?LinkId=32776*.

> **Note** For descriptions of the URL policy settings, see "URL Action Flags" on the
> MSDN Web site at *http://go.microsoft.com/fwlink/?LinkId=32777*.

Resultant Set of Policy

Group Policy Resultant Set of Policy (RSoP) reports Group Policy settings that are applied to a user or computer. Group Policy Results in GPMC requests RSoP data from a target computer and presents this in a report in HTML format. Group Policy Modeling requests the same type of information, but the data reported is from a service that simulates RSoP for a combination of computer and user. This simulation is performed on a domain controller running Windows Server 2003 and is then returned to the computer running GPMC for presentation. Finally, the RSoP MMC provides an alternative way to display this information, although Group Policy Results is generally the preferred method.

Changes to RSoP in SP1

In Windows Server 2003 SP1, Windows Firewall is not enabled by default. However, in Windows XP SP2, it is enabled by default. Windows Firewall blocks incoming requests against unopened ports. Enabling a firewall improves protection against many network-based attacks. For example, if Windows Firewall had been enabled, the recent MSBlaster attack would have had much less impact, even if users were not up-to-date with software updates.

> **More Info** For more information on Windows Firewall, see "Windows Firewall" in
> this appendix.

If you elect to use Windows Firewall, you should be aware of its effect on RSoP across the network. The following are two important changes to RSoP in Windows Server 2003 SP1:

- After Windows Firewall is installed on a computer, remote access to RSoP data no longer works from that target computer.

- When Windows Firewall is enabled, GPMC annot retrieve RSoP data using Group Policy Results or Group Policy Modeling.

Table B-1 summarizes the changes necessary to support remote RSoP tasks when running Windows XP SP2 or Windows Server 2003 SP1 with Windows Firewall enabled. The sections following the table provide additional information.

Table B-1   RSoP Task Reference

Task	Target Computer	Administrative Computer
Generate Group Policy Results	Enable Windows Firewall Allow Remote Administration Exception setting in Group Policy. This setting is located in Computer Configuration\Administrative Templates\Network\Network Connections\Windows Firewall\ [Domain | Standard] Profile\	GPMC with SP1 No action required RSoP snap-in Enable Windows Firewall: Define Program Exceptions. Configure the program exception list with the full path to Unsecapp.exe so the WMI messages can be transmitted. In a default installation, Unsecapp.exe is located in the C:\Windows\System32\ Wbem folder. Enable **Windows Firewall: Define port exception policy** to open Port 135
Delegate access to Group Policy Results	Enable Windows Firewall: Allow Remote Administration Exception setting in Group Policy. Configure the following DCOM security settings: DCOM: Machine access restrictions DCOM: Machine launch restrictions These policy settings are located in Computer Configuration\Windows Settings\Security Settings\Local Policies\Security Options	No changes necessary
Remotely edit a local GPO	Enable Windows Firewall: Allow File And Printer Sharing Administration Exception policy setting. This setting is located in Computer Configuration\Administrative Templates\Network\Network Connections\Windows Firewall\ [Domain | Standard] Profile\	No changes necessary

Administering Remote RSoP with GPMC SP1

The initial release of GPMC used a callback mechanism when waiting for the results of a Group Policy Results or Group Policy Modeling request. The administrative computer must be "listening" for this response; therefore, if Windows Firewall is enabled, Windows blocks these responses. Although opening the appropriate ports can address this issue, using the updated GPMC with SP1 removes the use of the callback mechanism. You should install GPMC with Windows Server 2003 SP1 to allow Group Policy Results and Group Policy Modeling to continue to work without opening up ports on the administrative computer.

> **More Info**   To install GPMC with Windows Server 2003 SP1, see "Group Policy Management Console with Service Pack 1" at the Microsoft Download Center at *http:// go.microsoft.com/fwlink/?LinkId=23529*.

To administer RSoP remotely, you must enable the Windows Firewall: Allow Remote Administration Exception Group Policy setting on target computers.

Delegating Access to Group Policy Results

By default, Group Policy Results and the RSoP snap-in can be used remotely only when the person originating the request is a local administrator on the target computer. Windows Server 2003 introduces a delegation model that allows this right to be delegated to users who are not administrators on the target computer. This is a common scenario when help desk personnel require access to computers without being made administrator on those computers.

In Windows XP SP2 and Windows Server 2003 SP1, the security model for DCOM authentication (on which RSoP relies) has been strengthened. Even if RSoP delegation has been configured correctly, this strengthening prevents local nonadministrators from retrieving RSoP information from a target computer.

> **Note**   This issue does not affect Group Policy Modeling because the request for simulated RSoP data is made against a domain controller running Windows Server 2003, which, by definition, is not running Windows XP.

You can manage the list of users and groups associated with DCOM authentication through Group Policy. To allow continued use of delegated RSoP, users to whom you want to grant this right must also have access through the DCOM authentication model.

Post-Setup Security Updates

Microsoft might have released security updates that mitigate virus threats since the release of the operating system files being installed. If the new server is connected to the network and a firewall is not enabled, the server might be infected with a virus before the security updates can be downloaded and installed. Post-Setup Security Updates uses Windows Firewall to mitigate this risk.

Post-Setup Security Updates is designed to protect the server from infection between the time the server is first started and time that the most recent security updates from Windows Update are applied. To protect the server, Windows Firewall is enabled during a new installation of any version of Windows Server 2003 that includes a service pack. If Windows Firewall is enabled and the administrator did not explicitly enable it using an unattended-setup script or Group Policy, Post-Setup Security Updates opens the first time an administrator logs on. Inbound connections to the server are blocked until the administrator has clicked the Finish button in the Post-Setup Security Updates dialog box. If the administrator set exceptions to the firewall through Group Policy or by enabling Remote Desktop during installation, inbound connections assigned to these exceptions remain open.

Post-Setup Security Updates applies to Windows server administrators who are performing a full installation of Windows Server 2003 that includes a service pack (such as a slip-stream version of Windows Server 2003 with SP1). This feature does not apply if either of the following cases:

- The administrator installed the operating system using an unattended-setup script that enabled or disabled Windows Firewall.
- Windows Firewall was enabled or disabled by application of Group Policy before Post-Setup Security Updates was displayed.

Post-Setup Security Updates does not apply if the administrator is updating an existing Windows Server 2003 operating system by adding a service pack or if the administrator is upgrading an existing Windows 2000 Server operating system to Windows Server 2003 with SP1.

Post-Setup Security Updates does not cause any applications to work differently. Manage Your Server is not displayed until Post-Setup Security Updates closes. However, Manage Your Server is available from the Start menu. Under the circumstances we've described above, Windows Firewall can now be enabled automatically until Post-Setup Security Updates is finished.

Security Configuration Wizard

The Security Configuration Wizard is a new feature in Windows Server 2003 SP1. This feature helps reduce the attack-surface for your server, which is a fundamental security best practice. Reducing the attack surface of Windows servers can minimize the number of servers that need to be immediately patched when a vulnerability is exploited because a given vulnerability will not necessarily be present in all configurations. The wizard is highly recommended for configuring Windows Firewall and creating security lockdown templates for servers based on their roles.

The wizard guides you through a series of questions to determine the functional requirements of your server. It then disables nny functionality that is not required by the roles the server is performing.

With the Security Configuration Wizard, you can easily do the following:

- Disable unnecessary services
- Disable unnecessary Microsoft Internet Information Services (IIS) Web extensions
- Block unused ports, including support for multihomed scenarios
- Secure ports that are left open using IPSec
- Reduce protocol exposure for Lightweight Directory Access Protocol (LDAP), LAN Manager, and Server Message Block (SMB)
- Configure audit settings with a high signal-to-noise ratio
- Import Windows security templates for coverage of settings that are not configured by the wizard

In addition to role-based security policy authoring, the wizard also supports the following:

- **Rollback**   You can return your server to its previous state (before you applied the Security Configuration Wizard security policy). This is useful if applied policies affect service in unexpected ways.
- **Analysis**   You can check whether servers are in compliance with expected policies.
- **Remote access**   You can use remote access for configuration and analysis operations.
- **Command-line support**   A command-line tool is provided for remote configuration and analysis of groups of servers.
- **Active Directory integration**   You can deploy Security Configuration Wizard policies using Group Policy.
- **Editing**   You can modify security policies created using Security Configuration Wizard—for example, when machines are repurposed.
- **XSL views**   You can view the data stored in the Knowledge Base, policies, and analysis results XML files.

The Security Configuration Wizard is an authoring tool that allows you to create a custom security policy by answering a series of questions. For settings that are not configured by the wizard, the administrator can import existing security templates.

Windows Firewall

Windows Firewall (previously called Internet Connection Firewall, or ICF) is a software-based, stateful filtering firewall for Windows XP and Windows Server 2003. Windows Firewall provides protection for computers that are connected to a network by preventing unsolicited incoming traffic through TCP/IP version 4 (IPv4) and TCP/IP version 6 (IPv6). Configuration options include:

- Configuring and enabling port-based exceptions
- Configuring and enabling program-based exceptions
- Configuring basic ICMP options
- Logging dropped packets and successful connections

Changes to Windows Firewall

In earlier versions of Windows, Windows Firewall was configured on a per-interface basis giving each network connection had its own set of firewall settings. For example, a network might have one set of settings for wireless and another set of settings for Ethernet. This configuration makes it difficult to synchronize firewall settings between connections. Also, new connections do not have any of the configuration changes that are applied to the existing connections. Nonstandard network connections, such as those created by proprietary dialers (for instance, ISP-configured dial-up networking connections) cannot be protected.

Global policy makes it easier for users to manage their firewall policy across all network connections and enables configuration through Group Policy. It also allows you to enable applications to work on any interface with a single configuration option.

With global configuration, whenever a configuration change occurs, it applies to all network connections in the Network Connections folder, including any non-Microsoft dialers. When new connections are created, the configuration is applied to them as well. Configuration can still be performed on a per-interface basis. Nonstandard network connections have only global configuration. Configuration changes also apply to both IPv4 and IPv6.

Changes for Audit Logging

To shorten your reaction time to attacks on your system, incorporate auditing the activity of Windows Firewall is part of your defense strategy. Use audit logging to track changes that are made to Windows Firewall settings and to identify which applications and services have asked your computer to listen on a port. When audit logging is enabled, audit events are logged in the security event log. Audit logging can be enabled on client computers running Windows XP SP2 and servers running Windows Server 2003 SP1.

To enable audit logging on your computer, complete the following steps:

1. Log on using an account that is a local administrator.

2. Click **Start**, **Control Panel**, and then click **Administrative Tools**.

3. In **Administrative Tools**, double-click **Local Security Policy** to open the **Local Security Settings** console.

4. In the console tree of the **Local Security Settings** console, click **Local Policies**, and then click **Audit Policy**.

5. In the details pane of the **Local Security Settings** console, double-click **Audit policy change**. Select **Success And Failure**, and then click **OK**.

6. In the details pane of the **Local Security Settings** console, double-click **Audit process tracking**. Select **Success And Failure**, and then click **OK**.

 Tip   You can also use Group Policy to enable audit logging for multiple computers in an Active Directory® directory service domain. Modify the Audit policy change and Audit process tracking settings at Computer Configuration\Windows Settings\ Security Settings\Local Policies\Audit Policy for the Group Policy objects in the domain system containers.

Changes for Netsh Helper

The Advanced Networking Pack for Windows XP introduced the firewall context of Netsh Helper. It applied only to IPv6 Windows Firewall. With the integration of Windows Firewall and IPv6 Windows Firewall, the firewall context of Netsh Helper no longer has an IPv6 context. This change accommodates the changes to Windows Firewall and integration of IPv4 filtering configuration options in the existing firewall context of Netsh Helper.

 Note   Any existing scripts that use the firewall context that appears with the addition of the Advanced Networking Pack will no longer work.

Windows Firewall New Group Policy Support

The administrator's ability to manage Windows Firewall policy settings enable applications and scenarios to work in the corporate environment. In earlier versions of Windows, Internet Connection Firewall had a single GPO: Prohibit Use Of Internet Connection Firewall On Your DNS Domain Network. With Windows Server 2003 SP1, you can set every configuration option through Group Policy. The following are some of the new configuration options:

- Define program exceptions

- Allow local program exceptions
- Allow ICMP exceptions
- Prohibit notifications
- Allow file and printer sharing exception
- Allow logging

Each of these objects can be set for both the corporate and the standard profile.

> **Note**   For a complete list of Group Policy options, see "Deploying Windows Firewall Settings for Microsoft Windows XP with Service Pack 2" at the Microsoft Download Center at *http://go.microsoft.com/fwlink/?linkid=23277*. An updated document that covers developments in Windows Server 2003 SP1 will be available before the final release of the service pack.

The IT administrator can now choose the default Windows Firewall policy set—that is, to enable or disable applications and scenarios. This gives the administrator more control, but the policies do not change the underlying functionality of Windows Firewall. Table B-2 lists the changes to Windows Firewall.

Table B-2   Windows Firewall GPO Changes

Setting	Location	Previous Default Value	Default Value	Possible Values
Protect all network connections	(Group Policy object) Computer Configuration\Administrative Templates \Network\ Network Connections\ Windows Firewall	Not applicable	Enabled	Enabled Disabled
Do not allow exceptions	(Group Policy object) Computer Configuration\Administrative Templates\Network\ Network Connections\ Windows Firewall	Not applicable	Not configured	Enabled Disabled
Define program exceptions	(Group Policy object) Computer Configuration\Administrative Templates\Network\ Network Connections\ Windows Firewall	Not applicable	Not configured	Enabled Disabled Program path Scope

Table B-2   Windows Firewall GPO Changes

Setting	Location	Previous Default Value	Default Value	Possible Values
Allow local program exceptions	(Group Policy object) Computer Configuration\Administrative Templates\Network\ Network Connections\ Windows Firewall	Not applicable	Not configured	Enabled Disabled
Allow remote administration exception	(Group Policy object) Computer Configuration\Administrative Templates\Network\ Network Connections\ Windows Firewall	Not applicable	Not configured	Enabled Disabled
Allow file and printer sharing exception	(Group Policy object) Computer Configuration\Administrative Templates\Network\ Network Connections\ Windows Firewall	Not applicable	Not configured	Enabled Disabled
Allow ICMP exceptions	(Group Policy object) Computer Configuration\Administrative Templates\Network\ Network Connections\ Windows Firewall	Not applicable	Not configured	Echo Request: On, Off Source Quench: On, Off Redirect: On, Off Destination Unreachable: On, Off Router Request: On, Off Time Exceeded: On, Off Parameter Problem: On, Off Mask Request: On, Off Timestamp Request: On, Off

Table B-2   Windows Firewall GPO Changes

Setting	Location	Previous Default Value	Default Value	Possible Values
Allow remote desktop exception	(Group Policy object) Computer Configuration\Administrative Templates\Network\ Network Connections\ Windows Firewall	Not applicable	Not configured	Enabled Disabled
Allow UPnP framework exception	(Group Policy object) Computer Configuration\Administrative Templates\Network\ Network Connections\ Windows Firewall	Not applicable	Not configured	Enabled Disabled
Prohibit notifications	(Group Policy object) Computer Configuration\Administrative Templates\Network\ Network Connections\ Windows Firewall	Not applicable	Not configured	Enabled Disabled
Allow logging	(Group Policy object) Computer Configuration\Administrative Templates\Network\ Network Connections\ Windows Firewall	Not applicable	Not configured	Enabled Disabled
Prohibit unicast response to multicast or broadcast requests	(Group Policy object) Computer Configuration\Administrative Templates\Network\ Network Connections\ Windows Firewall	Not applicable	Not configured	Enabled Disabled

GPMC Scripting

In this appendix:

GPMC Scripting Interface Essentials. 687

Using the GPMC's Prebuilt Scripts 695

The Group Policy Management Console (GPMC) is an excellent tool for managing Group Policy in Active Directory environments. It also provides a set of scripting interfaces for automating many Group Policy management actions. In fact, most of the tasks you can perform using the GPMC can be automated through its scripting interfaces. The GPMC installation also provides more than 30 prebuilt scripts that you can use to manage Group Policy right away. In this appendix, we will look at how to use those scripting interfaces to develop your own scripts for automating Group Policy management. We'll also review the prebuilt scripts provided with GPMC and describe how to use them to perform common Group Policy management tasks.

GPMC Scripting Interface Essentials

When you install the GPMC on your Microsoft® Windows XP or Windows Server™ 2003 computer, a set of subfolders is created under the installation folder (usually in %ProgramFiles%\gpmc). One of those subfolders is the scripts folder, and within that folder are a number of prebuilt Windows Scripting Host (WSH) scripts that leverage the GPMC scripting interfaces. There is also a help file (Gpmc.chm) in this folder that describes, among other things, all of the scripting interfaces and their associated methods.

Understanding the GPMC Scripting Object Model

The GPMC scripting object model provides a set of interfaces for performing tasks related to everything from creating and backing up GPOs to generating Resultant Set of Policy (RSOP) logging reports and modifying GPO permissions. However, the scripting interfaces provided by GPMC do now allow for editing of policy settings within a GPO. They provide only for management and reporting of GPOs as whole objects. Figure C-1 shows a map of the GPMC object model.

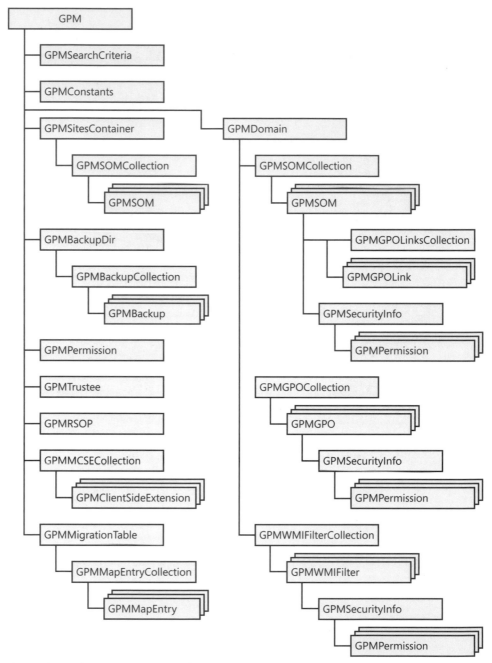

Figure C-1   The GPMC scripting object model

The GPMC object model is implemented within the file Gpmgmt.dll. As Figure C-1 shows, the root of the GPMC object model is an object called GPM, which is the starting for any scripts you write based on the GPMC. In fact, most anything you do with the GPMC scripting interfaces starts with creating an instance of the GPM object, then connecting to an Active Directory domain, then performing operations on one or more GPOs.

Creating the Initial *GPM* Object

Many of the methods on the *IGPMDomain* interface, when called, create instances of other interfaces that support most of the operations you will want to perform against your Group Policy infrastructure. If we were to write a VBScript-based WSH script, this initial instantiation of the GPM object would look like Listing C-1.

Listing C-1   Creating the Initial GPM Object

```
Set GPM = CreateObject("GPMgmt.GPM")
```

This command creates an instance of the *IGPM* interface, which has a set of methods that provide access to other interfaces that are useful for managing GPOs. For example, the next thing you usually need in your scripts to start managing GPO is to connect to an Active Directory domain so you can begin referencing GPOs within that domain. To do that, you need to create an instance of the *IGPMDomain* interface.

Referencing the Domain to Manage

The *GetDomain* method on the *IGPM* interface returns just such an instance. Once you've created an instance of *IGPM*, as just shown, you can call the *GetDomain* method on that instance to get a reference to *IGPMDomain*, as shown in Listing C-2.

Listing C-2   Creating an Instance of the *IGPMDomain* Interface

```
Set GPMDomain = GPM.GetDomain(DomainName, "", GPM_USE_PDC)
```

DomainName is the DNS domain name of the Active Directory domain you want to connect to, and the constant *GPM_USE_PDC* simply tells the command to connect to the domain's PDC emulator rather than another domain controller. You can optionally use a "" string parameter to specify a specific domain controller to connect to by DNS name. In most cases, the statement shown is sufficient.

Note   If you specify the domain name as a literal value, you must enclose it in quotation marks. See Listing C-3 for an example.

Creating and Linking GPOs

Once you have an instance of the *IGPMDomain* interface, you can call a number of methods to connect to a particular GPO, create new GPOs, search for a particular GPO, or restore a GPO from backup. For example, to create a new GPO with the name Desktop Configuration Policy, you can create a simple WSH script in VBScript, as shown in Listing C-3.

Listing C-3 Creating a New GPO Called Desktop Configuration Policy

```
Set GPM = CreateObject("GPMgmt.GPM")
Set GPMDomain = GPM.GetDomain("cpandl.com", "", GPM_USE_PDC)
Set GPMGPO = GPMDomain.CreateGPO()
GPMGPO.DisplayName = "Desktop Configuration Policy"
```

The first two lines create the familiar *IGPM* instance and use it to call the *GetDomain* method to connect to the Active Directory domain (cpandl.com). The third line calls the *CreateGPO* method on *GPMDomain* and creates an instance of the *IGPMGPO* interface, which holds the reference to the newly created GPO. When the GPO is created, it is created with a generic friendly name of "New Group Policy Object," so in the fourth line we set the *DisplayName* property on the *GPMGPO* instance to the desired name.

The new GPO is created unlinked to any container object. To link the GPO to a container object, you must specify a scope of management (SOM) using the *GetSOM* method on the *GPMDomain* object we created earlier. *GetSOM* returns a reference to the *IGPMSOM* interface, and that interface has a *CreateGPOLink* method that creates the actual Group Policy link on the SOM you specified. For example, if we modify the script shown earlier, we can create the Desktop Configuration Policy and link it to the Marketing OU within the Active Directory domain called cpandl.com, as shown in Listing C-4.

Listing C-4 Creating and Linking a New GPO

```
Set GPM = CreateObject("GPMgmt.GPM")
Set GPMDomain = GPM.GetDomain("cpandl.com", "", GPM_USE_PDC)
Set GPMGPO = GPMDomain.CreateGPO()
GPMGPO.DisplayName = "Desktop Configuration Policy"
Set GPMSOM = GPMDomain.GetSOM("OU=marketing,DC=cpandl,dc=com")
Set GPMLink = GPMSOM.CreateGPOLink(-1,GPMGPO)
```

Listing C-4 differs from Listing C-3 in the two additional lines at the end. The second-to-last line creates an instance of the *IGPMSOM* interface by calling the *GetSOM* method on the *GPMDomain* object. The parameter provided to the *GetSOM* method is the distinguished name (DN) of the container object you want to link to. This can be a site, domain, or OU. Site objects are stored within the configuration naming context rather than the domain naming context, so in the case of a site object the path to a site looks something like the following (where NewYork is the name of the site):

```
CN=NewYork,CN=Sites,CN=Configuration,DC=cpandl,DC=com
```

The last line of Listing C-4 creates the GPO link on the SOM using the *CreateGPOLink* method of the *GPMSOM* object. The first parameter indicates the order the GPO link should appear on the container object. As you know, a container object can have multiple GPOs linked to it, and the order in which the GPOs are linked affects the processing precedence and thus the effective policy for the computers and users within that container object. Passing *-1* to the *CreateGPOLink* method indicates that this GPO should be linked at the end of the list. Alternatively, you can link the GPO at a particular position by specifying that position in this parameter. The position numbering starts at 1, and if you specify a number that is greater than the number of GPO links that exist on that container object, an error will be generated. The second parameter is simply a reference to the GPO object that was created earlier in the script.

Unlinking a GPO is bit more complicated and involves a different set of interfaces. At a high level, you must first enumerate the links on a particular container (SOM) and then, after finding the correct link based on the GPO GUID, you delete the link using a method on the *IGPMGPOLink* interface. Listing C-5 shows the process for removing the link on the Marketing OU for the Desktop Configuration Policy we created earlier in Listing C-4.

Listing C-5 Deleting a GPO Link from an OU

```
Set GPM = CreateObject("GPMgmt.GPM")
Set GPMDomain = GPM.GetDomain("cpandl.com", "", GPM_USE_PDC)
Set GPMSOM = GPMDomain.GetSOM("OU=marketing,DC=cpandl,dc=com")
Set GPMLinkColl= GPMSOM.GetGPOLinks
For Each GPLink in GPMLinkColl
    If GPLink.GPOID="{5281266F-081E-4433-9218-22AEF9F313B0}" Then
        GPLink.Delete
    End If
Next
```

In Listing C-5, the first three lines are familiar from listing C-4. Line 3 provides an instance of the *IGPMSOM* interface that references the Marketing OU for which we want to delete the link. In line 4, we use the *GetGPOLinks* method on the *GPMSOM* object to return a collection of a links on that Marketing OU. Because a container object such as an OU can have multiple GPOs linked to it, the collection returns each of the links as an array of items that can be iterated through. In fact, in line 5 that is exactly what we do: we use the *VBScript For Each...Next* loop to iterate through each link. The current link is stored in the variable called *GPLink*. In line 6, we use an *If...Then* statement to find the link to the GPO we're interested in by using the *GPOID* property on that link object.

The *GPOID* must be the GUID of the GPO. A fast and easy way to find the GUID of a GPO is to use Gpotool, which is part of the Windows Server 2003 Resource Kit Tools. You use the following syntax with Gpotool to get the desired result:

```
gpotool /gpo:"GPOName" /domain:DomainName | find "Policy {"
```

GPOName is the friendly name of the GPO you want to work with, and *DomainName* is the name of the domain in which the GPO is stored. You pipe the output through the *find* command by using the search string *"Policy {"* to ensure that only the line of output containing the GUID of the policy is returned.

As an example, let's say you want the GUID of the Default Domain Policy GPO in the cpandl.com domain. You use the following syntax with Gpotool to get the desired result:

```
gpotool /gpo:"Default Domain Policy" /domain:cpandl.com | find "Policy {"
```

The output returned contains the GUID of the Default Domain Policy GPO, as shown here:

```
Policy {31B2F340-016D-11D2-945F-00C04FB984F9}
```

You can also find the GUID of a GPO in the GPMC. Select the GUID, and then click the Details tab. The Unique ID field on the Details tab provides the GUID of the GPO, as shown in Figure C-2.

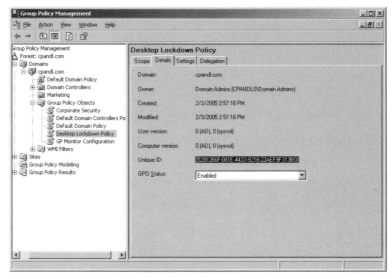

Figure C-2   Obtaining a GPO's GUID using the GPMC

After we locate the correct GPO link by its GUID, line 7 uses the *Delete* method to remove the link from the SOM. Note that the GPO itself is not deleted—just the link to the SOM. In addition to creating and deleting links, you can manage the properties on a link. For example, you can enable and disable links and set a link to Enforced. For example, instead of deleting the link to the Marketing OU as we did in Listing C-5, we can modify that script slightly to set the link to Enforced, as shown in Listing C-6.

Listing C-6   Setting a GPO Link to Enforced

```
Set GPM = CreateObject("GPMgmt.GPM")
Set GPMDomain = GPM.GetDomain("cpandl.com", "", GPM_USE_PDC)
Set GPMSOM = GPMDomain.GetSOM("OU=marketing,DC=cpandl,dc=com")
Set GPMLinkColl= GPMSOM.GetGPOLinks
For each GPLink in GPMLinkColl
   If GPLink.GPOID="{5281266F-081E-4433-9218-22AEF9F313B0}" Then
      GPLink.Enforced=True
   End If
Next
```

Listing C-6 differs from Listing C-7 in the last line. Instead of deleting the Group Policy link, we set the Enforced property on that link to True.

Automating Group Policy Security Management

The GPMC lets you manage security on GPOs by controlling which computers and users can process a particular GPO (referred to as *security filtering*) and which user groups can modify GPOs (referred to as *delegation*). You can also automate security management using the GPMC scripting interfaces.

The GPMC's prebuilt scripts include two scripts for setting permissions on a GPO: SetGPOPermissions.wsf and SetGPOPermissionsBySOM.wsf. No prebuilt scripts are provided for listing permissions on a GPO, but you can easily accomplished this task by using the GPMC scripting interfaces. Listing C-7 shows the script code that returns each permission entry on our Desktop Configuration Policy GPO object.

Listing C-7   Listing Permissions on a GPO Object

```
Set GPM = CreateObject("GPMgmt.GPM")
Set GPMDomain = GPM.GetDomain("cpandl.com", "", GPM_USE_PDC)
Set GPMGPO = GPMDomain.GetGPO("{5281266F-081E-4433-9218-22AEF9F313B0}")
Set Constants = GPM.GetConstants
Set GPMSecurity = GPMGPO.GetSecurityInfo

Wscript.Echo "Permissions on GPO: "+GPMGPO.DisplayName+VbCRLF
For Each GPMPermission in GPMSecurity
    If GPMPermission.Denied then
    AllowDeny = "Deny"
    Else
    AllowDeny = "Allow"
    End If
    If GPMPermission.Inherited then
    Inherit = "Inherited"
    Else
    Inherit = "Not Inherited"
    End If
    Select Case GPMPermission.Permission
      Case Constants.permGPOApply
        Perm="Read and Apply Group Policy"
      Case Constants.permGPOEdit
        Perm="Edit Group Policy"
      Case Constants.permGPOEditSecurityAndDelete
        Perm="Edit Group Policy, Modify Security and Delete Group Policy"
      Case Constants.permGPORead
        Perm="Read Group Policy"
    End Select
    Set GPMTrustee = GPMPermission.Trustee
    Trustee = GPMTrustee.TrusteeDomain+"\"+GPMTrustee.TrusteeName
    Wscript.Echo AllowDeny+", "+Inherit+", "+Trustee+": "+Perm
Next
```

Listing C-7 might seem long, but most of the code is used to set up the output of the permissions themselves. Let's look at what this script does. The first three lines should be familiar by now. Line 3 gets a reference to our Desktop Configuration Policy by using its GUID. (You could pass this into the script using a command-line parameter, of course, if you wanted to make the script more portable to other GPOs.) Line 4 is new. It calls the *GetConstants* method on the *GPM* object. *GetConstants* returns a reference to the *IGPMConstants* interface. This interface contains a set of properties that are used to manage various aspects of Group Policy from the GPMC scripting interfaces. For our purposes, we created this reference to leverage the permission constants that define the permission types that can be used on a GPO.

Line 5 calls the *GetSecurityInfo* method on the *GPMGPO* object. The *GetSecurityInfo* method returns the permissions on a GPO in the form of a reference to the *IGPM-SecurityInfo* interface. The *IGPMSecurityInfo* interface contains methods that let you enumerate each permission on a GPO. In line 6, we use the VBScript *Wscript.Echo* command to create a header for our output that calls the *DisplayName* property on the *GPMGPO* object to display the GPO's friendly name instead of the GUID in the output.

After setting up the header, we enter a *For...Each* loop to enumerate each permission on the GPO. The first line of the *For...Each* loop calls the *Denied* property on the *GPMPermission* object and tests for it to be true. A permission can be *Allow* or *Deny*, so we want to be able to know in the output if the permission is a *Deny*. If the *Denied* property is true, we set a variable called *AllowDeny* to "*Deny*"; otherwise, we set it to "*Allow*".

In the next statement, we call the *Inherited* property on *GPMPermission* to determine whether the permission is inherited. In most cases, a normal permission on a GPO should not be inherited, but returning this information can be useful in determining whether a particular GPO has permission inconsistencies. After we populate the *Inherit* variable with information about whether the permission was inherited, we use a *Select Case* statement to iterate through the *Permission* property on the *GPMPermission* object and compare it to the constants related to permissions (for example, *permGPOApply* or *permGPOEdit*.). When there is a match on the *Permission* property with the appropriate *Constants* property, we translate those constants into something more descriptive for the output and store that in the *Perm* variable.

The next command, *Set GPMTrustee = GPMPermission.Trustee*, is used to obtain trustee information about the permission. The trustee is basically the "who" of the permission. That is, it specifies which user or computer group or other security principal has the permission. This is, of course, important information to have in our script. The *GPMTrustee* variable that is returned on this command is actually an instance of the *IGPMTrustee* interface, which has methods that let us extract the trustee information from the *Trustee* property on the *GPMPermission* object. In fact, in the next line, we create the *Trustee* variable and form the string that will display the trustee by calling the *TrusteeDomain* and *TrusteeName* properties on the *GPMTrustee* object. *TrusteeDomain* returns the NetBIOS form of the domain name, so in that command we create the trustee variable by concatenating the NetBIOS domain name with the username and separating them with a backslash (\) to display the trustee using the familiar domain\group representation.

The next-to-last line in the script uses the *Wscript.Echo* command to output each permission to the screen or to the command line, using the variables that we defined within the *For...Each* loop. The *Next* command loops back to get the next permission and repeat the process. This script is best run using the command line–based Cscript.exe WSH processor because the script outputs each permission to the command shell if run that way. If it is run using Wscript.exe, each permission appears as a pop-up dialog box as the script is written, which is probably not as useful.

When the script is run, it returns a list of the permissions on a given GPO, as shown in Figure C-3.

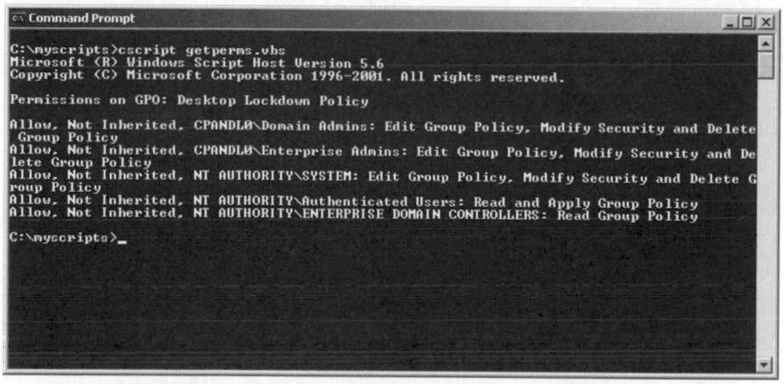

Figure C-3   Viewing the output from the GPO permissions script

Using the GPMC's Prebuilt Scripts

The GPMC provides a set of prebuilt WSH scripts that leverage the GPMC scripting interfaces that we just discussed to automate common Group Policy management tasks. On a standard GPMC installation, these scripts can be found in the %ProgramFiles%\GPMC\scripts folder. Most of the scripts have a .wsf file extension. The Windows Script File (.wsf) format is an XML-based scripting environment that lets you combine Jscript-based and VBScript-based scripts into a single .wsf file. It also allows for multiple jobs to be referenced so you can call a .wsf file and reference only a particular job or only a particular routine. Because these scripts are XML-based, they are normal text files that can be viewed in Notepad. However, they are probably best viewed using your favorite script editor.

In the next section, we'll review the key management tasks that the prebuilt GPMC scripts help you perform and provide details on how to use these scripts. Most GPMC scripts provide command line–oriented output, so they are best run using the command-line WSH script processor (Cscript.exe) rather than the Windows WSH script processor (Wscript.exe).

> **Note**   While the prebuilt GPMC scripts might work in most environments, Microsoft does not guarantee they will work in all cases. You might find that the scripts do not scale well in a large enterprise.

Creating GPOs

The CreateGPO.wsf script is used to create a single GPO. The GPO is created unlinked. The script has the following usage:

```
CreateGPO.wsf GPOName [/Domain:value]
```

The *GPOName* parameter is the friendly name of the GPO you want to create, and the optional *Domain* parameter lets you create the GPO in a domain other than the one where the GPMC is installed. Here's how you can create a GPO called Desktop Configuration Policy:

```
Cscript CreateGPO.wsf "Desktop Configuration Policy"
```

Deleting GPOs

The DeleteGPO.wsf script lets you delete a particular GPO. You can optionally keep all the links to the GPO. The syntax for this script is as follows:

```
DeleteGPO.wsf GPOName [/KeepLinks] [/Domain:value]
```

When you use this script, you supply the friendly name for the GPO. If you choose the *KeepLinks* parameter, the links to the GPO on container objects are kept when the GPO no longer exists. This might be a good strategy if you need to restore the GPO from a backup. In that case, with the links in place, you won't lose the references to the SOMs where that GPO was linked. You can also specify the domain name to perform the operation against. An example is shown here:

```
Cscript DeleteGPO.wsf "Desktop Configuration Policy" /KeepLinks
```

Finding Disabled GPOs

The FindDisabledGPOs.wsf script can locate any GPOs within a domain that have been disabled. The syntax is simple:

```
FindDisabledGPOs.wsf [/Domain:value]
```

If you run the script without the option *Domain* name, it returns all disabled GPOs within the domain where the GPMC is installed. The script returns GPOs that are completely disabled, ones that have only the computer side disabled, and ones that have only the user side disabled.

Finding GPOs by Security Group

The FindGPOsBySecurityGroup.wsf script lets you search for GPOs in which a particular group has a particular level of delegation. The syntax for the script is as follows:

```
FindGPOsBySecurityGroup.wsf GroupName /Permission:value [/Effective] [/None]
[/Domain:value]
```

For example, if you want to find all the GPOs in which the GPO Admins group has edit permissions on a GPO, you can run the script with the following parameters:

```
Cscript FindGPOsBySecurityGroup.wsf "GPO Admins" /Permission:Edit
```

If you use the *Effective* parameter, the script searches out effective memberships for the specified group. For example, if GPO Admins doesn't have direct Edit permissions on a GPO but has them by virtue of its membership in another group, the *Effective* parameter will track that down. If you specify *None*, the script searches for GPOs in which the GPO Admins group does not have Edit permissions.

Finding GPOs Without Active Links

The FindUnlinkedGPOs.wsf script lets you locate GPOs within a domain that have not been linked to any SOM. The script has the following syntax:

```
FindUnlinkedGPOs.wsf [/Domain:value]
```

The script returns a list of all GPOs within the specified domain that aren't linked to any containers in Active Directory.

Setting GPO Creation Permissions

The SetGPOCreationPermissions.wsf script lets you add or remove a groups ability to create GPOs in a domain. The syntax of the script is as follows:

```
SetGPOCreationPermissions.wsf Group [/Remove] [/Domain:value]
```

For example, if you want to grant the permission to create GPOs to the GPO Admins group, you call this script:

```
Cscript SetGPOCreationPermissions.wsf "GPO Admins"
```

To remove the permission from that group, simply add the */Remove* parameter to the command:

```
Cscript SetGPOCreationPermissions.wsf "GPO Admins" /Remove
```

Setting Other GPO Permissions

The SetGPOPermissions.wsf script lets you set or replace permissions on a GPO. These permissions include both security filtering (which computer or user can process a GPO) and delegation (who can read, edit, and delete a GPO). The syntax for the script is as follows:

```
SetGPOPermissions.wsf GPOName GroupName /Permission:value /Replace
[/Domain:value]
```

For example, if you want to change the existing permissions that the GPO Admins group has on the Desktop Configuration Policy from Edit to FullEdit, you call this script:

```
Cscript SetGPOPermissions.wsf "Desktop Configuration Policy" "GPO Admins"
/Permission:FullEdit /Replace
```

Backing Up All GPOs

You use the Backupallgpos.wsf script to back up all GPOs in a domain to a particular backup location—typically a folder on a file system somewhere. The script takes three input parameters—one mandatory and two optional—as shown here:

```
Backupallgpos.wsf BackupLocation [/Comment:value] [/Domain:value]
```

The backup location is the directory to which you want to write the backup data—it can be local or remote. The comment is stored with the backup so that when you choose the Manage Backups option in the GPMC interface, you see the comment associated with it, as shown in Figure C-4.

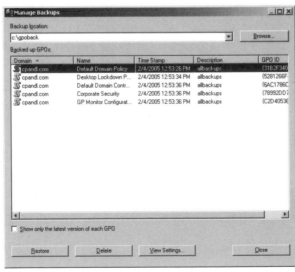

Figure C-4   Viewing GPOs backed up using BackupAllGPOs.wsf

As you can see from the figure, each GPO has the same comment when backed up using the */comment* option on this script. You can also optionally specify the domain in DNS format using the */domain* option if you need to back up a domain other than the one in which the GPMC is running. An example of usage for this script follows:

```
Cscript BackupAllGPOs.wsf c:\gpobackups /comment:"Backup of all GPOs"
/domain:cpandl.com
```

Backing Up Individual GPOs

The BackupGPO.wsf script lets you back up a single GPO at a time. Its usage is similar to the previous script, except that you need to specify the name of the GPO to back up:

```
BackupGPO.wsf GPOName BackupLocation [/Comment:value] [/Domain:value]
```

In this script, you can specify either the GPO's friendly name or its GUID. Either will be resolved to the correct GPO. An example follows:

```
Cscript BackupGPO.wsf "Desktop Configuration Policy" c:\gpobackups
/comment: "Backup of desktop lockdown before the change" /domain: cpandl.com
```

Copying GPOs

The CopyGPO.wsf script is used to copy one GPO to another, new GPO. When you copy a GPO, all of its settings are copied to the new target GPO. The copy feature in the GPMC is supported either within a domain or across domains within a single forest. It is not supported for copying GPOs across forests. The syntax for this script is as follows:

```
CopyGPO.wsf SourceGPO TargetGPO [/SourceDomain:value] [/TargetDomain:value]
[/SourceDC:value] [/TargetDC:value] [/MigrationTable:value] [/CopyACL]
```

As you can see, only the *SourceGPO* and *TargetGPO* parameters are required—the rest are optional. However, if you don't specify any options, the source GPO is copied to the same domain and all settings are assumed to be the same. Keep the following in mind:

- The *SourceDomain* and *TargetDomain* options let you specify a cross-domain copy. These should take the form of a DNS domain name (such as cpandl.com). The *SourceDC* and *TargetDC* options let you specify a particular domain controller to copy the GPO to and from when performing a cross-domain copy. This is typically not required unless you want the copy to happen from a particular domain controller.

- The *MigrationTable* option lets you specify the name of a GPMC migration table, which is used to translate security principal and path references embedded in GPOs during copy or import operations. The *MigrationTable* option is set as a file path to the location where the migration table resides.

■ The *CopyACL* option lets you specify to also copy the Access Control List on the source GPO to the target exactly as it appears. This means the DomianA ACLs will carry over to DomainB when the GPO is coped from DomainA to DomainB with this flag. If you don't choose the *CopyACL* option, the destination GPO that is created inherits the default permissions for any newly created GPO. The *CopyACL* option is useful if you have specific security filtering or delegation on the source GPO that you want to implement exactly on the new GPO.

An example of this usage is shown here:

```
Cscript CopyGPO.wsf "Desktop Configuration Policy" "Desktop Configuration Policy"
/sourcedomain:cpandl.com /targetdomain:east.cpandl.com
/MigrationTable:c:\migrationtables\east.migtable /copyACL
```

Importing GPOs

You can use the ImportGPO.wsf script to import a backed up GPO into a a specified target GPO. The script has the following syntax:

```
ImportGPO.wsf BackupLocation BackupID [TargetGPO] [/MigrationTable:value]
[/CreateIfNeeded] [/Domain:value]
```

BackupLocation is the folder where your GPO backups are stored, and *BackupID* is the friendly name or the GUID of the GPO to import. The *TargetGPO* parameter is the friendly name of the GPO into which you want to import the settings from the backed up GPO. The *MigrationTable* parameter lets you specify the location of a migration table to apply to the import process. The *CreateIfNeeded* parameter tells the script to create a new GPO to import the backed up one into if no *TargetGPO* is found. The *Domain* parameter lets you specify a different domain as the destination. An example of this script is as follows:

```
Cscript ImportGPO.wsf c:\gpoback "Desktop Configuration Policy" "New Lockdown
Policy" /MigrationTable: c:\migtables\lockdown.migtable
```

Generating RSoP Reports

The GetReportsForGPO.wsf script creates XML and HTML settings reports for a given GPO and saves them to a defined file system location. The syntax for this script is as follows:

```
GetReportsForGPO.wsf GPOName ReportLocation [/Domain:value]
```

GPOName is the friendly name for the GPO you want to report on, and *ReportLocation* is the folder where you want the reports to be saved. Note that both XML and HTML files will be created and will have the same name as the friendly name of the GPO (such as Desktop Configuration Policy.HTML).

Mirroring Your Production Environment

The CreateXMLFromEnvironment.wsf and CreateEnvironmentFromXML.wsf scripts are useful for setting up test environments that mirror your production environment. CreateXMLFromEnvironment.wsf is used to create a copy of your production domain environment, including its OU structure, users, permissions, and GPOs. That information is stored to an XML file. You can then use CreateEnvironmentFromXML.wsf within a new Active Directory domain to import the production structure and information so that the environments are identical in most respects.

The syntax for both commands follows:

```
CreateXMLFromEnvironment.wsf OutputFile [/Domain:value] [/DC:value]
[/TemplatePath:value] [/StartingOU:value] [/ExcludePermissions]
[/IncludeAllGroups] [/IncludeUsers]

CreateEnvironmentFromXML.wsf /XML:value [/Undo] [/Domain:value] [/DC:value]
[/ExcludeSettings] [/ExcludePermissions] [/CreateUsersEnabled]
[/PasswordForUsers:value] [/MigrationTable:value] [/ImportDefaultGPOs] [/Q]
```

The only mandatory parameters for each script are the location of the XML output file for CreateXMLFromEnvironment.wsf and the location of that XML file as input for CreateEnvironmentFromXML.wsf. In the CreateXMLFromEnvironment.wsf script, you can use the *Domain* parameter to specify which domain to capture, the *DC* parameter to specify which domain controller to pull the information from, and the *TemplatePath* parameter to specify the file system location where you want to store the GPO backups. If you don't want to capture the whole domain, you can use the *StartingOU* parameter to specify the DN of the OU where you want to start the capture.

If you choose the *ExcludePermissions* option, no permissions on either GPOs or container objects (SOMs) are captured for restoration. If you use the *IncludeAllGroups* option, all groups found in the Users container within the domain or at the root of the domain are included, as well as any other groups found in the domain. Otherwise, these groups are excluded. Finally, if you specify the *IncludeUsers* option, user accounts as well as groups are captured.

On the receiving side, the options that you can specify on the CreateEnvironment-FromXML.wsf script include the *Undo* parameter, which actually removes the objects found in the XML file rather than adding them to the new domain. The *Domain* and *DC* parameters let you specify the name of the destination domain and the domain controller, respectively, where want to import the captured information. *ExcludeSettings* and *ExcludePermissions* let you choose to not include GPO settings from the captured GPOs and to exclude GPO and SOM permissions, respectively. The *CreateUsersEnabled* option lets you create any captured user object as an enabled user instead of a disabled user, which is the default.

Using the *PasswordForUsers* parameter, you can specify a password that all newly created user objects will receive. The MigrationTable parameter lets you choose a migration table to apply to all GPOs as they are imported into the destination domain. The *ImportDefaultGPOs* gives you the option to import the settings captured in the Default Domain Policy and Default Domain Controllers Policy GPOs from the source domain into the target. Finally, the Q parameter lets you run the script quietly (without feedback). Here is sample usage for each script:

```
Cscript CreateXMLFromEnvironment.wsf c:\output\prodenvironment.xml
/Domain:cpandl.com /TemplatePath:"c:\gpoback" /
StartingOU:OU=Marketing,DC=cpandl,DC=com /IncludeUsers

Cscript CreateEnvironmentFromXML.wsf /XML: "c:\output\prodenvironment.xml"
/Domain:testcpandl.com /CreateUsersEnabled /PasswordForUsers:"P@ssw0rd"
/MigrationTable:c:\migtables\test.migtable
```

GPMC Prebuilt Script Review

The GPMC includes many prebuilt .wsf scripts. We've looked at the most frequently used ones. Table C-1 describes the remaining scripts.

 Note In Table C-1, a dash (-) has been added to the script name where needed to allow the line to break. The dash is not part of the script name.

Table C-1 Additional GPMC Prebuilt Scripts

Script	Purpose	Sample Usage
CreateMigration-Table.wsf	Automates the creation of a migration table for copies and imports, and lets you prepopulate some entries in the table using an existing GPO or a GPO backup.	Cscript CreateMigration-Table.wsf C:\migtables\test.migtable /GPO:"Desktop Configuration Policy"
DumpGPOInfo.wsf	Lists summary info for a specified GPO, including items such as GUID, version number, permissions, and when it was created.	Cscript DumpGPOInfo.wsf "Desktop Configuration Policy"
DumpSOMInfo.wsf	Provides a listing of information specific to a SOM, including any GPOs linked to that SOM, who has permissions to create new links, and who can generate RSoP logging and planning data.	Cscript DumpSOMInfo.wsf "Marketing" (Note that you can specify the display name of an OU, as in this example, or a DN.)

Table C-1   Additional GPMC Prebuilt Scripts

Script	Purpose	Sample Usage
FindDuplicateNamed-GPOs.wsf	Finds any GPOs in a domain with a duplicate friendly name.	Cscript FindDuplicate-NamedGPOs.wsf /domain:cpandl.com
FindGPOsByPolicy-Extension.wsf	Searches for GPOs that have implemented a particular policy area. For example, you can search for all GPOs in a domain that have implemented Security policy.	Cscript FindGPOsBy-PolicyExtension.wsf /"Folder Redirection" /domain:cpandl.com
FindGPOsWithNo-SecurityFiltering.wsf	Locates any GPOs that don't have Apply Group Policy permissions associated with them. Such GPOs are never applied to a user or computer.	Cscript FindGPOsWithNo-SecurityFiltering.wsf /domain:cpandl.com
FindOrphaned-GPOsInSYSVOL.wsf	Locates GPOs that have their Group Policy template (GPT) portion but don't have a corresponding Group Policy container (GPC) in Active Directory.	Cscript FindOrphaned-GPOsInSYSVOL.wsf /domain:cpandl.com
FindSOMsWith-ExternalGPOLinks.wsf	Searches all SOMs within a domain to determine if any GPOs linked to them reside in other domains.	Cscript FindSOMsWith-ExternalGPOLinks.wsf /domain:cpandl.com
GetReports-ForAllGPOs.wsf	Generates XML and HTML settings reports for every GPO in a domain and saves them to the specified folder.	Cscript GetReportsForAll-GPOs.wsf c:\reports /domain:cpandl.com
GrantPermission-OnAllGPOs.wsf	Adds or replaces a particular permission on all GPOs within a domain. For example, if you want to grant a special GPO Admins group the permission to edit all GPOs, you can use this script for that purpose.	Cscript GrantPermissionOn-AllGPOs.wsf "GPO Admins" /Permission:Edit /domain:cpandl.com

Table C-1   Additional GPMC Prebuilt Scripts

Script	Purpose	Sample Usage
ImportAllGPOs.wsf	Takes a folder of backed-up GPOs and creates new GPOs in the target domain, optionally using a migration table.	Cscript ImportAllGPOs.wsf c:\gpoback /Migration-Table: "c:\migtables\allimport.migtable" /domain:cpandl.com
ListAllGPOs.wsf	Lists details of all GPOs within a domain. You can use the /v switch to get a verbose listing.	Cscript ListAllGPOs.wsf /v
ListSOMPolicyTree.wsf	Lists all SOMs within a domain and shows what GPOs are linked to them.	Cscript ListSOMPolicy-Tree.wsf /domain: cpandl.com
QueryBackup-Location.wsf	Provides a listing of all backed-up GPOs within a given backup location.	Cscript QueryBackup Location.wsf c:\gpoback /verbose
RestoreAllGPOs.wsf	Restores the most recent backup of every GPO found within the specified backup folder.	Cscript RestoreAllGPOs.wsf c:\gpoback /domain: cpandl.com
RestoreGPO.wsf	Restores a specified GPO to its original state from backup.	Cscript RestoreGPO.wsf c:\gpoback "Desktop Configuration Policy" /domain:cpandl.com
SetGPOPermissions-BySOM.wsf	For a given SOM, modifies permissions on all GPOs linked to that SOM with a given group and permission level.	Cscript SetGPOPermissions-BySOM.wsf "Marketing" "GPO Admins" Permission:FullEdit /Recursive (Note that the *Recursive* parameter applies the permission change to GPOs linked to any child OUs below the specified OU—in this example, the Marketing OU.)
SetSOM-Permissions.wsf	Modifies GPO-related permissions on a SOM, including who can link GPOs to the SOM, who can perform RSoP logging on the SOM, and who can perform RSoP planning.	Cscript SetSOMPermis-sions.wsf "Marketing" "GPO Admins" /Permission:LinkGPOs /Inherit

Appendix D
Office 2003 Administrative Template Highlights

In this appendix:

Microsoft Access 2003 706
Microsoft Excel 2003 706
Microsoft FrontPage 2003 708
Microsoft Clip Organizer 2003 708
Microsoft InfoPath 2003 709
Microsoft Office 2003 709
Microsoft OneNote 2003 713
Microsoft Outlook 2003 715
Microsoft PowerPoint 2003 718
Microsoft Project 2003 719
Microsoft Publisher 2003 720
Microsoft Visio 2003 721
Microsoft Word 2003 722

The Office 2003 Administrative Templates contain over 2500 policy settings. In this appendix, we highlight some of the more commonly used settings in each template file. The options are listed with the relative path under that particular application's policy settings. For example, if the value in parentheses shows (Tools | Options...\View) and it falls under the Access 2003 policy settings, the full path within the Group Policy namespace is User Configuration\Administrative Templates\Microsoft Office Access 2003\Tools | Options...\View.

Note The Office 2003 Administrative Templates download for Office 2003 SP1 includes an Excel spreadsheet called "Office 2003 Group Policies.xls." This spreadsheet describes all of the settings available in detail. To obtain the Office 2003 Resource kit, visit *http://www.microsoft.com/downloads/details.aspx?FamilyID=4bb7cb10-a6e5-4334-8925-3bcf308cfbaf&DisplayLang=en*. The additional updates for Office 2003 SP1 are available at *http://www.microsoft.com/downloads/details.aspx?FamilyID=ba8bc720-edc2-479b-b115-5abb70b3f490&DisplayLang=en*. Additional resource tools and files for Visio 2003 and for Project 2003 can be obtained from *http://www.microsoft.com/office/ork/2003/tools/BoxA19.htm*.

Microsoft Access 2003

- Location in the Group Policy namespace: Access11.adm

- Relative path: User Configuration\Administrative Templates\Microsoft Office Access 2003

- Configuration options for the Tools | Options... menu settings including:

  - Whether the startup task pane appears at Access startup (Tools | Options...\View\Show)

  - General options, such as how many recently used files to show and what the default database path is on File, Open and File, Save (Tools | Options...\General)

- Configuration options for the Tools, Macro menu settings including:

  - Default macro security level (Tools | Macro\Security...)

  - Whether Access should trust all installed add-ins and templates (Tools | Macro\Security...)

- Configuration options for creating custom links to files within the startup task pane (New File Links)

- Configuration options for disabling items within the user interface including:

  - Command bar buttons and menu items. For example, you can disable certain menu items under the Tools or Help menu in Access (Disable items in user interface\Predefined).

  - Shortcut keys (Disable items in user interface\Predefined).

  - Custom command bar buttons, menu items, and shortcut keys. You can disable any of these from within the Access administrative template policies (Disable items in user interface\Custom).

- Configuration options for controlling the prompt to convert older databases (Miscellaneous)

Microsoft Excel 2003

- Location in the Group Policy namespace: excel11.adm

- Relative path: User Configuration\Administrative Templates\Microsoft Office Excel 2003

- Configuration options for Tools | Options... menu settings including:

  - View options, such as whether to show the startup task pane, whether to show multiple workbooks on the Windows taskbar, and whether to show formula or status bars in Normal or Full view (Tools | Options...\View)

❑ Edit options (Figure D-1), such as allowing cell drag-and-drop, alerting before overwriting cells, asking whether to update automatic links, and enabling AutoComplete for cell values (Tools | Options...\Edit)

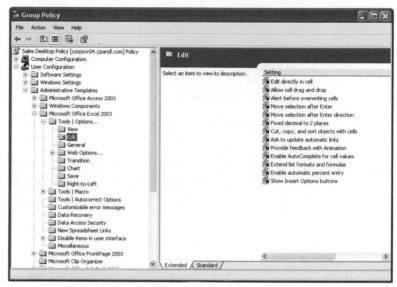

Figure D-1   Viewing Excel edit policy options within the Excel administrative template

❑ General options, such as the default file location, number of entries in the recently used file list, and standard font to use (Tools | Options...\General)

❑ Transition options, such as the default Excel file type for saving workbooks (Tools, |Options...\Transition)

❑ Save options, such as whether to enable AutoRecover, AutoRecover interval, and AutoRecover save location (Tools | Options...\Save)

■ Configuration options for Tools | Macro menu settings including the macro security setting level and whether to trust access to Microsoft Visual Basic projects (Tools | Macro\Security)

■ Configuration options for Tools | AutoCorrect settings, including whether to resolve Internet and network paths to hyperlinks as they are typed (Tools | AutoCorrect Options)

■ Configuration options for data recovery, such as what to do with corrupt formulas and whether to show data extraction options when recovering a corrupt workbook (Data Recovery)

■ Configuration options for data access security, such as whether to perform automatic query refreshes, whether to warn when connecting to an OLAP PivotTable, and whether to warn when connecting to an external data source (Data Access Security)

- Configuration options for creating custom links to spreadsheet files within the startup task pane (New Spreadsheet Links)
- Configuration of miscellaneous options, such as the default chart gallery path, whether to display four-digit year, and whether to locally cache network-based spreadsheet files when network problems occur (Miscellaneous)

Microsoft FrontPage 2003

- Location in the Group Policy namespace: fp11.adm
- Relative path: User Configuration\Administrative Templates\Microsoft Office FrontPage 2003
- Configuration option for the Tools | Options... menu setting that controls whether the startup task pane appears at FrontPage startup (Tools | Options...\General)
- Configuration options for creating custom links to FrontPage files and Web links within the startup task pane (New Page or Web Links)
- Configuration options for Optimize HTML On Publish check box (Miscellaneous)

Microsoft Clip Organizer 2003

- Location in the Group Policy namespace: gal11.adm
- Relative path: User Configuration\Administrative Templates\Microsoft Clip Organizer
- Configuration options for the Microsoft Office Clip Art Organizer feature
  - Disabling online access to clips from the Clip Organizer
  - Setting the Clips Organizer online URL to an alternative location
  - Disabling the File, Add Clips To Organizer, From Scanner Or Camera option
  - Hiding the various types of clip collections
  - Preventing automatic import of clips or prevent users from importing clips
  - Previewing of sound and motion in clips on Terminal Server
  - Searching clips based on a specific language

Microsoft InfoPath 2003

- Location in the Group Policy namespace: inf11.adm

- Relative path: User Configuration\Administrative Templates\Microsoft Office InfoPath 2003

- Configuration options for Tools | Options... menu settings including:

  - General options, such as controlling the size of the recently used file list (Tools | Options...\General)

  - Spelling and grammar options, such as whether to check spelling as you type, whether to hide spelling errors, whether to always suggest corrections, and whether to ignore words in uppercase letters (Tools Options...\Spelling & Grammar)

- Configuration options for Security settings, such as the ability to disable opening of solutions from the Internet Security Zone and disabling full access to a machine for installed solutions (Security)

- Configuration of miscellaneous settings, such as disabling the InfoPath designer mode, specifying a path to the InfoPath updater when a solution that is open in version 1 of the product is not compatible with that version, and controlling whether users can turn on or off printing of background colors (Miscellaneous)

Microsoft Office 2003

- Location in the Group Policy namespace: office11.adm

- Relative path: Computer Configuration\Administrative Templates\ Microsoft Office 2003 and User Configuration\Administrative Templates\Microsoft Office 2003

- Configuration options for configuring general application behavior that applies to all Office applications, on both a per-computer and a per-user basis including per-computer and per-computer security options

- Per-computer security options to allow Office Custom Maintenance Wizard files to be applied from any location for users who are not administrators. The Custom Maintenance Wizard is an Office Resource Kit utility that allows an administrator to change certain options within an Office installation after the application has been installed. (Custom Maintenance Wizard)

- Per-computer security options (Figure D-2) that include:

  - Controlling macro security levels across all of the Office 2003 applications. (Security Settings)

❑ Disabling Visual Basic for Applications (VBA) across all Office applications (Security Settings)

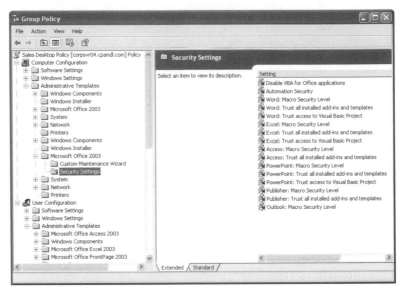

Figure D-2   Viewing Office general security policy options within the Office administrative template

> **Note**   These per-computer Office security policies override any conflicting per-user security policies that you have defined for the individual applications.

■ Per-user configuration options for Tools | Customize | Options menu settings in all Office applications, including whether to show full menus, whether to show screen tips on the toolbars, and whether to use menu animations. (Tools | Customize | Options)

■ Per-user configuration options for Tools | AutoCorrect Options... (Excel, Power-Point, and Access) menu settings in Excel, PowerPoint, and Access, including whether to show AutoCorrect options buttons, whether to correct two initial capital letters, and whether to replace text as you type. (Tools | AutoCorrect Options... (Excel, PowerPoint, and Access))

■ Per-user configuration options for controlling smart tag behavior. (Tools | AutoCorrect Options... (Excel, PowerPoint, and Access)\Smart Tags)

■ Per-user configuration options for Tools | Options | General | Web Options... menu settings that control how Office applications view and save Web pages.

❑ When saving a Web page, whether associated files are saved into a separate folder (Tools | Options | General | Web Options...\Files)

- ❑ Whether the Office application checks to see if it is the default editor for Web pages that are created using any Office application (Tools | Options | General | Web Options...\Files)

- ❑ Whether Office files that are opened from a Web server in Internet Explorer are automatically opened as read-write or read-only (Tool | Options | General | Web Options...\Files)

■ Configuration options for Tools | Options | General | Service Options... menu settings

- ❑ Access to online content on the Office Web site, such as templates and clips (Tools | Options | General | Service Options...\Online Content)

- ❑ Controlling how the document participates within shared workspaces in a Microsoft SharePoint Server environment (Tools | Options General | Service Options...\Shared Workspace)

- ❑ Setting the shared workspace URLs for the user to use when sharing a document in SharePoint (Tools | Options | General | Service Options...\Shared Workspace, Define Shared Workspace URLs)

■ Configuration options for Help menu settings including:

- ❑ Setting the Microsoft Office Online URL (Help)

- ❑ Enabling or disabling participation in the Microsoft Customer Experience Improvement Program (Help\Help | Customer Feedback Options...)

- ❑ Controlling Help | Detect & Repair... menu options, such as whether shortcuts are restored during a repair and whether user-customized settings are discarded during a repair (Help\Help | Detect & Repair...)

■ Configuration options for general security settings.

- ❑ Whether VBA is enabled in Office applications (Security Settings)

- ❑ Setting the level of automation security, which controls in what context COM objects can be called (Security Settings)

- ❑ Preventing Word and Excel from loading managed code (for example, .NET code) extensions (Security Settings)

- ❑ Preventing users from changing Office encryption settings (Security Settings)

■ Configuration options for setting shared paths to documents.

- ❑ Setting the path to user templates, workgroup templates, shared themes, and user queries (Shared Paths)

- Configuration options for the Office 2003 Save My Settings Wizard, an Office 2003 Tools utility that allows a user to save configuration settings associated with Office applications to an .ops file. This policy lets you set the default location for storing those .ops files. (Save My Settings Wizard)

- Configuration options for the Office Assistant, including:
  - Controlling which assistant is used (Assistant\General)
  - Controlling how long the tip light bulb remains on (Assistant\General)
  - Enabling or disabling the Office Assistant (Assistant\Options Tab)
  - Setting whether the Office Assistant makes sounds (Assistant\Options Tab)
  - Setting whether the Tip of the Day is shown at startup (Assistant\Options Tab)
  - Controlling whether a user searching for help in an Office application gets product and programming help (Assistant\Options Tab)

- Configuration options for Language settings.
  - Setting the language that menus and dialog boxes use (Language Settings\User Interface)
  - Setting the language that Office help uses (Language Settings\User Interface)
  - Setting the language of the installed version of Office (Language Settings\Enabled Languages)
  - Setting the language of Office on the Web (Language Settings\Other)

- Configuration options for Collaboration settings including:
  - Setting the maximum number of documents being reviewed using the send for review or ad-hoc review features (Collaboration Settings)
  - Enabling or disabling send for review or ad hoc review in Outlook 2003 Collaboration Settings)
  - Setting the default subject for a review request (Collaboration Settings)
  - Controlling the default message text for a review request and for a reply (Default Message Text For A Review Request and Default Message Text For A Reply)

- Configuration options for Web archiving including:
  - Saving Web archives in any HTML encoding format. Web archives are single files that contain the contents of an entire Web page. (Web Archives)
  - Configuring the Web archive encoding format to use. (Web Archives)

- Options for enabling or disabling the Smart Document feature in Word and Excel [Smart Documents (Word, Excel)]

- Configuration options for the fax service, such as disabling the Fax Over Internet feature and disallowing a custom fax cover sheet (Services\Fax)

- Configuration options relating to what appears in the person name Smart Tag menu in Office applications including:

  - Displaying a person's online status, Free/Busy time, phone number, etc. (Instant Messaging Integration)

  - Controlling how Active Directory is used to search for Instant Messaging name information, including whether Active Directory is searched and how fields such as e-mail address, office location, and telephone number map to Active Directory attributes (Instant Messaging Integration\Active Directory/Person Name Smart Tag Integration)

- Configuration options for Error Reporting in Office applications, including whether noncritical errors are reported to Microsoft or whether any error messages are reported to Microsoft. (Improved Error Reporting)

- Configuration options for Microsoft Information Rights Management service, which users can use to control how Office documents are used.

  - Whether the information rights management user interface is disabled (Manage Restricted Permissions)

  - Whether users are required to connect to the information rights management server to request permission to use an Office document (Manage Restricted Permissions)

  - Whether users can use groups to control permission access to an Office document (Manage Restricted Permissions)

- Configuration of miscellaneous options including:

  - Configuring the Provide Feedback With Sound option across all Office applications (Miscellaneous)

  - Disabling the track document editing time feature (Miscellaneous)

  - Controlling whether to show the paste options buttons (Miscellaneous)

  - Blocking updates from the Office Updates site from applying; this also disables the Check For Updates menu item (Miscellaneous)

Microsoft OneNote 2003

- Location in the Group Policy namespace: onent11.adm

- Relative path: User Configuration\Administrative Templates\Microsoft Office OneNote 2003

- Configuration options for Tools | Options menu settings including:

  - Controlling where on the OneNote window the page tab control appears— right or left (Tools | Options\Display)

  - Whether to show note containers (Tools | Options\Display)

  - Whether to create all new pages with rule lines (Tools | Options\Display)

  - Whether to permanently delete aged OneNote pages and the number of days before pages are deleted (Tools | Options\Editing)

  - Whether to empty the deleted folder on exit (Tools | Options\Editing)

  - Whether to enable automatic numbering and bulleting (Tools | Options\Editing)

  - Whether to mark spelling errors in notes (Tools | Options\Spelling)

  - Controlling pen use, including automatically switching between pen and selection tool (Tools | Options\Handwriting)

  - Whether to allow OneNote e-mail attachments and whether to allow attachment of audio recording files to e-mail messages (Tools | Options\E-mail)

  - Controlling the signature to use for OneNote e-mail messages (Tools | Options\E-mail)

  - Whether to copy an item when moving it (Tools | Options\Note Flags)

  - Controlling the use of the Linked Audio feature (Tools | Options\Linked Audio)

  - Specifying the number of bits and the sample rate to use when recording audio (Tools | Options\Linked Audio)

  - Setting the location of the My Notebook folder used to save OneNote files as well as the location of the backup folder (Tools | Options\Open And Save)

  - Specifying the location of side notes—which section they appear in (Tools | Options\Open And Save)

  - Enabling the Optimize OneNote Files On Exit feature and controlling how often OneNote files are optimized (Tools | Options\Open And Save)

  - Enabling automatic backup of My Notebook files at a given interval (in minutes) and specifying the number of backup copies to keep (Tools | Options\Backup)

  - Specifying the default unit of measurement used in OneNote (Tools | Options\Other)

❑ Controlling whether the OneNote icon appears in the Notification area on the System Tray (Tools | Options\Other)

❑ Configuring miscellaneous options, including specifying the AutoSave interval and whether OneNote should provide a tour the first time its started (Miscellaneous)

Microsoft Outlook 2003

■ Location in the Group Policy namespace: outlk11.adm

■ Relative path: User Configuration\Administrative Templates\Microsoft Office Outlook 2003

■ Configuration options for Tools | Options... menu settings including:

❑ Setting preferences such as how messages are read and replied to (Figure D-3) (Tools | Options...\Preferences\E-mail Options)

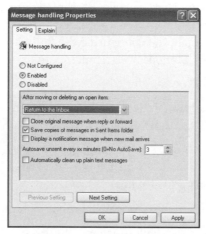

Figure D-3   Viewing message-handling options within the Outlook 2003 administrative template policy

❑ Enforcing whether e-mail is always read as plain text (Tools | Options...\ Preferences\E-mail Options)

❑ Configuring message Desktop Alerts feature—where a new message fades on the desktop (Tools | Options...\Preferences\E-mail Options\Advanced E-mail Options\Desktop Alert)

❑ Configuring e-mail tracking options, such as how to handle read receipt requests (Tools | Options...\Preferences\E-mail Options\Tracking Options)

❑ Configuring calendar options, such as the first day of the week, work week, and working hours (Tools | Options...\Preferences\Calendar Options)

❑ Configuring whether attendees are allowed to propose new times for meetings you organize (Tools | Options...\Preferences\Calendar Options)

❑ Configuring Free/Busy options, such as disabling the Microsoft Office Internet Free/Busy service or changing the URL to which Free/Busy information is published (Tools | Options...\Preferences\Calendar Options\Free/Busy Options)

❑ Configuring the default setting for how to file Contact objects (Tools | Options...\Preferences\Contact Options)

❑ Configuring the Journal feature, including whether to exclude or include certain types of Outlook items from journaling (Tools | Options...\Preferences\Journal Options)

❑ Configuring how Outlook notes appear in terms of color and size (Tools | Options...\Preferences\Notes Options)

❑ Configuring Junk E-Mail options, including whether to trust e-mail from people in your Contacts list, configuring the path to the safe senders, safe recipients and block senders lists, whether to permanently delete junk e-mail, and configuring the Junk E-Mail filter default protection level (Tools | Options...\Preferences\Junk E-mail)

■ Configuration options for e-mail setup including:

❑ Mail account options, such as sending messages immediately (Tools | Options...\Mail Setup)

❑ Dial-up options, such as hanging up when finished sending and receiving and automatically dialing during a background Send/Receive (Tools | Options...\Mail Setup)

■ Configuration options for e-mail format including:

❑ Setting the default e-mail editor (Tools | Options...\Mail Format\Message Format)

❑ Configuring Internet message formats, including how to encode plain-text messages, what to do with Outlook Rich Text Format messages that are sent to Internet recipients, and whether to send HTML messages with a copy of embedded pictures rather than the link to the picture (Tools | Options...\Mail Format\Internet Formatting)

❑ International options, such as the encoding type for outgoing messages and the use of English message headers and flags (Tools | Options...\Mail Format\International Options)

■ Configuration options for spell check behavior in Outlook messages, including whether to always suggest replacements for misspelled words and whether to ignore original message text in reply or forward when spell checking. (Tools | Options...\Spelling)

- Configuration options for Outlook security, including:

  - Whether to allow access to e-mail attachments and which file extensions are allowed (Tools | Options...\Security)

  - Disabling the Remember Password option for Internet e-mail (Tools | Options...\Security)

  - Preventing users from modifying the Outlook attachment security settings (Tools | Options...\Security)

  - Setting Outlook virus security settings (Tools | Options...\Security)

  - Configuring e-mail encryption options, including forcing all e-mails to be encrypted, minimum encryption key size, and forcing signing of all messages (Tools | Options...\Security\Cryptography)

  - Configuring automatic picture download settings to control whether images are downloaded within HTML messages (Tools | Options...\ Security\Automatic Picture Download Settings)

- Configuration of miscellaneous options including Empty Deleted Items Folder On Exit (Tools | Options...\Other)

- Configuration options for the behavior of the preview pane (Tools | Options...\Other)

- Configuration options for enabling e-mail logging for troubleshooting (Tools | Options...\Other\Advanced)

- Configuration options for reminders to play a sound and to be displayed (Tools | Options...\Other\Advanced\Reminder Options)

- Configuration options for automatic archiving and retention behavior, including how frequently to autoarchive, what to archive, and what the retention criteria are (Tools | Options...\Other\AutoArchive)

- Configuration options for Smart Tag behavior, including enabling or disabling Instant Messenger names and displaying a user's Messenger status in the From field of an e-mail (Tools | Options...\Other\Person Names)

- Configuration options for Macro security settings, including the default macro security level for Outlook (Tools | Macro\Security)

- Configuration options for whether to display the Exchange Over The Internet user interface (Tools | E-mail Accounts\Exchange Over The Internet)

- Configuration options for cached Exchange mode behavior, including allowing/ disallowing download of full items or headers, disallowing downloading only headers on slow network connections, and configuring the time interval between uploads and downloads of changes (Tools | E-mail Accounts\Cached Exchange Mode)

- Configuration options for the default authentication mechanism with the Exchange server (Exchange Settings)

- Configuration options for Offline Address book synchronization behavior and allowing or preventing the creation of .ost files (Exchange Settings)

- Configuration of miscellaneous options, such as preventing a user from changing his Outlook profile and preventing users from creating new e-mail account types (Miscellaneous)

- Configuration options for the .pst default location and maximum file sizes (Miscellaneous\PST Settings)

Microsoft PowerPoint 2003

- Location in the Group Policy namespace: ppt11.adm

- Relative path: User Configuration\Administrative Templates\Microsoft Office PowerPoint 2003

- Configuration options for Tools | Options... menu settings including:

  - Whether to show the startup task pane and whether to show the status bar (Tools | Options...\View)

  - Setting the size of the recently used file list (Tools | Options...\General)

  - Editing options (Figure D-4) such as whether to allow drag-and-drop text editing, setting the maximum number of undos, setting the maximum number of slide masters within a presentation, and whether to enforce password protection of PowerPoint documents (Tools | Options...\Edit)

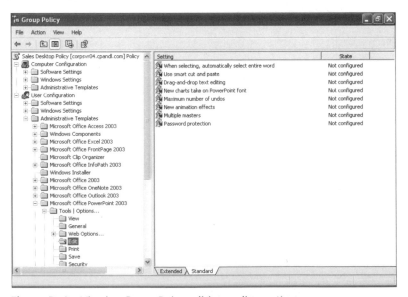

Figure D-4   Viewing PowerPoint editing policy options

❑ Printing options such as whether to enable background printing, whether to print inserted objects at the same resolution as the printer, and whether to print TrueType fonts as graphics (Tools | Options...\Print)

❑ File Save options such as whether to enable fast saves, the default file location for saving PowerPoint files, and the AutoRecover interval (Tools, Options\Save)

❑ Whether to make hidden markups visible (Tools | Options...\Security)

❑ Spell check options such as whether to always suggest corrections, whether to check spelling as you type, and whether to check writing style (Tools | Options...\Spelling And Style)

❑ AutoCorrect options such as whether to replace straight quotes with smart quotes (Tools | AutoCorrect Options...\AutoFormat As You Type)

■ Configuration options for Tools, Macro settings, including the macro security setting level and whether to trust access to Visual Basic projects (Tools | Macro\Security...)

Microsoft Project 2003

■ Location in the Group Policy namespace: proj11.adm

■ Relative path: User Configuration\Administrative Templates\Microsoft Office Project 2003

■ Configuration options for Tools | Options... menu settings including:

❑ Default date format and default project view, such as Gantt chart, calendar, etc. (Tools | Options...\View)

❑ General options such as displaying help on startup and opening the last file used on startup or enforcing the prompt for project info for new projects options (Tools | Options...\General\General Options For Microsoft Office Project)

❑ Setting the default standard and overtime rates (Tools | Options...\ General\General Options For 'Project1')

❑ Edit options such as allowing cell drag-and-drop and enabling editing directly in cells (Tools | Options...\Edit\Edit Options For Microsoft Office Project)

❑ Setting the display of time units (Tools | Options...\Edit\View Options For Time Units In 'Project')

❑ Calendar options such as days in a month, default start and end times, fiscal year start month, hours per day, and hours per week (Tools | Options...\Calendar)

- Configuration options for File, Save, including:

    - The default Project file format for a Save As operation (Tools | Options...\Save)

    - The default file locations for workgroup and user templates and projects (Tools | Options...\Save\File Locations)

    - AutoSave options such as the save interval and whether to prompt before saving (Tools | Options...\Save\Auto Save Options)

- Configuration options for the default macro security level (Tools | Macro\ Security)

Microsoft Publisher 2003

- Location in the Group Policy namespace: pub11.adm

- Relative path: User Configuration\Administrative Templates\Microsoft Office Publisher 2003

- Configuration options for default publishing and pictures locations (Default File Locations)

- Configuration options for Tools | Options... settings, including:

    - Displaying the new publication task pane at startup and showing a rectangle for text in the Web graphic region (Tools | Options...\General)

    - Editing options such as automatically selecting the entire word when selecting text, and configuring the use of Chinese font sizes (Tools | Options...\Edit)

    - User assistance options such as using the Quick Publication Wizards for blank publications and showing tip pages (Tools | Options...\User Assistance)

    - Setting automatic display of the printing troubleshooter (Tools | Options...\Print)

- Configuration options for File, Save such as allowing background saves (Tools | Options...\Save)

- Configuration options for spell checking such as whether to use the user dictionary for spelling correction suggestions and whether to flag spelling errors in words that look like URLs or e-mail addresses (Tools | Spelling)

- Configuration options for the default macro security level (Tools | Macro\ Security...)

- Configuration options for formatting and prompting the user when reapplying a style (Format)

- Configuration options for spell checking such as whether to flag repeated words and whether to check spelling as you type (Spelling)

- Configuration of miscellaneous options such as whether to enable type-and-replace and setting the default Publisher direction (Miscellaneous)

Microsoft Visio 2003

- Location in the Group Policy namespace: visio11.adm

- Relative path: Computer Configuration\Administrative Templates\Microsoft Office Visio 2003 *and* User Configuration\Administrative Templates\Microsoft Office Visio 2003

- Per-computer settings for security settings such as the default security level, whether to trust access to Visual Basic projects, and whether to disable VBA. These options override conflicting per-user settings (Visio:Security Settings).

- Per-user settings for Tools | Options... menu settings including:

  - Whether to show the startup task pane, smart tags, and stencil window Screen Tips (Tools | Options...\View\Show)

  - Configuring undo levels and the size of the Recently Used File list (Tools | Options...\General\General Options)

  - Drawing window options such as whether to zoom a drawing when using an Intellimouse, enabling connector splitting, and whether to automatically zoom when editing text (Tools | Options...\General\Drawing Window Options)

  - Whether to use AutoRecover and at what interval, and whether to prompt for document properties the first time the document is saved (Tools | Options...\Save\Save Options)

  - Whether to show file save and file open warnings (Tools | Options...\Save\Warnings Options)

  - Regional options such as the language to use during file conversion (Tools | Options...\Regional)

  - Configuring the search parameters when searching for a shape (Tools | Options...\Shape Search)

  - Security settings such as whether to allow VBA or allow COM automation events (Tools | Options...\Security\Macro Security)

  - Advanced options, including whether to run Visio in developer mode and whether to record all Visio actions in an Outlook Journal (Tools | Options...\Advanced\Advanced Options)

❑ Configuring default file paths for stencils, templates, Visio drawings, startup documents, help, and add-ons (Tools | Options...\Advanced\File Paths)

❑ Configuring color settings for various backgrounds, including stencils, drawing, and Print Preview windows (Tools | Options...\Advanced\Color Settings)

❑ AutoCorrect options such as displaying fractions with fraction character, replacing straight quotes with smart quotes, and replacing hyphens with a dash (Tools | AutoCorrect Options...\AutoFormat As You Type)

❑ Configuring the default macro security level (Tools | Macro\Security)

Microsoft Word 2003

■ Location in the Group Policy namespace: word11.adm

■ Relative path: User Configuration\Administrative Templates\Microsoft Office Word 2003

■ Configuration options for Tools | Options... menu settings including:

❑ Configuring Word documents as they appear in the taskbar, whether the startup task pane should appear in documents, whether ScreenTips should appear, whether animated text should be enabled and documents should include picture placeholders (Tools | Options...\View\Show)

❑ Whether documents should show formatting marks, including tab characters, spaces, optional hyphens, or all marks (Tools | Options...\View\ Formatting Marks)

❑ General options such as the size of the Recently Used File list, whether to enable navigation keys for WordPerfect users, the standard unit of measurement on a page, and whether to start Word in Reading layout (Tools | Options...\General)

❑ Editing options such as whether to use the Insert key for paste, whether to allow Ctrl+click to activate a hyperlink, and which application to use for editing pictures (Tools |Options...\Edit)

❑ Printing options such as whether to enable draft output, background printing, and automatic A4-to-letter paper resizing (Tools | Options...\ Print\Printing Options)

❑ File, Save options such as the default format for saving Word files, whether to enable AutoRecover and what the interval is, whether to always create a backup copy on a save operation, and whether to automatically make a local copy of files stored on network drives or removable media (Tools | Options...\Save)

- ❑ Security options such as enabling a warning before printing, saving or sending a file that contains tracked changes, and making any hidden markups visible (Tools | Options...\Security)

- ❑ Spelling and grammar options such as whether to correct for grammar or grammar and style, whether to show readability statistics, whether to check spelling and grammar as you type, and whether to always suggest corrections (Tools | Options...\Spelling & Grammar)

- ❑ Configuring default file locations for startup documents, documents, tools, clip art pictures, and AutoRecover files (Tools | Options...\File Locations)

- ■ Configuration options for AutoCorrect such as whether to replace text as you type, correct accidental use of the Caps Lock key, and always capitalize names of days (Tools | AutoCorrect...\AutoCorrect)

- ■ Configuration options for the default macro security level (Tools | Macro\Security...)

- ■ Configuration options for language settings such as enabling automatic detection of language (Tools | Language\Set Language)

- ■ Configuration of miscellaneous options such as whether to convert a drive letter reference to a UNC path or vice-versa and whether to automatically generate a legal blackline document when using the Compare and Merge Documents feature (Miscellaneous)

Index

A

Aaxa.adm file, Internet Explorer .adm files, 518
Access 2003
  Administrative templates, 706
  default database folder location, 391
Access Control Entries (ACEs), default
    permissions, 479
Access10.adm file, Office XP, 382
Access11.adm file
  Office 2003 .adm files, 517
  Office 2003 Administrative Templates, 377
Account Lockout Duration setting, Account
    Policies, 143
Account Lockout policy, 15
  account policies, 555
  security template, 142
Account Lockout Threshold setting, Account
    Policies, 143
Account logon events setting, Local Policies,
    144–145
Account management events setting, Local
    Policies, 144
Account Policies
  configuring, 16
  Default Domain Policy GPO, 15
  linking GPOs at domain level, 122
  security templates, 142–143, 210, 554–555
accounts
  Administrator, disabling, 641
  computer and user, verification, 585–586
  Guest account status setting, Local Policies, 145
  verification, 583–584
ACEs (Access Control Entries), default
    permissions, 479
Act as part of the operating system setting, Local
    Policies, 145
ACTIONLIST syntax, Group Policy Object Editor
    interface updates, 546
Active Directory
  convergence, troubleshooting, 643–645

database corruption, troubleshooting, 640–641
design considerations, 100
  database storage location, 100
  directory replication, 101
  OUs (organizational units), 101–103
  sites, 103–104
  system file storage location, 101
directory tree, 23–26
domain-based Group Policy, 6, 32–38
ESE (extensible storage engine), 473
GPO creation permissions, 478–479
Group Policy, 10–11
inheritance, 11–12
linking GPOs, 121–122, 633
local logons vs., 641
replication, 586, 643–645
viewing GPO security settings, 477–478
Active Directory Services Interface (ADSI), 10
ActiveX controls, Internet security zones, 307
Add Group Or User dialog box, 49
Add Item dialog box, 394
Add Recovery Agent Wizard, 419
Add Standalone Snap-In dialog box, 30, 151, 414,
    476
Add Upgrade Package dialog box, 342
Add workstations to domain setting, Local
    Policies, 145
Additional Rules policy, Software Restriction
    Policies, 361
  Certificate rules, 361–362
  hash rules, 362–363
  Path rules, 364–365
  Trusted Zones rule, 363–364
Add/Remove Snap-In command (File menu),
    214, 476, 563
Add/Remove Snap-In dialog box, 214, 414, 563
Add/Remove Templates dialog box, 378, 520
address books, Internet Explorer default
    programs, 299

.adm files, 516
  adding to GPO, 520
  best practices, 550–551
  creating custom files, 525–526
  default files, 516–518
  file language, 527
    comments, 547
    EXPLAIN syntax, 547–548
    Group Policy Object Editor interface update
      syntax, 534–546
    #if version syntax, 529–530
    MAXLEN syntax, 547
    registry updating syntax, 530–534
    REQUIRED syntax, 547
    string and tab limits, 549
    structure, 527–529
    SUPPORTED tag, 548, 549
  importing
    into GPO, 518
    tips, 519–520
  installed defaults, 518–519
  managing
    controlling updates, 522–523
    operating system releases, 523–524
    service packs, 523–524
    working tips, 523
  policies vs. preferences, 524–525
  removing files, 521–522
Adm subfolder, GPTs, 485
administration
  cross-domain GPO linking, 110
  privileges, GPO deployment, 128
  troubleshooting GPOs, 626–638
Administrative Files, Office XP, 270–271
administrative installations, 320–321
Administrative Templates, 9–10, 516, 705
  Access 2003, 706
  adding to GPO, 520
  .adm file, 485
  Clip Organizer 2003, 708
  creating custom files, 525–526
  customizing
    best practices, 550–551
    settings, troubleshooting, 627–630

default files, 516–518
example of simple file, 526–527
Excel 2003, 706–708
file language, 527
  comments, 547
  EXPLAIN syntax, 547–548
  Group Policy Object Editor interface update
    syntax, 534–546
  #if version syntax, 529–530
  MAXLEN syntax, 547
  registry updating syntax, 530–534
  REQUIRED syntax, 547
  string and tab limits, 549
  structure, 527–529
  SUPPORTED tag, 548–549
FrontPage 2003, 708
GPOs (Group Policy Objects), 29
importing
  into GPO, 518
  tips, 519–520
InfoPath 2003, 709
installed defaults, 518–519
managing files
  controlling updates, 522–523
  operating system releases, 523–524
  service packs, 523–524
  working tips, 523
Office 2003, 377–380, 709–713
OneNote 2003, 713–715
Outlook 2003, 715–718
policies vs. preferences, 524–525
PowerPoint 2003, 718–719
Project 2003, 719–720
Publisher 2003, 720–721
removing files, 521–522
troubleshooting, 394–395
Visio 2003, 721–722
Word 2003, 722–723
Administrative Templates policy, storage setting,
  496
administrators
  account, disabling, 641
  group, Restricted Groups security, 148
  Group Policy, 8–10

administrators, *continued*
  hardening clients, 206–207
    local group configuration, 208
    security settings, 207
    services and software, 207–208
  MMC (Microsoft Management Console), 226
    blocking author mode, 227
    designating prohibited or permitted
      snap-ins, 227–228
    requiring permissions for snap-ins, 228
Adprep.exe, Windows Server 2003, 670
ADSI (Active Directory Services Interface), 10
ADSI Edit
  viewing defaultSecurityDescriptor attribute,
    480–482
  viewing gPLink attribute, 490–491
Advanced Features command (View menu), 475
Advanced Security Settings For dialog box, 268
Advanced settings, profile folder redirection,
  277–279
Advanced Software Deployment Options dialog
  box, 338
Advanced View option (RSoP), 594, 597–598
advertisements, Windows Installer packages, 327
Aer_1033.adm file, Office 2003 .adm files, 517
Allow Anonymous SID/Name Translation policy,
  Default Domain Policy GPO, 17
Allow Audio Redirection setting, Terminal
  Services device mapping, 457
Allow Authenticated IPSec Bypass policy,
  Windows Firewall policy, 425
Allow Logging policy, Windows Firewall policy,
  437–438
Allow Reconnection From Original Client Only
  setting, Terminal Services connections,
  455–456
Allow User Installs option, Prohibit User Installs
  policy, 240
Always Use Local ADM Files For Group Policy
  Editor policy, 522
Animated Bitmap Creator, 291
Animated Bitmap Previewer, 291
animated logos, Internet Explorer, 291
antivirus software, Attachment Manager, 221
Any policy settings setting, Account Policies, 143

Application Compatibility, Microsoft Windows,
  218
  configuring additional settings, 219–220
  optimization, 218
Application Data
  profile folder redirection, 272
  user profile, 254–255
applications. *See also* software
  adding to categories, 340
  defining categories, 338
  event logs, 365
  filtering policy settings, 55–56
  logging, configuring, 610–611
  modifying categories, 339
  Windows compatibility settings, 218
    configuring additional settings, 219–220
    optimization, 218
application-specific settings, Office-related policy,
  384–385
asynchronous processing
  configuration, 119–120
  GPO design, 110–111
  vs. synchronous, 502
Attachment Manager, Microsoft Windows
  configuring risk level and trust logic, 221–224
  security risk assessment, 220–221
attachments, Windows Attachment Manager
  configuring risk level and trust logic, 221–224
  security risk assessment, 220–221
attributes, groupPolicyContainer object, 476–477
Audit policy
  Default Domain Controllers Policy GPO, 18
  Local Policies, 143, 556
  Security Configuration Wizard, 157
  security templates, troubleshooting, 211
  Windows Firewall, 681–682
Audit the access of global system objects setting,
  Local Policies, 145
authentication
  IPSec policy creation, 403–404
  public key certificates
    basics, 415–416
    managing public key policy, 418–420
    public key policies, 416–418
  users, Internet security zones, 307

author mode, MMC (Microsoft Management Console), 227
automatic removal, Windows Installer packages, 328
Automatic Updates, 243
  automatic download and installation process, 246
    detection frequency setting, 246
    notify user installs, 247
    optimizing scheduled installs, 248–249
  blocking access, 249
  configuring, 243–246
  designating update server, 249–251
  Windows, 243
    automatic download and installation process, 246–249
    blocking access, 249
    configuring, 243–246
    designating update server, 249–251
automation, GPMC, security management, 693–695

B

Back up files and directories setting, Local Policies, 145
Back Up Group Policy Object dialog box, 90
back ups, GPOs, 89–90
background policies, processing, 78–79, 501–505
Backup dialog box, 90
Backup Operators group, Restricted Groups security, 148
Backupallgpos.wsf script, GPMC prebuilt scripts, 698–699
BackupGPO.wsf script, GPMC prebuilt scripts, 699
baseline file cache, usage, 237–238
Basic settings, profile folder redirection, 274–276
block inheritance, gPOptions attribute, 491
Block Policy inheritance, 655
Block Policy Inheritance option, GPOs, 125–126
blocking
  inheritance, 65–66
  port filtering via IPSec policy, 412

Browse For A Group Policy Object dialog box, 31, 343
Browse For Folder dialog box, 91, 298
Browser Title dialog box, 290
Browser Title policy, 290
Browser Toolbar Button Information dialog box, 293
Browser Toolbar Customizations dialog box, 293–294
browsers, Internet Explorer
  connection settings, 301–303
  customizing interface, 290–294
  global default programs, 299–300
  options policies, 313–316
  proxy settings, 303–306
  security, 306–313
  URL customizing, 295–299
buttons, Internet Explorer, customizing, 292–294

C

calendars, Internet Explorer default programs, 299
captions, Internet Explorer, customizing, 292
categories
  adding applications, 340
  defining for applications, 338
  modifying for applications, 339
CATEGORY syntax
  .adm file structure, 528
  Group Policy Object Editor interface updates, 535–536
CDs, burning feature prevention, 234
Certificate Rules, Software Restriction Policies, 361–362
Change the system time setting, Local Policies, 145
Chat.adm file, Internet Explorer .adm files, 518
CHECKBOX syntax, PART syntax, 539
Choose Computer Container dialog box, 82
Choose User Container dialog box, 82
CLASS MACHINE, .adm file structure, 528
CLASS syntax, .adm files, 530–531
classes, groupPolicyContainer object, 474

clients
    best practice security settings, 194–205
    hardening, 192–205
        Help Desk staff, 208–210
        IT staff and administrator computers, 206
        required ports, 205–206
        restricted groups, 206
    Terminal Services encryption levels, 450
client-side extensions. *See* CSEs (client-side extensions)
CLIENTTEXT keyword, PART syntax, 539–540
Clip Organizer 2003, Administrative templates, 708
.cmw file
    deploying new Office configuration, 375–376
    updating Office configuration, 375
CMW File Viewer, Office 2003 Resource Kit, 372
color icon files, Internet Explorer, customizing, 293
COMBOBOX type, PART syntax, 540–541
commands
    File menu, Add/Remove Snap-In, 214, 476, 563
    Tools menu (Word 2003), Options, 387
    View menu
        Advanced Features, 475
        Filtering, 55
        Toolbars, 294
Common.adm file, Administrative Templates, 516
communications, networks
    IPSec policy, 398–400
    managing IPSec policy, 401–415
    managing Windows Firewall policy, 424–438
    public key certificates, 415–420
    Windows Firewall policy, 420–424
compatibility, Microsoft Windows application settings, 218
    configuring additional settings, 219–220
    optimization, 218
Compatws.inf template, security template default, 137
Component Status (RSoP Summary tab), 595
components
    verification, 586–587
    Windows, Administrative Templates, 10

Computer Configuration policy
    GPO linking, 107–108
    GPT Machine subfolder, 485
    setting override, 218
computers
    configuration
        GPOs, 649
        policies, 661–664
        searching policy objects, 57
        setting refresh, 68–80
    filtering, 59–61
    hardening, 164
        closing unnecessary ports, 164–165
        disabling unnecessary services, 165–166
        tools used, 166–167
    Local Group Policy access, 29–31
    policies, 5
    remote, Local Group Policy access, 31–32
    scripts, 282
        administration, 8
        controlling visibility, 285–286
        execution, 287
        startup and shutdown, 283–284
        timeout, 286–287
    searching policy objects, 57
    user account verification, 585–586
Conf.adm file, Administrative Templates, 516
configuration
    Application logging, 610–611
    core verification, 582–586
        computer accounts, 583–584
        computer and user accounts, 585–586
        computer trusts, 583–584
        network configuration, 583
        network connection, 583
        time synchronization, 584
    GPMonitor.exe, 605–606
    Internet security, 309
        Local Intranet security zone, 310–311
        Restricted Sites security zone, 312–313
        Trusted Sites security zone, 311–312
        zone settings, 309–310

configuration, *continued*
    Microsoft Office, 370
        Office-related policy, 383–395
        resource kit tools, 371–383
    Office-related policy, 385–386
    options
        Clip Organizer 2003 Administrative
            templates, 708
        InfoPath 2003 Administrative templates, 709
        Microsoft Access 2003 Administrative
            templates, 706
        Microsoft Excel 2003 Administrative
            templates, 706–708
        Microsoft FrontPage 2003 Administrative
            templates, 708
        Microsoft Office 2003 Administrative
            templates, 709–713
        Microsoft OneNote 2003 Administrative
            templates, 714–715
        Microsoft Outlook 2003 Administrative
            templates, 715–718
        Microsoft PowerPoint 2003 Administrative
            templates, 718–719
        Microsoft Project 2003 Administrative
            templates, 719–720
        Microsoft Publisher 2003 Administrative
            templates, 720–721
        Microsoft Visio 2003 Administrative
            templates, 721–722
        Microsoft Word 2003 Administrative
            templates, 722–723
    policy setting, filtering, 55
    profile folder redirection, 274
        Advanced setting, 277–279
        Basic setting, 274–276
        Settings tab, 279–281
    user profiles, 260
        data access, 266–268
        limiting profile size, 269–271
        update and change modification, 265–266
        ways utilized, 260–265
    Userenv logging, 614
Configure Slow Link Speed setting, slow link
        detection, 466–467

Confirm File Replace dialog box, 380
Connection Settings dialog box, 302
connections
    Internet Explorer, setting deployment,
        301–303
    slow network links, 461–463
        Configure Slow Link Speed setting, 466–467
        CSE (client-side extension), 467–468
        default Group Policy application, 462–463
        Do Not Detect Slow Network Connections
            setting, 465–466
        Group Policy Slow Link Detection setting,
            464
        Prompt User When Slow Link Is Detected
            setting, 466
        RAS connections, 463
        Slow Network Connection Timeout for User
            Profiles setting, 465
    speeds, design considerations, 104
    Terminal Services, 448
        Allow Reconnection From Original Client
            Only setting, 455–456
        Limit Number Of Connections setting,
            448–449
        Secure Server (Require Security) setting, 451
        Set Client Connection Encryption Level
            setting, 449–451
        Set Rules For Remote Control To Terminal
            Services User Sessions setting, 452–453
        Set Time Limit For Active Terminal Services
            Sessions setting, 454–455
        Set Time Limit For Disconnected Sessions
            setting, 454
        Start A Program On Connection setting,
            451–452
        Terminate Session When Time Limits Are
            Reached setting, 455
contact lists, Internet Explorer default programs,
        299
Control Panel, Administrative Templates, 9
convergence
    Active Directory problems, 643–645
    SYSVOL problems, 643–645
Cookies folder, user profile, 254

CopyGPO.wsf script, GPMC prebuilt scripts, 699–700

copying policy object settings, 85–87

core configuration, verification, 582–586
    computer accounts, 583–584
    computer and user accounts, 585–586
    computer trusts, 583–584
    network configuration, 583
    network connection, 583
    time synchronization, 584

Create Data Recovery Agent option, 419

CreateEnvironmentFromXML.wsf script, GPMC prebuilt scripts, 701–702

CreateGPO.wsf script, GPMC prebuilt scripts, 696

CreateMigrationTable.wsf script, GPMC prebuilt scripts, 702

createTimeStamp attribute, groupPolicyContainer object, 476

CreateXMLFromEnvironment.ws script, GPMC prebuilt scripts, 701–702

Cross-Domain Copying Wizard, 86

cross-domain linking, GPOs, 110

CSEs (client-side extensions), 492
    logging, 617–623
    network slow link detection, 467–468
    processing architecture, 492–494

Custom Installation Wizard, 319, 352, 372–373
    administrative install of .msi file, 373
    configuring Office installation, 374
    Microsoft Office management, 370
    Office 2003 Resource Kit, 372
    transform file deployment, 374

Custom Logo dialog box, 291

Custom Logo policy, 291–292

Custom Maintenance Wizard, 375
    deploying new Office configuration, 375–376
    Microsoft Office management, 370
    Office 2003 Resource Kit, 372
    updating Office configuration, 375

Customizable Alerts, Office 2003 Resource Kit, 372

Customize Toolbar dialog box, 294

customizing
    Administrative Templates

    bets practices, 550–551
    file language, 527–549
    files, 525–526
  GPOs
    loopback processing, 440–443
    slow network links, 461–468
    Terminal Services, 444–461
  Internet Explorer
    connection settings, 301–303
    global default programs, 299–300
    logos, 291–292
    proxy settings, 303–306
    security, 306–313
    title bar text, 290
    toolbar, 292–294
    URLs, 295–299
  Microsoft Office, 371
    Administrative Templates, 377–380
    configuration GPOs, 380–381
    Custom Installation Wizard, 372–374
    Custom Maintenance Wizard, 375–376
    managing multiple versions, 381–383
    Web site, 371–372
  security templates
    copying, 563–564
    creating new, 564
    Sceregvl.inf file, 564–572
    services, 572–574

D

DACL (Discretionary access control list), security descriptor, 559

data, folder redirection administration, 9

databases, Active Directory
    replication, 101
    storage location, 100
    troubleshooting corruption, 640–641

DC security.inf template, security template default, 137

DCGPOFIX fix, 14

debugging
    Folder Redirection Policy, 620–622
    Security Policy logging, 622–623
    Windows Installer Policy logging, 617–620

Default Domain Controller Policy GPO, 7, 14,
      17–18
Default Domain Policy GPO, 7, 14–17
Default Response Rule, IPSec policy, 403
defaults
   linked GPOs, 13–14
      Default Domain Controllers Policy GPO,
         17–18
      Default Domain Policy GPO, 15–17
   Office-related policy, folder and file locations,
      391–393
   programs, Internet Explorer, 299–300
   security settings, viewing and modifying,
      479–482
   security templates
      Compatws.inf, 137
      DC security.inf, 137
      Hisecdc.inf, 139
      Hisecws.inf, 140
      Iesacls.inf, 137
      Notssid.inf, 140–141
      Rootsec.inf, 141
      Securedc.inf, 138
      Securews.inf, 138–139
      Setup Security.inf, 141
   software deployment, global, 346–348
defaultSecurityDescriptor attribute, 479–480
   modifying, 482
   viewing, 480–482
delegation
   administration, Active Directory OU design,
      102
   restrictions, GPMC troubleshooting, 631–638
Delete Cached Copies Of Roaming Profiles
      settings, 261, 264, 461
DeleteGPO.wsf script, GPMC prebuilt scripts,
      696
deleting
   GPOs (Group Policy Objects), 51
   installed software, 355
Deploy Software dialog box, 329, 333
deployment
   design considerations, 100
      Active Directory, 100–104
      GPO application, 106–114
      GPO performance, 115–121

   network topology, 104–105
   remote access connection, 105–106
GPMonitor.exe, 605–606
GPOs
   best practices, 121–129
   testing, 129–133
IPSec policy, 399
Office 2003 Administrative Templates, 377
   initial deployment steps, 378–379
   updates, 379–380
security templates, 161
   importing in GPOs, 161–162
   secedit.exe tool, 162
   Security Configuration and Analysis tool,
      162
   Security Configuration Wizard and scwcmd
      command, 163–164
software
   global defaults, 346–348
   management, 354–368
   non-Windows Installer package files,
      330–334
   planning, 322–326
   Windows Installer packages, 326–330
Designated File Types policy, 359
Designated File Types Properties dialog box, 359
designs, 100
   Active Directory, 100
      database storage location, 100
      directory replication, 101
      OUs (organizational units), 101–103
      sites, 103–104
      system file storage location, 101
   GPO application, 106–107
      cross-domain linking, 110
      custom settings, 114
      Fast Logon Optimization policy, 111–112
      inheritance modification, 112
      monolithic vs. functional, 113–114
      site, domain, OU linking, 107–109
      synchronous and asynchronous processing,
         110–111
   GPO performance, 115
      asynchronous processing configuration,
         119–120
      common issues, 115–116

designs, GPO performance, *continued*
   configuring script timeout, 119
   disabling unused sections, 118
   filtering based on group membership, 120–121
   limiting loopback processing, 120
   linking to OUs, 117–118
   optimizing background refresh interval, 118–119
   reducing settings, 117
  network topology, 104–105
  remote access connection, 105–106
Desktop
  Administrative Templates, 9
  profile folder redirection, 272
  user profile, 254
Details dialog box, 297
detection
  frequencies, Automatic Updates, 246
  slow link settings, 463
   Configure Slow Link Speed setting, 466–467
   CSE (client-side extension), 467–468
   Do Not Detect Slow Network Connections setting, 465–466
   Group Policy Slow Link Detection setting, 464
   Prompt User When Slow Link Is Detected setting, 466
   Slow Network Connection Timeout for User Profiles setting, 465
devices, mapping using Terminal Services, 456
  Allow Audio Redirection setting, 457
  Do Not Allow Client Printer Redirection setting, 457
  Do Not Allow COM Port Redirection setting, 457
  Do Not Allow Drive Redirection setting, 458
  Do Not Allow LPT Port Redirection setting, 458
  Do Not Set Default Client Printer To Be Default Printer In A Session setting, 458
Devices, Prevent users from installing printer drivers setting, 145
DFS (Distributed File System), 586–587

DHCP servers, allocating incorrect DNS information, 646
dialog boxes
  Add Group Or User, 49
  Add Item, 394
  Add Standalone Snap-in, 30, 151, 414, 476
  Add Upgrade Package, 342
  Add/Remove Snap-in, 214, 414, 563
  Add/Remove Templates, 378, 520
  Advanced Security Settings For, 268
  Advanced Software Deployment Options, 338
  Back Up Group Policy Object, 90
  Backup, 90
  Browse For A Group Policy Object, 31, 343
  Browse For Folder, 91, 298
  Browser Title, 290
  Browser Toolbar Button Information, 293
  Browser Toolbar Customizations, 293–294
  Choose Computer Container, 82
  Choose User Container, 82
  Confirm File Replace, 380
  Connection Settings, 302
  Custom Logo, 291
  Customize Toolbar, 294
  Deploy Software, 329, 333
  Designated File Types Properties, 359
  Details, 297
  Edit Rule Properties, 408, 412
  Favorites And Links, 297
  Filter Properties, 409–411
  Filtering, 55
  Find Users, Contacts, And Groups, 671
  Internet Properties, 300–302, 311
  IP Filter List, 409
  Local Area Network (LAN) Settings, 303
  Local Intranet, 311
  Manage Backups, 91
  New Certificate Rule, 362
  New GPO, 41, 87
  New Hash Rule, 363
  New Organizational Unit, 43
  Permissions Entry For, 268
  Policy Settings, 234
  Policy Templates, 378–380, 520

dialog boxes, *continued*
  Programs, 300
  Proxy Settings, 304
  Remove Software, 355
  Restore, 92
  Restricted Sites, 313
  Run, 8, 563
  Search For Group Policy Objects, 58
  Security Settings, 60, 268, 310
  Select Computer, 31, 93
  Select Users, Computers, Or Groups, 46, 268,
    346, 671
  Show Contents, 389
  Software Installation Properties, 339, 347
  Trusted Publishers, 360
  Trusted Sites, 312
  Windows Firewall, 426–427
Directory service access setting, Local Policies,
  144
directory trees, 23–26
disabled state, policy settings, 8
disabling
  Administrator account, 641
  GPO processing, 72–73
  inherited policy, 64
  slow-link detection, 76
Disallowed and Unrestricted modes, Software
    Restriction Policies, 360–361
Discretionary access control list (DACL), security
    descriptor, 559
Disk Quota policy, storage setting, 496
Disk Quota Policy Processing policy, 76
displayName attribute
  groupPolicyContainer object, 476
  Sceregvl.inf file, 566
DisplayType, Sceregvl.inf file, 566
DistinguishedName attribute,
    groupPolicyContainer object, 476
Distributed File System (DFS), 586–587
DNS (Domain Name System), 10, 586
  GPO application problems, 645–646
  Group Policy, 10–11
Do Not Allow Client Printer Redirection setting,
    Terminal Services device mapping, 457

Do Not Allow COM Port Redirection setting,
    Terminal Services device mapping, 457
Do Not Allow Drive Redirection setting, Terminal
    Service device mapping, 458
Do Not Allow Exceptions policy, Windows
    Firewall, 427
Do Not Allow LPT Port Redirection setting,
    Terminal Service device mapping, 458
Do Not Detect Slow Network Connection
    settings, 261, 264, 465–466
Do Not Set Default Client Printer To Be Default
    Printer In A Session setting, 458
documentation, GPOs, 129
domain controller focus, 37–38
Domain Controller Security Policy tool, 29
domain controllers
  Active Directory, directory replication, 101
  Domain Controller Security Policy tool, 29
  hardening servers, 187
    required ports, 189–190
    security environment, 187
    security settings, 188–189
  logon, Group Policy, 588–589
  PDC Emulator, troubleshooting, 626–627
  troubleshooting unavailability, 639–640
Domain member
  Digitally encrypt or sign secure channel data
    (always) setting, Local Policies, 145
  Digitally sign secure channel data (when
    possible) setting, Local Policies, 145
Domain Name System. *See* DNS (Domain Name
    System)
Domain Profile, Windows Firewall policy
    operation, 421
domain-based Group Policy, 6
  forest function level, 6
  management, 32–33
    accessing additional domains, 37
    connecting to additional forests, 35–36
    domain controller focus option setting,
      37–38
    GPMC installation, 33–34
    running GPMC, 34–35
    showing connected forest sites, 36

domains, 6
  enforcing inheritance, 67
  GPO linking, 41, 107
    Computer Configuration and User
      Configuration, 107–108
    creating and linking separately, 41–42
    interaction, 108–109
    single operation, 42–43
  GPOs (Group Policy Objects)
    creation rights, 45
    Terminal Services, 445–446
  linking GPOs, 122–123
downloads
  Internet security zones, 307
  Microsoft Office Web site, 371–372
drives
  mapping using Terminal Services, 456–458
  Windows Explorer
    hiding, 232–233
    preventing access, 233–234
DROPDOWNLIST syntax, PART syntax,
    541–542
DumpGPOInfo.wsf script, GPMC prebuilt scripts,
    702
DumpSOMInfo.wsf script, GPMC prebuilt
    scripts, 702
DVDs, burning feature prevention, 234
Dw20.adm file, Office 2003 .adm files, 517

E

Edit Rule Properties dialog box, 408, 412
editing GPOs, 636
EDITTEXT syntax
  .adm file structure, 528
  PART syntax, 542–543
EFS Recovery Policy Processing policy, 76
e-mail
  Internet Explorer default programs, 299
  Outlook, configuring security options,
    393–394
Enable Automatic Configured policy, NetMeeting
    configuration, 229
enabled state, policy settings, 8

enabling
  GPO processing, 72–73
  inherited policy, 64
encryption, Terminal Services connections,
    449–451
END CATEGORY, .adm file structure, 529
END PART, .adm file structure, 528
END POLICY, .adm file structure, 528
Enforce Password History setting, Account
    Policies, 142
Enforced option, GPOs, 125–126
Enforcement policy, 358
enforcing GPOs, 654
enforcing inheritance, 66–67
enterprise environments, 6
ESE (extensible storage engine), Active Directory,
    473
event logs
  accessing, 611
  Application configuring, 610–611
  event IDs, 611–613
  event sources, 611
  troubleshooting, 212
  security template, 146–147, 556
  Userenv configuring, 614
Event Viewer, Microsoft Windows
  customizing, 225
  using information requests, 224
events, Group Policy, 611–613
Excel 2003
  Administrative templates, 706–708
  default file location, 392
Excel10.adm file, Office XP, 382
Excel11.adm file
  Office 2003 .adm files, 517
  Office 2003 Administrative Templates, 377
executables, Internet Explorer customizing, 293
EXPLAIN syntax, .adm files, 547–548
Explorer
  Administrative Template files, 517–518
  security, Windows Server 2003 Service Pack 1,
    672–674

Explorer, *continued*
 URL Action settings, Windows Server 2003
   Service Pack 1, 674–675
 Windows, 231–232
  CD and DVD burning prevention, 234
  hiding drives, 232 233
  limiting Recycle Bin size, 235–236
  preventing drive access, 233–234
  removing Security tab, 235
extensible storage engine (ESE), Active Directory,
  473

F

Fast Logon Optimization policy, 111–112
Favorites And Links dialog box, 297
Favorites folder, user profile, 254
favorites lists, customizing URLs, 296–297
 creating, 297–298
 importing, 298–299
Feature Control policies, Internet Explorer
   security, 673
File menu commands, Add-Remove Snap-in, 214,
   476, 563
File Replication Service (FRS), 587
File System, security template, 150, 560
files
 attachments, Windows Attachment Manager,
   220–224
 GPMon.cab, 605
 GPMonitor.adm, 605
 GPMonitor.chm, 605
 GPMonitor.msi, 605
 Office-related policy, location default, 391–393
 server, hardening, 190–191
 sharing, Windows Firewall, 427–428
 system troubleshooting, 213
 SYSVOL
  GPO application failures, 642–643
  troubleshooting replication/convergence,
    643–645
 Windows Explorer, 231–232
  CD and DVD burning prevention, 234
  hiding drives, 232–233
  limiting Recycle Bin size, 235–236

 preventing drive access, 233–234
 removing Security tab, 235
Filter Properties dialog box, 409, 411
filtering, GPOs
 ACLs, 126
 based on group membership, 120–121
 security, 656
Filtering command (View menu), 55
Filtering dialog box, 55
filters
 computer, 59–61
 IPSec policy
  actions, 411–414
  defining rules, 406–407
 policy settings
  operating system and application
    configuration, 55–56
  techniques, 54–55
 security group, 59–61
 user, 59–61
 Windows Firewall, basics, 420–421
 WMI (RSoP Summary tab), 595
Find Users, Contacts, And Groups dialog box,
   671
FindDisabledGPOs.wsf script, GPMC prebuilt
   scripts, 696
FindDuplicateNamedGPOs.wsf script, GPMC
   prebuilt scripts, 702
FindGPOsByPolicyExtension.wsf script, GPMC
   prebuilt scripts, 703
FindGPOsBySecurityGroup.wsf script, GPMC
   prebuilt scripts, 697
FindGPOsWithNoSecurityFiltering.wsf script,
   GPMC prebuilt scripts, 703
FindOrphanedGPOsInSYSVOL.wsf script,
   GPMC prebuilt scripts, 703
FindSOMsWithExternalGPOLinks.wsf script,
   GPMC prebuilt scripts, 703
FindUnlinkedGPOs.wsf script, GPMC prebuilt
   scripts, 697
Flags attribute, groupPolicyContainer object, 476
Folder Redirection Policy, debugging logging,
   496, 620–622
Folder Redirection Policy Processing policy, 76

folders
    Office-related policy, default location, 391–393
    redirection administration, 9
    shared, Administrative Templates, 10
    user profiles
        limiting, 270–271
        redirecting, 271–281
Force Logoff When Logon Hours Expire policy,
        Default Domain Policy GPO, 16
Force shutdown from a remote system setting,
        Local Policies, 145
foreground processing, 501–505
forests, enforcing inheritance, 66
Fp10.adm file, Office XP, 382
Fp11.adm file
    Office 2003 .adm files, 517
    Office 2003 Administrative Templates, 377
FrontPage 2003, Administrative templates, 708
FRS (File Replication Service), 587
functional design approach, GPOs, 113–114

G

Gal10.adm file, Office XP, 382
Gal11.adm file
    Office 2003 .adm files, 517
    Office 2003 Administrative Templates, 377
general deployment properties, software
        deployment, 334–335
General option (RSoP Summary tab), 594
GetDomain method, 689
GetReportsForAllGPOs.wsf script, GPMC
        prebuilt scripts, 703
GetReportsForGPO.wsf script, GPMC prebuilt
        scripts, 700
global defaults
    programs, Internet Explorer, 299–300
    software deployment, 346–348
global settings
    Office-related policy, 384–385
    user profiles, 255
global software, installation options, 334
    adding applications to a category, 340
    defining application categories, 338
    deployment type and installation options,
        335–337
general deployment properties, 334–335
global deployment defaults, 346–348
modifying
    application categories, 339
    security on installer file, 344–346
package customization with transforms, 344
upgrades, 340–343
gPCFileSysPath attribute, groupPolicyContainer
        object, 477
gPCMachineExtensionNames attribute,
        groupPolicyContainer object, 477
GPCs (Group Policy containers), 644
    checking for errors, 473–475, 600–602
    syncing, 644
gPCUserExtensionNames attribute,
        groupPolicyContainer object, 477
gPLink attribute, 488–491
GPMC (Group Policy Modeling), 648–649
    creating GPOs in, 632–633
    domain-based Group Policy
        accessing additional domains, 37
        connecting to additional forests, 35–36
        domain controller focus option settings,
            37–38
        installation, 33–34
        running, 34–35
        showing connected forest sites, 36
    filtering policy settings, 55–56
    GPOs (Group Policy Objects), creating OUs, 43
    installation, 22
    navigating GPOs, 22
    scripting, 687
        automating security management, 693–695
        creating GPOs, 689–693
        creating initial GPM object, 689
        linking GPOs, 689–693
        object model, 687–688
        prebuilts, 695, 704
        referencing domain to manage, 689
    searching objects, 56–57
        beginning, 58–59
        techniques, 57–58
    troubleshooting, delegation restrictions,
        631–638

gpmc.msc command, 75
GPMon.cab, 605
GPMonitor.adm, 605
GPMonitor.chm, 605
GPMonitor.exe
  components, 604
  configuring, 605–606
  deploying, 605–606
  installation, 604–605
  reports, 607–609
  troubleshooting Group Policy, 604–609
GPMonitor.msi, 605
GPOs (Group Policy Objects), 6–7
  back up, 89–90
  copying settings, 85–87
  creating
    GPMC, 632–633, 689–693
    software deployment planning, 322–323
  customizing
    loopback processing, 440–443
    slow network links, 461–468
    Terminal Services, 444–461
  deleting permanently, 51
  deployment best practices, 121–129
    administrative privileges, 128
    designing based on categories, 125
    limit enforced and block policy inheritance,
      125–126
    linking, 121–123
    naming and documenting, 129
    network topology, 127–128
    security filtering, 126
    software installation, 124–125
    source file servers, 124
    WMI filters, 126–127
  design considerations, 106–107
    cross-domain linking, 110
    custom settings, 114
    Fast Logon Optimization policy, 111–112
    inheritance modification, 112
    monolithic vs. functional, 113–114
    site, domain, OU linking, 107–109
    synchronous and asynchronous processing,
      110–111
  disabling processing, 72–73

DNS problems, 645–646
editing, 636
enabling processing, 72–73
enforcing, 654
filtering, 59–61
GPMC
  backing up, 698–699
  copying, 699–700
  creating, 696
  deleting, 696
  finding by security group, 697
  finding disabled, 696
  finding unlinked, 697
  generating RSoP reports, 700
  importing, 700
  permissions setting, 697–698
  scripting object model, 687–688
importing settings, 87–89
inheritance, 13, 654–656
intersite replication, 645
intrasite replication, 645
linking, 12–13, 39
  Active Directory, 633
  default policy, 13–18
  domains, 41–43
  GPMC, 689–693
  OUs, 43–45
  removing, 51
  sites, 39–41
  troubleshooting problems, 650–651
loopback processing status, 592
management, 28–29, 634–635
  Active Directory–based Group Policy, 32–38
  Local Group Policy, 29–32
management privileges, 45
  creation rights, 45–46
  delegating control, 49
  GPMC permissions, 47–48
  link management, 50–51
Microsoft Office, configuration, 380–381
modeling, RSoP (Resultant Set of Policy),
  93–95
navigating, 22
  creating and linking, 22–23
  RSoP (Resultant Set of Policy), 23–28

Office 2003 Administrative Templates, 377
  initial deployment steps, 378–379
  updates, 379–380
performance considerations, 115
  asynchronous processing configuration,
    119–120
  common issues, 115–116
  configuring script timeout, 119
  disabling unused sections, 118
  filtering based on group membership,
    120–121
  limiting loopback processing, 120
  linking to OUs, 117–118
  optimizing background refresh interval,
    118–119
  reducing settings, 117
permissions, troubleshooting, 591–592
policy setting options, 39
restoring, 91–92
RSoP Summary tab, 594
searching policy objects, 57
settings
  applying to groups, 652–653
  conflicting settings, 653–654
slow links, 592
troubleshooting
  administration problems, 626–638
  application failures, 642–643
  conflicting settings, 653–654
  implementation problems, 647–656
  incorrect settings, 647–650
  infrastructure problems, 638–646
  inheritance, 654–656
  linking, 650–651
verbose output, 602–604
verification, Gpotool, 602
viewing, 636–638
Gpotool, troubleshooting Group Policy, 600–604
  GPC errors, 600–602
  GPO verbose output, 602–604
  GPO verifications, 602
  GPT errors, 600–602
  SYSVOL errors, 602
GPRESULT, 648–649
Gpresult tool, troubleshooting
  Group Policy, 599–600
  security settings, 214

Gpt.ini files, GPT subfolders, 485
GPTs (Group Policy templates), 473, 483–488,
    644
  checking for errors, 600–602
  syncing, 644
gpupdate command, 80
GrantPermissionOnAllGPOs.wsf script, GPMC
    prebuilt scripts, 703
grayscale icon files, Internet Explorer
    customizing, 293
Group Policy, 3
  administrator use, 8–10
  basics, 4
  domains, 6
  GPOs (Group Policy Objects), 6–7, 12–18
  infrastructure
    Active Directory, 10–12
    DNS (Domain Name System), 10–11
  logging, 609–623
    accessing event IDs, 611–613
    accessing event logs, 611
    accessing event sources, 611
    configuring Application logging, 610–611
    CSE logging, 617–623
    Userenv logs, 614–617
  processing, 5
  settings, 7–8
  troubleshooting, 581–592
    core configuration verification, 582–586
    GPMonitor.exe, 604–609
    GPO permissions, 591–592
    Gpotool, 600–604
    Gpresult, 599–600
    infrastructure component verification,
      586–587
    link status, 589–590
    logon domain controller, 588–589
    loopback processing status, 592
    order, 589–590
    RSoP (Resultant Set of Policy), 593–598
    slow links, 592
    status states, 587–588
    versions, 587–588
  workgroups, 6
Group Policy containers (GPCs), 473–475
Group Policy Editor settings, troubleshooting,
    627–631

Group Policy Modeling. *See* GPMC (Group Policy Modeling)

Group Policy Modeling Wizard, 81, 444

Group Policy Monitor. *See* GPMonitor.exe

Group Policy Monitor Administrative template, 604

Group Policy Monitor console, 604

Group Policy Monitor service, 604

Group Policy Object Editor, 14
  navigating GPOs, 22
  syntax for updating interface, 534
    ACTIONLIST syntax, 546
    CATEGORY syntax, 535–536
    PART syntax, 537
    POLICY syntax, 536–537
    STRINGS syntax, 534–535

Group Policy Object Editor snap-in, 441

Group Policy Objects. *See* GPOs (Group Policy Objects)

Group Policy Results, Windows Server 2003 RSoP, 678

Group Policy Results Wizard, 93, 395, 443, 593

Group Policy Slow Link Detection policy, 76–78

Group Policy Slow Link Detection setting, slow link detection, 464

Group Policy templates. *See* GPTs (Group Policy templates)

groupPolicyContainer class, defaultSecurityDescriptor attribute, 479–480
  modifying, 482
  viewing, 480–482

groupPolicyContainer object
  attributes, 476–477
  class, 474
  security, 477–478

groups
  applying GPO settings to, 652–653
  GPOs (Group Policy Objects), creation rights, 45

GUID, searching policy objects, 58

H

hardening clients, 192–205
  Help Desk staff, 208
    local group configuration, 209–210
    security settings, 208–209
  IT staff and administrator computers, 206–207
    local group configuration, 208
    security settings, 207
    services and software, 207–208
  required ports, 205–206
  restricted groups, 206

hardening computers, 164
  closing unnecessary ports, 164–165
  disabling unnecessary services, 165–166
  tools used, 166
    Netstat tool, 166–167
    Portqry tool, 167

hardening servers, 168
  domain controllers, 187
    required ports, 189–190
    security environment, 187
    security settings, 188–189
  file server, 190–191
  member servers, 168
    OU design considerations, 168–170
    required ports, 187
    security environments, 170
    security settings, 171–186
  print server, 190–191
  Web server, 191
    required ports, 192
    security settings, 191–192

hash rules, Software Restriction Policies, 362–363

Help Desk staff, client hardening, 208
  local group configuration, 209–210
  security settings, 208–209

Hide Properties Pages policy, Task Scheduler, 231

Hide User Installs option, Prohibit User Installs policy, 240

high risks, file attachments, 220

Hisecdc.inf template, security template default, 139

Hisecws.inf template, security template default, 140

history data, processing storage, 508–509

History folder, user profile, 255

home URLs, customizing, 295–296

HTML editor, Internet Explorer default programs, 299

I

ICMP
  exceptions, Windows Firewall, 434–435
  pings, 586

icon files, Internet Explorer customizing, 293

IDs, event, 611–613

IEAK (Internet Explorer Administration Kit), 291, 674

IEM (Internet Explorer Maintenance), 674

Iesacls.inf template, security template default, 137

#if version syntax, .adm files, 529–530

IGPM interface, 689

IGPMDomain interface, 689

IIS (Internet Information Services), 225
  Application Compatibility, 219
  Prevent IIS Installation policy, 225

implementation
  GPOs, troubleshooting, 647–656
  Group Policy
    domains, 6
    GPOs (Group Policy Objects), 6–7
    workgroups, 6

Import Settings Wizard, 89

ImportAllGPOs.wsf script, GPMC prebuilt scripts, 703

ImportGPO.wsf script, GPMC prebuilt scripts, 700

importing
  .adm files
    into GPOs, 518
    tips, 519–520
  Internet Explorer, security zone settings, 313
  links, 298–299
  policy object settings, 87–89

Inetcorp.adm file, Administrative Templates, 516

Inetesc.adm file, Internet Explorer .adm files, 518

Inetres.adm file, Administrative Templates, 516

Inetset.adm file, Administrative Templates, 517

.inf file, raw security template files, 563

Inf11.adm file
  Office 2003 .adm files, 517
  Office 2003 Administrative Templates, 377

InfoPath 2003, Administrative templates, 709

information requests
  Windows Event View, 224
  customizing, 225

infrastructure
  component verification, 586–587
  GPOs, troubleshooting, 638–646
  Group Policy
    Active Directory, 10–12
    DNS (Domain Name System), 10–11

inheritance, 61–62
  Active Directory, 11–12
  Block Policy, 655
  blocking, 65–66, 491
  enforcing, 66–67
  GPOs, 13
    modification considerations, 112
    modifying default, 654–656
  link order precedence, 62–63
  overriding, 64
  policy settings, 8

initial processing, 5

installation
  GPMonitor.exe, 604–605
  Microsoft Office, 349
    administrative vs. nonadministrative installation, 349–351
    computer assignment method, 352
    configuration, 374
    service packs and patches, 353
    transform files, 351–352
  software, 318
    advanced options, 334–348
    basics, 318, 319
    customizing installation package, 319–320
    GPO deployment best practices, 124–125
    limitations, 321–322
    location setup, 320–321
    managing deployed applications, 354–368

installation, *continued*
  Windows Installer, 236–237
    baseline file cache, 237–238
    elevating user privileges, 239–240
    logging configuration, 241–242
    preventing removable media sources, 241
    Prohibit User Installs policy, 240
    rollback file creation, 238–239
    System Restore checkpoint control, 237
  Windows service packs, 354
Installer
  files, Windows Installer packages, 328–330
  Windows, 236–237
    baseline file cache, 237–238
    elevating user privileges, 239–240
    logging configuration, 241–242
    preventing removable media sources, 241
    Prohibit User Installs policy, 240
    rollback file creation, 238–239
    System Restore checkpoint control, 237
install-on-first-use, Windows Installer packages, 327
Instlr11.adm file, Office 2003 .adm files, 517
Interactive logon, 145
interfaces
  GPMC scripting
    automating security management, 693–695
    creating GPOs, 689–693
    creating initial GPM object, 689
    linking GPOs, 689–693
    object model, 687–688
    referencing domain to manage, 689
  Internet Explorer customizing, 290–294
International Information, Office 2003 Resource Kit, 372
Internet, Security zone, 220
Internet Explorer
  administration, 9
  Administrative Template files, 517–518
  connection settings, 301–303
  customizing interface
    logos, 291–292
    title bar text, 290
    toolbar, 292–294
  global default programs, 299–300

linking GPOs at domain level, 123
options policies, 313–316
proxy settings, 303–306
security, 306
  deploying configuration, 309–313
  importing zone settings, 313
  restricting setting changes, 308
  Windows Server 2003 Service Pack 1, 672–674
  zone settings, 306–308
URL Action settings, Windows Server 2003 Service Pack 1, 674–675
URL customizing, 295
  favorites, 296–299
  home search and support, 295–296
  links, 296–299
Internet Explorer Administration kit (IEAK), 291, 674
Internet Explorer Maintenance (IEM), 674
Internet Explorer Maintenance policy, storage setting, 497–498
Internet Explorer Maintenance Policy Processing policy, 76
Internet Information Services. *See* IIS (Internet Information Services)
Internet Properties dialog box, 300–302, 311
intersite replication, 645
intervals, refresh, changing default, 70–72
intrasite replication, 645
IP Filter List dialog box, 409
IP filter lists, IPSec policy, 408–411
IP Filter Wizard, 409
IP security, administration, 9
IP Security Filter Action Wizard, 412
IP Security policy, storage setting, 500–501
IP Security Policy Processing policy, 76
IPSec (IP Security) Policy, 397
  activating and deactivating, 401–402
  Allow Authenticated IPSec Bypass policy, 425
  basics, 398
  creating policies, 402
    assigning, 402–404
    defining rules and actions, 404–408
    filter actions, 411–414
    IP filter lists, 408–411

deployment, 399
IPSec basics, 398
vs. IPSec Policy, 399–400
linking GPOs to Active Directory sites, 121
monitoring, 414–415
IT staff, hardening clients, 206–207
local group configuration, 208
security settings, 207
services and software, 207–208
iwearucmpvo value, 242

J–K

Java applets, Internet security zones, 307
Kerberos Policy, 15
account policies, 555
security template, 142
KEYNAME syntax, .adm file structure, 528, 531

L

L2TP (Layer 2 Tunneling Protocol), IPSec, 399
languages, Office-related policy, 394
LANs (local area networks), 405
Layer 2 Tunneling Protocol (L2TP), 399
LDAP (Lightweight Directory Access Protocol), 10
legacy policy settings, filtering, 55
legal notices, linking GPOs at domain level, 122
LGPOs (Local Group Policy Objects), 7, 12, 511
License Server Security Group setting, Terminal Services licensing, 448
licensing, Terminal Services, 447–448
Lightweight Directory Access Protocol (LDAP), 10
Limit Number Of Connections setting, Terminal Services connections, 448–449
Limit The Bandwidth Of Audio And Video policy, NetMeeting configuration, 229
Limit The Size Of Sent Files policy, NetMeeting configuration, 229
linking
customizing URLs, 296–297
creating, 297–298
importing, 298–299

GPOs (Group Policy Objects), 12–13, 39, 58–59
Active Directory sites, 121–122, 633
cross-domains, 110
default policy, 13–18
domains, 41–43, 122–123
OUs (organizational units), 43–45, 117–118, 123
removing, 51
site, domains, and OUs, 107–109
sites, 39–41
troubleshooting linking problems, 650–651
inheritance precedence, 62–63
searching, 56–57
beginning, 58–59
techniques, 57–58
slow networks, 461–463
Configure Slow Link Speed setting, 466–467
CSE (client-side extension), 467–468
default Group Policy application, 462–463
Do Not Detect Slow Network Connections setting, 465–466
Group Policy Slow Link Detection setting, 464
Prompt User When Slow Link Is Detected setting, 466
RAS connections, 463
Slow Network Connection Timeout for User Profiles setting, 465
speeds, design considerations, 104
status, Group Policy, 589–590
structure
gPLink attribute, 488–491
gPOptions attribute, 491
security, 491–492
ListAllGPOs.wsf script, GPMC prebuilt scripts, 704
LISTBOX PART component, PART syntax, 543–545
listings
Enumerating Items on Menu, 389
Sample ZAP File, 332
ListSOMPolicyTree.wsf script, GPMC prebuilt scripts, 704

local area network (LANs), 405
Local Area Network (LAN) Settings dialog box,
  303
local computers, Local Group Policy access,
  29–31
local environments, 6
Local GPO (LGPO), 7, 12, 511
  management, 7
    local computer access, 29–31
    remote computer access, 31–32
Local Install Source feature, Microsoft Office
  2003, 350
Local Intranet dialog box, 311
Local Intranet security zones, configurations,
  220, 310–311
local logons vs. Active Directory, troubleshooting
  corruption, 641
local policies
  IPSec policy, 399
  security template, 555–556
Local Policies section, security template, 143–146
local profiles, 254–257
local security, administration, 9
Local Security Policy tool, 13, 30
log files, troubleshooting Software Installation
  policy, 365–366
    common issues, 367–368
    steps, 366–367
Log on as a service setting, Local Policies, 145
Log on locally setting, Local Policies, 145
Log Users Off When Roaming Profile Fails
  settings, 262–264
logging
  Group Policy, 609–623
    accessing event logs, 611
    configuring Application logging, 610–611
    configuring Userenv logging, 614
    CSE logging, 617–623
    event IDs, 611–613
    event sources, 611
    Userenv logs, 614–617
  Security Policy, debugging, 622–623
logoff scripts, 8, 284–285
logons
  domain controllers, Group Policy, 588–589

events setting, Local Policies, 144
  scripts, 8, 284–285
logos, Internet Explorer customizing, 291–292
logs
  events, troubleshooting, 212
  Windows Event Viewer
    customizing, 225
    using information requests, 224
  Windows Installer, 241–242
loopbacks
  customizing GPOs, 440, 441
    Merge mode, 442–443
    Replace mode, 441–442
    troubleshooting, 443
  processing
    limiting, 120
    status, GPOs, 592
low risks, file attachments, 221
LPGOs
  creating, 511–512
  managing, 512–513
  restricting access, 513–514
  structure, 512

M

Machine subfolder, GPTs, 485
maintenance, 80–81
  copying policy objects settings, 85–87
  GPO back up, 89–90
  importing policy objects settings, 87–89
  modeling for planning purposes, 81–84
  restoring GPOs, 91–92
Manage Backups dialog box, 91
managed software, 318
management, GPOs (Group Policy Objects),
  28–29, 634–635
  Active Directory–based Group Policy, 32–38
  Local Group Policy, 29–32
MAPI (Messaging Application Programming
  Interface), 10
mapping devices, Terminal Services, 456–458
Maximum Password Age setting, Account
  Policies, 142
Maximum Retries To Unload And Update User
  Profile setting, 266

MAXLEN syntax, .adm files, 547
member servers, hardening, 168
  OU design considerations, 168–170
  required ports, 187
  security environments, 170
  security settings, 171–186
membership data, processing storage, 511
menu items (Office)
  disabling options with custom options, 388
    custom disable policy, 389–390
    determining unique ID, 388–389
  disabling options with predefined options, 387
  notification for disabled options, 390
Merge mode, customizing GPO loopback,
  442–443
Messaging Application Programming Interface
  (MAPI), 10
Microsoft, security template settings, 574–577
Microsoft Access, default database folder
  location, 391
Microsoft Access 2003, Administrative templates,
  706
Microsoft Clip Organizer 2003, Administrative
  templates, 708
Microsoft Excel, default file location, 392
Microsoft Excel 2003, Administrative templates,
  706–708
Microsoft FrontPage 2003, Administrative
  templates, 708
Microsoft InfoPath 2003, Administrative
  templates, 709
Microsoft Management Console. *See* MMC
  (Microsoft Management Console)
Microsoft Management Console (MMC), Service
  Pack 1 administrative tools, 671–672
Microsoft Office
  Administrative Templates files, 517–518
  configuration management, 370
    Office-related policy, 383–395
    resource kit tools, 371–383
  deployment, 349
    administrative vs. nonadministrative
      installation, 349–351

computer assignment method, 352
    service packs and patches, 353
    transform files, 351–352
  Web site, 371
Microsoft Office 2003, Administrative templates,
  709–713
Microsoft OneNote 2003
  Administrative templates, 713–715
  default folder location, 392
Microsoft Outlook, configuring security options,
  393, 394
Microsoft Outlook 2003, Administrative
  templates, 715–718
Microsoft PowerPoint 2003, Administrative
  templates, 718–719
Microsoft Project 2003, Administrative templates,
  719–720
Microsoft Publisher 2003
  Administrative templates, 720–721
  default folder location, 393
Microsoft Visio 2003, Administrative templates,
  721–722
Microsoft Windows
  Application Compatibility, 218
    configuring additional settings, 219–220
    optimization, 218
  Attachment Manager
    configuring risk level and trust logic,
      221–224
    security risk assessment, 220–221
  Automatic Updates, 243
    automatic download and installation
      process, 246–249
    blocking access, 249
    configuring, 243–246
    designating update server, 249–251
  Event Viewer
    customizing, 225
    using information requests, 224
  Explorer, 231–232
    CD and DVD burning prevention, 234
    hiding drives, 232–233
    limiting Recycle Bin size, 235–236
    preventing drive access, 233–234
    removing Security tab, 235

Microsoft Windows, *continued*
  Installer, 236–237
    baseline file cache, 237–238
    elevating user privileges, 239–240
    logging configuration, 241–242
    preventing removable media sources, 241
    Prohibit User Installs policy, 240
    rollback file creation, 238–239
    System Restore checkpoint control, 237
  MMC (Microsoft Management Console), 226
    blocking author mode, 227
    designating prohibited or permitted
      snap-ins, 227–228
    requiring permissions for snap-ins, 228
  NetMeeting, 228–230
  Prevent IIS Installation policy, 225
  Server 2003 Service Pack 1
    administrative tools, 671–672
    Adprep.exe, 670
    Internet Explorer security settings, 672–674
    Internet Explorer URL Action settings,
      674–675
    Post-Setup Security Updates, 678–679
    RSoP (Resultant Set of Policy), 676–678
    Security Configuration Wizard, 679–680
    Windows Firewall, 681–685
  Task Scheduler, 230–231
*Microsoft Windows Command-Line Administrator's
  Pocket Consultant,* 230
Microsoft Windows Server 2003 Inside Out, 226
*Microsoft Windows XP Professional Administrator's
  Pocket Consultant,* 218
Microsoft Word 2003
  Administrative templates, 722–723
  default folder location, 393
Migration Table Editor, 132
migration tables, 130–131
  domain-specific GPO settings, 131
  structure, 132
    destination names, 133
    source name, 133
    source type, 132
Minimum Password Age setting, Account Policies,
  142

Minimum Password Length setting, Account
  Policies, 143
MMC (Microsoft Management Console), 226
  blocking author mode, 227
  custom console, 226
  designating prohibited or permitted snap-ins,
    227–228
  requiring permissions for snap-ins, 228
  snap-ins, Group Policy editing, 494
  Windows Server 2003 Service Pack 1,
    administrative tools, 671–672
modeling, 80–81
  copying policy objects settings, 85–87
  GPO back up, 89–90
  importing policy objects settings, 87–89
  planning purposes, 81–84
  restoring GPOs, 91–92
  RSoP (Resultant Set of Policy), 93–95
moderate risks, file attachments, 221
monitoring, IPSec policy, 414, 415
monolithic design approach, GPOs, 113–114
.msi file, administrative installation, 373
Msi.log, 241–242
MST File Viewer, Office 2003 Resource Kit, 372
multiple containers, linking GPOs, 650–651
My Documents folder
  profile folder redirection, 272
  user profile, 254
My Recent Documents folder, user profile, 254

N
Name property, software general deployment
    properties, 334
naming
  GPCs, 475
  GPOs, 129
native Windows Installer files, 328
navigation
  GPOs (Group Policy Objects), 22
    creating and linking, 22–23
    RSoP (Resultant Set of Policy), 23–28
  link structure
    gPLink attribute, 488–491
    gPOptions attribute, 491
    security, 491–492

navigation, *continued*
  logical structure
    GPCs, 474–475
    GPO creation permissions, 478–479
    groupPolicyContainer object attributes,
      476–477
    groupPolicyContainer object security,
      477–478
    viewing and modifying default security
      settings, 479–482
  physical structure
    GPT permissions, 488
    GPTs, 483–486
    versioning, 486–488
NetHood folder, user profile, 254
NetMeeting, 228–229
  configuring, 229–230
  Internet Explorer default programs, 299
Netsh Diag, 324
Netsh Helper, Windows Firewall, 682
Netstat tool, hardening computers, 166–167
networks
  access, 146
  Administrative Templates, 9
  configuration, verifying, 583
  connections
    deploying settings, 301–303
    proxy settings, 303–306
    verifying, 583
  GPO deployment, 127–128
  Group Policy design, 104–105
  secure communications
    IPSec policy, 398–400
    managing IPSec policy, 401–415
    managing Windows Firewall policy,
      424–438
    public key certificates, 415–420
    Windows Firewall policy, 420–424
  security section, Security Configuration
    Wizard, 146, 157
  share, roaming profile configuration, 258
  slow link connection, 461–463
    Configure Slow Link Speed setting, 466–467
    CSE (client-side extension), 467–468
    default Group Policy application, 462–463

    Do Not Detect Slow Network Connections
      setting, 465–466
    Group Policy Slow Link Detection setting,
      464
    Prompt User When Slow Link Is Detected
      setting, 466
    RAS connections, 463
    Slow Network Connection Timeout for User
      Profiles setting, 465
  slow-link detection configuration
    background policy processing, 78–79
    basics, 75–77
    policy processing, 77–78
New Certificate Rule dialog box, 362
New GPO dialog box, 41, 87
New Hash Rule dialog box, 363
New Organizational Unit dialog box, 43
newsgroups, Internet Explorer default programs,
  299
non-Windows Installer package files, 330–334
not configured state, policy settings, 8
notify user installs, Automatic Updates, 247
Notssid.inf template, security template default,
  140–141
NUMERIC syntax, PART syntax, 545

O

Object access setting, Local Policies, 144
objects, GPOs (Group Policy Objects), 6–7
  management, 28–38
  navigating, 22–28
  searching, 20–23
Oe.adm file, Internet Explorer .adm files, 518
Office
  configuration management, 370
    Office-related policy, 383–395
    resource kit tools, 371–383
  deployment, 349
    administrative vs. nonadministrative
      installation, 349–351
    computer assignment method, 352
    service packs and patches, 353
    transform files, 351–352
  installation configuration, 374
  Web site, 371
Office 2000 Resource Kit Web site, 371

Office 2003
  Administrative templates, 705, 709–713
    Access 2003, 706
    Clip Organizer 2003, 708
    Excel 2003, 706–708
    files, 517–518
    FrontPage 2003, 708
    InfoPath 2003, 709
    Microsoft Office 2003, 709–713
    OneNote 2003, 713–715
    Outlook 2003, 715–718
    PowerPoint 2003, 718–719
    Project 2003, 719–720
    Publisher 2003, 720–721
    Visio 2003, 721–722
    Word 2003, 722–723
  Resource Kit
    tools overview, 372
    Web site, 371
Office Information, Office 2003 Resource Kit, 372
Office Installation Wizard, administrative install of .msi file, 373
Office XP, Administrative Files, 382
Office XP Resource Kit Web site, 371
Office10.adm file, Office XP, 382
Office11.adm file
  Office 2003 .adm files, 517
  Office 2003 Administrative Templates, 377
Office-related policies, 383
  basics, 383–384
  configuring, 385–386
  default file and folder locations, 391
    Access 2003, 391
    Excel 2003, 392
    OneNote 2003, 392
    Publisher 2003, 393
    Word 2003, 393
  global and application-specific settings, 384–385
  language settings, 394
  Outlook security options, 393–394
  preventing user changing configuration
    controlling application options, 386–387
    disabling menu items and options with custom options, 388–390
    disabling menu items and options with predefined options, 387
    notification for disabled menu items, 390
    troubleshooting, 394–395
Office-related policy, Microsoft Office management, 370
offline files
  caching, 258
  redirected folders, 274
OneNote 2003
  Administrative templates, 713–715
  default folder location, 392
Onent11.adm file
  Office 2003 .adm files, 517
  Office 2003 Administrative Templates, 377
Only Allow Local User Profile settings, 261, 461
operating systems
  .adm files, 523–524
  filtering policy settings, 55–56
OPS File Viewer, Office 2003 Resource Kit, 372
options
  Group Policy, 7–8
  Sceregvl.inf file, 570
  software installation, 334
    adding application to category, 340
    defining application categories, 338
    deployment type and installation options, 335–337
    general deployment properties, 334–335
    global deployment defaults, 346–348
    modifying application categories, 339
    modifying security on installer file, 344–346
    package customization with transforms, 344
    upgrades, 340–343
Options command (Tools menu – Word 2003), 387
order, Group Policy, 589–590
OUs (organizational units), 101
  Active Directory design, 101–103
  GPO linking, 43, 107
    Computer Configuration and User Configuration, 107–108

creating and linking separately, 43–44
creating in GPMC, 43
interaction, 108–109
single operation, 44–45
hardening servers, 168–170
linking GPOs at domain level, 123
linking to GPOs, design considerations,
117–118
user accounts, troubleshooting, 651–652
Outlk10.adm file, Office XP, 382
Outlk11.adm file
Office 2003 .adm files, 518
Office 2003 Administrative Templates, 377
Outlook
configuring security options, 393–394
Internet Explorer default programs, 299
Outlook 2003, Administrative templates,
715–718
Ownership, security descriptor, 559

P

Package Definition Files, Office 2003 Resource
Kit, 372
package files, Windows Installer, 326–330
PART, .adm file structure, 528
PART syntax, Group Policy Object Editor
interface updates, 537–539
CHECKBOX syntax, 539
CLIENTTEXT keyword, 539–540
COMBOBOX type, 540–541
DROPDOWNLIST syntax, 541–542
EDITTEXT syntax, 542–543
LISTBOX PART component, 543–545
NUMERIC syntax, 545
TEXT syntax, 546
Password Must Meet Complexity Requirements
setting, Account Policies, 143
Password Policy, 15
account policies, 555
security template, 142
patches
Microsoft Office deployment, 353
software upgrades, 341
Path rules, Software Restriction Policies, 364–365

PDC (primary domain controller), 22
PDC Emulator, troubleshooting, 626–627
performance
cross-domain GPO linking, 110
GPOs, 115
asynchronous processing configuration,
119–120
common issues, 115–116
configuring script timeout, 119
disabling unused sections, 118
filtering based on group membership,
120–121
limiting loopback processing, 120
linking to OUs, 117–118
optimizing background refresh interval,
118–119
reducing settings, 117
permissions
Active Directory on GPCs, 477–478
GPOs, 478–479, 591–592
GPTs, 488
Group Policy management, 45
delegating GPOs control, 49
GPMC, 47–48
GPO creation rights, 45–46
GPO links and RSoP management, 50–51
Permissions Entry For dialog box, 268
pings, ICMP, 586
planning
modeling Group Policy, 81–84
software deployment, 322
configuring, 324–326
creating GPOs, 322–323
plug-ins, Internet security zones, 307
policies
Group Policy, 3
administrator use, 8–10
basics, 4
domains, 6
GPOs (Group Policy Objects), 6–7, 12–18
infrastructure, 10–12
processing, 5
settings, 7–8
workgroups, 6

policies, *continued*
objects, searching, 56–59
processing settings, 5
settings
filtering, 54–56
forced refresh, 78
POLICY, .adm file structure, 528
Policy change setting, Local Policies, 144
Policy Events tab (RSoP), 597
Policy Settings dialog box, 234
POLICY syntax, Group Policy Object Editor
interface updates, 536–537
Policy Templates dialog box, 378–380, 520
Portqry tool, hardening computers, 167
ports
exceptions, Windows Firewall, 435–436
hardening clients, 205–206
hardening computers, 164–165
hardening servers
domain controllers, 189–190
member server, 187
Web server, 192
troubleshooting, 213
Post-Setup Security Updates, Windows Server
2003, 678–679
Power Users group, Restricted Groups security,
148
PowerPoint 2003, Administrative templates,
718–719
Ppt10.adm file, Office XP, 382
Ppt11.adm file
Office 2003 .adm files, 518
Office 2003 Administrative Templates, 377
prebuilts scripts
GPMC, 695
Backupallgpos.wsf script, 698–699
BackupGPO.wsf script, 699
CopyGPO.wsf script, 699–700
CreateEnvironmentFromXML.wsf script,
701–702
CreateGPO.wsf script, 696
CreateXMLFromEnvironment.ws script,
701–702
DeleteGPO.wsf script, 696

FindDisabledGPOs.wsf script, 696
FindGPOsBySecurityGroup.wsf script, 697
FindUnlinkedGPOs.wsf script, 697
GetReportsForGPO.wsf script, 700
ImportGPO.wsf script, 700
SetGPOCreationPermissions.wsf script, 697
SetGPOPermissions.wsf script, 698
precedence, link order inheritance, 62–63
Prevent IIS Installation policy, Microsoft
Windows, 225
Prevent License Upgrade setting, Terminal
Services licensing, 448
Prevent local guests group from accessing
application log setting, Event Log security,
147
Prevent local guests group from accessing
security log setting, Event Log security, 147
Prevent local guests group from accessing system
log setting, Event Log security, 147
Prevent Removable Media Source For Any Install
policy, 241
Prevent Roaming Profile Changes From
Propagating To The Server setting, 266
Prevent Task Run or End policy, Task Scheduler,
231
primary domain controller (PDC), 22
printers
Administrative Templates, 9
mapping using Terminal Services, 456
Allow Audio Redirection setting, 457
Do Not Allow Client Printer Redirection
setting, 457
Do Not Allow COM Port Redirection setting,
457
Do Not Allow Drive Redirection setting, 458
Do Not Allow LPT Port Redirection setting,
458
Do Not Set Default Client Printer To Be
Default Printer In A Session setting, 458
server, hardening, 190–191
sharing, Windows Firewall, 427–428
PrintHood folder, user profile, 255
Privilege use setting, Local Policies, 144

privileges
  administration, GPO deployment, 128
  Group Policy management, 45
    delegating GPOs control, 49
    GPMC permissions, 47–48
    GPO creation rights, 45–46
    GPO links and RSoP management, 50–51
  users, Windows Installer, 239–240
  Windows Installer packages, 327
problems. *See* troubleshooting
Process tracking setting, Local Policies, 144
processing, 68–69
  asynchronous vs. synchronous, 502
  background, 501–505
  changing default interval, 70–72
  CSEs (client-side extensions), 492–494
  data storage, 507–508
    history data, 508–509
    membership data, 511
    state data, 509–510
  enabling/disabling GPO, 72–73
  foreground, 501–505
  GPOs, linking at domain level, 123
  manually, 80
  preference change, 73–74
  security policy modification, 507
  server-side extensions, 494–495
    Administrative Templates policy, 496
    Disk Quota policy, 496
    Folder Redirection policy, 496
    Internet Explorer Maintenance policy,
      497–498
    IP Security policy, 500–501
    QoS Packet Scheduler policy, 497
    Scripts policy, 497
    Security policy, 499
    Software Installation policy, 499–500
    Wireless Network policy, 495
  slow link detection, 505–506
  slow-link detection configuration
    background policy processing, 78–79
    basics, 75–77
    policy processing, 77–78

Product Information, software general
    deployment properties, 334
production forest, 130
Profile Wizard, Office 2003 Resource Kit, 372
profiles
  roaming
    configuring user accounts, 258–259
    network share configuration, 258
  users, 254–257, 260
    data access, 266–268
    limiting profile size, 269–271
    redirecting folders and data, 271–281
    update and change modification, 265–266
    ways utilized, 260–265
Program Compatibility Wizard, 218
programs, Internet Explorer global defaults,
    299–300
Programs dialog box, 300
Prohibit Drag-and Drop policy, Task Scheduler,
    231
Prohibit New Task Creation policy, Task
    Scheduler, 231
Prohibit Notifications policy, Windows Firewall
    policy, 437
Prohibit Task Deletion policy, Task Scheduler,
    231
Prohibit Unicast Response To Multicast Or
    Broadcast Requests policy, 438
Prohibit User Installs option, Prohibit User
    Installs policy, 240
Prohibit User Installs policy, 240
Proj11.adm file, Office 2003 Administrative
    Templates, 377
Project 2003, Administrative templates, 719–720
Prompt User When Slow Link Is Detected
    settings, 262, 466
proxy settings, Internet Explorer, setting
    deployment, 303–306
Proxy Settings dialog box, 304
Pub10.adm file, Office XP, 382
Pub11.adm file
  Office 2003 .adm files, 518
  Office 2003 Administrative Templates, 377

public key certificates
    basics, 415–416
    managing public key policy, 418–420
    public key policies, 416–418
public keys
    policies, 416–420
    security administration, 9
Publisher 2003
    Administrative templates, 720–721
    default folder location, 393

Q–R

QoS Packet Scheduler policy, storage setting, 497
QueryBackupLocation.wsf script, GPMC prebuilt
    scripts, 704
RAS (Remote Access Services), linking GPOs to
    Active Directory sites, 122
recoveries, default GPOs, 14
Recycle Bin, limiting maximum size, 235–236
references
    computer configuration policies, 661–664
    user configuration policies, 664–667
refreshing, 5, 68–69
    changing default interval, 70–72
    enabling/disabling GPO processing, 72–73
    manually, 80
    preference change, 73–74
    slow-link detection configuration
        background policy processing, 78–79
        basics, 75–77
        policy processing, 77–78
registries
    Administrative Templates, 516
        adding to GPO, 520
        best practices, 550–551
        creating custom files, 525–526
        default files, 516–518
        example of simple file, 526–527
        file language, 527–549
        importing into GPO, 518
        importing tips, 519–520
        installed defaults, 518–519
        managing files, 522–524
        policies vs. preferences, 524–525
        removing files, 521–522

processing data storage, 507–508
    history data, 508–509
    membership data, 511
    state data, 509–510
    Security Configuration Wizard settings, 157
    troubleshooting, 212
Registry, security template, 559
registry keys, approved locations, 524
Registry section, security template, 149–150
RegistryPath, Sceregvl.inf file, 566
RegistryType, Sceregvl.inf file, 566
remote access, connection design considerations,
    105–106
Remote Access connections, defining IPSec policy
    rules, 405
Remote Access Services (RAS), linking GPOs to
    Active Directory sites, 122
remote administrative operations, Windows
    Firewall, 429–430
remote computers, Local Group Policy access,
    31–32
Remote Desktop feature, Windows Firewall,
    430–431
remote installation, administration, 9
Removal Wizard, Office 2003 Resource Kit, 372
Remove Program Compatibility Property Page
    policy, 219
Remove Security Tab policy, 235
Remove Software dialog box, 355
Rename Administrator Account policy, Default
    Domain Policy GPO, 16
Rename Guest Account policy, Default Domain
    Policy GPO, 16
Replace a process level token setting, Local
    Policies, 145
Replace mode, customizing GPO loopback,
    441–442
replication
    Active Directory, 101, 586
    Active Directory problems, 643–645
    intersite, 645
    intrasite, 645
    SYSVOL problems, 643–645
reports, GPMonitor.exe, 607–609
REQUIRED syntax, .adm files, 547
Rerun Query option (RSoP), 594

Reset account lockout counter after setting, Account Policies, 143

resource kit tools, Microsoft Office, 371
    Administrative Templates, 377–380
    configuration GPOs, 380–381
    Custom Installation Wizard, 372–374
    Custom Maintenance Wizard, 375–376
    managing multiple versions, 381–383
    Web site, 371–372

Restore dialog box, 92

Restore files and directories setting, Local Policies, 145

RestoreAllGPOs.wsf script, GPMC prebuilt scripts, 704

RestoreGPO.wsf script, GPMC prebuilt scripts, 704

restores
    default GPOs, 14
    GPOs, 91–92

Restrict Terminal Services Users To A Single Remove Session setting, 461

Restricted Groups
    security template, 147–148
    troubleshooting, 212

Restricted Groups settings, security template, 557

Restricted Sites, Internet Security zone, 220

Restricted Sites dialog box, 313

Restricted Sites security zones, configuration, 312–313

Resultant Set of Policy. *See* RSoP (Resultant Set of Policy)

Retention method for security log setting, Event Log security, 147

risk levels, configuring Attachment Manager, 221–224

roaming profiles
    configuring user accounts, 258–259
    data access, 266–268
    limiting profile size, 269–271
    network share configuration, 258
    redirecting folders and data, 271
        basics, 272–274
        configuration, 274–281
    update and change modifications, 265–266

ways utilized, 260
    Delete Cached Copies Of Roaming Profiles setting, 261
    Do Not Detect Slow Network Connection setting, 261
    Log Users Off When Roaming Profile Fails setting, 262
    Only Allow Local User Profiles setting, 261
    Prompt User When Slow Link Is Detected setting, 262
    Slow Network Connection Timeout For User Profiles setting, 263
    Timeout For Dialog Boxes setting, 264–265
    Wait For Remote User Profile setting, 265

Rootsec.inf template, security template default, 141

RSoP (Resultant Set of Policy), 23–26, 93, 415, 648–649, 676
    basics, 27–28
    management privileges, 50–51
    managing logs centrally, 604–609
    modeling policy settings, 93–95
    troubleshooting Group Policy, 593–598
        Advanced view, 597–598
        Policy Events tab, 597
        Settings tab, 596–597
        Summary tab, 594–596
    troubleshooting security settings, 214
    Windows Server 2003 Service Pack 1, 676
        administering, 677–678
        changes, 676–677
        Group Policy Results access delegation, 678

RSoP logging mode, 593

Run dialog box, 8, 563

S

SACL (System access control list), security descriptor, 559

SAM (Security Accounts Manager), 10

Save Report option (RSoP), 594

Sceregvl.inf file
    computer registering, 571–572
    customizing, 570–571
    structure, 564–570

Scheduled Tasks Wizard, 230
schedules, Task Scheduler, 230–231
scope of management (SOM), 508
screen savers, linking GPOs at domain level, 122
scripts
    computer, 282
        controlling visibility, 285–286
        execution, 287
        startup and shutdown, 283–284
        timeout, 286–287
    configuring timeout, 119
    GPMC, 687
        automating security management, 693–695
        creating GPOs, 689–693
        creating initial GPM object, 689
        linking GPOs, 689–693
        prebuilts, 695, 704
        referencing domain to manage, 689
        scripting object model, 687–688
    Internet Explorer, customizing, 293
    Internet security zones, 307
    linking GPOs at domain level, 123
    users, 282
        controlling visibility, 285–286
        execution, 287
        logon and logoff, 284–285
        timeout, 286–287
Scripts policy, storage setting, 497
Scripts Policy Processing policy, 77
scwcmd command, security template
        deployment, 163–164
Search For Group Policy Objects dialog box, 58
search URLs, customizing, 295–296
searches, policy objects, 56–57
    beginning, 58–59
    techniques, 57–58
secedit.exe tool
    security template deployment, 162
    troubleshooting security settings, 213
Securdc.inf template, security template default,
        138
Secure Server (Require Security) setting, Terminal
        Services connections, 451

Securews.inf template, security template default,
        138–139
security
    administration, 9
    client hardening, 192–205
        Help Desk staff, 208–210
        IT staff and administrator computers,
            206–208
        required ports, 205–206
        restricted groups, 206
    computer hardening, 164
        closing unnecessary ports, 164–165
        disabling unnecessary services, 165–166
        tools used, 166–167
    defaultSecurityDescriptor attribute, 479–480
        modifying, 482
        viewing, 480–482
    file attachments, Windows Attachment
        Manager, 220–221
    filtering, 126, 656
    GPOs
        creation permissions, 478–479
        linking, 491–492
    GPT permissions, 488
    groupPolicyContainer object, 477–478
    groups
        filtering, 59–61
        searching policy objects, 57
    Internet Explorer, 306
        deploying configuration, 309–313
        importing zone settings, 313
        restricting setting changes, 308
        security zone settings, 306–308
    management, GPMC automation, 693–695
    network communications
        IPSec policy, 398–400
        managing IPSec policy, 401–415
        managing Windows Firewall policy,
            424–438
        public key certificates, 415–420
        Windows Firewall policy, 420, 424
    options, troubleshooting, 212
    policy refresh, 78
    privileges, Group Policy management, 45–51

security, *continued*
  server hardening, 168
    domain controllers, 187–190
    file server, 190–191
    member servers, 168–187
    printer server, 190–191
    Web server, 191–192
  settings, linking GPOs at domain level, 123
  software installation, modifying on installer
      file, 344–346
  templates, 136
    Account Policies section, 142–143
    Compatws.inf, 137
    copying, 563–564
    creating new, 564
    customizing services, 572–574
    DC security.inf, 137
    deployment, 161–164
    Event Log security area, 146–147
    File System section, 150
    Hisecdc.inf, 139
    Hisecws.inf, 140
    Iesacls.inf, 137
    Local Policies section, 143–146
    Microsoft settings, 574–577
    Notssid.inf, 140–141
    overlap with GPOs, 561–562
    raw security .inf files, 563
    Registry section, 149–150
    Restricted Groups security, 147–148
    Rootsec.inf, 141
    Sceregvl.inf file, 564–572
    Securedc.inf, 138
    Securews.inf, 138–139
    Security Configuration and Analysis snap-in,
      151–152
    Security Configuration Wizard, 152–160
    Security Templates snap-in, 151, 562
    Setup Security.inf, 141
    structure, 554–560
    System Services section, 148–149
    troubleshooting, 630–631
  troubleshooting, 210
    areas of potential problems, 210–213
    tools, 213–215
Security Accounts Manager (SAM), 10
Security Configuration and Analysis snap-in,
    151–152, 214
Security Configuration and Analysis tool, security
    template deployment, 162
Security Configuration Wizard, 152
  accessing, 152
  best practices, 159–160
  incorporating templates into policies, 158
  sections, 153–157
  security templates, deployment, 163–164
  Windows Server 2003, 679–680
Security Group Membership When Group Policy
    Was Applied option (RSoP Summary tab),
    595
Security Options
  Default Domain Controllers Policy GPO, 18
  Local Policies, 143, 556
Security Policy
  debugging logging, 622–623
  processing modification, 507
  storage setting, 499
Security Policy Processing policy, 77
Security Rule Wizard, 405
Security Settings dialog box, 60, 268, 310
Security tab, Windows Explorer, 235
Security Templates snap-in, 151, 554, 562
Security Zones And Content Ratings policy, 313
Select Computer dialog box, 31, 93
Select Users, Computers, Or Groups dialog box,
    46, 268, 346, 671
SendTo folder, user profile, 255
servers
  Automatic Updates, 249–251
  hardening, 168
    domain controllers, 187–190
    file server, 190–191
    member servers, 168–187
    Web server, 191–192
  Security Configuration Wizard, 153–157

server-side extensions, processing architecture, 494–495
  Administrative Templates policy, 496
  Disk Quota policy, 496
  Folder Redirection policy, 496
  Internet Explorer Maintenance policy, 497–498
  IP Security policy, 500–501
  QoS Packet Scheduler policy, 497
  Scripts policy, 497
  Security policy, 499
  Software Installation policy, 499–500
  Wireless Network policy, 495
server-to-client communications, IPSec, 400
server-to-server communications, IPSec, 399
service packs
  .adm files, 523–524
  Microsoft Office deployment, 353
  Office 2003, Administrative Templates, 379–380
  software upgrades, 341
  Windows, 354
  Windows Server 2003
    administrative tools, 671–672
    Adprep.exe, 670
    Internet Explorer security settings, 672–674
    Internet Explorer URL Action settings, 674–675
    Post-Setup Security Updates, 678–679
    RSoP (Resultant Set of Policy), 676–678
    Security Configuration Wizard, 679–680
    Windows Firewall, 681–685
services
  disabling, hardening computers, 165–166
  security templates, 572
    acquiring syntax, 572–573
    displaying correct services, 572
    manually updating, 573–574
  system troubleshooting, 212
Set Call Security Options policy, NetMeeting configuration, 229
Set Client Connection Encryption Level setting, Terminal Services connections, 449–451

Set Path For TS Roaming Profiles setting, Terminal Services user profiles, 459
Set Rules For Remote Control To Terminal Services User Sessions setting, 452–453
Set The Intranet Support Web Page policy, NetMeeting configuration, 229
Set Time Limit For Active Terminal Services Sessions setting, 454–455
Set Time Limit For Disconnected Sessions setting, Terminal Services connection, 454
SetGPOCreationPermissions.wsf script, GPMC prebuilt scripts, 697
SetGPOPermissionsBySOM.wsf script, GPMC prebuilt scripts, 704
SetGPOPermissions.wsf script, GPMC prebuilt scripts, 698
SetSOMPermissions.wsf script, GPMC prebuilt scripts, 704
settings
  filtering
    operating system and application configuration, 55–56
    techniques, 54–55
  GPOs
    applying to groups, 652–653
    conflicting settings, 653–654
    troubleshooting, 647–650
  Group Policy, 7–8
  Group Policy Editor, troubleshooting, 627–631
  policies, forced refresh, 78
  searching, 56–57
    beginning, 58–59
    techniques, 57–58
Settings tab (RSoP), 596–597
Setup Security.inf template, security template default, 141
SetupCommand key, 332
shadow copies, redirected folders, 274
shared folders, Administrative Templates, 10
Show Contents dialog box, 389
Shut down the system setting, Local Policies, 145
shutdown scripts, 8, 283–284

sites
   Active Directory design, 103–104
   GPO linking, 107
      Computer Configuration and User
         Configuration, 107–108
      interaction, 108–109
   GPO links, 39–41
slow link detection
   configuration
      background policy processing, 78–79
      basics, 75–77
      policy processing, 77–78
   disabling, 262
   Group Policy refresh, 5
   processing behavior, 505–506
Slow Network Connection Timeout For User
      Profiles settings, 263, 465
snap-ins, MMC
   prohibition or permitted designation, 227–228
   requiring permissions, 228
software. *See also* applications
   deployment
      non-Windows Installer package files,
         330–334
      planning, 322–326
      Windows Installer packages, 326–330
   installation, 318
      administration, 9
      advanced options, 334–348
      basics, 318–319
      customizing installation package, 319–320
      GPO deployment best practices, 124–125
      limitations, 321–322
      linking GPOs at domain level, 123
      location setup, 320–321
   management, 354–355
      redeploy an application, 356
      Software Restriction Policies, 356–365
      troubleshooting Software Installation policy,
         365–368
      uninstall deployed applications, 355
   Microsoft Office configuration, 374
   Microsoft Office deployment, 349

      administrative vs. nonadministrative
         installation, 349–351
      computer assignment method, 352
      service packs and patches, 353
      transform files, 351–352
   restriction, 9
   Windows service packs, 354
Software Installation policy, 318
   basics, 318–319
   customizing installation package, 319–320
   limitations, 321–322
   location setup, 320–321
   managing installed software, 354–355
      redeploy an application, 356
      Software Restriction Policies, 356–365
      troubleshooting, 365–368
      uninstall deployed applications, 355
   Microsoft Office deployment, 349
      administrative vs. nonadministrative
         installation, 349–351
      computer assignment method, 352
      service packs and patches, 353
      transform files, 351–352
   storage setting, 499–500
   Windows service packs, 354
Software Installation Policy Processing policy, 77
Software Installation Properties dialog box, 339,
      347
Software Restriction Policies, 356–357
   Additional Rules policy, 361
      Certificate rules, 361–362
      hash rules, 362–363
      Path rules, 364–365
      Trusted Zones rule, 363–364
   configuration, 357
   Designated File Types policy, 359
   Disallowed and Unrestricted modes, 360–361
   Enforcement policy, 358
   Trusted Publishers policy, 359–360
Software settings, GPOs (Group Policy Objects),
      28
Software Update Services (SUS), linking GPOs to
      Active Directory sites, 122
SOM (scope of management), 582

Sp1shell.adm file, Internet Explorer .adm files, 518
SRV records, troubleshooting, 646
Standard Profile, Windows Firewall policy operation, 421
Start A Program On Connection setting, Terminal Services connections, 451–452
Start Menu folder
  Administrative Templates, 10
  profile folder redirection, 273
  user profile, 255
startup scripts, 8, 283–284
state data, processing storage, 509–510
stateful port filtering, Windows Firewall basics, 420–421
static logos, Internet Explorer, 291
status states, Group Policy, 587–588
Store passwords using reversible encryption setting, Account Policies, 143
STRINGS syntax, Group Policy Object Editor interface updates, 534–535
structures
  LGPOs, 512
  link
    gPLink attribute, 488–491
    gPOptions attribute, 491
    security, 491–492
  logical
    GPCs, 474–475
    GPO creation permissions, 478–479
    groupPolicyContainer object attributes, 476–477
    groupPolicyContainer object security, 477–478
    viewing and modifying default security settings, 479–482
  physical
    GPT permissions, 488
    GPTs, 483–486
    versioning, 486–488
  security templates, 554
    account policies, 554–555
    Event Log settings, 556
    File System, 560
    local policies, 555–556
    Registry, 559
    Restricted Groups settings, 557
    System Services, 558
Subs.adm file, Internet Explorer .adm files, 518
subsequent processing, 5
Summary tab (RSoP), 594–596
Support Information, software general deployment properties, 334
support URLs, customizing, 295–296
SUPPORTED tag, .adm files, 548, 549
SUS (Software Update Services), linking GPOs to Active Directory sites, 122
synchronization, time verification, 584
synchronous processing
  vs. asynchronous processing, 502
  GPO design, 110–111
syncing, 544
System access control list (SACL), security descriptor, 559
System events setting, Local Policies, 144
System Restore, checkpoint control, 237
System Services
  security template, 558
  troubleshooting, 212
System Services section, security template, 148–149
System.adm file, Administrative Templates, 517
systems
  Administrative Templates, 10
  configuration, policy setting filtering, 55
SYSVOL files
  checking for errors, 602
  GPO application failures, 642–643
  troubleshooting replication/convergence, 643–645

T

Take ownership of files or other objects setting, Local Policies, 145
Task Scheduler, 230–231
taskbars, Administrative Templates, 10
TCP/IP NetBIOS Helper service, 586

techniques
  filtering, policy settings, 54–55
  searching policy objects, 57–58
Temp folder, user profile, 255
templates
  Administrative, 9–10, 705
    Access 2003, 706
    Clip Organizer 2003, 708
    custom settings, 515–551, 627–630
    Excel 2003, 706–708
    FrontPage 2003, 708
    InfoPath 2003, 709
    Microsoft Office 2003, 709–713
    OneNote 2003, 713–715
    Outlook 2003, 715–718
    PowerPoint 2003, 718–719
    Project 2003, 719–720
    Publisher 2003, 720–721
    Visio 2003, 721–722
    Word 2003, 722–723
  GPTs, 483–486
  Group Policy Monitor Administrative, 604
  Group Policy template (GPT), 473, 483–488
  Office 2003 Administrative Templates,
      377–380
  security, 136
    Account Policies section, 142–143
    Compatws.inf, 137
    copying, 563–564
    creating new, 564
    customizing services, 572–574
    DC security.inf, 137
    deployment, 161–164
    Event Log security area, 146–147
    File System section, 150
    Hisecdc.inf, 139
    Hisecws.inf, 140
    Iesacls.inf, 137
    Local Policies section, 143–146
    Microsoft settings, 574–577
    Notssid.inf, 140–141
    overlap with GPOs, 561–562
    raw security .inf files, 563
    Registry section, 149–150
    Restricted Groups security, 147–148
    Rootsec.inf, 141
    Sceregvl.inf file, 564–572
    Securedc.inf, 138
    Securews.inf, 138–139
    Security Configuration and Analysis snap-in,
        151–152
    Security Configuration Wizard, 152–160
    Security Templates snap-in, 151, 562
    Setup Security.inf, 141
    structure, 554–560
    System Services section, 148–149
    troubleshooting, 630–631
Templates folder, user profile, 255
Temporary Internet Files, user profile, 255
Terminal Services, customizing GPOs, 444
  connection configuration, 448–456
  controlling on individual computers, 444–445
  device mapping, 456–458
  domain controlling, 445–446
  licensing, 447–448
  order of precedence configuration, 446
  user profiles, 459–461
  user properties, 446–447
Terminate Session When Time Limits Are
      Reached setting, 455
test forest, GPO migration to production, 130
testing, GPOs, 129
  migration tables, 130–133
  migration to production, 130
  production forest to production forest, 130
text, Internet Explorer title bars, 290
TEXT syntax, PART syntax, 546
time synchronization verification, 584
Timeout For Dialog Boxes setting, 262–265
timeouts, scripts, 286–287
title bars, Internet Explorer, customizing text,
      290
toolbars, Internet Explorer, customizing,
      292–294
Toolbars command (View menu), 294
Tools menu commands (Word 2003), Options,
      387
ToolTip text, Internet Explorer customizing, 292

transform files, 319
   Microsoft Office deployment, 351–352, 374
   software installation, package customization, 344
   Windows Installer packages, 327
troubleshooting
   Active Directory
      convergence, 643–645
      database corruption, 640–641
      local logons vs. Active Directory, 641
      replication, 643–645
   cross-domain GPO linking, 110
   domain controllers, 639–640
   DNS, 645–646
   GPMC, delegation restrictions, 631–638
   GPOs
      administration problems, 626–638
      application failures, 642–643
      conflicting settings, 653–654
      implementation problems, 647–656
      incorrect settings, 647–650
      infrastructure problems, 638–646
      inheritance, 654–656
      linking, 650–651
   Group Policy, 581–592
      core configuration verification, 582–586
      GPMonitor.exe, 604–609
      GPO permissions, 591–592
      Gpotool, 600–604
      Gpresult, 599–600
      infrastructure component verification, 586–587
      link status, 589–590
      logging, 609–623
      logon domain controller, 588–589
      loopback processing status, 592
      order, 589–590
      RSoP (Resultant Set of Policy), 593–598
      slow links, 592
      status states, 587–588
      versions, 587–588
   Group Policy Editor settings, 627–631
   loopbacks, 443
   Office-related policy, 394–395

   OUs, 651–652
   PDC Emulator, 626–627
   security settings, 210
      areas of potential problems, 210–213
      tools, 213–215
   Software Installation policy, 365–366
      common issues, 367–368
      steps, 366–367
true policies, 524
trust logic, configuring Attachment Manager, 221–224
Trusted Publishers dialog box, 360
Trusted Publishers policy, 359–360
Trusted Sites
   Internet Security zone, 220
   security zones configuration, 311–312
Trusted Sites dialog box, 312
Trusted Zones rule, Software Restriction Policies, 363–364
trusts, verification, 583–584
TS User Home Directory setting, Terminal Services user profiles, 460
tunnels, defining IPSec policy rules, 405
Turn Off Application Compatibility Engine policy, 219
Turn Off Automatic Updates Of ADM Files policy, 522
Turn Off Program Compatibility Wizard policy, 219
Turn On Application Help Log Events policy, 220

U
updates
   .adm files, 522–523
   Automatic Updates, 243
      automatic download and installation process, 246–249
      blocking access, 249
      configuring, 243–246
      designating update server, 249–251
   Office 2003, Administrative Templates, 379–380

upgrades
  software installation, 340–341
    new version deployment, 341–343
    patches and service packs, 341
  Windows Installer packages, 327
UPnP Framework exceptions, Windows Firewall, 431
URL Action settings, Internet Explorer, 674–675
URLs, customizing, 295
  favorites, 296–299
  home, search, and support, 295–296
  links, 296–299
user accounts, OUs troubleshooting, 651–652
User Configuration policy, GPT User subfolder, 485
User Configuration section, GPO linking, 107–108
user configuration settings (GPOs), 649
user data, user profiles, 256
User Group Policy Loopback Processing Mode policy, 75
user profiles, 254–257, 260
  data access, 266–268
  limiting profile size, 269–271
  redirecting folders and data, 271
    basics, 272–274
    configuration, 274–281
  update and change modifications, 265–266
  ways used, 260
    Delete Cached Copies Of Roaming Profiles setting, 261
user profiles, 254–257, 260
    Do Not Detect Slow Network Connection setting, 261
    Log Users Off When Roaming Profile Fails setting, 262
    Only Allow Local User Profiles setting, 261
    Prompt User When Slow Link Is Detected setting, 262
    Slow Network Connection Timeout For User Profiles setting, 263
    Timeout For Dialog Boxes setting, 264–265
    Wait For Remote User Profile setting, 265

User Rights Assignment policy
  Default Domain Controllers Policy GPO, 18
  Local Policies, 143
User Rights Assignment settings, local policies, 556
User subfolder, GPTs, 485
Userenv logs
  configuring, 614
  Group Policy, 614–617
users
  authentication, Internet security zones, 307
  configuration
    refresh, 68–80
    searching policy objects, 57
  configuration policies, 661–667
  controlling Terminal Services profiles, 459
    Delete Cached Copies Of Roaming Profiles setting, 461
    Only Allow Local User Profiles setting, 461
    Restrict Terminal Services Users To A Single Remove Session setting, 461
    Set Path For TS Roaming Profiles setting, 459
    TS User Home Directory setting, 460
  filtering, 59–61
  GPOs (Group Policy Objects), creation rights, 46
  policies, 5
  rights troubleshooting, 211
  scripts, 282
    administration, 8
    controlling visibility, 285–286
    execution, 287
    logon and logoff, 284–285
    timeout, 286–287
  searching policy objects, 57
  Terminal Services properties, 446–447

V

VALUENAME, .adm file structure, 528
VALUENAME syntax, .adm files, 532
VALUEOFF/VALUEON syntax, .adm files, 532–534
verbose output, GPOs, 602–604

verification GPOs, Gpotool, 602

versioning, 486–488

versionNumber attribute, groupPolicyContainer object, 477

versions, Group Policy, 587–588

View menu commands
  Advanced Features, 475
  Filtering, 55
  Toolbars, 294

viewing GPOs, 636–638

Virtual Private Network (VPN), IPSec, 399

Visio 2003
  Administrative templates, 721–722
  policy settings, .adm files, 521

Visio11.adm file, Office 2003 Administrative Templates, 377

VPNs (Virtual Private Networks), IPSec, 399

W

Wait For Remote User Profile settings, 265

Web servers, hardening, 191
  required ports, 192
  security settings, 191–192

Win32_Product class, 383

Windows
  Application Compatibility, 218
    configuring additional settings, 219–220
    optimization, 218
  Attachment Manager
    configuring risk level and trust logic, 221–224
    security risk assessment, 220–221
  Automatic Updates, 243
    automatic download and installation process, 246–249
    blocking access, 249
    configuring, 243–246
    designating update server, 249–251
  components, Administrative Templates, 10
  Event Viewer
    customizing, 225
    using information requests, 224
  Explorer, 231–232
    CD and DVD burning prevention, 234

    hiding drives, 232–233
    limiting Recycle Bin size, 235–236
    preventing drive access, 233–234
    removing Security tab, 235
  Installer, 236–237
    baseline file cache, 237–238
    elevating user privileges, 239–240
    logging configuration, 241–242
    preventing removable media sources, 241
    Prohibit User Installs policy, 240
    rollback file creation, 238–239
    System Restore checkpoint control, 237
  MMC (Microsoft Management Console), 226
    blocking author mode, 227
    designating prohibited or permitted snap-ins, 227–228
    requiring permissions for snap-ins, 228
  NetMeeting, 228–230
  Prevent IIS Installation policy, 225
  Server 2003 Service Pack 1
    administrative tools, 671–672
    Adprep.exe, 670
    Internet Explorer security settings, 672–674
    Internet Explorer URL Action settings, 674–675
    Post-Setup Security Updates, 678–679
    RSoP (Resultant Set of Policy), 676–678
    Security Configuration Wizard, 679–680
    Windows Firewall, 681–685
  service pack deployment, 354
  Task Scheduler, 230–231

Windows 2000, Terminal Services control, 446

Windows Explorer, 231–232
  CD and DVD burning prevention, 234
  hiding drives, 232–233
  limiting Recycle Bin size, 235–236
  preventing drive access, 233–234
  removing Security tab, 235

Windows Firewall
  IPSec policy, 400
  Windows Server 2003 changes, 676–677
  Windows Server 2003 Service Pack 1, 681
    audit logging, 681–682
    changes, 681
    Netsh Helper, 682

new Group Policy support, 682–685
Windows Firewall dialog box, 426, 427
Windows Firewall policies, 420, 424
  Allow Authenticated IPSec Bypass policy, 425
  Allow Logging policy, 437–438
  allowing exceptions, 426–427
    defining program exceptions, 432–434
    Do Not Allow Exceptions policy, 427
    file and printer sharing, 427–428
    ICMP exceptions, 434–435
    port exceptions, 435–436
    remote administrative operations, 429–430
    Remote Desktop feature, 430–431
    UpnP Framework, 431
  basics, 420–421
  enabling and disabling, 425–426
  Prohibit Notifications policy, 437
  Prohibit Unicast Response To Multicast Or Broadcast Requests, 438
  utilizing, 421–424
Windows Installer, 236–237
  baseline file cache usage, 237–238
  deploying new Office configuration, 376
  elevating user privileges, 239–240
  installation packages, 319
  logging configuration, 241–242
  preventing removable media sources, 241
  Prohibit User Installs policy, 240
  rollback file creation, 238–239
  System Restore checkpoint control, 237
Windows Installer packages, software deployment, 326–330
Windows Installer Policy, debugging logging, 617–620
Windows NT, creating additional domains, 11
Windows NT System Policy, 7
Windows Server 2003, CSEs installed, 493–494

Windows Server 2003 Security Guide, 171
Windows settings, GPOs (Group Policy Objects), 28
Windows.adm file, Administrative Templates, 517
Winnt.adm file, Administrative Templates, 517
Wireless Network policy, storage settings, 495
wireless networks, administration, 9
Wireless Policy Processing policy, 77
wizards, Group Policy Results Wizard, 593
WMI
  filters
    GPO deployment best practices, 126–127
    RSoP Summary tab, 595
  searching linked filters, 57
Wmp.adm file, Internet Explorer .adm files, 518
Wmplayer.adm file, Administrative Templates, 517
Word 2003
  Administrative templates, 722–723
  default folder location, 393
Word10.adm file, Office XP, 382
Word11.adm file
  Office 2003 .adm files, 518
  Office 2003 Administrative Templates, 377
workgroups, 6
Wuau.adm file, Administrative Templates, 517

Z

ZAP files
  creating, 331–332
  deploying software, 332–334
zones, Internet security, 306–308
  deploying configuration, 309–313
  importing settings, 313
  restricting setting changes, 308

Microsoft Press

Security resources and guidance
—direct from Microsoft

Microsoft® Windows® Security Resource Kit, Second Edition
ISBN: 0-7356-2174-8   Suggested Retail Price: $49.99 U.S., $72.99 Canada

Get the in-depth information and tools you need to help protect your Windows-based clients, servers, networks, and Internet services—with definitive technical guidance from the Microsoft Security team and two industry veterans. You'll learn how to plan and implement a comprehensive security strategy, assess security threats and vulnerabilities, configure system security settings, and more. You'll also find new coverage of service packs, Microsoft Office 2003 Editions, and Internet Information Services (IIS) 6.0. The CD provides must-have tools, scripts, templates, and other key resources.

Assessing Network Security
ISBN: 0-7356-2033-4   Suggested Retail Price: $49.99 U.S., $72.99 Canada

Don't wait for an attacker to find and exploit your security vulnerabilities—take the lead by assessing the state of your network's security. This book delivers advanced network testing strategies, including vulnerability scanning and penetration testing, from members of the Microsoft security teams. You'll find detailed information on how to perform security assessments, uncover security vulnerabilities, and apply appropriate countermeasures. The CD includes time-saving tools and scripts to reveal and help correct security vulnerabilities in your own network, plus a complete eBook.

Microsoft Windows Server™ 2003 PKI and Certificate Security
ISBN: 0-7356-2021-0   Suggested Retail Price: $59.99 U.S., $86.99 Canada

Capitalize on the built-in security services in Windows Server 2003—and deliver your own robust, public key infrastructure (PKI)-based solutions at a fraction of the cost and time. This in-depth reference cuts straight to the details of designing and implementing certificate-based security solutions for PKI-enabled applications. Get the inside information, real-world solutions, and best practices you need to avoid common design and implementation mistakes, help minimize risk, and optimize security administration. You'll find timesaving tools and scripts, plus an eBook, on the CD.

To see more Microsoft Press® products for IT professionals, please visit:
microsoft.com/mspress

What do you think of this book? We want to hear from you!

Do you have a few minutes to participate in a brief online survey? Microsoft is interested in hearing your feedback about this publication so that we can continually improve our books and learning resources for you.

To participate in our survey, please visit:

www.microsoft.com/learning/booksurvey

And enter this book's ISBN, 0-7356-2217-5. As a thank-you to survey participants in the United States and Canada, each month we'll randomly select five respondents to win one of five $100 gift certificates from a leading online merchant.* At the conclusion of the survey, you can enter the drawing by providing your e-mail address, which will be used for prize notification *only*.

Thanks in advance for your input. Your opinion counts!

Sincerely,

Microsoft Learning

Learn More. Go Further.